DOING IT RIGHT

By Jim O'Brien

The Steelers of Three Rivers And Four Super Bowls Share Their Secrets For Success

In Memoriam

Fifty percent of the profits from this book were donated to the Arthur J. Rooney Memorial Scholarship Fund. It provides financial aid to needy youngsters who want to go to college who are residents of Pittsburgh's North Side, Mr. Rooney's beloved neighborhood community.

Copyright © 1991 by Jim O'Brien

James P. O'Brien — Publishing
P.O. Box 12580
Pittsburgh, PA 15241
Phone (412) 221-3580

Portions of some of the articles were originally published in The Pittsburgh Press, and are reprinted here with permission.

First Printing, July 1991 by Wolfson Publishing
Second Printing, May 1995

Designed by Marty Wolfson and Jim O'Brien

Photos by Mike Fabus and others

Manufactured in the United States of America

Printed by Geyer Printing Company, Inc.
Pittsburgh, PA 15213
Typography by Cold-Comp
Pittsburgh, PA 15222

Photo reproductions by Modern Reproductions, Inc.

ISBN Number 0-916114-09-0

Dedication

To the memory of my father and my brother — both named Dan O'Brien — whom I miss.

To my wife Kathleen and our daughters — Sarah and Rebecca — whom I love.

To my mother, Mary O'Brien, who always believed me, even when she shouldn't have. To my brother, Richard, and my sister, Carole, who care.

To the memory of Art Rooney and Frankie Gustine, two gentlemen who knew more than any of us about the game of life.

—Jim O'Brien

Books By Jim O'Brien

COMPLETE HANDBOOK OF PRO BASKETBALL 1970-71

COMPLETE HANDBOOK OF PRO BASKETBALL 1971-72

ABA ALL-STARS

PITTSBURGH: THE STORY OF THE
CITY OF CHAMPIONS

HAIL TO PITT: A SPORTS HISTORY OF
THE UNIVERSITY OF PITTSBURGH

DOING IT RIGHT

WHATEVER IT TAKES

MAZ AND THE '60 BUCS

REMEMBER ROBERTO

PENGUIN PROFILES

To order copies directly from the publisher, send $24.95 for hardcover
edition and $14.95 for softcover edition. Please send $3.50 to cover ship-
ping and handling charges per book. Pennsylvania residents add 6%
sales tax to price of book only, Allegheny County residents add an additional 1% sales tax, for total of 7% sales tax. Copies will be signed by
author at your request. Discounts available for large orders. Contact
publisher regarding availability of all books in *Pittsburgh Proud* series.
Several of them are sold out.

Contents

"When you win, you have all the answers."
—Art Rooney

*"The Pittsburgh Steelers are an
organization that does try to do it right.
Doing it right is important to us.
We want to be something special to our people.
That's how we view the Steelers;
they are special."*

— Dan Rooney
President
Pittsburgh Steelers

*"If the Steelers won on Sunday,
the sun came up on Monday."*
— Myron Cope

*"Reality never repeats. The
exact same thing is never taken
away and given back . . . There
are cigars in heaven. For that
is what we should all like. The
happy past restored."*
— C.S. Lewis

The Long Black and Gold Line
"They looked larger than life"

It was Photo Day, July 20, 1979, and the Steeler veterans had to report that day to join the rookies and free agents at training camp at St. Vincent College in Latrobe, about 40 miles east of Pittsburgh.

I was as eager as anyone to see them. I had been away from Pittsburgh for ten years, covering the Miami Dolphins for one year, in 1969, for *The Miami News,* and then just about all the teams in New York, including the Giants and the Jets, for nine years with *The New York Post.* I had remained a fan of the sports teams in my hometown. While I was away, the city had earned a national reputation as "The City of Champions."

The Steelers had won three Super Bowls during the previous five years, the Pirates had won the World Series in 1971 and 1979, and the Pitt football team had won the national championship in 1976. I felt as if I had missed out on something special. So I had come back home to work for *The Pittsburgh Press,* where I had worked on weekends while in high school, and in the summer after my sophomore year at Pitt.

I was standing on the upper field at St. Vincent, talking with other members of the media. We were in an area that was roped off to keep the thousands of fans who had assembled under control. They were close enough to take their own pictures, but the ropes and security guards were there to see that the fans were not in all the pictures to be taken that day. It is an annual rite of training camp, a morning set aside for the media and the club's publicity department to take pictures of all the players.

I can still see the scene that day. The players started coming out of the locker room in single file. They were dressed mostly in black. The crowd was parted to make way for the Pittsburgh Steelers.

They looked larger than life. I had covered sports on a big-time level for about 15 years, yet I could not get over how I felt. I could not get over how huge Mean Joe Greene appeared. I had met and interviewed the likes of Joe DiMaggio, Joe Louis and Joe Namath, yet I was standing there staring at Joe Greene like he was a giant from another planet.

Then came Mel Blount, Lynn Swann, Terry Bradshaw, Jack Ham, Jack Lambert, Donnie Shell, Franco Harris, Mike Webster, Mike Wagner, Dwight White, Larry Brown, Steve Furness, John Banaszak, J.T. Thomas, and it was something to see. So many outstanding players. I had covered and interviewed Wilt Chamberlain and Julius Erving, Muhammad Ali and Joe Frazier, Jimmy Connors and Billie Jean King, Bobby Hull and Jean Beliveau, Willie Mosconi and Minnesota Fats, Willie Hartack and Eddie Arcaro, Ted Williams and Mickey Mantle, and thought I had become a big-time professional, too cool to get too excited about this sort of stuff. Yet I felt like a little kid in the presence of the Pittsburgh Steelers. Some of the newcomers to the team, I was to learn in researching this book, felt the same way. Deep down inside, I think some of the other sportswriters felt that way, too.

1

Those Steelers I saw that day had worn the ring. The Super Bowl ring, the symbol of being the best there was in the National Football League. They had a passion to succeed again. That summer scene still runs on in my head like a movie that never stops.

I had watched these super Steelers many times on TV, even caught them in person a few times over the years while covering Monday Night Football, which was my beat one year at *The New York Post*, and when they played the Giants or the Jets, but this was somehow different.

I will always remember those Super Bowl Steelers streaming out of that locker room and snaking their way down the hillside to get their pictures taken. Whenever I am at the Steelers' camp, I can still conjure up that image. And I do not even have to close my eyes to do so.

To do this book, I visited many of those Steelers who filed out of that locker room that day, and found out where they are and what they are doing now, what their struggles and successes have been since their glory days with the Steelers.

I have come to them from a different perspective than when we had last spoken. We were not worried about the next game, the next test, who they were lining up against, the next deadline. We were looking back, and reflecting upon what we had experienced, what we had learned. I wanted their personal reflections, what they had gained from it, the highlights, the disappointments. We had lived a little longer, and learned a little more.

I re-read Roger Kahn's great book, "The Boys of Summer," as a guideline. He had covered the great Brooklyn Dodgers teams of the '50s as a beat reporter for just two seasons, to my surprise on this second reading, less than half as much as I had covered the Steelers on a daily basis. Whereas he visited only certain players from the Dodgers' best days, I decided I also wanted to interview some players who had joined the team when it went into decline after all those Super Bowl successes, and some of today's players, to get insights into what it was like to play in the shadows of Terry Bradshaw, Franco Harris, Joe Greene, Jack Ham, Jack Lambert and Mel Blount, and be held up to their standards. I wanted the book to deal with today, the contemporary Steelers' scene, so it would be as relevant as possible.

I learned so much from talking to the Steelers who have played at Three Rivers Stadium, who have contributed to the successes and failures for the past 20 years. I learned so much that I did not know when I was reporting on the team for *The Pittsburgh Press*. It was an adventure, an educational experience. I learned how they leaned on each other so much, how they needed support systems, how they were afraid to fail, how they worried so much about their status at the start and finish of their careers, and sometimes in between. There was a spiritual side to the Steelers, which might surprise some who think only in terms of the latest odds, and how often the Steelers beat the spread.

They spoke about their teammates and told stories they had never disclosed publicly before. They related stories about behind-the-scenes incidents, in-the-locker room exchanges, and disclosed secrets, such as players who were long at odds with one another, or the coaches. Some were stormy, some were telling sad stories, some were outrageous. None was boring. I went through their files at the Steelers' offices to make sure I did not miss anything, and I was pleased when I did not find any traces of the anecdotes and tales they were telling me now. They seemed more relaxed, more honest with their feelings, and they were not afraid of what their coaches might say if they saw these opinions expressed on paper. They spoke, for instance, of their respect as well as their disenchantment with Chuck Noll, the only coach these Steelers had known at Three Rivers Stadium. I wanted this book to be upbeat and positive, but I also wanted it to be balanced and fair. Some of them made some remarkable decisions and did some unique things in their youth that helped you to understand how they grew and matured in such a special manner. Most of all, they seemed determined to make you aware that they were more than just football players.

It helped you understand what was so special about those Steelers of the Super Bowl era, what they had in common. So many of them grew up the hard way, but benefitted from having supportive parents, two parents in most cases. Both parents usually worked, not in the yuppie sense, but because they had to in order to make ends meet. Some of the parents had several jobs. So did the Steelers when they were youngsters. Many of them had responsibilities, chores to look after. They learned about teamwork early. Many of them made sacrifices along with their families. Many of them came from large families. Many of them were caring individuals. Most came from strong spiritual backgrounds, where the families went to church regularly, and it was an important part of their lives. It still is. Many of them overcame adversity while they were with the Steelers. Many of them have been successful since they retired as ballplayers and got on with what Noll has always referred to as "their life's work." Many of them are great role models.

It is interesting to study how these men responded to challenges in their lives. What motivated these people to such a high level of performance? How have they sustained that performance? They can teach you how to successfully compete in all phases of life.

It made you realize how superficial the usual coverage of a club, any club in sports, often is because of the different focus, the emphasis on the outcome of the next contest, the won-loss column, the latest statistics, the latest injury list, the latest draft signings, the latest opinions expressed on sports talk shows, the reluctance to get into any subject that is too deep or too sensitive, or too close to home.

Some of the interviews were so intense I came away emotionally exhausted. I learned, the hard way, that I should not interview two ballplayers in the same day. Sometimes it was like group therapy, and there was just myself and one of the Steelers sharing stories.

Hopefully, the reader will learn something about life and teamwork from this book. It is more about life than it is about football. It is an up-close and personal look at one of the greatest sports teams of all time. It should give you some revealing insights into the real Steelers of Three Rivers Stadium. They were brothers in black and gold.

"You think about that team," Joe Greene once said to Bob Oates, Jr., a sportswriter from Los Angeles. "There were some first-class men playing for the Pittsburgh Steelers. Take Jack Ham — I'd trust him implicitly in any sort of dealing. Or Blount. Or Harris, or Swann, or Kolb, or Webster, or L.C., or White, or Donnie Shell. You can just keep naming them. They were men of character.

"That was the reason we were able to survive at the top of a very competitive game. We did not have the type of guys that were going to punch the time clock before the game was over. Nobody was looking for any freebies. It was a tremendous experience to be part of that group. We had some very upstanding gentlemen on the Pittsburgh Steelers ballclub."

Swann, who played ball in Los Angeles for the University of Southern California, and grew up in San Mateo, was eager to convince another Californian about the merits of his adopted city.

"One thing I've really enjoyed is the fact that the team has always been a strong part of the city. We are Pittsburgh's Steelers, not just some team with the name of a city. And another thing that I'll keep longer and cherish more than anything is the warmth and friendship and the strength of character of this team."

Oates reminded Swann that Greene had said something like that.

"It's a powerful thing," said Swann. "I consider it an extraordinary privilege to have been able to know these people. It's been so encouraging, so satisfying, to see guys grow and develop, to see people who have always been good become even better. Pittsburgh is a special town, and the Steelers are a special team."

Christopher Passodelis, one of Pittsburgh's biggest boosters, has been a fan of the Steelers and Pirates and Pitt teams throughout his life. He is a mover and shaker, with interests in the restaurant, insurance and real estate development business.

He is close to Andy Russell, Mike Wagner, Rocky Bleier, Mel Blount, Sam Davis, Ray Mansfield and so many other Steelers. He was a great admirer of Art Rooney. There is a spectacular view from his Christopher's Restaurant, high above Grandview Avenue on Mt. Washington, and he often finds himself staring through the gleaming windows at the city and the three rivers and the stadium below. Passodelis is a wise Greek philosopher and historian.

"It was like a happening," said Passodelis of that period in the '70s. "Something special and different was going on here. It's unlikely to ever happen again. It was like an Irish rainbow. I can remember seeing a rainbow one day stretching from downtown Pittsburgh to Three Rivers Stadium right before they won their second back-to-back Super

4

Bowl. The Steelers pulled Pittsburgh together. We have more ethnic groups here than anywhere else, yet we were all one behind this football team. It melded us. We were all citizens of the City of Champions. People came early to the stadium, and they had their cookouts, and they stayed late. They didn't want to go home. Our football team was fun and it made us smile.

"The Steelers have been diplomats for this city. They have represented the city with such great pride. And they loved each other. I remember Franco picked up the tab for a retirement party for Joe Greene here at Christopher's. They showed some highlight films of when they were playing. I saw these massive men crying, watching films of their youth, when they were so great. And they're still so great."

Three Rivers Stadium

5

Bruce Van Dyke, Ray Mansfield and Larry Gagner in 1969.

Ray Mansfield
"Ol' Ranger" rounds up Class of '78

Sunday came up cool and windy and it was not the kind of day when you would want to be hosting a big party in a big tent. The sky over Pittsburgh kept changing from bright and sunny to dark and gray, darker and grayer than usual. The Monongahela River was muddier than usual. Ray Mansfield frowned as he studied the scene. It was before noon and the party was to start at 5 o'clock. Mansfield fretted.

"Gawd, those rain clouds look ominous," he observed.

He stood in an opening of the Melody Tent at Station Square this Sunday, June 10, 1990, and watched as the workers from Bobby Rubino's and Subway set up barbeque grills and hero sandwich stations out of cover. He could see pennants and flags flapping in a frenzy on the Gateway Clipper sternwheeler moored nearby.

"Why today? Why me?" Mansfield must have wondered.

Mansfield, who played center in the National Football League for 14 seasons, one with the Philadelphia Eagles (1963), and 13 for the Pittsburgh Steelers (1964-76) and still holds the Steelers' record for consecutive games played (182), felt like he did when he was snapping for a punt and looked up and saw a scowling Dick Butkus of the Chicago Bears looming over him.

People responsible for graduation parties and proms, weddings, reunions and outdoor picnics that same weekend knew how Mansfield felt. June seemed hell-bent on matching May for record rainfall and cool temperatures.

Mansfield and his business partner, Chuck Puskar, their staff and a group of volunteer workers had put together a Steelers' reunion, bringing back many of the members of the 1978 Super Bowl championship squad thought to be maybe the best NFL team of all time, plus other former black and gold veterans.

The schedule included this Sunday night get-together, a chance for fans to mingle with their favorite Steelers, and an NFL Alumni golf tournament the following day at the Oakmont Country Club. Mansfield also raced out to Oakmont that same Sunday morning, checking out last minute details.

It was all for a good cause, the Sudden Infant Death Syndrome (SIDS) Foundation of Western Pennsylvania. Mansfield, the mover and shaker behind the Pittsburgh chapter of the NFL Alumni, was the tournament director.

"That's what I'm really worried about," said Mansfield, the furrows in his brow as deep as the once-infamous sand traps or bunkers of Oakmont's championship course.

There had been some snafus in lining up the alumni for the events, and most of the publicity had centered around the negative news that Terry Bradshaw, who was to be a featured guest, would not be coming back to kiss and make up with Pittsburgh and its fans.

Bradshaw had been advertised as one of the returning heroes, the tickets referred to an "Evening with Terry Bradshaw," after Bradshaw's personal secretary had said he would be here. But Mansfield, weeks earlier, had felt in his arthritic bones — like a river captain on the Gateway Clipper fleet can predict when it will rain — that Bradshaw would not show up. "It's too bad," he said. "Terry ought to be here. He was a big part of all this."

It reminded me of something another blond bomber from the Southwest once said while in retirement. Bobby Layne, who quarterbacked the Steelers (1958-62), said, "What I miss most is the guys."

Mansfield's mouth broke into a thin smile under his broad walrus mustache. "I just hope the other guys show up," he said. "I hope the fans show up."

A few days earlier, Mansfield sat behind his desk in his office at Diversified Group Brokerage of Pittsburgh, which offers insurance and group health plans, at a building on South Central Avenue in Canonsburg and made one phone call after another to try to get everybody together. A huge mural of John Wayne provided the background. The decor could best be described as early western, as the "Ol' Ranger" rounded up his former teammates.

"You have to call and remind them," offered Mansfield. "Athletes are tough to deal with. They're unreliable. I've always known that."

Why does Mansfield do this every year? This was the 11th golf tournament he has organized at Oakmont, all for SIDS, ever since Bryan Patrick Puskar, the three-month old son of his partner, died inexplainedly in his crib in 1976.

"He enjoys it," said Ray's wife, Janet, an energetic soul herself. "It's doing something nice for a group. He likes groups. Besides, no one else will do it. He enjoys the challenge of it."

The Melody Tent and the fans proved to be as durable as Mansfield was as a ballplayer and as formidable and strong as the "Steel Curtain" defense in its heyday — only a few rain drops leaked through the tent later in the day during a hard but brief storm — and the event turned out fine. The food and drink and company were all-pro.

There were some disappointments, for sure. A relentless rock band made sure nobody could talk to anybody, and some notable Steelers were not there — Franco Harris was in Italy with his mother and Joe Greene got lost somewhere — and the weather was shaky all day.

But some of "the best of the best" showed up, such as L.C. Greenwood, Rocky Bleier, Mike Webster, Sam Davis, Moon Mullins, Jon Kolb, Mike Wagner, Steve Courson and Roy Gerela. Stars from other years were also on hand, such as Hall of Famer John Henry Johnson, Andy Russell, John "Frenchy" Fuqua, Bob Kohrs, Bill Hurley, Rick Woods, Lloyd Voss and John Reger.

Some had new kids, some had new wives and new girl friends. Some had new stories, most had old stories.

One fan asked Fuqua a question he has been asked umpteen times. "Did you touch the ball on Bradshaw's pass that ended up as the Immaculate Reception for Franco, or did Jack Tatum (the Raiders' defensive back) touch it first?" Back then, the rules would have nullified Franco's catch if the ball was tipped by Fuqua rather than Tatum. Now that's OK.

Fuqua did not fumble the question this time, either. He just smiled and replied, "Somebody touched it."

Ted Petersen, who has been living in Bridgeville for quite awhile now, had recently been named the head football coach at Washington's Trinity High School after serving as an assistant coach at Canon-McMillan High School.

J.T. Thomas of Monroeville and Larry Brown of Carnegie were looking forward to opening their new restaurant, Applebee's, in Green Tree's Bourse Shops, the next day.

John Banaszak, who lives in Peters Township, told teammates why he sold his string of speedy auto service outlets, and about his latest business ventures. Banaszak also talked about Mansfield, a fixture in Upper St. Clair.

"I'm sure this is all a labor of love for him," said Banaszak, who enjoys these get-togethers. "I'd have to question whether I could donate that much time and effort to this. I've run a golf tournament and I know the sacrifices involved."

Bleier put it this way: "The role the Ol' Ranger played and continues to play is that of the historian and storyteller about our teams. He is the keeper of the memories. He was the offensive leader of our team the way Andy Russell was the defensive leader of our team. He settled down the young players. And he's still looking after us."

As Steelers' veteran play-by-play announcer Jack Fleming, who was there with his family from Mt. Lebanon, was introducing the players to an enthusiastic crowd of about 1,000 Steeler die-hards, he said, "I hope I didn't miss anyone. I'm not responsible for this list."

At that point, only one former Steeler had not been introduced on stage. From the wings, Mansfield slipped through a crack in the Steelers' lineup, and made his way to the microphone. "You forgot me!" he said. "But I didn't forget me!"

Mansfield played football for 25 years, and never missed a game. No matter how banged up he was, he played, in junior high, high school, in college and in 13 seasons with the Steelers.

Mansfield, a popular after-dinner and business workshop/seminar speaker, loves to spell out his list of injuries. They include broken ribs, broken fingers, broken thumbs, broken neck bones, torn rib cartilage, stretched knee ligaments, mangled hands, numb arms and ankles swollen twice their normal size. None of them could keep him off the field.

Mansfield and his best buddy, Andy Russell, both turned 50 early in 1991. It was hard for anyone who followed their careers to accept that. Mansfield did not feel 50, for sure. Then again, there were days he felt much older.

9

He has been told he has the neck of a 90-year old man and can't play tennis with neighbors, though he would love to, because his shoulders hurt so badly afterward. It is not worth it. The iron man has grown old and fragile. And nobody, according to Andy Russell and Jack Ham, loves to compete more than Mansfield.

Russell says Mansfield came from a difficult environment as a youngster. Mansfield tells stories about his youth, when his family moved from Arizona to California to Washington, looking for work picking fruit. He tells stories that sound right out of John Steinbeck's "The Grapes of Wrath," riding around in the back of a flatbed truck as his folks looked for the next field where they needed a few more hired hands. So Mansfield enjoyed the good life of professional football. It was easier than picking fruit, and a lot more rewarding. Mansfield missed it more than most when he had to hang up his cleats.

"I had a lot of withdrawal problems," Mansfield admitted, when discussing how difficult it had been for him to retire from pro football. "Nothing I ever did was as satisfying as playing football. I think we all go through some emotional problems the first couple of years (after retiring). Sometimes players don't like to admit that."

Mansfield played in 182 consecutive games, still a Steelers' record. Even Chuck Noll couldn't keep Mansfield off the field.

In the 1971 finale, Noll had claimed Bobby Maples off waivers from the Houston Oilers and started him at center.

Mansfield told a funny story to Steve Hubbard of *The Pittsburgh Press* for a story in August of 1986 when Mike Webster was nearing Mansfield's consecutive game record, but eventually came up short.

"I sat on the bench, no special teams, no nothing," said Mansfield. "I had about 120 games in my streak and I started getting nervous, so I put myself in on special teams without his permission.

"I just went in on the kickoff return team and for an extra point. I told the guy, 'I'm coming in to relieve you,' and he didn't know any better. I don't think Chuck noticed. Coaches don't give a damn about those streaks, especially Chuck, but to a player in them, they're important.

"I broke a rib when I cut-blocked John Matuszak in 1973. In '74, (Jon) Kolb and (Lyle) Alzado fell on me, my knee went forward, my body went back, and I stretched some ligaments.

"I had a broken transverse process in my neck; that's the bony projection in the back of your neck. That was the year I had a lot of pain and numbness down my left arm whenever I hit somebody. I didn't know about it until the next year when I went to Latrobe Hospital and asked what was wrong and they said, 'Nothing but this old break'. I think that was '72.

"I had hundreds of minor stuff that hurt like heck, but you play through them. I had a thumb so bad, I thought Joe Greene broke it off. I couldn't open a door, but I could slam into defensive linemen all day. I split cartilage in my ribs; I couldn't laugh, couldn't do anything. I'd have to hold my breath while I was hitting people.

10

"Webster's first year, I sprained my ankle and he came in and stuffed the nose tackle. My ankle was dark blue and twice the normal size, but I knew if I didn't get out there, I'd never get back in. It hurt so bad afterward that night, I couldn't put (bed) covers on it.

"But I wanted to be out there every play. I never wanted to be off the field. Even if we were crushing a team, I wanted to be out there."

Ray Mansfield, as president of Pittsburgh chapter of the NFL Alumni Association, presents team president Dan Rooney with $5,000 check for the Art Rooney Memorial Scholarship Fund following annual NFL Alumni golf tournament at Oakmont.

Canton, Ohio
Home of the Pro Football Hall of Fame

Canton, Ohio is a mid-size midwestern city without tall buildings that has been somewhat bypassed by progress if not inner city highways. It takes special pride in being the birthplace of professional football, so to speak, and the home of the Pro Football Hall of Fame, which you can see while speeding along I-77. Its population is about 90,000, down from a high of 120,000 some years ago.

Its claim as the birthplace of pro football, by the way, is hotly disputed by people who follow the Steelers back at St. Vincent College in Latrobe, and by others from Pittsburgh proper.

After all, one of the first displays one sees upon entering the Pro Football Hall of Fame is that featuring a photograph of Dr. John K. Brallier, a dentist who was paid the munificent sum of $10 plus expenses to play quarterback for the Latrobe A.C. in a game against a sandlot team from nearby Jeannette back in 1895 and, for many years, he was thought to be the first professional football player. The Latrobe team was sponsored by the local YMCA who hired Brallier when he was a 16-year-old student at Indiana Normal (now Indiana State University of Pennsylvania) to play for their team. Other members of the team were on some sort of profit sharing basis —probably a split of the collection taken among spectators. They beat Jeannette, 12-0.

There is a plaque referring to this event at Latrobe Stadium, where the Steelers have scrimmaged other NFL teams in recent seasons.

The Timken Roller Bearing Company made the most important donation of $100,000 to get the Pro Football Hall of Fame off the boards and into a bona fide building in Canton. Ironically enough, Timken now has a plant in Latrobe.

In 1960, however, a man named Nelson Ross visited the offices of Pittsburgh Steelers executive Dan Rooney and presented him with a 49-page research paper in which it was determined that William "Pudge" Heffelfinger — not Brallier — was the first pro.

The Ross paper detailed many events that led up to a football game played on November 12, 1892 between two Pittsburgh amateur teams, the Allegheny Athletic Association and the Pittsburgh Athletic Club. According to Ross, this was the game in which Heffelfinger became the first pro. He was paid $250 to play by the Allegheny team. That was a lot of money when you consider that Johnny Unitas was paid just $7 a game to play for a Pittsburgh semi-pro team in 1955. The Pro Football Hall of Fame now recognizes Heffelfinger as the first pro.

Possibly encouraged by the success of Latrobe and the Pittsburgh clubs, additional professional football teams began to pop up in the East. The more successful included the Duquesnes of Pittsburgh, the Olympics of McKeesport and the Orange A.C. of Newark, New Jersey. It wasn't until 1920 that the Huppmobile Agency in Canton enters history as the meeting place of the founders of the American Professional

Pudge Heffelfinger

Football Association, including George Halas. Eleven teams came up with the $100 membership fee and they included the Canton Bulldogs.

In any case, Canton takes its role as the birthplace of the first real professional football league quite seriously, and gets tremendous community support to stage its special week, when pro football fans, especially those in nearby Pittsburgh and Cleveland, come to participate in the parties and celebrations surrounding the induction of each year's class into the Pro Football Hall of Fame. Canton gets cleaned up pretty good, but somehow it is like polishing and shining old shoes once too many times and the luster is lost. The people of Canton put on their best faces for the big show, however, and they make good things and good times happen.

"There are some great, great football players here tonight," first-year National Football League commissioner Paul Tagliabue would say at a dinner in the Canton Civic Center on the eve of the induction ceremonies. "This is fun.

"Pete Rozelle used to say the two greatest weekends of the NFL season were the Super Bowl and the Hall of Fame. When I was coming here today, when I thought about the Pro Football Hall of Fame, I thought about Jack Lambert and Franco Harris and I had to think about The Chief, Art Rooney. Memories . . . these people make you think of other people . . . the memories roll upon the memories."

Earlier that day, Friday, August 3, 1990, I was standing on a corner in Canton, trying to catch the spirit and enthusiasm of the city on its big weekend, wanting to catch the local sights and sounds and smells, to discover a little more about the heart and soul of this town that reminded me so much of McKeesport, my wife's hometown, or other industrial communities back home in Western Pennsylvania — Homestead, Ambridge, Charleroi, Aliquippa, Midland, Hazelwood, Monessen, Monongahela, Braddock, Rankin, Uniontown, Johnstown — that are poorer because the action and active steel mills and allied industries have moved elsewhere, leaving too many empty downtown department stores, too many tired storefronts, too many young people and old people standing on street corners and in strip malls, and too few jobs in a tough transition period.

This particular corner was at the intersection of Third Street and Cleveland Avenue. The parade through the city that precedes the induction ceremonies takes place on Cleveland Avenue. It was set for 7:30 the next morning. Imagine people getting up that early to see a parade. But, as I would discover, there would be early-birds arriving about 1:30 a.m. to stake claim to the best seats in the bleachers that are put up along the parade route that leads to the Pro Football Hall of Fame.

I was standing alongside the downtown branch of the Carnegie Library. On the other corners were the police station, the Federal Building, and the Ohio Power Building. It was the latter that caught my eye. The building was surrounded by a display celebrating the special week. It read "A Touch of Class," which was the theme for 1990. In front

14

of the building were larger-than-life black-and-white placards of the players and coach who were to be inducted the next day into the Hall of Fame. Pictured to the right of the main entrance was Tom Landry, the only coach the Dallas Cowboys had known in the first 29 years of their existence.

On the other side of the stairway was Jack Lambert of the Steelers, menacing as ever. Between Lambert and Landry, over the doorway, was a mural depicting the legendary likes of Jim Thorpe, Red Grange, Bronko Nagurski and George Halas. A banner read "The Legends Go On and On. . ." I wondered how Lambert might feel if he were standing where I was standing, seeing himself alongside Jim Thorpe, Red Grange, Bronko Nagurski and George Halas, four of the most famous football greats of all time. Could Lambert have imagined such a sight in his wildest dreams back in nearby Mantua, Ohio? He had come to Canton as a kid. He was fascinated by its football atmosphere. He liked seeing all the football stars on display, their plaques, their likenesses, their bronzed busts. Now he was there with Thorpe and Grange — the "Carlisle Indian" and "The Galloping Ghost" — and Nagurski and Halas — "Bronko" and "Papa Bear." That is the beauty of Canton, the company you are keeping.

The faces of the former pro football greats positively beam from the time they hit town till they leave, and so do their many admirers who show up to share in their glory. It puts a special glow on the city. A sunny day helps.

Standing outside the Civic Center, waiting for a big dinner and more Hall of Fame festivities to start, I found myself rubbing shoulders with George McAfee, a great running back for the Chicago Bears under George Halas. McAfee reminded me of my dad, and he did not look much bigger. McAfee, I learned later, was 72. He had been listed as 6-0, 177, from Ironton, Ohio, and had been a great breakaway runner. He had shrunk a few inches in the interim.

Nearby was Dante Lavelli — what a great name — who had been such a gifted receiver for Ohio State University and the Cleveland Browns. He had been one of Otto Graham's favorite targets for so many years, along with Mac Speedie and Dub Jones.

There was Eddie Robinson, the legendary coach of the football team at Grambling College, who was in Canton, no doubt, to witness the induction of one of his former players, Buck Buchanan, who went on to become a great defensive lineman for the Kansas City Chiefs.

Seeing two of Buchanan's former teammates, Bobby Bell and Lenny Dawson, brought back memories of my one-year (1965) stint at the U.S. Army Home Town News Center in Kansas City, Missouri where I spent many Sundays that fall in the press box at Municipal Stadium spotting and providing stats for network TV announcers Charley Jones and Paul Christman. The Chiefs were one of the best teams in the American Football League back then. Five years later, when they defeated the Minnesota Vikings in the Super Bowl, they proved they were one of the best teams in all of pro football. I covered that game, at Tulane Stadium in New Orleans, for *The Miami News*.

15

Seeing Bob Griese, the non-plussed general of the Miami Dolphins, did the same. I spent one year (1969) in Miami covering the Dolphins, shortly after they and the Chiefs had come into a merged National Football League, and they posted a 3-10-1 record under George Wilson. I left the next year for New York and *The New York Post*. The Dolphins, under Don Shula, went 10-4 and then began a reign as one of pro football's greatest teams, winning two of three Super Bowls in which they played in the early '70s, and posting the only perfect (17-0) season in NFL history.

So this was a special weekend. I had watched up close and interviewed and shared some special moments — good and bad — in the lives of Lambert and Harris, two of the Steelers I had reported on from 1979 to 1983 for *The Pittsburgh Press*, and Buchanan and Griese. Ted Hendricks, the linebacker for the Baltimore Colts, Green Bay Packers and Oakland Raiders, was a contemporary. Bob St. Clair of the San Francisco 49ers was a bubble gum card from my childhood come to life in Canton. He was 6-6 and bigger than anybody else in pro football back in the '50s, and he ate raw meat. I would never forget that note on the back of his bubble gum card. And Landry had been an especially surprising and pleasant interview through the years, not at all like the stern, unfeeling fellow with the stiff hat and stiff demeanor he appeared to be on TV when the Cowboys were celebrated as "America's Team," and were on TV more than any other NFL team.

When you go to a sports hall of fame, whether it is in Canton or Cooperstown — where the Baseball Hall of Fame is located — or Springfield, Massachusetts, the birthplace of basketball, you go on a journey into your own past as well as whatever sport is featured. That is the fun of it.

Exhibits, busts and films have different meanings to different people. It is like entering a time machine.

It is exciting stuff to see pros you watched or had an opportunity to interview, as well as your old bubble gum card collection come alive before you, at the dinner at the Canton Civic Center on the eve of the induction.

Among those introduced were Herb Adderly, Bobby Bell, George Connor, Bill Dudley, Weeb Ewbank, Tom Fears, Frank Gatski, Frank Gifford, Lou Groza, Lamar Hunt, John Henry Johnson, Deacon Jones, Dick "Night Train" Lane, Willie Lanier, Bob Lilly, Hugh McElhenny, Ray Nitschke, Jim Otto, Pete Pihos, Gale Sayers and Gene Upshaw. Two former roommates on the Steelers, Joe Greene and Mel Blount, showed up the next day for the induction ceremonies.

When former pro football star and ABC-TV analyst Dan Dierdorf introduced Steelers' president Dan Rooney, he offered, "We're going to need a new wing for his team at the Hall of Fame . . . there are so many Steelers in there." Canton is Dierdorf's hometown.

It is a place where the bands play songs like "God Bless America" and "Stars and Stripes Forever," and "Battle Hymn of The Republic."

And those bands might be from high schools in such storied towns as Masillon, East Palestine, Warren, Alliance and Canton.

Canton's citizens turn out strong for the annual activities. Each year the new enshrinees are honored at an extravaganza dubbed "Football's Greatest Weekend." There's a game that kicks off the NFL's pre-season schedule that draws a capacity crowd to Fawcett Stadium, right next to the Hall of Fame.

A middle-aged woman who identified herself as being from Alliance, Ohio, said she had gone to high school with Hall of Famer Lenny Dawson. "I wasn't part of the jock crowd, so he wouldn't know me," she said. "I wasn't part of the college crowd. I was just in between, nothing special."

About 40,000 swarm into downtown Canton to enjoy a Ribs Burn-off, and over 200,000 turn out for the fireworks show and concert. Thousands — it's a tough ticket — turn out for the Mayor's Breakfast and Fashion Show Luncheon. The Enshrinees Civic Dinner, on the eve of the induction, attracts more than 3,000. The Festival Parade, which precedes the induction, is watched by over 200,000 people. They bring in the stars of TV soaps and sitcoms to appear in the events. Norman Fell, the ornery neighbor in "Three's Company," was the grand marshal of the 1990 parade. It was one big soap opera.

Honored players have been known to break down and cry at the enshrinement ceremonies on the Hall of Fame steps, with crowds of 10,000 in attendance, even more when some Steelers are inducted. Then you would think you were in Pittsburgh.

The local daily newspaper, *The Repository*, was celebrating its 175th anniversary, and sponsored a float in the parade. On the front page of its sports page, there was a story about a local favorite, Percy Snow, a former star of the Canton McKinley Bulldogs, and more recently an All-American at Michigan State University.

The story was about his holdout from the Kansas City Chiefs. He was their No. 1 draft choice, and thought to be a real stud at linebacker, but he was balking about the $600,000 per year the Chiefs were offering him. I wondered what Lambert would think when he saw that story. Lambert held out one summer camp to get a contract for more than $100,000 and created a real stink. What are the odds that Percy Snow will be coming to his hometown someday to be inducted into the Pro Football Hall of Fame?

The only Canton native ever to be so honored was Alan Page of the Minnesota Vikings, a tremendous success story. A Notre Dame graduate, Page is now a practicing attorney, and he continues to remain involved in civic activities in his hometown. Marion Motley, a bruising fullback and linebacker for the Cleveland Browns, grew up in Canton, and is also honored in its Hall of Fame.

Bob Stewart, the sports editor of *The Canton Repository,* saw Motley and Page playing pro football. He had been on the sportsbeat in Canton for 33 years when the paper was celebrating its 175th birthday.

He went to West Virginia University and is a fan of the Cleveland Browns. I have a neighbor like that, Jim Hesse, and I get claustrophobic when I am in Hesse's home, with all those WVU and Browns pennants, posters and memorabilia all about the family room and game room. Stewart smiled when I told him about my neighbor, an executive at Wheeling-Pittsburgh Steel.

"You're a Pitt guy and you grew up with the Steelers, so you wouldn't understand," said Stewart.

Asked about economic conditions in Canton, Stewart said, "It's better than Youngstown. We're better off than Youngstown because it was almost completely dependent on steel. Canton is a blue collar community, supported over the years by the Timken Roller Bearing Company, and the Ford Motor Co., Republic Steel, which is now LTV, the Hoover Company. It's mostly basic industry, and now it's a little more diversified. In some ways, we were like a smaller version of Pittsburgh.

"I remember Pittsburgh when it was called, and justifiably so, the Smoky City. You couldn't see across the rivers. There was no Golden Triangle or Point State Park then."

Asked to describe the scene in Canton when one or two of the Steelers are inducted into the Pro Football Hall of Fame, Stewart said, "They're dancing in the streets, like on Super Bowl Sunday, when the Steelers make it.

"The Steeler fans are something else. I have a great love for them. When I was growing up in West Virginia, I was a Steeler and Pirate fan. I remember when Jock Sutherland was the coach, and they used the single-wing formation. I remember when John Michelosen succeeded Sutherland as coach. I remember when Fran Rogel played.

"But Steeler fans have been a little hard to live with in Canton in recent years. They don't quite treat it like a Browns' game, but it's close. They tend to take over the enshrinement.

"They come down the night before, or early in the morning — it's only a hundred miles away — so they start showing up at the Hall around 8 a.m. That's when the commotion starts.

"For Pittsburgh, it's a holiday. Canton people, for the most part, are Browns' fans. When the Browns play in the Hall of Fame game it's a tough ticket. They sell out for all the Hall of Fame games, but it wasn't always that way. They used to draw about 9,000 fans to Fawcett Stadium for it back in the early '60s, and a week or two later they'd draw 20,000 for a high school all-star game."

Stewart covered the Browns and traveled with them for several years, and he has seen the Steelers-Browns rivalry up close in both cities. "It's pretty intense," he said.

So it was double trouble in the summer of 1990 as the Browns were playing the Chicago Bears in the Hall of Fame game, which attracted all the Browns' fans to the city. The night before, everybody in the streets seemed to be wearing either Browns or Steelers jerseys.

18

"Art Rooney and the Bears all voted to have the Hall of Fame in Canton," recalled Stewart. "I don't know if Mr. Rooney's friends in Latrobe ever forgave him for that."

Chris Berman and Tom Jackson were in town with the ESPN crew, and Jackson seemed eager to share a story about a visit to the Steelers' offices at Three Rivers Stadium to do a feature before the Hall of Fame induction ceremonies.

"I was so excited about seeing Mr. Rooney's office, which is now a library," said Jackson, a former standout performer for the Denver Broncos, a linebacker who once intercepted Terry Bradshaw in a major upset of the two-time Super Bowl champion Steelers in the first round of the playoffs back in 1977. "There's a big portrait of him, and the secretary showed me that if you stand in a certain place with the light just so it looks like he's in the room now. It's a reflection.

"One of the things about the game of football is that you gain a respect for other people. It's always amazed me how so many players I met have felt the way they do about Mr. Rooney. I've talked to players and they have said, 'Hey, the Hall of Fame is a great honor, and the Super Bowls were great, but the thing I'll cherish the most was playing for Art Rooney.'

"I always wondered what it would be like to play for a team and a guy who bought the team and kept it all those years. There were 40 some years of mostly losing seasons, and now Mr. Rooney is known as one of the great winners of all time. It was just a thrill for me to be in the same room where he had worked, and to see all those pictures."

Pro Football Hall of Fame

19

Art Rooney, Lenny Dawson and Purdue coach Bill Daddio after 1957 NFL draft.

1987 Hall of Fame Class included, left to right front row, Larry Csonka, Lenny Dawson, Don Maynard and, rear, Joe Greene, Jim Langer, John Henry Johnson and Gene Upshaw.

20

Lenny Dawson
"Their defense could shake you up"

L enny Dawson stood in the center of the Canton Civic Center and spoke at length with George Young. Dawson was still a handsome figure at age 55, with dark brown hair combed perfect, as always. He still looks like a college coverboy. Like Dick Clark, he looked like he had just come off the studio set he shares each week during the season with Nick Buoniconti on HBO's NFL Report. Young, by contrast, is a huge man, a Charles Dickens' character, a bald-headed roly-poly playful sort, who is the general manager of the New York Giants and a key factor in returning the Giants to glory again.

Both Dawson and Young have close ties with the Pittsburgh Steelers. Dawson was the Steelers' No. 1 draft pick out of Purdue in 1957, and spent three seasons as a reserve with the Steelers. Young was a scout for many years, going back to his days with the Baltimore Colts, and remains close friends with Art Rooney, Jr., who once headed the Steelers' scouting department. Young and Rooney were frequent companions on the road, especially at college all-star games. Dawson and Young are both fond of the Steelers' front-office people.

Dawson symbolizes all that was wrong with the Steelers before Chuck Noll came along in 1969. In Kansas City, Dawson will always be considered a great quarterback. In Pittsburgh, he remains a Steelers' mistake, one of many in those days.

The Steelers won a coin flip with the Cleveland Browns before the 1957 draft to get a crack at the first pick. Both teams wanted Dawson. Walt Kiesling chose Dawson. The Browns had to settle for Jim Brown. All three parties found their way to the Pro Football Hall of Fame. Kiesling did not make it, however, on the strength of his wisdom for getting rid of Johnny Unitas. Dawson sat on the bench for Buddy Parker who came in from Detroit as the coach of the Steelers.

Dawson was inducted into the Pro Football Hall of Fame in 1987 in a class that included John Henry Johnson and Joe Greene of the Steelers. Dawson had grown up in nearby Alliance, and he was the seventh son of a seventh son, so there was a big crowd with just his relatives alone. Plus, he had played for the Browns early in his career, after his stint with the Steelers, so he had plenty of support from the local fans.

In Canton in the summer of 1990, Dawson was wearing a corn-yellow blazer, the kind worn by all the members of the Pro Football Hall of Fame when they come back to Canton. He was one of the best. He had come a long way since he was a seldom-used Steelers' backup for Earl Morrall and Bobby Layne.

I used to see Dawson play with the Chiefs when I was stationed at the U.S. Army Home Town News Center in Kansas City during the 1965 season. Roger Valdiserri, who became the assistant director of athletics at Notre Dame and oversaw the school's award-winning sports information department, was the publicity director of the Chiefs that year. He was from Belle Vernon, and was a long-time friend of Beano

Cook, with whom I had worked as a student sportswriter at the University of Pittsburgh. So Valdiserri put me to work in the Chiefs' press box, spotting for network TV announcers Charlie Jones and Paul Christman. I would come back home to Pittsburgh and I would stop in the Steelers' offices, then in the Roosevelt Hotel, and I would tell them about how good the Chiefs were in the American Football League.

Art Rooney and Fran Fogarty, the team's business manager, would smile at me — a young punk sports writer home on leave, and what did I know? — and I remember on one visit that Bill Burns, a good friend of Rooney and a fixture on KDKA-TV as a news anchorman for over 30 years, was also present. I mentioned Dawson, and Burns said, "How good could he be? We got rid of him!"

"Hey, that doesn't mean anything!" I answered smartly. "You got rid of Johnny Unitas, too. So that's not the bottom line."

In those days, the Chiefs included Buck Buchanan, Willie Lanier, Bobby Bell — who have all made it to the Pro Football Hall of Fame — and Johnny Robinson, Wendell Hayes, Otis Taylor, E.J. Holub, Jerry Mays, Abner Haynes, Ed Budde, Jim Tyrer, Jan Stenerud, Fred Williamson and Fred Arbanas. It was a pretty fair team. Hank Stram was the coach. They got to the Super Bowl in 1966, way before the Steelers, where they lost to the Green Bay Packers, 35-10, in Super Bowl I.

In 1970, I covered Super Bowl IV for *The Miami News* and recall Dawson being the focal point of attention before and after the game at Tulane Stadium in New Orleans. That week was a nightmare for Dawson. He says it was one of the worst weeks of his life.

On the Tuesday before the game, Dawson was alleged to have been connected with a gambler earlier in his career and, while the charges were proven to be totally without foundation, Dawson still can't shake the memory. I remember getting into an argument with my boss over the story, and the way we were handling it — I thought Dawson was getting a raw deal — and left *The Miami News* a week after getting back from New Orleans because of that spat. So it was a bad week for both of us. Maybe that is why I have always been a big fan of Dawson.

The Chiefs defeated the Minnesota Vikings, 23-17, in the last game ever played by an AFL team. Dawson was named the game's MVP.

Dawson was one of two quarterbacks who played for the Steelers in 1957 who went on to make it big in the AFL. The other was a fellow named Jack Kemp, a free agent from Occidental College, who is now a cabinet member as U.S. Secretary of Housing and Urban Development.

Earl Morrall was the Steelers' starting quarterback in 1957 and 1958, succeeding Jim Finks as the team's leader. Morrall represented the Steelers in the 1958 Pro Bowl. The other stars of the Steelers in those days were Jack Butler, Dale Dodril, Jack McClairen, Fran Rogel, Ernie Stautner, Frank Varrichione, Bill McPeak and Elbie Nickel.

Buddy Parker had become coach of the Steelers for the 1957 season. In 1958, Parker traded Morrall to his former team, the Detroit Lions, to get Bobby Layne. Two years after they got Layne, the Steelers dispatched Dawson to the Cleveland Browns. After just one season with the Steelers, Kemp ended up with the San Diego Chargers, back when they had an assistant coach named Chuck Noll.

The Steelers were always combative under Layne, an old-fashioned leader and one of the most legendary players in Pittsburgh sports history, but they might have been smart to hold on to Dawson and see him develop. He did not do much better with the Browns, however, and needed the AFL to find the opportunity he needed to prove himself.

He always had good friends in Pittsburgh, especially Joel Litman, who had been his roommate at Purdue. Litman's dad, Archie "Tex" Litman, was a businessman and sports entrepreneur in Pittsburgh. He was the founding owner of the Pittsburgh Rens of the American Basketball League. The star of his team was a 19-year-old college dropout named Connie Hawkins, and the publicity director and later general manager, at age 23, was Joe Gordon. Gordon later became the publicity director of the Pittsburgh Hornets of the American Hockey League and then the Pittsburgh Penguins of the National Hockey League. He joined the Steelers in 1969, the same year that Noll became the head coach, and one year before the Steelers moved into Three Rivers Stadium. Like Dawson, Gordon had been a friend of Joel Litman.

"When the Chiefs were in the Super Bowl," Dawson said, "I used to get nice notes from Mr. Rooney. He'd congratulate me and tell me how proud he was of me. He'd mention that the Steelers had also let go of John Unitas and Jack Kemp and Earl Morrall and Bill Nelsen, and that they didn't have all the answers.

"I ended up playing 19 years of professional football. Morrall played 20 or 21. Kemp 13 or 14. Unitas, of course, might have been the greatest quarterback of all time. He was the first famous quarterback the Steelers cut."

Maybe not. The Steelers had a crack at Sid Luckman of Columbia in the draft back in 1939, and they traded his rights to George Halas and the Chicago Bears. Luckman is also in the Pro Football Hall of Fame.

"I knew most everyone in the Steelers' organization," Dawson said. "So I was rooting for them when they got to the Super Bowl. I lived in Pittsburgh for six years, and I still have a lot of friends there.

"I was there when things weren't so hot. I remember 'Hi, Diddle, Diddle, it's Rogel up the middle.' I knew that stuff. I was there."

He was on the opposing side in the '70s when the Chiefs and Steelers were among the best teams in pro football. The Chiefs went on the decline about the same time the Steelers started their rise.

Seeing Jack Lambert and Franco Harris at the Hall of Fame events, along with the likes of Joe Greene and Mel Blount, brought back memories, mostly unpleasant ones, for Dawson.

"Lambert wasn't the usual size for a linebacker, weighing about 215 pounds, if that, but he was tall and rangy and so competitive," recalled Dawson, forcing a smile. "He caused me all sorts of problems. Nobody was tougher on Sundays. I don't know of too many people who played with the intensity that he did."

I mentioned to Dawson that somebody had told me that when Lambert was a kid in Mantua, Ohio, he often pedaled his bike five miles to the Browns' training camp in Hiram, Ohio, and that most of the journey was up hills. "A lot of kids in his neighborhood thought he was crazy," I said.

Dawson smiled in earnest on that note. "They probably still think he's crazy," he came back, smiling at his own joke.

"With Lambert at middle linebacker," the former leader of the Chiefs continued, "they could double up on your wide receivers and let him cover your tight end. Sometimes he'd even drop back into the deep coverage. He could cover a lot of territory, and he could come back upfield fast to stop your runners, or a receiver out of your backfield. Their defense could shake you up and make things happen. Lambert had that speed and skills, and he really caused problems. Today, though, at 215, you wonder whether he'd get the opportunity to play in the pros. Their defensive guys said they couldn't afford to let up, or he'd be all over them in the huddle.

"I'd see Lambert a lot when we were lining up, but before I could think of him, I'd have to worry about ol' No. 75 (Joe Greene). He was a little closer. One game, Mo Moorman, our starting guard, was hurt and George Daney was in for him. Daney tried holding Greene and grabbing him. And Greene was still getting to me before I could hand the ball off to anyone. It seemed unfair, as far as I was concerned.

"Offensively, Franco was the key. You could stop him, you could stop him, you could stop him, and then he'd break one, and go 70 or 75 yards. All of a sudden, he'd just break it. When Franco came to the team, he fit right into what Chuck Noll wanted to do. But the key was the defense. They intimidated. It began with their defense."

INSIDE THE NFL 1990 lineup: Cris Collinsworth, Lenny Dawson and Nick Buoniconti provide weekly expertise for fans.   Craig Blankenhorn/HBO

The Pro Football Hall of Fame
"Remember living those moments"

Jack Lambert and Franco Harris, heroes of the Steelers' Super Bowl triumphs, were among the seven men to be inducted into the Pro Football Hall of Fame on Saturday, August 4, 1990.

The others were Bob St. Clair of the San Francisco 49ers, Buck Buchanan of the Kansas City Chiefs, Bob Griese of the Miami Dolphins, Tom Landry of the Dallas Cowboys, and Ted Hendricks, a rare bird in that he played for the Baltimore Colts, Green Bay Packers and Oakland Raiders.

But it was strictly a Steelers' showcase, almost boorishly so at times, as the fans from Western Pennsylvania poured into Canton, Ohio — just over 100 miles away for most of them — and took over the town in the manner of Attila the Hun. It was the fourth straight year that Steelers from that era were similarly honored, and the fans felt it was becoming an annual pilgrimage — similar to when they used to visit St. Vincent College each summer, or follow their beloved ballclub to cities such as Cincinnati, Philadelphia, Cleveland, Buffalo, New York, Baltimore, Tampa and Miami during the glory years.

The crowd was dominated by Steeler loyalists, men and women, wearing black and gold and white football jerseys, caps, jackets, some of which had been in mothballs in recent years. They wore faded jerseys with No. 58 — Lambert's old number — and No. 32 — which had been Harris's number — and it wasn't hard to determine whose side they were on. They were ready with their uniforms and game faces. "Here we go, Steelers, here we go. . .," they hollered.

The scene was reminiscent, only on a much smaller scale, of the scene at Super Bowl XIV, when Steelers' fans were so much more evident than those of the Los Angeles Rams, even though the game was staged at the Rose Bowl in Pasadena, California. The crowd contributed mightily that day in January of 1980 to the Steelers winning their fourth Super Bowl in six years, and that spirit was resurrected for the enshrinement ceremonies in Canton.

"How about those Pittsburgh fans?" said Hank Stram, when he was called upon to introduce Buchanan. Miami's Don Shula said similar things before introducing Griese, but also chided the Pittsburghers a bit, and left them in a feisty mood. "I wish to thank Coach Shula for getting the Steelers' fans all fired up for me," said Griese in jest.

Al Davis, the Raiders' owner, always likes to take on the Steelers, and he warned the fans to behave, or he would have the Hall of Fame moved to California. He did not specify which city, probably because he was not sure where he could make the best deal.

"If you carry on, we might have to move Pittsburgh to the West Coast," he said. "It's always great to be with an audience that loves you, that respects you and, like the Pittsburgh Steelers fans, is scared to death of you."

True to form, Davis drew the loudest and longest boos of the afternoon, which brought a droll smile to the familiar face of Davis. He got exactly the response he was seeking.

Buchanan was the best of the speakers, in our opinion, and Joe Greene agreed with that judgment. Buchanan was humble, and thanked all the right people: family, friends, proper influences such as teachers and coaches, from those in high school to his college coach, Eddie Robinson, at Grambling, to Stram with the Chiefs.

Buchanan mentioned that there were many men honored in the Hall of Fame who had been told earlier in their careers that they were too small, too slow, or lacking in some respect. "To the young people," said Buchanan, "never give up your hopes and dreams of success."

St. Clair was the opening act, and that was not easy because the Steeler fans were already impatient to get their own players in the spotlight. St. Clair spoke about the good old days, and the importance of the camaraderie, which he felt had waned in pro sports because of the big money and different attitudes and approaches. "You're missing something," he said.

Griese was more glib than usual, and bounced back and forth between serious and not-so-serious offerings, and was self-effacing about his own athletic limitations, while taking pride in what he accomplished.

"I never dreamed I'd be here," said Griese. "I never dreamed of playing college football. I never dreamed I'd be playing pro football.

"You don't have to be the biggest or the strongest, the most skilled, or the prettiest. If you have drive and determination, the heart, the enthusiasm . . . yes, maybe you can be successful in athletics, and successful in life."

Landry allowed people to see that he is a wonderful gentleman, with a sense of humor, and not the stone-faced straight arrow he appeared to be when seen on the sidelines at Cowboys' games for a quarter of a century. Like Chuck Noll, his public image has not always been true to the man.

Hendricks had no idea, it seemed, of what he wanted to say. Once called "The Mad Stork" because he loomed over most of his opponents, and was a legend for his off-the-field antics, Hendricks had not changed much. There was a movie playing at one of the downtown Canton theaters called "Bird on a Wire" that weekend, and it could have been a fitting title for Hendrick's life story.

Lambert and Harris had the most attentive audience, however, and both made the most of the occasion. Lambert was like an Irish politician out to win votes for an upcoming election. Lambert would hate for anyone to call him political, because that was not his style as a ballplayer, but he has a political genius, like it or not. Art Rooney would have been proud of him. Lambert left time for applause at the end of each point he made. He was good, very good. Harris had a different style, as always. Harris sounded like a Baptist minister, and he had the crowd chanting everything but "Amen" as he spoke about the special times they had all enjoyed together. It was a toss-up as to which one of them had been most effective. But they provided insights into their own greatness as well as those of their teammates, and why it was such a special era in Pittsburgh sports.

Harris and Lambert had been two of the most popular of the Steelers from those special teams, and there were even more fans in Canton than had been there for earlier inductions featuring Joe Greene, John Henry Johnson, Jack Ham, Mel Blount and Terry Bradshaw. All of the above but Bradshaw, of course, were present for the 1990 Class induction, along with Andy Russell, Rocky Bleier, John Banaszak, Dwight White, J.T. Thomas, Larry Brown and Lynn Swann, of those I could spot in the crowd, and Steelers' president Dan Rooney and business manager Joe Gordon and their wives.

Swann was the one who introduced Harris. He himself had been a serious candidate for induction in the Pro Football Hall of Fame, but came up short in the voting. "All the fans in Pittsburgh said that someday I'd make it to the Hall of Fame," said Swann. "Maybe I'm half-way there. Maybe next year. But you know in Pittsburgh we never believed in next year. We believed in today.

"Franco was never a man who gave you a lot of conversation. He gave us pride by his work ethic. Every day in practice he'd take a handoff, and he'd run down the field 40 yards. He'd come back and take another handoff and go another 40 yards.

"I lived with this man. He would talk about how badly he needed a championship. He'd walk back and forth in the locker room before a big game, and everybody got charged up from that. We won four Super Bowls on the shoulders and legs of Franco Harris.

"In that fourth Super Bowl, it was Franco Harris who got us ahead, and it was Jack Lambert who kept us there."

Always a soft-spoken individual, and sometimes a difficult, reluctant interview, Harris had a smile from ear to ear when Swann surrendered the microphone to him, and Harris really played to the crowd. All he needed was a tent to turn it into a revival meeting.

"Here we go, Steelers, here we go," the fans began to chant. Harris had to smile some more. "That brings back some memories . . . the Army is here," he said, referring to "Franco's Italian Army."

"OK, Steelers fans, I just want to get this over with," Harris began. "You know, I had to leave the Steelers in 1984, but now I'm back . . . Yes, I'm back.

"And I'm thrilled and honored to join my teammates once again, but this time to join them as a member of the Pro Football Hall of Fame. God, I was with the right teammates. They were great.

"During that era, each player brought his own little piece with him to make that wonderful decade happen. Each player had his own strengths and weaknesses. Each his own thinking. Each his own method. Each had his own. But it was amazing because it came together, and it stayed together to forge the greatest team of all time."

That got the fans going again. "Here we go, Steelers, here we go. Here we go, Steelers, here we go. . ."

"I'm going to savor this for a minute," said Harris, shaking his handsome head, and smiling more than ever.

"Here we go Steelers, here we go. . ."

"My teammates were men of character, with a lot of heart and soul," he continued. "This was the team I belonged to, a team that will live forever. So I want you to remember. Remember living those moments. Do you realize how great those moments were?"

The Steelers' fans screamed "Yeah!"

"Did you savor them?"

"Yeah!"

"Did you see Lynn Swann in Super Bowl X?"

"Yeah!"

"Unbelievable. Rocky Bleier in Super Bowl XIII, leaping 15 feet and catching that ball in the end zone. Do you remember?"

"Yeah!"

"Do you remember John Stallworth catching that pass in Super Bowl XIV over his shoulder for a touchdown?"

"Yeah!"

"It was great. We remember, but while we were playing we never knew what the future would bring. We were just trying to win the next game. We tried to give you the best we had each week. Then, by trying to give you the best each week, we never knew we were building a Steelers' wing to the Hall of Fame."

"Yeah!"

"But now you'll always know that you saw the best. You will know because it says so right here in Canton, for all to see. The Pittsburgh Steelers are here, and here to stay. Remember.

"We didn't know that at that time we were building such a dream, but now the results are in. Any way you look at it, it is truly immeasurable and certainly unforgettable. Don't forget us! Don't forget us!"

Lambert was introduced by Dennis Fitzgerald, who had coached him at Kent State University and with the Steelers. Fitzgerald was the least familiar of all the men who served to introduce the inductees, but it was true to Lambert's style of always looking after the little people.

Lambert was as thrilled as anybody ever has been about being inducted into the Hall of Fame, but he had to have a laugh or two or he would not be Lambert. So he rode in the morning parade down Cleveland Avenue, wearing Bermuda shorts, and kept lifting his bared legs to make sure all the parade-watchers saw them, as he waved to them from the back of a convertible automobile.

This was a tamer Lambert, however, a family man and the tip-off to that change came at a breakfast meeting I had with Doug Dieken of the Cleveland Browns. "Times have changed," declared Dieken. "I was with Jack Lambert last night and we spent the night showing each other baby pictures."

Lambert knew this was a home crowd. He could see the handwriting on the walls of Fawcett Stadium above, to his right. He could see signs that read "Jack We're Proud Of You — Your Kent State Teammates" and "I'm A Lambert Lunatic," which was from McKeesport, Pa., and others that read "Steeler People IX X Super Bowl XIII XIV."

"I was so fortunate to have played on some of the greatest teams of all time," Lambert began. "And, arguably, the greatest defense ever assembled. And, finally, how fortunate I was to have played for the Pittsburgh Steelers fans. A proud and hard-working people, they love their football and their players.

"If I could start my life all over again, I would be a professional football player, and you damn well better believe I would be a Pittsburgh Steeler."

Lambert let the crowd cheer for awhile, and smiled a thin smile as he squinted into the sun.

"To my family, to all of my teammates at Crestwood and Kent State, to all of you fans out there who will never be in any Hall of Fame," Lambert continued, "at the risk of sounding a bit pretentious, I give this day to you. This is your day, and this is your Hall of Fame.

"I would like my wife, Lisa, and my daughters, Lauren and Elizabeth, to stand. There, ladies and gentlemen, is *my* Hall of Fame."

Franco Harris, Pete Rozelle, Jack Lambert at Hall of Fame game in 1983.

Jack Lambert
"The man behind the Steel Curtain"

Jack Lambert was a big football fan when he was growing up in Mantua, Ohio, about 35 miles from the Pro Football Hall of Fame. It was five miles from Hiram College, where the Cleveland Browns conducted their summer training camp. He rode his bicycle to the camp just about every chance he got.

"I was a big Cleveland Browns' fan," recalls Lambert. "I've still got autograph books at home filled with Jim Brown and Milt Plum and Jim Ninowski and all those guys. Leroy Kelly."

What did he remember best about his boyhood visits to the Hall of Fame?

"I was probably around 12 years old," he said. "The thing that stood out most in my mind was probably the old uniforms they had there — what they wore for pads when they first started the game. Back when men were men!"

Lambert had to laugh at his own line, pure Lambert. Big, bad and having fun all the way. To get a reaction, Lambert was always likely to let the single tooth in his partial plate dangle out of his mouth. With him, you never knew when he had on his Halloween mask.

When Dennis Fitzgerald introduced Lambert for his induction into the Pro Football Hall of Fame in July of 1990, Lambert's former coach at Kent State and with the Steelers referred to him as "The man behind the Steel Curtain." He could just as easily have called him "The man behind the steel mask." You were never sure whether the real Lambert was before you or not.

Lambert hated to do public speaking for the Steelers, but he may have been the best on the team at it. He was always prepared, and you never knew whether he was going to get into a serious tirade on some subject — something like kids fooling around with drugs — or whether he was going to be the most humorous delegate at the dais — detailing "the true story" of Rocky Bleier's wartime heroics. He took his speaking seriously, however, no matter his subject, and always did his homework and frequently came in appropriate costume or with props. Anything for a good show.

"I can still see my mother at night down in the basement washing my football pads," Lambert recalled of his youth during induction ceremonies at Canton. "Ma thought it was right that I wear the whitest of football pants.

"I got my athletic skills and temperament from my dad's side of the family. Most of the time was spent throwing and catching a baseball or throwing and catching a football. My dad bought football helmets — this was before the days of NFL Properties — and he bought helmets and painted them. He chose to paint a Pittsburgh Steeler helmet for me. Thank you, Dad.

31

"And, of course, Chuck Noll, who will one day be standing on these very same steps to join Coach Landry in the Hall of Fame ... thank you, Coach Noll.

"I want to thank the Steelers organization and the National Football League for enabling me to realize a childhood dream. How fortunate I was to play for Art Rooney and his family. How fortunate I was to be associated with the entire organization."

Lambert then thanked some of the not-so-familiar members of the Steelers' organization — "the little people" — which was so like Lambert. He mentioned Ralph Berlin, the team's trainer, and Tony Parisi, the team's equipment manager, who had been with the Steelers over 20 years. He cited Rodgers Freyvogel, the field manager, and his predecessor, the late Jackie Hart. He went through a list of team doctors. "I have to thank the trainers and team doctors for putting me back together again after tough games," he said.

Lambert and Franco Harris were the fifth and sixth representatives of the Steelers' four Super Bowl champion teams of the 1970s to receive pro football's greatest honor. Both were elected in their first year of eligibility.

Lambert had been the Steelers' leading tackler in each of nine straight seasons (1975-83) before he had to retire prematurely because of a serious toe injury following the 1984 season, and he was the only linebacker in the league voted to all nine Pro Bowls during that span.

A second round draft choice in 1974, he was named the Steelers' MVP twice (1976, 1981) and NFL defensive player of the year twice (1976, 1979). Lambert was the only rookie starter on the Steel Curtain defense in 1974, and later served as the defensive captain for his final seven years. By that time Lambert had accumulated 23 1/2 sacks and had 28 career interceptions to lead all active NFL linebackers.

After he was drafted, Lambert drove from Kent to Pittsburgh on several occasions, and asked the Steelers' linebacker coach, Woody Widenhofer, to review films and the team's defensive strategies with him. That's when the Steelers knew they had somebody special.

But Lambert didn't look at himself that way.

"I guess I'm from the old school," he said. "When I went into the locker room at Three Rivers Stadium for the first time, I didn't say anything to anybody. I just sat in front of my locker and looked at everyone. I was awed. I always wanted to play pro football and here I was with all these guys I'd always looked up to. Some people are different. Some rookies come in and feel they belong ... they take right over. I wasn't like that."

On Tuesday, July 4, Lambert came to Three Rivers Stadium for a pre-Hall of Fame press conference with the local media. Asked what he had been up to, Lambert allowed, "I've been on 125 acres of woods up in Worthington, Pa. What have I been doing? I've been changing lots of diapers. I have a two-year-old and a five-month-old little girl. Their names are Lauren and Elizabeth. You can't see me changing diapers? Well, I do it. Keeping busy. I do some promotions for some different companies and make some appearances. Play a little golf."

Lambert had always looked after his money carefully because he lived a simple lifestyle, nothing flashy, and wanted to make sure he was secure and able to do just what he wanted to do when he could no longer play football.

Following his eighth year with the Steelers, he had once told us, "You go out and play the best you can and, hopefully, at the end of the season you have a Super Bowl ring to show for it. I'd like to finish my career here. I consider myself a Steeler.

"I'd like to play until I'm 65, and retire like you guys do. I really enjoy the challenge of it. This is a great life. You have six months of the year to play football, and six months to do whatever you want to do. One of the reasons they're asking you to come to speak is because we won four Super Bowls. Some people forget this. It's easy to do."

Lambert never let his focus get off football too long. But now that he was retired, he came out of his retreat once in a while to make some public appearances.

"I have bills to pay, too," he said. "I have to do a little bit of work out there. If people come along and ask me to represent a product or something of theirs I'd be happy to do it if it's something I believe in. That goes along with it."

Lambert was looking forward to going to Canton for many reasons: "Well, it's the ultimate honor that a football player can receive. But I think that when it's all said and done, I'll be glad when it's over. I can get back to my normal routine. Like I said, the thing I'm really looking forward to is seeing a lot of people I haven't seen in a while. That will be nice.

"My family took me down there the first time I went there. I walked around the last time I went down for Jack Ham's induction. It had been a long time since I'd been there, but it's always a thrill to walk in there and see all the great players that have played the game."

Franco Harris
"He dreamt of long runs"

When Franco Harris was inducted into the Pro Football Hall of Fame, he spoke a little about his roots, his beginnings, his family.

"It all started back in Mt. Holly, a little town in New Jersey," he said.

"My mother, Gina, at first she didn't understand football. And now she loves it. It's a shame my father can't be here, but I know he's upstairs and he's smiling."

That scene in Canton, Ohio brought to mind a scene at St. Vincent College a decade earlier, during the summer of 1980, late July to be more specific. Franco's father, Cad Harris, died just a few days before the Steelers were to open training camp in quest of their third straight and fifth Super Bowl championship, at least that was their goal and certainly Franco's goal. I talked to Franco for a feature story that first appeared in *The Pittsburgh Press:*

"This was the part of the year he always enjoyed," Franco said of his father following the first day of practice back then, as he relaxed between workouts in his dormitory room at Bonaventure Hall, a room he shared with Lynn Swann.

"He was proud of us and what we accomplished. All of us. He'd be excited about a lot of things right now.

"My mother is writing a book about her life, going through the war in Italy — they had to flee to the mountains for their lives and two of her brothers were brutalized and cut to bits by the Nazis — and then marrying a black soldier from America. Her name was Gina Parenti and her village was destroyed during the war."

By his performance those first few days in camp, one would never know that anything disturbing had happened to Harris, but it had, indeed. "It sets you back some, sure," he said of his father's unexpected death. "It always hurts. Time will help ease the hurt. You can't let that take away from other parts of your life."

The Steelers were still a big part of his life. "I feel good, and I still enjoy playing this game," said the 30-year-old Harris, who was beginning the ninth of his 12 pro seasons. "I'm excited about this season. I've been excited about things this year.

"I'd like to win a third Super Bowl in a row. I'd like to get another ring. No doubt about it, me and some other guys here would like to go down in history as part of the best football team ever assembled."

Franco said his mother was dedicating her book to her late husband and, without spelling it out, it seemed that Franco would be dedicating his season to his dad. He was a special man, a humble man, a quiet man, and to hear Franco reflect on him provided insight into why the Steelers' star running back is the way he is.

Franco Harris

Asked how old his father was when he died, Franco smiled and wagged his handsome head. "He was 59 or 61. He didn't have a birth certificate." He didn't have a lot of things, it seemed, and on the other hand he had a great deal. What he didn't have, Franco tried to provide.

"I know how proud he was of me playing ball," said Franco. "He never said much at all. But my mom would always tell me how happy he was or how he'd feel."

Franco does not like to talk about football or himself, and has often been difficult to interview, he is so sparse in his comments. But he enjoyed talking about his father and his family, and why he enjoyed taking them places, nice places, good places, and going first cabin.

"Football afforded me that opportunity," he said. "As a child, we never went to a restaurant. I mean never. We never went on a vacation. We always had what we needed, and we were never without essentials, but there were no extras. It feels good to give them something back."

Cad Harris — he had no middle name — was a military man, a 20-year man in the U.S. Army. Franco, the third oldest of nine children, was born at Fort Dix, New Jersey. "He was definitely a military man all the way," Franco recalled. "Instead of saying, 'Hurry up,' he'd say, 'Make ace!' You ever hear that expression in the Army? He loved the Army and being part of the Army.

"Coming from a situation where he didn't have an education — he really couldn't read or write — and my mother having only an eighth grade education, well, when it came to school they were very strict about it. We had to show him our report card. If we got anything less than a "C" it was whipping time. I remember one time my sister did it, and how he tore her up. Man, my dad didn't play."

There were four other brothers, and four sisters in the Harris family, a closely-knit family. "But one thing," Franco continued, "he was always there. He worked two jobs to make ends meet. He worked hard. He had his certain way. When you have nine kids, I guess you've got to have rules. It's funny, but with all those kids he still controlled the total situation in the home. He controlled everything. He only said something once, and you better do it.

"I'd have to say it was because of him and the way he controlled the house that none of us ever went astray in any way. There could have been opportunities when I was young, of being on that thin line when I could've done something bad, and I thought of my dad and the consequences, and I didn't do it."

Born of a black father and an Italian mother, Franco's upbringing and background were unique. He is the best example that it was a good blend, a good marriage, a good family. His wife, Dana, is white, and they have a son, Dok, who is 12. Franco will help Dok find his way in the world. Dana's maiden name is Dokmanovich, which is Serbian. She is a former Eastern Airlines attendant. They have never been officially married, but she is Franco's wife, no doubt about that.

They live in a townhouse on the North Side, not far from Three Rivers Stadium and Art Rooney's old house. It is in an old neighborhood known as the Mexican War Streets (because its streets were laid out during that conflict). Harris is happy in such a neighborhood. "It has interesting people," offers Franco. He seems to always be surrounded by kids.

"Franco has a charisma with people; he's always there for them, when there's a need," said Joe Gordon, the Steelers' publicist through Franco's career and now one of the team's top executives. "He's especially good with kids."

"I really had a happy childhood, relating to other people, other kids," said Franco. "My father was great with people. He didn't care about color. He knew all kinds of people. When I was three or four, we moved into this project area of Mt. Holly. I guess we were like the second black family to move into that area. Soon the street was full of families with mixed marriages, blacks with European wives, Italian and German. There was quite a bit of that.

"At the funeral for my dad, I saw a lot of them. I hadn't seen some of them since between the time I was five and ten. A lot of the old Italian ladies who came over with my mom were there. They were all shipped over together, and they had stayed together."

His mom must have had some say in the Harris household. After all, his name is Franco, and he has a brother, Pietro, and another brother named Giuseppi, and both of them followed Franco to Penn State to play football for Joe Paterno there.

His younger brother, called Pete, who tried out unsuccessfully for the Steelers, said, "I never saw Franco much when we were kids. He was always at Fort Dix shining shoes and bagging groceries. Too many kids to help support."

When Pete's story was relayed to Franco, he frowned at first, and then smiled.

"I think it helped, coming from a family like I did," said Franco. "I really do. My mom, she thought European. She was strict and conservative. The children always came first. They would do without certain things for us.

"One thing they had a dream of doing. They wanted to get out of that project area. When I was nine, my mom went out, by herself, and bought a piece of land. She had to go by herself. My dad couldn't go; they wouldn't have sold it to him. It was seven years later before they had the money to build a home on that piece of land.

"They did it and we moved into a new house. They had accomplished that dream."

Franco has fulfilled his own dreams and then some, even if he never did get that fifth Super Bowl ring.

When Franco reflects on his football career, he says, "Records are nice, but sharing them with your teammates is the best part. I'm sure there are other guys who will rush for 12,000 yards and break any records I might set. But I don't think there will ever be another team that wins four Super Bowls in six years, or has the kind of unity we had. Those things go beyond the numbers.

"There have been no empty spots in my career. I don't think anything could make me feel I haven't had a worthwhile career. I'd say I'm probably not as recognized as Jim Brown or O.J. Simpson, but if you look at it, they've accomplished more than I have. They're my idols, too."

And so are the Steelers he played with, some of whom have beaten him to the doors of the Hall of Fame, and some of whom are still waiting their turn.

"It all started with the coming of Joe Greene," Harris said as he stood on the steps of the Hall of Fame during induction ceremonies in the summer of 1990. "He was a great leader, and a man who anchored a great defensive line.

"Joe was joined by Jack Ham. What can you say about Jack Ham? But that he was the greatest linebacker. Then Mel Blount and Terry Bradshaw were inducted into the Hall of Fame. Mel was the cornerstone of our defensive secondary."

He took time to call attention to J.T. Thomas, who was in the audience, and also played in that same defensive secondary. It was a nice gesture, so typical of Harris.

"Bradshaw had a will that was second to none. And, on the other side, Jack Lambert wouldn't let anybody play anything less than their best. Truly, the best guys were on that team. With Lammie, my teammate, going in today, it's something. Thanks, Lammie, for setting the tone for our defense.

"Thanks, Lammie, for teaching us to run out of bounds by always chasing me in practice (he allowed time for laughs on that line). What makes your talent come through? What makes you work? God, I was with the right teammates. They were great. They brought out the best in me. They made me a better ballplayer."

Then he smiled in the direction of Rocky Bleier, his running mate for so many seasons with the Steelers.

"The next guy, I can't say enough about. Thanks, Rocky. Thanks for leading the way here. Thanks for being unselfish. This guy shows you what playing from the heart is all about.

"Lynn Swann and John Stallworth were the best. Thanks, guys, you made it easy to run. We were the best."

"Hi, diddle-diddle, Rogel up the middle."
— Popular chant, 1955

*"I can never be a Steeler fan as long as they
have Franco Harris on their team."*
— Complaint, 1980

Franco Harris always did it his way, just like Frank Sinatra, who was the honorary general of Franco's Italian Army, and once came to practice and drank a glass of wine with Franco at Myron Cope's urging.

38

The man who made the critical remark about Franco Harris, keep in mind, is from Dallas. He moved to Pittsburgh in 1975, he is a pro football fan, and he would like to side with the Steelers.

Franco Harris, he said, kept him from switching allegiances. "I hate the way he runs," he said.

Even more surprising, another man nearby agreed with the man from Dallas. The second fellow was from the Pittsburgh area and was a stalwart Steelers' fan — "though they cost me money every week because they never cover the spread." But he did not like Franco's style, either.

To knock Harris, after all he had done for the Steelers, might seem like heresy to some, but his sideline-to-sideline forays, his stutter-step, his "jiggle," as it was put by Paul Brown of the Cincinnati Bengals, his stop-and-go, his step-out-of-bounds when it gets too busy on the sideline, his willingness at times to go down without a fight, or sticking his helmet in there, well, it all added up to drive some hard-nosed fans to distraction.

Pat Livingston, the former sports editor of *The Pittsburgh Press*, asked Paul Brown, who had been the founder and head coach of the Cleveland Browns, to compare Harris and his ace running back, Jimmy Brown.

"He's not like Jimmy Brown at all," said Paul Brown. "He doesn't have Brown's power or straight-ahead speed. Brown would take the ball and go. Franco's different. He gets to the same place, but he does it in a different way.

"They're hard to compare. Franco's a great back, though, and he's been one for a long time. He's one of those unusual runners who don't come along every day."

In a sense, Harris was damned if he did, and damned if he didn't. Because for him to be effective he had to stick with the style that gained him all those yards. Harris was the Steelers' first round draft pick in 1972 and he rushed for 1,055 yards to lead the team to its first-ever division title. "We never won nothing here until Franco came," said Joe Greene, another Hall of Fame performer, who came to Pittsburgh three years ahead of Harris, but felt Franco was the key star.

"On a football field, you don't have time to stop and think. But Franco thinks out everything. You watch Franco run. He's not dancing. He's making decisions."

Harris was the only NFLer voted to every Pro Bowl from 1972 to 1980. He was one of only two NFL players to rush for 1,000 yards eight times. When his career ended in 1984, Harris ranked second on the all-time ground gaining list with 12,120 yards, just 192 yards behind all-time leader Jim Brown. He was named MVP of Super Bowl IX. He holds virtually every team rushing record in addition to many post-season and Super Bowl records. Walter Payton of the Chicago Bears and Tony Dorsett of the Dallas Cowboys and Denver Broncos have since passed Harris on the rushing list.

His place is secure in sports. Harris is one of the few sports figures — Oscar, Wilt, Kareem, Reggie are among them — whose first names suffice. His "Immaculate Reception" catch against the Oakland Raiders in the AFC playoffs in 1972 shows up weekly on TV highlight films. Yet his style never went down right with many Steeler fans. "What's his story?" they'd scream when he would scoot for the sidelines and avoid a tackle.

"It takes its toll," Harris has said on more than one occasion. "Sometimes you have to know when it's time to go in there and take all those bumps, and when it's best not to fight it and go down or out of bounds."

He even spoke about his policy at practice sessions when he insisted that no one tackled him or hit him unnecessarily. "The other guys joke about that," he said when he was still playing for the Steelers, "but frankly, I feel that I take enough punishment during the season, and I don't want to get hurt when we're playing among ourselves. It doesn't make no sense to me."

Others recognized his genius for the game. Ernie Stautner, a long-time assistant to Tom Landry with the Dallas Cowboys and that team's defensive coordinator for many years, a Hall of Famer and a former tackle with the Steelers, said, "He can be running toward the hole he's supposed to go to and if the hole is closed, he'll stop, change directions very quickly, find another hole and get through it."

Or, as Dick Hoak, a fellow Penn State alumnus, and the Steelers' offensive backfield coach throughout Franco's career, put it: "He has a great sense of where he is on the field and where everybody else is."

Franco was not one to worry about his own stats, or where he ranked on the latest rushing list. "I don't think about that at all, not when I'm getting ready for a game," he said. "I'm glad I'm doing it, and it's nice and all that, don't get me wrong. I just don't worry about it.

"It's not the most important thing on my mind right now," he said before a big game at Three Rivers Stadium against the Cincinnati Bengals when he had a chance to pass San Francisco's Joe "The Jet" Perry, and move into fourth place on the all-time list. "If those things happen as we go along, that's great. If we can accomplish all the things we want to accomplish as a team while I'm doing that, then that's great.

"If you do what you're supposed to do, and just work hard at it, those other things will come. If they come as a result of doing other things, fine. Now is not the time to sit back and pat myself on the back."

His teammates were always willing to do that. Said Lynn Swann, his roommate the many years he was with the Steelers, "Franco knows he's very good. He just doesn't find it necessary to think of himself as being great. We know he's great."

Jack Ham, who was a teammate for three seasons at Penn State, as well as with the Steelers, and met him as a high school All-American at Rancocas Valley High School in Mt. Holly, New Jersey "I knew him then, when Penn State was recruiting him," said Ham, "and he has never changed. I think that's what I admire most: that despite all the publicity and all the good things that have happened to him, he never has changed."

Rocky Bleier, his running mate in the Steelers' backfield, made this observation: "Someday I'll be boasting to my children and grandchildren that I played next to Franco Harris. In a steady, quiet way he's accomplished what he's accomplished. He could care less about the criticism. He could give a damn. And look what he's accomplished. He's special, but he's never asked for special treatment around here. We have too many other great players, and that's not his style anyhow."

His style. Harris has always had his own style. He never sought the spotlight, but he was among the most active Steelers when it came to civic and community charities and the associated activity.

Once, when I was in charge of lining up sports celebrities for a father-son banquet at The Press Club, I sent an invitation to all the Steelers. A few agreed to attend. I did not expect to hear from Harris. One day, he poked his head into a room where I was speaking to someone at the Steelers' offices, and he said, "Hey, I'll be at your banquet Thursday night. I'm not going to eat. I'll be there at eight o'clock, and I'll stay for an hour, and sign as many autographs as I can in an hour." Then he was gone. He showed up just as scheduled and his appearance was the highlight of the evening. There were about 40 other local sports celebrities present on that particular program, but Harris was the highlight. Just for an hour. He never stopped signing autographs for young people during that hour.

Franco always was at his best in the big games. "It's a do-or-die situation," he said of his penchant for post-season production. "You either win or you lose. I don't like to be a loser. I always like to come away with something. I always feel we should win and I go out to make that happen. If you don't win, you go home."

Hoak was asked to explain how Harris always came up big in the playoffs and Super Bowls. "He doesn't prepare any differently for a playoff game," Hoak said. "It just seems like when we're playing in a must game, and we need a big game from someone, he has it.

"I remember the year (1976) after we had won our second Super Bowl, and we were playing Cincinnati. We were 1 and 4 and they were 4 and 1 and we had to win. We gave Franco the ball some 40 times and he gained 160 some yards (143 to be precise). He was like that. Harris has to carry the ball 20 times to be effective. He has to get a feel for the game.

"One thing he has over other runners is that he can sense things happening around him that most runners can't. O.J. Simpson did that real well. Earl Campbell is a good runner, but he relies on speed and strength. Franco senses something and changes directions."

"Everybody's a star
in the movie of their life."
— Ted Turner

When Harris thought about running, long runs danced in his head. "I dream of long runs — the extinct species," he said. "No negative stuff.

Most of the time I think about the team we're playing that week, and I'm running plays through my head. If we do certain things, I think about what I want to do in response.

"Sometimes I think about those things when I'm sleeping, too. It's nice dreaming about them, anyway."

Toasting with Frank Sinatra

With wife Dana

Sam Davis (57) and Moon Mullins (72) open hole for Harris.

My Dad and the Hazelwood Steelers
"The same old Steelers"

When I was about 13 years old, and an eighth grader at St. Stephen's Grade School in the Hazelwood section of Pittsburgh, I used to watch some Steelers games on television with my dad and my brother Dan. There were only a few games on TV in those days, back in 1955, and I remember it was mostly the Steelers or the Baltimore Colts that we could watch. The Steelers and the Colts had some sort of deal with the Dumont network to televise games in the same region.

Televised football in those days came out like scouting films, if you have ever seen them, a view of the field from high atop the stadium or ballpark, and the kind of shot where you could see all 22 players on the field, and they all appeared small because the camera — and there was only one camera back then, for the most part — was positioned so far away. There were no close-ups, zoom lenses, slow motion, instant replays, fancy graphics or esoteric statistics. There was no Howard Cosell or John Madden.

The games on TV were all in black and white, too, just like the football bubble gum cards I had in stacks in the closet upstairs in the bedroom I shared with my older brother Dan. There always seemed to be snow in the picture, too, but I think that was because we had poor reception. I blamed it on the fact that our TV was in the middle of our mantel, right above a fake fireplace. Some fast-talking salesman, like a Danny DeVito, no doubt, had talked my parents into putting in a fancy mantel with a TV in it. Dust and soot from the nearby steel mills used to fall down our chimney and cling to the picture tube, which couldn't have helped the reception, either. That is when the steel mills were open, and flames and smoke shot up from the huge smoke stacks and lit up the skies over Pittsburgh. That is when Pittsburgh was the steel capital of the world, and that is how the Pittsburgh NFL franchise got its nickname. But space was at a premium in what we called our "front room," so it seemed like a good idea to have the TV out of the way.

The Pittsburgh Steelers were our team, even if they were not very good back then. They always played hard, and we always heard the other teams hated to play them, even if the other teams usually won. You knew when you had played the Steelers, so they said, because you could see the bruises on your body the next morning.

It was back then that I became a Steelers' fan. It was there that a life-long interest in the team was born. Wherever I lived — whether it was Louisville, Kansas City or Fort Greely, Alaska, when I was in the Army — or Miami or New York, where I worked as a sports writer, before coming back home again, I was always interested in finding out how the Steelers had fared in their most recent football game. It has not always been easy to be a Steelers' fan.

43

But in 1979, after working elsewhere for ten years, I returned home to cover the Steelers for *The Pittsburgh Press*, and did so for the next five years. In my first year covering the team, they won their fourth Super Bowl and became acknowledged as one of the greatest football teams of all time.

But it was not always like that. When I was growing up, the Steelers had a reputation as losers. It was like that when my dad, brother and I were watching them on TV.

The Steelers' record was 4-8 in 1955. The next year, with Walt Kiesling as coach, the Steelers would improve to 5-7, the same record they had in 1953 under Kiesling. The Steelers always seemed to be 4-8 or 5-7 in those days. In the first 25 years of their existence, or since the franchise was founded in 1933, the Steelers had a winning record only twice — at 8-4 in 1947 under the former Pitt legend, Jock Sutherland, and at 7-4 in 1942, the year I was born, under Kiesling. That's right. Kiesling coached the Steelers in two separate spans, as did Joe Bach, and no other National Football League franchise can, or would want to, make that claim.

Steelers' owner Art Rooney liked both of those fellows, you see, and it was no big deal. No matter who was coaching the Steelers back then, the results always seemed the same, mediocre for the most part. The plays always seemed the same. That is why the fans called them S.O.S., for short, or the Same Old Steelers, a term that originated with Rooney himself. The team's fullback was Fran Rogel, who had played at Penn State, and was from nearby North Braddock, another steel town, or at least it was in those days.

My dad never took me to see the Steelers play at Forbes Field, yet it was only four miles from our house. He was never really into sports. He still had a few swimming medals from local parks competition as a kid tucked away in a drawer somewhere in my parents' bedroom, but that was about it as far as fun and games. But I do remember one day, when I was eight or nine, being hoisted up by my dad onto a bar stool in Frankie Gustine's Restaurant, across the street from Forbes Field, so I would be eye-to-eye with Fran Rogel. It was a big deal to my dad, and I didn't know any different.

Back then, Steelers' fans, and everyone else in the ballpark, knew that the Steelers would start the game by handing the ball off to Rogel for a plunge up the middle. As the Steelers quarterback, who was Jim Finks, now the front office boss of the New Orleans Saints, would call out the signals for that first play, the Pittsburgh fans would often holler out in a chorus, "Hi, Diddle, Diddle, Rogel up the middle!" The opposition did not need any scouts to alert them to that game-opening play. Or so it seemed anyhow. Those early coaches included the likes of Jap Douds, Luby DiMeolo, Johnny Blood, Buff Donelli, Bert Bell (later the NFL commissioner), Greasy Neale, Jim Leonard and John Michelosen, and they all put losing teams on the field. Under Michelosen, in fact, who had been a disciple of Sutherland, the Steelers were the last NFL team to employ the single-wing offense.

The stars on the Steelers in the mid-50s were Finks, Rogel, Lynn Chandnois, Elbie Nickel, Ernie Stautner, Dale Dodril, Jack Butler, Bill Walsh, Jerry Shipkey, Bill McPeak, Ray Mathews, Frank Varrichione, Pat Brady and Johnny Lattner.

There were others, who were there for shorter stints, but stick in the mind for one reason or another, such as George Tarasovic, Paul Cameron, Bobby Gage, Earl Morrall, Goose McClairen, Jerry Nuzum, Jim "Popcorn" Brandt, Ed "Little Mo" Modzelewski, Joe Geri, Gary Glick and Willie McClung.

So it was a genuine thrill, during the time I was covering the Steelers for *The Pittsburgh Press* in the early '80s, to be invited to a dinner with some former Steelers one evening at the Pittsburgh Athletic Association (PAA), just across Fifth Avenue from Pitt's Cathedral of Learning, and a block away from where Forbes Field once stood. I was invited by Jerry Nuzum, who had been the team's best running back in 1949, and had once lived in my hometown of Hazelwood while he was playing for the Steelers. He had also invited Chandnois, Joe Gasparella and "Bullet Bill" Dudley and their wives, as well as Rogel, a bachelor. "Bullet Bill" remains one of my all-time favorite football nicknames, right up there with Charley "Choo-Choo" Justice and Dick "Night Train" Lane.

We had a sandlot football team for young men 18 to 25 in Hazelwood in the mid-'50s called the J.J. Doyles, and they were one of the best in the Pittsburgh area on that level, usually playing for a championship against the Sto-Rox Cadets or the Rox Rangers or the Greenfield Preps. When my dad and I would watch the Steelers on TV in those days, and they were doing poorly, he would invariably tell me, "I think the J.J. Doyles could beat the Steelers. And I mean it."

I figured fathers were saying the same thing to their sons about the Carrick Merchants, the Homewood-Brushton Bulldogs, Millvale Indians, Pitcairn Mohawks and the Bloomfield Rams. There were lots of so-called heavyweight sandlot football teams in the area in the '50s and '60s. The names still spark memories for many long-time football fans. They include the Library Tigers, Saline Street Merchants, Greenfield Preps, St. Rosalia's, Crafton Vets, Butler Cubs, Crunkleton Bears, Knights of Equity, Pittsburgh Trojans, Trafford Alumni, Duquesne Ironmen, Millvale Ameci, Pittsburgh Eagles, Bellevue A.A. and Beechview Legion. Just to make a few more sandlot football fans happy, here are some others from that same era: Valley Tigers, West End Ponzis, St. Peter Preps from the Hill, J. Scott Morgan of Homewood, Shaler A.C., East End Chiefs, South Side Polechaks, New Kensington Firemen, Westinghouse Alumni, Mt. Lebanon Wildcats, Garfield Eagles, Arnold Preps, Aliquippa Indians, Port Vue Quakers, Broadway Mounts, Soho Oakleafs, Etna Sycamores, South Side Sooners, Corpus Christi of East Liberty, Goose Goslins of Carrick, Mt. Oliver Civics, Glen-Hazel Boys Club. And the inmates at Western Penitentiary and the Workhouse in Blawnox always fielded ballclubs, but played only home games.

I played for a midget football league team in the mid-50s called the Hazelwood Steelers. In 1955, in fact, I played for the Steelers on

Saturday afternoon, after playing for St. Stephen's in the City's Catholic Grade School Football League in the morning. I played center and linebacker for the Steelers, and halfback for St. Stephen's. You were not supposed to play for both teams, and it did not help when I wore the red pants of St. Stephen's by mistake one afternoon instead of the gold pants of the Hazelwood Steelers. I wanted to play quarterback, which I did one season with the Steelers, but I was too small, too slow and too near-sighted to amount to anything. But I could remember the plays. I was born to be a sportswriter.

I wore No. 19 because Johnny Unitas, who had grown up in Pittsburgh and been rejected as a player by both the University of Pittsburgh and the Pittsburgh Steelers, was the star quarterback of the Baltimore Colts, the other team that we got to see on TV. Unitas had been cut by Kiesling at training camp. The Steelers kept three quarterbacks that year, and anyone who followed the Steelers back then can still name them: Finks, Ted Marchibroda and Vic Eaton. The Steelers developed a habit of passing up great quarterbacks. Earlier in their history, the Steelers had allowed Sid Luckman to get away and later on they would cut Lenny Dawson, and both are in the Pro Football Hall of Fame, along with Unitas. They also cut Jack Kemp who became a star in the American Football League as well as the U.S. Congress. They also traded away Bill Nelsen, who became a big success with the Cleveland Browns. "We're experts on quarterbacks," said Art Rooney.

HBO's "NFL Report" did a looking-back feature on Unitas during the 1990 season in which he said, "I tell my kids I don't want the word 'can't' in their vocabularies. I tell them to try; you never know what you can do." Unitas has since declared bankruptcy, in debt for over $3 million.

I remember one night the Hazelwood Steelers were playing the Bloomfield A.C. at Arsenal Field in the Lawrenceville section of the city. Arsenal Field is 80 yards long, not uncommon for inner-city football fields and was coated with oil to keep the dust down. You got dirty when you played on those fields. During the game, after you had advanced the ball past midfield, the referee would move the ball back 20 yards farther from the end zone, to make up for the field's shortcomings.

What excited me was that this was the same field that Unitas had played on, for $7 a game, so the story goes, for the Bloomfield Rams in a senior sandlot league, after he was cut by the Steelers. It was where he was playing when George Shaw was sidelined with an injury, and Weeb Ewbank went searching for an emergency replacement in his quarterback ranks in Baltimore. Unitas turned the Colts into champions, along with Lenny Moore, Raymond Berry, L.J. Dupre, Alan Ameche, Buddy Young, Art Donovan, and the likes. (While researching this book, I learned that Unitas and Moore were Hall of Famer Mel Blount's favorite players when he was a boy.) I got into the game late that night, in relief of Rick Reagan, our regular quarterback. Our coach, Bill Fleming, told me to take the snap and fall on the ball three times and run out the clock. I did what I was told, but this was hardly what

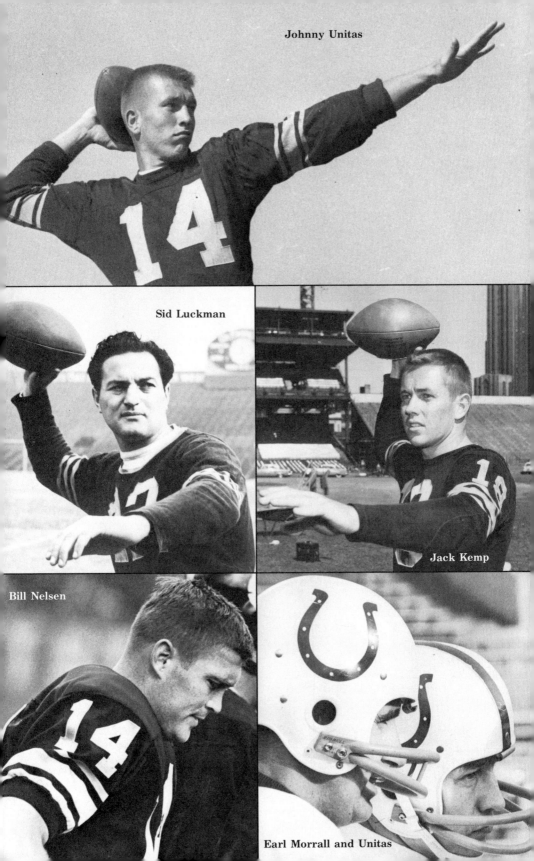

Johnny Unitas

Sid Luckman

Jack Kemp

Bill Nelsen

Earl Morrall and Unitas

Dale Dodril

John Henry Johnson

Jim Finks

Justice Byron "Whizzer" White and President Kenn

Ernie Stautner

Jim Thorpe in Art Rooney's office

e Greene, Fran Rogel, Jim O'Brien,
hn Brown in the Allegheny Club

John Henry Johnson, Chuck Noll, Lynn
Chandnois, Bill Dudley

Jerry Nuzum

Jack Butler, Art Rooney, Elbie Nickel, Pat Brady,
Dan McCann at Curbstone Coaches luncheon

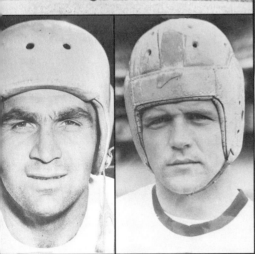

Elbie Nickel   Bill McPeak   Bobby Layne

I had in mind. Unitas never would have gotten his chance with the Colts if Bill Fleming had been his coach, and told him to do what he told me to do. My mother now lives three blocks away from that field.

Fleming had a nephew who was the star of our team. His name was Davey Fleming, and he was our top running back. He was later the star of the newly-formed Gladstone High School football team in the late '50s and early '60s. He never went to college, but starred for a semi-pro team called the Pittsburgh Valley Ironmen in the Atlantic Coast Pro Football League. I was the publicity director of that team. Fleming was good enough to rate a tryout with the Steelers, and shined in some of their pre-season scrimmages, but had trouble learning the plays, and lacked the experience to get more serious consideration. He wrapped his wrists with tape and wrote some of the plays on the tape, like a circular cheat sheet. He should have been a Steeler. He went on to play ten years as a defensive back with the Hamilton Tiger Cats of the Canadian Football League. The other running back for the Hazelwood Steelers was a young man named John Sklopan, who played quarterback and led South High to a City League championship. Sklopan later played for Southern Mississippi and the Edmonton Eskimos in the CFL. So we had quite a backfield on the Hazelwood Steelers.

I went to Pitt in 1960, following the lead of my brother Dan, who preceded me by five years. He had graduated with a degree in engineering, and I was going to be an English writing major. I wanted to be a journalist. I joined *The Pitt News,* the student newspaper, before I even signed up for my classes. *The Pitt News* offices were located in the Student Union, which used to be the Schenley Hotel, where visiting baseball and football teams stayed when they were playing the Pirates or Steelers across Forbes Avenue at Forbes Field. In my second month at Pitt, the Pirates won the World Series in seven games against the New York Yankees when Bill Mazeroski hit a ninth-inning home run over the brick wall in left field, and started a city-wide victory celebration. It was an exciting way to start college.

I remember seeing the Steelers play at Pitt Stadium and Forbes Field while I was a student at Pitt. Two games come to mind, mostly because of one play in each of them. I remember seeing Y.A. Tittle, the bald-headed quarterback of the New York Giants, kneeling on the field after his helmet had been knocked off by John Baker of the Steelers. Tittle was stunned, and a trickle of blood streamed down his forehead. That was at Pitt Stadium. The other occurred at Forbes Field. I watched the game that day from atop the right-center field roof of the double-decked ballpark. I saw a play quite unlike any other I have since witnessed. Mike Ditka, a former Pitt All-America, caught a pass for the Chicago Bears and broke about six tackles as he zig-zagged back and forth across the field for a long run in which he traveled twice as far as he was credited for in the scorebook. Then again, I wonder whether I remember both of those plays because great pictures had been taken of those special moments.

50

I have some other special memories involving Steelers, Hall of Famers, in fact, when I was a college student at Pitt.

I frequented bars, like Frankie Gustine's on the campus, before I was of legal age, so I could hang around sportswriters from the local dailies, so I could soak up the atmosphere, learn how to behave like a sportswriter, and often begged them to critique my latest writing efforts for *The Pitt News,* or for a tabloid called *Pittsburgh Weekly Sports,* which I founded my senior year (1963) along with Beano Cook, then the sports information director at Pitt and, in more recent years, a college football analyst on ESPN. When I was drafted into the U.S. Army, Bob Smizik filled in for me as editor of *PWS.* He had also succeeded me earlier as sports editor of *The Pitt News.*

I cannot remember the exact circumstances, but one night I bumped into John Henry Johnson, who was in his last years of a distinguished pro football career and had a hard-earned reputation as one of the fiercest competitors in the game. We bumped into each other in downtown Pittsburgh, and he invited me to tag along with him to an after-hours spot called the Aurora Club in the Hill District, near the Civic Arena.

John Henry drew a lot of attention, and catcalls, when we entered the Aurora Club. His was obviously a familiar face there. I was happy I was with John Henry. The place was packed, and I was the only white person in the place, and probably the youngest, too. John Henry ordered some drinks for us both. After we had about three rounds of drinks, and I thought it time I ought to be getting home, an impatient waitress pleaded with John Henry for payment.

"How about taking care of your tab, John Henry?" she begged.

John Henry shrugged his wide and round shoulders, and smiled up at the waitress, signalling that she was wasting her time, as if he had no money in his wallet.

"Don't pull this on me again, John Henry," she hollered. "You better pay up this time!"

"Who's going to make me?" said John Henry, as he picked up his trench coat, and bid the barroom crowd goodbye. Most of them laughed aloud at John Henry's shenanigans.

We backed out of the club, like Nick Nolte and Eddie Murphy in "48 Hours." Thank God I was with John Henry Johnson that night.

Later on, when I was 19 or 20, I used to occasionally visit a bar called Dante's in Whitehall. It was owned by a gentleman named Dante Sartorio, and someone was usually playing a piano near the bar. They took requests. Several Steelers frequented Dante's on a nightly basis. The contingent was headed by two future Hall of Famers, quarterback Bobby Layne and defensive tackle Ernie Stautner. Running back Gary Ballman, defensive lineman Lou Cordileone, and defensive end/placekicker Lou Michaels were among the other regulars. They were a tough group, all throwbacks to a more rough-and-tumble era. Jim Boston, now the chief negotiator for the Steelers, moonlighted there as a bartender after working on the sidelines with the Steelers at their practice sessions.

51

Several sportswriters also hung out at Dante's, including Myron Cope, Pat Livingston and Bob Drum, along with some radio-TV, public relations and advertising types. To me, it was a great place for an aspiring sportswriter to get to know the right people.

I was not that crazy, however, about keeping company with Layne. He liked to give people a tough time, and could be verbally abusive. Layne drank a lot and it showed in his behavior. I found him boorish. Myron Cope thought he was the greatest. Once, when I begged off accompanying Cope into the back room where Layne was holding court, Cope criticized me by saying, "Layne is like Leif Ericson. You have a chance to be with one of the legendary figures of football."

I declined, and stayed behind. "You go with Leif Ericson," I said sharply. "To hell with Leif Ericson and Bobby Layne!" I'd had my fill of Layne. He and Stautner liked to play a bar game called "buzz," and I will never forget the rules for that pastime.

Extra drinks were purchased and put on the table. And everybody had his own drink in addition to that.

People counted off around the table. The idea was not to say the number "seven" or any numbers that contained "seven" or any multiples of "seven." If you did, you had to down a drink from the table in a single swallow. Fraternity stuff, but Layne loved it. And, of course, the more mistakes you made the more you had to drink. And the more you drank the more mistakes you were likely to make.

Instead of saying the forbidden numbers, you were to say "buzz," and then the order of announcing the next number would be reversed. So the order of calling out your number would go in one direction, and then come back, and go back the other way. You had to pay attention.

If you hesitated before you said your number, which, as a novice, I often did, Layne would loudly swear at you to get you up to speed. He cursed me a lot, and made me nervous. He liked that.

On the eve of a Steelers' game once, Layne was out late at night, drinking too much as usual, and he drove his car into a trolley car, and nearly knocked it off the tracks in downtown Pittsburgh. Layne told the magistrate the trolley car was in the wrong lane.

On another night, I traveled to Dante's with my brother and father, both named Dan O'Brien. My dad had a tendency to drink too much, so I cautioned him as we approached Dante's. "Look, Dad, we're going to be out for quite a while tonight, and we can have a nice time, so take it easy. Start slow. Pace yourself. We're in no hurry."

No sooner were we seated in Dante's than my dad instructed the waitress, "Bring me an Iron City and an Imperial." That was the classic shot and beer combination that Pittsburgh became famous for when visitors were noting local customs. It was no way to pace yourself. It was a good way to get drunk. And dumb. And daring. And destroyed.

At one point in the evening, my brother came to me, and he was visibly upset. "Stautner's giving Dad a bad time," he told me. "We're not going to put up with that! Let's go!"

I grabbed my brother by the shoulder and spun him around. I pulled him close, and looked him in the eye, and whispered to him. "Dan, yes we are going to put up with that."

I talked some sense into both of them, and we went home. Dealing with my mother would be enough of a mismatch for the pack of us, without getting into a scuffle with Ernie Stautner.

So when Layne was elected to the Pro Football Hall of Fame in 1967 and Stautner was similarly honored in 1969, it was special to us. My dad died in between those enshrinement ceremonies, in 1969. My mother moved out of the house where we had always lived on Sunnyside Street in Glenwood. Somehow I felt freer to move myself after that, and a few months later I left Pittsburgh with Kathleen Churchman, my bride of a year and a half, and moved to Miami. I was going there to cover the Miami Dolphins of the American Football League for *The Miami News*. It would be the AFL's swan song.

I got ribbed in Pittsburgh for that, too, especially when I went to the Steelers' offices to say goodbye. I got the same sort of abuse I heard when I had come back from Kansas City during my Army stint and told them how good I thought the Chiefs were. Many of those Chiefs and many of those Dolphins are now in the Hall of Fame, and wearing Super Bowl rings as well.

During my years in Miami and New York, I had an opportunity to meet Muhammad Ali and Joe Frazier, and the likes of Mickey Mantle, Willie Mays, Ted Williams, Joe Namath, Bill Bradley, Julius Erving, Willis Reed, Jerry West, Oscar Robertson, Tom Seaver, Nolan Ryan, Pancho Gonzalez, Bobby Hull, Jean Beliveau, Joe Louis, Jimmy Connors, Joe DiMaggio, Ralph Kiner, Billie Jean King, John McEnroe, Jack Dempsey, Toots Shor and other celebrities. I visited the boyhood home of Babe Ruth, and went to the homes of Henry Aaron and Bill Mazeroski to do magazine interviews. It was a kick. I often wondered what my dad would have thought if he had been along for the ride.

I wish my dad had met Art Rooney, the best person I ever met in sports. I would have liked him to have learned for himself what a humble, guileless man this was, and why he was so special. And why the Steelers, for better or for worse, were always so special. So unique. It has been a trip.

Art Rooney always remembered where he came from, and he always reminded you of where you came from. Years later, I would come walking into the Steelers' offices wearing a new suit and feeling special, and Mr. Rooney would call out to his oldest son, "Hey, Dan, come out here! Get a look at this dude from Hazelwood!"

The good things started to happen to the Steelers when they moved to Three Rivers Stadium. "We were never really a big league team," Rooney often remarked, "until we moved into Three Rivers Stadium. Now we had a place to call our own, and we had our own offices. We had finally arrived."

Just as I will always remember being hoisted onto a bar stool at Gustine's to get an eye level look at Fran Rogel, perhaps my children will someday recall their earliest memories of being around the Steelers.

Once, when I was covering the Steelers, I took my oldest daughter, Sarah, to St. Vincent College with me for an overnight stay. I remember little things, little kindnesses. Ed Kiely, a public relations man who had been associated with the Steelers since 1951, came out of nowhere the next afternoon and placed a ballcap on Sarah's head, smiled and moved on. It was a black ballcap with 'Steelers' in gold script across the front of it. I remember Joe Greene and Rocky Bleier going out of their way to walk over and say hello to Sarah in the cafeteria, to offer complimentary remarks and they made her smile. I remember when we left, I asked Sarah what she liked best about the Steelers' training camp and she made my week by replying, "Having you all to myself."

I remember another day that same season when I took Sarah and her little sister, Rebecca, with me to a Steelers' practice at Three Rivers Stadium. They sat on a rolled-up tarp on the sideline in their winter parkas. They posed for pictures with owner Art Rooney. L.C. Greenwood, who was 6-6, 240, and wore a dark shield over his eyes, sneaked up on them and hollered "boo" and scared the hell out of both of them. They squeezed between my legs when he hollered. Later, after L.C. apologized profusely, he became one of their favorites.

Steelers descend to practice field at St. Vincent College.

Joe Greene
"Living the king's life"

Joe Greene just grinned that great grin of his, and then he let loose that throaty laugh of his, and the room got even warmer on a summer's eve at St. Vincent College in Latrobe.

That great grin belies the image of Mean Joe Greene, as he was called at North Texas State University and with the Steelers during the decade of the '70s when he was the most dominant and feared defensive lineman in the National Football League. He was the leader of the Steelers when they won four Super Bowl championships, something no team had ever done before them, he was the man in the middle of the much-vaunted Steel Curtain.

His words this particular night, however, were definitely those of Mean Joe Greene. "Guys like me were fortunate to be playing football," said Greene, giving you his best thoughtful look. "Football was an outlet, a release.

"It was a joy to be able to hit somebody in the mouth and not go to jail. I tell my guys they're living the king's life. They can get out and kick ass and not get in trouble. Hey, it's football; it's not tennis; it's not golf."

Yet Greene had a soft side, too. He could feel for another player who was injured and unable to play, even if others thought that particular player should tough it out, and get out on the field.

"You never know another man's pain," said Greene.

Greene was 45 and in his fifth season as an assistant coach on Chuck Noll's staff, looking after the defensive line. Five months after he took the job he was inducted into the Pro Football Hall of Fame.

As a player, Greene was the guru of the Steelers, the team philosopher, a favorite of the media because he always had something to say — and he still says what's on his mind — and he commanded everyone's attention and respect on the squad. A rookie who did not know all the rules would turn down his radio quickly, and without complaint, after getting a baleful look from Greene clear across the expansive clubhouse.

Greene was still a formidable figure, even if there was more paunch to his stomach then when he suited up in the black and gold, and he still demanded respect from the Steelers.

"To me, football was a war," said Greene. "It took me a few years in college before I learned to play football. Before that, I was just beating up everybody all the time. It starts in high school . . . not wanting to be embarrassed in front of your friends . . . or the girl you met last week who you invited to come to the game . . . or not wanting to be embarrassed in front of your family. I always had respect for authority and for people, but, yes, I was in the vice-principal's office a lot in high school for disciplinary action. Somebody's got to be top dog, and I wanted to make sure it was me.

55

"You kill to win. When I was in college, it took me a year to quit fighting and start playing football. My idea was just to beat the hell out of the other guy."

Joe Walton was the only other coach in the room that evening, and he smiled at Greene's remarks. He, too, was enjoying a post-practice beer in a room reserved for the coaches, staff and media to take a break after a day on the practice fields. This was prior to a special outdoor barbecue dinner for the team on a hillside next to Bonaventure Hall, where everyone was housed for the Steelers' summer stay at St. Vincent.

Walton was back home again, after a long absence. He is from Beaver Falls, and was a football star there before they ever heard of Joe Namath. A clutch touchdown receiver under John Michelosen at the University of Pittsburgh, and with the Washington Redskins and the New York Giants — in the early '60s when they were one of the most successful teams in NFL history — Walton was marking his 30th year in the league, the last 20 as a coach. He was head coach of the New York Jets the previous seven seasons, and was in his first year as offensive coordinator of the Steelers.

"When I think of playing against Joe Greene, I think of how he was going to mess up our game plans," said Walton. "Guys like him dominate the game. If you want to do something, you've got to make sure you take care of him. He was like Lawrence Taylor of the Giants. When Lawrence Taylor wants to play, you can't block him."

"He stops the players in your offense," interjected Greene. "You can't run."

"There's somebody else like that," Walton went on. "Andre Tippett's like that. When we played New England, you couldn't block him. You couldn't run at him.

"You can't win a Super Bowl unless you have a dominating offensive player or without a dominating defensive player, and the Steelers had that, and then some, with Terry Bradshaw and Joe Greene.

"Teams that are good know it. They carry themselves differently. They have a different outlook on a game. They expect to win. When they don't, they figure the other team got lucky or they didn't play their best game. The good teams never get beat, not in their mind, anyhow. When you're around a team that knows it's good the atmosphere is altogether different. I played for a good college team at Pitt, and I played for a bad team with the Redskins in Washington. Then I went to a good team, the Giants. Frank Gifford and Sam Huff said to me, 'We always win.' And they wanted everyone to think that way."

That is the way Walton and Greene want to get the current Steelers to think. "You've got to get to the point where you win, and then you expect to win," said Greene.

Later that same evening, Greene was having a good time at the dinner table, tackling some barbecued pork and corn on the cob, and chewing out the Steelers at large for what he considered a gross oversight.

Two weeks earlier, Franco Harris and Jack Lambert had been inducted into the Pro Football Hall of Fame. They were the fifth and sixth

Joe Greene is flanked by Keith Gary and Gabe Rivera.

Mike Fabus

Steelers in a four year period to be so honored, starting with Greene in 1987. "We should have all been in Canton for the ceremonies," growled Greene. "It would be inspirational for the guys on the team now. I could see if you were the Seattle Seahawks and not being able to make the trip to Canton. But we're in Pittsburgh, and it's a two-hour ride. It doesn't make sense to me. What's one more practice?"

At that, Pat Hanlon, the young publicist of the Pittsburgh Steelers who has since left the organization to become the public relations director for the New England Patriots, started moving fast in the other direction. "Ah, Joe, don't get started on that again!" Hanlon pleaded in retreat.

"I felt like that the first year I went back after I'd been inducted," said Greene. "I was there when Jack Ham got in. I was there when Mel Blount and Terry Bradshaw got in. And I was there this year for Franco and Lambert."

Just then, as if on cue, Ralph Berlin and Tony Parisi passed the table on their way back to their chores. Berlin was starting his 22nd season as the team's trainer, and Parisi his 26th year as the team's equipment manager. Lambert had thanked them both, as well as all the other clubhouse workers, in his acceptance speech on the steps of the Pro Football Hall of Fame. "Those two guys should have been there," said Greene. "It hurt them that they weren't there. It's a big moment in their lives, too."

Noll had been sitting diagonally across the table from Greene, but he and team president Dan Rooney were out of earshot now as Greene continued his dissertation on a sore subject.

"It's a once-in-a-lifetime thing," said Greene. "We should make the most of it for our organization. It would pump up our players, and show them what we can accomplish here in Pittsburgh. When I first came to Pittsburgh, the attitude wasn't very good. It was a losing atmosphere. It took Chuck ten years to build a winning attitude. Look at the standards he set."

Tunch Ilkin, an offensive tackle and the team's offensive captain who had represented the Steelers in the Pro Bowl the previous two years, was sitting within striking distance of Greene. Greene jabbed him in the bicep, and said, "You don't get Tunch to try and live up to somebody else's standard, but you want to show him the way. You have to do it without keeping your feet stuck in the past."

Ilkin nodded in agreement and continued eating. Starting his 11th season with the Steelers, Ilkin was not about to interrupt Greene.

"When we were struggling, they'd say S.O.S. — it was a carryover from the previous regimes — and it stood for the Same Old Steelers," Joe Greene went on. "That's how we were stigmatized. We were the armpit of pro football."

Joe Greene goes back to the beginning, those dark days of 1969 when he was the Steelers' No. 1 draft choice and Chuck Noll was the No. 1 hope of a franchise that had floundered for nearly 40 years.

"I remember the first meeting," said Greene. "Coach Noll said our goal is to win the Super Bowl. And I didn't believe that. I was thinking of that team and the present. Coach Noll was looking down the road."

And what a road it was: six consecutive AFC Central championships, eight straight playoff appearances, four Super Bowl championships (IX, X, XIII and XIV) and the recognition as the "Team of the Decade" in the '70s, and one of the greatest teams in the history of sports.

The Steelers won their first game that season under Noll, and then lost the next 13. The winning did not happen overnight.

Greene gained a reputation as the fiercest, and often the nastiest No. 75 in the league, looking to kill quarterbacks with a single blow and leap over opposing linemen in a single bound, hellbent on terrorizing everybody and everything in his path. Today, Greene would only grin at such an Attila the Hun image.

He was known as Mean Joe Greene and he came by it honestly, though he was never comfortable with the tag.

"I've enjoyed the whole journey," said Not-So-Mean Greene back in February of 1982 at a luncheon in the Allegheny Club of Three Rivers Stadium to mark his retirement. "But it has come to an end." Thinking better about that, he added, "It's the beginning."

In a sense, it was both. It has been said that athletes die twice, when their athletic careers come to an end and, like the rest of us, when their heart stops beating.

At age 35, and after 13 mostly glorious seasons for the Steelers, Greene was going into the restaurant business back home in Duncanville, Tex. He and Cincy Powell, a former pro basketball player, were opening a restaurant called "Partners." Some of the Steelers party stopped there for dinner on the eve of an exhibition game with the Dallas Cowboys the next season.

It was a nice place and it was busy that Friday night. But it didn't make it. Greene had an opportunity to work as a network analyst on NFL games, but he was not good at it. Whereas Ham has an ability to offer quick insights, and Lynn Swann is stylish, and Bradshaw has an old country boy appeal, Greene needed more time to make his observations than the flow of the game permitted. The offers for TV commercials stopped coming, and Greene needed to get back to what he did best — lead young men onto a football field — to be successful again.

"I'm optimistic," Greene had said at his retirement, when asked if he were afraid of the future. "I've been wanting to do something else for years, but I've always been a one-track person and my mind was strictly on football.

"I'm going to miss the thrill of tackling somebody; that'll be murder. That was always a very satisfying feeling, unless it was Earl Campbell or Pete Johnson I was tackling.

"The Super Bowl experiences were above my wildest dreams. I walked on clouds, all four times. It was just a wonderful, wonderful feeling.

"I'm going to miss the fans, too, and seeing them filling the stadium and waving their 'Terrible Towels' and screaming and shouting and understanding when I didn't sign or did sign an autograph, or frowned or smiled at them. Joe Greene wasn't always at his best. But he tried."

Greene was having a hard time saying goodbye, even to the forever persistent sportswriters who surrounded him. "I'll come back next year and conduct a press conference after every game," he said to cheer them. "We respected one another . . . the sharing of ideas."

He had a glad and firm hand for everyone, a goodbye that would be remembered by each. That wonderful wink. "It's time," he said. "Right now I think I'm ready to go out in the real world and live.

"The other day my mother showed me an old scrapbook and there was a picture in there of Dan Rooney and me when I signed my first contract with the Steelers. I looked at it and said, 'Wow, that looks like my son.' So I'm sure it's time."

He may not have believed Noll at that first meeting when the new coach spoke about Super Bowl ambitions, but Greene was confident he could do it with the right supporting cast. Noll and club president Dan Rooney and the Steelers' scouting staff made sure Greene got what he needed. But Joe Greene was, indeed, the first block in building a dynasty for the next decade.

Following practice at the South Park Fairgrounds where the Steelers worked out in those days, Greene was asked how he regarded the veterans. "They're here, I'm here," he responded. "What they can do, I can do."

From the start, he knew his role. "I'm hoping to start right off the bat," he said. "I've never taken a back seat in football. I'm ready to play with the so-called big boys.

"I've spent the last ten years learning to play this game. Football is my life, my career. I've got to make myself succeed."

No one succeeded any better, which is why he is regarded as one of the greats of the game. At Greene's retirement party, Joe Gordon, then the team's publicist and now Rooney's right-hand man, made this observation: "Joe will be in the Hall of Fame with the Class of 1987. And if Joe Greene doesn't get in the first year he's eligible there's no justice." Gordon was in Canton, of course, in the summer of '87 to witness one of Greene's greatest moments in sports.

"That's something that happens after you've played, something that goes with the territory if you're good enough to qualify," said Greene back then.

Those days at South Park seemed like yesterday. "Those fleeting 13 years," said Greene, letting that phrase sail for awhile. "I enjoyed myself. I challenge anyone to say they had as much fun as I had here. I came here as a boy, and I leave as a man. I think of it as a graduation. I've had 13 years of post-graduate work. It has gone by so fast."

During the formal part of the program, he said, "I'd like to thank the Pittsburgh Steelers, but I don't think that's possible." He looked down the dais toward Art and Dan Rooney and Noll. "Mr. Rooney and Dan and Chuck and the staff . . . they allowed a country boy to come up from Texas and be himself, and say what he wanted to say, good or bad. I'm grateful for being able to be myself.

"I could have been labeled as a radical or misfit. I bumped on all the boundaries. I pushed on them, not for any particular purpose. That was me, and they allowed me to be myself."

He was thrown out of a game early in his rookie season for a late hit on Fran Tarkenton, the quarterback of the New York Giants. Tarkenton, a scrambling type, had frustrated him all afternoon and Greene was out to level him.

Greene talked about it the following day at a Curbstone Coaches luncheon at the old Roosevelt Hotel, where the Steelers' offices were located before Three Rivers Stadium opened in 1970. "It's the way I play football," he said. "I really get angry at an opponent for being on the same field with me."

He said that back in high school in Temple, Texas, it had been the same way. "I got thrown out of my first game my freshman year for fighting," he said.

He was asked if he had been talking to Tarkenton throughout the game, as one of the players revealed. "I may have said, 'I'm going to get you!' I often tell quarterbacks that," said Greene.

When Greene was banished for playing overly-aggressive football, Noll dismissed it by saying, "It's a first for the Steelers."

Greene's rule of thumb on going after quarterbacks: "My theory is that when you kill the head, the body dies."

He was thrown out of another game later that season, at Minnesota, when he belted Viking lineman Jim Vellone with a forearm across the face. "I don't relish getting thrown out of a game," Greene said. "The true mark of a champion, I know, is to shake off adversity and keep playing football. I hope to be like that from now on."

He tried. But sometimes his basic instincts got the best of him, or somebody across the line from him. Listen to Joe DeLamielleure of the Buffalo Bills talk about him.

"You're not going to block Joe Greene 100 percent of the time; it's a give and take thing," said DeLamielleure, an outstanding offensive guard. "You just hope he doesn't embarrass you. I had a teammate tell me a story once about how Joe had ripped a facemask off an All-America center while he was playing at North Texas State so he could impress the pro scouts. I had a nervous stomach that night, and we were playing the Steelers the next day.

"I was in awe the first time I played him. Of all my memories in football, playing against him and Merlin Olsen for the first time were my biggest thrills."

The second time against Greene was quite a thrill, too, as the Bills knocked off the Steelers in the second game of the 1975 season. Former Bills' center Mike Montler had a story about that one.

"It was late in the third period and we were driving on the Steelers — just running, no throwing — six yards a clip until we got to about their 12-yard line," Montler recalled.

"When we broke the huddle, there was Mean Joe Greene standing with one foot on top of the football that I was supposed to snap.

"He was screaming and hollering like a man possessed: 'You

61

wanna see a football player? Well, I wanna show you. Come on, here I am!' All sorts of ranting and raving about the savage things he was going to do to us.

"I finally asked an official to remove the guy's foot from the ball. As soon as I snapped it, Greene teed off and really coldcocked me. . .

"When we huddled up again, Joe D says to me, 'Hey, Mike, was he talking just to you?' And I said, 'No, Joe, I think he was talking to both of us. It looks like he's going to get everybody.' "

DeLamielleure delivered this tribute: "He played when other guys would have sat out because he knew how much he meant to that team. When I think of the Pittsburgh Steelers, I think of Joe Greene and I think the average fan in the crowd does. That's a real tribute to a defensive player."

Maybe that's why Dan Rooney remarked at the retirement luncheon, "Joe Greene has been exciting and brought exciting times since the first day he came here. I was talking to Chuck and he said this is quite a transition. The day after we drafted him, the *Post-Gazette* had a headline that said, 'Steelers Draft Joe Who?' Joe never liked that, and he said so. He said many things in the 13 years he's been here and they were all positive."

At least it seemed so over lunch that day. There were times that not everyone concurred with Dan Rooney's remarks. There was the time Greene blasted the game officials and vowed, "If I get half a chance, I'll punch one of them out and it'd give me a whole lot of satisfaction."

He drew a fine from NFL Commissioner Pete Rozelle for that remark. Early in his career, he got into an argument with Pat Livingston, the sports columnist of *The Pittsburgh Press*, and he spat in Livingston's face.

During the 1975 season, Paul Howard of Denver and Bob McKay of Cleveland both claimed that Greene kicked them. Greene's response was to smile and say, "I think I've been too nice lately."

Two years later, he was fined $5,000 for punching Howard in the stomach in the midst of the madding war in the trenches.

When the Steelers were warring with the Oakland Raiders, both on and off the field, when George Atkinson and Jack Tatum were street-talking all the time and leveling Lynn Swann every time he ran down and across the field, Greene issued an at-large warning: "We have the kind of guys who can play it dirty. I won't shy away from the dirty stuff. In fact, you might say I'm capable of leading the way."

Noll, on the other hand, was unhappy with what he was reading in the newspapers back then, what he thought was negative writing about the Steelers. "It could have an effect," Noll ventured. "People put it in there that we're dirty. We're clean. We hit hard. If you don't hit hard, it's basketball."

When Noll went to court after Atkinson sued him for statements Noll made about his aggressive style, he listed Greene, Mel Blount and Ernie Holmes, as well as several Oakland players, as belonging to a "criminal element" in the league. Noll later insisted his attorney made up the list to prove a point. Blount sued Noll, but Greene chose to turn his cheek this time. He didn't see how any good could be accomplished by getting into an argument with his coach. He had good timing, too, and a sense of what was good for the Steelers.

During a players' strike in the summer of 1974, Greene stayed home. "I didn't want to carry a picket sign against the Rooneys," he explained then. "They're the nicest people I know. If the other owners were like the Rooneys, there wouldn't be a strike."

After the Steelers had won four Super Bowls, an independent promotion was launched featuring Greene, showing him wearing four Super Bowl rings on the fingers of his right hand, and a bare thumb thrust outward, with the theme "One For The Thumb in '81" emblazoned across T-shirts and such.

At a dinner to launch the promotion, Art and Dan Rooney were present. "Joe Greene is a great player," said Art Rooney, a man of few words, at the event in a ballroom at the Downtown Hyatt. "Joe Greene is a great man."

When Greene got up, he said, "Why do I play? The organization. Mr. Rooney gave me a job, and I enjoy working for him. Then there's Dan. He's not only an outstanding boss, but a friend.

"There's Chuck Noll. This is a guy who's created an environment for us football players to use our talent in the proper way. There are two sides to everyone's personality, a positive side and a negative side. He's created an environment for us to bring out the positive side.

"Any type of losing is something we as players don't accept. So when our backs are to the wall, and we're losing, we know we can turn it around. Everything is positive. It's all because of the tutelage of Chuck Noll."

It is the summer of 1990 at the Steelers' pre-season camp at St. Vincent. It is almost midnight, but Greene is huddled in the beer room with John Fox, the Steelers' defensive backfield coach, and John Guy, an assistant to Bill Curry at the University of Kentucky, and before that at the University of Alabama. Guy is there as part of an NFL development program for minority coaches.

They are going over defensive alignments, discussing the x's and o's of football, just to make sure they are ready for the next morning's session.

Prior to joining the Steelers the previous season, Fox had been an assistant and defensive coordinator for three seasons on Mike Gottfried's staff at Pitt. He had coached college ball a total of ten years at seven different colleges, and somewhere in there put in a year with the Los Angeles Express of the short-lived United States Football League. He and his wife, Robin, a beautiful former airline stewardess, lived in four different cities in one year early in their marriage.

Fox is fascinated with Noll and the success of the Steelers, and is always seeking more information about what makes Noll and the Steelers tick, so he can be a better coach and so his players will be better players. He thinks guys like Greene have the serum.

63

"I couldn't believe how Coach Noll handled things after the first two games last year when we just got blown off the field," said Fox, referring to 1989 season-opening losses by 51-0 to the Cleveland Browns and 41-10 to the Cincinnati Bengals. "He never got down. I felt pressure, but it wasn't coming from him. I'd seen coaches go crazy and blame the players and all the assistants, and be screaming at everyone under less dire circumstances. That doesn't help. Chuck never got down on any of us. He's amazing."

Greene just grinned, and nodded. "That's Chuck, he's always the same, win or lose," said Greene.

Greene grabbed a can of Iron City beer that had Franco Harris' image and stats on the side. They had just been issued the week before at a special promotion at the Steelers' camp, to coincide with Harris going into the Hall of Fame. Jack Lambert declined an offer to be similarly honored because he is associated with a rival beer company. Harris was paid $10,000 for the endorsement.

"We never won nothing until Franco came," said Greene, going back to the 1972 season, the first year the Steelers went to the playoffs. "He made the difference. Lambert . . . he was quiet, at first, and paid us all proper respect as a rookie. But he was never really a rookie. He belonged right away. He and Lynn Swann and Mike Webster all came the same year (1974) and we had some players by then. I wonder how they would have fared if they'd have come before we had any players.

"All those guys in the Hall of Fame are on beer cans but me," said Greene, ruefully, but in a theatrical way. "Maybe because I'm a coach they can't have me on there." The beer can was a reminder of something that had happened at the camp at the same promotion. At that press conference, Harris had said some things critical about his relationship, or lack of same, with Noll.

"Chuck is Chuck," Greene continued. "He's not going to grab you and congratulate you and tell you how great you are. You have to accept him for the way he is. When you did something special, he'd give you that little smirk, just a little change in his face, the slightest change. You had to recognize it. It was his way of acknowledging a good play. He cares about the guys. They are his guys."

Fox was also puzzled by the poor relationship that was so well chronicled between Bradshaw and Noll. "Chuck was the quarterback coach back then, that was it," said Greene.

"When did you know you were good, Joe?" Fox persisted, switching the subject to safer ground. "Did a light come on? When did you know?"

Greene recalled some tough games when the Steelers rallied to win, and when he recognized that the team had the right stuff. "You have to believe," he said. "You have to know you'll win, that you're better than anybody else.

"The fans and the media beat these guys down with all that talk about the Super Bowl Steelers. The players don't look at it the way they should. These guys should emulate those great players, use them as models. But they're tired of hearing about it. I was on those teams. I know what it was like, how we struggled to find ourselves.

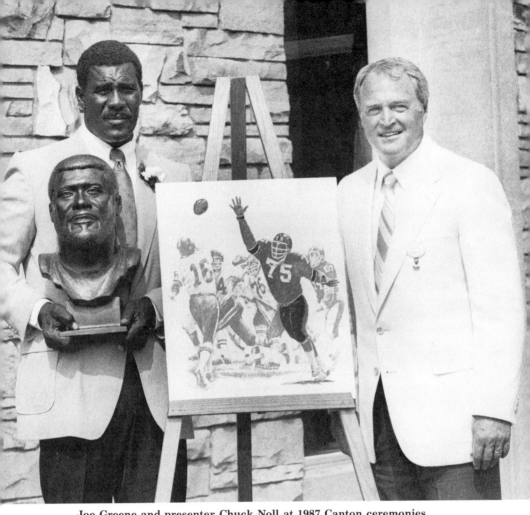

Joe Greene and presenter Chuck Noll at 1987 Canton ceremonies

Showing Keith Willis what's up   Defensive coach John Fox

"There were days when we couldn't buy a sack. We couldn't bribe a sack. They just weren't there. But we turned things around and we became the best. These guys could be great like that. In the playoffs last year (1989), we were playing Steeler football. All those gut checks . . . and the people loved it. I had at least ten people tell me we were playing like we did when I was on the team. It was there."

Fox offered a thought: "There's a tradition and a mystique and they know all about that. And that's good. Why can't Bubby Brister be another Terry Bradshaw? It can happen again."

"He can, that's just it," said Greene. "Sometimes I see these guys do something, and it reminds me of one of the guys on our great teams. That kid Chris Calloway came across the middle today and made a catch — just the way he leaped, just the way he looked, the size (5-10, 180), the way he went up for it — it was Swann. Yes, Lynn Swann came to mind. Just for a moment."

John Guy got up the gumption to offer a thought on this matter. "You have to be careful how you do it," he said. "When we were at Alabama all we heard about was what it was like when Bear Bryant was the coach. That's all we heard. Coach Curry couldn't succeed; they never gave him a chance. We'd win, but it was never good enough. We were always being compared to Bear Bryant."

"But that's also why guys went to Alabama," offered Fox. "The team's tradition was a magnet. The Steelers should still mean something special to young players."

Greene gave Fox a grandfatherly look, and assured him that it could happen again. "These guys could be great like that. Some of our greatest players struggled at the start, and it took a few seasons for them to find themselves.

"Take Terry Bradshaw, for instance. He was booed in the beginning, and he's never forgiven the fans for that. Look how he turned out! What showed me what Terry Bradshaw was all about was the fourth Super Bowl. When they talk about quarterbacks or field generals, that's when he showed why he was so special. The Rams had our ass. They were so pumped up and they were handing our helmets to us. Jackie Slater knocked me down on one play, and he was standing over me, hollering, 'Thank you, Jesus, thank you, Jesus.' I knew then they were fired up. But Bradshaw, Lambert, Stallworth and Swann — those were our heroes that day — turned it around.

"We were down 13-10 in the second half when Swann went up high to make that great touchdown catch to put us ahead. Then the Rams took the lead back. And Lambert made that big interception. The fans stood up and started hollering, 'Dee-fense . . . Defense . . .' and they really picked us up. When Stallworth made that tough over-the-shoulder catch (73-yard TD pass) in full stride it was my greatest moment in football. That's the day we really showed what sort of stuff we were made of. That was the real Steelers."

St. Vincent
"Field of Dreams"

There was a freshly-dug grave behind Bonaventure Hall, where the Steelers reside while they are at St. Vincent College. I came upon it the afternoon of August 10, 1990. The Steelers had played their opening pre-season game in Montreal the night before against the New England Patriots and had come away winners. It is unlikely any of the Steelers knew what was going on outside their dorm rooms while they were away. They had no idea that another body had been buried outside the windows where they sleep most of the summer.

The gravesite was unmarked. It was next to one that read: Rev. Richard Gick, O.S.B., Born July 26, 1912, Died Sept. 28, 1989. The gravesite was the 454th belonging to Benedictine monks — priests and brothers — that border the rim of the hill behind Bonaventure Hall. There had been 67 monks buried there since the Steelers started training at the school in 1966. The tombstones are all similar in style, going back to 1890. They are all topped by the St. Benedict Cross, an ornate cross that has origins in the early days of the Catholic Church in Europe. They provide a unique pattern to the skyline as seen from the Steelers' rooms in Bonaventure Hall. It is a cross that is seen on school seals and such at St. Vincent.

The new grave, I was to learn, belonged to Father Edmund Cuneo, who died on Monday, August 6, 1990, and was buried on Thursday, August 9. He had once been president of St. Vincent College. "He was one of the absolute key people here in the '40s, '50s and '60s, very important and very active," said Father Bennett Crowley, a 38-year-old Benedictine priest at St. Vincent.

"He was known popularly as 'Mr. St. Vincent.' He was involved in our prep school, which has since closed. He used to get pre-med students into med school, and personally visited the director of admission offices or deans at med schools. He'd leave here with a list and went to visit med schools. He didn't drive, so he had to have someone drive him. But he was very successful in getting placements. He was a charming story-teller and good company. I used to like to visit his room and talk to him. He developed Alzheimer's Disease, however, and during the last five or six years he was out of it. He had no idea as to what was going on."

Following the Steelers' first game of the 1990 season, while walking down a hallway toward the Steelers' locker room, I bumped into Brother Pat Lacey, who has been at St. Vincent's as long as the Steelers have trained there and is a personal favorite of many of the players. I mentioned Father Cuneo to him, and he told me that Father Cuneo had once served as a priest at St. Mary's Church on the North Side.

Brother Pat told me how Jack Lambert had befriended a Father Raymond Balko. "It was for father that Jack stayed in the pros," said Brother Pat. "They became friends in Jack's first year. Father would see him walking around, looking like a bit of a lost soul, and started to talk to him. They got to be friendly, and Jack would go to his room to talk with him. Jack was thinking of quitting the team at one point, but Father talked him into staying. He believed in Jack. Jack came back to our school when Father died, and Jack read one of the homilies at the funeral service. Jack said it was more scary than playing in the Super Bowl. They were very close. He always went to Father's room and talked to him when he wasn't feeling so hot. Jack would be down and out, and Father was an inspiration to him."

Once upon a time, there were plans to bury the priests and brothers in crypts under the basilica at St. Vincent College — almost like in catacombs — but state health officials urged college officials to do otherwise.

That basilica, by the way, is an awesome church, an old-fashioned church, with marble everywhere, ornate statues and symbols, stained glass windows, with a strong religious presence. It is an impressive place. Most of the Steelers have never seen it.

As I passed through it I came upon a statue of the Blessed Virgin Mary. It reminded me of my father. No one else was in the basilica, so I thought it was all right to say something.

When I was walking through it, I found myself talking to the statues, especially the one of the Blessed Virgin Mary. "My dad was always a big fan of yours," I said in a whisper, or maybe I just thought aloud. "He always said you never let him down when he was praying for somebody else. Look after him and my brother Dan."

Old fashioned churches can do that to you. I don't know if the ghosts of any of my childhood teachers, the Sisters of Charity, were pulling strings or what. It seemed natural enough.

St. Vincent College prides itself as being a strong liberal arts college where young men and women can get a good education, and the school is especially proud of its academic record in preparing young people for graduate school acceptance and professional careers. It believes it does an excellent job in pre-law, pre-medicine and business administration. It went coed in 1984, and has about 1200 students, evenly divided between men and women.

The 1990 season marked the 25th summer stay of the Steelers at St. Vincent College. It has been a mutually rewarding relationship. Art Rooney Jr., the second oldest son of the late Steelers' owner, went to school and was graduated from St. Vincent in 1957. He was a "participant," as he puts it, on the school's football team.

St. Vincent once had a fine football team under Coach Al DeLuca, highlighted by a 1950 victory over Emory and Henry of Virginia in the Tangerine Bowl. But the program grew too expensive for the school, and a nice campus stadium was leveled to make room for a science building when the program was dropped in 1963.

Before the Steelers conducted their training camp at St. Vincent, they had trained at Rhode Island University, and before that at California (Pa.) State University, Slippery Rock University, West Liberty (West Va.) College. Even earlier, they trained for several years at St. Bonaventure University in Olean, New York, where Father Silas (Dan) Rooney, the brother of the Steelers' owner, was the athletic director.

"Some of those places were logistical nightmares," related Art Rooney Jr., who worked with his brother, Dan, and the Steelers' business manager at the time, Fran Fogarty, to bring the Steelers to St. Vincent College in 1966. The school had built new dormitories, and the religious retreats the school sponsored for laymen in the area were not drawing as well as they had once upon a time. So there was room for the Steelers at St. Vincent College.

The Steelers had practiced at St. Vincent for a period back in the 1930s, and had an eye on the campus for some time before they were able to work things out to the mutual satisfaction of the Steelers and St. Vincent officials.

Oland "Do Do" Canterna, a former Pitt athlete and teammate of Lou "Bimbo" Cecconi, was the athletic director and basketball and baseball coach back then, and helped sell the Steelers on St. Vincent College. Now Canterna is more concerned with fund-raising at the school, but he is still pitching its plusses.

"It's been a wonderful association," he said. "We're happy with it, and I hope the Steelers are still happy with it. My feeling is 'Who's going to watch them up in Rhode Island?' The fans who watch them every Sunday can come up here to see them practice. We're not that far from Pittsburgh. And if they need anything, it's not that far to send a truck."

Canterna recalls the days before the Steelers came to St. Vincent, back when he was a student at Pitt, and playing varsity basketball games in a gym under Pitt Stadium, and later when he was coaching at St. Vincent. "I saw them losing at Forbes Field and at Pitt Stadium," said Canterna. "Unless they were playing the Browns, you could get a good seat on the day of the game. I remember walking up the hill.

"Then they got good and everybody's attitude and expectations changed. We started to get down on the Steelers when they didn't win that big."

I believe the Steelers have stayed so long at St. Vincent College because they are comfortable there, especially the Rooneys and their coach, Chuck Noll.

St. Vincent College was founded in 1846 by Boniface Wimmer, a Benedictine monk from the Bavarian abbey of Metten, who came to America in order to educate the sons of German immigrants and to train a clergy for the German-speaking people of the United States.

"Settling in Westmoreland County, at the site of a parish founded in 1789 for English and Irish Catholics," according to a booklet on the history and heritage of St. Vincent College, "Wimmer established at St. Vincent the first Benedictine monastery in North America."

69

Noll is a German Catholic and he was graduated from St. Benedictine High School in Cleveland. From there, he went to the University of Dayton, another Catholic college. He played football at both schools in a distinguished manner. In 1953, as a 21st round draft choice, he stuck with the Cleveland Browns and began a rewarding career in professional football.

For Noll and the Steelers, St. Vincent College is something of a summer retreat, a place to go to get their act together, to reflect on football on a full-time basis, and get their heart and souls in order for the challenge yet to come.

"It's a good working place," said Noll. "The facilities are adequate and we can accomplish what we want here, and it's close enough to Pittsburgh so we can get what we need, and for our fans to come see how we're coming along. It doesn't wear on you, and when you get some time off you can get back home for a break.

"The old Giants used to go to Oregon for two months. When I was playing for Cleveland, we used to go to St. Mary's College in California. They had a big cross on the top of a church steeple. Abe Gibron used to say, 'This is really living at the foot of the cross.' It's hard work, and you can get a concentrated effort at a place like this. And you can still have a good time."

One of Noll's top assistants during the Super Bowl era was George Perles, a smart football man and a good coach, who used to engage in constant chatter during practice with another assistant coach, Rollie Dotsch. They were much noisier than any of Noll's recent aides.

"People will be coming here to take baths," Perles once said as he stood on a grassy knoll and overlooked the plush green campus. "Everybody's always looking for the Fountain of Youth, and it's here, at St. Vincent — a religious place, too. They already hold retreats here, but it'll be even bigger. We'll have the most talked-about college in the world."

Sometimes, during the best of times, there would be traffic problems at St. Vincent during the early weeks of training camp simply because there were too many people on the campus. "It can be a problem," acknowledged Noll, "but it sure beats not having anybody here."

St. Vincent's locker rooms and dorm rooms certainly are not as fancy as some of the more modern facilities other professional football teams have built for themselves, like those of the Dallas Cowboys and Kansas City Chiefs. The players are isolated from the big city lights.

"I look at training camp a lot different from many guys," the veteran L.C. Greenwood once observed. "I don't come here to have a good time or to be out with the boys. If I have to leave home to go to St. Vincent, I'm coming here to work on football. I really get into football here.

"I put everything else out of my mind. St. Vincent is a great place to get ready. You can go through hell for five weeks, and then come back to the big city."

Some players look back to St. Vincent with mixed emotions. There were good times and bad times. Swann liked mixing with some of the special fans who came there each year, but there were days he didn't enjoy.

"Take cutdown day," said Swann. "I don't even like to be around the locker room when guys are saying goodby. They're shaking hands, trying to smile, because that's what you're supposed to do.

"But if you're a person, it hurts. You hear voices quivering, you see the look in a friend's eyes. You wish you were someplace else. Then, maybe an hour later, you're back on the practice field, preparing the way you always do. It's the nature of the profession."

Dick Hoak has special memories of St. Vincent College. He grew up in nearby Jeannette, and used to come to the campus when he would come home from Penn State to play basketball on Sundays in Kennedy Hall. He also was married to Lynn in the basilica there. He likes it because he is able to go home at night to nearby Greensburg when the Steelers are in training camp.

The monks once farmed the land, but they have turned over the fields on a lease basis to others in more recent years. The fields where the Steelers practice run parallel to those farm fields, and a corn field runs along the horizon across the way from the campus buildings.

It is some setting.

Why do the Steelers stay at St. Vincent?

"Just look at it," demanded Dan Rooney, as he strolled across one of the practice fields. "It's perfect."

Larry Brown and little boys at St. Vincent practice session

71

Joe Walton

Chuck Noll

Chuck Noll
"Singing in the rain"

*"If they are lucky, good coaches can become
the perfect unobtainable fathers that young
boys dream about and rarely find in their
homes. Good coaches shape and exhort and urge."*
— Pat Conroy in "The Prince of Tides"

C huck Noll is never more at peace with the world than when he is at training camp at St. Vincent College in Latrobe. He is like a man in his workshop, eager to use all his tools, tinkering with what he has made, happy within himself.

When Noll strolls across the campus, whether it is before or after practice, he always looks like he has just gone to heaven. Camp is a time for optimism, when everybody can dream about going to the Super Bowl. Noll despises negativism.

This was after lunch one day in the summer of 1990 when Noll retreated to his suite on the first floor of Bonaventure Hall. His home away from home consisted of an outer room that served as an office, a bedroom, and a private bathroom. During the school year, the floor counselor resides there.

It was not Hilton Head, where Noll has a nice getaway condominium, but it suited him just fine for another summer.

Noll sat on one chair and put his heels up on another chair, and looked like a man who knew how to relax.

The year before, 1989, Noll had taken the Steelers to the playoffs for the first time in five years, and he was rewarded by being named the AFC Coach of the Year for the first time by the Professional Football Writers of America. It was an honor long overdue for a man whose professional football career spans five decades, and four Super Bowl titles.

Noll is not one to dwell on the past. He likes history, but feels it is best to wait until retirement before you start writing any chapters. He's not ready to do that yet. He likes to read how-to and fix-it books, so he can learn something new, and maybe it will help him rebuild the Steelers to the glory he and the team once knew.

"I try to stay away from fiction," said Noll.

After 21 years as head coach of the Steelers, his record placed him fifth among the winningest coaches in NFL history, right up there with George Halas, Don Shula, Tom Landry and Curly Lambeau. Noll is also not one to toot his own horn, but he knows he is one of the best.

It had rained during both of the practices that day, and Noll looked drenched, but undaunted when he came off the field. He was asked if it bothered him to be out in the rain like that. Had he tired of that sort of thing?

"When you get into something," said Noll, "success is kind of what you expect. If you haven't had any success, the rain will bother you.

"You have to have a kind of vision. You have to see the light at the end of the tunnel. If you haven't got those things, the rain becomes a real pain. You focus on the rain. If it becomes something that bothers you, well, then you should do something else.

"You have to pay attention to what's going on right now. It's a big key. The key word is focus. When you're in this business, you have to reduce the distractions. You can't lose sight of what you want to attain. If you allow other things to occupy your mind you can't focus on what you need to do in order to win.

"I don't enjoy training camp any more than any football game. I enjoy the games; I don't particularly enjoy the aftermath."

In short, he likes to coach football, but he does not particularly relish being questioned about his every decision in the wake of a game, especially after difficult defeats. Then again, he does not go out of his way to dwell on past successes or failures, either, even Super Bowl victories.

"You have a lot of people who want to live in the past," noted Noll. "When I was growing up, we used to go to a donut shop. It was called the Mayflower Donut Shop. It had a sign on the wall which I thought was sound advice. It read: 'As you wander on through life, brother, whatever be your goal, keep your eye on the donut and not on the hole.' I thought it was a sage thing. That's something you always have to ask yourself: What is the donut and what is the hole?"

Noll was asked what went through his mind that morning when he was awakened by the sound of rainfall.

"I thought about what we'd have to do," said Noll. "We have to get into this sort of weather during the season, and it would be a chance to work on things out in the elements. You play the game in those kind of conditions, you have to practice in them, too.

"Later on, it will be good for us. You know you can function in this kind of situation. It's not something you want to do everyday.

"Somebody told me a long time ago and I have tried to get our squad thinking this way. You have to be an actor, not a reactor.

"If it's raining, you have to take care of your own attitude. Because it's raining you don't put yourself in a snit. I have to make them consider this an opportunity, not a bummer of a day.

"What a bore it would be to practice in perfect weather all the time. You can't change the rain. I want to get myself to where I can handle it."

One of Noll's goals at training camp each year is to keep distractions to a minimum, so he and the players can concentrate on what really needs to be accomplished. He works with tunnel vision.

"It's become a habit. As a player, when you first start into it, there are a lot of things that distract you. If you're worried about being hit, you screw everything up. You try to get a program established, and try to get everybody into their own niche to make it whole.

"You want to focus on what you want to do, what you want to get achieved on a particular day. The people who want to play are the people who are here. People who retire want to be remembered for the way they were when they were producing. So people ought to be the best they can be while they're able to function at the fullest capacity."

At night at St. Vincent, Noll stays in his room for the most part, whereas his assistant coaches used to run down the road to the local watering holes as fast as they could. Now some of them go down. They are a lot tamer and better behaved these days.

"It's become a habit for me," said Noll. "It's the same way when we're at the stadium, or after a game. You come here and you work late, and by the time you're ready to go to bed your motor is still running. You come home and you're still wired and you can't go to sleep. So I'll read for awhile. It slows me down. Then I'm able to sleep.

"I can't be out late at night. I work hard all day. I need sleep. I can't function if I slept as little as some of the people up here. You have to practice what you preach.

"I have a philosophy as far as team sports go. If you want to function as a team and you start talking about blame or credit you get things out of whack. You don't use a measuring stick to measure people's contributions.

"You have a lot of individual parts. I have to look in the mirror. What the hell am I doing? Did I cause this to happen? If you see somebody doing something wrong you want to correct it. You want to help them be the best they can be. Sometimes you have to holler, 'Hey, you're dipping your head when you're tackling people. Don't do that.'"

Noll believes in "synergism" — that the whole is greater than the sum of its parts. He does not think it is his job to motivate players. "It is my job," he said, "to direct motivated individuals."

The Steelers worked out for a while in the gym that day. Just walking through plays, mostly slow-motion stuff. It did not look like much fun. "It's a necessity," said Noll. "It's a dull way to reinforce what you've given them in a meeting. It's one of the things I learned early on. You tell somebody something, but it's not established in their minds. You have to give them a recognition and an appreciation of what you're talking about. You try to speed up the process. So you go through it several times at practice until they understand exactly what you want done, and why. You teach through technique. You want to reduce the mistakes. You want them to think their way through it. So you go slowly."

Noll had brought in a new offensive coordinator in Joe Walton, a former Pitt All-American and Pro Bowl performer with the Washington Redskins and New York Giants who had been the head coach of the New York Jets the previous seven seasons. Walton brought in a new playbook. It was confounding many of the players.

I asked Noll why Walton was not asked to learn the Steelers' terminology, and be permitted to drop what he did not like, and add what he liked to do that was not in the system. It seemed like it would be easier for an experienced and wise head like Walton to make the adjustment rather than have everyone else, including the coaches, learn a new system.

That system, by the way, would become an early-season controversy, when the Steelers struggled at the start and could not score touchdowns.

"After talking with Joe, we decided it was best done in his system," said Noll. "We were changing a lot of things in our passing game. I had to learn it, too, and it's tough to teach an old dog new tricks. We were going to change, anyhow, and Joe just made it easier to do so.

"As far as my personal philosophy goes, this does not represent a change for me, contrary to public opinion. There's no best way to do something. If there's a more efficient way, I'm all for it. Football grows. It's not the same thing. It's always evolving. So you have to constantly adjust to the changes, trying to get a flexible system.

"Joe's pretty much running the offense. Maybe I'm an assistant. Coaching is coaching. You don't say, 'Do it because I say it.' There's a great deal of searching around that's done in coaching, trying to get your players comfortable with what they're doing, wanting them to be confident in what they're doing, and you listen to them, too. You don't say, 'Hey, I'm the boss. My way is the only way.' Some of the players have good ideas, too.

"We needed to make a rational transition in our thinking. What we were doing was not getting us where we wanted to be. It's normal to go through life repeating what you've done before, and resenting change. It's probably as bad as wishing your life away."

Noll is known to freeze players with a stare. He could stare men into submission. As Pat Conroy wrote of a general in his "Lords of Discipline" book, "he was an athlete of the stare; he enjoyed the sport."

Noll was asked what coaches he had or worked with who influenced him the most.

"When you've got good teachers, and Paul Brown was certainly one, and I had them even in high school and college, you pick up things without realizing it. It's tough to pinpoint where you learn something.

"Like most things in football, it's a team effort. They all contributed in some way to what I am today, whatever that might be. I've never said, 'Hey, I'm a genius. I thought about that myself.' There's an osmosis. That's just a reality. You absorb stuff as you go along, and you work it out to suit what you do best.

"The biggest thing I learned from all of them is attitude. I've been lucky to have been around a lot of talented people, a lot of people with physical abilities. I've learned that you have to be demanding. You only get what you demand.

"There are a lot of things you can't coach. When you get a team together you have varying personalities. Everybody is not the same. One of the things I learned in dealing with human beings is that they are not machines.

"They don't have a limit. You can't sit down and figure the force they can handle. That's why you can't put a mechanical formula on it. There are some things you can't measure. You can't measure mind and heart. Different people make different kinds of contributions to the whole. You're trying to find out if someone fits into what you're trying to do. You try to give each one of them an opportunity. That's all you can do. The rest is up to them."

What's Chuck Noll really like? Why don't his players like him better? How come he was never named Coach of the Year when the Steelers won those four Super Bowls?

How come Franco Harris and Terry Bradshaw have been saying bad things about him?

Why do sportswriters pick on him?

Chuck Who?

Noll has always raised questions by his demeanor, public posture, private ways, stubbornness, Dutch sense of humor, some of the things he has been quoted as saying, his style. Noll is an enigma to some. A sphinx to some. To others, he is simply good company. A good man. A good family man. A man who has his priorities in order. Above all, he should be regarded as a great coach. One of the greatest in the game, that is, in the history of the game.

No other coach can boast that he coached a team to four Super Bowl championships. But Noll would never make such a boast. He concerns himself with what needs to be done to win another NFL title. He worries about today, not yesterday, not tomorrow. He suffers most sportswriters as if they are mere fools. His players have said he has often warned them to be wary of the press, and to be careful about what they say in interviews.

Noll does not even wear a Super Bowl ring. During the glory years, some of his players and coaches wore a Super Bowl ring on each hand, and on all four fingers of one hand for picture-taking purposes — remember how they wanted to win one for the thumb? — but Noll has always been content with wearing just his wedding ring.

When the Steelers were winning all those Super Bowls, and bringing back bonus checks, many of the players and assistant coaches and administrative staff people went out and bought bigger homes and moved into fancier neighborhoods.

Noll still lived in the same attractive, but unassuming, green house he purchased when he became the coach of the Steelers back in 1969. It is the same house Steelers' president Dan Rooney showed him when he hired him. A few years ago, Noll caused a stir in the neighborhood by putting an addition on the back of the house. You can be sure it is not a trophy room.

I have lived in the same community, Upper St. Clair, in the suburbs just 10 miles south of Three Rivers Stadium, for the past 12 years, but I have never seen Noll anywhere in Upper St. Clair. I live just over a mile from his house. I spotted him once in his frontyard, tending to his roses, one of his interests, and that is it. I have never seen him shopping, or at a school or community event. Noll sightings at local stores still stir conversation. They are as rare as some birds. Alison Conte of Tambellini's Pasta & Yogurt in Norman Centre, near Noll's home, said Georgia peach and chocolate are his favorite flavors of frozen yogurt. Store owners I know, such as pharmacist Marshall Goldstein of the Pinebridge Apothecary, tell me Noll's wife, Marianne, does all the talking, while Chuck quietly drifts around the aisles. Noll keeps a low profile. In some respects, Noll is a bit of a recluse.

One of his best friends, John "Red" Manning, was the basketball coach and then the athletic director at Duquesne University. He has been with Pittsburgh National Bank the past nine years. Manning was a good coach, but he was never comfortable in the public arena. Like Noll, he was wary of the press.

Manning's wife, Pat, is often mistaken for Marianne Noll. They look like sisters. The Mannings live in Bethel Park, within two miles of the Nolls' home.

Dan Rooney introduced the Nolls to the Mannings soon after he hired his new coach, and the couples have gotten along famously.

"Chuck is an interesting guy," said Manning in March, when I ran into him at South Hills Village. "He's so smart. He'd make a great military general. He'd have been great if he had been involved in the war in the Persian Gulf. He sets his mind to doing something and he does it. He can really focus on what he wants to do. Plus, he's a great leader.

"He's into boats now. He has all kinds of books on boats. He'll fix things for me around my house. He knows something about a lot of things. He's easy to like. He has a good sense of humor, and he knows how to have fun. Hey, he'll do the Charleston, or something like that, on the spur of the moment. He knows how to get a laugh out of you.

"One of the things that impresses me about him is that I have never heard him rap a player or anybody associated with the Steelers. Never. I've met a lot of good people in sports in my time, and he's one of them. And my Pat is very close with Marianne. We've had a lot of fun together."

Noll shuns sports banquets. He does not have his own TV show. He did a few commercials, at first, but felt uncomfortable in the role, and felt it would be better if the players got the commercials. They could benefit more from the exposure, the extra money. "The glory should go to the players," he said. He will not appear on sports talk shows. Who needs the aggravation, the abuse? His time is too important to squander on a sports talk show. He likes to keep the crazies and critics at a safe distance.

He has said the same things week after week for 21 years at his press conferences, refusing to go after the bait offered to him by the local news media. The Steelers could be playing The Little Sisters of the Poor, and Noll would say, "No matter what you guys think, we have a lot of respect for their folks."

At one press conference in particular during the 1990 season, Noll was asked two questions that stick in my mind. He was asked about the playing status of Aaron Jones. "I don't know yet," said Noll. "I saw Aaron in the hallway this morning, and he was on crutches. I'll have to check with the doctor." Rookie running back Barry Foster had flubbed a kick return assignment, and backed away from the ball which was, in turn, picked up by an opposing player and it set up a touchdown on the ensuing play. It was a major goof. Noll was asked what was going through Foster's mind on that play. "I don't know what was going through his mind," he snapped. "I can't see into his head."

But I wondered why he had not asked Foster what he was thinking, or talked to him personally and made sure it never happened again. And why didn't he ask Aaron Jones about his status? It seemed natural enough to ask one of your players how he was doing, or to ask him what the doctor told him.

"That wouldn't be Chuck," said Joe Greene. "That's not his style."

Noll is old fashioned. He has his own stubborn set of values. He acquired them in Cleveland, long before he ever met Paul Brown. He is not in favor of faking injuries to stop a clock in order to compete with the hurry-up offense, say, of Sam Wyche and the Cincinnati Bengals, because he is above that sort of trickery. And he does not like his players to put on a show or song-and-dance act after scoring a touchdown, or doing something right. "I'd like our people to act like they've been there before," he said.

When the Steelers are at St. Vincent College, Noll may as well be on one of the religious retreats that are held there for Catholics of the nearby communities. Noll would never go out with his assistant coaches or the sportswriters to the local watering holes on Rt. 30 in the Latrobe-Greensburg area. Noll is not much of a mixer. Maybe dinner with some special friends, but no all-night drinking marathons. Noll's too smart for that.

"I couldn't function if I didn't get a certain amount of sleep," he says. "I couldn't coach and do my job."

He wanted the players to get their sleep as well. Gerry Mullins, a guard on the great Super Bowl teams, was from Southern California, and was regarded as an easy-does-it, laid-back Californian, afraid of no one or anything.

"Chuck took curfew seriously," said Mullins. "When we went over the wall at camp, we feared finding Chuck Noll standing in the hallway when we got back after hours. The idea of it still scares me."

Noll does not believe in spending the entire day on football, or in sleeping at Three Rivers Stadium. He believes in reasonable working hours, and that there is a point of no return as far as preparing for a football game.

He does not make as much money as some other coaches, but he is still at it, and comfortable with his station in life, whereas some other super coaches such as John Madden, Bill Walsh, Dick Vermeil and Tom Landry have gone to the great broadcasting booths in the sky. Noll does not believe in "burnout" and you can make book that he will not leave the sideline to become a football analyst.

His critics claim that Noll has stayed too long — that the game has passed him by — and that he would be better to retire, and enjoy his laurels, to enter the Pro Football Hall of Fame. Noll is not ready for retirement. He will pick his own time.

It is a shame more Steelers' fans do not have an opportunity to see Noll off stage because he is a most likable fellow. He can be as warm as a winter's fireplace. He is easy to talk to, especially if the subject is not the Steelers or football. Some complain, however, that he is an expert on too many subjects.

He is an accomplished airplane pilot, a deep sea diver and underwater photographer, a gourmet cook who knows fine wine and tends his garden. He also enjoys classical music and tennis, though he will not play tennis with sportswriters. I suspect he would not want to lose and have them think they were superior in some respect. His latest interest is boating.

"Did you ever notice how Noll is full of advice on how to raise children?" a sportswriter once sniped. "He has one child. Dan Rooney has nine children and he never suggests he knows the best way to raise kids. But Noll's an expert on everything."

Sportswriters have an opportunity to get closest to Noll at the team's training camp each summer. He is accessible to them at Three Rivers Stadium, but he is more accessible and relaxed, and usually in better spirits when the team is at training camp, before the games count in the standings.

It would have been insightful for most, for instance, if they had seen and heard Noll following the second practice session of the day, back in the summer of 1990, when Noll appeared in "the beer room" at St. Vincent College. It is a room reserved for coaches and staff and sportswriters, where post-practice gatherings are a relaxed, let-your-hair down affair. A beer or two before dinner, and some off-the-record discussions.

It had rained all day long on this particular day. The sportswriters had not strayed from their rooms much, except for lunch, to watch the practice sessions. It was a good day to write. It seemed a bad day to be out on the football field. Not for Noll, though.

He had showered and had a well-scrubbed look, a positive shine on his face. He had just combed his hair, and he looked fresh as can be. He walked into the room as though he were in an Easter Parade. He was cheerful, downright sunny. "Nice day, huh?" he asked of no one in particular.

"It can't be too much fun to be out there on a day like today," said Norm Vargo, the sports editor of *The Daily News* in McKeesport, a sports writer who is completely comfortable in Noll's company, since he has been on the Steelers' beat nearly as long as Noll has been coaching the club.

"That's not so," said Noll. "We got some things done today. We've got to play in this stuff, so you need to practice in it, too. It worked out fine."

Vargo asked Noll how his 32-year-old son, Chris, was doing. Chris had worked one summer as an intern in the sports department of *The Daily News*.

"Chris just bought a 163-year-old house in Elkins, New Hampshire that needs a lot of work," said Noll. "He and his wife have their work cut out for them with that place. I told him to trash it."

Chris is a teacher, a trade Noll has often said he would have pursued if he were not a coach. Noll's wife, Marianne, has been a teacher. Her mother was a teacher. "There are a lot of good teachers in the family," noted Noll.

"It makes me feel old to think that Chris is married," said Vargo, "and has his own home."

"If he makes you feel old," Noll came back, "what do you think he does to me?"

"Are you looking forward to being a grandfather?" asked Vargo.

"Oh, sure," said Noll, with a smile and a wink. "I'm looking forward to that."

"Then you'll retire," said Vargo.

"No, I haven't been in pro football long enough," Noll shot back. "This is only my 38th training camp."

Noll began his NFL career as a 21st round draft choice of the Cleveland Browns out of the University of Dayton back in 1953. He played guard and linebacker for seven seasons when the Browns won two NFL championships. He retired prematurely, at the age of 27, and began his coaching career in 1960 as an assistant to Sid Gillman with the Los Angeles Chargers of the American Football League.

In 1966, Noll joined Don Shula's staff with the Baltimore Colts for a three-year stint in which the Colts lost only seven regular season games, plus a Super Bowl III loss to the New York Jets and Joe Namath. It was shortly after that setback that Noll was named head coach of the Steelers, succeeding Bill Austin.

I remember being in that same "beer room" when Austin was the coach of the Steelers. His biggest sin was that he tried to be like Vince Lombardi, with whom he had worked as an assistant coach on the great Green Bay Packers teams. He mimicked Lombardi, but the ballplayers saw right through his charade. Noll never tried to be like Paul Brown, Shula or Gillman, some of the greatest coaches in the game. He learned a lot about football and life from them, but he is his own man. Noll is just Noll, take it or leave it.

81

Noll has never been what the sportswriters wanted him to be, more open, more critical, more quotable, more of a personality, more colorful. He is just Noll. Very vanilla.

The Steelers' record in the first of Austin's three seasons as head coach was 5-8-1. It was 4-9-1 the next season, and 2-11-1 in his final season. It did not seem like the Steelers could get any worse.

In Noll's first season, the Steelers won their first game. The players and fans got excited. Then the Steelers lost the next 13 games. It was the franchise's worst record since the World War II year of 1945, when the Steelers-Cardinals merged unit compiled an 0-10 record.

"He lost all those games," Art Rooney often reflected about Noll's first year, "but he never lost the team. That's when I knew we had ourselves a good coach."

Rooney always respected Noll, but he never fully understood him, either. A people person, Rooney was always happiest when he had a good cigar and a good conversation going at the same time. He loved to talk to people, especially sportswriters. If he had not been a pro sports entrepreneur, he often said, he would have wanted to be a sportswriter, to be where the action was.

"You see how you're sitting there and just talking to me," Rooney once told me. "You come here often and just plop down in that chair, and we talk. I like that. In 17 years, Noll has never just come in here and sat there and talked to me. When he came in, it was on business."

Once, during an NFL owners' meeting in Rancho Mirage, near Palm Springs, California, I questioned Joe Gordon, then the publicity director of the Steelers, about why Noll never suggested that my wife, Kathleen, and I join him and his wife, Marianne, for breakfast or lunch, or just a drink, for a little light-hearted socializing. It seemed natural enough.

"If you're waiting for Noll to do that," said Gordon, with a grin, "you've got a long wait coming. I've been here as long as Chuck, and he's yet to ever invite me to lunch or breakfast."

Myron Cope has been there just as long, as the analyst on the Steelers' radio broadcasts, and as a sports talk show host who has often stuck a long needle into Noll's backside. That day it rained all day at the Steelers' training camp, and Noll came in beaming afterward, I mentioned to Cope how great Noll appeared.

"Noll's amazing," Cope came back as only Cope can. "He looks fantastic for a guy who's never had any fun in his life. A big day for him is when he goes shopping with Marianne."

As Noll neared his 200th career victory in early December, 1990, he was interviewed by Steve Hubbard of *The Pittsburgh Press*, who probed him to find out how he had managed to survive 22 seasons as the head coach of the Steelers when coaches like Vermeil and Madden succumbed to stress, and quit the sidelines.

Chuck Noll's family at their home in Upper St. Clair: his wife, Marianne, their son, Chris, and daughter-in-law, Linda.

Mike Fabus

City of Champions Mayor Richard S. Caliguiri presents citation to Chuck Noll in 1979.

With Mark Malone and Terry Bradshaw on sideline.

As player for Cleveland Browns

lanked by Joe Greene and Jerry Olsavsky

With Howard Cosell at 50 Seasons banquet

lanked by Rollie Dotsch and Terry Bradshaw

"There's pressure, but you have to deal with that," Noll told Hubbard. "Usually, the biggest pressure comes — at least in my case — from myself, not from the exterior. Because I learned a long time ago you have no control over other people, what they think, what a writer writes or anybody.

"The only control you have is over yourself and what you do. I made up my mind a long time ago to do what I think is right and go from there. The pressure is making the decision you think is right. You do it and let the chips fall.

"Because as you go through life, one thing is certain: If you ever make decisions, you're going to make mistakes and you're going to be second-guessed.

"If that's stressful, you're in the wrong profession. You should go to a place where you don't have to make decisions.

"Pressure to get something done, pressure to make the right decision — that knocks out that procrastination and gets you going. If you have to do it, it is a stimulant and it should be a stimulant."

According to Hubbard, Noll stays stimulated because he works maybe the National Football League's sanest hours. His typical in-season day begins at 8:30 a.m. and ends at 9 p.m. Monday, 11-12 p.m. Tuesday, 7-8 p.m. Wednesday, 6 p.m. Thursday and Friday, 1-1:30 p.m. Saturday (if no travel is involved).

"I can't function without proper rest," said Noll. "If I go too long, which you do on some occasions, you're not worth a damn the next day and you're cheating the people you're trying to help prepare for a game.

"When we go to 2 and 3 (a.m.) . . . it's very inefficient. You end up getting bleary-eyed, don't get enough sleep and you can't make good judgments."

Noll takes a six-week vacation just before the season begins to recharge his battery, and then it's football seven days a week from July to January.

"I guess there are a lot of times I say, 'Why am I doing this? I could be having fun somewhere?' That happened to me as a player. You're running along, you're not quite in the shape you want to be in, and you think, 'What the heck am I doing here when I'd like to be sitting under a tree?'

"Those thoughts crop up into everybody's mind at one time or another. Then you make your decision. 'I want to be here. I want to be doing this.' "

After Noll notched his 200th career victory, in a 24-3 victory over the New England Patriots at Three Rivers Stadium, one of his assistants and former stars, Joe Greene gushed, "To win 200 games you've got to be a little good, a little lucky and a little old."

Noll would buy that. He did not want to make a fuss over the milestone, but he conceded, "It makes you stop and think a little bit. Stop and think about how long you've been around, more than anything else," said Noll, just a month away from turning 59.

"To try and keep your focus on what's ahead, you try to think about now and tomorrow. You don't look back very much. That's training. I've been trained for years . . . since way back in high school.

"When you start looking at those kinds of things, you put it on one guy. There are a lot of people who are involved, past and present, and actually you feel like you have a few more than 200. Sure, I'm proud of it. I'm proud to have been in it this long. I guess that's what it takes.

"If you spend all your time reflecting about the past, I guess that's a sign of old age. If you wish your life away by worrying about the future, you're frittering away the most important time you have, which is now."

Noll was asked how he celebrated his 200th victory. "It was not outrageous," he assured the assembled media at his weekly press conference. "I went out to dinner with my wife — just the two of us."

Chuck Noll's boss and biggest booster, Dan Rooney, reflected on what the 200th win meant.

"Just to be in that group of people — Halas, Shula, Landry and Lambeau — is phenomenal. He has done it with class and dignity. That really makes it special. Hopefully, he'll keep doing it for a long while. He's enjoying himself and he's doing the job.

"I can see him coaching until he's 65 — easy. And come 65, I might say I can see him coaching until he's 70."

The Pittsburgh Post-Gazette polled several football people who knew Noll and printed their observations before he won his 200th NFL victory.

Don Shula, Miami Dolphins coach, for whom Noll had served as an assistant coach with the Baltimore Colts: "I know Chuck better than anybody and I have just so much confidence in his ability. I was very, very happy last year when he damn near took his team to the Super Bowl. He went through the struggle at the same time all of us were — the Raiders, Cowboys, Dolphins, the teams up there year-in and year-out. He survived and got it turned around. I'm just glad the Rooneys continued to show that confidence in him, to give him a chance to turn it around."

Sid Gillman, former NFL coach for whom Noll had served as an assistant with the San Diego Chargers in his first coaching assignment: "He's no different now than he was with the Chargers as I observe him on the sidelines. Details mean so much to Chuck. He's a drillmaster. He takes people and takes nothing for granted and drills them until they do a good job. That's what makes a coach. He's a disciplinarian."

Al Davis, Los Angeles Raiders owner, who was interested in Noll when he was looking for a coach and ended up hiring Madden after the Steelers signed Noll in 1969: "He's not afraid. He's firm in his beliefs. I've always admired that. That's part of his success. He was always destined to be excellent. We both had our dreams, and thank God his have come true."

Paul Brown, Bengals owner and founder and former coach of the Cleveland Browns, where Noll spent his NFL playing career: "He's smart, he's a disciplinarian. The players know there's no monkey business there. He's made it his life's work, which means he isn't trying to sell automobiles on the side. I admire the fact he doesn't blink an eyelash when somebody goes after him. You always know they (the Steelers) will be physical. Nothing fancy. They'll come after you and stay with you until the final whistle blows. He's a tacit, quiet man and I'm not exactly effusive. I think we sort of understand each other."

George Perles, former Noll assistant and now head football coach of Michigan State University: "He works at it. He doesn't want to speak, doesn't want to be at the head of the table. He won't wear any of the rings. You talk about a clean-cut straight arrow. Everybody should have the opportunity to work for him. He's the best thing that ever happened to me."

Noll is often portrayed as a cold and calculating individual, devoid of human emotions. Bob Labriola of *Steelers Digest* shot down that idea in a column he wrote after Noll's 200th victory.

"In 1971, Walt Hackett, then Noll's defensive line coach, died of a heart attack while on a scouting trip on the West Coast," wrote Labriola. "Noll and his wife, Marianne, made the funeral arrangements, were there to console Hackett's two young daughters, and they remain in touch with the family today. Don Shula's wife has battled cancer for some time, and outside of their family, two people constantly are in contact to express concern and boost her spirits. Chuck and Marianne Noll." The Nolls attended Dorothy Shula's funeral in March when she died, at age 57.

"But that is his private life. He doesn't care to talk about it, and so he won't. He also doesn't talk about himself, his accomplishments, his goals, his plans. Those who get Noll to talk find he discusses ideas, principles, philosophies. He is, evermore, a teacher."

Talking with players who have been around a long time, or a short time, you get the same thoughts about Noll's posture toward his players.

"You know when he's happy, when he's ticked off and when he's really ticked off," said Dwayne Woodruff, who had been with the Steelers for 11 seasons. "He doesn't holler or scream. I can't ever remember Chuck losing it, but he makes sure he portrays exactly how he feels about a situation.

"He treats you like a professional. You're paid to do a job and he expects you to do it. His expectations are extremely high, but I think that's why the Steelers have done so well over the years."

Carnell Lake, a second year safety from UCLA, was in the Steelers' clubhouse at Three Rivers Stadium when he said, "I don't think anyone in here, except for the quarterbacks, has ever talked to him longer than two minutes."

Dick Hoak has been with Noll as both a player and coach for over 20 years, and he says Noll has never been to his home in Greensburg. Hoak has been to Noll's house in Upper St. Clair, however, and he came away with his feelings reinforced about his boss.

"If you went to his house, you probably couldn't tell he was the coach of the Steelers by looking around. And if you were looking for trophies and things like that, you'd have a hard time finding any."

Bill Priatko is a pal of mine and a great admirer of Chuck Noll. Priatko credits Noll as the No. 1 reason the Steelers won all those Super Bowls.

Priatko is in charge of academic support services for the student athletes at Robert Morris College in Coraopolis, where I teach a twice-weekly class in sports information. Priatko is a good man, in the spirit of the Steelers' late owner Art Rooney, whom he also greatly admired, and I visit him as often as possible because he is the same sort of decent, caring inspirational man of great faith. He has a wonderful family.

He takes great pride in being an alumnus of the University of Pittsburgh and of the Pittsburgh Steelers. He is a positive person.

Priatko played linebacker for one season with the Steelers in 1957. The year before that, he was with the Green Bay Packers. He was never a star, just a survivor. In 1959, he went to the training camp of the Cleveland Browns at Hiram College and made the team.

"It was Chuck Noll's final season with the Browns, and I learned right away all you needed to know about Noll and why he is such a special person," said Priatko.

"Paul Brown was the coach of the Browns and he used to give all the players a test during training camp. You had to diagram all the plays and formations, and you had to indicate what each of the 11 players did on that particular call. I'd like to see some of the guys do that today. You didn't just have to know what you were doing on a particular call, but you had to know everybody else's assignment, too.

"It took most of the players about an hour and 15 or 20 minutes to complete the test. There was a test for the offensive players and there was a different test for the defensive players. Now Noll played guard on offense and linebacker on defense. He was one of the few who played both ways.

"Noll was in the same room where I was taking the defensive test. He got up from his seat after about 25 minutes and went to the front of the room and turned in his test. Then he went into another room and took the offensive test. He had a hundred per cent on both tests. He's the only one who had a hundred per cent on either test. He aced them both!

"He was something. We'd sit around after a meal, and he talked about so many different things. He had so much knowledge. It was obvious he was an intelligent person. He knew so much about so many things. He was a learned man. He was just different from the rest of the guys on the team. He was not just a football player."

Priatko played his high school ball at Scott High in North Braddock, where he befriended Fran Rogel who went on to be the Steelers' starting fullback from 1950 to 1957. They see each other at Steelers' alumni affairs.

Franco Harris, Terry Bradshaw and Gerry Mullins in heyday.

Priatko doesn't miss any reunions. In the summer of 1990, Priatko was one of several former Steelers who were organizing some alumni activities that were to feature the 1978 Steelers' squad, thought to be perhaps the greatest NFL team of all time.

He recalls a meeting in an upstairs room at Froggy's, a famous watering hole on Market Street in downtown Pittsburgh owned by Steve Morris and favored by sports enthusiasts. He recalls that Ray Mansfield called the meeting, and that Lloyd Voss, Leo Nobile, Ernie Bonelli and Gerry Mullins were among those present.

Terry Bradshaw was not returning phone calls made by Mansfield. Bradshaw had already been billed as the featured attraction at this two-day event, a barbecue dinner at the Melody Tent at Station Square, and a golf outing at the Oakmont Country Club. But it looked like he was not going to show up, which is exactly what happened.

"I'm tired of that hot dog," Mansfield said, according to Priatko. "When I go out and speak now, I bring up Bradshaw. I tell people what I think. I don't care if Terry is upset with the Steelers, or the front office, or Pittsburgh or the fans. But he shouldn't be taking it out on his teammates. We were teammates. That's what pro football is all about: the togetherness among teammates. It's your teammates that count. He ignores Andy Russell and me. And we were his teammates." He said Mullins, who was once regarded as Bradshaw's best friend on the team, seconded the motion. "Everyone knows we were close," said Mullins, "and he doesn't pay any attention to me, either."

Priatko had played at Pitt and with the Steelers with Richie McCabe, a scrawny fellow from the North Side who surprised people by playing football at Pitt and in the pros. McCabe had once been the waterboy for the Steelers while attending North Catholic High School. Priatko recalled telephone conversations with McCabe when McCabe was an assistant coach with the Denver Broncos.

"He said he talked every week with George Allen of the Washington Redskins, and that Allen thought Chuck Noll was one of the few coaches who could deal with Bradshaw. A lot of the coaches thought he was a hot dog, too. They didn't think they could put up with him. But they thought Noll handled him well, and got the most out of him. It's a shame Bradshaw doesn't understand or appreciate that."

90

Keith Willis
The commuter from Newark

Keith Willis is a huge man with a huge heart. He works hard at standing tall and flattening opposing quarterbacks. He is listed at 6-1, 263 pounds. He is a graduate of Northeastern University in Boston. His hometown is Newark, New Jersey.

Willis walks tall because he did his homework and he did graduate from college, and because he came from the dreary projects of Newark, where not walking tall was perceived as a weakness. The wrong kind of guys took advantage of such weaknesses. It is no different from the Steelers' practice fields or any playing sites in the National Football League.

Northeastern is not a pro football farm team. It is not a big time football program. Willis wanted to play pro football, but he was ignored in the 1982 draft. None of the 28 franchises in the National Football League felt that Willis was worth drafting. He signed with the Steelers as a free agent. He commuted by bus to practice at Three Rivers Stadium his first few seasons with the Steelers.

Willis still feels like a free agent. As far as he is concerned, he will always be a free agent. His status with the Steelers has never changed. It worries Willis. He has never made the big money, the real big money. He does not forget that he has done much better than anybody he knew growing up in those projects in Newark, but he also knows he is worth more than the rookies who get those half-million dollar signing bonuses.

He is a respected defensive lineman. He led the team in sacks three times in a six-season stretch. In 1983, he broke the team record with 14 sacks in a sensational season. The record was broken the following year by Mike Merriweather with 15, but it remains the second best in Steelers' history.

That is worth something. He has improved his pay to the point where he is making more money than he ever dreamed of making.

He and his wife, Maxine, and their two children, Jasmine and Keith Jr., live in a beautiful home in Wexford, a fashionable suburb to the north of Pittsburgh, an easy 15 to 20 minute drive to Three Rivers Stadium.

He is certainly better off than his kid brother who died from an overdose of drugs, done in by the perils of the project in Newark. That never leaves Willis when he starts feeling sorry for himself.

In 1990, during his ninth summer stay at St. Vincent College, Willis was walking away from the second football workout of the day. It was not easy for him to stand tall, try as he might. When the Steelers leave the practice field, they must walk up a hill to get to the field house locker room. The grade on that hill gets steeper as one nears the top. The more tired one is the steeper it seems.

91

Near the top it is steep enough that someone thought it would be a good idea to construct a stone stairway. There are 19 steps in the stairway. On the 18th step on this particular sunny day, Willis hesitated awhile. Sweat beaded on his shaven skull, and his head glistened in the afternoon sun. And he just stood there, as if he were seeking the strength to advance one more step. He had just turned 31, which is when pro athletes start feeling old. Willis worried about where he stood with the Steelers, but that was no different from his first camp when he was 22 years old.

"On a professional level, I didn't know what I was getting into," Willis would say of that first summer at St. Vincent, after he had showered and cooled down and collected his thoughts.

"A lot of guys gave me the impression I was nothing more than a dummy — for people to beat up on me. I put that notion aside in a hurry. I was here to make the team."

Now Willis was back at his first camp, at least in his mind's eye. "The vets . . . telling me to go in there . . . 'Get in there, rookie!' I didn't appreciate that. I didn't want anybody bossing me around, except the coaches. But I thought, OK, I'll do it. I'll get on the film; it's a chance to impress the coaches.

"My upbringing is this: Don't boss me around. You kindly ask me to do something. My response to you shouting at me is that you don't respect me. These guys were walking around with chips on their shoulders.

"The big problem was I came in as a free agent. These are guys you just use and abuse. I wasn't for that. That's not the way I was raised.

"I had no inkling of what would happen to me after my senior season at Northeastern. I sat in the Prudential Building in Boston and watched the NFL draft on a big screen that had been set up there by the Patriots. I was expecting to get drafted. I left the building around the seventh pick. No one had picked me. I felt saddened.

"My wife — she was my girl friend back then — and I talked about it that same day. She said, 'What if you don't get drafted, but you get a trial with the Steelers?' She was from Pittsburgh, from the South Side. She was more upset than I was that I didn't get drafted. She was coming up with all kinds of what-ifs. But she had good vibes and she believed in me. We got married here my first year."

For the most part, free agents at training camps are fodder for the veterans and draft choices who enjoy a higher status, no matter what the general managers and coaches might say. Free agents come and they go. Ten years later, those free agents who stayed around a few days, maybe for a scrimmage session or two, like to tell people they once played for the Pittsburgh Steelers. Their names do not show up on any official lists of former Steelers, however, because they never made the final roster and they didn't play in any regular season games. But once they were Steelers.

The free agents who succeed often become legends and are pointed to by club officials as perfect examples of how you can beat the system, how there is, indeed, a genuine opportunity to make the team, to stick with the Steelers.

In Pittsburgh, they pointed to Donnie Shell, a defensive back out of South Carolina State, who was one of five rookie free agents to make the team in the strike year of 1974. Shell became a Pro Bowl performer, collected four Super Bowl championship rings, and stayed with the Steelers for 14 seasons. Sam Davis, Tony Dungy, Randy Grossman and John Banaszak were all free agents who made their mark with the Steelers' greatest teams, but they were all gone, except Banaszak, by the time Willis came to camp in 1982. Banaszak was cut that summer, which opened a spot for Willis.

"I never knew what to expect when I first got here," said Willis. "But it's been rewarding. Donnie Shell was a motivating force in my success. I talked to Donnie a lot.

"Donnie, in the most significant way I'll never forget . . . he said, 'There's not a guy on this team that's better than you. When we go in the locker room every guy puts on his pads the same way. When we go onto the field, we do it the same way. The only unfortunate thing is you didn't get drafted.' He said, 'When you step on the field, make yourself known.' I said, 'That's one thing I'm good at . . . making myself known.' And I wanted to be known in a positive light."

When Willis looks back, he credits his mother, and teammate Dwayne Woodruff for showing him the way. He remembers the kindness and personal interest of people like Tony Parisi, the Steelers' equipment manager, for making the journey a lot easier.

"My mother kept me out of trouble. I'm afraid of cops. It costs too much to get out of trouble. In high school, during my first year, I came to recognize that. I grew up with guys who always got in trouble. I knew that the system didn't win. I saw them get whopped and beat up by the cops. I never wanted anyone beating me up."

When Willis was a rookie, he shared a story with me for *The Pittsburgh Press*. He remembers today that it was the first story that was written about him. He was doing well in pre-season games in the summer of 1982. Steeler coaches were advising sportswriters on the beat to watch Willis. Mary Willis used to tell people to watch Keith Willis, too. She worried about him, the fourth of her five sons. One already had died, at age 16, from a drug overdose. She worried that Keith, who was a few years younger, was traveling with a similar crowd, and that he would end up the same way.

"We were totally different," Keith said confidently that day at St. Vincent College. "The only thing we had in common was that we came out of the same woman."

At first, Keith was not willing to say what happened to his brother, just that he died young. "It was such a tragedy in my life," he said. "I try to put it out of my mind.

"It had a profound effect on my life. That derived from my mother thinking I was like my brother."

From the start, since he has been with the Steelers, Willis was always eager to call home and tell his mother how well he was doing. "She's happy as hell. Me and my mother can sit down and talk about everything now, like friends, not just a mother-son relationship," said Willis.

Anybody who knows Newark, or who has spent any time there, or heard much about it, knows a lot about what Willis went through in his youth. "It was very tough," he said. "The part of town that I grew up in could be compared to the wilderness. Everybody was out for himself. They would do anything to get the necessities of life."

It was called the Central Ward. Willis said he was glad his mother got under his skin the way she did, so he didn't put a needle under his skin the way his brother did. His mother has gone from having heroin to a hero in her home. But she did not realize this early on.

"You're just like your brother," Mary Willis would holler a decade before Willis joined the Steelers, and Keith would simply shudder.

"One day, when I was 12," recalled Keith, "this old man who lived in our project called and asked my mother if I could go to the store for him. She said I would, and I got mad because I didn't want to do it. 'You're just like your brother — heartless and mean,' she screamed."

Keith could still hear that remark ringing in his ears. "My brother was a follower," he said. "He'd do anything anybody would offer."

Willis tried to follow the right pack, and went out for the football team in his sophomore year at Malcolm X Shabazz High School. "I ran in the backfield, but I didn't like that," he said. "I went back to being the old Keith, just roaming the halls. In my junior year, a coach saw me wandering around and — to make a long story short — told me I should come out for football, and see if I could develop my talent."

Willis was given a second opportunity and took advantage of it. He earned a scholarship as a senior to Northeastern, where he was a four-year starter, co-captain as a junior and senior, and led the team in tackles his last three seasons.

At Northeastern and with the Steelers, Willis has kept the best kind of company. Woodruff, who overcame much personal adversity, and went to law school at Duquesne University and became an attorney while playing for the Steelers, has been Keith's closest friend on the Steelers.

"Dwayne and I have developed a relationship over the years. It's pretty concrete. We always are together. His wife and my wife are good friends. We go out together," said Willis.

"I know all the adversities he went though. When I came here, he was the guy who lent me his wife's car so I could go get furniture for my apartment. I would have been taking a taxi or riding a bus. Those things you don't forget."

He puts Parisi in the same category.

94

"Tony put some wheels under me, and I'll never forget him for that," said Willis, who laughed when asked about the first car he drove during his early years with the Steelers. "My first car with the Steelers was something else. I'm glad I can sit here and laugh about it. I took the bus from Bellevue to practice for my first five years with the team.

"Tony Parisi came up to me after training camp had broken up, before maybe the second or third game, one day when we were at the stadium. Parisi felt bad about me not having any car. Tony took me to a friend who had an Oldsmobile dealership. He got me a big Delta 88. My teammates called it The Green Monster. Walter Abercrombie and some of the guys on the team really hammered me about that. That's why I took the bus to practice. It was easier than taking any more abuse."

Those early days help keep Keith humble, and at the same time they make him resent the rookies, especially the high-priced rookies, who come to camp each year, some of them out to steal away his job.

"More money is being made by younger guys. That's mind-boggling. They're making $600,000 or $700,000. I think it needs to be adjusted. A guy can come in here and get $600,000. You know he'll get a signing bonus and at least a three year commitment from the club. That's a bad system. Some of them figure they've already got it made. Why kill themselves?"

Hall of Famer Joe Greene made good money in his days with the Steelers, first as a No. 1 draft choice in 1969, and then as a perennial All-Pro performer, but nothing like the players of today. Greene was coaching the Steelers' defensive linemen, and he had little patience with anybody who was not as ambitious to work hard and to win as he was when he was playing.

"The thing that upsets Joe Greene more than anything is lack of effort," said Willis. "He's working and coaching with approximately 12 guys each year. He knows each individual has potential to play on a professional level. The most frustrating thing for Joe is the guy who has potential and doesn't play up to it.

"He wants to see a guy practice at a level of 110 per cent or more. That's the way I live. There's no way you can play this game at less than 110 per cent.

"Joe Greene gets after guys. He does get pissed off. Keith Gary and Darryl Sims really pissed him off. He'll get out there and go through different drills with us, but he's not that young stud he once was. That makes him even madder.

"What Joe preaches is that you have to demand respect. You have to get their respect. Don't let up. Don't give them any room for disrespect. If you do, they'll take full advantage of it."

Greene was gone from the Steelers when Willis first reported to the Steelers. He had retired after the previous season. But he had set the standard for defensive linemen with the Steelers. During his heyday, Greene was thought to be the best defensive lineman in the game.

Growing up in Newark, Willis was not a big sports fan. "I wasn't a fan of no one," he said. "I wasn't really into professional sports. There was no specific team I followed.

"I went to see the Yankees and Mets play a few times. I didn't go to see the Jets or Giants. The first professional football game I saw in my life was between the New England Patriots and the Pittsburgh Steelers. It was steaming hot; I was stripped to my shorts. It was in my first year at Northeastern and the coaches took us to a game at Foxboro Stadium.

"But I never had a particular team as a favorite. But I was impressed when I first joined the Pittsburgh Steelers. I had seen these guys on TV. To be in the same locker room and be sitting next to L.C. Greenwood and Lynn Swann and Terry Bradshaw and Jack Ham, John Stallworth and Donnie Shell. It was amazing. Here I am with all these guys who once won four Super Bowls. Something that had then been achieved by only one team in history. It was a mind-boggling experience.

"I held Mel Blount's four Super Bowl rings. It was quite an experience, something I truly want to experience before I leave the game."

As he spoke, Willis knew he was running out of time to achieve that accomplishment. But he had come close. Greene had never gotten "the one for the thumb" he had sought before he retired. But Willis thought the Steelers still had enough talent to go all the way.

"I thought then that these guys are now old in the game, but they're well-experienced. They know what it takes to win. I thought, 'Hey, I'll be a part of that and get to the Super Bowl.' That's what I expected, anyhow.

"In my second year here, we went to the playoffs. We had Miami 21-10 in the AFC championship game and I just knew we were on our way to the Super Bowl. But Dan Marino got hot and they killed us in the second half.

"I was disappointed that one time. I was extremely disappointed when we went down to Miami and we had them down. We were ahead at halftime and we totally forgot what we did in the first half. I was so disappointed we didn't win that game and go to the Super Bowl."

Asked what the difference was from his first camp till now, Willis was quick to say, "We had great attendance at all our practice sessions back then. There were people all over the place; it was hard to move around. We get a couple thousand now on a good day. Back then, it seemed like there were 15,000 people running around here. That was also a mind-boggling experience in itself. Back at our college, on game day we didn't have a third of the people at our home games that we had here. I thought I'd have to do better with all these people watching. Here I was practicing before crowds that far exceeded what we had at our home games in Boston.

"It was great being with the Steelers. I knew nobody had any more respect than the Steelers. It was a great feeling. Everyone respected the Steelers. It was Steeler Mania from the first day."

After he made the Steelers, Willis still felt insecure. He knew he needed to go back to Northeastern. "I went back and got my degree.

Once a free agent, you're always a free agent. Nine years, and I'm still being treated like a free agent. So it's best to have something to fall back on."

Did Willis really still feel like a free agent?

"Absolutely, I find that I can't think otherwise. I can't think I have this team sewed up. It can be taken from me that quickly.

"I have to be focused. This is my job. Everybody says you should think about your life after football. I know there has to be a life after football. I'm thinking about the life after, but right now I'm concentrating entirely on football.

"It's different for me now. Some of the older players feel the same way I do. I used to know everyone. The other day, during a scrimmage, I saw one of our guys do something well. I hollered out 'great play,' but I didn't know his name. I thought maybe I better sit down and get into the roster and get to know these guys."

Keith Willis

Mark Malone
He had a tough act to follow

M any people in Pittsburgh may owe an apology to Mark Malone. This personable young man is as good as they come and then some — a super person if something less as a quarterback — and he tried so desperately hard to be what the Steelers and their fans wanted him to be. That was something close to the second coming of Terry Bradshaw. But he came up short. And so did the fans.

They were so tough on Malone. So was the media. To them, he simply was not good enough — nothing personal, mind you — and they criticized and booed him unmercifully. It got very personal. Some of the signs and banners that were unfurled at Three Rivers Stadium got very close to home. Malone's home.

He was an easy target. He was big and strong, a look-alike for Tom Sellick, the movie star, with a ready white-toothed smile to match. He was tall, dark and handsome, always bronzed, it seemed, a bona fide California beach boy.

One fan who felt compelled to let Malone know that he had his admirers asked me to forward a letter to him this past year. Here's an excerpt from a letter from Judy Wolfram from Eighty Four, Pennsylvania:

"I just want you to know that not everybody in Pittsburgh who is a die-hard Steeler fan is not totally unfeeling, ignorant or nasty. I knew from the beginning that you were not Terry Bradshaw. I knew that you were Mark Malone and I liked and accepted you as Mark Malone. I think that you deserved much better than you got. But I want to congratulate you on your poise. You didn't let them drag you down to their level. You kept your cool and your dignity. That's class, baby, real class. You are a class act, no doubt about it."

I always liked Malone, too. He and I had shared a dais at many fund-raising charity-related dinners. He spoke well and represented the Steelers well. There was a seriousness about him, a suaveness about him, a sincerity about him. In short, he was always a class act. But Malone never fit the mold.

"In a blue collar town like Pittsburgh, they want to beat the other team physically, it seems," offered Malone. "In California, they get caught up with long touchdown passes and big scores. They like their quarterbacks: Joe Montana, John Brodie, Y.A. Tittle, Dan Fouts, Roman Gabriel, guys like that. Here, they want shutouts, and they want dee-fense, dee-fense. They love Jack Lambert and Mean Joe Greene and Ernie 'Fats' Holmes. Here, they like the tough guys. Did you beat the hell outta the other guy?"

Like Bradshaw, but in a different way, Malone was a sensitive young man. It hurt when they booed him. But he did not brood about it. He just pressed. He pushed himself harder, but it did not help. Bradshaw had simply set too high a standard for quarterbacks in Pittsburgh,

Mark Malone sets up behind Craig Wolfley   Mike Fabus

make that the National Football League. It was impossible to be as good as Bradshaw, and so many of the Steelers who starred for the Super Bowl teams were gone from the scene, too, so the teams Cliff Stoudt and Malone commanded simply were not as good as the Steelers of the '70s. That did not matter to many of their detractors.

"I wasn't Bradshaw and I wasn't Joe Montana," said Malone, "but I was in the NFL for ten years, so I must've been pretty good. I can't complain when I was able to play ten years, not when you consider the average career span. Obviously, there were some goals I set for myself and for the team that weren't attained. That's disappointing. I gave everything I had during those ten years. That's all I could do."

When Malone made that remark, he looked up, like he might have looked up in a huddle after he had called a play, to make sure you understood what he was saying.

Talking to Malone was a draining experience. We shared stories of personal setbacks. We talked easily and freely. It was like a group therapy session.

Malone spent seven of his ten NFL seasons with the Steelers, and finished up in backup roles with the San Diego Chargers and the New York Jets. Joe Walton was the head coach of the Jets, and worked closely with his quarterbacks. In 1990, Walton was fired after seven seasons in New York, and became the offensive coordinator of the Steelers.

Walton was asked whether it hurt Malone that he was such a sensitive, emotional guy. "It could have," Walton said. "I'm not saying it did, but it's a tough business. We had a fine quarterback in New York with Richard Todd, and he struggled at the start, but got much better. But he had a stuttering problem when he was a kid, and he had to get special help for it. Sometimes, when we were in a pressure situation, that stutter came back."

During his stay with the Steelers, Malone had some great moments, some great games, even a terrific season, but there were more disappointing days and nights than there were good ones, and the Steelers were not nearly as good a team as they had been when Bradshaw was behind center. Those four Super Bowl trophies cast a long shadow over Malone and his teammates.

"The impact it had on me and the teams I played with was both positive and negative," said Malone, a visitor to the Steelers camp in 1990 to interview players for a pre-game show on Pittsburgh's WPXI-TV during the pre-season schedule.

"You felt as if you had a tradition to live up to and a standard that was set. The downside is that nobody will ever attain what the teams of the '70s did. Those teams were unique," said Malone.

"The kids on the team today don't know enough about what it was like here to feel the same kind of pressure that we did. And the fans don't seem to know how lucky this city was, or how fortunate they were. It was a glorious decade. It will probably never happen again. Some of the younger guys here haven't played enough to know what it takes, or how auspicious an achievement it was.

"When I was the quarterback, there was desire to bring about the continuance of that reign. But that fell short. And you know you will be associated with that fall. The Super Bowls were still fresh in everyone's mind when I took over.

"Hey, in 1984, we were in the AFC championship game. We were that close, and then the Miami Dolphins just exploded in the second half and beat us. Danny Marino had one of the greatest performances in his career to beat us. The fans here expected us to be in the Super Bowl in 1985. But we just didn't have the talent to be in the Super Bowl.

"The fan doesn't know that, how complicated things are behind the scenes. I had been handed the legacy of one of the greatest quarterbacks of all time. I had the responsibility of carrying that on, no matter how unrealistic that was."

On this particular visit to the Steelers' camp as a TV commentator, Malone arrived just hours after the team had released a veteran backup quarterback in Randy Wright.

It was weird. I had just mentioned Malone's name in a conversation with sportswriters, and within two hours he appears in the same room. Many of the media present that morning felt the Steelers were still short on reliable relief pitchers. "Who else could they get?" somebody asked.

"They should've gotten Joe Ryan before the Browns got him," suggested one sportswriter. "He would have been the perfect backup. Plus, he'd been with the Jets all those years, and he knows Walton's offense."

"Maybe they'll get Mark Malone," I interjected. They all smiled, as if it was a ridiculous idea. "He played under Walton last year. I'll bet he knows the offense better than Bubby Brister right now. And he's never going to cause you a problem."

Then Malone makes the scene. Unreal, I thought. I had forgotten he was doing a TV show during the pre-season. And I'd seen him just two weeks earlier describe a televised scrimmage between the Steelers and the Washington Redskins in Latrobe. Malone was asked if he might be a candidate for the job. "You couldn't pay me enough money," he said.

That wasn't always the case. Malone was a surprise No. 1 pick of the Steelers in the NFL draft on April 29, 1980. After all, the Steelers seemed set at quarterback with Bradshaw in his prime, plus reliable backups in Mike Kruczek and Cliff Stoudt.

Of course, a few years later they were similarly set when they passed up Danny Marino of the University of Pittsburgh, and they have been criticized ever since for not taking Marino. In short, you are damned if you do, and damned if you don't. No one knows that better than Malone.

At Arizona State, Malone had set school records with 148 completions in 289 attempts, and passed for 12 touchdowns and ran for 12 touchdowns. Art Rooney Jr., who was director of the team's player personnel department at the time, likened Malone to former Heisman Trophy winner Paul Hornung as an athlete. Hornung, a quarterback at Notre Dame, ended up as a running back with the Green Bay Packers.

At 6-4, 223 pounds, Malone was similar in size to Bradshaw. The scouting report said: "with 4.6 speed (in the 40), he runs like a fullback." That sounded like Bradshaw, too. Asked if Malone had "a Bradshaw-type arm," Chuck Noll smiled and said, "You won't find too many 'Bradshaw-type' arms around." From the first hour, the comparisons were inevitable.

Soon after Malone was drafted, Bradshaw telephoned the Steelers' offices from his Circle M Ranch in Grand Cane, Louisiana, and cried out light-heartedly, "Are they trying to run me out of town?"

Pittsburgh fans may have booed Bradshaw at the start, when he was struggling like a colt trying to get its legs under it, but they did not run him out of town. They saved that for his two successors, Stoudt and Malone. "Stoudt said he'll never set foot in this town again, or in Pennsylvania for that matter," said Malone.

Stoudt had spent the 1989 season, ironically enough, as a backup to Marino in Miami. Stoudt never threw a pass in a regular season game the entire season.

When Malone was playing college ball, Bradshaw was his idol. As a student at Valley High in El Cajon, California, just outside San Diego, Malone had been an All-American in football and in track and field. Like Bradshaw, he was a javelin thrower. For the record, though, Bradshaw threw the javelin farther. In fact, Bradshaw once held the national scholastic javelin throw record. Again, Malone came up short in the comparison test.

Malone never suggested he was better than Bradshaw at football, or any sport. But when he came to Pittsburgh he hoped he would someday get an opportunity at quarterback. He also worked harder than Bradshaw ever did in the public relations and community service activities endorsed by the Steelers. Along with his pretty wife, Mary Ellen, Malone was involved in many local charities, including Multiple Sclerosis, Children's Hospital, Ronald McDonald House, West Penn Burn Unit, Literacy Foundation and Epilepsy Foundation.

On some Sundays, however, the Sundays when he disappointed Steeler fans with his performances, none of it meant a damn thing. One of the signs even made a disparaging remark about Mary Ellen and a well-publicized concern about cancer. How cruel. What makes it even more disturbing for Malone is that Bradshaw, who enjoyed so much success with the Steelers and won over the hearts of Pittsburghers with his play, has chosen to spit tobacco back in the faces of those who boosted him.

"Terry Bradshaw has crapped all over the Pittsburgh Steelers organization and the city and the fans," said Malone. "I've never seen a guy enjoy so much success and be so miserable. And people here still love him. He has forsaken the city, and he says he'll never come back. Of course, he came back a few days after he said that, I'm told, to film some segment for his network TV show. He said some things about me and other players in his autobiography. It's really a shame. Frankly, I really don't understand the guy."

While Malone is trying to make it on a local market, Bradshaw's star was rising at CBS as a network analyst. After several seasons of covering games for CBS, he was assigned an in-studio slot for the 1990 season. "I don't understand how he could forsake this town, the people and the guys who won four Super Bowl titles with him. He owns the town. He's as big a part of this team as anyone. But he's miserable. He refuses to make peace with Pittsburgh and Chuck Noll, yet the people here still love him.

"There are some things he doesn't consider, either. As strong an arm as he had, the timing was still right for him in Pittsburgh. Without the guys who were on his team, he wouldn't have had a prayer. This is a team sport. People think it's track and field. This isn't just throwing a javelin — throw it farther than anyone else and you win."

Neither Malone nor the supporting cast in the '80s was as good in Pittsburgh as the team was during the '70s. Even so, Malone got more than his share of scorn and criticism for the club's collapse.

"It's funny," remarked Malone. "I have yet to meet one person on the street or in, say, a hardware store who — young or old — hasn't had good things to say to me. Obviously, there were some people out there who were booing me, but I never meet them."

Just then, as if on cue, a young man who had been standing nearby during this conversation, not sure what he should do, stepped forward and extended his hand to Malone. "My father has season tickets," he said, for openers, "and, even though you had some bad times, we still rooted for you." Malone smiled and shook the young man's hand, and returned to his dialogue with a see-what-I'm-saying smile in his eyes. "That's what I get all the time," he said. "Or they tell me they never booed me.

"I'm a firm believer that the only thing that matters to most people is wins and losses. It also bothered me that so many people in the media here hit on me pretty hard. Yet I don't think there was one media guy who disliked Mark Malone, the person. Most guys liked me and respected me. Cliff Stoudt hated the whole thing. I've handled it 180 degrees differently than he has. It might have bothered me as much as it did him. He challenged the crowd and made gestures to them. I made a promise to myself to be as diplomatic and as professional as I can be. I prepared myself for it. It was probably more difficult for Mary Ellen. She had to sit in the stands and hear all that stuff.

"It had to be tough for her. She loved me and she supported me. She'd ask me how I was feeling. What did I see in the future? We talked alone or in private a lot back then. My how things had changed."

It had been some time since that night in Seattle in November of 1981 when he made his first start — it was as a wide receiver — and caught a record 90-yard touchdown pass from Bradshaw. The Steelers' airplane got fogged in that same night, and, when players retreated to some local watering holes that evening, Stoudt broke his right hand throwing a jab into a mechanical punching bag in a local playpen. So Malone became the No. 2 quarterback that same night.

There were times Malone thought Stoudt was a tough act to follow. "So many quarterbacks went through difficult beginnings before they went on to have great careers," Malone said at the time. He mentioned some examples that would strike a familiar note with Pittsburgh football fans: Johnny Unitas, George Blanda, Bill Nelsen and even Terry Bradshaw, as well as Norm Van Brocklin, Sonny Jurgensen, Lenny Dawson, Y.A. Tittle, Billy Kilmer and Brian Sipe.

"If there wasn't frustration at first," said Malone back then, "you wouldn't enjoy the success so much. If you're not frustrated at one point, you're one in a million."

Malone sat out most of the 1982 season following major knee surgery, and played in just two games the following season while still in rehabilitation. He was never as mobile or speedy after that.

Yet Malone made his mark in the Steelers' record book, and not just for that record distance TD catch that still stands. Only Bradshaw, Bobby Layne and Jim Finks had better career passing stats than Malone in Steelers' history to that point.

Only Bradshaw completed more passes (2,025) than Malone (690) — but the difference is so vast because Bradshaw was so superior to anyone who ever quarterbacked this ballclub. Only Layne had more single game passing yards (409) than Malone (374). Bradshaw is third in that category with a 364-yard game, but Malone, which may surprise many, is also fourth with a 351-yard effort. Malone once completed 11 consecutive passes in a game against his hometown San Diego team. So there were some momentous times in Malone's career with the Steelers.

Yet, Malone was never sure where he stood in the Steelers' organization. In college, he had a fiery coach in Frank Kush, who came from Windber, Pennsylvania. "Chuck Noll and Dick Hoak, our backfield coach, are opposites of Kush," he said. "They don't say too much. You don't know if things are good, bad or indifferent. You don't know what to make of things."

But, Malone was getting good vibes from the fans, too good maybe.

"In '84, we went to the AFC championship game, and I was the golden boy in town. I was going to bring the team back to glory. For a time, I felt great being here.

"In '85, I dislocated my toe, and all of a sudden it became apparent that we weren't going to be that good. It became more and more difficult. There came not only the boos, but the media became critical as well. At the same time, my wife was diagnosed as having a cancerous tumor. I was in and out of the hospital to visit her. They took her thyroid out, and learned that it was a non-malignant tumor. That Sunday we won the game."

It did not last, however. The Steelers had stumbled at the start, losing four of their first six games, righted themselves at midseason and won three in a row, but finished by losing four of their last five for a 7-9 record. "I found myself in the huddle, and guys looking at me to see if it was going to break me or affect me," Malone remembered. "It was something I sensed.

"I'm a very emotional person. Like my mom, my dad always told me. He said I got that from her. My wife and I are taking a course in the Lamaze method of delivery for our first baby. They showed a film of a baby being born, and as soon as I saw that baby appear I started crying. I just started to cry. It doesn't make me any less of a man. I'm just like that; it's me. But it may have worked against me."

Maybe his dad would not have approved, that is the thought that comes to mind. Malone's old man must have been a tough cuss, a macho guy who built racing stock cars, a mechanical-minded man who was a perfectionist. Get it right or get somebody killed must have been his motto.

Malone had two heroes when he was a kid. One was Willie Mays, the Hall of Fame outfielder for the New York and San Francisco Giants. "The other was most definitely my father," said Malone. When Mark was eight years old, his parents were divorced. "There was a great deal of animosity between my mother and father at the time of the divorce. They put me in a who-do-you-love-the-most? game. My dad was traveling everywhere on the grand national stock car circuit, and I didn't see a helluva lot of him.

"He came back to San Diego toward the end of my high school career. He saw me play in one high school game, and it was a high school playoff game that we lost. I didn't play particularly well. It devastated me to know he was watching me that way. My dad had so much success, and I'd really had a storybook high school sports career. But he comes to the one game where we lose. He was a perfectionist. I had had some tremendous games. Why now?

"I can remember him hollering to me. He called me over. I felt so embarrassed. He grabbed me and hugged me. I remember crying. I wanted so badly to please him. The next year, I was a freshman at Arizona State and we became real good friends. That year, at age 38, my dad died. He had a massive heart attack and died. We had become such great friends, best buddies. After all those years, it was becoming such a great relationship."

Malone remembers seeing the movie "Field of Dreams," in which a man builds a baseball field because a voice tells him to, not knowing exactly why, but thinking maybe it was to be a magnet to lure back the greatest baseball players of all time, including "Shoeless Joe" Jackson — "build it and he will come" is the command he kept hearing — and, in the end, his deceased father shows up and starts playing catch with him.

"It's like a wave comes over you when you see that," said Malone. "Something like that can happen between a father and a son. That's the way the movie ends. My dad and I never played catch. Not once. Like a lot of guys, I cried at the end of that movie.

"I thought about my dad telling me I was too emotional. 'You get that from your mom,' he'd always say. He was a big, brawling guy. But he also told me that the women in your life are going to love you for it. My dad would be 52 right now. He'd have been a great grandfather. He didn't hug me when I was a kid, but he did when I was in college.

I was big and I was expected to be strong. He was always pushing me to be strong. He was the benchmark.

"You know, you play football for a long time. I gave it everything I had. I didn't have the flamboyant success of Bradshaw or Joe Montana. But I also knew that some day I would have to quit playing football. But I have to go on being a human being."

Mark Malone and Danny Marino go back a ways, to when Malone was the big man on campus at Arizona State, and he was asked to entertain Danny Marino, a hot prospect who was being recruited out of Pittsburgh's Central Catholic High School.

"Our coach, Frank Kush, wanted him in the worst way," Malone recalled. "I was told I'd have to give up my condo and my car," he joked, "whatever was necessary to get Danny Marino to come to Arizona State.

"Our baseball coach wanted him, too, because he was such a great pitcher. So I picked him up at the airport and took him to a place to shoot some pool.

"We played to see who'd buy the beer. Danny beat me ten straight games of pool. I thought I was playing Willie Mosconi. I let him walk back to the hotel. The next thing I heard, he was going to Pitt."

Marino smiled over Malone's story, but had a better one of his own.

"I was supposed to see this college quarterback and I see this guy wearing a blousy silk shirt, open to the navel, with all this jewelry hanging from his neck. He had this thing on his hip — I thought it was a gun — but I found out it was a disco purse. A disco purse, can you imagine that?

"I thought is this guy a quarterback or is he John Travolta? I didn't know what to make of him."

Mark Malone, Joe Paterno and Danny Marino at Allegheny Club

Bubby Brister
"Like John Wayne and Bobby Layne"

It was Photo Day, July 18, 1990, and Bubby Brister was the center of attention for the majority of the thousand or so Steelers fans in attendance for the opening of the team's 24th summer training camp at St. Vincent College in Latrobe.

During the glory days of the '70s, you could not move around too easily on Photo Day because the crowds numbered better than 5,000. While the enthusiasm for the Steelers had not returned to those days of old, it was reportedly better than the year before. Things were getting better.

Bubby Brister had led the Steelers to the second round of the playoffs the year before, and pumped up Pittsburghers and Western Pennsylvanians, giving them a glimmer of hope that the team might yet get that one for the thumb — that fifth Super Bowl ring the team had been after the entire decade of the '80s.

The year before, on this same camp-opening day, Brister had boldly predicted that the Steelers would win ten games, and be back in the playoffs again, after a five-year absence.

So the sportswriters and sportscasters were coveting more of the same, something with punch, to get their camp coverage off to a stirring start, something to offset the fact that the Steelers had not signed their No. 1 draft choice, Eric Green, a tight end from Liberty University. Noll would not talk about anybody who wasn't at camp, the reporters knew for sure.

The Steelers had a new offensive coordinator in Joe Walton, a one-time All-America tight end at Pitt and in the pros with the Washington Redskins and New York Giants, and they were going to have a new offensive system that featured a control-passing offense. The Steelers were going to pitch passes to their tight ends — and sometimes employ two of them at the same time — and this was a radical departure from the way Chuck Noll had gone about his business when he was winning all those Super Bowls, as well as when the team was disappointing with its offensive production ever since those much-missed days of glory.

But Bubby came into camp as conservative as the new offense. He would not be tossing many bombs during the season, something he dearly loved to do, so he was not going to toss any bombs at the Photo Day press conference, either. Bubby did his best to keep himself and his lips — which were as quick and usually as strong as his release — under control. At least that was the idea, but he strayed from the protective pocket after a while, as he is wont to do in a game.

"It's all business now," began Bubby, as he strode confidently toward Bonaventure Hall, where he would be putting his handsome dark-haired head on a pillow for the next six weeks. "I'm all football and nothin' else.

Bubby Brister

Mike Fabus

"I'm not going to make any predictions. We're going to make the playoffs; we're good enough. I think people know that now because this team earned a great deal of respect last season."

Although Brister would later write "think Super Bowl" on a chalkboard in the team's dressing room at Kennedy Hall, he declined to publicly predict that the Steelers would make it to the Big Party for the first time in a decade.

"All I'll say is getting to the Super Bowl is why we're up here," said Brister, having a difficult time completely putting a cap on his motor mouth. "That's what counts, what it's all about. But every other team feels the same way right now.

"We know we're good, but we want to be the best. I'm not going to be satisfied until we win our division and the Super Bowl. We want to go to the playoffs, but we want to do it on our home field, not somebody else's. We need our fans."

The Steelers had withstood one of the worst starts in NFL history in 1989, losing their first two games by a combined score of 92-10, to win five of their last six games. They beat Houston in overtime in a first round playoff game, then lost at Denver, 24-23, in the final two minutes. They had come so close to the AFC title game.

"We've been to the playoffs now and we've played on other people's fields," said Brister. "We want to play in Pittsburgh, on our field and in front of our fans. We want them to have to play us before all those screaming Steelers' fans in January.

"I think the '90s are going to be a very nice time for Pittsburgh."

Brister was unhappy with his own passing performance of the previous season. He was confident of his leadership ability, but felt he had to do more to put points on the board.

"I have to laugh when people tell me I had a great year," he said. "Because I thought I was mediocre. I definitely think when my number is called, I have to make the big play more often. When Louis Lipps is open deep, I have to get him the ball . . . I just need to be a little more consistent and a little more patient. I'm not talking totally patient because I'm still going to be wild out there. I'm still going to go nuts at times. I just have to pick my spots."

Just to lighten things up a little, Brister started talking about baseball. Before he reported to St. Vincent College, he had taken some batting practice during a Pirates' workout at Three Rivers Stadium.

A former farmhand in the Detroit Tigers' system, Brister is the answer to the trivia question: Who's the only player to play for both Chuck Noll and Jim Leyland?

Leyland, who would be named the Manager of the Year for his work with the Pirates in 1990, managed Brister one year in the Florida Instructional League. Leyland threw batting practice to Brister a few days before. When Brister missed a round-house curve, Leyland hollered, "There's the pitch that sent him to the huddle."

Brister replied: "If I'd seen hanging curve balls like that, I'd still be playing baseball . . . I never could hit that damn curve."

When this tale was related to Noll, he smiled and said, "I'm glad."

"Bubby Brister has become a cult hero, thanks to one of the most refreshing shticks in years," wrote Ron Cook, the columnist for the *Pittsburgh Post-Gazette.* "He is brash. He is cocky. He talks like a winner when he isn't screaming at officials, opponents and even teammates."

Brister, like Terry Bradshaw before him, appealed to a broader-based audience than just football fans. He was a cowboy hero come to town. Bradshaw once brandished a Stetson when he came to camp, and labeled himself "The Midnight Cowboy." The name was even more appropriate for Brister.

He was tall, dark and handsome as all get out, with a fashionable young man's haircut. He walked with a swagger, and swore like a steelworker. He had to be bleeped on just about every interview he has done since he came to Pittsburgh. He says whatever's on his mind, and that mind has been subject to the same scrutiny — and stage whispers — as Bradshaw's was before him. If he were, indeed, a "dumb" quarterback, the faithful were hoping he was as dumb, and undeniable, as Bradshaw.

Brister and Myron Cope were both among the local celebrities lampooned in a satiric review staged by Don Brockett called "Son of Forbidden Pittsburgh '90," which I saw twice at the Green Tree Marriott during the summer months.

Cope got the needle with a song called "Yoy To The World," in which Cope is called the "sex god of Pittsburgh broadcasting."

Brister was blistered by show-stopper Phyllis Stern and her soul sisters and soul brothers, six of them in all, in a song that went like this: "Though I've not seen his face, I'd know him any place . . . we're watching Bubby's buns."

The song's message was that Brister, by far, had the best-looking backside on the Steelers. That won't win you a Super Bowl ring, but it might help your popularity at some of Pittsburgh's watering holes.

He had not won the big one yet, but already Brister was being parodied on stage in Pittsburgh. There was a locally distributed candy bar called the "Bubby Bar" and he was featured on posters and T-shirts throughout the area. He could sell maps to young women showing them the way to his home deep in the woods of Wexford, just to the north of Three Rivers Stadium. "I could shoot deer off my back porch," boasted Brister.

He had star quality, no doubt about it, even though, like the young Bradshaw, he had his critics who did not think he was the answer to the Steelers' passing problems.

From the first day, the day he was drafted by the Steelers, on April 29, 1986, Brister's name has often been mentioned in the same breath as Bradshaw. Sometimes by mistake, as if the names are interchangeable or tag along with each other in some fans' minds.

"If you miss Terry Bradshaw, you're probably going to love Walter Brister," wrote Dave Fennessy of the *McKeesport Daily News.* Fennessy noted, as did the other reporters covering the draft that day, that Brister was from Louisiana and talked funny — and a lot — just like Bradshaw.

How did he get that nickname "Bubby" to begin with?

"I have five older sisters and none of them liked Walter," said the new kid on the block. "Bubby was their version of Brother, or something like that. So I've been stuck with Bubby ever since I was two. I've gotten into a lot of fights because of having a girl's name like that."

Beautiful. Bubby Brister could not have gotten off to a better start. Bubby might have been a softie-sounding name for an NFL quarterback, but Walter was worse. How about his full handle — Walter Andrew Brister? Just like Boomer Esiason of the Cincinnati Bengals never wants you to call him Norman, Bubby does not want you to call him Walter or Andrew.

Brister also disclosed that his sports hero was Sammy Baugh, which had to please Art Rooney who always regarded Baugh as the greatest quarterback ever, just ahead of Sid Luckman, Johnny Unitas and Terry Bradshaw.

Brister had been a well-traveled quarterback who finished up in a strong style as a senior in his hometown of Monroe at Northeast Louisiana University, and became the Steelers' third round draft pick, after linemen John Rienstra of Temple and Gerald Williams of Auburn.

"I'm very familiar with Terry Bradshaw," said Brister over the telephone that first day. "I've attended some of his clinics down here, watched him throw, and I've talked with him several times. I'll be playing for his old team.

"I'm no Terry Bradshaw," Brister felt the urge to say. "He was a great quarterback. The greatest. I used to watch him on television when I was growing up. My uncle was one of his coaches (at Lousiana Tech). But I never tried to play like him. He wasn't my hero. John Wayne was my hero.

"My high school colors were black and gold, and I'm tickled to death to be wearing them again. When they (the Steelers) called me to tell me I'd been drafted by them, I told them if I have half as much success there as Terry Bradshaw did, we'll win two Super Bowls."

Dick Haley, the Steelers' player personnel director, shared Brister's enthusiasm over the soon-to-be-consummated marriage. Brister had worked out for Tom Moore and Tom Modrak, a Steelers' scout, and they were both impressed with his arm strength and his mobility.

They rated him right behind Purdue's Jim Everett and Iowa's Chuck Long as pro quarterback candidates. "He's an excellent athlete with a very strong arm and he's very mobile, just like another quarterback from 30 miles down the road who did pretty well in this league," said Haley. "At this point, we couldn't afford not to take Brister."

Coming out of high school in Monroe, Brister was all set to go to Alabama, where he had been recruited by Bear Bryant. But the Tigers got into the picture, and offered Brister a signing bonus of $50,000 and he took the money.

"I spoke with Coach Bryant about it," Brister said, "and he told me all he could give me was three hots and a cot. He said if he was me, he'd do the same thing."

When Brister became disenchanted with his chances to make it big in baseball — he had been moved from the pitching staff to the outfield, which bored him — he turned to Tulane to resume his football and school activity. Brister did not think he was getting a fair shot at the starting job at Tulane — the coach, Wally English, went with his son instead — so he transferred back home to Northeast Louisiana.

Despite the gypsy background, Brister was confident about his opportunities in the National Football League. "There's no doubt in my mind," he said on draft day, "I can start in the NFL some day."

When Mark Malone sprained a thumb in December of 1986. Brister became the first rookie quarterback to start for the Steelers since Mike Kruczek in 1976.

Fans began calling every sports talk show in town saying they wanted Brister to start the next game instead of Malone. "The only poll that counts around here is Chuck Noll's," said Brister, catching on fast. "I'm flattered by how the fans feel, but it doesn't matter."

Malone did not think he should lose his starting job to Brister. "If I put the numbers up on the board that Bubby put on the board," Malone said, "people would still be screaming at me. But with a new face, new blood, people go crazy.

"People aren't going to support any quarterback here until he wins the Super Bowl. They'll support Bubby for a while. Bubby might play a year or two, but if he doesn't win a Super Bowl, they'll be on him. If you're not winning Super Bowls, people will boo you. It's just the way it is in pro football in this city."

Before the start of his third season as a starter, Brister sounded even more confident than the day he was drafted.

"I have no reason to think I won't be one of the top quarterbacks in the league in the next year or two," he said. "I'm going to keep getting better and better."

On another day at St. Vincent, Bubby bubbled, "I'm sort of a blue collar worker. I'll block, I'll run. If you want to (bleep) with me, I'll fight you."

Noll and Walton wanted him to be less emotional, more in control of himself and the team, and talked to him about it. But the good-looking quarterback with the quick lip was not listening too closely.

"I don't put up with any bullshit," he said, "from any players, from the referees, from anybody."

As for the Steeler fans, he offered: "Football is very important. They don't tolerate losing."

Back then, Brister believed he was just the man the fans were looking for to lead the team back to the top of the NFL heap.

"I think that's what I bring to this team," he said. "We can't lose. We gotta shoot for perfection. We gotta be winners. We gotta win the Super Bowl. That's how I grew up."

112

Brister grew up as a big fan of movie actor John Wayne, a no-nonsense hombre, a passion he shared with two former Steelers, Mike Webster and Ray Mansfield.

"I liked John Wayne," Brister said, "because he didn't take no shit off anybody. His word's all you needed."

If the same were true of Bubby Brister, the Steelers would have won another Super Bowl or two with him behind center. Brister, who has a gold pendant No. 6 hanging from a gold chain around his thick neck, says, "I don't play to lose. If I'm shooting a game of pool, checkers, whatever. If you get in my huddle, you better be there to win the ballgame."

Brister is actually brasher than Bradshaw. He is more of a throwback to Bobby Layne, who had a fiery tongue, and a lash that cracked hard on the backs of his teammates in practice and in the games. So Brister is like John Wayne and Bobby Layne.

Layne would take his teammates out at night, however, and soothe their wounds with scotch and soda, or some beer and hamburgers. Whereas Layne loafed with Ernie Stautner and Tom "The Bomb" Tracy, Brister's best friend on the Steelers was Merril Hoge, from Idaho State, who didn't smoke or drink or dance. Brister branded Hoge "the Stormin' Mormon." Off the field, the Steelers all loved Layne. Layne was a winner, in Austin, Detroit and Pittsburgh. Ballplayers tend not to run in groups like that these days, however.

It would be tough for most of them to keep up with Brister's nocturnal travels, though he says reports of his carousing are exaggerated. "About 25 percent of those stories are true," Brister said.

"I think it's normal to go out and have a couple of beers and dance with a lady. For damn sure, I don't want to be categorized as something else."

Brister has always been all-boy. Back in Neville High in Monroe, Louisiana, his baseball coach Joe Coats recalls, "He was very diligent. He knew he wanted to make the pros and he was committed to what he wanted to do." Brister was a two-time all-state pitcher, and averaged 15½ strikeouts a game over a three-year span.

Brister was back in his home area when the Steelers played the New Orleans Saints at the Superdome in the 14th game of the 1990 schedule. Brister watched the Saints play in the Superdome and on TV when he was growing up. The Steelers won a tough one, 9-6, thanks to three field goals by Gary Anderson.

Brister still managed to create most of the post-game excitement, even if he was not to blame, when a female reporter gave him a kiss and a hug as he stood in front of his dressing stall with a white towel wrapped around his midriff.

It was all innocent enough, but there had been an ugly incident in the New England Patriots locker room earlier in the season when several players exposed themselves and taunted a woman reporter named Lisa Olson, and that incident caused shock waves throughout the sports world. The media tied Brister's locker room embrace back to that controversial story.

Shari Warren, a reporter for KSLA-TV in Shreveport, had been a classmate of Brister at Northeast Lousiana. She asked Bubby what he wanted for Christmas, and that set off the "bad boy" spirit in him.

"I just want to keep winning for Christmas," Brister began. "That's all I want. Maybe you for awhile. How about that?"

"You can have me for awhile," said Miss Warren, who then hugged Brister.

"We were teasing around," she explained later. "That's what we've always done. I hugged him like an old friend."

Teammate Louis Lipps, who personally turned the football program from a big loser to a big winner at East St. John's High in Reserve, La., is one of the Steelers who believes in Brister. "Bubby is the sparkplug for us," allows Lipps. "He gets us going. He rubs off on everybody — in the huddle, on the sideline, in the locker room. He's our quarterback. He's our leader."

Hoge says, "He's a wild Cajun. He's a stallion. You just have to turn him loose."

"He's dramatic," says Tunch Ilkin.

Mike Mularkey, a veteran tight end who had previously played at Minnesota, said, "Bubby is a take-charge guy, one who makes things happen instead of waiting for them to happen. I personally like the cockiness in him, because you need that in a quarterback. Even when we're losing, if the guy comes in the huddle and tells you it can happen, I believe it. Some quarterbacks say that and don't mean it. I believe it when Bubby says it."

Noll believes in Bubby, too. But please don't ask him to compare Brister to Bradshaw. "I really like this type of question, and my standard answer applies," he said at one of his weekly press conferences. "There are no two guys the same, and obviously he is not the same as Terry. They are two different and unique people. I'm sure Bobby Layne was unique, but everybody has to be themselves and their leadership comes from that."

Walton became a Bubby fan in a hurry. "Bubby has everything he needs to become a great quarterback in the NFL," said the Steelers' offensive coordinator. "He's plenty big enough, quick enough and intense enough. The big thing is that the Steelers, every player, believe in Bubby. That's more than half the battle.

"Leadership is a hard word to define, but it's necessary to be a good quarterback. The team has to feel you. They have to feel your emotion, they have to feel your command. That's where everything starts.

"It starts with the way a quarterback calls the plays in the huddle, the way he calls the signals, an emotion he has. And the team feeds off what he does. If you don't have it. . ."

Tom Donahoe, the director of pro personnel and development, told Bob Labriola of *Steelers Digest*, "The main thing is he's a team guy first, and a lot of quarterbacks aren't. A lot of quarterbacks are me-first guys, always concerned about stats and pass ratings. Genuinely, I don't think that's Bubby's priority. He's always talking we. His priority is he wants to get to the Super Bowl, and he'll do whatever is necessary for us to achieve that goal. That makes him a leader."

Bubby believes everybody who is behind him. "When I'm in the huddle," he said, "I don't take no bull. If guys are dragging, or we're not playing together, I get on their butt. It fires me up because I know I'm getting to those guys. Then they get fired up, and it snowballs."

Bubby Brister got off to a bad start in September. The Steelers had lost three of their first four games, and Brister was getting most of the blame for the sorry showings.

Following the second game, a 20-9 victory over the Houston Oilers in the home opener at Three Rivers Stadium, I sat in on a post-game press conference at which Brister said: "The same people who were cheering me last year are booing me now.

"I'll tell you this: we're going to have the last laugh. The players and coaches here have told me they are backing me. Joe Greene said to be patient. He said it takes awhile when you change things around. Hey, I'm doing my best. I've been frustrated, too. It's all tough right now.

"We were having some success toward the end of last year, and now it's hard for all of us. What am I going to say to you guys each week? Whatever I say, I better be careful so I don't upset too many people. We've got a great defense, and we've got to get our offense to the same level.

"We're trying. God, we're trying. We're giving 100 percent. There's no reason to bitch and moan and gripe about it. I know I'm good. I can shed it (the criticism) off, like water off my back. One day we're going to turn it around. The same people who are bitching and moaning will someday be saying, 'I told you so. I told you he was a great one!' Hey, the way things have been going lately, I'd probably boo, too. I know we don't look like San Francisco.

"I want to be good. I want to win. That's the only reason I'm here. Believe me, we'll be a team to reckon with."

Noll stuck his nose into the room, and trying to lighten up the atmosphere, he asked Brister in front of the assembled media, "Are you working overtime? Are you getting paid time and a half?"

Brister: "Coach, I'm not saying anything bad about you."

Noll: "If you're going to say something bad, say it to me."

Brister: "No, I'll be playing Canadian Football if I do."

On another day, Brister was scheduled to be interviewed by Mark Malone, who had preceded him as quarterback of the Steelers, and had a good idea of how he must be feeling, as they talked off camera before the taping for "Steelers' '90," a pre-game show co-hosted by Malone for WPXI-TV in Pittsburgh.

"I told Bubby to just hang in there and try to keep focused on what he was doing," Malone told Bob Labriola of *Steelers Digest*. "You have to try not to take all the stuff that's coming at you to heart. Nobody wants to help you in those situations, nobody wants to throw you a rope and pull you out."

Brister needed a big brother, and Malone fit the bill that day. "I was down, probably more than I ever have been since I've been playing football, which is 20 years," said Brister. "The fans were booing us, and a lot of it was at me, but early in the season it was hard for us to do anything about it. They don't understand we have a lot of new things to learn and a whole bunch of stuff in the game plan. So you have to swallow your pride, keep working hard and hope you come out of it.

"I was down. My parents now live in Pittsburgh, and they're about the only ones I could talk to. Some of my close friends called, but everybody else alienated themselves from me. I'd just go to the store and people would say things."

Brister was balking about the changes, the same changes he had applauded at the start of training camp.

Back then, he was saying, "I think we needed a change. We needed some spice in it. Even if I do have to take a couple of steps back, it's going to make me a better quarterback in the long run. Tough times don't last, but tough guys do."

He had forgotten about that, however, in the interim. He was critical of the play-calling, substitution rotations, the messenger system, all the short passes, you name it. He ripped into Walton's offense following a season-opening 13-3 loss to the Browns in Cleveland. "I'm about to become unglued," he said. He ticked off Noll in one post-game session, and drew a critical comment from his coach at Noll's weekly press conference the following day.

"Our quarterback has to get himself straightened out, too," said Noll. "Pointing the finger someplace else is not going to get it done." Noll's message to Brister was simple, like a T-shirt saying: "Just get it done."

Malone tried to make light of that, too. "Bubby's got a history of speaking out and saying things that a day later he probably wished he hadn't said," Malone said. "But I think that's just Bubby."

Brister, who backed up Malone in 1986 and 1987, said he was not sorry. Of course, he said this after he bounced back and was on his way to leading the Steelers to four victories in their next five outings. He was named the AFC's outstanding offensive performer for the month of October. Talk about a turnaround. That is just what Walter Brister — ah Bubby — did.

"I don't ever regret anything I say, because if I say something it's for the benefit of the team," said Brister.

"I'm not a selfish person, I don't give a damn about statistics. I just want to win football games. I don't regret saying things. I took the lashing.

They said I was a crybaby, but I know what works. I know what wins for us because I'm out there playing with these guys every day. I said what I said, and some of it was true."

Malone had more to say on the subject: "Bubby has gone from coming in as a kid to starting off terribly in his second year to turning it around and going to the playoffs. I find that a lot similar to when I came in and got things turned around and we went to the championship game in 1984. Everybody thought I was the golden boy, the future of the franchise. I remember the reception on the return trip from Miami.

"A lot of times," Malone continued, "right or wrong, when there's blame to place it's going to be placed on you, the quarterback. When you're winning, you're the greatest guy in the world.

"But Bubby realizes those things are beyond your control, and the bottom line to fend all those things off is to win football games and get your butt in the playoffs."

Brister had just come off some much-needed victories and was feeling better. "Things are good now," he said. "That's how fast it turns around, but that's how fast it can go back down, too. Everybody loved us last year, everybody hated us at the beginning of this year. That's the life and times in the NFL — you're either at the top or the bottom. I try to keep a balance, but it's tough in the public eye, because you're either great, or you're sorry."

Joe Walton was an intruder, as far as Brister and some of the other ballplayers were concerned. He had been fired as head coach of the New York Jets, and had been picked up by Chuck Noll to replace Tom Moore as the team's offensive coordinator. Moore had gone to the Minnesota Vikings during the off-season. He had been an assistant once before at Minnesota. If Walton was so smart, some of the Steelers whispered, how come he had been a big loser in New York?

Walton came in with an intricate system that initially taxed Brister's patience and confidence. Malone could have warned Bubby about how difficult it was going to be. Malone had finished up his career as a back-up quarterback to Ken O'Brien in New York. And Malone was a much quicker read than Brister, everybody knew that.

A sample play would go like this: "Deuce split right tight two short motion short sprint left 49 2 hide X go one two."

Now repeat that.

"There are a lot of new things," Brister said at the outset of camp. "Thank God for the pre-season games."

But they weren't enough, as it turned out.

Brister quickly became a basket case, publicly blasting Chuck Noll, Walton and whatever else he didn't like. Walton was shuttling in plays, formations and motions with wide receivers and tight ends, for the most part. Often there would be something lost in the translation.

"The plays would come in with 16 or 18 words, the receiver was out of breath, and by the time I'd decipher the play, we'd be running out of time," complained Brister. "There was chaos in the huddle."

Noll would not buy Brister's arguments. "I think it was a language thing more than anything else," he said. "I don't think it was the system. He was used to calling a lot of the same things by different terminology. That's all."

To which Brister came back saying, "It's the same old story. If you win, the quarterback's the greatest, and if you don't the quarterback's the problem."

What Brister fails to acknowledge is that this is one of the reasons the quarterback is usually the best paid player on a pro football team. Brister had signed a three-year contract through the 1991 season that called for a base salary of $875,000 in 1990 and $950,000 in 1991.

When the Steelers defeated the Denver Broncos in The Mile High City by 34-17 in mid-October, Brister did a complete turnabout. He had passed for 353 yards and four touchdowns. "It's the most fun I've ever had playing football in my life," he said. "If it's going to be like this, look out."

He would go on to throw four touchdown passes in wins against the Los Angeles Rams and against the Cleveland Browns before the end of the season. He had never thrown four touchdown passes in a game before he teamed up with Walton.

With Brister and Walton, it was, however, either feast or famine. "Bubby's either all-world or all-Allegheny," is the way one Steeler associate put it.

Brister was a bit devious in what he did to overcome his uncomfortable feeling with what Walton wanted him to do. After a touchdownless first month, and a 1-3 start, Brister developed a signal system with backup quarterback Rick Strom without the coaches' knowledge. Later, he met with Walton and Noll and asked if some portion of the plays could be waved in from the sideline.

"They sat us down and gave us a quiz on the signals, and we got it all right," Brister said. "We haven't had a problem since. I figured somewhere down the line, we'd just have to do that. It was just too tough on the receivers to bring in all that bullshit.

"They don't know a slot-split from a slot-A-wide. Right now, we're signalling in the formation and the motion. So all the receiver has to do is bring in the play. It's not that tough."

Brister says he doesn't study the stat sheet after the game, or check out the league listings. "Stats don't mean much, except at contract time," he said. "If we can win, the team will be happy, I'll be happy and I hope some of my folks will be happy.

"We found out what it takes to get to a Super Bowl," said Brister. "And we won't be satisfied till we get there. And I believe I'm one of the guys who'll take us there. I'm not Elway and I'm not Montana, but I'm me. I want to win it all."

At mid-season, Brister was interviewed at length for a WPXI-TV special by Sam Nover in which he made some interesting observations:

"I'm all out," said Brister. "I've been doing this since I was a little kid. I hate to lose. You better put it all on the line. Losing bugs me."

That is one of the things that bugged him about baseball players, and one of the reasons he abandoned baseball and being in the Detroit Tigers chain to go back to college and play football again.

"My temperament is football, no doubt about it," said Brister. "Baseball players were always talking about their (bleeping) stats. I'd say, 'Hey, fellas, we lost.'"

On his role as the Steelers' offensive leader:

"I want to get my team fired up. I don't feel I act too macho when I feel I need to do something different. If somone isn't getting the job done, I'll tell them."

On his roommate Merril Hoge:

"He works hard and takes it serious. That's why I like him. I like to hang around with a guy who wants to be the best."

Asked why he swears so much during interviews, Brister said, "My coaches all used the F-word a lot when I was coming along. It's the way people in pro football talk. No one says, 'Gosh, darnit, I missed a block.' There's not a whole lot of room for nice guys. I don't mean to offend anybody by it. I get letters telling me kids can read my lips during a game. I just do it out of second nature."

When Nover noted that Brister was 28 and single, Brister smiled before Nover finished talking. "I'm living a normal bachelor life," said Brister. "I'm a red-blooded American male. I like to drink beer and go and dance with a pretty girl. I'm normal."

How does he think the fans feel about him in Pittsburgh?

"It's like anything in life. It's not going to be rosy all the time. Tough times never last, but tough people do. I feel like I'm a better quarterback. But when I'm bad, people who were cheering us start booing us. All of a sudden you're nothin'. I've gone from the penthouse to the outhouse in a hurry."

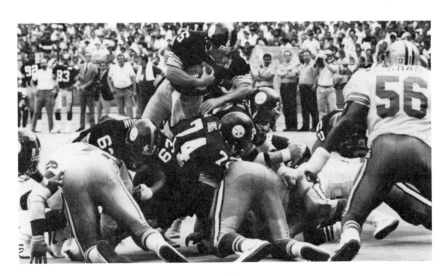

Myron Cope
Custodian of "The Terrible Towel"

There are no western saloon-style swinging doors at the entrance to the Baggy Knee, a neighborhood bar-restaurant in Greensburg, the next big town west of Latrobe, but you would have sworn there were the way Myron Cope came into the place one July night during the Steelers' summer training camp of 1990.

He started firing before anybody at the bar could draw a breath, let alone a gun, as he moved swiftly into the midst of a media gathering midway through the room. Cope was wearing a bright red sweater, and he was in the best of spirits, fresh-scrubbed, bright-eyed and bushy-tailed as usual. At 5-6 and age 62, he was both the shortest and senior member of the Steelers' media tribe. He was still its most enthusiastic and excited member. Cope's chemistry has always amazed me. Every show is like his first show. Every conversation is a show.

"Did you guys catch my show tonight?" cried Cope for openers. "I really gave it to Ralph Cindrich and Eric Green tonight! I know Cindrich listens to my show, so I spoke directly to him — like he was right there in the studio.

"I told him he better get that Eric Green signed real soon before he blows the millions he's going to make playing for the Steelers. I told him this Middle East crisis is going to get worse; it's going to heat up in the Middle East. I told him that Eric Green is going to get drafted into the Army before you know it, and he'll be playing in Kuwait or Iraq instead of Pittsburgh and the National Football League. You laugh, but this is serious stuff. If he signs, he'll still get his money, even if he gets drafted into the Army. It may seem far-fetched, but I don't think so. I'm serious! 'Listen up, Cindrich,' I said. I like Cindrich, so I'm trying to help him. I told him. . ."

Cindrich is a sports attorney who lives in Mt. Lebanon, a suburb six miles south of Pittsburgh, who used to play football for Pitt and the Houston Oilers and New England Patriots. He is now one of the most respected sports agents in the game. He was representing the Steelers' No. 1 draft choice, a giant of a tight end named Eric Green, 6-5, 275, who had played for former NFL coach Sam Rutigliano at Liberty University. Green had skipped the entire training camp, holding out for a better contract than the Steelers were offering. He would miss the entire pre-season schedule and the first two games of the regular season as well before becoming a big impact player on the team. Cope coined his nickname "Greenhouse" after he started catching TD passes. It would have been nice if Cope had managed to get Green into camp, but even Cope comes up short sometimes.

Cope railed on, to the amusement of most of the media types. This was a gathering, just before camp would break up for the summer, of most of the beat reporters. Present were Ed Bouchette of the *Pittsburgh*

Steelers' broadcasters Myron Cope and Jack Fleming in broadcast booth at
Three Rivers Stadium, where fans wave "Terrible Towel."

Post-Gazette, Ron Musselman of the *Valley News Dispatch*, Mike Prisuta of the *Beaver County Times*, Norm Vargo of the *McKeesport Daily News*, Mike Ciarochi of the *Greensburg Tribune Review* and Bob Labriola of *Steelers Digest*.

The only holdovers from my days on the beat (1979-83) were Vargo, 56, who had been my running buddy on the road, and Ciarochi, 36, who was then with the *Uniontown Herald-Standard*. I had been away from this scene for seven years, and felt out of it. I had been brought to the Baggy Knee by Pat Hanlon, the public relations director of the Steelers, who had been my right-hand man when I was the assistant athletic director and sports information director at the University of Pittsburgh from 1983 to 1987. He was my protege and my pal. He had since, at age 30, taken a new job as director of public relations for the New England Patriots. He and I had been to dinner earlier that evening at DeNunzio's in nearby Jeannette with lifelong friends of local product Dick Hoak, who had been with the Steelers as a player and coach for the past 29 years. Tony DeNunzio and Aldo Paulone had been gracious and generous hosts. Tony's son, Ron, owns the restaurant. We had V.I.P. treatment. So it was becoming a long day.

No one had enjoyed this ritual of training camp any more than I had when I covered the club. It was part of the schedule, or so it seemed, to cut out of the campus of St. Vincent College at night, after writing the day's stories for *The Pittsburgh Press,* and join the other reporters, as well as several of the Steelers' assistant coaches, at some favored watering holes on Rt. 30.

The Steelers' assistants who were regulars back then, especially at a tavern named Pete's, were Woody Widenhofer, George Perles, Rollie Dotsch and Paul Uram. Sportswriters in search of a beer, the inside story on the Steelers — perhaps the next cuts — spirited company, camaraderie, could find it on Rt. 30. At three in the morning, when cuts were to be announced in about five hours, you could usually succeed in prying a few names, with a Deep Throat kind of code, out of the coaches. It gave you a head start on the next day's work, if not a scoop. Cope and Vargo seldom missed one of those get-togethers. Cope was always the catalyst for such good times. He knew how to have fun. And the customers loved him. "Hey, Myron, let me buy you a drink!" one after another of the locals would holler out, pronouncing Myron the way they did Iron in Iron City Beer. Cope was always courteous and cheerful, and played to the crowd. He loved the attention, though he would swear he didn't.

Cope had been the color man to Jack Fleming's play-by-play broadcast of Steelers' games on WTAE Radio since 1970, the year that the Steelers moved into Three Rivers Stadium. He also had a nightly sports talk show on WTAE, and was easily the most popular sportscaster in the city. During the Steelers' glory days, he had invented "The Terrible Towel," had encouraged fans to form booster groups for Steeler players such as Franco's Italian Army and Lambert's Lunatics, to bring banners and signs to Three Rivers Stadium — even suggesting the wording or messages sometimes — and gained national notoriety for his uniqueness. He may also have had the worst voice in radio history, but it played well in Pittsburgh if not Peoria. But Cope had charisma and chutzpah and he had the city and its citizens by the back of the neck. No one worked harder at his trade than he did. He did his homework and he had a network of tipsters — "birdies" he called them — who gave him the latest gossip in the games that Pittsburghers played.

I had first met him when I was 14, back in 1956, when he was covering the Pittsburgh Golden Gloves for the *Post-Gazette,* and I was covering the best team in the amateur boxing tournament, the Glen-Hazel Boys Club, as the sports editor for my hometown *Hazelwood Envoy,* a bi-weekly. He was nice to me and encouraging from the start. He has remained a mentor.

At age 19 and 20, I frequented a bar in the Baldwin-Whitehall section of town known as Dante's, where Cope, and other sports media types went to mix with the likes of Bobby Layne, Ernie Stautner and other Steelers. It was part of my college education, even though I received no credit for the course at the University of Pittsburgh.

Cope preceded me by about 15 years as the sports editor of *The Pitt News,* and his picture appears today in several Pitt publications as one of its distinguished alumni.

I skipped out of the Baggy Knee early, eager to get back to my dorm room at Bonaventure Hall and get a good night's sleep — I had aged considerably since I last attended training camp, I thought. Cope joined the others at a late-night retreat known as The Tin Lizzie.

Despite the late night, Cope was running on all cylinders the next day. Soon after he got up, he learned that Randy Wright, an off-season acquisition who had played quarterback for the Green Bay Packers for the previous five seasons, had been cut from the squad by Chuck Noll that very morning. The news made Cope's day, if not Wright's day.

"See, see what I told you guys," said Cope, coming up swinging as soon as he arose from his bed at Bonaventure Hall. "I told you that Randy Wright was messing with the wrong guy when he took on Cope. I knew he wasn't right for this team. How can a guy who can't stand cigaret smoke expect to quarterback in the National Football League?"

Cope couldn't contain himself. He had a story to tell. This was before breakfast, and most of the sportswriters were scrambling to get dressed so they could catch Wright before he left the camp, so they could get his reaction to what happened.

"Let me tell you what happened with me and Wright," said Cope. "I'm smoking a cigaret on the plane on one of our trips this summer and I see Wright waving his newspaper in the air in front of me, and he keeps doing it.

"Finally, I say to him, 'Hey, Wright, am I bothering you by smoking?'

"He says, 'Yes, you are.' But I keep smoking. Then he turns around, and he says, 'Would you please put out that cigaret?' I keep smoking. He keeps waving his newspaper. He asks me again to put out my cigaret.

Finally, I said, 'Are you allergic to cigarets?' He said, 'Yes, I am.' So I snuffed it out. Then I told him, 'Hey, I've been smoking cigarets in this seat for 20 years and I've had some pretty great players bum cigarets from me. Like John Stallworth.' To which Wright says, 'That's fine, but I'd appreciate it if you didn't smoke.'

"I turned to Bubby (Brister), who was behind me, and I said, 'He's in imminent peril of death.' Bubby laughed. Then Bubby leaned over top of me and told him, 'Hey, Randy, the last guy who told Cope that got cut.'

"When we were getting off the plane, I said to Bubby, loud enough for Wright to hear, 'Hey, Bubby, let me put on a uniform for one play and let me play wide receiver. I want to go in the huddle and blow smoke right in Wright's face.'

"I wanted Wright to hear me, and he turned and said, 'I've heard worse from better people.'

"To which I said, 'That's fine.'

"Imagine that. How the hell can you play quarterback in the NFL if you can't stand cigaret smoke? Can you imagine what Bobby Layne would have said to him. He'd have said, 'You jerk. Where the hell are you coming from?' Bobby Layne would ream his butt out good."

Cope was bleary-eyed and in need of a cup of coffee. But the coffee pots were all empty. "Can anybody around here make a cup of coffee?" he pleaded.

I volunteered, but told him it was a simple procedure to make the coffee. I asked him to come over so I could show him how to do it. "This way you won't be dependent on anyone else," I preached to him. "You'll be able to make your own coffee." Cope protested as only Cope can. "It's the last day of camp," he railed. "It's a waste of time." Once I showed him how to do it, however, he snapped, "I knew it couldn't be that complicated if you could do it!" I had to smile. "See, you're all set for next season up here," I said. "You'll be able to make your own coffee from the first day on."

With Wright gone, and his feelings already known about Eric Green, and a freshly-brewed cup of coffee in hand, Cope turned his attention to Tim Johnson, a fourth year defensive lineman from Penn State, who was also holding out for a new contract.

"That Johnson's always quoting the Bible, saying The Lord will provide," said Cope. " I guarantee you he's never been through a Depression."

Word would come down later in the day that the Steelers had traded Johnson to the Washington Redskins for a future draft choice. That completed Cope's day.

"You did the right thing today," Cope told Chuck Noll as they crossed paths outside the dining room at St. Vincent. "That Randy Wright was wrong for the Steelers." Then Cope repeated his Randy Wright story for Noll's sake, since he had missed the many other renditions Cope had already offered that morning.

"You know what I like about you, Myron," said Noll with a smile. "You make all your decisions so personal."

124

It was the Friday before the big Sunday showdown with the Cincinnati Bengals at Three Rivers Stadium in November of 1990. If the Steelers won they would take over first place in the AFC Central Division, and Chuck Noll would notch his 200th NFL career victory. Myron Cope had just come away from interviewing Noll for the weekly pre-game radio show.

Cope was moving through the Steelers' offices in a hurry, as always, leaning forward like a pile-driving fullback. Cope came into Art Rooney's old office to be interviewed himself about his 21 years as the Steelers' radio color commentator.

Over the past few weeks, Cope had revived his "Terrible Towel," and told the fans to bring them to Three Rivers Stadium. This game was that big, as far as Cope was concerned, and the time was right. Pittsburghers were becoming excited about their football team again.

Two weeks earlier, after the Steelers had been blown out by the Bengals, 27-3, Cope commented on the radio about the presence of so many Pittsburghers at Riverfront Stadium in Cincinnati. "It's like the '70s all over again!" Cope cried out in his own caricature style. It was quite a turnabout from the first four weeks of the season, when the Steelers lost three of their four games, prompting Cope to comment on the air, "It looks like it could be a grim season."

When I asked him about that, Cope was calmer in reply. "This team is not bristling with the kind of Hall of Fame performers you had in the '70s," he said. "Maybe they know that comes along once in a lifetime, if you're lucky. But people are reacting to this team in a positive manner.

"I think it's a young football team that is on the improve. I'm the custodian of the 'Terrible Towel,' and I've resisted all these years when people wanted me to bring it back.

"My decision came after they beat the Atlanta Falcons (21-9). The Steelers had two games on the road, followed by a week off in the new schedule set-up. It gave us the time we needed to get new towels into the stores." A percentage of the money spent on "Terrible Towels" at Kaufmann's department stores was sent to the Allegheny Valley School for mentally and physically handicapped children. Cope has been active for many years in raising funds through various promotions for the school, as well as other charities.

"I said to myself, 'I have three weeks to get out the message.' The bye week was a bonus that wouldn't have happened normally in the past. But I'm only on my show two days a week now and I don't have as many opportunities as I used to in order to promote it."

When Cope talks about the "Terrible Towel," he talks about it as if he were talking about a grandchild. He takes tremendous pride in coming up with what became a symbol of the enthusiasm and craziness of Steelers' fans. "He's a he," Cope says of the towel.

During the broadcast of the Steelers-Bengals game at Three Rivers Stadium, Cope mentioned that Keith Willis had gotten on his case when he came through the training room. "Willis was giving me a bad time about bringing back the Terrible Towel," said Cope. "He hollered out, 'Hey, Cope's in here looking around for old towels.' I said, 'Listen, Willis,

I told The Towel what you said, and he put a curse on you. But I told The Towel you have no brains and that you didn't mean it. I told him to look after you.' And see what happens! On the fourth play of the game, he catches a deflected pass for his first interception of his career. He'll never knock The Towel again."

Cope had cut back on his work schedule, and went from doing a morning commentary and nightly two-hour talk show five days a week to just two days, Monday and Tuesday. It was his own decision. He wanted to relax a little, have some fun, play golf, and not push himself so hard.

I kidded him about calling himself "the custodian of the Terrible Towel." Cope has always been a catalyst for the fans at Three Rivers Stadium. During a broadcast, he might say something like, "let's hear it from you loyal listeners with your transistors in the stadium." Asked how he saw his role in the Steelers' scheme of things, Cope paused.

"I've never attempted to define my role," he said. "I have spent 21 years having a lot of fun with this stuff, and I go where my instincts take me. I'm a fan in that sense."

Cope's love affair with the Steelers and Pittsburgh sports teams, in general, goes back to his youth. He grew up in Squirrel Hill, just two miles from Forbes Field, where the Pirates and Steelers played in those days.

"When I was a kid," recalled Cope, "I would walk to Forbes Field to see games. I loved baseball. I even went to a tryout there. I got two cuts at the plate and I was out of there.

"I used to go out there and work as a vendor, so I could make a few bucks and see the games at the same time. All the young guys would report to the park before the game, and they'd lock us up in an area. If they picked you, then you got to work that night. If they didn't, they tossed you out.

"I'd go out there on Sundays when the Steelers were playing, and I had no intention of working on Sundays. After they locked us up, I knew there'd be an opportunity to get out of there through a break in a chain fence. When no one was watching, I'd shoot through and run up into the right field stands, as far up as it was possible to go. I'd hide in the bathroom up there, so nobody would spot me in the stands. I'd take the Sunday paper with me, and I'd go over the lineups. I'd wait until the fans started coming, and then I'd go out and get lost in the crowd. I used to watch right from the 50-yard line. There were more people standing there than there were people sitting on the 50-yard line. Forbes Field was built for baseball, and the best seats were high in the right-center field stands. I'd do that every Sunday the Steelers were at home, sitting in the toilet, reading the sports section."

Nowadays, Cope comes just as early, only he doesn't have to hide anymore. And now he has a seat on the 50-yard line, one of the best in the house. And people bring him all the sports notes and lineups he can ever use. And hot coffee.

Having grown up in Pittsburgh, he can appreciate why the Steelers were important to the people of the area back in the '70s.

"I think they were important for two reasons," claimed Cope. "This has always been great football territory. High school football was so big around here. Football became even more important here when the steel industry went down the tubes, and so many people were out of work, when the mills were closing down for good. The Steelers gave them something to be happy about, something to cheer. You could look forward to the games on Sunday, and it helped you get started on Monday. It was a psychological shot in the arm. People in Pittsburgh had fallen on hard times, and they needed to feel like a winner in some way.

"So we had the great Steeler teams, and we became known as 'The City of Champions,' and we were celebrated on national TV, and we had lots of fun things like the 'Terrible Towel' that set us apart from other pro football fans, and we just swarmed into other cities, and everybody knew it when the Pittsburghers came to town. Everybody was wearing their black and gold, and waving their towels. If the Steelers won on Sunday, the sun came up on Monday.

"It's much more fun when you win than when you lose. But I never considered it to be a matter of life and death. I wasn't going to take the gas pipe because the football team lost a game."

Cope and Noll lived about a mile or five minutes from each other in the suburban community of Upper St. Clair, nine miles south of Three Rivers Stadium, during the '70s and '80s.

"If I have something that needs fixing or adjusting, I know Noll can do it," said Cope, with a mischievous look on his face. "I'll drop the hint to Noll like, 'Geez, Chaz, I'm having trouble hooking up the stereo.' The next thing I know he's there, and he's got his bifocals on, and he has it fixed. He can't resist showing me what he can do.

"When something goes wrong at the house, I tell Mildred, 'I think I'm gonna have to say something to Noll and get him over here.' He's more reliable than any plumber or electrician I ever dealt with. And he doesn't cost as much."

Imagine having Chuck Noll as a handyman at your house?

"I think I understand Noll pretty well, and have now for awhile," commented Cope. "I don't think he's nearly as complicated as people make him out to be. Noll is a guy who, for one thing, has things figured out. When he does a press conference, for instance, he knows what constitutes a story. He knows how to get points across with his players, with the press, with the league office, with the opposition.

"He's a guy of very measured thinking. It takes a long time for him to trust you. I think I was doing my show with Noll for about a half dozen years before he trusted me. Before he wasn't asking himself, 'Whose side is this guy on?' It was twelve years before he trusted me to tell me things off the record. He'll level with me now. With most coaches, by mid-year of their first season, he knows he can trust you.

"I wouldn't classify him as a friend of mine. We live a mile away from each other, but we don't move in the same social circles. He's been over to my house a lot. Sometimes I'll catch him on his way to work.

"Why is he so good at what he does? He knows his stuff. He knows his football. He knows the x's and o's. He has enough confidence in himself to stay with those things that have been successful for him. In bad times, they say he's stubborn. But I have noticed other coaches talking about stubbornness these days in a more positive light. With Noll, he simply believes in what he has learned.

"From time to time, he'll make changes. Like with Joe Walton's offense. It's not like his mind is totally closed. He knew the Steelers' offense had become predictable, and that it was not as productive as in the past. So he brought in somebody he thought could turn things around for the better.

"He pays not one shit's worth of attention to what guys like us say or write. He has total blinders on.

"What works for one coach doesn't necessarily work for another coach. He's from the school that's not given to pep talks. He wants people to motivate themselves. But you have a different brand of ballplayer today, and they're not as apt to motivate themselves. Maybe it does require more motivation from the head coach. But if he does it, he will not tell you about it.

"He recently told me about sitting down with a ballplayer and talking over things. He knows when something's on the record or off the record; he doesn't have to spell it out with me. Yet, he added, 'This is very much off the record.' He didn't want any one thinking he had sat down with a ballplayer. That's so unusual for him."

Two weeks later, at his weekly press conference, Noll was asked by someone on the Steelers' beat if he thought the players were any different today than they were when he won the first of his 200 victories. Noll responded, "No, they're the same."

Cope was asked about Art Rooney, and his impact on the Steelers during the '70s when they were winning all those championships.

"The affection with which he was held by the players is unique in pro sports," said Cope. "They all felt like they were his guy. He said 'how are you?' to each and every one of them, and made them feel important. The Chief is not here now, but the team is responding to Chuck Noll. The Chief will always be missed, but his spirit is still here."

Tragedies
"I feel closer to them"

Tragedy was a frequent visitor to the Steelers' training camp at St. Vincent College. The Latrobe school was a great place for getaways, for retreats, the religious and the sports camp kind, but it was not so far outside the real world that people there could not be pulled back, and forced to face difficulties in their lives.

Sometimes it was an illness or death back home, sometimes an auto accident, and memories of such setbacks remain for those familiar with the Steelers' history.

Back in the summer of 1977, for instance, Cliff Stoudt lent his car to fellow rookies Randy Frisch and Dave Grinaker to drive from the camp in Latrobe to Pittsburgh for a pre-season game against the Buffalo Bills.

On the way back to camp, Frisch was driving on a rain-slicked Route 30 in North Huntingdon Township, and he was driving much too fast, especially for the weather conditions, according to witnesses. The car spun out and struck a guard rail, and then a pole. Grinaker got out of the wreckage alive, but Frisch was killed. Grinaker suffered multiple fractures which ended his football career.

Stoudt, who was performing well at camp up until that point, was shaken up badly by the accident. His mind was not in the huddle the rest of the summer, and he was waived from the squad. No one else picked him up, so Stoudt stayed with the Steelers' organization, and got a second chance. There were also accidents elsewhere.

On Nov. 17, 1978, Randy Reutershan was traveling north on Washington Pike near Bridgeville when his auto went out of control, crashed through a guard rail, sheared off a utility pole and landed in a field. Reutershan, a rookie who had previously played at Pitt, suffered a severely fractured skull, and was unconscious for several days. He failed his physical exam the following summer and was finished as far as pro football was concerned.

There were close calls, too. In Lynn Swann's rookie year of 1974, he and Franco Harris had just returned to Pittsburgh from playing in a Monday Night Football game in New Orleans.

It was about 2 a.m. in Pittsburgh, and there was snow on the road as Swann drove in to the city on the Parkway West. Being a Californian, he had no experience driving in the snow. "The road was a sheet of ice in one place, and I slammed on the brake," said Swann. "The car spun into a guard rail. I thought I was going to kill Franco and myself, that we'd be laying out on the street and a car would run over us."

129

In late June, 1979, John Banaszak and Ray Oldham flipped over in a golf cart while playing on a course during a Steelers' vacation sojourn to Puerto Rico. Oldham jumped free and landed in a lake, while Banaszak was pinned under the cart in marshy land surrounding the lake.

"Ray saw my legs sticking out from under the cart," said Banaszak, "and he started crying, 'Banny, Banny, you all right?' "

With Oldham's help, Banaszak slid out from under the golf cart and escaped with bruises, cuts and an embarrassed look because he had been the driver.

"It happens in everyday life to everyday people," observed Banaszak. "Just because we're athletes we're not exempt from accidental death. It just seems more of a shock when we're involved.

"We were very fortunate. Both Ray and I could have been badly hurt. I was under the cart in a foot and a half of mud as it was. I could've been pinned under water. Ray had a hard time moving the cart because he couldn't get traction in the mud. It scared the hell outta me, and Ray more so because he didn't know what shape I was in under the cart."

On August 28, 1979, three Steelers — Mike Kruczek, Steve Courson and Gary Dunn — just missed being struck by a steel-carrying flatbed truck which lost its brakes on Green Tree Hill.

Two autos burst into flames in front of them after a spectacular chain-reaction crash involving 13 vehicles on the Parkway West at the height of the morning rush hour. There were 10 people injured, but none seriously in something of a miracle.

"We could see the truck coming right at us, but we couldn't do anything," recalled Courson, who was at the wheel of an auto he had purchased only four days earlier. "Your life passes in front of your eyes real fast," Courson sighed.

"Mike hollered, 'Look out!' And I see this 18-wheeler coming at us. I couldn't do anything. There was no time to react. It was going 60 miles an hour and its brakes were squealing.

"It missed us by a foot, and we had a bird's-eye view as it pinballed through 12 cars. We saw a guy trying to run out of his car, and the truck was pulling the car along with it.

"We got out of our car and we couldn't believe that no one was badly hurt. Bennie Cunningham and Larry Brown were in a car behind us, and Ted Petersen and Tom Beasley were back of them. So we all got out and came together.

"It was the day for final cuts and if there's one day you don't want to be late for practice it's that day. But, thinking about it, we were lucky to get to practice at all."

When Dan Rooney was reminded of all these auto accidents, he said, "It's one of the reasons insurance rates are so high for young males."

Vic Ketchman, the sports editor of the *Observer-Reporter* in Irwin, reminded me of two other situations from 1980, my second year at the Steelers' training camp.

The father of Franco Harris died before the camp opened, and a shaken Franco came to camp and said he was going to dedicate the season to the memory of his father. At that same summer camp, Jack Lambert broke down one day while discussing the death of Steelers' field manager Jack Hart, who had been a favorite of Lambert. Hart had a drinking problem and frequently disappeared for a day or so and, finally, got fired by club president Dan Rooney for his absences. Everyone said Hart, who had been with the Steelers for so many years, died of a broken heart.

The 1982 camp was marked by the accidental death of the father of Frank Pollard. Frank Pollard was a fine pile-driving running back for the Steelers for nine seasons. He was never a star, just a reliable running back, the other back in the backfield. He ran and he blocked, and he did whatever he was called upon to do. He was a plugger, a reincarnation of Fran Rogel.

When Pollard was released before the start of the 1989 season, only Franco Harris and John Henry Johnson had rushed for more yards in a Steelers uniform. Harris was in his own league with 11,950 yards, Johnson a distant second with 4,383 and Pollard third with 3,989, just ahead of his backfield coach his entire career, Dick Hoak, who had 3,965. It was Hoak primarily who made sure Pollard gained the ground he needed to get the bronze medal in the Steelers' record books.

The likes of Rocky Bleier, Walter Abercrombie, Rogel, Frenchy Fuqua, Tom Tracy, Terry Bradshaw, Preston Pearson, Lynn Chandnois, Earnest Jackson, Sidney Thornton, Bill Dudley. Joe Geri and Merril Hoge round out the all-time rushing list, so Pollard's marathon performance is impressive in retrospect.

Here's a story I wrote about Pollard's plight in the August 18, 1982 issue of *The Pittsburgh Press:*

LATROBE — There are days when it becomes difficult for Frank Pollard to practice. There are nights when he finds it difficult to sleep. Yesterday was one of them.

It wasn't because a thunderstorm forced the Steelers to conduct the first hour of their afternoon practice in the gym at St. Vincent College, or that the field was mushy when the rain let up enough for them to go outdoors.

Practice was longer than usual yesterday, but Pollard likes to play football, and he has some catching up to do at camp because he reported late. He wasn't complaining.

It wasn't the pass he dropped, the hamstrings that are as tight as harpstrings and kept him from playing against the New England Patriots in Knoxville, Tennessee, last Saturday night. Nothing like that.

During practice, he finds it difficult to concentrate on what Dick Hoak, the backfield coach, is telling him about a particular play. Or what to expect Saturday night when he should see action against the New York Giants.

During the night, Frank often gets up and walks the hall, even though he is supposed to stay in Room 141 after curfew.

"It usually happens around 3 o'clock," said Pollard. "I start dreaming about my father, and I go downstairs and sit."

Pollard's father was in a tragic accident the day before Frank was to report to the Steelers' training camp July 23. Pollard stayed home while his 52-year-old father was in the hospital, fighting for his life, burns searing 60 percent of his body.

Frank Pollard Sr. owned an auto-wrecking firm in Meridian, Texas, and he was removing a fuel tank from a friend's truck when a spark caused an explosion.

"My father caught the full brunt of the explosion," Pollard said last night, between dinner and a team meeting here. "He rallied in the hospital, and seemed to be getting better. The doctors thought he had turned the corner. I was all set to come to camp."

But the Steelers' young running back had to stay home longer than he had anticipated. He didn't show up at St. Vincent until August 4, two days after his father's funeral.

"I thought he'd be in bad shape physically," said Hoak, "but he surprised me. It's a good thing he came to our mini-camp, where we worked on a lot of our new offense. Otherwise, he would've been so far behind. But Frank's a worker; he'll be all right."

Pollard's physical shape is one thing, his mental shape is something else, something the coaches can't measure with their stopwatches, charts or scales.

This is a tough kid. When he came to camp for the first time two years ago, he had to leave after the opening day of practice. His wife and baby were in a bad auto accident.

"My little girl was only three months old, and this pickup truck hit my wife's car on the same side where my little girl was lying on the seat," recalled Pollard. "It knocked her to the floor, and my wife thought she was really hurt bad. She sounded scared on the phone when she called me."

But it wasn't as bad as feared, everybody was fine in a short time, and Pollard returned to camp and stuck with the Steelers, quite an achievement for an 11th-round draft choice.

This time, however, he brought a burden back with him and it's heavier than rain-soaked shoulder pads.

"It's getting worse," the former Baylor running back confided. "I'm thinking about it more and more. But I'm getting a lot of support from the guys. They know it's on my mind."

Several Steelers spent extra time with Pollard, including Ron Johnson, Tyrone McGriff and Sidney Thornton. "Ron and Sidney have both lost their mothers," said Pollard. "Tyrone lost his father."

It points up another side of the Steelers, and what goes on behind the scenes at Bonaventure Hall. Donnie Shell and Mel Blount have urged Pollard to join them at the prayer meeting each morning, and Pollard planned to take them up on their offer today. That would please his mother, Katherine.

132

"She told me to hold on," Frank explained. "She said, 'You'll have many bad moments, but your dad wouldn't want you to grieve.' She told me to go to church, to read my Bible. I know my mother is hurting. There was nothing but love between those two people. "

Even so, Pollard gets down. His chin drops like the weeping willows that line the lower field at St. Vincent; and they were drooping lower than ever during yesterday's hard rain.

The Laurel Mountains looked like the Smoky Mountains of Tennessee, and a haze brooded over the landscape. Lightning lit up the sky. The storm dimmed the lights in the campus gym and dorm. Pollard's moods shifted as dramatically.

"Why?" he said. "I keep asking myself that all the time. I questioned it. I had a lot of hate when he died. I felt a lot of disappointment.

"I keep seeing my dad. When I was at home, all we talked about was what my life was like here with the Steelers. I keep hearing his voice, talking about what we used to talk about."

Pollard is the second oldest of five children. He said his father was emotional and happy when he made the grade with the Steelers two seasons ago, right after their second straight Super Bowl triumph, their fourth in six seasons.

"He hugged me hard," said Pollard. "He's been to every game within driving distance. He saw me play in Dallas and Houston.

"We were real close. When we were together, he talked a lot about the team. It meant a great deal to me to have him feel about me the way he did, because I respected him more than anyone else in the world.

"He sacrificed a lot to put me through college. He did a lot just to make my life better. I just regret not having been able to help him as much as I could've. Whatever I do this season is going to be for him.

"My first year at camp, I called him every day on the telephone. Last year, I called him every other day. Now I call my mother. I want to ask her where he is. I catch myself. I say, 'Let me speak to. . .,' and I catch myself."

Sometimes Pollard smiles, like he smiled when he walked off the practice field yesterday alongside Coach Chuck Noll. Sometimes he snarls.

Linebacker David Little leveled him just as he was reaching up to pull in a pass in a drill yesterday. As Pollard lay there, Little bellowed, "Get off your butt!" Pollard responded sharply, "Shut up!"

He has often been moody on the football field in the past, but now it's worse.

"My buddies will get on my back when that happens, and joke to me. But it's hard. The other night in Tennessee, I saw Sidney with his dad and Bennie Cunningham with his folks, and I felt bad.

"I know he wanted me to do well," said Frank. "I think it has given me added incentive. I'll make it."

And he has learned something about some of the Steelers. "I feel closer to them, some that I didn't know much about before. I know what they're about now."

Gabe Rivera

Mike Fabus

I was nearly killed in an auto mishap just before my third birthday, back in the summer of 1945. I was riding in the back of a taxi cab with my family. We were riding across the Glenwood Bridge in the rain and the wooden floor of the bridge, which also had steel streetcar tracks on it, was quite slippery. The taxi cab driver was drunk and driving too fast for conditions, I have been told, and the cab swerved sharply, and I was thrown out of the back seat in a sling-shot manner. I soared head-first into the top rail of the sidewalk on the bridge. A foot higher and I would have soared right into the Monongahela River below. As it was, the top of my head hit the steel railing, and I bounced back into the streetcar tracks. I was lucky no streetcar or auto traffic was coming in that lane. Doctors at Mercy Hospital told my parents they didn't think they could save me. I required 48 stitches to close the wounds in my head, and had to have a piece of skin from my knee used as a patch for a hole the size of a quarter under my nose. But I came out of it OK, I think, and returned home in time for my birthday.

Eighteen or nineteen years later, when I was 21 or 22, I'm not sure of the exact year, I was driving home one night by myself after having too much to drink at Dante's, a bar-restaurant in Whitehall where several of the Steelers and several sportscasters hung out regularly.

I was driving back to Hazelwood on Beck's Run Road, a serpentine stretch, and I dozed off. I went across the road into the other lane, and woke up to the sound of my car striking several construction horses. I was knocking them over like a heavy-legged hurdler, but I stopped in time to avoid crashing into an unyielding utility pole. I was lucky. This all came to mind when I was doing some research about Gabe Rivera, the Steelers' No. 1 draft choice in 1983, whose career and walking days came to an abrupt halt when he was badly injured in an auto accident in his rookie season. It happened five weeks into his first NFL season, and he had already shown enough to hint that he could be a great one.

On October 20, 1983, Rivera was thrown through the rear window of his sports car after it collided with another car on Pittsburgh's North Side.

On that fateful night, when it was raining hard, Rivera was driving a Datsun 2802X, and was not wearing his seat belt. He crossed Babcock Boulevard and struck a 1978 Ford LTD driven by 48-year-old Allen Watts, who had a Steelers' license plate on the front of his vehicle. Watts was wearing his seat belt. Rivera's 290-pound body was jettisoned through the rear window of his car and landed in the woods 20 feet from the point of collision. He was unconscious.

Rivera suffered broken ribs, a bruised heart and a bruised lung, nerve damage to the right shoulder and, most seriously, a crushed spinal cord.

Pittsburgh police charged Rivera with drunken driving, speeding, reckless driving and driving on the wrong side of the road. Rivera remained in the hospital for more than a month. Twenty three days after his accident, Rivera's wife, Kim, gave birth to a son, Timothy.

Then Rivera was transferred to the Harmarville Rehabilitation Center, 15 miles northeast of Pittsburgh, to a unit for quadraplegics — those who have paralysis in all four limbs.

Throughout his rehabilitation and recovery, Rivera has done his best to be positive and to work hard to improve his condition. "The important thing," said Rivera, back home in Texas, "is to strive to try to get better in a different way . . . while it's not the kind of life-style I want, it's the way I want to go about it right now, so that maybe there will be a cure or that someday I might be walking."

He admitted that it has been difficult, and that he has suffered from depression from time to time. It didn't help that his wife, Kim, left him, along with their son, Timothy, shortly thereafter.

"For some people it's hard," related Rivera, "and for some people, it's not hard. That's what is so weird when you have a traumatic accident. Some people keep a tremendous attitude toward life. Then there's some that just don't care really. For me, it's hard."

Gabe's father, Juan Rivera, said there was a Mexican saying that goes something like this: "If something bad will come, something good will come later."

In time, Rivera regained some feeling in his arms, and was able to drive a specially-equipped van. He was able to brush his teeth, go to the bathroom, and take a bath. The Steelers paid Rivera for his full rookie season even though they didn't have to because his injuries were not football-related. They offered him a job as a scout, but he was not interested.

Rivera had played football for San Antonio's Jefferson High School and went on to play for the Texas Tech Red Raiders. In college, he was known as "Señor Sack." He made 19 tackles in one game against Houston. He could bench press 480 pounds, clean jerk 310 pounds and had a vertical jump of 27 inches. He wrecked Texas A&M all by himself, according to Jackie Sherrill, their coach who had previously been the head coach at the University of Pittsburgh. "He was the difference," said Sherrill. "If he's not on the field, we win."

Dick Haley, the director of Steelers' player personnel, saw Rivera in action against the University of Washington. "He went up against two 285-pound tackles and just tore them up. It's uncommon, a guy that big who can run and move like that."

The Steelers were among the teams in that draft who bypassed Pitt's Danny Marino, who was the 27th pick and the sixth quarterback taken in the first round.

Once before, Chuck Noll had reached into Texas for a dominant defensive lineman for his No. 1 draft choice, and that, of course, was Mean Joe Greene of North Texas State in 1969. The Steelers also got Ernie Holmes and Dwight White from Texas schools.

Noll liked what he saw in Rivera, who was 22, 6-2, 293 pounds. Rivera wore a size 54 coat, had a 20-inch neck, size 13EE feet. "He's quick," Noll said the day of the 1983 draft. "You can't teach quick."

He was quick in a car, too, and had picked up a series of moving violation tickets for speeding while a student at Texas Tech.

He had an enormous appetite. One night, he ate 13 hamburgers in a single sitting. On another night, he ate 23 enchiladas, and another time, on a special diet, he ate 23 cans of tuna for a snack. He had ballooned as high as 320 pounds while in college. Some Steelers had labeled him "Señor Burrito."

Rivera had been both a legendary defensive lineman and a prodigious eater in more light-hearted days. After his accident, he was the subject of more somber conversation. Everything was different. It would never be the same again.

"When you are a teenager, you figure out what you are going to do with your life," remarked Rivera. "You make some choices. I did that once. Now, I have to do it again.

"I think about how good I might have been. Then again, I might have been a flop. But we'll never know, will we?"

Craig Colquitt was the Steelers' punter when I covered the club. Like most punters, he was different, and he had a lot of time on his hands. So he did a lot of thinking, probably too much thinking. He thought he would like to be a writer someday.

"I fantasize a lot," he said.

One of his favorite fantasies went like this: "We're in the Super Bowl and I make a good punt. Their guy settles under it, and he fumbles it. The ball bounces up high and, like a flash, I grab it, and I run 30 yards into the end zone for a touchdown that wins the game."

Not bad, as fantasies go. "I've actually dreamed it," commented Colquitt back in the fall of 1980. "I dreamed it before the last Super Bowl. But, of course, it didn't happen.

"Instead of spiking the ball," continued Colquitt. "I kick it into the stands. Another fantasy of mine is playing quarterback. I'd really enjoy being at the helm."

In addition to dreams, there were also nightmares in Colquitt's career with the Steelers.

The images of the night of May 7, 1979, flashed before his mind as well. That was the night when he lost control of his new sports car and went off a winding road near Knoxville, where he had been a student athlete at the University of Tennessee. He had crashed his car into a tree.

Holly Bryant, a 21-year-old student at Tennessee, whom Colquitt had been dating for several months, suffered permanent head injuries in that crash. Colquitt had administered mouth-to-mouth resuscitation to Miss Bryant. She was left in a coma and had suffered, according to expert testimony in a court case that followed the incident, irreparable brain damage.

Colquitt was cleared of drunk-driving charges which were leveled against him after the accident. Earlier, his insurance company made an out-of-court settlement on a $3 million suit that had been brought against him by the guardian of Miss Bryant.

In June of 1980, Colquitt was married to Anne Davis, whom he met and commiserated with in the aftermath of the accident. Miss Davis, it developed, had been dating Atlanta Falcons' linebacker Andy Spiva at the time he was killed in an auto accident. Spiva also played at the University of Tennessee, and Colquitt met Miss Davis on the campus. They helped pull each other out of an emotional tailspin.

"Spiva was driving a car, and he had a teammate with him," recalled Colquitt. "He was driving on a terrible night, I'm told, and he went through a large puddle, and the car hydroplaned. He went off the road and hit a tree. The car wrapped itself around the tree. There was no drinking involved. It was just an accident."

With Spiva, who grew up in Atlanta, was Garth TenNapel, another young linebacker for the Falcons. Spiva received hard blows to the head and chest in the accident and died from the injuries. TenNapel was in a coma for a long time and was permanently disabled.

"Anne and I met and started talking and we found out we had shared a similar experience and had a lot in common. It brought us together," said Colquitt.

Sounds like a soap opera, right? Craig and Anne are still married, and quite active in their church.

"I've been trying to lift myself above that," he said. "I have depressing thoughts that her (Miss Bryant's) life is at a standstill. I'm trying to climb above that."

Craig Colquitt

Frank Pollard

Tom Ricketts
Growing up with the Steelers

Tom Ricketts had come a long way in one year. Here he was toe-to-toe with Chuck Noll, which would have made him nervous only 15 months earlier when he first met the man he had looked up to all his life. Now it was Noll who was looking up to him.

Noll had his hands on his hips. Ricketts had his hands on his hips. It was nearly noon, but this was no showdown or duel. Noll was simply offering some advice to Ricketts, on how he ought to block on a particular play-action pass. Noll speaks softly, so he needs to be near you.

Ricketts was a second-year pro out of the University of Pittsburgh, a hometown boy who made good, and he was still wearing a bright blue and gold warmup suit with "Pitt" in script across his broad chest. He also had a ballcap on backwards, and his curly brown hair was sprouting out of the front and back of the cap like plumes.

Ricketts had been the second of two first round draft picks of the Steelers the year before, following Tim Worley, a high-speed running back from the University of Georgia, into the fold. Both had their share of difficulties and setbacks as rookies, and would have more of the same in their second seasons, but both had contributed to a club resurgence and a 9-7 record, the team's best record in five years, and 10-8 overall counting two playoff outings in the 1989 campaign.

Ricketts nodded as Noll offered instruction. Noll was wearing clean-pressed beige shorts, a white jersey, and a black windbreaker with the Steelers' insignia over his heart. They stood, strangely enough, at the top of the key at the north end of the basketball floor in the field house on the campus of St. Vincent College in Latrobe.

It had rained all day the day before, and during the night and through the morning, so the Steelers took what they call their "walk-through" practice indoors on this gray day. They were all in sneakers, some in shorts, some in jeans, wearing all kinds of T-shirts and sweatshirts, and looking like they were at a company picnic.

"It's where we reinforce what we talk about at team meetings," noted Noll afterward. "It's where you show them just exactly the way you want it done. No one gets it right the first time; you've got to go over it again and again."

Noll was not only the head coach at the Steelers' summer training camp in 1990, he was also the offensive line coach because a bad back had sidelined Ron Blackledge, one of his assistants, for the entire summer. Noll likes the one-on-one stuff. He is a hands-on coach, no coaching towers in the end zone for him, just the team's cameraman, Noll could not have had a better student than Tom Ricketts.

Tom Ricketts

"I was more impressed about meeting Chuck Noll the first time," related Ricketts later, relaxing on a couch in the media room at St. Vincent, "than I would have been anybody else — even the President of the United States.

"I never had a problem communicating with anybody. No matter how big a personality they were, or what power they had. But I was nervous when I first met Chuck Noll.

"I guess it was from growing up in this city, and knowing so much about him, but not knowing him personally. It was different; it was a strange experience. I thought it really was something. I'm rarely impressed, but I was impressed."

If Ricketts had a tobacco wad pressed under his lower lip that day, as he did when he was talking about it, he might have swallowed it.

Ricketts, a 6-5, 295-pound left tackle for the Steelers, grew up like no other kid in the neighborhood in Murrysville, a suburb just east of Pittsburgh, halfway between Three Rivers Stadium and St. Vincent College. "I was always the biggest kid," he remembers.

He was born in 1965, when Noll was yet a young assistant to Sid Gillman with the San Diego Chargers of the American Football League. It was four years before Noll would be named head coach of the Pittsburgh Steelers.

Ricketts said he saw only one Steelers' game when he was a kid, back in 1974 when he was nine years old. It was the final game of the regular season, against the Cincinnati Bengals at Three Rivers Stadium. The Steelers won that game 27-3 to finish the schedule with a 10-3-1 record.

"Steeler tickets were very hard to get, and if my dad or uncle ever got any, well, little Tommy was going to be the last to go," recalled Ricketts. "So this was a big day. I really liked the atmosphere. The stadium was filled with people, and they were making lots of noise, and I was all caught up with seeing the big-name guys like Joe Greene, Jack Ham, Jack Lambert, Lynn Swann, John Stallworth, Rocky Bleier, Franco Harris and Terry Bradshaw. It was just an exciting time."

The Steelers went on from there to beat the Buffalo Bills in an AFC playoff game, and they beat the Oakland Raiders on the road in the AFC championship game and, finally, they beat the Minnesota Vikings in Super Bowl IX in New Orleans. It would be the first of four Super Bowl triumphs by the Steelers.

"When I was growing up, the Steelers were at their peak," said Ricketts. "There was no other team better. I started playing football when I was about ten for a midget league team in the Franklin Regional School District. I was a freshman in high school when the Steelers won their fourth Super Bowl. It was the best of times.

"Over the years, all four of those Super Bowls, the teams just got so special. It was a great thing for a team to do. They gained so much respect from everyone."

At Franklin Regional, Ricketts was a standout in football — as a senior, he was named first team all-state by both the Associated Press and United Press International — and he also lettered in basketball and baseball.

He picked Pitt as his college choice. "I wanted to go to a team that was successful in the past and had a great tradition," he said. "When you say you went to the University of Pittsburgh, and played football there that opens people's eyes. This was my hometown and Pitt was the school I always heard about."

He wanted to play for Foge Fazio and Joe Moore. Fazio was the head coach at Pitt, and Moore the offensive line coach, a grizzled guy who had turned out a succession of great offensive linemen who made their mark in college and in the National Football League.

They included the likes of Mark May and Russ Grimm of the Washington Redskins, Jimbo Covert and Rob Fada of the Chicago Bears, Jim Sweeney of the New York Jets, Jerry Boyarsky of the Cincinnati Bengals and New Orleans Saints, and Emil Boures of the Pittsburgh Steelers. With the exception of May, who was from New York, all those guys had grown up in Western Pennsylvania. The Pitt team then included a three-time All-American tackle named Bill Fralic, who was from Penn Hills, a community on the border of Murrysville. Fralic went on to become a Pro Bowl performer with the NFL's Atlanta Falcons. Ricketts was recruited to take the place of Fralic at Pitt.

"It had to be one of the top schools for offensive linemen in the country," said Ricketts.

It took awhile — Ricketts was not Fralic — but Ricketts developed into an outstanding college tackle. He played one year under Moore, who was fired by the athletic department, and two years under Fazio, who was fired a year later. Mike Gottfried became the head coach. He was sidelined with an injury in Gottfried's first year. He preferred Fazio to Gottfried, but got along fine with Gottfried. "He was the head coach, so I figured he must know what he's doing, that he'd be a good coach," said Ricketts.

The Pitt people have always boasted about the school's tradition, and there were always pictures and posters and mementos hailing the team's triumphs in past seasons. "I thought it was a positive thing that so many people had been successful there," said Ricketts.

Ricketts even met his wife, Sandy Albright, at Pitt. She was a record-breaking All-American swimmer from South Park.

"My wife's grandfather, Dr. Charles Hartwig, had been an All-American (in 1934) at Pitt, and he had been an assistant coach there when they had their greatest teams. I saw so many people who were such a success, not just a handful of people.

"When you go into a program, and see maybe four people have made it, you think that maybe you can do it, too. But when you see so many people who could go to Pitt and succeed, it gave you a better feeling. It makes you feel like your chances are much greater to fulfill your goals.

"If you're at a mediocre program that has no tradition . . . no matter how well you do there's no one saying you have a reputation to hold up. But it brings out the best in an individual, and in a team, if you have high standards that have been set for you to match or top."

Led by Heisman Trophy winner Tony Dorsett, Pitt won the national championship in 1976, the year after the Steelers had won the second of their four Super Bowls. The Pirates had won the World Series in 1972 and again in 1979. Pittsburgh was hailed as "The City of Champions."

Ricketts says the fallout from that successful decade, unmatched in any city in this country during that span, is still raining down on the present-day Panthers and Steelers.

"The people who've gone through that think that no season is successful unless you're No. 1, unless you win the national championship, unless you win the Super Bowl. They've been spoiled."

Each year Chuck Noll tells his team that their goal is to get to the Super Bowl. It has been that way from his start in 1969.

"The first time I met him," said Ricketts, "I mean I had so much respect for that man. I had seen him on the news on TV, and I had read about him in the papers. He seemed like such a tough man. It seemed like he had so much more authority than anyone else in the Pittsburgh area.

"It was a great feeling to know that I was going to be playing under him."

Ricketts realized Noll was something special after the Steelers, ironically enough, had been absolutely crushed in their opening two games of his rookie season: by 51-0 to the rival Cleveland Browns at Three Rivers Stadium, and by 41-0 by the Bengals in Cincinnati.

"That's where I learned what he was really all about," said Ricketts. "A lot of coaches would just go nuts, really. The way he handles pressure is amazing. Pressure just does not bother Chuck. Whether that comes from time, from having been in so many big games, from having been so successful for so long, I don't know.

"Chuck has proven himself and I think that's why he reacts the way he does to bad situations. He's just so level-minded. If you have a coach who says, 'Let's figure out what's wrong,' it helps you not to panic. If he can't handle himself, how can he handle you?

"Chuck's way makes it easier for a player and for the other coaches. It makes it easier for a player to accept. He is never looking for somebody to blame. Nor does he put the blame on anybody. He looks for the right answers.

"With a guy like Mike Gottfried, he was trying to prove himself in every game. There was so much pressure. He'd get hot, and he'd holler at everyone. We were all to blame. Noll is not like that. That's probably what separates the great coaches — like himself — from the average and mediocre coaches.''

The 1990 campaign was a season of growth for Ricketts. He received lots of attention, and more playing time than the previous season, because Tunch Ilkin missed most of the pre-season recovering from shoulder surgery, and then was in and out of the lineup during the regular season with several ailments, including a four-week stint on injured reserve with a dislocated elbow.

"I got a lot of time at camp, and I had to win my time in the lineup," remarked Ricketts. "Tunch went down, and I thought I did well under the circumstances. Now I have to keep getting better. I have goals here to become a starter. Those things should come through if I continue to work at it. The important thing is to stay healthy, and to keep a good frame of mind."

When Ilkin was out, Ricketts shared time in a few games with Justin Strzelczyk, an 11th round draft choice out of Maine. This brought more criticism of Ricketts, whom some thought was a No. 1 draft choice who was not panning out. Some even labeled Ricketts a ''stiff'' and that had to hurt.

"Deep down, I know I can do it," said Ricketts. "I've been building up confidence the last few weeks. There's a lot of pressure in the world. The important thing to do is to concentrate on what you have to do as a player. I can't fulfill everybody else's expectations. I feel I'm moving in the right direction.

"Tunch is one of the best offensive linemen in the NFL. He's been a Pro Bowler. Tunch is the heart and soul of our offensive line. If he can play, I'm sure he'll be in there. But I'm ready to go if needed.

"I'm more confident now. It's been frustrating for me because I want to play. I started at Pitt. I'm not used to standing on the sideline and watching other people play.

"I hope that changes. I feel I've showed people I can do the job. Chuck told me I've got to be more patient. I guess he's right. My time will come."

A night game with the Oilers
Strange evenings in the press box

"I can see Daniel waving goodbye. God, it looks like Daniel must be the clouds in my eyes."
"Daniel"
—Elton John

Somehow I sensed that it was going to be a strange day. I had watched "Ghostbusters II" on TV with the kids in the afternoon, and now I was driving in town, taking my mother to her apartment in the Lawrenceville section of the city, and I was going to go to Three Rivers Stadium from there, to see the Steelers' 1990 opener against the Houston Oilers. It was a night game with an 8 p.m. start.

I took a different route than I usually take, to avoid the early stadium traffic. Instead of going through the Fort Pitt Tunnel, I drove down West Liberty Avenue and through the Liberty Tunnels. The Pittsburgh skyline looked like the city skyline in "Ghostbusters I" and "Ghostbusters II," like something strange was in the offing.

The sun was going down in the west, and only half of it shone above Mt. Washington. So the top half of the buildings basked in the sunlight and the bottom half were dark in the shade, giving the buildings a strange eeriness. I did not tell my mother what I was thinking because I did not want to upset her. But my brother Dan was uppermost in my thoughts that evening. The last time the Oilers and Steelers had played a night game at Three Rivers Stadium was on October 26, 1981. I will never forget that day. It is branded into my brain like the insignia on the side of the Steelers' helmets. No one in my family will ever forget that day. That is the day my brother Dan committed suicide.

I did not know he had done this when I went to work that day and covered the game for *The Pittsburgh Press*. I did not learn of Dan's death until I returned home at about 2 a.m., and my wife told me the shocking news. "Your brother Dan is dead!" she cried. "He killed himself!"

Life would never be quite the same for anyone in our family after that fateful day, and it was all coming back to me as I drove my mother home before the Steelers' 1990 home opener. My mother had had two boys die at birth, both within a two-year period after I was born. Now Dan was dead, too, and my mother had three sons to mourn, another anniversary to note on her crises calendar.

I dropped off my mother at the senior citizens residence where she had been living the past 13 years and headed back toward the downtown area. She was 83, but in good health and good spirits. She lived in a building where deaths were a daily point of conversation and reflection. Indeed, there is a list in the lobby of all the former tenants who have died. Their death anniversaries are noted on a calendar of events that is posted on a bulletin board each month. Right along with all the birthdays and anniversaries. It has to make you wonder when your number is going to come up, just like in the bingo games they play nightly in the nearby recreation room. My mother had suffered a lot of heartache in recent years, but she was a strong woman, and had bounced back well. She calls out the bingo numbers at her residence and enjoys card games there.

Traffic was backing up on the bridges, and I decided to park my car downtown rather than get caught in the traffic near the stadium. I parked my car on the street in the middle of a complex of buildings called the Gateway Center, near KDKA's studios, and walked through Point State Park.

Other people were making the same journey. It was a pleasant, rather mild September evening, and it was an opportunity to take in the scene before a Steelers' game at Three Rivers Stadium. The huge fountain at the tip of Point State Park was spraying water high into the dusk-lit skies. To the left of it, Fort Pitt was being refurbished. George Washington once slept there and worked there. I crossed the Fort Duquesne Bridge, filing across it with many fans, and took in the sights and the boats in the Allegheny River below me, and could see the Monongahela River and Ohio River on the near horizon. Some fans were coming across the rivers from Station Square on the Gateway Clipper sternwheeler boat, which docked at Roberto Clemente Park. It was pure Pittsburgh.

I went through the parking lots where the tail-gating activity was in full swing. People were cooking on grills. I saw people grilling ham, and steak and eggs. Smoke and good smells filled the air. Many were reading the Sunday *Press* to pass the time, and listening to loud music. The fans were getting revved up for the action to follow. Live bands were playing music at an ear-splitting level. Some people had huge TV sets next to their cars. Many of the men and the women were wearing black and gold football jerseys, the unisex uniform of the day, and other Steeler paraphernalia. I saw some men urinating in the parking lot, much to the amusement of the company they were keeping. It was the usual wild scene. I saw the Little Steeler Car, owned by the Ultimate Steeler Fan, filled with all sorts of Steeler souvenirs. I looked to see if I recognized any of the tail-gaters, but I did not see any familiar faces. I used to know many of them when I was covering the club from 1979 through 1983. I had eaten their potato soup, hot sausages, pierogies, hamburgers, hot dogs, and had even partied with some of the people in similar set-ups at Super Bowl sites in California and Florida. I liked talking to them and finding out what was on their minds, rather than spending all the pre-game time with other sportswriters in the stadium, hearing the same stories and complaints, something I thought was hardly productive.

Back on October 26, 1981 I had spent some time before the game with friends from McKees Rocks and the Montour area who were tail-gating before the Steelers-Oilers game. It was raining, but they had put up an awning over their dining tables. A few weeks later, they told me that all I talked about that night was my brother Dan and how I was so concerned about him. When I arrived at the funeral home where my brother was laid out, the first floral basket I noticed had a card on it that read: "From Jim's Tailgate Friends." Among those who called on our family at the funeral home was Art Rooney, the owner of the Steelers. He moved among the people there like a bishop, and stopped to talk to individuals, and appeared to have a calming effect on everyone.

When my father died back in 1969, Rooney had dispatched several club officials to attend the funeral.

Joe Gordon, the business manager of the Steelers and previously their publicity director for nearly 20 years, was then the publicity director of the Pittsburgh Penguins. When he learned of my father's death, he called and asked me if there was any way he could be of assistance. We were going to be burying my father on a Tuesday, the same day I normally completed the work at the printing plant for my newspaper, *Pittsburgh Weekly Sports*. Gordon went to the print shop in my place and proofread a 12-page tabloid and put it to bed. It had a circulation of 9,000. But Gordon always treated me as if I were an editor of *The New York Times*.

Jim Boston, now the chief negotiator for the Steelers, and the man who handles their travel arrangements among other chores, came to the funerals of my father and brother. But he was a friend of my brother. Boston, during his early days with the Steelers, had moonlighted as a bartender at Dante's, the Steelers' hangout in Dan's neighborhood of Baldwin-Whitehall. Boston had been with the Steelers since 1949, when he joined classmate Richie McCabe of North Catholic, helping out on the sidelines. Boston grew up in a neighborhood on the North Side, just a few blocks from where Three Rivers Stadium is now located.

Dan had been depressed most of that year, 1981, and I had talked to him on many occasions, trying to lift his spirits. I had read self-help books to get the information I needed to pep him up. All I succeeded in doing was pepping up myself. On the day of his death, I was reading a book called "The Sky's The Limit" by Dr. Wayne Dyer, America's self-proclaimed No. 1 problem solver and life enhancer. He is good. I never felt better. Dan never felt worse. He felt badly about changing jobs, and leaving Mesta Machine Company in Homestead. When Pittsburgh was celebrated as the "Steel Capital of the World," Mesta had built steel mills all over the world. They were a world leader in the manufacturing of mill machinery. In his work, my brother had traveled to Europe, the Orient, South Africa and Australia. Pittsburgh had put some of those places back together after world wars, or, in the case of Third World nations, helped them get started, and had prospered as a result. But the steel industry was in decline, so were all associated businesses, and Pittsburgh was experiencing hard times. It was depressing.

Many people lost their jobs as the mills started closing down. The fire that lit up the skies, and the smoke that darkened the skies were missing from the landscape along the three rivers, and Pittsburgh would never be quite the same again. The spirits of the disenfranchised steelworkers were sagging. Many of the displaced workers turned to the Steelers to lift their spirits. When business in Pittsburgh was good the Steelers were bad. Conversely, when Pittsburgh business was going down the tubes, the Steelers started winning. I am sure the Steelers saved some people in Pittsburgh. But even the Steelers could not keep a smile on my brother's face, or his chin off the sidewalk.

He often followed me and the Steelers to road games, in places like Tampa, Miami and New York. Once, he traveled to San Diego and stayed in my room before a Steelers' game there. I remember him coming to the room, and telling me I had to go out by the swimming pool. He said I wouldn't believe what I would see there. Once there, I came upon Jack Lambert of the Steelers who was on roller skates. Lambert always said he would have been a helluva hockey player, and here he was showing us all how well he could skate — on roller skates, anyhow. Lambert skated in a frenzied rush right up to me, and stopped on the dime at my shoetips. If he had been on ice skates he would have sprayed ice shavings on my slacks. "How do you like this?" asked Lambert. Then he skated into the dining room of a nearby restaurant, right up to a table, and took hold of the team's field manager, Jack Hart, and kissed him on the cheek. Anything to get a rise out of people. My brother had a good laugh about that. But it did not last. We stayed up late that night, and didn't get enough sleep. In the morning, when I woke up, Dan was not in the room. He had walked, without a word to me, to a nearby church for Sunday mass. Always the altar boy.

Dan was the treasurer of Mesta Machine Company, and a tremendous success story in our community and at Mesta. My father had worked at Mesta for over 35 years, as a drill press operator before he died in 1969. He drilled holes in steel plates, and took pride in the fact that he was often given jobs with a minimum tolerance for error. Two of his brothers, my Uncle Rich and my Uncle Robbie, had also worked there over 35 years, Rich as a metal polisher, a dirty job where he came home each night with a carbon-blackened face, looking like Al Jolson, and Robbie as a helper who shoveled steel chips most of his work career, and came away with a bad back. That was also a dirty job. None of them made good wages. None of them enjoyed his job. It was strictly a paycheck. I never even visited Mesta Machine Company when my dad was working there. I was afraid I would have to stay and work there someday. I never wanted to work there. My brother Dan went to the University of Pittsburgh on a Mesta-sponsored scholarship, and earned a B.S. in mechanical engineering. While working as a draftsman and later in sales at Mesta, he earned a master's degree in business administration (MBA) at Pitt's night school. He became one of the company's top executives. He was handsome and had a lot of friends. He had a nice family, a wife and a daughter and a son.

Mesta was having some financial difficulties, some personnel problems, and it was tearing at my brother. He thought some funny stuff was going on, and felt helpless. I remember driving past the company one day with him, and seeing workers on strike. They were screaming and swearing that they would shut down the company. "They won't be happy until they do," Dan said. "And they will." He had left the company at one point, and came back, feeling he had made a mistake. "Your brother thinks Mesta Machine is a family business," one of his friends told me. "He thinks it's your family's business." In 1981, Danny left Mesta once again and took a position with an engineering firm in downtown Pittsburgh. When Danny discussed his daily ritual, he made traveling from Baldwin to a building in midtown sound like a trip to the Orient. For him, it became that difficult. Like he was traveling the Burma Road. It was torture. And he used to fly to Australia without a second thought. I remember him telling me about how big the Steelers were in Sydney, and he had me send some posters of the Steelers to some fans he had met there. I still have some of the postcards he sent me from Sydney, one with the world-famous opera house pictured on it.

He started second-guessing his career decision, and felt he had made a mistake. He felt he had fouled up his future, and that his family would suffer from his decision. He was also having some health problems, which may or may not have been related to the obvious stress he was experiencing in his job. He had some vision difficulties, like there was a black shade drawn across the bottom half of his eyes, and he felt tired a lot. He went to see a priest for help, but, like a lot of people, he did not recognize he really needed some professional counseling, some psychiatric or psychological help. People tend to deny that they really need that kind of help. They do not want to risk anyone saying, "He's going crazy." Or "He's a head case."

I remember a day when Dan came to St. Vincent College to spend some time with me at the Steelers' training camp in the summer of 1981. We went to play golf that day at a nearby par 3 nine-hole course along Rt. 30 called Statler's. I had been told that Terry Bradshaw and some other Steelers often played there. After about six holes, my brother Dan was dragging. I could not believe it. He was only five years older than I; he had just turned 44, and he was tiring. He looked like he was walking in quicksand instead of a grassy golf course. I asked him what was wrong, and he got defensive. "I don't know," he snapped. "Something's wrong; my legs are like jelly. But I don't know what's wrong!"

Later that night, we stopped at one of the Rt. 30 bars frequented by the sportswriters and assistant coaches. Midway through the second drink, Dan slid off his stool onto the floor. "My god, Dan, you've had two drinks and you're falling on the floor," I cried. "What's wrong with you?"

At first, he was argumentative. Then Dan looked at me like a boxer who was getting up from a knockdown, with a worried look in his eyes. Like he was begging me to throw in the towel.

The last time I saw Dan alive was three days before he died, at lunch at a midtown restaurant called The Rusty Scupper. We were joined by one of Dan's lifelong buddies, a commercial artist named Paul Belic, who had been a pitcher on a sandlot baseball team in our hometown of Hazelwood, and still had clippings from when I wrote about him in *The Hazelwood Envoy.*

There was a lifesize photo mural on the wall at The Rusty Scupper which caught our eye. It showed Billy Mazeroski of the Pirates racing toward home plate after he hit the ninth inning homerun in the seventh game of the World Series to defeat the Yankees in 1960. We had to laugh because a fellow who had gone to school with my brother and Belic, a sports enthusiast named Fred McCauley, was pictured chasing after Maz with his dark blue blazer flapping. McCauley has been immortalized by that act of chasing Maz home that October day. I have never seen McCauley in a sportcoat or suit since then.

I criticized Dan's decision on ordering a plain hamburger in a restaurant that boasted of a dozen or so different hamburger concoctions. "C'mon, live a little, Dan," I said. "Be a little daring. You don't come here to get a plain hamburger." Dan was always a plain eater, but it seemed to point up how bland his life had become for him. I hated to see him that way, so down on himself and his job and his life. Now, of course, I wish I had not criticized him. It is the last thing I can remember saying to him. I would be happy if I could take him today to some fancy restaurant for a plain hamburger.

In the summer of 1990, when I traveled to the Steelers' training camp at St. Vincent to begin work on this book, I thought of my brother Dan and Terry Bradshaw as soon as I saw Statler's Golf Course and some of the bars we had frequented along Rt. 30. Lots of things bring my brother to mind: funerals, football games, church services, sunny days, cold beers, good times, bad times, the Pitt campus, prayers, certain songs. I get messed up when I hear Elton John singing "Daniel" or anybody singing "Danny Boy." Today, there is an amusement park — Sand Castle — where much of Mesta Machine Company used to stand. There are lots of times when I wish Dan were with me, having a good time. He should be here, I will think aloud.

He was five years older than I. My sister, Carole, was five years older than him, and my oldest brother, Dick, was five years older than Carole. We had a strange lineup in our family. Everyone was five years apart. Dick was 17 and serving as a cook in the U.S. Navy, somewhere in the South Pacific, when I was two years old in 1944. He married as soon as he came out of the military service, so I do not remember being in the same house with him at all. He always seemed like a cousin or an uncle to me. Now he seems like a brother to me. Carole has become more important in my life.

Dan and I hung out with different crowds in our youth. He liked to go fishing, which I never did. He played sandlot football for a team called the Tecumseh Street Indians. I remember they had strange jerseys, mostly purple with orange and yellow striped sleeves, like old-time football or rugby jerseys. He was not a very good athlete, but he liked sports. I always kidded him about the way he walked. We shot a little basketball together, and tossed a baseball once in a while. I remember going out with him on many evenings, especially a trip to the Playboy Club in New York.

He and Dick really loved sports, though, more than I ever did, I think. They talked a lot about the upcoming games, and bet on sports events, something I was never into. My dad was not into sports much, but my mother liked to listen to the ballgames on the radio while she did her ironing. She thought boys should be involved in sports. I enjoyed playing sports more than I did talking about sports.

As kids, Dan and I shared a bedroom most of our youth. There was a time we even shared a bed, a big one that had belonged to my parents previously, but that set-up did not work. Dan was always punching me for not getting a bath, or for kicking him as we slept in the middle of the night. That is why I think I love big bedrooms now. I like my space. I have a tendency to sleep on the right edge of the bed.

Dan was always an excellent student, and much better behaved at St. Stephen's Grade School than I was. He was always being held up to me as a model. "If you were only as good a boy as your brother," the Sisters of Charity would say, all too often. He was an altar boy. I got kicked out of altar boy class because of my behavior or misbehavior during the school day.

He was a good kid and everybody liked him. He never got into fights or mischief. He defended me in more fights than I would like to count, but punched me once during such a squabble, breaking my eyeglasses with a shot in the nose, because he thought I had gotten overly zealous in a fight in front of our home. Dan did not approve of my tactics. Dan never got into any difficulty in the neighborhood. No mothers called our mother to complain about him.

We were the best man in each other's weddings. I was the godfather for his first-born child. We had our fights, our differences, but we were friends. I loved him.

I admired him and boasted about him and his success to my school friends. He did the same about me in my sportswriting career. When I worked in Miami and in New York, anytime I got something new, an apartment, a house or a baby daughter, Dan would be on the doorstep the same day to see it. Friends of his told me he thought I was the successful one in the family. I knew he was proud of me.

He liked to tag along with me on some assignments, and he always did when the opportunity presented itself. I had a summer internship at *The Pittsburgh Press* in the summer of 1962, and I was assigned to do an advance story on the Police Circus which was ready to open at Forbes Field, where the Pirates and Steelers played in those days.

During the interviews, I was invited, along with my photographer, Al Herrmann, Jr., to come back later in the day for a pre-circus party outside the walls of Forbes Field. We were told we could bring a guest. Al brought fellow photographer Don Stetzer of *The Press*, and I brought my brother Dan.

It was a terrific party with circus performers from all over the world putting out culinary delights from their native countries. There was lots of food and drink, and some of the circus performers did acrobatics with their children right by our tables. It was a circus within a circus.

At one point, I remember Dan and I decided we needed to take a leak, and went over behind some trees and circus wagons, and urinated on the wall of Forbes Field. Does that sound sacrilegious? Suddenly, a lion roared right behind us, and I thought we were both going to bolt through the wall at the same time.

Dan regained his composure in time to ask a beautiful young woman who was part of the aerial trapeze act if she would accompany him on a date the next day. We were both bachelors at the time. He was going to take her to Kennywood Park.

She was a beautiful Bulgarian redhead, I recall, and she accepted Dan's invitation. When Dan showed up the next day, however, to his surprise, he learned that the young woman's father — a very muscular "catcher" in the trapeze act — would be chaperoning his daughter on the date. It was a European custom. We both had some laughs over that.

When I delivered Dan's eulogy at his funeral mass, I likened him to "The Daring Young Man On The Flying Trapeze." In my New York days, I had met William Saroyan, the flamboyant author from Fresno, who wrote that story. Dan had done well, and his friends and family had enjoyed watching him soar in his successful career. We all took pride in a local boy doing well. He was flying high for all of us. When he died the way he did, I remember a retired fireman, Buss Bradley, who was our friend asking this question: "If that's what success does to you, is it worth it?" We all wondered about that.

Dan always thought I was the one who had it made, being a sportswriter and traveling with all the big-time teams, and mixing with all the celebrities. He thought my job was such a big deal. I guess a lot of people would like to be a sportswriter.

It was Sunday, September 16, 1990 and I was surrounded by sportswriters and sportscasters, almost nine years after Dan's death. I was watching the Steelers and Oilers, but my mind kept going back to their meeting on that Monday Night Game of October 26, 1981.

Bob Smizik, a sportswriter at *The Pittsburgh Press* who had worked with me during our student days on *The Pitt News* and with *Pittsburgh Weekly Sports,* and had been a close friend, was sitting next to me in the press box that dark day in 1981.

Smizik was informed by the press box p.a. announcer that there was a phone call for him. This was highly unusual. Some sportswriters started kidding Smizik about the nature of the call. I scolded them when Smizik was out of earshot. "You shouldn't do that," I said. "His dad has been sick, and you don't know what the call is all about. Suppose someone died in his family?"

But, no, someone had died in my family. My wife, Kathie, was calling Smizik to tell him what had happened to my brother Dan, and asking him to make sure I came straight home after writing my stories that night. She asked him to stay with me in case I somehow learned of my brother's death from someone else.

Dan did not go to work that day. He stayed home. At some point in the afternoon, he took a rifle he had in his home — I had advised him many times to get rid of it; I was always afraid of rifles — and shot and killed himself. My sister-in-law found him when she came home from work that day.

Smizik did not say anything to me when he returned from talking to Kathie that night. When we were working at the office back at *The Press* after the game, I had gotten done before him. But I hung around the office for some reason, in no hurry to leave. And talked. Finally, Smizik suggested I go home, saying he would be OK, and that he would finish up soon.

I do not remember anything special about the ride home that night. But I remember the scene well when I got home. I have looked at life and a lot of other things, especially sports, a lot differently from that night on. Neither sports nor life should be taken too seriously.

After Dan died, I became a more positive writer and a more positive person. I had seen what negative thinking can do to a person. I wanted none of it. I slip up once in a while. I am too competitive for my own good at times. But I try my best to be upbeat. I try not to be negative.

Dan O'Brien, treasurer, Mesta Machine Company

Dwight White

Bill Amatucci

Dwight White
"Smarter than the average bear"

Times change. Images change. Dwight White wanted me to know that when I telephoned him to arrange a visit with him.

I was thinking about that as I walked from Three Rivers Stadium through some sidestreets on the North Side, and across the Sixth Street Bridge on my way to see White at Center City Tower, a relatively new building at Smithfield and Seventh.

I had begun my journey by walking on a sidewalk paved with Belgian block, or cobblestone, which has been a trademark of Pittsburgh's streets from its earliest days. It was familiar looking, as I grew up five houses away from a street that was built with Belgian block.

One of the appealing things about downtown Pittsburgh is that you can walk from one end of it to the other in a half hour. You have to like the scale of the city, as it is manageable. It has a subway line, but it is more a matter of convenience than necessity. From the stadium where White worked as a defensive lineman for the Steelers for ten years (1971-80) to the 24th floor office where he stored his briefcase, it was a pleasant 20-minute walk on a balmy made-to-order October morning.

I walked over the Sixth Street Bridge that spans the Allegheny River. En route, I bumped into Mike Wagner, who was the free safety on the Steelers' Steel Curtain defense. Small world.

On the other side of the bridge, the Fulton Theatre, which used to be a majestic first-run film house, had a sign on the marquee that promoted an upcoming Gay and Lesbian Film Festival Week. Nearby, on the same side of Sixth Street, is the City Club, a health and fitness club which included some Steelers and Pirates among its original investors and appears to be still going strong. I remembered shooting baskets there once with Dave Parker of the Pirates, who confused such activity with off-season conditioning. I remembered the Steelers' Jack Ham and his wife, Joanne, hosting a grand opening party there. He was among the club's original investors.

At the next corner stands the Roosevelt Hotel, or what used to be the Roosevelt Hotel. Now it is a residence for senior citizens, and it is called the Roosevelt Arms. Before the Steelers moved into Three Rivers Stadium in 1970, the team's front office and ticket office were located on the first floor of the Roosevelt. Art Rooney was reported to be paying the hotel rent for a half dozen of its older residents.

Rooney shared a small office there with Fran Fogarty, the team's business manager. I remembered being with them one day when a gentleman came rushing in from the lobby, pulling the fly down on his trousers, mistaking the door for the men's room. "Next door!" cried out Rooney, not missing a beat. It was easy enough in those days to mistake the Steelers' offices for a public restroom.

Franco's Restaurant, on the first floor of the Roosevelt these days, does not belong to Franco Harris.

There was a bearded black man, wearing a black windbreaker with the Steelers signature over the breast pocket, selling roses and other floral bouquets in front of the parking lot next door. He looked chilled, standing in the shadows.

I went down Liberty Avenue, which soon becomes seedy and the city's sin strip — adult film, peek shows, and Doc Johnson's marital aids are advertised in bright twinkling neon lights — and made a right at Seventh Street, where the Stanley Theatre has become Benedum Center. Othello and Swan Lake were among the coming attractions.

After spending several hours with Dwight White it would not surprise me if he had the role of Othello, or that he would have season tickets for the opera and ballet. White remains a powerful presence, and his voice is boisterous and loud, and his complaints many. He sings many sad songs. He is full of rage.

Ed Kiely, longtime public relations executive with the Steelers, told me about talking to Roy Blount Jr., after he had written a book on the Steelers called "Three Bricks Shy of a Load" back in the early '70s. "I asked Roy which player impressed him the most, and he said Dwight White," recalled Kiely. "He said White was smart and easily the most candid of the players he interviewed." Nothing's changed in that respect. White, by the way, told me that Kiely was the one Steelers' executive who saw something special in him, and served as something of a mentor in calling White's attention to books and magazine articles he ought to read. Kiely was the Steelers' office intellectual.

White was known as "Mad Dog" during his playing days at East Texas State University and with the Steelers. He was always going around describing his job thus: "It's a dog's life." And he barked and howled on the football field and in the locker room, anything to antagonize or amuse anybody, and he lived up to his nickname. With a gap-toothed smile. His gold-colored practice jersey was often blood-stained, and White wanted it that way.

"There's a saying," said White, "that if it looks like a duck and it walks like a duck it must be a duck. But that ain't necessarily so."

Now White was in a handsome gray flannel suit, still a huge man at 6-4, 257 pounds — he said he weighed himself that morning; just a pound or two over his playing weight. He wore a muted pinstriped dress shirt with a burgundy paisley tie. He looked the part of a successful businessman. He provided a striking contrast to the simple shifts worn by the Southern black women in the Romare Bearden prints that flanked him on the office walls.

White is a partner and principal operator of the Pittsburgh office of W.R. Lazard and Co., a black-owned investment banking firm whose headquarters are in New York City. Impressive stuff. His secretary's name is Mary Smith. She's from Mars, Pennsylvania and she had been with White for the past ten years, assisting him at three different investment firms.

She was with him when he was working for Bache-Halsey, then Prudential-Bache in the USX Building, and later with Daniels & Bell, where he succeeded the founding owner Travers Bell as president and chief executive officer. Daniels & Bell was the only black-owned firm on Wall Street, said White.

White has come a long way from his Steeler days. To some, he may be one of the most surprising success stories of all the Steelers' alumni. Some rank him right up there with Andy Russell for personal success in the business world. But White's saga is a true rags-to-riches story, whereas Russell's story was simply a riches-to-riches story. And White's success is no surprise to White.

"I knew I was smarter than the majority of the players in our locker room," said White. "I knew I was bigger than football. Football was a part of my life, but football was not my life. Let's just say, like Yogi Bear used to say, I'm smarter than the average bear."

White likes to spin some southern lines like that from time to time. "I came from nothing. I had to reach up just to hit bottom," is another. "When the world hands you a lemon, make lemonade out of it." Or, a blue line like "The white man's pissing on you and telling you it's raining."

Former teammate Dwayne Woodruff recalls White's role in the clubhouse. "You talk about the life of the party," said Woodruff, "that's Dwight White. No matter how bad you were feeling he could make you feel better."

Times change. Images change. I mentioned something about how Jack Lambert was really different from his image as a mean bloodthirsty football player, how well he handles himself publicly, how much calmer he appears as a more mature, married man than the hellraiser he was once thought to be.

"I'm impressed with Lambert," allowed White. "It wasn't always that way. You know we went most of our time together on the Steelers without speaking to one another." I had covered the club on a daily basis for nearly five years, but I did not know that. Neither of them ever mentioned it, nor did anybody else.

"We wouldn't even look at each other in the huddle, or talk to each other in the huddle," said White. Imagine that. Two key members of the Steel Curtain with a steel curtain between them through those glory days. Most of their teammates were unaware of the rift.

"Here's why: one day at St. Vincent College, Lambert and I were both in the training room after practice," said White. "I was in my third year and he was a rookie. He was getting his thigh wrapped by Ralph Berlin. I hear Lambert holler, 'Hey, White!' When I looked up, he threw his jock strap across the room, and his jock hit me right in the face. Right in the nose.

"I hollered, 'Come here, Rook.' And I gave it to him right in the middle of the room. I told him I didn't appreciate what he'd done, and that if he pulled a stunt like that again I'd kick his ass right on the spot. 'Don't ever do that shit again,' I told him. I still think I can kick

Lambert's ass. Everybody in the locker room heard it, and I had embarrassed him. He didn't appreciate that. We didn't speak to each other after that.

"He didn't care for me and I didn't care for him. If we did speak, it was to say 'Screw you, White,' or 'Screw you, Lambert.' I didn't like his whole act. I'd be in the locker room listening to a black radio station like WAMO, and Lambert would come in and holler, 'Jesus Christ, turn off that damn African music.' I could see where he was coming from.

"He had a bumper sticker on his truck that said 'I DON'T BRAKE FOR LIBERALS.' Shit like that. And he was always wearing those black leather jackets and police ballcaps, law and order shit. I saw him as a right-wing, conservative white bullshit artist.

"He was being macho, I was being macho. He was stubborn, and I was stubborn. I went to the Hall of Fame ceremonies again this year — I'm happy for those guys getting in — and I thought Lambert made the best speech at his induction. I have changed my mind quite a bit about Lambert. He's a good example, to me, of another guy who really isn't what he was made out to be.

"He's a private person, he has values, and he's very positive. But he was seen as Mean Jack Lambert, just like Mean Joe Greene, and he was supposed to be Dracula in cleats. Lambert and I could get along fine now. I've been married for 13 years, and I know that to argue can be wholesome. As long as you put the arguments aside and behind you.

"I always respected Lambert as a ballplayer. He was for real. He always gave you his best effort, and he expected the same from everybody else on our team.

"Jack has showed me some sensitivity. What he did during his playing days was not unlike what I did. We were both playing the role. We were both trying to convince everybody what a badass we were. We wanted everybody to think we were mad men."

White is still mad about a lot of things. He remains critical of Chuck Noll and some members of the Steelers' front office, whom he believes merit criticism for the handling or mishandling of issues involving Joe Gilliam and Franco Harris, for starters.

"Where's Chuck Noll come off with his Franco Who? bullshit? Or Terry Who? Or Joe Who? Who the hell was Chuck Noll before he came to Pittsburgh and teamed up with some of the greatest football players of all time?" snapped White.

"I'll tell you why the Steelers went from being big losers to being big winners. They got lucky, that's why. They got the greatest players in the draft for several years."

Dwight White describes himself as having been an angry young man. He has tempered his act considerably, but certain subjects get him riled up easily. He grew up the hard way in tough neighborhoods in Hampton, Virginia, and Dallas, and says he still has the scars to show for it.

Overall, he is proud to have played for the Steelers, feels a kinship with the city of Pittsburgh "because I have prospered here in so many ways," and is thankful he had the opportunity to contribute to

Dwight White goes after live ball.

Front Four (left to right): Dwight White, Ernie Holmes, Joe Greene, L.C. Greenwood on Photo Day at St. Vincent

so many championship teams. On the wall of his office there is a framed cover of the December 8, 1975 issue of *Time* magazine, in which he was pictured along with the other members of the Steelers' famed front four: Joe Greene, L.C. Greenwood and Ernie Holmes. They were as formidable and durable as Belgian blocks. That framed cover certifies that White had a special role with a special team. But some things still bother him about his days with the Steelers.

"Everything I say isn't going to be syrupy stuff," warned White. "One thing that sticks in my craw, one of the most disappointing things I experienced...and it stirred up the pit of blackness in me — was what they did to bring about the ruination of Joe Gilliam, who was a good man and a good friend of mine.

"For all the great things that Chuck Noll did and the Rooneys did, the Gilliam episode brought all that boyhood bullshit back to me, that I was still in a pit of snakes. And that's what happened with Joe Gilliam.

"I was brought up to believe that you work hard and you'll win in the long run. And I bought into that. I bought into the Steelers' philosophy. I was a loyal, dedicated employee, proud to be a Pittsburgh Steeler.

"I remember Bradshaw having problems in his early days, and I remember Noll benched Brad. Joe Gilliam took over and he got on the cover of *Sports Illustrated* for being a talented, up-and-coming black quarterback in pro football. We were winning (Gilliam led the 1974 Steelers to a 4-1-1 record before he was replaced by Bradshaw).

"I remember the *Pittsburgh Post-Gazette* — and they've got to take some of the blame for what happened, too — running a ballot on the front page of the paper, asking their readers to vote for the quarterback of their choice: Terry Hanratty, Terry Bradshaw or Joe Gilliam. And we were winning...

"I remember Chuck coming into the locker room soon after that ballot and giving Brad back the job. I had to believe that the public pressure got to him. The guys on the team just looked at each other in disbelief."

Told about White's gripe, Andy Russell said, "It wasn't quite that way. When people say that they're forgetting something. Joe lost his job because he wasn't doing what the coaches wanted him to do, and that was to hand the ball off to No. 32 (Franco Harris). Joe was just throwing passes, the farther the better, and he had a real bad game in which he had about four or five passes intercepted. And Chuck turned to Bradshaw for the next game."

Mel Blount, who believes no good will come of holding any grudges or looking back too much, said, "Certainly, Joe was hurt by his demotion, but you can't blame Chuck Noll or anybody else in the organization for Joe's drug problem. That didn't start in Pittsburgh. He had that problem at Tennessee State, scouts talked about it, and it just worsened when he got to Pittsburgh. He had more money in Pittsburgh. If you were into clothes, you'd be able to buy more clothes and more expensive clothes. If you were into drugs, in the first place, well, you know what happens.

160

"I think Noll put the best players on the field, the players he felt he could win with. Noll played the hot player; he put his best people on the field. There may have been a double standard as far as salaries for black and white players — I think it still exists — but Chuck didn't care about color when he made up the starting lineup. That's why he was so successful."

That's not the way White saw it: "I thought what the Steelers did in taking his job away from him had a lot to do with the demise of Joe Gilliam. Joe was doing fine up until that time. I know that. He was cocky and confident, but he was an OK guy. His dad had been his coach at Tennessee State. He got depressed after Noll took his job away from him. And that's when he turned to the hard stuff.

"I thought that was rotten. Joe legitimately won the job. He had worked hard for the opportunity. But they took his job away from him and it wasn't fair. Chuck and Dan may say it was something else. But that's the way it looked to me. We were winning, and the following week they pulled the rug out from under Joe.

"That was a big disappointment to me. It made a statement to me about Pittsburgh. It put me back in Virginia in the mid '50s when all the racist stuff was going on.

"We were very proud of Joe. Not that we had anything against Terry Bradshaw. But it was typical white folks' bullshit. Noll told us Brad would be starting, and the black ballplayers just looked at each other. It was not consistent with fair play.

"Joe did a lot of things after that that hurt him. He didn't help himself. He just went off. Joe may have ended up in the street, anyhow, but I think Chuck Noll has to take some credit for that."

White was only pausing here to take a deep drag on a cigaret. "I smoke too much," he said, making a face.

"I also think they could have handled the Franco Harris fiasco a lot better. For Noll to have the audacity to say 'Franco Who?' when he was asked about Franco's status during summer training camp is unacceptable.

"In Franco's situation, and his dispute over his contract, I felt it was resolvable. Just get it done, whatever you have to do. Don't let it fester. He turned the franchise around; don't forget that. The sense of fair play was not there."

White knows what is right and what is wrong. His eyes are always wide open.

He looks out at the view from his 24th floor office and he can see the Civic Arena, with the Hill District right behind it, and the University of Pittsburgh on the distant horizon. "How do you have a black ghetto between downtown and the University community?" he asked. "That's where the bulldozer stopped."

When he retired at age 30, he had spent more than half of his life — about 19 years — playing football. In an interview with *Pittsburgh* magazine, he made the following statement:

"The Steel Curtain is what really started it back in '72 and '73 — four black guys from the South. I can't relate to you what it was like.

We'd be in the huddle and I'd look over at Ernie Holmes and see the sweat and blood on his face and we knew we all had to do the job. You don't find that kind of intensity anywhere else. It was a very intense level of maleness and you know you have to be somebody to compete on that level.

"I've seen a lot of guys finish the game, sit around and expect a fat cat to come around and take care of them. You know, it's like you've been living in a bubble. It's very easy to get rocked to sleep and think you'll play forever, or that you'll be fixed for life. But even with the Super Bowls, them being the best case, you have to think ahead, think about investing in life and developing other areas. You have to retool your head."

While he was playing for the Steelers, White sampled some job opportunities opened to him by his stature with the Steelers. He worked for the U.S. Department of Commerce, then H.J. Heinz Co., then a small investment banking firm based in New York.

He laughs about the idea of him frequently going to business luncheons in the hallowed halls of the Duquesne Club, on Sixth Street, just around the corner from his offices. But he also notices that there is a soup kitchen at the Trinity Cathedral, just across the street from the city's most elite club. He could dine in either place and fill his belly.

White has worked both sides of the tracks, and he can smell a rat before he sees one. His office reception area may have stacks of such trade publications as the *Wall Street Transcript, Pennsylvania Bulletin, Futures — The Magazine of Commodities,* and such, but he can remember when his relatives thought comic books were the most important publications in the world.

"I'm still playing catch-up, but I try to continue to educate myself. My wife has been a big positive in my life. She quieted me down, and she's domesticated me. I was out of focus with reality for awhile there. She comes from a good family out in Rochester, Pa. — yeah, the hometown of Babe Parilli — and she's a much better person than I am. Her name is Karen, and she teaches at Allegheny Community College. She has her undergraduate and master's degrees from Pitt, and she's working on her dissertation now for her doctorate at Pitt. She's in education and she educates me."

At the time I visited, they had been married 13 years and had a nine-year-old daughter, Stacey. Karen and Stacey keep White away from Three Rivers Stadium on Sundays when the Steelers are at home. He plays at home, too.

"I have something else to do on weekends, that's why I don't go to the Steelers' games. I save the weekends for my family. I don't have a problem working the crowd — I can handle that — but I don't need the traffic and hassle. I don't want to go there and drink beer and then feel loggy on Monday. I have a routine and I stick to it.

"I walk five miles a day. I lift weights. I take a lot of steam baths. I don't eat red meat anymore. I get my sleep at night. I smoke too many cigarets.

"In order to get an accurate focus, or a picture of Dwight White," he volunteered, "you have to go back before I came to Pittsburgh. It has been a constant evolution. When Dwight White came to Pittsburgh I wasn't just born. There was always a driving force. I always wanted to get somewhere.

"We all think we're complicated. I feel I'm a very complicated person. It comes, I feel, from living all those years in Virginia and Texas. The scarring effect from some of the negatives and distorted views I had of the world going into my 20s. Growing up in the projects. I can clearly remember incidents that were crossroads in my life. I could've gone the other way. So close. I could've gotten into real trouble.

"I had great, great parents. I was the oldest of three children. You'd have to know my parents' background to understand where I'm coming from. My father was in the Navy, and he went to Hampton Institute. He went broke, so he had to stay there. My mother had to move there from Texas, and that is where I was born.

"My father was from Dallas, and my mother was from Smithville, about 30 miles south of Austin. My mother was one of 21 children. She had 19 brothers and one sister. They chopped cotton, all of them. They were not what you'd call migrant workers, but they never had much in the way of money.

"My father had 13 brothers and two sisters. My grandfather died when my dad was 12. So I never knew that grandfather at all. As a kid, I didn't know my relatives. They were all in Texas and we were in Virginia, just our family.

"There was an intensely racist atmosphere in Virginia. My dad had many difficult times there. I remember when we came back to Texas. One of the most vivid days I'll never forget. It bonded all the hostilities I had ever experienced in Virginia.

"I remember going with my parents and relatives on a Sunday evening to a place; I don't remember the town. It was a few hours from Dallas. We were going to pick up my mother's parents at a cotton field. All the brothers and sisters had put up some money to buy them a house in Dallas and bring them there.

"I remember they were staying at this big house in the middle of cotton fields. It was just like we were riding into somebody's plantation. When you went in the house, there were thin mattresses, or cots, all over the floors. Nothing else in the way of furniture. There were personal belongings, purses and coats and towels, in piles by the mattresses. That whole sordid scene really bothered me. I was a very angry young person, quiet and shy, a virtual volcano.

"I'd just come from Virginia. I felt the color thing in Virginia. I remember sitting in on strikes. I remember segregated beaches. The same water, but the beaches were sure different. The white beach was always maintained just so. There was a pier down the middle of the two beaches. This was in the '50s."

I told White that when I was a youngster, growing up in Pittsburgh, I recall going swimming in South Park, and passing Sully's Pool, which was just for the blacks — both in the same Allegheny County park.

Blacks were not allowed at the one pool in South Park or at Kennywood Park's swimming pool in those days.

"My uncles were all there that day. I remember this one uncle. He was a grown man, but the big thing he wanted to know was if I had any comic books. He was the last of 21, and that was my Uncle Johnny. He just died at 46. I'm 42." White went on.

"He was just out of high school, and he was asking did I have any comic books. 'Where's his head?' I thought then. 'Boy, is this a dead end.' I didn't say anything, though. But I told myself, 'I'm going to do more than this.'

"I can't forget it. We told our grandparents, 'You don't have to do this anymore.' They were so old, but they looked relieved. Some of my uncles back there became successful businessmen. They made money with liquor stores and barbecue restaurants.

"My dad was very religious. He was a deacon at our church. He never had a drink. I drink beer, but not hard stuff. But that wasn't the case with my mother's brothers. There's only about four or five of them left. They all died from too much drink and too much barbecue. Eating that burnt shit every day will kill you, ruin your insides.

"When I came to Dallas, though, it was much better than it had been in Hampton. It was a bigger city and there was more to do. I couldn't believe they had such facilities — like gyms — for black people.

"I've overcome a lot of things. But I'm still trying to overcome the effect of being treated like a second-class citizen. It was such an ugly situation in Virginia.

"By 1967, they still had not desegregated the schools in Dallas. The first time I ever got close to a white person was as a freshman at East Texas. I had an awful lot of hate. I was mean. I was growing up in a place where being mean helped you to get your way.

"When I moved to Texas, I was in seventh grade. I came out for the football team. I saw that as something I could do. It would give me a chance to vent my frustrations. I lived in a pretty tough neighborhood, and you lost a lot of clout among the boys, and became something to laugh at if you weren't on the team. Well, I was cut in the seventh grade. It was terrible. I cried all the way home. And my mother wasn't too happy, either, because she paid $14 for a pair of football shoes so I could play. It was one of the most humiliating things to happen to me. Kids can be very cruel, you know. I got very upset. Duane Thomas was in the eighth grade at that school when I was in seventh grade. He later played for the Dallas Cowboys and we played against each other in the Super Bowl. I think Thomas had a lot of hostility in him, too, and that's why he had a difficult time with the Cowboys.

"We moved out of the projects in Dallas, and moved to a different school district. I wasn't going to get involved. I wasn't going to risk any embarrassment again. I was a lady's man, hanging out on the corners in front of the liquor stores at night. I was now at Madison High School. Up until my last year, I had no desire to play football. I was going to go into the military service and see the world.

164

"The coach came after me a couple of times, and finally got me to come out for spring practice at the end of my junior year. I played tight end. The next year I'm the starting tight end and we played in a state championship game, the Negro Interscholastic League, that is, against Herbert High School of Beaumont, and they beat us. Oh yeah, they had a section called Negro Sports Capsule in the *Dallas Morning News* in those days. I've still got the clippings? You ask yourself, 'Did this every really exist?' And it did.

"I received two scholarship offers. One was to Prairie View A&M, and East Texas, in Commerce, Texas. I went to East Texas. When I got there, the first building I went into had a floor that was so shiny you could see your face in it. Wow? What a place! To have a brand new book was something. In high school, we had to use books that white kids had used for years. They were scribbled in and pages were missing. We had air-conditioned dorms at East Texas, and all the food you could eat.

"But the first few years were a bad experience. There were 27 blacks in the school that first year — it had been mandated by federal law — and 24 of them were athletes. There were blacks from New York and New Jersey, because the entrance standards were lower, and they had a real impact on me. I was the first black captain of the school football team my senior year at East Texas, but before that it was rough. The white guys on the team said that I had a chip on my shoulder. They weren't too happy to see me.

"I was ill-prepared to compete with them in the classroom, but I could compete with them on the football field."

I reminded White of what he had said about those days of playing football at East Texas in an earlier meeting, when he was regaling everybody in the back of a bus on a trip from Cleveland back to Pittsburgh after beating the Browns, 51-35, during the 1979 season, before the Steelers won their fourth Super Bowl. It was a 270-mile bus ride and it reminded White of his schooldays.

"We played in the Lone Star Conference, and Harvey Martin of the Cowboys was a teammate of mine," White recalled back then. "We'd go 400 and 500 miles on the bus sometimes, and we'd get off the bus along the way and practice in any field we could find. If you got hurt, we didn't even have ice.

"Harvey and I used to work on our coach's farm during the summer. We'd sit on the back of the plow to weigh it down. We were getting paid $10 an hour just for being heavy. Hey, what else was I going to do with myself during the summer?

"Harvey used to caddie for the coach when he'd go golfing and pick up another $3. I used to have to get by on about $15 a month when I was going to school."

But White believes everything turned out OK for him.

"I feel I'm a good person. I know the difference between right and wrong. I've been fair. I'm not a rotten person. I'm not a mad dog."

That was something one of his former teammates, Jon Kolb, now an assistant coach on Noll's staff, took exception to during an interview when I was on the Steelers' beat back in 1980, writing for *The Pittsburgh Press.*

165

"People talk about him or write about him like he's some kind of dog," said Kolb. "I take that personally. I can remember Dwight White getting out of a sick bed in a hospital and helping us win our first Super Bowl. Nobody should forget that."

That is when White, after losing 30 pounds when he was sick, played in Super Bowl IX against the Minnesota Vikings and recorded the first safety in Super Bowl history when he trapped Fran Tarkenton for the first score of that game. White remembers it well.

"I was playing here four years and I get to the biggest game of my life down in New Orleans, and during practice I fall out deathly sick and end up in the hospital. But I came back. I draw on that. I've always come back.

"I've been behind the eight-ball. But I come back. I was a very slow developer. I had more success with the Steelers than anywhere I'd ever been. It all started when I got to Pittsburgh. I can't forget that."

In his last days with the team, he once said, "The Steelers success has meant a lot to me, to the city, to the fans. It's easy to become consumed by it. As great as this team and this game has been, we have to deal with our own identities, and a future outside of football. Don't worry about Dwight White. He'll bounce back.

"I try to keep this whole thing in perspective. I saw a movie called 'Rollerball' in which James Caan was an aging sports star in a violent game in which the idea was to maim or even kill an opponent. He was called into the front office and told he was finished. The executive told him, 'Hey, it's time for you to go. No one player is bigger than the game.'

"But I beg to differ with that. I have a lot more life to live beyond this game. A lot of good things are going to happen to me in the future. I'm optimistic. I'm a survivor."

White has kept his word, and then some.

"I knew I was bigger than their game. But I'm also proud that I played that game. I'm proud of what we achieved here. Knowing how we started from being the worst team in the league. Being part of a team that kicked everybody's ass for ten years. We lifted the esteem of everyone in this city. That's a great feeling," said White when we talked in his office.

"But a lot of things went down on that team that were wrong and I didn't think they were decent. I put a lot of emphasis on right and wrong."

Of all the players we spoke to, White was the most strident and pedantic in his speech. He was not the lone voice of dissent, but he was the most persistent and passionate. He kept taking off a Super Bowl ring, one of the four massive rings he collected as a member of their championship team, and then putting it back on again, like he was not sure if he still wanted to wear it.

"He's not hard to get going," said Roy Gerela, a former teammate on the Steelers. "All you have to do is mention the Pittsburgh Steelers organization to get Dwight going."

White wants to soften his image a bit: "Hey, I'm not Rap Brown, or Stokeley Carmichael or Angela Davis, but I have my views on these things," he said.

White was asked if Bradshaw was speaking for more of his teammates than most people might realize when he knocked Noll, the Steelers' organization and Pittsburgh, in general. White responded, "Terry's right about some things, but he could be more diplomatic. He's being an asshole, basically. Bradshaw didn't help the cause with all his criticism.

"I feel different. I'm a Pittsburgher. I do owe this city and its people something. I came so far, and it never would have happened if I hadn't come to Pittsburgh."

Early line included (left to right) Dwight White, L.C. Greenwood, Lloyd Voss and Joe Greene.

167

All-Pro linebackers Jack Ham, Jack Lambert, Andy Russell

Andy Russell
"I could make the comparisons"

A ndy Russell reminded me of Bill Bradley as he analyzed the game he played so well and the people he played it with. In 1970 I had gone to New York from Miami just in time to be named to a four-man reporting staff that stayed with the New York Knicks throughout the NBA playoffs — at home and on the road — and the Knicks included Bradley, Willis Reed, Dave DeBusschere, Walt Frazier, all Hall of Famers now.

But Bradley was the brainy one, the cerebral one from Princeton, the one who arched one eyebrow just so, looking like a biologist checking out a caterpillar, when he dissected his sport. Russell and Bradley both came from Missouri, and maybe they were used to dealing with people from the "Show-Me" state. They both had to smile at the way they loved to play their game, while reminding you that it, indeed, remained a game. They had a different perspective than most athletes.

"The game of football is very complex, a very complicated game," Russell said with a straight face. "It's like chess with 22 pieces."

It is the 22 pieces that make the difference in football, if not in chess, and Russell realizes that as well as anyone, well, maybe not as well as Chuck Noll, the coach who finally made winners of the Steelers, a team that had been a loser most of its life.

Russell, at 49 in the fall of 1990, had gone gray, as they say. But his gray hair was cut short, and he retained his handsome boyish appearance, and his smile and the gleam in his green eyes. He was dressed for Wall Street, not Sixth Street, and he looked quite successful in his spacious second floor office at Two North Shore Center. He was the oldest and wisest of the Steelers when they won their first Super Bowl. He went back the farthest, to Forbes Field and Pitt Stadium and South Park, and felt he could appreciate the team's rise more than anyone else on the squad. He could make comparisons.

Russell remembers the first time Noll spoke to the squad at large. Russell sets up the story well, as if he were playing chess. Russell says he is not positive about every word of the dialogue, as he recalls it, but that it is in the proper spirit of the occasion:

"The club had gotten rid of Bill Austin after we'd gone 2-11-1 in 1968, and here's this new guy. No one knew much about him. We had some good guys in terms of attitude and commitment — good people who've been real successful in business since their Steeler days — and we had team meetings all the time. 'Why are we lousy?' we'd ask ourselves every week. The problem with football is that, from your first exposure to it, there's a theory that if you're not winning it's because you don't try hard enough. Nothing may be further from the truth. We had a terrible sense of frustration.

"With this in mind, Noll says, as best I can remember, 'I've been studying the films for five months and I can tell you guys why you've

160

been losing.' The room fell into a hush. 'We just don't have enough good football players in this room, that's why you've been losing. And I'm going to get rid of most of you. You're not good enough. You're not good enough athletes. It has nothing to with your heart or your motivation. It has to do with your talent, with your genes. You're not fast enough, you can't jump high enough, and you don't have the athletic skills needed to be a winner in this game.

" 'It's not your fault. It's not because you have some psychological inferiority.' I remember him saying.

"That got everybody's attention in a hurry," related Russell. "And he kept his word. Three years later, there were only seven of us left. That was Ray Mansfield, Bobby Walden, Sam Davis, Rocky Bleier, Bruce Van Dyke, Ben McGee and myself."

Five of those became the bedrock for the revamped Steelers of the '70s, the team that was to become the most dominant in pro football during that decade. What the San Francisco 49ers were to the '80s, and the early '90s, the Steelers were to the '70s.

"Why did we win in the '80s?" Russell asked a rhetorical question. "Sheer talent. It's that simple.

"People always posed the question: Why did you win? We didn't win it because some magical chemistry came together. It wasn't because we tried any harder. Or because we had a better atittude.

"We were losing with good people. Look at what's happened to them since. I thought Paul Martha played so hard for someone his size. He wasn't afraid to stick his nose in there. But Noll didn't think we could win with guys like Martha. Today, Martha's the head of the Civic Arena Corporation, is reponsible for the Penguins, and was a real force in helping settle the strike in the NFL a few years back. They didn't come any tougher or smarter than Paul. He was always such an over-achiever. But it wasn't enough in Noll's eyes.

"We won in the '70s because we had the best talent. I remember lining up in a huddle in the Pro Bowl in 1976 (following the 1975 season) and we had eight Steelers in the defensive huddle. How's that for talent?"

Besides Russell in that huddle, there were Mel Blount, Glen Edwards, Joe Greene, L.C. Greenwood, Jack Ham, Jack Lambert and Mike Wagner. Offensively, the Steelers were represented in that same game by Franco Harris, Terry Bradshaw and Lynn Swann. That's a total of 11 players — from one team!

If Russell says it was a matter of sheer talent, then how does Chuck Noll fit into the picture?

"He's a pretty interesting dude," remarked Russell. "Maybe it's oversimplifying, or a mistake when I say talent was the reason we won. He is a great coach and he put a great coaching staff together.

"Chuck Noll got you to play your best. He respected you. He understood your position, but then he let you know that he expected the best from you. There was an extraordinary amount of pressure on you, but you really did it yourself. You just didn't want to let him down.

"The coaches gave you a significant input into game plans. You weren't just on the field doing what they told you to do. They might say, 'Andy, how do you think you could stop him?' And they'd listen. Bud Carson was like that, and so was George Perles and Woody Widenhofer. Sometimes they'd show me that I was wrong. And vice versa.

"It was very exciting. There was an unusual chemistry. I never played on any football team that had that kind of chemistry. We had a system for fines among the linebackers if we made mental mistakes. You had to pay a $5 fine. If you did something great, everybody else had to kick in. We had a great party with that money at the end of the season."

The offense had a system, too, and the defense found it at fault. There were games when the opposition seemed to know exactly what the Steelers were going to do offensively.

"For ten years we had the same 'live' color when we were audibilizing a change of call at the line of scrimmage," Russell explained. "The 'live' color was always brown. When Terry Bradshaw would shout 'brown' it meant he was going to change the play. Maybe he'd say 'brown 39 ride U.' That meant that the 3 back would go in the 9 hole. Ride was the way the ball would be handed off by the quarterback, and U was the blocking scheme. Sometimes it didn't matter if the other team knew what we were doing because Franco would go into the wrong hole and he'd make ten yards.

"But there were games when the opposition knew what we were going to do and they'd plug it. We asked Terry about it and he said he knew. 'But sometimes I'll tell them in the huddle to ignore the audible.' I asked Mike Webster and Ray Mansfield about it and they said he never said that in the huddle.

"As a defensive player, I knew what kind of an edge that could give you. I was always listening to the signals. If I found something that could impact position I sure took advantage of it. It was Terry's fault; he wasn't using the ignore-the-audible approach. Even so, we won four Super Bowls in six years, so it's hard to fault Terry for that.

"But in 1974, we had two games left, and we had to win one of them to make the playoffs. We were playing Houston and New England. We played the Oilers, and they weren't half as good as Pittsburgh, and they beat us, 21-17.

"They shut down our offense. Ralph Cindrich, the Pitt guy who is an attorney now, was playing linebacker for the Oilers. He was a rookie, and he was making all the tackles. We made him look like an All-Pro. I asked him about it afterward. He said, 'We knew every play you were running. We knew the live color.'

"Joe Greene was so upset after that game. He was going home, quitting the team. This was a few weeks before we won our first Super Bowl and Joe Greene was going home. People forget stuff like that. He left the field in the fourth quarter he was so upset with the way we were playing. He was going home to Texas.

"We played New England the next week and beat them. Then we played Buffalo here, and they had a good team, and we crushed them. Then we won at Oakland and then we beat Minnesota in the Super Bowl.

"To me, the game in Oakland was the most exciting football game I ever played in. That was maybe the best team I ever played against. We went out there like 22 guys against the world. It was a hostile situation. There were 75,000 people waving black socks at us, and that game got us into the big game.

"We went out to Oakland intense and hopeful we could win. The intensity was unbelievable. The Raiders were so good. They'd beaten Miami the week before, and Miami was the defending league champion.

"John Madden, the Oakland coach, made a big mistake. He was quoted after the game as saying what a great game the Oakland-Miami game had been, and how the two best teams had already played. Oakland had handled us pretty easily earlier in the year (winning 17-0 in Pittsburgh in the third game of the schedule), and they thought they could do it again.

"It was the most excited I ever saw Noll. Joe Greene got real emotional, too. Noll got up at a team meeting on Tuesday before the Oakland game. We were all sitting around in a classroom-like setting, sitting in those chairs that have a writing surface curling around your legs.

"Noll got up and told us what Madden had said. That the two best teams had already played. Noll started to shout. I don't remember his exact words, something like we're going to show them who's the best. So while Noll is shouting, Greene jumps up, and he's wearing the desk like a skirt, and he starts shouting. Joe just got so excited. We were ready on Tuesday.

"In fact, I was fearful that we were going to peak too soon. On Wednesday, we were wild. I was worried about an emotional dip. But that was the most exciting game we ever played."

Then Russell volunteered a thought we found hard to swallow. "I think the guys on the current team are better; I think if everything stayed the same, today's team could beat us."

How could he say that?

"They have better conditioning and training. They're bigger and stronger and more powerful. They may not be as talented, but I still think they could beat us because of their superior physical training."

Hey, you don't have to buy everything Russell wants to sell you.

Believe him, however, when he says, that it wasn't any more fun playing for all those winning teams after so many years of losing.

"No, it wasn't any more fun. In fact, the old days were more fun. All the humor was in the bad old days. When we got to the top we didn't do anything funny. We just kicked people's butts."

Russell was sharing his stories while sitting on the other side of a round table in his spacious and beautifully appointed office of the investment securities firm of Russell, Rea, Zappala & Gomulka Holdings, Inc. at the North Shore Center. It is just up the Allegheny River from Three Rivers Stadium, on the same side of the riverfront.

There were lots of windows in Russell's office, and he had a wide picturesque view of the downtown office building complex, on the other side of the Allegheny, whose waters were glistening on the sunny day we visited. "I have to fight sitting here and staring out the window all day," Russell confessed. "It's a spectacular view at night." There was a small park with a fountain outside his windows, and he could see the larger fountain spraying forth from a distance at The Point. He could not see Three Rivers Stadium — it was hidden by other riverfront buildings — but he did see Steelers running by on a path below, getting themselves in shape, at other times during the year.

Russell, Rea, Zappala & Gomulka began as investment bankers, but they have branched out considerably. They still provide financial services and money management, they still underwrite bond issues, but they now seek more investment opportunities for themselves as well, real estate development, and are quite involved these days in the waste disposal business.

Russell was called out of his office several times by his business associates, such as Sam Zacharias of the Gateway Financial Group from the floor above, to approve financial deals they were working on, and to confer with his partners on business matters. I had a chance to check out the room, and it looked familiar, the abundance of earth tones — the browns, beiges, peaches, creams — with a hint of blue here and there. There are plants everywhere, an oriental print opposite a fiber arts work his mother had done. The room looks like it has been done by a professional decorator, yet there is a touch of home with big framed photos of the Russell children, Andy, 24, and Amy, 21.

"Did your wife, Nancy, decorate your office?" I asked Russell upon his return, and he nodded in the affirmative. "How'd you know that?" he asked. "I've seen this same look when we checked out your house, remember?" I responded.

Back in 1979, when my wife and I moved to Pittsburgh from New York, we were shown Russell's home in Upper St. Clair. He was moving cross town to Fox Chapel. We were shown his home by a real estate salesperson named Annie Hall. Because I was a sportswriter, Hall pointed out homes owned by sports people, such as Chuck Noll's home and one that happened to be for sale that had belonged to Dave Schultz, the enforcer for the Penguins after he had been one of the leading Broad Street Bullies for the Philadelphia Flyers for so many NHL seasons. Imagine wanting to buy a house because Dave Schultz had lived in it?

So I scolded Annie Hall and told her not to tell me who owned these homes she was showing me. "I'm looking for a house," I said, "not a sports souvenir." So she said nothing when she showed me this terrific-looking house where the Russells resided. They were not home. But I started seeing weights and barbells in the basement and Pro Bowl plaques in the family room, and recognized that the plaques belonged to Andy Russell. We nearly bought the place. But the impressive thing about the house was the way Nancy had decorated it. There was a great look to the whole house. The Russells have always been a class act. "My perspective is totally impacted by my whole experience with the Steelers, not just the Super Bowl years," said Russell. "I started with a team that almost won the NFL championship in 1963. That was when we played at Forbes Field. I was the only player on the championship team who went back that far. Ray Mansfield and I both started our pro careers in the same season, but he was with the Philadelphia Eagles that first year."

As Russell related his stories, I had to smile. I was a senior at Pitt that fall. Paul Martha was one of my classmates. Martha was an All-America running back on a Pitt football team that went 9-1 and did not go to a bowl game. President Kennedy was killed that November. Pitt's sports information director Beano Cook and I had started a newspaper called *Pittsburgh Weekly Sports* that fall. And I wrote stories about the Steelers in Russell's rookie season. I, too, had memories of the games he talked about.

"I'd just come from the University of Missouri where we had eight practice fields," related Russell, who knows most of his stories by rote he has told them so often. "And now I was at West Liberty (West Va.) College, where between practices the rookies combed the fields for rocks. Your conditions are a great step down from what you knew in college.

"You're now practicing at South Park. Our dressing room was in the basement of an old building that was the Red Cross unit at the park. There's a hole in the wall, and snow is filtering down on the equipment. It was unbelievable. The toilets didn't have any seats on them. Talk about primitive.

"Our coach, Buddy Parker, closed the training room once because we had so many injuries. He just closed it, and sent the trainer home.

"Yet, in the final game of the season, at New York, we were playing the Giants in a game to determine who'd finish first in our division. We hadn't lost in the previous four games, winning two of them and tying two of them. We tied the Chicago Bears at Forbes Field, 17-17, but we should've won. They called back a touchdown by Dick Hoak."

I remembered that game as the one in which Mike Ditka, a former Pitt All-America tight end from Aliquippa, had broken about five or six tackles on a spectacular run. "Sloppy tackling," said Russell. "I wasn't one of the ones who missed him.

"We had beaten New York easily (31-0) early in the season. I thought we were going to the championship game. I was starting as a rookie linebacker and was so proud of what we'd done. But we came out in cleats and they came out in tennis shoes on a frozen field. Ed Brown was our quarterback and he was shaky all day. He kept misfiring on passes to Buddy Dial who was wide open. We blew it. We lost (33-17) and we shouldn't have. We finished with a 7-4-3 record.

"To this day, the classiest act I ever saw Art Rooney do came after that game. We came that close to winning a championship for him, and let it get away. Yet he went around the locker room in Yankee Stadium and shook hands with each player, and wished us all a good off-season. To this day, that's the singlemost classy thing he ever did. It was not a pretty game. The coaches coached it badly and we played it badly.

"So I almost started my career on a championship team. We had a lot of outstanding and skilled players, people like Buddy Dial, Preston Carpenter, Clendon Thomas, Lou Cordileone, Joe Krupa and Lou Michaels.

"I went into the military service the next season, and missed the next two years. The Steelers fixed some things to keep me out of the service, but I was upset about that. I didn't want any special favors. I'd been in ROTC in college and I had an obligation. I went to Europe as a first lieutenant.

"When I came back to the Steelers, Buddy Parker was gone, and so was Mike Nixon, who succeeded him for one season. I came back with Bill Austin, who had played for the Giants when they had great teams and had been an assistant to Vince Lombardi with his great teams in Green Bay. The team was devastated. He was dealing with a team with relatively little talent. We had three straight losing seasons under Austin. It was awful. Then they got Noll."

Russell still takes pride in the fact that he was invited to participate in ground-breaking ceremonies for Three Rivers Stadium.

"That's another reason I can appreciate what we accomplished more than most. Hey, Lynn Swann joined our team in 1974 and we won the Super Bowl that year. He knew nothing but success with the Steelers, but, of course, he was one of the big reasons we were so successful.

"Guys like him hadn't been in that building at South Park, hadn't dodged the snowballs at Pitt Stadium or heard the boos at Pitt Stadium, or picked up the stones at West Liberty. That's why our success meant more to Mansfield and me. We were involved in all the Steelers' war stories. We were there when the players used to leave the practice field at South Park and everybody went to the Parkside Inn and ate hamburgers and drank beer together. We weren't as successful in those days, but we had more fun. And it's a lot more difficult to be a good linebacker on a bad team than it is to be a good linebacker on a great team."

What changed everything? Why did the players stop socializing as a team?

"Winning made the break," explained Russell. "Losing teams are much closer than winning teams. Losing teams pull together. They feel vulnerable. They don't want to go out in public alone. They're afraid people will scream at you: 'You guys are bums.' It happened. We had a lot of team parties in those days.

"When you win the whole city embraces you. You were welcome everywhere. There were more job opportunities and openings for everyone. Everyone wanted a Steeler on their side. We all went our separate ways. As big money came in, we separated even more."

Russell always had an eye on other interests. When he was playing for the Steelers, he was always working for someone, laying the groundwork for his business success. He was a model for many of the

Steelers, and advised them on what was best for their off-the-field success. He was a mentor to many of them. He was always carrying an attache case. He always looked the part of the young business executive.

That is what Russell's father had in mind in the first place. "My dad went to the Harvard Business School, and he ran Monsanto Chemical Company's European operation. The family lived in Brussels. I didn't grow up wanting to close off an opposing tackle. My father made me promise not to play pro football. 'I want a son who's serious about life,' he said.

"But I loved football. I was going to play a year, and even my wife, Nancy, was against that. Then I was going to play two more years while I went to graduate school. I crammed 20 credits into a term during the off-season and got my master's in business in two years. Then I was going to play one more year so I could qualify for an NFL pension. I ended up playing 14 years with the Steelers.

"I could have stayed longer. They asked me to come back. But I had reached my team goals and my personal goals. I was trying to hold onto that. But I didn't want them to tell me when it was time to go. I didn't want Noll to say, 'I don't think you can help us anymore.' I wanted to tell him. The guy was great to me, but I wanted to be the one to say goodbye."

Russell's parents were both living in Pittsburgh as we spoke, but in separate senior residence facilities. His father was at Canterbury Place. "He's sicker and he needs more care," said Russell. His mother resides at Friendship Village in Upper St. Clair. "I see them more than I ever did," he said. "There was a long period in my life, when they were living in Europe, and I was lucky to see them once a year." Russell spoke to the residents of Friendship Village earlier in the year. "I thought he was going to talk about football," one of the residents told me, "but he talked about life. He was just great."

Because of the nature of his father's business, Russell said, "I didn't really have a hometown." He was born in Detroit, but his father was transferred by Monsanto to Chicago, then to New York, and then to St. Louis, the company's headquarters. Russell went to high school and played ball in St. Louis. During Russell's freshman year at the University of Missouri, his dad was asked to go to Europe to oversee Monsanto's operations there. His mother and father lived in Europe for eight years. Russell had an opportunity to visit them when he was over there as a first lieutenant in the U.S. Army in 1964 and 1965.

"That influenced my decision to get involved in international business," related Andy Russell. His son, Andy, was working in Germany with a German Venture Capital Group in Frankfurt. His daughter, Amy, was in her senior year at Ohio U.

During December of 1990, I spotted Russell and his son Andy attending a Pitt basketball game against Toledo at Pitt's Fitzgerald Field House. Russell walked by the bleacher crowd and did not seem to turn a single head. Russell simply does not look like a football player, and that is fine with him. He dropped weight immediately upon retiring, and stays in great shape. Then, too, he looks different with white hair.

When we spoke, Russell was getting set to go on an annual nature-challenging trip with Mansfield. "This year we're going for a hike in the Grand Canyon," said Russell.

"We try to do one great test a year since we retired as players. The year after we retired, we did our first one just when training camp for the Steelers was starting. We had always gotten ready for that challenge, and now we needed another one.

"We both started in pro football the same year, and we both retired the same year. Our wives call this annual trip a 'rite of passage,' our way of growing away from the game. A lot of our well-meaning friends would say, 'Now that you've retired, you're never going to have that excitement again. You'll never perform in front of two million people again.' We pretty much agreed those people were wrong. We were 35 or 36 years old, and we both felt pretty strong.

"So we went up to northern Minnesota, on the Canadian border, and entered a 165-mile non-stop canoe race. It took us 63 hours and 47 minutes to do it. It was a gut test. We were up in the wilderness of Minnesota and Canada, running through the woods in the darkness carrying a canoe over our heads. Ray was about 270 pounds then, and had never been in a canoe before. I was about 185 pounds and I was in the back of the canoe. Sometimes I'd dip my oar to row and I didn't hit water because the back of the canoe was sitting up so high.

"It was called the Boundary Waters Canoe Area. Old French fur trappers used to travel this route, covering 48 lakes that were connected by what they call portages. It was something. We were both hallucinating. The fatigue factor was unreal. The locals said we couldn't do it. They said this was 'real man' stuff.

"Hey, the record for completing the course was 48 hours, and that was done by two guys about 165 pounds who were members of the Outward Bound group. But we completed it. We had no choice, as we saw it. Where were you going to stop? You were still out in the wilderness. There were no other canoes, just us. There were all kinds of times we wanted to quit.

"We got back in a ranger station, and Mansfield said, 'That experience was every bit as thrilling to me as any Super Bowl.' Now maybe if he had thought about that awhile he wouldn't have said that. But at that moment that's the way we both felt.

"Mansfield is something; now there's a tough guy. He's the only guy I know who intimidated Fats Holmes. You know Ray grew up under difficult circumstances. His father was sort of an itinerant fruit picker, and they lived out of camps and hotels, and traveled around Arizona and California and finally ended up in Washington. That's where he went to college.

"We made a pact that every year we'd get back to that physical side of ourselves. Every year we work out in advance of it. We've climbed mountains, you name it. We went to Nepal once on a gut test with Mel Blount. That was something. The people there had never seen a black man before. They just came around and stared at Mel.

"Ray and I have been around the world eight times. We've done it all. Maybe it's not the same as one of those games with the Raiders when Kenny Stabler, their quarterback, would wink at you, and tell you he was coming your way, and you wanted to be ready for that challenge. But it's still a good feeling."

Russell was reminded of a touch-tag football game he and Mansfield had put together a few years earlier at Three Rivers Stadium with the Dallas Cowboys, sort of a rematch of their Super Bowl confrontations.

Russell injured his Achilles tendon in that contest, and came away on crutches. He was hobbled by that injury for quite awhile, and he was embarrassed by what he had done to himself. "I put my ego in front of my brain," he said. "I had my shoe taped on, and my tendon just popped in the second half. That was a shock. I can run around, and it feels OK. But if I have to push off it too quickly, I can feel it again. It's there. I quit playing racquetball. I wanted to win too badly, and I pushed myself too hard. I couldn't just let the other guy win. I'd exert myself too much. A friend of mine had a heart attack. I decided it wasn't worth it. I stick to golf now. Maybe I'm getting smarter. Or maybe I'm just getting older."

The big five-oh was winking at Russell now instead of Stabler, as we spoke. Andy Russell, 50, no way.

Andy Russell and Ray Mansfield explore the Grand Canyon.

178

Danny Marino
Another quarterback who got away

D anny Marino should have been a Steeler. He was born to be a Steeler. He set all-time passing records during his All-America days at the University of Pittsburgh, and drew the fervent admiration of Steelers' owner Art Rooney among others, but he got away.

Twenty-six teams in the National Football League, including the Steelers, who had the 12th selection in 1983, passed on Marino before the Miami Dolphins drafted him. The Steelers instead drafted a defensive tackle from Texas Tech named Gabe Rivera. Rooney grumbled into his cigar about that decision.

Rivera was in an auto accident in his rookie season, and was left paralyzed by his injuries, which included a broken back. Marino became the most prolific and productive quarterback in NFL history with the Dolphins, even if he hasn't enjoyed the Super Bowl success of the San Francisco 49ers' Joe Montana, who is from Monongahela, Pa. Marino passed important passing marks faster than anybody before him.

Foge Fazio, Marino's coach at Pitt, said Don Shula, the coach of the Dolphins, was the only NFL coach to personally call him on the phone to check out the rumors about Marino's alleged misconduct and drug usage. "Danny was a good kid," offered Fazio, "and a great quarterback. You couldn't go wrong with Danny Marino. He's a winner."

No one had to tell that to the owner of the Steelers. Rooney had sat in Pitt Stadium on several occasions and seen Marino perform in standout fashion, and watched him in games on TV on even more occasions. "He's super," The Chief would often say. "We've got to find a way to keep that kid in Pittsburgh."

He said that first following Marino's junior season at Pitt, when Marino led the Panthers to an 11-1 record, including a sensational 24-20 victory over Georgia in the Sugar Bowl when Marino threw a last-minute TD pass to John Brown for the game-winner at the Superdome in New Orleans.

Rooney repeated it after Marino's senior season, when his numbers and reputation slipped, when there were whispers that Marino was messing around with drugs, and when the Pitt record dropped off to 9-3, including a disappointing season-ending 7-3 loss to SMU in the Cotton Bowl.

The biggest difference from Marino's junior to senior season was the number of touchdown passes and victories he produced. Otherwise, his stats were strikingly similar. As a junior, he completed 226 of 380 passes. As a senior, the numbers were 221 of 378. He had 23 passes intercepted both seasons. Total passing yardage as a junior was 2,876 compared to 2,432 as a senior. He threw 37 touchdown passes as a junior and just 17 as a senior.

"People complain that he was 9-3 as a senior," said Rooney. "Hey, I'd take 9-3 every year. He's still a winning pitcher."

179

Danny Marino

Dave Cross

Rooney often made references to baseball, his first love. It had been Marino's first love, too. He starred in both football and baseball at Central Catholic High School and was drafted by the Kansas City Royals, but turned them down to play football at Pitt. He didn't play baseball at Pitt.

Three days before the Dolphins came to Pittsburgh to play the Steelers early in the 1990 season, I had lunch with Art Rooney Jr., the second oldest of five sons of the late Steelers' owner, and the former player personnel director and head of the scouting department during the Steelers' glory years. He had been deposed from his position two years earlier by his older brother, Dan, the president of the Steelers, in a move that saddened their father deeply.

"My father never forgave me for not drafting Danny Marino," said Art Jr., who had lost a great deal of weight at his doctor's orders and was but a shadow of his former hefty and hearty self. "He was still critical of me about that even when he was essentially on his deathbed. I have to share some of the blame for that, but it was not my final call."

I remembered once discussing Dan Marino with Art Jr. prior to the 1982 draft. He told me how impressed he had been with the way Marino had handled himself in talking to pro scouts at a pro evaluation session at the Pontiac Silverdome during his senior year at Pitt. "He was definitely the No. 1 prospect in the lobby," said Art Jr. back then. "He's a real handsome kid, and he knows how to handle himself. He walks tall. And he talks tall."

Marino had always been that way. He was always into sports. He was the only boy of the three children of Dan and Veronica Marino. Both his parents are sports fans. And his dad drives a delivery truck for the *Pittsburgh Post-Gazette*, and helped spawn his son's interest in sports. His dad was often the only spectator in the stands at Pitt Stadium during practice sessions.

Dan first starred at Frazier Field, just down the street from his family's home on Parkview Avenue at the southern tip of Oakland. From the field, an 80-yard oil-coated ballyard, not uncommon in Pittsburgh's inner-city, Marino could overlook the J&L Steel (now LTV) complex where the smoke stopped coming out of the smokestacks while he was a teenager. Nobody had a better view of the decline of Pittsburgh's steel industry than Dan Marino.

He was the quarterback for the St. Regis Grade School football team in the City Catholic Grade School League. Later, he would matriculate to Central Catholic High School and then the University of Pittsburgh, both within a mile or so of his home, both within walking distance. Forbes Field, where the Pirates and Steelers played when he was a kid, was even closer. People would park their cars in his neighborhood and walk to the ballpark.

Earlier in 1990, Frazier Field had been renamed in Marino's honor. The same week his No. 13 jersey was retired at Central Catholic. He had been similarly honored at Pitt upon graduation in 1982. Someday, his No. 13 jersey will be hanging in the Pro Football Hall of Fame.

Many of the groundskeepers and ushers and front-office workers at Forbes Field lived in Marino's neighborhood. So did some of the ballplayers. Pirates' Hall of Famer Willie Stargell lived near Marino's grandmother, and Danny caught ball with Stargell in the street several times in his youth. Many of those same groundskeepers are still working at Three Rivers Stadium, and they still tell tales about Marino as a kid. They still grumble about him getting away.

No one talked to the groundskeepers any more than Art Rooney. He, too, rued the day the Steelers failed to draft Danny Marino, and his view was supported strongly by those groundskeepers.

Western Pennsylvania has produced many great quarterbacks. They include Hall of Famers such as Joe Namath of Beaver Falls, George Blanda of Youngwood, and Johnny Unitas of Pittsburgh, and future Hall of Famers like Marino, Joe Montana of Monongahela, and Jim Kelly of East Brady. The standards have always been high for quarterbacks in Pittsburgh.

Montana and the San Francisco 49ers failed to get to the Super Bowl after the 1990 season, but Kelly did, coming back from disabling injuries to lead the Buffalo Bills to the big game for the first time.

Another Western Pennsylvania product, Jeff Hostetler, who had been a reserve quarterback for most of seven seasons with the New York Giants, did the same. Hostetler was born in Davidsville, and played for Conemaugh Township High School and West Virginia University, where he married the daughter of Coach Don Nehlen.

He took over late in the season for the injured Phil Simms. Before long, some Giant fans were saying, "Phil Who?"

After he had directed the Giants to a victory over the San Francisco 49ers for the NFC title, Hostetler told reporters, "Everybody can make their own history. There were so many people doubting me, doubting the Giants. Everybody has their own opinion, but you guys have never seen me play. How can you say I can't do it? They keep on telling me I can't. And I'm going to the Super Bowl."

A lot of great quarterbacks grew up within a 60-mile radius of Pittsburgh. They included Johnny Lujack of Notre Dame (Connellsville), Arnold Galiffa of Army (Donora), Richie Lucas of Penn State (Glassport), Matt Szykowny of Iowa (North Catholic in Pittsburgh), Freddie Mazurek of Pitt (Redstone), Tommy Clements of Notre Dame (McKees Rocks), Chuck Fusina of Penn State (McKees Rocks), Terry Hanratty of Notre Dame (Butler). Willie Thrower of Michigan State (New Kensington), Dick Vidmer of Michigan State (Hempfield), and Major Harris of West Virginia (Brashear in Pittsburgh).

Roy McHugh, the former sports editor of *The Pittsburgh Press*, wrote an article for *The New York Times* (January 20, 1991), about all the quarterbacks from Western Pennsylvania in a pre-Super Bowl section.

McHugh hinted that football was in decline around Pittsburgh, and was not aware of any future quarterback prospects from the area. Nor was the head of the Steelers' scouting department aware of a current college quarterback with local roots who was regarded as a pro prospect.

"Not that the Steelers have ever thought about drafting one," wrote McHugh, sticking a long needle into the Steelers' backside.

McHugh also suggested that the change in Pittsburgh from an industrial town to a service and high-tech community might have something to do with the decline. Pittsburgh used to be a tougher town with tougher people, he ventured.

At least a half dozen head coaches in the National Football League in recent years came from the area, namely Mike Ditka, Marty Schottenheimer, Chuck Knox, Joe Bugel, Bud Carson and Joe Walton.

"Steelworkers and coalminers are vanishing Americans," wrote McHugh. "As the mills and the mines shut down and the population dwindles and school mergers eliminate rivalries, a football-centered ethos is breaking up. No longer is Western Pennsylvania football superior or even equal to the football in several warm-weather states, or in certain other parts of the North."

He wrote that Marino and Kelly, for instance, come from shot-and-a-beer neighborhoods.

Bob Smizik, a columnist for *The Pittsburgh Press*, who covered Marino during his Pitt days, offered the opinion in November of 1990 that the talent pool in Western Pennsylvania was drying up.

Asked to explain this, Jack McCurry of North Hills High School, one of the most successful football coaches in Greater Pittsburgh, said, "At one point in time, football was a way of life in this area. It was a way to get out of the mill or be a celebrity in your hometown. You were a member of a winning team and that was something. It's not that way anymore. There are so many other avenues for kids to go. It's not the focal point it once was."

Don Yannessa, the head football coach of Baldwin High School, said, "There are a lot of cases where athletes are not coming out in the same numbers as they once did."

I remember seeing Marino and Kelly paying visits to the Steelers' offices during the Super Bowl years because they were big fans of the Steelers and of Terry Bradshaw. Bradshaw enjoyed having them come around, and he offered tips to them.

The Steelers are still Montana's favorite team, aside from the San Francisco 49ers that is. Before the Steelers played in San Francisco during the 1990 season, Montana told a sportswriter, "I'm still a Steelers fan until we play them. I've always been one. I would have loved to have played for the Steelers, growing up there and having feelings that I had about the team. It would have been nice to play there."

But the Steelers still had one of the greatest quarterbacks of all time in Bradshaw when Marino came out of Pitt. Bradshaw, indeed, had been one of Marino's biggest boosters. The Steelers thought Bradshaw was in his prime, and didn't realize that a shoulder injury was worse than anyone thought, and that he was on the downside of his career. Then, too, in 1980 they had made Mark Malone, a quarterback from Arizona State, their No. 1 pick, and capable Cliff Stoudt was still on the sideline. So Chuck Noll thought he was well stocked and in good shape at the QB slot.

But Marino, like Bradshaw, was a once-in-a-million prospect. Maybe he was too close for the Steelers to see how special he really was, the old can't-see-the-forest-for-the-trees tale.

During the 1990 off-season, Marino had grown unhappy in Miami, mostly because the Dolphins didn't have enough talent to be serious contenders, and were a mediocre 8-8 the previous season. Marino made noises about wanting to be traded, and mentioned Pittsburgh as one of the teams he'd prefer. The same sort of stirring had come up before with another area hero, Tony Dorsett, an All-America who set national running records at Pitt, who spoke about becoming a Steeler after his career had gone sour with the Dallas Cowboys.

Marino's well-publicized lament stirred up some excitement and controversy in Pittsburgh. Some fans still weren't convinced that Bubby Brister was the real thing, while others thought the Steelers would have to pay too dearly to get Marino, and it would mess up a team that seemed to be turning things around and was headed in the right direction.

On the morning of the game on Sunday, Sept. 30, Pittsburgh sports writer and radio sports talk show host Bruce Keidan asked Dolphins' owner Tim Robbie on a pre-game show whether he would ever consider sending Marino back home where he belonged. Robbie chuckled and said Marino was in a good frame of mind about playing for the Dolphins and that he hoped to have Marino spend his entire pro career in Miami.

A few nights before the game, Marino did a live shot from Miami with sportscaster John Steigerwald on KDKA-TV and he looked positively splendid in a sharp black suit. He was still the most handsome of heroes. On the eve of the game, Marino visited with family and friends. After the game, he was surrounded by same. He had dissected the Steelers' defense and helped the Dolphins defeat his one-time favorite team, 28-6.

He upped his pitching record to 5-2 against the Steelers. At one time, he was 4-0 against them, and that's when the Steelers' fans fretted the most about the Steelers not drafting him.

Several years back, before one of those games at Three Rivers Stadium, Dolphins' coach Don Shula spotted Art Rooney walking through the halls outside the locker rooms. Shula asked Rooney to come into the Dolphins' dressing room, to say hello to Marino. "I don't go into our own locker room before a game; I don't belong in there," Rooney begged off. Shula persisted, however, and brought Marino out to a lobby-like entry to see the Steelers owner. "Beware of newfound friends and acquaintances," Rooney advised him. "Good luck."

Marino beat the Steelers that day, and brought more misery upon Steelers' fans in follow-up performances.

Never was that disappointment keener than after the AFC championship game of 1984. The Steelers were up by 21-10 against the Dolphins in Miami, and seemed destined to advance to the Super Bowl. But Marino personally rallied the Dolphins and put on one of the greatest performances of his career to lead his team to a 45-28 victory.

Marino completed 21 of 32 passes for 421 yards and four touchdowns that day. The Dolphins ended up losing to the San Francisco 49ers, 38-16, in Super Bowl XIX, but it had been the greatest of years for Marino.

"When I first got here, we won a lot, and I kind of took it for granted," said Marino. "We went to the Super Bowl and we lost.

"I wanted to win so badly, but after the game, I remember saying to myself, 'Hey, we'll be able to come back and do this every year.' But it just doesn't work that way."

He passed for an NFL record 5,084 yards that year. He also set a league mark with 48 touchdown passes.

In eight seasons with the Dolphins, Marino passed for 31,416 yards and 241 touchdowns. In 14 seasons, by comparison, Bradshaw passed for 27,989 yards and 212 touchdowns.

"At this stage," said Shula, "Dan has far better statistics than anyone who has ever played the game. When you project that out over a period of time, and throw in some championships, there is no question of where he will rate."

Or, as Howie Long of the Los Angeles Raiders put it during the 1990 NFL playoffs, "Any time you put the ball in the hands of Danny Marino, he has the ability to break your heart. Believe me, I know."

Yes, he should have been a Steeler.

Dave Cross

Terry Bradshaw and Ahmad Rashad of CBS chat with Danny Marino.

Pittsburgh
At its best for Art Rooney

Pittsburgh does not get any better than it was on Sunday, October 7, 1990. The sky was mostly blue, with white-white cirrus clouds streaking it, and the Goodyear Blimp was hovering over Three Rivers Stadium where the Steelers were playing the San Diego Chargers in a National Football League contest.

It was a good picture to televise out west to the folks in sunny Southern California. This could not be Pittsburgh, the Smoky City, they must have thought.

The temperature was 77 degrees, the humidity was 59 percent, and the winds were blowing at 13 miles per hour to the south. It was easy to sweat, but the breeze provided a refreshing relief. So did the Steelers.

It was 1:40 p.m., in the first minute of the second quarter, and the Steelers had just scored a touchdown. In the fifth game of what had already been a frustrating campaign, the Steelers' offensive unit had scored its first touchdown of the season. That's right, it took five games for the offense to finally score a touchdown.

A new offensive system and a new offensive coordinator, Joe Walton, an All-America at Pitt and an All-Pro receiver for the Redskins and Giants in the NFL, had come home to Beaver Falls, or at least nearby Beaver, and to serve the Steelers as an offensive coordinator, and he was catching the same kind of flak he had endured for most of his seven seasons as head coach of the New York Jets. Things were not going well, and Walton and the Steelers, and head coach Chuck Noll, were all under fire from the media and the fans for a season that seemed doomed already.

Eric Green, the Steelers' No. 1 draft pick out of Liberty University, a controversial choice who had worsened his already shaky status by holding out the entire training camp in a contract dispute, had caught a pass as a tight end from quarterback Bubby Brister for an eight-yard touchdown and enabled the Steelers to take a 10-7 lead over the Chargers. It was the first of two touchdown passes Green would grab on this afternoon as the Steelers outscored the Chargers, 36-14, to improve their record to 2-3.

Bobby Bonilla and Barry Bonds of the Pittsburgh Pirates were standing on the sideline during the game, and cheering on the Steelers. Bonilla looked like he could play tight end, and Bonds could be a wide receiver or defensive back. The Pirates would be playing the Cincinnati Reds the following day in the third game of their National League Championship Series. The day before, Bonilla and Brister and their teammates had fooled around playfully on the field at Three Rivers Stadium, the Pirates playing catch with a football, and the Steelers swinging baseball bats. It was all in good fun, sports at its amateur best.

Pittsburghers were excited about the Pirates, who would go on to lose to the Reds, the eventual World Series Champions.

Pittsburgh certainly was not yet ready to reclaim its status as "The City of Champions," which it was called in the '70s when the Steelers won four Super Bowl championships, the Pirates two World Series titles, and Pitt a national championship in 1976, and had native sons such as Johnny Unitas and Joe Schmidt inducted into the Pro Football Hall of Fame, but it was getting close to the real thing. It was a lot better than the week before when the Steelers and Pitt both suffered embarrassing losses.

The night before, some of the Steelers' best ballplayers from the past, especially stars of those Super Bowls teams, club officials, civic leaders and members of the Rooney family had gathered for a dinner at the Rooneys' boyhood home, just a few blocks from Three Rivers Stadium. It was part of a weekend celebration to mark the unveiling of a memorial statue of Art Rooney, the late owner of the Steelers, before a big early-arriving crowd in a park-like setting just outside Gate D at Three Rivers Stadium. Rooney had resided on the North Side all his life, refusing to leave a neighborhood that had become an inner-city ghetto because he was comfortable on its streets.

When Green grabbed that first TD pass, I left the press box at Three Rivers Stadium and drifted out to a walkway on the third level of the stadium. I wanted to see what was going on outside the stadium, in the area just below where Art Rooney's statue was now on permanent display.

There was nobody near the statue. What a stark contrast to the scene a few hours earlier.

The background to the statue showed off Pittsburgh at its best. There were about thirty pleasure boats of as many different sizes bobbing up and down in the water of the three rivers — the Allegheny, the Monongahela and the Ohio. The huge water fountain at Point State Park, where Fort Pitt and Fort Duquesne once stood in the earliest days of this city, was blowing back toward the downtown section. All the water was glistening. A sternwheeler called the Gateway River Belle went by in the brown-green water, just about 50 yards from Rooney's statue, alongside the riverbank stretch called Roberto Clemente Park.

Across the way, on the South Side of town, a freight train stretched all the way from the Fort Pitt Bridge to the West End Bridge, about a mile apart. The Duquesne Incline was in operation, one cable car going up the steep side of Mt. Washington, and another cable car coming down. All that was missing was a tug boat pulling coal barges. It's a scene that can't be duplicated anywhere else in America.

Those hills, foothills to the Allegheny Mountains, spanned the horizon. From left to right, there is Mt. Oliver, then Beltzhoover, then Mt. Washington, then Sheraden, and then the hills overlooking McKees Rocks. They once mined coal in those hills. Mt. Washington was once known as Coal Hill. George Washington was supposed to have kept watch up there to see if anyone was approaching Fort Pitt by the rivers.

The coal from those hills was sent up and down the rivers on barges pulled by tug boats, and fed the furnaces of the once-fiery steel mills, which are no more for the most part in the Pittsburgh area. There is very little smoke over the mills in Pittsburgh or Western Pennsylvania these days.

They also mined football players from those hills. Joe Schmidt came out of Mt. Oliver and the University of Pittsburgh to become a Hall of Fame linebacker for the Detroit Lions. The Steelers should have drafted him, but messed up, which was their history in those days. Another Hall of Famer, Johnny Unitas, grew up on Mt. Washington, and was cut by the Steelers soon after leaving the University of Louisville for their tryout camp. Steelers' president Dan Rooney used to play against Unitas in the City Catholic Football League, and felt from the start that coach Walt Kiesling should not have cut him. Ted Kwalick came out of McKees Rocks and starred as a tight end at Penn State and with the San Francisco 49ers and Oakland Raiders. Art Rooney rooted for all of them.

In hills and valleys beyond those hills, other football players grew up to greatness, such as Hopewell's Tony Dorsett, Mt. Lebanon's John Frank, Aliquippa's Mike Ditka, Youngwood's George Blanda, Monongahela's Joe Montana, Beaver Falls' Joe Namath, Rochester's Babe Parilli and Jim Mutscheller, Homewood's Tony Liscio, Oakland's Dan Marino, East Brady's Jim Kelly and Sewickley's Chuck Knox.

Art Rooney knew them all and counted them all as friends. They liked to tell people the same.

The view from Three Rivers Stadium on this particular Sunday afternoon was stunning. It was a view Art Rooney enjoyed on many days at the ballpark.

For awhile, there had been no one around the Art Rooney statue. Now, three youngsters appeared, two girls and a boy, riding bicycles. They drove up to within about five feet of the statue and stopped. They just sat there, and stared at the statue. Then they drew nearer to it and touched it, and hung around it for awhile.

Ed Kiely had come up behind me and was observing the same scene. Kiely had been a Steelers' public relations representative for 35 years. Kiely had remained a constant companion of Art Rooney, accompanying him to most civic functions and sports events.

"The Chief would have liked that," said Kiely, "kids coming up to him like that."

They could not have picked a better day to unveil the statue of Art Rooney. The event started at 10 a.m., three hours before the kickoff, and would last about an hour.

The show was about to begin, and the Bethel Park High School marching band played an appropriate attention-getting overture. Ceremonies commenced for the unveiling of the Art Rooney statue.

It was a perfect day on the North Side, the sort of Sunday morning Art Rooney would have relished, when he would have been mixing with the people outside St. Peter's Church after mass, the sort of sunny day when he would have been looking forward to the afternoon game with the San Diego Chargers, and the Pirates' playoff games with the Cincinnati Reds in the week to come.

Mr. Rooney died August 25, 1988, following a stroke at the age of 87. But his legend lives on, and the statue will serve as a reminder of what a wonderful man we were lucky to have among us.

"Dad would not have been comfortable with all this attention," declared Dan Rooney, the team president and the oldest of five sons of the Steelers' founder. "But he'd be happy here, listening to the stories about the Pirates in the playoffs, the Steelers and (for a laugh) the offense. He'd be happy just loafing on the North Side."

Fans and friends and former ballplayers and associates all gathered together to mark this special day. Pittsburgh's retired bishop, Father Vincent Leonard, who had officiated at the funeral mass for Art Rooney, referred to him as "a great sportsman and a great citizen."

"We all knew and loved The Chief," said Sophie Masloff, the mayor of Pittsburgh. "He stopped to talk to everyone. To Art Rooney, everyone he met was someone special. He made you feel important."

Jean Caliguiri, the wife of the late mayor, Richard S. Caliguiri, attended the ceremonies. A month later, a statue of her husband would be unveiled in front of the City-County Building on Grant Street.

Mayor Caliguiri died soon after Art Rooney, and the city grieved over the loss of two of its most beloved and admired citizens. They were both boosters with a ready smile for everyone. They were the heart and soul of Pittsburgh.

At the Steelers' 50 Seasons Celebration in 1982, Art Rooney had remarked, "I never had a player I didn't like. I never had a player I didn't think was a star." And the feeling was mutual. Many had returned to pay tribute to their old boss.

The stars of recent seasons, the Super Bowl seasons, the glory years, attracted the most attention, and stirred the Steelers' fans who sought their autographs once again. They included the likes of recent Hall of Famers Jack Lambert and Franco Harris, along with Joe Greene, Rocky Bleier, Donnie Shell, Ted Petersen and John Stallworth. They even got hugs and kisses from the most fervent of Steelers fans.

"My fondest memory of playing for the Pittsburgh Steelers," allowed Lambert, "was the twinkle in Arthur J. Rooney's eyes. When we pass the statue, we will be forever reminded of that twinkle."

Harris, he of "the Immaculate Reception" fame, offered this tribute: "This remarkable and grand man has made a lot of special times for all of us. He was always there to help and to give. And this feeling filtered down to the players. I think the Steelers' players give more to their community than any other team in professional sports."

Some Hall of Famers from earlier years were familiar to older fans, the likes of Bullet Bill Dudley, Ernie Stautner and John Henry Johnson. And Jack Butler, who should be in the Hall of Fame, and who was so close to The Chief. They were also there.

There were others from teams that struggled through mostly difficult days at Forbes Field and Pitt Stadium like Charlie Scales of

West Mifflin (1960-61), John Brown (1967-72) and Bruce Van Dyke (1967-73). Lloyd Voss (1966-71), who lives in Scott Township, played at Pitt Stadium and Three Rivers Stadium, but retired before the Steelers became a playoff contender.

Ralph Berlin of Bethel Park, the team trainer for 22 seasons, was hugging all of them. The family of Joe Carr, who died earlier in the year and who had served the Steelers for so many years as ticket manager, was there from Mt. Lebanon. So was Ray Downey of Mt. Lebanon, the long-time p.a. announcer. Baldy Regan, a City Councilman from the North Side, and a long-time friend of the Rooneys, was there to make sure everybody was properly introduced to each other.

You had to be a real Steeler fan to recognize other former Steelers who stood in the crowd. Most of them played their college ball locally, back in the days when Art Rooney always had a lot of Pitt and Duquesne guys on his team.

Some stayed a long time, like Dick Haley, who lives in Bridgeville. He was in his 24th season with the Steelers, four as a player (1961-64), and 20 as the Steelers' director of player personnel.

Gene Breen (1965-66), who grew up in Mt. Lebanon, was also present, along with Joe Zombek (1954) of McDonald, Carl Nery (1940-41) of Scott Township and Ernie Bonelli (1946) of Mt. Lebanon. and their families. Rudy Andabaker (1952-54) of Donora, Jerry Nuzum (1948-51) of Wilkinsburg and Bill Priatko (1957) of North Braddock and North Huntingdon were all smiles, as usual. Joe Cibulas (1945) of the North Side and Ray Kemp (1933) of Cecil and Bellevue, two former Duquesne University players, were among the oldest alumni there. Art Rooney's door was always open to them and they cherish the relationship they enjoyed as much as any of the Steelers sporting Super Bowl rings.

"His philosophy was to treat each and every person the way they'd all want to be treated," said Allegheny County Commissioner Tom Foerster, a life-long friend and admirer of Art Rooney, who had also grown up on the North Side and played football, as did Dan Rooney, at North Catholic High School.

It was also a big day for my next-door neighbor, public relations executive Boris Weinstein, and his wife, Sandy, and their son, Carl, who came in from Seattle, where he is director of promotions for the Seattle Mariners. "The idea for this statue was brought to me by Boris Weinstein," said John Howell, WPXI-TV vice-president and general manager, who was the general chairman of the statue fund committee.

Howell reported that over 7,000 individuals, including more than 100 Steelers' alumni, contributed a total of $371,000 to the statue fund. It is a beautiful sculpture by Raymond Kaskey, who grew up in Carrick and attended Carnegie Mellon University. A former Steeler, Joe Gasparella (1948, 1950-51), served as architect for the project.

The seated figure of Art Rooney is about 7 feet tall. If the figure were standing it would be 10 feet tall. It is at eye level, which is nice because people can get close to it, and pose for pictures with Art Rooney's likeness.

"He wouldn't want to be put on a pedestal, you know that," Dan Rooney said when I told him I liked how the statue was positioned alongside a park bench.

"It's nice that people can come and sit with him. If there was anything you could say about our father, it's that he was a man of the people. The people can come and sit with him and share that feeling. It's something special."

I had seen pictures of the statue a week earlier, sort of cheating. Mike Rooney, the son of Art Jr. and Kay of Mt. Lebanon and a grandson of Art Rooney, had traveled to a foundry in Chester, Pennsylvania, and seen the statue before it was shipped to Pittsburgh. A fine arts graduate of Washington & Jefferson College, Mike wanted to see how the statue was created. Mike had his arm draped around his grandfather's shoulder in my favorite photo.

Eric Green, the star of the Steelers' victory that day, never met Art Rooney. He missed out on one of the great perks of being a Pittsburgh Steeler. Somebody will have to tell Eric Green about Art Rooney, so he can fully appreciate what wearing a Steelers' uniform means.

"We meet so few truly great men in our lifetime," Lambert said. "As members of the older generation, it is our duty to tell the stories of Art Rooney, to tell of his acts of generosity.

"Most of all, tell them how he cared not whether his players were black or white, Catholic, Protestant or Jew. We were all his boys. And, in this day and age, what a beautiful legend to leave behind."

For all we know, the statue of Art Rooney might be located at a site where the Steelers' patriarch nearly drowned during a flood when he was a youngster.

Listen as Art Rooney relates the tale, as he did many times, during the summer of 1972.

"That water looks pretty peaceful now," he said, pointing out toward the three rivers. "But that's because it's August and not April. You know, once, a long time ago, I darned near drowned here, right near this spot.

"I tell you it was something. In those days — that was back before they had flood controls — if you spit in these rivers, the flood came up. It wasn't unusual to paddle our way to school in a boat.

"Well, right here on this spot, right where this new stadium is built, there used to be a park called Expo Park. The Pirates played there before Forbes Field opened in 1909. My dad's saloon was right over there, across the street.

"This one year there was an awful flood and three of us were paddling our way to school in a canoe — a kid named Squawker Mullen, my brother Dan, and me. We were taking that canoe right through the outfield in old Expo Park. Squawker was moving around in the canoe and I told him to sit down. Sure as shooting he was going to upset it — and sure as shooting he did. Squawker and Dan didn't have boots and a coat on, so they made it easily to a safe spot. But me, I had on boots and an overcoat. I'll tell you, it was my last gasp when I reached out and grabbed hold of that grandstand."

amateur boxer

Art Rooney

With John Michelosen and Jock Sutherland

With Billy Conn

With Buddy Parker and Pete Rozelle

With Bobby Layne

With Ernie Stautner at Hall of Fame

With grandson Art II

With his wife Kathleen Rooney

With Frank Sinatra

With son Dan Rooney

With Arnold Palmer.

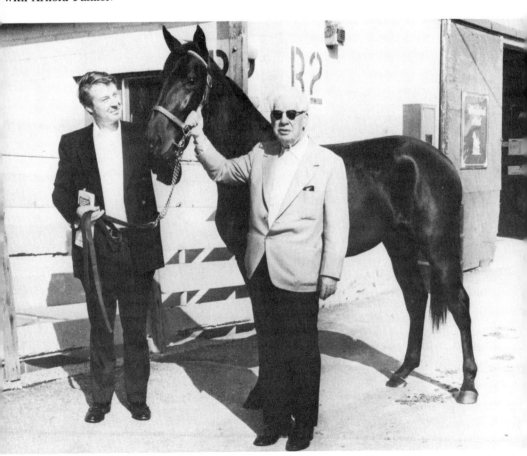

With son Tim Rooney at the racetrack

With Pirates owner John Galbreath

With Johnny Blood

With Woody Hayes

With Jack Lambert

Bill Nack, now with *Sports Illustrated*, once wrote in *Newsday*, the Long Island newspaper, before the Steelers won their first Super Bowl championship in 1974, "Art Rooney is the very symbol of the Steelers, as much a part of Pittsburgh as the Allegheny and Monongahela Rivers, which join to form the Ohio River not far from where he grew up."

Rooney was born in Coultersville, Pennsylvania, east of Pittsburgh, on January 27, 1901.

"My mother's people were all coal miners and my father's people were all steel workers," Rooney remarked. "They all worked in the mills."

Rooney's roots were always important to him, and he did not stray far from them.

"We lived on the second floor of my father's saloon — Dan Rooney's Saloon," he said. "He owned it for years and years. It was a rough neighborhood, in a way, but in those days kids were on the playground from the time the sun came up to the time it went down. We played baseball and football and boxed."

And no one did it any better in the neighborhood than Art Rooney. Unless it was his friend, David Roderick, who was also a pretty fair amateur boxer, and grew up to be the president and chairman of the board of U.S. Steel, later called USX.

Rooney's boyhood home above the bar was on a site where Three Rivers Stadium now stands. As an adult, Rooney and his family resided in an 11-room high-ceilinged mansion, now over 140 years old, in what was once the most fashionable neighborhood of Pittsburgh's North Side. One of Dan Rooney's daughters was living there with her family. It is right next door to a house once owned by Harry Thaw, who killed architect Sanford White in a celebrated scandal years ago, and across the street from a home once occupied by Lillian Russell. The neighborhood got old and deteriorated while the Rooneys lived there, but Art never considered moving. He was at home there and he liked the people in the neighborhood. It is where he belonged. "We were rich and he had us living in a ghetto," said Art Rooney Jr.

Baseball was Art Rooney's first love and when he founded his pro football team he called them the Pirates. They were the Pirates from 1933 until 1941 when he changed the name because his club kept getting confused with the baseball team. "We figured Steelers was the proper name because Pittsburgh is the steel capital of the world." It was back then, anyhow.

The Steelers were not always successful and did not always draw well, so there were always overtures from other cities to move the franchise. Some of the offers were quite lucrative. But Rooney rebuffed them all.

"I could have made moves to Baltimore, New Orleans and Atlanta," he said, "but I'm a Pittsburgher and I like the town. Great people live here. Friendly people."

As he grew older, he complained that too many of his friends were dying. "I probably attend more wakes than anyone in Pittsburgh," he said with a mixture of pride and remorse.

He especially liked people he met at the ballpark. The members of the ground crew were among his favorites. At his insistence, the Steelers have always taken two members of the ground crew on each of their chartered airplane trips to road games. "They do a good job," said Rooney, always looking after the little people. "They made me an honorary member of the ground crew." That was as important to him as any awards he won when the Steelers were winning Super Bowls.

He wished he had worked harder at the football business in the franchise's formative years. "I really didn't spend the time on this like I should have, like George Halas and Curly Lambeau did. It was my fault. There is not any doubt about that. I was at the racetrack. I was doing what I could do.

"I have made tremendous bets on horse racing," Rooney once said. "That's the only game I ever bet on. Never football. I've enjoyed betting on horses and winning. If I'm losers, I don't enjoy it at all. If I'm winners, I really enjoy it and I make a good player, as good a player as there is. If I lose, I back off."

It was on a hot betting streak, at Saratoga and other upstate New York tracks, that Rooney made a killing, for a reported $250,000, and was then financially able to bankroll a pro football team. Thus the Pittsburgh entry in the National Football League was born.

It was Art Rooney himself who first referred to his team as "the same ol' Steelers." The fans shortened it to S.O.S.

Speaking at a sports dinner late in his life, and speaking so softly it was difficult for many to hear him, Rooney said he regretted ever making that remark. Larry Werner, the executive vice-president of Ketchum Communications, cannot help but smile when he recalls what Mr. Rooney said that night: "Of all the things I ever said, that's the one thing I wished I had never said. It came back to haunt us."

"We're losers in a country where winning means you're great, you're beautiful, you're moral. If you don't make a lot of money, you're a loser."
— Bill Veeck

Ed Ryan has a lot in common with Art Rooney. Ryan's roots are in the steel and coal mining business of Western Pennsylvania. He built a business — Ryan Homes — from humble beginnings and it became a national homebuilding conglomerate.

Ryan has been a great admirer for many years of Rooney, with whom he shared a passion for sports, horses, racing, Ireland, the Catholic Church, the Little Sisters of the Poor, and people who need a helping hand.

"When Art Rooney's name was mentioned in my house, my dad always paid him special respect," said Sue Gillespie, Ed Ryan's daughter. "Everyone has somebody they look up to, and Art Rooney was my dad's hero. My dad used to tell me about seeing Mr. Rooney in places like Phoenix, and seeing him in the lobby on Sunday morning, getting ready to go to mass. My father admired that."

In 1988, Ryan received the Harness Track Association Art Rooney Award for sportsmanship and dedication to harness racing, and it is proudly displayed on his desk at his Mt. Lebanon real estate development office.

Ryan treasures correspondence he had with Rooney. He remembers having Rooney out to The Meadowlands, which he owned along with Joe Hardy of 84 Lumber and Del Miller, the Hall of Fame harness racer and breeder. "It would be wonderful," wrote Rooney to Ryan in one of his letters, "if every night at The Meadows would be like last Friday night."

Ryan remembers once asking Rooney if he would appear in a TV commercial for The Meadows. "How much would you want to do it?" Ryan asked him. To which Rooney replied, "I wouldn't do it for a million dollars. But for my good friend Del Miller I'll do it for nothing." And he did. And it was a big hit.

Reflecting on Rooney, Ryan got emotional. "He lived and he was in contact with all these great people," remarked Ryan. "He lived the best of what I would hope to be, but will never be. He was a national treasure."

In a book called "Pittsburgh Steelers: The First Half Century," by Bob Oates, Jr., published by Rosebud Books in 1982, Art Rooney reflected: "Everybody in this town had a part in it," he said of the Steelers' unparalleled success in the '70s.

"I've always liked people. I've heard people say that one of the reasons we won so big recently is that we treat our players well, that we treat them as individuals. Well, maybe that's true, but that's not why we do it. If you like people, that's just your nature. You can't try to like people to help your team win or something. It can't be false. It has to be a spontaneous thing. You just like them. And that's how it was around here.

"Think about Rocky Bleier. When he came back from the war, I wasn't sure he could make it. That first year his wounds were still so bad, the trainer and the equipment manager were coming to us and saying we had to make him stop. He was killing himself, but he would never quit. He wanted to do it so badly, and we wanted to give him a full shot. So we kept him around for that year, and he had another operation, and the next year he made the team. I've never known anybody but Rocky who could have done it.

"And Chuck Noll. What a tremendous person. An honorable person and a great coach. People think he's hard, but I'm not sure. He may not like me to say it, but he has sentiment. He has a lot of charity. He gives a player a long time to show what he can do and he takes a long time to make up his mind whether a fellow is over the hill. He's a good man; he cares.

"We've just had great people here. And somehow, here in Pittsburgh, it seems like that's the way it ought to be. The people in this town are good people. They're friendly; they don't put on airs. The working people don't try to act like corporation executives. The executives are like the workers, just regular people.

"And what fans the Pittsburghers have been! They were patient through all the losing years, and then we started to win, they just picked the team up. You can talk to any of the players. They'll tell you how important the fans have been to our success.

"And when we finally did win those Super Bowls, I honestly can't tell you if I was happier for the Steelers or for the whole town of Pittsburgh. I know the wins helped to give the people here some pride in their town — I know because so many have told me.

"It just feels right. I was born and raised here, and I believe if you have lived in a town for most of your life, you become part of that town. The town itself is you.

"I've lived here 80 years and the Steelers have been here 50. By now I feel that I am Pittsburgh.

"And Pittsburgh is the Steelers."

The view from the 40th floor of One PPG Place is spectacular. From there, you can see the statue of Art Rooney, Three Rivers Stadium, the three rivers, Point State Park, the rooftops of Gateway Center, Mt. Washington, the whole panorama of Pittsburgh.

It was a rare sunny day in mid-February and Vince Sarni was standing near the wall-to-wall windows of his office suite, pointing out different landmarks. Sarni was the chairman and chief executive officer of PPG Industries, Inc. at the time.

"It's some view," said Sarni. "When people come here from all over the world, they're fascinated by it. They are intrigued by seeing the Ohio River formed by the meeting of the Monongahela and Allegheny Rivers, and how the Ohio River runs north. Not too many rivers in the world do that."

In 1990 the CYO of Pittsburgh selected Sarni as the winner of the Arthur J. Rooney Award for his outstanding citizenship and leadership role in the community. Among his many civic activities, Sarni was a major fund-raiser for the Greater Pittsburgh Guild for the Blind in Bridgeville, not far from his home in Mt. Lebanon.

"Art Rooney was an example of why this is a great community," said Sarni. "This was a man who was truly a good person. He was very successful, but in a modest way.

"He never forgot where he came from. In fact, he stayed in the same house where he raised his family for his entire adult life.

"He did all the things that helped make this country great. There are good people who care about their neighbors, and want to make it a better place to live. That's how it was with Art Rooney.

"I've never heard anybody say anything bad about Art Rooney or his family. That's rare. He was the patriarch of a family that worked together, and supported each other. I've heard great stories about him.

200

"I was very lucky. I moved to Baltimore in the '50s and saw the Colts come from the bottom of the barrel to become the best team in pro football. I remember the team we hated to see come to Baltimore the most was the Steelers. They couldn't beat us, but they beat us up. When they left town, there were always three or four of our guys who couldn't play the next week. I was at the game at Yankee Stadium where they beat the New York Giants (23-17) in sudden death overtime on a touchdown by Alan Ameche."

Sarni said he used to take his family to a swim club in Baltimore that was owned by Art Donovan, an All-Pro defensive lineman for the Colts. Sarni was a big fan of Johnny Unitas. I told him Unitas was my hero when I was growing up. I pointed to Mt. Washington, where Unitas grew up. Only the day before, I had driven past Arsenal Field in Lawrenceville, where Unitas had played sandlot football before becoming a Baltimore Colt. Sarni reminded me that the Steelers had once conducted their pre-season training camp at the University of Rhode Island, where he once played football as a college student.

"I came to Pittsburgh in 1968 and the Steelers were so bad back then," he said. "And I saw them come along under Chuck Noll and become the biggest winners. I saw all four Super Bowls. I'm a big fan and defender of Chuck Noll."

There were pictures in Sarni's magnificent office showing him with President Ronald Regan and with President Bush and his wife, Barbara. But the ones he pointed out to me showed him with his brothers, and with his grandchildren. "I've been lucky," said Sarni. "But the bottom line, as to where you learned what made you successful, and where your values and ethics were formed, is your family. Family is the most important thing in your life. The Rooneys and the Steelers have always understood that."

Steelers' grass practice field on North Side

Family Album

Steelers' owner Art Rooney poses with Jim O'Brien and his daughters, Sarah, 7, and Rebecca, during 1980 visit to Three Rivers Stadium for a team practice session.

Terry Bradshaw
"The Prodigal Son"

This was outside Three Rivers Stadium on Sunday, Oct. 7, 1990, and Terry Bradshaw was taking a verbal beating from two women who were in the crowd that had gathered to witness the unveiling of the Art Rooney memorial statue.

"I see a lot of the Steelers are here, but not Terry Bradshaw," said the one woman.

"He never comes here for anything anymore," said her friend.

"What's with him? Why is he so down on Pittsburgh these days? What did we do to him?"

"I don't know, but he says he's not coming back. He wasn't even here for Art Rooney's funeral. He said he didn't want to create a circus."

"He didn't show up this summer for that Steelers' reunion they had, either. He must see himself as something special. Like he's above it all."

"It doesn't surprise me. Didn't you hear what he said on that show Ann Devlin did?

"Oh, yeah, I heard about that."

"Well, he really took off on this town, the team, just about everybody in Pittsburgh. Mr. Rooney may have been the only one he said nice things about."

Terry Bradshaw should still be the toast of the town in Pittsburgh. After all, he quarterbacked the Steelers to four Super Bowl titles in six years. No other quarterback in the history of the NFL can make such a boast. He was so good, and came up big in the big games, and led a very good and very talented team to many victories. When Pittsburgh was called "The City of Champions" in 1979, Bradshaw shared the Sportsman of the Year award from *Sports Illustrated* with Willie Stargell of the Pirates. Things could not have been better in Pittsburgh.

When I first came on the Steelers' beat in 1979, one of the veteran reporters, Norm Vargo of *The Daily News* in McKeesport, told me, "You won't believe Bradshaw. Win, lose or draw, he's always there for us after the game. He'll talk till you're blue in the face. Terry Bradshaw will always give you a story. He'll never disappoint you."

I had already had some positive experiences with affable and thoughtful athletes, outstanding performers who understood what a writer was looking for and needed to do his or her job, such as Mercury Morris of the Miami Dolphins, Julius Erving of the New York Nets, Walt Frazier and Willis Reed of the New York Knicks, Muhammad Ali in boxing, and Tom Seaver and Bud Harrelson of the New York Mets, and Joe Namath of the New York Jets, and Denis Potvin and Bryan Trottier of the New York Islanders, but Bradshaw, was indeed, a rare treat. He was one of the easiest athletes I ever had to deal with in my career.

So it seemed out of character for him to be coming down so hard on his former employers, former co-workers and teammates, Pittsburgh and its fans. Bradshaw said his former coach, Chuck Noll, did not have the same fire in the '80s as he had in the '70s. He called for Noll's firing. All of a sudden, everybody was fair game.

His former teammates were as confused as the fans. "All that the city of Pittsburgh has done for him. . ." said Donnie Shell, not finishing his sentences, but letting you know how he felt. "All that Pittsburgh gave to him. . ."

Shell is familiar with the Biblical story of "The Prodigal Son," and, in a sense, that is what Bradshaw has become. So there is hope for reconciliation.

"I could carry that football team. I knew I was the only one who could carry that football team," Bradshaw was saying on a much-ballyhooed WTAE-TV special called "Bradshaw: Out of Bounds," in which he was interviewed at length by Ann Devlin during the 1990 season.

Devlin had a daily TV show called "Pittsburgh's Talking" in which she prided herself on posing penetrating questions for national and local celebrities on all kinds of timely stories and issues, and she enjoyed good ratings and good reviews. Judging by the fallout, she had quite an audience for her interview with Bradshaw.

Bradshaw had been taking shots here and there through the years at the Steelers and Dan Rooney and Chuck Noll, in particular, and being critical of players such as Mark Malone and Bubby Brister, who succeeded him.

The show opened with sound bites on Bradshaw saying things like "fans are fans, I hated and loved them, hated and loved them, hated and loved them." And, "No one will ever win four (Super Bowls) in six years. It won't happen. You can chisel that sucker in stone."

There was a replay of the famous "Immaculate Reception" touchdown pass from Bradshaw to Franco Harris that enabled the Steelers to knock off the Oakland Raiders in the AFC playoff game in 1972, the first playoff appearance in the Steelers' 40-year history.

Steelers' announcer Jack Fleming offers the play-by-play call of one of the most famous plays in pro football history. "And Bradshaw is back and looking . . . Bradshaw runs out of the pocket . . . he's looking for someone to throw to. He fires it downfield. And there's a collision . . . it's caught out of the air . . . the ball is pulled in by Franco Harris . . . Harris is going for a touchdown for Pittsburgh. Harris is going for. . ." Viewers were expected to fill in the rest of that scenario at Three Rivers Stadium themselves.

Cut to Ann Devlin delivering the first of many incisive questions: "Do you owe Pittsburgh anything?"

"I don't owe them anything," Bradshaw said. "I don't want to be harsh and cold. Why am I such a focal point here? Why is it me?"

Bradshaw is reminded that he remains very big in the minds of the Steeler faithful, that he was still one of their favorites, despite his protests to the contrary.

"That's great," Bradshaw said. "I told them in my Hall of Fame speech. I love you, Pittsburgh. I don't want to live here, there's nothing for me to do here. There's nothing for me to go back to. They had the Hall of Fame thing at Three Rivers Stadium (during the 1989 season). But I felt uncomfortable going back and getting my Hall of Fame ring."

"Why?" interjected Devlin.

"I was scared to go back and get it. I was afraid of how I'd be treated. So I didn't go."

"Afraid of who?" Devlin came back.

"The people," Bradshaw said. "The fans. Because of the friction that we'd had with Chuck and I and the Steelers. I hadn't heard from Dan or nobody and Chuck. I felt uncomfortable. You see, I felt uncomfortable. If I'm uncomfortable, I won't go. The Steelers have not made me feel comfortable. Because I started doing the KDKA show and that really created a lot of problems."

"With them," asked Devlin, "and your old teammates?"

"Yeah, yeah. Then when I did the Hall of Fame speech and I didn't ask Chuck (to introduce him). Then Gerry Mullins and a few of the other guys started saying, you know, some things that were getting back to me.

"That's all it is. I felt I had to ask somebody, at that point, that I was close to. I couldn't have somebody I couldn't hug and shed a tear with." So Bradshaw selected sportscaster Verne Lundquist of CBS-TV to introduce him at the Hall of Fame.

"Verne and I are like brothers," Bradshaw said. "I asked my brother and he couldn't do it. I asked my dad and he couldn't do it. Mr. Rooney had passed away, and those are the people I could have asked.

"I thought about asking Mike Webster. I thought about asking John Stallworth. I thought about a lot of people. Then I just thought the best thing to do here . . . There were two people — Buddy Martin and Verne — I thought about. Buddy was going to write the book (on Bradshaw) and Verne and I were so close at CBS. I thought he would do a good job. He did a great job. It's not a slap at anybody. It's just I'm like a little animal. I tend to do things to protect myself — it's just natural."

Bradshaw was asked why he wasn't closer to the Steelers' organization. "Because I don't ever hear from the Steelers. You never hear from them. I never hear from Chuck. I didn't mean to turn my back on Pittsburgh. But life goes on."

But he seemed to be trying to pick a fight with Noll. Why? "I was just having fun with Chuck," Bradshaw said. "I was digging Chuck."

Why?

"Just to be mean . . . because I thought he was being mean. I thought he was insensitive."

Bradshaw was doing his best to be cool, but he looked uncomfortable, and kept rubbing his dimpled chin, and scratching the back of his neck.

"If Dan Rooney called you tomorrow. . .," began Devlin.

"What could he say?" interrupted Bradshaw before she could finish her question.

"He asked me at the Hall of Fame, 'When are you coming back?' And we both had a big laugh. That's the gospel."

Later, switching subjects, Devlin asked Bradshaw how he felt about Mean Joe Greene. "Love him," Bradshaw said. "Probably closer to him than anybody. He's a big ol' teddy bear. Tender heart. He always stood up for me. He was always there. He always supported me. Geez, I sound like I'm at the Academy Awards."

"What about Mike Webster?" said Devlin.

"He used to fart in my hands all the time," Bradshaw said of his center, getting a bleep from the censors at WTAE-TV. "Nah, we had no jerks on our football team. He didn't do that."

Devlin asked Bradshaw what it would take to get him back to Pittsburgh for a Steelers' game. "The only way I'd ever go back to Three Rivers Stadium," he said, "is if they have the entire Super Bowl team at halftime. I'll go back. I promise. On my word."

He was asked about his love-hate relationship with the fans. "In the beginning, I really did hate them," he said. "Near the end, it didn't matter. The last five or six years, the fans had no effect on me. They drink their Iron City beer; women fight the cops; they don't know how to dress and they talk funny. But they have a blast. Sometimes they blast the ballplayers. I guess they don't mean any harm."

He was asked if he thought Pittsburgh was a great sports town.

"I don't think Pittsburgh's a great sports town. A great sports town supports its teams whether they're winning or losing. Chicago's a great sports town; so is LA. They support their teams no matter how high they finish. Pittsburgh is a nice sports town. Nothing great about it."

Bradshaw was asked if he still pulls for the Pittsburgh Steelers.

"I pull for the Saints," he said. "I go back home. I grew up with the Saints. I haven't turned my back on Pittsburgh. My gift to you people was the four Super Bowls. We all gave that to you. What more do you want from me? I'm not going to live there. Isn't that enough? Let Bubby win one."

Ah, Bubby Brister. He, too, comes from Louisiana. He didn't succeed Bradshaw as the Steelers' quarterback, but he had operated in his long shadow. He had come up short of Bradshaw's standards, just like Cliff Stoudt and Mark Malone did. None of them has been Bradshaw.

Bruce Keidan, the sports columnist of the *Pittsburgh Post-Gazette* was jousting with a first-time caller to Keidan's sports talk show on WTAE Radio during the 1990 season. Keidan did this show on Wednesday, Thursday and Friday nights, while Myron Cope continued to do it on Monday and Tuesday. On these sports talk shows, people often call and say "Bradshaw" when they mean "Brister," and vice versa.

There's a lot of Bradshaw in Brister as far as his country twang, his boldness, his flair for cutting up, and saying the most outrageous things. But Brister is not Bradshaw.

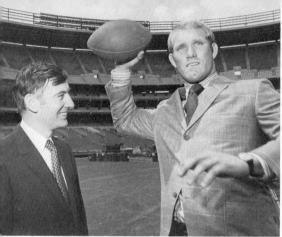

Dan Rooney with rookie Terry Bradshaw

With Joe Gilliam and Terry Hanratty

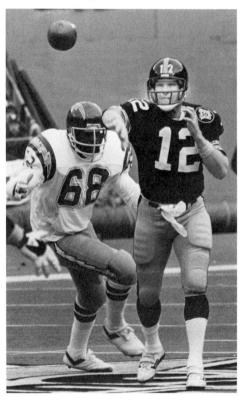

With Johnny Blood and Lynn Swann

Getting instructions from Chuck Noll

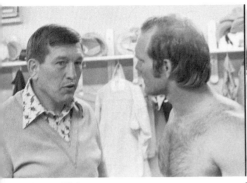

th Johnny Unitas

With Hanratty and Noll

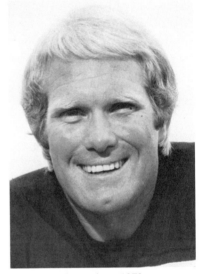

gratulating Gary Anderson

With hairpiece circa 1979

th Mark Malone and Cliff Stoudt

As CBS studio host 1991

"It's odious to compare Brister to Bradshaw," commented Keidan. "I'm doing Brister a disservice. Brister has a strong arm. Bradshaw had a rifle. Brister doesn't need to be as good as Bradshaw for the team to win. It's a different time, a different team. We shouldn't hold all quarterbacks up to the standard set by Bradshaw."

On May 28, 1990, Terry Bradshaw's No. 12 jersey was retired at Woodlawn High School in Shreveport, Louisiana. His red and blue No. 12 jersey had been retired in 1970 at Louisiana Tech.

"This is where it all began," Bradshaw said to the 3,000 students who gathered at an assembly. "This is where my dream to become a pro quarterback one day began.

"I dreamed I wanted to be in the NFL one day. And then I dreamed that I could, one day, maybe quarterback a team to the Super Bowl. And then I dreamed that, one day, I could help my team win the Super Bowl. All of those dreams have come true."

"If you knew Terry," Bradshaw wrote in his book, *Looking Deep,* which he did with sportswriter Buddy Martin, "you'd know he was just a big kid . . . At an early age, he saw that by being silly he could make people laugh. And he got a kick out of people enjoying his performances."

That is what Bradshaw did as a ballplayer, and that is what he has been doing ever since as a TV commentator. He was a big hit when he had his own show on KDKA-TV in Pittsburgh, and was an even bigger success when he became a member of the CBS "NFL Today" cast.

"Some people have it and some don't," said KDKA-TV's John Steigerwald. "And he has it. He just jumps through the screen at you."

For the 1990 season, Bradshaw was moved into the CBS studios for Sunday's "NFL Today" package, but seemed uncomfortable. He was better being where the action was — at the game sites.

Some of Bradshaw's problems with Pittsburgh and the Steelers started with some of the smart aleck comments he made about his former coach, Chuck Noll, especially on a weekly special he did during the football season on KDKA-TV in Pittsburgh.

He called Noll "a jerk" on one show — "a jerk who seems to have lost it all."

Later, Bradshaw felt badly about that remark, and tried to place the blame elsewhere. He said was he was told to be critical of the Steelers on the show, and to speak his mind.

In a more apologetic way, Bradshaw offered more double talk to try and make peace:

"I'd like to throw my arms around Chuck right now and tell him I love him, say to him, 'Thanks, you taught me how to play, how to read defenses, how to be tough, how to win. I love you.' But I'm not going to seek him out to say those things."

210

When Noll was asked what was bugging Bradshaw, and what was the source of the differences, Noll cut it off short. "There's nothing to patch up," he said. "Nothing will ever take away all of the good things that he did for the Steelers."

Dan Rooney responded similarly: "Terry was a great player and a rare talent. His enthusiasm and confidence were big factors in our success. We will always think of him as a Steeler."

Then, in defense of his coach, Rooney continued, "I know Chuck has had great players, but ask yourself, how many coaches have you seen that screw things up? A coach has an awful lot to do with the development of players. One of the things I'll always say is that Terry Bradshaw might have been the best physical quarterback that ever played, but if he had played for someone less demanding than Noll he might not have wound up being the player he was, a four-time Super Bowl champion and a Super Bowl MVP."

But Bradshaw didn't quit knocking Noll or Rooney on KDKA-TV. In late 1988, Bradshaw suggested strongly that Rooney get smart and realize he had to replace Noll as the coach. "I have to question his commitment — at the age of 56," Bradshaw said.

Bradshaw was frequently quoted criticizing his former coach. "Knowing how he treated us when we could no longer win football games for him still upsets me," said Bradshaw. He was angry about the way Noll had handled him, Franco Harris, Joe Greene and L.C. Greenwood when their careers came to an end.

Back in January of 1986, Bradshaw attacked Noll: "He just doesn't appreciate the people he had. That hurts. I wouldn't deal with my players like that. He pretends like we didn't exist. To kick Franco out, to kick L.C. out, and Joe Greene and myself — like we did not exist.

"People say to me, 'How can you forget?' Hey, no one was criticized more than I was. I haven't forgotten that."

The much-publicized conflict disturbed teammates and anybody else who had thrilled to the Steelers' successes.

"Terry was a big part of that team we played on in the '70s," Mike Webster said at the Steelers' reunion in 1990. "We achieved a lot together. My underlying hope is that one day Terry and Chuck can get together and resolve, uh, whatever differences they have had. It's very important because those two guys achieved a great deal together, and I want them both to be able to enjoy it."

Jack Ham had a hard time taking Bradshaw seriously about anything he might say. "Talk to him tomorrow, and he'll tell you something else," said Ham. "Sybil had fewer personalities than Bradshaw."

Players change their opinions as they get older and mature. Perspectives change. As young players, Ham and Franco Harris were often critical of Joe Paterno, their coach at Penn State. Gerry Mullins was critical of John McKay, his coach at the University of Southern California. Later in their careers, they all learned to appreciate their college coaches, and allied themselves with their former mentors in alumni or fund-raising activities.

When Bradshaw announced his retirement from the Steelers after the 1983 season, he certainly spoke from a different perspective. "It took a long time, but when we got to the mountaintop, it was glorious," Bradshaw said of his struggles-to-success story with the Steelers.

"We had so many great things happen for the city of Pittsburgh, which for so long had been a loser. It was great to not only play with a great football team, but to play a part in rebuilding the image of the city."

Bradshaw had set some impressive records for others to shoot at in the Steelers' record books.

Bradshaw ranked 9th on the NFL's all-time list with 212 touchdown passes, 12th in pass attempts with 3,901, 15th in completions with 2,025 and 13th in passing yards with 27,989. He was particularly productive in the playoffs, passing for 3,833 yards and 30 touchdowns in 19 post-season games.

During a TV interview in 1988, Bradshaw said if he were playing today, he would probably be making $3 to $3½ million." Since Joe Montana makes $4 million, Bradshaw might be doing even better than that. Looking back, Bradshaw was probably underpaid in Pittsburgh, but he's done OK for himself, and no one will have to hold any fund-raisers on his behalf.

When he was inducted into the Pro Football Hall of Fame Bradshaw said, "one of the things athletes never think about is how they'll feel when something like this happens in their life. As a child, I dreamed of being in the NFL. Once you get in the NFL, and once you realize that you are throwing for a lot of touchdowns and a lot of yards, and then you find out you'd kill to win a Super Bowl. Then you win a Super Bowl, and you say, 'Gosh, this is really good.' And everybody forgets about the bad years, the bad games and the bad stats. And then you win four, and nobody had ever done that before.

"Thank you, Franco Harris. Thank you, Rocky Bleier. Without you and the other guys, I couldn't have done it." Then, with a laugh, he added, "It'd be great now to put my hands under Mike Webster's butt one more time.

"I can remember the coin flip in 1970 between George Halas of the Bears and Art Rooney of the Steelers. I can laugh now, but back then I had no idea of what it meant to be the No. 1 draft choice in the NFL."

On another occasion, trying his best to be humble, Bradshaw said, "Anybody could have quarterbacked the Steelers and been a winner, and I'm being honest about that. I was a good quarterback . . . and at times I showed signs of brilliance. And at other times I gave people an upset stomach or a headache."

There were struggles at the start, when he was trying to find himself, and at the end of his career with the Steelers, when he tried his best to overcome a series of injuries to prolong his stay with the Steelers.

"The Steelers were very patient with me," Bradshaw said sometime between the beginning and the end.

Earlier in his Steelers' career, Bradshaw tried to sort out his difficulties. "I've sought and needed approval from everyone," he said. "I always wanted everyone to like me. I wanted the City of Pittsburgh to be proud of me. I really do need approval. I need it. I want it. I function better with it.

"My first few seasons, I used to count the number of people on my bandwagon every day. I had people call me a dummy and a hick. I had a lady stop me outside the stadium and tell me I stunk. I heard the people cheer when I got hurt. Rub up against enough briar patches and your hide will get pretty tough. Mine did."

Back then, he appreciated what his coach did for him. "Our coach, Chuck Noll, may be tense and all that," he said, "but he doesn't show it. Maybe that's why he's such a great coach."

Looking back, for instance, to the Steelers' first Super Bowl performance. "I remember the crowd noise just scared the daylights out of me, and that's all I could think about," Bradshaw said. Noll and some of his assistants had a knack for settling Bradshaw done before such big games.

His teammates believed in Bradshaw. Larry Brown, a soft-spoken giant of an offensive tackle, said, "It's going to be a long time, if ever, before a quarterback will come along to approach Bradshaw's greatness. He was a personality, a key to many things. Terry made things go. He did things on and off the field to help our team."

Bradshaw's career was interrupted in 1980 when he suffered a broken thumb, and then a broken hand sidelined him for much of 1981. He passed for 1,768 yards and 17 touchdowns during the strike-shortened 1982 campaign before suffering the elbow injury that eventually ended his career.

It is the early years, however, that stuck with Bradshaw the most, it seems, and they stuck in his craw.

"My rookie year was a disaster," he said. "I was totally unprepared for pro ball. I'd had no schooling on reading defenses. They'd never blitzed me, and I'd just run away. I had never studied the game, never looked at films the way a quarterback should.

"I had never been benched before. I'd never played on a team that had another quarterback besides me. I had no idea how important I was to the team. I'd never been to Pittsburgh, never even seen the Steelers play on television.

"We had another good quarterback in Terry Hanratty. He was an All-American at Notre Dame, and he was from Western Pennsylvania (nearby Butler, in fact). He related well with the other players. He had polish. He was one of the guys. And the people were pulling for him.

"I was an outsider who didn't mingle well. There were no cowboys on the team, no one who liked to fish or do the things I liked to do. The other players looked upon me as a Bible-toting Li'l Abner."

No sooner had Bradshaw put aside the challenge offered by Hanratty than another came along in the presence of a quarterback from Tennessee State named "Jefferson Street" Joe Gilliam. He was black and that became an issue.

Bradshaw said the low point of his career came in 1975 when he temporarily lost his starting job to Joe Gilliam. If that was not it, certainly it was the time he was booed in Pittsburgh after he had been injured and was being helped off the field. The fans were glad to see him out of the game.

Nowadays, Bradshaw doesn't like to look back on those days. "No, I don't drift back too far," he said. "If I drift, I drift back to the good times. I don't want to feed my brain all that bad stuff. I'm like an alcoholic — if you get off the damn sauce, you sure don't want another drink. Let that past lie, let it sleep."

Terry Bradshaw always had something to say. If you did not like what he had to say, several of his teammates have often said, come back an hour later and he will say something different.

Anyone checking back on Bradshaw will see statements that are completely contrary on subjects from one week to another, let alone one year to another, or one decade to another.

When he was more upbeat on the subject of the Steelers, and Chuck Noll and Dan Rooney, and his teammates, Bradshaw had a biography called "Terry Bradshaw: Man of Steel." It was published by Zondervan Publishing House of Grand Rapids, Michigan, which also prints Bibles, and his book was a guide-to-better-living book. It is important to reflect back on what he said then just to keep a balanced scoreboard.

"I'm convinced that a team of good characters — and by that I mean a bunch of guys who are morally sound and who really care about each other — will win the close games and come through in the clutch and perform well under adverse circumstances. Basically, I think that's the makeup of our team."

Bradshaw was smart enough to know that was not the generally-accepted public perception of the Steelers, especially outside of Pittsburgh.

"They see the Steelers as a bunch of rowdy, tough-talking guys who take pleasure in beating up on other people once a week from September to December and, it is hoped, on into the month of January."

When Bradshaw would introduce his religious beliefs into any of his pre-game or post-game thoughts, some sportswriters would tell him to skip that stuff. But in his book, Bradshaw could say whatever struck his fancy.

"Maybe I'm a little old-fashioned," he wrote back in 1979, "and maybe a bit square, like if families were doing things together instead of flying off in a hundred different directions, we'd have a lot fewer problems, not only in the home, but around the world.

"Peace of mind — that's what it's all about. Thank God I was raised in a good Christian home with lots of love, where people cared about one another, about what happens to each other, where to good times and the bad times are shared by every member of the family."

Some strong-armed pitchers last longer than others. On May 8, 1991, Nolan Ryan of the Houston Astros, at age 44, pitched the seventh no-hitter of his baseball career. On that same May day, another 44-year-old right-handed thrower, Terry Bradshaw, seven years retired, gave a motivational talk at the American Business Press convention in Naples, Florida.

Speaking in an animated fashion at the Ritz Carlton Hotel, Bradshaw, said, "Everything in your life will end. . . will kind of fade away. It comes. It goes. Then you sit back. You've got the memories.

"My success came from hard work and overcoming adversity. Folks, you don't know what it's like having your name on the front page talking about how dumb you are."

Bradshaw smiled at his own remark, and used it to make a point. "If you can smile at somebody, you can change them and if you touch them you win them over.

"I had to get in a huddle with 10 huge men. Massive, huge, crazy human beings. I had to manage these guys. I had to lead these men. . . I had to stimulate and motivate 10 brain-dead, steroid-crazed men. . . If I had to call a play, I found the best way to sell a play was with my face. I could convince them by smiling that this was a great play.

"I'm telling you, until you've been to the Rose Bowl (site of Super Bowl XIV), until you've gone down into a huddle, until you've heard that crowd roar, until you've had your name introduced on the loudspeaker, until you've run out and seen the Terrible Towel waving and the pompons going and you've seen your mom and dad in the stands.

"Until you've looked into the TV cameras, until you've talked to reporters, until you've experienced that moment before the big game and put on those pads and that jersey and strapped on those shoulder pads and heard that Knute Rockne speech and got up and talked to yourself and sat there and thought and concentrated and gone over a game plan.

"Until you've heard the roar of the crowd, until you've pulled up in a bus and felt your stomach going inside out, until the hair on your back not on your head, because there's not much up there, crawls up and down your spine, you have no earthly idea what it feels like.

"It's overpowering. It is overwhelming. I loved playing pro football. I loved it. It was in my heart and soul and my mind. I lived it, breathed it. I loved it with all my fiber.

"Let me hear my name called out one more time. . . Let me look over at the sidelines and see Chuck Noll. Let me see Arthur J. Rooney, now in heaven. . . Let me get back in my arena where I'm comfortable. Put me back on a football field."

Dwayne Woodruff

Mike Fabus

Dwayne Woodruff
Working the graveyard shift

Dwayne Woodruff was waiting for me in his room at Bonaventure Hall, following a morning practice and lunch during the 1990 summer training camp at St. Vincent College. The door to Room 244 was closed, so I knocked on it, and Woodruff hollered to come in. He was lying on one of the two beds he had pushed together to form a king-size sleeping area, and he was talking on the telephone to his wife. He motioned to me to pull up a chair.

The television was on, and so was a large fan. He turned off the television with a remote control device as soon as I sat down, but he continued talking on the telephone. I checked out his surroundings. The room was sparsely furnished, part of a student dormitory during the school year. It looked, perhaps by design, like a monk's cell.

His room was located at the base of a steep hill. Through the windows you could see a graveyard. The top of the hill, about 40 yards from Woodruff's windows, was lined with black Benedictine crosses, marking the graves of hundreds of Benedictine monks — priests and brothers — and it provided an eerie edging to the horizon. There were bits of blue sky and the boughs of green trees filling the top of the windows.

"I don't think anyone in the NFL has a training camp quite like ours," said Woodruff when he set the phone aside, and turned to talk to his visitor. "We're not a team that makes many changes. I've been looking at that graveyard for 12 years. I can visualize that picture anywhere I am, seeing that cemetery . . . running down the hills to football practice . . . the whole scene here. It would be a shock to be anywhere else.

"There are a lot of funny stories about that cemetery. I never looked at it as being eerie. Maybe it's there to keep the evil spirits from us."

This was Woodruff's 12th summer at St. Vincent College, the summer camp of 1990, but he had spent the first of those summers in a room — Room No. 251 — on the other side of the building. It has a different view, one of the practice fields and the field house and other brick buildings on the campus. That room faces the playing fields and the afternoon sun, on what the players call the "hot side" of the building. Now, as an elder statesman on the team, he rated his own room on the "cool side" of the building, protected from the sun by a hillside, lots of trees and those tombstones. As a rookie, he hadn't brought an electric fan. He did not know any better back then.

Some things had changed. The phone he had been talking on was a cordless model, for example, and he stuffed the antenna before he began to talk. He not only had a television set, but he could switch channels from the comfort of his beds. But he was 33 now, not 22. He had three children, not one. He had a wisdom, which comes to some with age. He had a Super Bowl ring, which he picked up at the end of his first season with the Steelers, and he had a law degree from Duquesne

University, which he picked up while moonlighting at law school during his latter seasons with the Steelers. He was now a practicing attorney for Meyer, Darragh, Buckler, Bebenek, Eck & Hall in Pittsburgh. But he was not ready to be a full-time attorney.

He wanted to stick with the Steelers, at least for one more season. Nothing had changed in that respect. As a rookie, he did not know where he stood with the Steelers. As the lone link to the Steelers' Super Bowl years, as a former team MVP, as a returning starter, he still did not know where he stood with the Steelers, or in the scheme of things with Chuck Noll and his plans for a different decade. Joy and their daughters, Jillian and Jenyce, and son, John, would still have a Steeler in the family for whom they could root.

"It's no different than any other year," said Woodruff. "As for the way I approach it, I still approach it the same way. I don't say, well, if I don't make it I can become a full-time attorney. The other career is something that's out there for me. But I can't think about it now. I can't use it as another pillow. It's always the same: you put all your energies into it, and give it your best shot."

Woodruff had to wonder where he stood with the Steelers. During the previous spring, he had not been protected in the Class B free agent draft. They protected 37 players, but he was not one of them. Wasn't he good enough? But that had been done the year before, too, and the Steelers retained him and he even started at his left cornerback position in his 11th pro season. The Steelers, in a sense, were playing a game, making sure they protected certain younger players with potential, while gambling that no other team would want Woodruff at his age and salary.

Woodruff had been offended and had been angry about the Steelers leaving him up for grabs. "I think I deserved better than that," he said of the slight when he spoke to a class of students in the Sport Management Program at Robert Morris College during the off-season. "The Steelers have always preached about loyalty, but I think it's a two-way street." For the record, it was the Steelers who had the connections to get him into Duquesne's Law School and into the local law firm. He was advised not to get into a feud with his employers. It was not in his best long-range interests.

So he was back at St. Vincent College for his 12th summer stay — he had missed the entire 1986 campaign with a knee injury he suffered in a pre-season game at Dallas — and he was relaxing. At least that had been his original intention.

We talked a little about that first year with the Steelers, about his family, about his friends, about former and present teammates, about special insights he had gained during his long stay with the Steelers, about his coaches, about his current status, shaky as it was, and Woodruff was able to smile through most of his stories, even the tragedies that have challenged him from the start. There is a warmth about Woodruff that makes anybody comfortable with him. It had been that way from the start.

"You learn persistence, patience and dedication," said Woodruff. "You become a lot closer to the Lord. Even though you have those ups and downs, I still believe I've been blessed. The lows have been very low, and the highs have been very high. You learn to survive. Thank God for that."

Back in 1979, we were both in our first year with the Steelers at St. Vincent College. In those days, he left his door open. "You always want to know who's at the door," said Woodruff in the way of explanation that first day we met. Only the day before, his roommate, a defensive end from Syracuse University named Bernard Winters, was put on waivers.

Woodruff wondered then whether the caller would be "The Turk," maybe a field manager or ball boy who would be assigned to go tell players to report to Bill Nunn Jr., the camp director, who would tell them they had been cut from the squad. "The Turk" was thought to wield a huge sword, with which he cut off your head, figuratively speaking.

Woodruff was a sixth round draft choice, the 161st player taken in the draft. "Just being in camp is exciting," Woodruff said back then. "Like Lynn Swann comes in, and all these old pros here, all the people I used to watch on TV. And all of a sudden, here I am trying to make the same team. You have to say, 'Hey, this is for real, you're finally here.'" He didn't come with the greatest credentials. "Louisville isn't Alabama," he said.

There were some problems back home, and Woodruff was willing to share his concerns. His father, who had been a career man in the U.S. Army, was confined to a wheelchair. His mother was not feeling well. Woodruff would later learn that she was stricken with stomach cancer.

Dwayne had gotten married after his junior year at Louisville and he and his wife, Joy, were the parents of a 10-month-old daughter named Jillian.

Reflecting on his father, Woodruff said, "He was a tanker and he played on the camp football teams. When he got back from Vietnam he got sick. They found a ruptured disc in the back of his neck; they're not sure if he got it from playing football or from being in those tanks.

"He's slightly paralyzed; he can't walk. He played halfback and wide receiver in high school in Temple, Texas. That's Joe Greene's hometown. He knows Joe's oldest brother. They all went to Dunbar High School."

Coming from the University of Louisville linked Woodruff with another former Steeler, or near-Steeler. "One of the coaches told me when I got here, 'We only ever had one other player from the University of Louisville and that was Johnny Unitas. And we cut him! We want to make sure we don't make the same mistake twice.' I thought, geez, they cut Unitas and he turned out to be a Hall of Famer. Everybody at Louisville was aware of Johnny Unitas. We had a building named after him on the campus. And the Steelers cut him. It made me wonder and worry," Woodruff said.

Woodruff was in his room playing solitaire that first day we met. He was asked to reflect back on that first camp.

"I had been red-shirted while I was at Louisville and I had another year of eligibility when I was drafted," he said. "They told me at Louisville I could go to grad school and play football. But we were married and had a child, and it was not a difficult decision to make, once I got drafted, that I should go to the NFL.

"But, from the start, I was homesick. I'd been in college and away from home so long, to begin with. I had gotten so used to being with my Joy and Jillian. I didn't like being away from them. We didn't have much time for a honeymoon. We didn't have the time to get away together. There were so many school demands. But I think the way it started off helped us pull together.

"I was playing all the positions, the corners and the safety slots. Mel Blount was established at the right corner. Ron Johnson and Larry Anderson were both in their second year. Tony Dungy and J.T. Thomas and Donnie Shell and Mike Wagner and Ray Oldham were all here. It was an interesting group, some real characters.

"Mel was the oldest guy in the defensive backfield. He was not a rah, rah kind of guy. He had the same kind of temperament I had. He settled you down. He'd say, 'Just relax. Forget the last play. Just remember what you did right or wrong.' The majority of the people on that team, the veterans, were willing to answer any questions you might have. J.T. rambled on all the time, and you had to say, 'OK, J.T., I have it; that's enough.'

"You want to be the best you can be, and you want to beat out the best possible player. So you helped the competition. Then when you beat him out you knew you had beat him out at his absolute best. It's still like that."

Woodruff was asked if he gave much thought to just how great the Steelers surrounding him were in those days. After all, they had won the Super Bowl the year before, and had won three Super Bowls altogether the previous five years. "I think about it more now than I did then," he answered. "Then I was more concerned with making the team.

"It was more than being a part of the Steelers and all those great legends of the game. You had the opportunity to play with some great players. I'll be old and gray and telling some great stories about those guys, but I haven't had the time to sit back and think much about it. It will be fun.

"I knew I was fortunate then. I had the opportunity to play on a great football team with some great players. It was a matter of being in the right place at the right time."

He remembers being befriended by a woman named Myrd Milowicki and some of her girlfriends, all housewives in Westmoreland County, who brought their children to camp almost daily to watch practice.

"I guess they just adopted us," said Woodruff. "I came into camp and they were there, from the first day. Everyone on the team knew who they were. I was walking by them one day, and I was tired, and

I had my head down, and they hollered out to me, 'You're going to make the football team. You don't have anything to worry about.' And I said to someone on the team, 'Who are these ladies?'

"Joy came up to camp one day. It had been raining. And she wasn't dressed for a rainy day. Her heels kept sinking into the ground on the field, so she went up to the sidewalk, and Myrd and her friends spotted her in the crowd. We were new in town, but they just took her in and she stayed at Myrd's house for a couple of days. I'd stay there when we'd get a night off. That just showed me they were special people. It would be a funny feeling if they weren't here.

"They invited us into their home. They didn't really know us. Myrd had a daughter named Becky and she was just a little tyke when we first came here. We watched her grow up year after year. She was part of the family. She got killed in an automobile accident last year. It's difficult for all of us that she's gone. We'd gone through tragedies in our immediate family — with both of my parents dying — and Myrd had become part of our family. It was difficult for her."

What was never difficult for Myrd was becoming close with the Woodruffs. "I don't see different color," she said during the summer in 1990, sitting in her usual place between the dining hall and the dormitory. "I just see good people."

Woodruff needed all the support he could find that first year. He just had so many doubts, so many disappointments, and he magnified them, like most rookies. "I was lonely and I'd stay right here in my room most nights," he said. "We were still in two-a-days (practice sessions in the morning and afternoon). I was dead tired. My rookie year was tough. My hamstrings were sore, my groin was sore. I was like a walking mummy out there, but I had to keep going. There were so many people at our practices, but I tried not to get caught up in the commotion over the team. I just wanted to make the squad.

"You have so many questions. You always have questions. That first year they kept seven defensive backs. There were four or five Pro Bowlers on the defensive unit, and they'd just won the Super Bowl the year before, and you ask, 'What the hell am I doing here?'

"Every so often, we'd get some guys and go down to Bobby Del's Bar, or the 19th Hole, and we'd get a couple of beers. We'd come back and I'd get on the phone a lot. I'd talk to Joy. She'd hear me complaining about all my aches and pains and tell me to come on home. 'I'll take care of you.' Then I'd call my dad. He was the opposite. 'I've been through that. You hang in there. You stick it out.' I'd hang up and go to sleep. I'd always have to call him after I talked to Joy. Now I usually talk to her more, and Joy says, 'Hey, it's tough for everybody. You have to stick in there.' She calls it tough love."

Those two also had a positive influence on Woodruff when it came time to undertake law school studies at Duquesne University a few years back. "The Rooneys and the organization were all behind me," he said. "Dan Rooney wrote a letter to the school for me. I didn't go that year, but I enrolled the following year. Being an attorney was something I had been intrigued with for a number of years.

"My father and Joy were my two greatest influences. My dad said, 'You have a family and you need to prepare yourself for the future, to be able to take care of your family. You can't play football forever.' Joy told me I could do it if I wanted to. I got yesses from both of them."

Woodruff remembers another strong presence in his pro football life, that of Joe Greene. "I was only here a few weeks, just before training camp would be over. And I already knew we'd be going to the Super Bowl. Joe Greene would say things that made you feel that way. We had the players we wanted, there was no concern about the offense or the defense. All that was set. We just had to wait to get to the first game and get going. It was already a formality that we'd be in the Super Bowl. It's just something that grows.

"Joe Greene had that good presence. He was special for the team. I would go for days just saying hello, but I didn't think he really knew me. I remember we had just finished the regular season and we were getting ready to go into the playoffs. He came by and said, 'Woody, now you're going to see some real football.' I was wondering what I'd been seeing for 14 games. I knew that instant we were going to win the Super Bowl. He didn't just say that. He never said anything just to say it. It was always well thought out.

"You could be in a room with a hundred people and you'd be thinking of what to say and you'd just shut up when Joe Greene got up. He commanded that kind of respect.

"Athletes are different from people who aren't involved in athletics. They know that they're good. Some players come here wondering why they're here. They don't stay long. The ones who stay know they're good. They observe different things, and learn what they have to do. They've always been that way.

"In the middle of my career here, I hurt my knee, and they drafted two or three defensive backs in the early rounds right after that. In the last few years, you don't have the good moves you had, the speed, but you're smarter and you wonder how long you can last and be effective."

After all these years, and seeing some special friends leave the franchise, Woodruff knows there will not be any special treatment as far as staying with the Steelers.

Asked about his coach, he replied, "The relationship that Chuck and I have has always been the same. It's a player-coach relationship. Period.

"Athletes, at least the older ones, don't have any trouble with that. The younger ones, or the quarterbacks and kickers — they're more emotional — have a different feeling about that. I look at Chuck as a person and as a coach. I don't expect anything else from him. We don't have a problem at all.

"Any comments that are said have been some things that have been said before, or after games. We get along just as good now as we ever did."

Asked if Noll ever surprised him, he said:

"Never. But I really think Chuck is different outside the game.

I think Chuck will sit down and talk to you. From what you see here and at the stadium, you'd think he didn't have any friends. That's not true. Outside the game, he has his own friends. In my mind, Chuck is like some of my old high school coaches. They put things in their proper place. It's all football here, and you have your family life there, and your social life there, and you don't mix them up. That's why he's here.

"He stays at the same level from the beginning of the season till the end of the season. And he wants his players to do the same. He wants to get you to a level. He's not going to get high when you're good and go the other way when you lose. He's the same every football game. He wants you to know what's expected. He doesn't want any surprises.

"When you can get all these people together to think the same thing, that's a real talent. It's very rare that you can get people to all want the same thing. It's something that grows.

"We talk more about the team and the way things are now. I don't talk about the way the team used to be. We talk about the way it is and the way it's going to be.

"History has a way of repeating itself. For this team to get back on that level, which I talk about sometimes, you have to grow up as a person."

Does he find himself sounding like Blount when he talks to the younger players these days?

"I'll say things he said. I find myself repeating what he told me."

When it's over, will Woodruff have any problems with getting on with his life's work?

"I think a lot of players think of still playing the game. They don't want to let go of it. That's a tough way to feel. If you don't let go of the past and you don't move forward you've got a problem. You have to untie that rope and keep going. You move forward. You can't sit back and think about the past."

Does he ever find himself standing on the walkway above the practice fields, on a foggy morning or evening, when there is a surrealistic look to the place, like it has been airbrushed, and reflecting on the first days of training camp, when he saw all those great Steelers coming out of the locker room in a single file on Photo Day? One great player after another. Do they ever reappear for him on that field? Like the great baseball players of the past appeared out of nowhere in the movie "Field of Dreams"?

Woodruff smiled. "No, they don't," he said, "When I look out there and see that, I'll know my playing days will be over."

Mel Blount

Mike Fabus

Mel Blount
Mr. Mel and his boys

Mel Blount may have been the most impressive physical specimen of all the Steelers in their glory days, unless you hold out for Joe Greene, who was his roommate at St. Vincent. Theirs was a formidable room that drew respect from the rest of the tenants.

Blount (pronounced Blunt), at 42, and seven years away from playing cornerback for the Steelers, remained a formidable figure, especially the way he appeared as I approached him on his horse and cattle farm in Taylortown, Pa., a rural community just outside Washington, about 35 miles south of Pittsburgh on the way to Wheeling, West Virginia.

He looked like a longrider. Always one of the tallest of the Steelers, at 6-3, and among its sleekest, at 205 pounds, with a 33-inch waist, he looked even taller, standing in front of a white barn that was being renovated by workmen.

Blount wore a spotless, stiff beige cowboy hat atop his always clean shaven skull, and a long black dust-stained coat with a cape that made his broad shoulders even broader, and reached clear down to his mud-covered boots. He wore spurs on his boots, and riding chaps or leggings atop his freshly-laundered and pressed blue jeans. He had on a black and red checked flannel shirt. He looked like a larger-than-life version of Lou Gossett, Jr., like something right out of a movie. You could provide your own appropriate background music.

Blount has always carried himself like a proud show horse. Blount is still a blue-ribbon champion.

You wouldn't want to mess with Mel Blount, everybody always said on the Steelers' set, and the advice was still merited. But Blount, at heart, is a peaceful man, when out of uniform and removed from the football field, not looking to hurt anyone. Just the opposite of his image. He is a Baptist who always knew his Bible as well as his playbook. "I think people miscategorized a lot of us, especially the black guys," Blount offered early in our conversation. "I think we were better and smarter people than we were given credit for."

His own coach, Chuck Noll, had once included Blount in testimony he offered in a California court case as a member of the "NFL's criminal element" for the hell-bent destructive way he played the game. Blount was a tough customer, no doubt about it. When I worked in New York during nine years of the Steelers' dominant decade in pro football, I viewed Blount as a thug. The Steelers, like their arch rivals, the Oakland Raiders, all seemed like dirty ballplayers from a distance.

Once I came home to cover the Steelers' beat for *The Pittsburgh Press* in 1979, however, Blount became one of my favorite Steelers. There is a strength, a sensitivity, a kindness, a respect for his fellow men and women, a strong religious bent, a desire to do something worthwhile with his life, that again sets Blount apart from the pack. He is a load, all right, sent special delivery from someplace special. I am biased about Mel Blount.

"You always did like me," he said with an even smile.

This was a late October day in 1990, when there was frost on the pumpkins that had been put out on the nearby porches of mostly white frame houses in preparation for Halloween. Blount seemed to draw strength from the briskness in the air. It only chilled me.

"I'm glad I don't have to work outdoors," I said. "I had my fill of this kind of weather when I was in the Army in Alaska."

He smiled when a workman turned off a power drill and said, "It feels like snow's in the air."

Blount seemed happy at the Mel Blount Youth Home he had established less than two years earlier, a hostel for troubled kids who need a place and respite to help them get their acts together, so they can get on with the rest of their lives.

There were five young boys, all from different communities in Pittsburgh, in residence when I visited. They were from Homewood, Westgate, East Liberty, Wilkinsburg and the Hill. Two more were to come the following week, Blount said, and there would be room for an eighth youngster. They were housed in a beautiful brand-new pre-fab log cabin. Two similar structures were under construction nearby. "These are built to last," boasted Blount, knocking on wood.

Each cabin can accommodate eight boys comfortably, and 24 will be the maximum, for the time being anyhow, for the enrollment at the Mel Blount Youth Home.

Blount showed me their rooms. The boys had made their beds, something they are expected to do each day. There are two beds to a room. Each boy has his own chest of drawers, a closet, a desk, a small bulletin board for notes and family photos — they do get homesick — and a bathroom for each four-bed unit. Everything was neat.

There are chore assignment lists, anti-drug messages and house rules posted on a larger community bulletin board. The first house rule is: no lying, cheating or stealing. The second is: no fighting. The third: no arguing or verbal abuse. It goes on like that. Blount seems to command their earnest attention. "We're not here to baby-sit them," he said. "They have to learn to look out for themselves."

He showed off a recreation room, and another room soon to be turned into a weight room, talked about a gymnasium that was on the drawing boards, pointed out an area where a golf driving range will be established, and took me to an area where a half dozen IBM computers and accompanying software were set up.

"Everything we need to do for kids," said Blount, "we can do fine right here."

The boys were involved in a classroom discussion when I was escorted into their domain. They had just read a poem about Jesse Owens, the Olympic track legend. Denitia Blount, the wife of Blount's 24-year-old son, Norris, was teaching the children. She and her husband are both graduates of Baylor University. Norris was busy with chores elsewhere on the farm. They have two children, Natasha, four years old at the time, and Tyler Nicole, eight weeks. Mel Blount is a grandfather. Oh, my.

The boys in residence sprang out of their seats, in turn, and introduced themselves. They had a spark, a gleam in their eyes. "We teach them to greet a person by looking in their eyes, and don't be looking like you're guilty," said Blount. The boys all address their host as "Mr. Mel," and everybody else as "sir" and as "ma'am." Mel will make southern gentlemen out of all of them.

Blount was the youngest of 11 children in a "typical southern farm family" back home near Vidalia, Georgia, where they grow those sweet onions, about 100 miles from Atlanta. Until late in his playing career, he had always gone home to the farm, to ride his horses, to be in the southern sun he felt was conducive to better workouts.

His grandfather, a former slave, had pieced together a 2,600-acre spread, assembling the realty at 50 cents per acre. Blount's family still looks after the farm.

He has had another youth home for several years back in Vidalia as well, and pays an occasional visit to check on things there, and with his family.

For six years, between the time he retired from playing for the Steelers and shortly after he was inducted into the Pro Football Hall of Fame, he had worked in player relations for the National Football League, visiting regularly with all the teams and talking to the players, trying to present a blueprint for personal success, and proper conduct on and off the field. He represented the league at many functions, both at home and abroad. He was a tremendous goodwill ambassador, and he always drew respectful attention — from ballplayers and businessmen. But he backed off that full-time assignment, and now takes his pick of promotional appearances from NFL headquarters. "Now I have the best of both worlds," he said. "This is such a big project. I had to focus more on this."

NFL Commissioner Paul Tagliabue paid a visit to Blount's farm before the 1990 season, and was impressed. "We want to be good citizens and good role models to instill in our young people how important it is to be productive," said Tagliabue. The commissioner's wife would later send each of the boys a dictionary for their desks.

"It has impressed me to see what Mel is doing here," said Tagliabue.

With his body and handsome countenance, Blount always looked better than most men in a business suit. But he always felt a little out of place in downtown Pittsburgh or midtown Manhattan. The skyscrapers stifled him, the sidewalks were too hard and too hot. "I had on my business suit, but I still wore my cowboy hat and cowboy boots, and I was still a cowboy," he reflected. He felt a little like TV's McCloud in the big city. "But I was still myself. I'm comfortable with myself."

He prefers the pace, the sounds and smells — yes, the rich smells — of the farm. "Here, I can be an honest cowboy. A farm brings you back to earth. It smells good." It brought to mind a visit I had made many years before to Kansas State University in Manhattan to interview a quarterback named Lynn Dickey for *Sport* magazine. I was driving by a corral when I smelled something. "That's not manure you smell," said our guide, "that's money you smell."

Blount thought about what he had said, and added, "I could stay on the farm for years and be happy. I have no hangups, no bitterness, no hunger for anything else. I learned how to adjust from being a cornerback in the NFL. I can make adjustments on the run, at full speed. I don't have any hangups. Nothing that's happened in my life that I'm ashamed of."

Now Blount was sitting behind the wheel of a Ford Bronco II, a four-wheel drive van. It was black with gold lettering on the door. What other colors would you expect? The license plate read "MBYH 47." That's for the name of his place and the number he wore proudly during his 14 seasons with the Steelers.

Blount allowed his Bronco II to idle at the top of the hill, overlooking the 246-acre spread in a Christmas card-like bucolic setting.

From this viewpoint, the dark rail fences that had been erected outlined various segments of the farm, from the riding arena just to the left of the barn at the bottom of the hill, an area where black angus graze directly behind the dormitories — the boys can look out their windows and watch them — and the boundaries near the roads. Everything seemed in place. To the right, you could see the Buffalo-Blaine Elementary School, and you could hear the boisterous, high-spirited voices of children in the playground at lunch break. "That's one of the things they tried to use not to allow us to locate our boys home here," said Blount. "They thought we were too close to their school."

Such obstacles were overcome, however, and now his teachers and counselors use the same curriculum as the McGuffey School District, which monitors the classroom efforts of the Mel Blount Youth Home.

Horses were running about, and Mel said there were eight of them, his own, which he had brought there from his farm in Georgia. He loved to ride horses, and so did the kids. Blount has won riding championships, and likens the thrill to winning the Super Bowl.

"The kids love all these animals," he said. "That's probably one of the biggest therapeutic aspects of the program here. There's something about kids and animals that just click. Animals can sense love and these kids are so innocent. It's good therapy for the kids. They love these horses. They're always after me to let them ride them.

"Everything out here is designed for the kids. This can be a life-long experience for them, something they can take with them when they leave. They're here for a half year to a year, and they can build on it for the rest of their lives."

To me, his spread seemed big, but he said, "This is small. My family's place in Georgia is nearly 3,000 acres." He pointed out where his workers — there were nine workers on the staff — had harvested three acres of sweet corn over the summer. "We sold that to Giant Eagle," he said. "We are developing things here, like produce and the cattle, and some other things, that will be revenue producers to eventually help support the place."

There is natural spring water on the farm that fills a tub that the horses drink from. There are natural gas pumps about the fields. The water belongs to Blount. The gas belongs to Pennzoil. "They have the mineral rights on all these farms out here," said Blount. I smiled because I had bought a quart of Pennzoil oil at a service station just down the road at the crossroads between Prosperity and Taylortown.

Only a few days earlier, a fire had broken out in a coal mine in that same Washington County area, spewing out dangerous fumes and smoke into the atmosphere. It took nearly a week to get that under control. To the 400 miners who lost their jobs, the place seemed like hell. To Blount, it was still heaven.

"I'm convinced that God brought me to this place, and I'll tell you why," continued Blount. "After I had been named to the Pro Football Hall of Fame, I appeared on the Ann Devlin TV show here on WTAE. When she was introducing me, she was talking about all the Super Bowls and Pro Bowls I'd been in, and going on about my accomplishments and that stuff, and she posed this question: 'Where do you go from here?'

"I told her I'd been looking for a place in Washington County to start a boys' home, but that I hadn't found what I was looking for yet.

"I told her the Hall of Fame gave me a great platform to work from and I wanted to help young boys. The show was on right before I went to Hawaii to be introduced with the new Hall of Fame class at halftime of the Pro Bowl.

"The guy who owned this place — he's about 70 some years old — started calling me at the Steelers' office while I was away. When I came back, he and I got together. We had breakfast one morning at King's in Bridgeville, and then I came out here to see the place. It was a bit rundown, but I could see what I could do here. I knew it was made in heaven.

"He wanted $450,000 for it, and I told him he had a deal. I didn't have any real money at the time. I hadn't even begun a fund-raising effort for the home. I gave him $5,000 hand money. I had to have $95,000 more at the closing.

"The Youth Home didn't have a penny then. But I had enough faith in myself and the Lord. I knew I was doing God's work. He's just using me. I'm just a tool. We have Bible study here every Thursday night. Last night, we had Rev. Hollis Halft here. Do you remember him?

"He used to conduct prayer meetings and Bible study sessions for the players when I was with the Steelers."

Not many people were aware of it, but when the Steelers were winning all those Super Bowls about half the squad used to regularly get together for religious purposes. "Rev. Hollis was talking about Solomon and his Book of Proverbs last night. He was talking about wisdom. Wisdom is what you need to succeed in life. That's why this place is so important."

Pro Bowlers in Hawaii in 1980 include (left to right, kneeling) Donnie Shell, Mike Webster and John Stallworth, (standing) Franco Harris, Joe Greene, unidentified hostess, Jack Lambert, Mel Blount and L.C. Greenwood.

All-time interception leaders Jack Butler and Mel Blount

Blount bought the property on Feb. 29, 1989. "We had no money only a few weeks before that," he recalled. "But Bill Blair came to the rescue. Bill Blair owns Mountaineer Park, the race track which used to be Wheeling Downs, and he knew I loved horses, and he liked my profile as a former Steeler, and we struck a deal for me to be a spokesman for the track. It takes me an hour to get there from here. I got a $200,000 signing bonus to work for him. So I was able to lend more money to the Youth Home to get this thing going.

"I had no money when I said I'd take this place, but I had a vision. We have a goal — to raise $2.4 million — and we're getting some great support. As soon as I got here, I knew I had been led to this place.

"You sit up here at night and it's like being on a mountain and you can see all those lights in the village. Just little lights. Taylortown has a tiny downtown, so to speak. I tell people that this is my Mt. Washington. It's a wonderful view."

To get to Taylortown, you head west coming out of downtown Pittsburgh. You pass through the Fort Pitt Tunnel and take the Parkway West to I-79 South, following the signs to Washington, or what has always been called Little Washington. It is about a 35-mile trip to Taylortown.

You go by Bridgeville, the exit Chuck Noll could take to his home in Upper St. Clair, about ten miles out of the city. Then you pass Canonsburg, the hometown of long-time popular singers Perry Como and Bobby Vinton and the Sarris Candies chocolate store where their framed autographed photos can be found on display.

There had been a commotion in Pittsburgh only a week earlier involving Vinton. He had come home and sung the National Anthem — at least, that was the idea — during the National League championship series between the Pirates and the Cincinnati Reds. But he forgot some of the lyrics.

CBS broadcaster Jack Buck, just having a little fun, said on the air, "I guess if you're Polish and you're from Pittsburgh you can sing the National Anthem any way you like." Buck, whose wife is Polish, laughed at his own Polish joke.

Sophie Masloff, the mayor of Pittsburgh, the city council and the Polish Falcons all blasted Buck in the media, and demanded a public apology for his remark, which they thought inappropriate and racist in nature. Other Pittsburghers felt it was much ado about nothing.

Next came an exit to Houston or Eighty Four, thought to have been named after a mail stop on the local railroad. Take your choice. Then came the Meadowlands, a breeding farm and harness racing track developed by legendary harness racing great Del Miller and his friends, Ed Ryan and Joe Hardy.

Then you take 70 West, toward Wheeling, and you see signs for Washington & Jefferson College and for Jessop Steel. There is also Millcraft Industries. It is still a steel town that is coming back from hard times, just like Pittsburgh. You get off 70 West at Exit 4, and turn right at the first stop sign. If you turn left, interestingly enough, you will go into a town called Prosperity. Blount told me to look for the dark fences that border his property. They set the place apart from the rest of the countryside.

I noticed some cows and a stream to my left, mail boxes and similarly-sized boxes for copies of the *Washington Observer-Reporter*, the county daily, and then an entrance, a magnificent entrance to the Mel Blount Youth Home, big black letters on a bright new white wall heralding the facility.

It took me about 50 minutes to get to Blount's place. It took Blount a lot longer to get there. Taylortown is in Buffalo Township, and some of the people there did not take too kindly to having a black man, Steelers' star or no Steelers' star, four Super Bowl rings or no Super Bowl rings, bringing misbehaving black kids into their peaceful community.

Objections were raised at community meetings, and there were months of public debate about the issue. Blount won out, but at a high price. Soon after he and his staff moved in, there had been racially-motivated violence by some of the area's white neighbors. There had been trouble.

"We feel that's basically behind us," Blount said, hopefully, of the gunshots, attempted arson and other shows of hostility by neighbors. The Klu Klux Klan had come and gone, leaving burning crosses behind them.

It reminded us of a statement Blount's teammate Dwight White had said, "I always say you can go down South, or you can go up South."

Blount observes: "Obviously, there will always be racism and there will always be segregation and prejudice."

At noon, Blount suggested we go get some lunch, and we left the farm and rode into Taylortown's main shopping district. We entered a restaurant-lounge there, with Blount leading the way. We entered a dimly-lit restaurant. Everyone was white and everyone, or so it seemed, was looking at Blount. It is no wonder. He has to be the the biggest, blackest cowboy in town. He could not have attracted more attention if he had a gun belt on his hip. Damned if I didn't feel like an old gunslinger come to town.

Soon after my wife and I moved back to Pittsburgh in 1979, I had written a newspaper story about a teenage death in our community that was tied up with a controversial school issue, and soon after my dream house was vandalized, with awful graffiti spray-painted on its bricks, right below my daughters' bedrooms. It took a long time to get over that.

For a year, at least, every young person I saw in the neighborhood was a suspect. I kept wondering who did it. Were you the one? I figured Blount had to be thinking the same thing when he walked into that restaurant.

A man with a friendly smile came over to our table, and told Mel where they had met, and then told me where we had met, at two different fund-raising banquets. He inquired about Mel's daughter. He knew her name, Tanisia. "Believe it or not," Blount told the man, "she'll be 21 soon. She has a birthday coming up next week — October 24th."

That brought up another sore subject. Blount had been divorced from his second wife, Leslie, an attendant with USAir. I had bumped into her on a business trip to New Orleans, her hometown, two years earlier. "She said she was still in love with you," I told Blount. To which he replied, "That was difficult. I still care about her, too. But there were some basic philosophical differences. She's a Catholic; I'm a Baptist. It wasn't working. But that's personal."

So was a sign Blount spotted on one of his fences on the way back to his farm. He backed up his Bronco II to make certain he saw what he thought he saw. There was a hand-painted sign — in yellow print — on one of the horizontal slats: It read: "Mel Blount Sucks!"

Blount shook his head. "You have to be a little sick to do something like that," he said, sighing.

His former teammates come by on occasion for a visit, like Franco Harris or Jack Lambert, who had just been inducted into the Pro Football Hall of Fame, or J.T. Thomas. Even contemporary Steelers, such as Terry Long, have been out to the farm.

"It's great to see somebody's dream come true," said Harris, "and he's making a lot of other people's dreams come true."

"I think it's terrific," said Lambert, always a man of few words. "I'll be back."

"I've always been a big fan of Mel Blount," said Thomas, who grew up in Macon, Georgia, an hour and a half drive from Vidalia. "Mel and I understand each other; we speak the same dialect. I know where he's coming from."

Blount lives on the farm in a stately white brick house that was built in 1810, and the rec room has all kinds of trophies, plaques, paintings, pictures of him with teammates, and artifacts and assorted football paraphernalia on disorderly display. Blount was, indeed, one of the best, and the room provides testimony to that.

He was a third round draft choice in 1970, right behind quarterback Terry Bradshaw of Louisiana Tech, and Ron Shanklin, a wide receiver out of North Texas State. He struggled at the start, like one of the newborn colts in his barn, to find his legs in the National Football League.

"I remember a game in his second season," recalled Andy Russell, who was the defensive captain in 1971, "when Paul Warfield of the Miami Dolphins burned Mel for three touchdowns (for 12, 86 and 60 yards in a 24-21 Dolphins' victory). Mel was in shock. I used to feel like a camp counselor in those days, convincing the young guys that they'd get better."

Blount, sitting in that Taylortown restaurant, could smile at the memory. It only reminded him of his good fortune.

"That was early in my career," he said. "Yeah, I thought about quitting after my second season. I thought a lot about it. The greatest education I got was with the Steelers. I learned from my mistakes. It was strictly on-the-job training.

"When I came to the Steelers, it was a blessing from the Lord. When I went to the Steelers, I knew nothing about football. I had no football knowledge. I couldn't recognize offensive formations. At Southern University, I just had to go out and cover somebody.

"I was fortunate to have Chuck Noll and the Rooneys and the assistant coaches to bring me along. Charley Sumner was my first defensive backfield coach. He'd ask me to identify formations at team meetings, and I couldn't do it. I was lost. I nearly got cut a couple of times my rookie year. I just had raw talent. Then Bud Carson came in, and he really brought me along, taught me what I needed to know.

"It took me longer, just like it took Bradshaw time to become comfortable, and to know what we were supposed to be doing. I was just a young country kid from an all-black high school and an all-black college. I was thrown into a world dealing with white people. I worked for my daddy on the farm. That was my background, the only world I knew."

But he got better in a hurry. He played for 14 seasons before retiring after the 1983 season. During his career, he was hailed as the prototype cornerback of his era and a major reason why the Steelers were the dominant team of the NFL in the 1970's. When the NFL outlawed the bump-and-run tactics of defensive backs, it was thought that Blount was the biggest reason. He simply shut down opposing receivers.

"I didn't want to be second to anyone," he once said. "I wanted to set standards for my position."

He set a club record by playing in 200 games, which has been broken. He left as the Steelers' all-time interception leader with 57.

His teammates were his biggest admirers. "When you create a cornerback, the mold is Mel Blount," said Steelers' linebacker Jack Ham, who went into the Hall of Fame the year before Blount. "I played in a lot of Pro Bowls. I never saw a cornerback like him. He was the most incredible athlete I have ever seen. With Mel, you could take one wide receiver and just write him off. He could handle anybody in the league."

Another former teammate, Notre Damer Terry Hanratty, had this to say about Blount: "Size, speed, quickness, toughness — that's what Mel had. If you gave Blount free rein to hit you, you were in trouble because, if he missed, he had the speed to catch up. A lot of receivers got short arms when they were in Mel's territory."

Hanratty's remark reminded me of my first impression of Blount back at St. Vincent in the summer of 1979. It was the first day of camp for the veterans, and Noll wasted no time in having them scrimmage.

On the first play, a reserve running back named Jack Deloplaine took a pitchout and swept to the left side. Up came Blount from his right cornerback position, and dove at Deloplaine's legs. He missed. Other Steeler defenders came up in support, and Deloplaine slowed down to look for some daylight. Wham! Deloplaine was leveled by a hard tackle from behind. It was Blount who made the big hit.

Blount had just come off his eighth pro season in which the Steelers had won their third Super Bowl, and he had played in the Pro Bowl twice, yet he had made a second effort like that on the first play at training camp.

After practice, I asked him about it. "I learned a long time ago," he said, "that you can't get anything accomplished by pounding your fist on the ground."

That incident has always served me like a parable, and Blount remembers a lot of parables. But not that one.

"I don't remember that one," he said. "I'm like a boxer who's been punched too many times. I forget a lot of things. But I do know you've got to get up after you've been knocked down, and get going."

Blount was eager to tell me a story of his own, one he felt needed to be told. "Nobody really knows the background on this one," he said. "It's time it was told. It explains why I had some troubles with the Steelers midway through my career, and how I ended up in a court battle with the team.

"People always say I sued Chuck Noll, but that was not really the case. I sued Chuck Noll and the Steelers. In 1975, I was the NFL's Defensive MVP and the Steelers' team MVP and led the league in interceptions (with 11). I was the MVP in the Pro Bowl that followed the 1976 season. I was making under $50,000, and I thought I should be making more. The Steelers told me to wait until the season was over, and they'd take care of me. This was before the 1977 season. Jim Boston, who handles their contract negotiations, came down to New Orleans to meet with me. He offered me a $5,000 raise. 'I can't accept that,' I told him. 'I can't take it.' He got mad, and he said, 'You either take this or you'll starve to death.'

"That put such a bad taste in my mouth. I thought it was a racist remark. I thought he was talking to me like I was some sort of slave. I made up my mind that I could make it without football, if I had to someday. Then, right after that, Noll got sued by George Atkinson of the Oakland Raiders (for $2 million in damages for slander). Atkinson had beat up on Lynn Swann pretty good the year before, and Noll had blasted his tactics, labeling Atkinson as a member of 'the criminal element in the National Football League,' stuff like that. At the court hearing out in San Francisco, they showed Noll a film clip of me slamming Cliff Branch of the Raiders to the ground, and one of Joe Greene punching Paul Howard of the Denver Broncos in the stomach. They asked Noll what he thought of our brand of play. He said we were also in that same 'criminal element,' and that set me off. I was holding out, to begin with, and I was still upset with the Steelers for the way Boston had treated me. That's the same summer Lambert held out for more money. I was just mad at the Steelers. I wasn't suing just Noll."

That case was settled out of court to Blount's satisfaction. He quickly put it behind him, and so did Noll and the Steelers. Blount had been after a $100,000 a year, but didn't get it.

By the time Blount and the Steelers were playing in Super Bowl XIV, going for their fourth NFL title in January of 1980, Blount was the best-paid player at his position, making $142,000 a year, according to the NFL Players Association survey. And he was about to pick up another $18,000 as the winner's share.

His pre-game remarks were typical Blount. Before the Steelers' first Super Bowl, he had been critical of the Minnesota Vikings' quarterback, Fran Tarkenton, to the consternation of his coaches. Noll banned him from the press room interviews after his outburst. Blount was never the strong, silent type. In 1980, he was still vocal.

"There's no use coming here and losing," Blount said at the Steelers' headquarters in Newport Beach, California. "I'm never satisfied with second best, and neither is this ballclub. We have the kind of ballclub that should be on the top. And we should be on the top for a long time. I'm ready to do what's necessary to beat the Rams. I play rough, but I think I play the game hard and clean."

He still plays the game that way, only he talks a kinder, gentler game these days. "In Proverbs, chapter 12, verse 18, it says 'A reckless tongue pierces like a sword, but a tongue of the wise brings healing.' I don't want to hurt anybody any more," he said.

That wasn't always the case. In his early days with the Steelers, Blount was outspoken, and critical of a lot of people, opposing players, coaches, club officials and the media. Mel was mad at everybody back then. He was accused of giving himself the nickname of "Supe" — short for Super. He was also labeled "Motormouth Mel" by the Pittsburgh media.

He was thought to be a bad actor, overly cocky, argumentative, and many thought he would be traded after early feuds with his coaches and management.

He attacked the local media for lack of publicity. He criticized Bud Carson, the Steelers' backfield coach, for benching him late in the 1974 AFC title contest with the Oakland Raiders after he had been burned by Cliff Branch one too many times. Blount labeled the yanking as "stupid," which did not go down well with Chuck Noll.

Even though he had three years remaining on a $50,000 per year contract that had been extended the year before, Blount held out until the first week of the season in 1977. He filed a $5 million dollar suit against Noll and the Steelers over the "criminal element" comment.

Noll was defending himself against a law suit by the Raiders' George Atkinson, and claimed he was "coerced" by the prosecuting attorney into admitting that Blount, Greene, Ernie Holmes and Glen Edwards were part of the "NFL's criminal element" along with the Raiders' Atkinson and Jack Tatum. Blount dropped the law suit against Noll and the Steelers when he signed a new contract and came to camp.

His career has been checkered in other ways. His ambitions have changed from year to year. At various times, he has been a tobacco farmer in Georgia, raised horses on a 10-acre ranch in Louisiana before he was forced to declare bankruptcy because he could not meet the payments on the mortgage, went to Hollywood to see if he could get into acting in movies, operated an employment agency, campaigned for fellow-Georgian Jimmy Carter when he ran for the Presidency in 1976, said he should have majored in agriculture in college, talked about going to law school.

This was all before I met Mel Blount. "You wouldn't believe how much he's grown since he first came here," said Joe Gordon, the team's publicist throughout Blount's playing career. "He's the best example I know of about how an athlete can benefit from the exposure to professional sports and the doors it can open for you. He's come a long way."

There are 19 head of black angus cattle on the grounds at the Mel Blount Youth Home, and Blount believes they will someday help pay the mortgage. He mentioned some rich men, such as Edward J. DeBartolo and his son, Eddie, Jr., the shopping mall magnates who owned the San Francisco 49ers and Pittsburgh Penguins among other things, as being breeders of black angus, as well as Armand Hammer. In short, there is money to be had with black angus, or maybe you need money to raise black angus.

He took me into the barn, and showed me a recently-born black angus — "he's a good-looking animal" — and his eight horses. He was particularly proud of two red horses. "This one is what they call an 'own daughter' of Secretariat, and this one is Secretariat's granddaughter," he said. "Yes, Secretariat. There's some royal bloodlines in this barn."

The boys had finished their classroom work by now, and they were all out in the barn, sweeping out the stalls, doing their daily chores. Blount was going to let them ride the horses when they were done.

"We go out on treks on the farm," said Blount, "and we see squirrels and foxes and groundhogs and I have to tell them what they are; you don't see those in the city streets. I tell them about the different types of trees, and what you can do with them.

"I like to take them with me to all the banquets I go to now. I had them in the city recently for a meeting that local black business leaders had with Governor Casey at the Rivers Club. They would never get exposure like that in their lives if they hadn't come here. They got to shake hands with the governor. Experiences like that will stay with them."

One of the boys was having trouble pushing a wheelbarrow up a ramp to dump the contents into a wagon. It was too heavy for him. Blount did it for him. "Don't load it up so much next time," he said. "Fill it half way up so you can handle it." The boy smiled back.

One of the smallest and youngest of the boys was wielding a pitchfork, and turning straw and what they had just swept out of the stalls. "You know what this is?" he asked me.

"It's what the horses and cows leave behind," I said.

"It's manure," he said, happy to tell me that. "Mr. Mel wants to make sure we call it that. He doesn't want us calling it something else."

Blount smiled, and got back in his Ford Bronco II. He bid me goodbye, and rode off into the sunset.

Roy Gerela
"Sometimes you have a bad day"

Only Terry Bradshaw put more points on the scoreboard for the Steelers during their glory years, with his passes and runs for touchdowns, than did Roy Gerela.

Gerela was a little guy with a big heart, the smallest of the Steelers — at 5-10, 185 pounds — and their placekicker when they won three of their four Super Bowls. Kickers determine the outcome of more games than anybody else, but Gerela was in awe of the athletic skills and speed of the biggest guys on the team.

Growing up near Vancouver, British Columbia, Gerela had been quite the athlete himself, excelling as a forward who could score goals in both hockey and soccer as a schoolboy, for starters, then adding baseball to his repertoire before he ever tried to play football. He was always a scrappy soul.

Gerela (pronounced Jur-el-ah) once thought he could become a major league baseball player. He was a catcher who was fearless when it came to blocking the plate against a sliding baserunner hell-bent on scoring a run.

With all that behind him, Gerela still marveled at men like Joe Greene, Ernie Holmes, L.C. Greenwood, Dwight White, Steve Furness, John Banaszak and Gary Dunn, the gigantic fellows who labored on the defensive line for the Steelers, when he watched them play touch football games at Three Rivers Stadium.

Gerela got a kick out of these games that the general public never witnessed, and most of the media simply smiled at. These were games the big guys organized among themselves to break the tedium, and to get a chance to touch the football like only the quarterbacks, running backs, wide receivers and players at the so-called "skilled positions" got to do in the real games.

"Every Tuesday we'd have a team meeting, then go out and run a mile to loosen up, and the defensive linemen would pick teams and play touch football," said Gerela. "They wanted to have some fun. I'd kneel down on the sideline and watch them. I couldn't get over how well some of them could throw the ball, the foot speed, the way they could move. I was in awe of their athletic skills.

"Our team was blessed with so much talent — even the backups like Steve Furness and Ed Bradley, who could have started for other teams — had so much ability."

Since he paid so much attention to the big guys, Gerela was asked who he thought was the toughest of the bunch. Gerela gave us a surprise answer. "If you're talking about a street fight, I'd have to pick Preston Pearson," he said.

Preston Pearson? The versatile running back who went from the Steelers to the Dallas Cowboys, and played on Super Bowl teams for

239

Roy Gerela

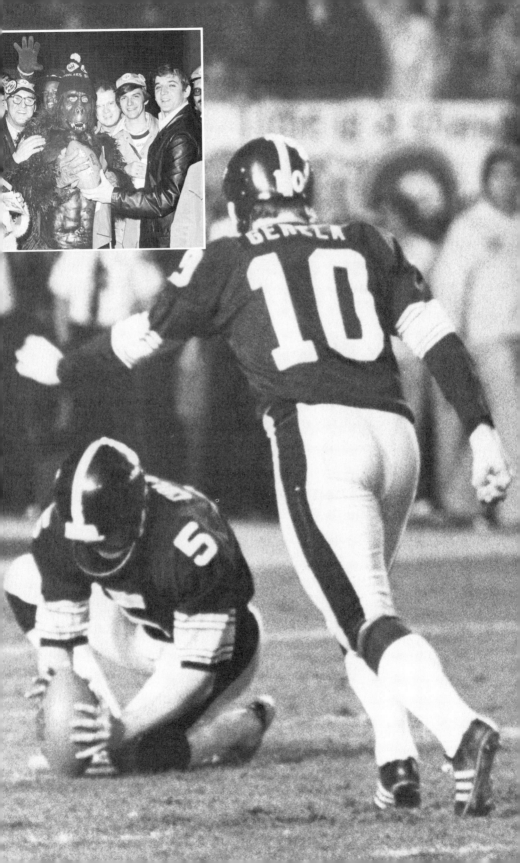

both clubs? "That's right, Preston Pearson," said Gerela. "I thought Preston could whip a lot of those big linemen. Guys like Terry Bradshaw and Mel Blount were both tough customers, too.

"Why don't you ask me who was the craziest? We had a lot of characters on that team, too, like Dwight White, Jack Lambert and Ernie Holmes."

None of those agile big guys, however, was any more valuable to the Steelers than was the strong-legged Gerela. When he was going well, and splitting the uprights regularly with his kicks, and booming kickoffs deep into the enemy endzone, Gerela was as popular as any of the Pittsburgh players.

His most ardent fans called themselves "Gerela's Gorillas," and one of them donned a gorilla costume and carried on in the stands at every Steelers' home game. That was Bob Bubanic of Port Vue, whom some thought became a factor in the Steelers' home field advantage. "Gerela's Gorillas" were as much a part of the spectacle that was the Three Rivers Stadium scene for Steelers as were "Lambert's Lunatics," and "Franco's Italian Army," ("Go, Paisan, Go," a banner read), Jack Ham's "Dobre Shunka" (Slavic for "Great Ham"), "Bradshaw's Boosters," "Rocky's Flying Squirrels," Myron Cope's "Terrible Towels," "The Steeler Stinger" and "The Terrible Fan."

It didn't get any better than that as far as an exciting and formidable pro football atmosphere was concerned. Toward the end of his career, however, when Gerela started hooking his kicks and missing critical three-pointers, the cheers turned to boos.

Gerela accepted both with the equanimity that seems to be part of the make-up of field goal kickers. You win some, you lose some. "Sometimes you have a bad day," said Gerela with a grin.

Chuck Noll never changed in the way he dealt with Gerela during his eight-year stay (1971-78) with the Steelers. "I could have kicked five field goals in a game or missed three, and he was more or less the same," said Gerela.

"I can't say enough good about the man. He gave me my chance to play for the Steelers, and he stuck with me at the end, and gave me a chance to recover from an injury, which I never did. He never singled me out for losing a contest."

When Gerela was asked to give up the ghost, he was the all-time leading scorer for the Steelers with 731 points to his credit, but he has since been surpassed in that statistical category by Gary Anderson. Gerela once held the record for most field goals in a season with 29 in 1973, and for most career extra points with 293. "I always," he said, "gave the Steelers my best shot."

Gerela had a wise old owl look as he peered over eyeglasses and spoke about his days with the Steelers. He was wearing a tight-fitting sport coat, and had gotten heavier. He was sitting at a table at Applebees, an eclectic restaurant in the brand-new Bourse Shopping Center near his home in Scott Township, a suburb just a few miles south of Three Rivers Stadium. He shared a home in Scott Township with his friend of 15 years, Helen Kickel. It is ironic that Gerela would have a girl friend named Kickel.

Gerela was enjoying a two-fisted hamburger with all the fixings, french fries and about eight cups of coffee as he chatted about his career. He is a nervous sort, something that seems to go with his trade. His concentration would wander. He would be turning 45 in April of 1991, when he would be eligible to start collecting on his NFL pension if he so desired — at $600 a month, he figured — and he was involved in several pursuits that kept him busy.

He had been selling insurance as an independent agent for seven years — he mentioned that he had sold the insurance to former teammate Mel Blount at his Youth Home out in Washington County. He was also selling a newly-developed energy conservation lighting apparatus to companies and schools around the city. In the evenings and on weekends, he was serving as an assistant coach on the football staff at Baldwin High School. In short, he was staying out of trouble. Gerela gave you the impression he was still looking for the right job, and he later was hired as an assistant coach at his alma mater, New Mexico State University.

When he was with the Steelers, Gerela roomed on the road with Andy Russell for a spell. Talk about an odd couple. Russell has become one of the biggest success stories in Steelers' history in his business enterprises. Russell always counseled younger players to prepare themselves for their post-playing days. "I wish he had talked to me more about that," said Gerela.

Gerela wanted to be coaching on a collegiate or pro basis, but had never been able to land a job. I had seen coaches take advantage of him, asking him to spend an afternoon working with their kickers, but when it came to getting a job, these same coaches became elusive. Gerela had certainly tried. He had called on coaches on every level, looking for an opening, but had been frustrated.

"A lot of doors you think were open when you play become shut when you retire," said Gerela.

I had caught up with Gerela after a high school football game a few nights earlier, when Baldwin lost to Upper St. Clair, my community team that had won the WPIAL title under coach Jim Render the previous two seasons, and the PIAA championship the year before. Gerela was in his second season as an aide to Don Yannessa, who had gained national attention for the outstanding championship teams he had turned out for years in Aliquippa, the area that bred both Mike Ditka and Tony Dorsett.

"Don works hard, and he knows there are no short-cuts," said Gerela. "He's going to have a good team in a few years at Baldwin. He's building a solid program from the ground up. Don's practices are so well organized. When you're around Yannessa, just like being around Noll, you know why they've been successful. Yannessa has a different personality than Noll — he is much more public-relations conscious and at ease in public and more humorous — but he has the same work ethic. Don's knowledgeable in all areas of the game."

Gerela helped Yannessa by working with the special teams, the wide receivers and sometimes with the secondary. The year before he hooked up with Yannessa, Gerela helped Dan McCann, the head coach of the football team at Duquesne University, who was also a successful sales executive for The Pittsburgh Brewing Company.

"I thought I had some good contacts to get a college job; I don't want to go to any rinky-dink program," said Gerela. "It's hard. Trying to get into coaching on a higher level is somehow so damn hard. Nothing is going to be given to you, but you'd just like a chance to show what you can do."

Spoken like a true place-kicker.

Gerela grew up the hard way, like so many of the Steelers on those Super Bowl teams. He took a circuitous and unlikely road to get to Pittsburgh, and it seemed he was content to stay there. He was probably tired from a lifetime on the road. But, as a salesman, he was still on the road.

Some Steelers thought Gerela was a cheapskate. "He has yet to buy his first drink for anybody," one said. "He still has the first dollar he made as a Steeler." Learning about Gerela's background might provide some insight into that behavior. "Usually guys who grow up poor are the first guys to buy a drink," said a Steelers' teammate who should know, shooting down my theory.

Gerela was born in Sarrail, Alberta, spent his early years in Powell River, British Columbia, went to high school in Honolulu, Hawaii, to college in Las Cruces, New Mexico, and played two years for the Houston Oilers before the Steelers claimed him for the waiver price of $100.

Sarrail is a tiny farm community, and Gerela was the youngest of six boys in a family of 11 children. His dad was a mechanic, and the family moved when Roy was about four months old to Powell River, about 150 miles north of Vancouver, where his father got a job as a laborer in a paper mill. Bill Gerela was a burly, gregarious guy who liked to play the violin and to drink, not necessarily in that order, and to have a good time. Roy's mother, Olga, did laundry at the Powell River General Hospital to help make ends meet. There was never enough money.

The Gerelas lived in a small wooden house on Sutherland Street that had three bedrooms and a kitchen, a vegetable garden in the backyard and an outhouse beyond that. "We were the last house at the end of a road that ran along the coastline," recalled Gerela. The Gerelas made all their own clothes from the cheapest of materials, made all their own Christmas gifts, and sometimes went hungry.

"We didn't have any money to go to movies or buy things," said Gerela. Roy's dad liked to watch his boys play sports, and was a big booster from the sidelines. "I was 13 when my dad died."

The day after his father's funeral, Roy kissed his mother goodbye and left Powell River with his older sister and her American husband to live in Tacoma, Washington.

"It was the saddest day of my life," said Gerela. "My father had just died and I was leaving my mother and going to a strange country."

Roy's brother-in-law worked for IBM, and he was soon transferred to Rockville, Maryland, and from there to Honolulu. That is where Roy started playing football as a defensive back and a punter. "I was a minority there, too," Gerela said of his schooldays in Hawaii, "and I never felt wanted by the native kids."

His brother Ted was playing football at Washington State University, and would become the best place-kicker in the Canadian Football League for the hometown British Columbia Lions.

Roy was recruited to play at New Mexico State University, where he continued as a defensive back and punter. It was not until his senior year, however, that he began fooling around with place-kicking. He did it soccer style, and says he really taught himself how to do it.

He did well enough that final year to rate being the fourth round draft pick of the Houston Oilers. He kicked for the Oilers for two seasons before he was cut by a new coach named Ed Hughes. The Steelers claimed him from the waiver list.

Asked to select the highlight of his career with the Steelers, Gerela just smiled and said, "Probably when I made the team. I can remember when I first came in. The Steelers had a guy named Paul Rogers (an eighth round draft pick out of Nebraska) and a guy named Allen Watson, who had been their kicker the year before. He wasn't bad. All I kept hearing was that we didn't have a kickoff man. They had a kickoff (contest) between the three of us at Three Rivers Stadium. And I finished dead last.

"Coach Noll came over to me and put his arm around my shoulder and walked me out to midfield. I figured he was going to say goodbye. We got halfway across the field, and he said, 'Roy, you're going to be my kicker this year. I don't care what you do every week in practice. I just want you to be ready on Sunday. I like what you did in Houston.'

"Now, the way I saw it, here's a guy who's taking a shot in the dark with me. That's why I've always been a big fan of Chuck Noll. I've always been grateful that he gave me that kind of break. To him, one day didn't mean anything. It never did."

Asked why he was so successful as a place-kicker, Gerela grinned and replied, "More fear than anything else. It's what he (Noll) wanted. I had something I really wanted for a long time, and I didn't want to give it up. The dividends were too great.

"When you were on the sidelines it was horrible. The twisting and turning of your insides. You just want to come through and contribute. Everyone takes it for granted that you should make it all the time. I had one chance. The guys on the line can screw up three times in a row and come back and make a great play. I'm not allowed to do that."

245

Gerela was wearing one of the three Super Bowl rings he owns. "It's from the first one," he said. "It's the most important, like the first time you do anything. I won the league scoring title that year, and I won the Golden Toe Award, played in the Pro Bowl and, of course, we won the Super Bowl. Everything just fell into place. Plus, it's the nicest of the rings I have. It's less gaudy than the other two."

Gerela won the scoring title that year with 93 points, hitting 33 of 35 extra-point attempts and 20 of 28 field goal attempts. The year before, he set Steelers' records with 123 points, 29 field goals, 43 field goal attempts, and 36 extra points. He had 119 points the year before that. Gary Anderson has since erased most of Gerela's club kicking records. "I have the other two rings," said Gerela. "Every ring has a story."

When Gerela was going good, he was one of the team's most popular players. A group of fans from Port Vue, a hillside community overlooking McKeesport (the home of Lambert's Lunatics), adopted him. That's how "Gerela's Gorillas" got started.

In Gerela, 5-9 or 5-10, take your pick, and then 185 pounds, the steel workers saw a shoulder-padded version of themselves, a blue collar worker they could identify with. This was during a time when steel workers — many of them out of work and watching the mills along the river close up one after another — really needed something positive to rally round. The Steelers and Pirates and Pitt and Penn State football teams of the '70s provided a much-needed boost to these otherwise disappointed people. They loved the Steelers, in general, and guys like Lambert and Gerela, in particular.

"Gerela's Gorillas" always assembled in one of the end zones at Three Rivers Stadium, and waved disparaging signs aimed at unnerving the visiting place-kickers. They screamed and shouted and distracted Gerela's counterparts any way they could. Incredible things happened to visiting kickers, and some seemed to come apart at the seams at Three Rivers Stadium.

Myron Cope used to provide instructions to "Gerela's Gorillas" on his nightly sports talk show on WTAE Radio, even suggesting the wording on their signs for the next game. Cope got caught up in his role with "Gerela's Gorillas," and once told Chuck Noll that the group was responsible for the Steelers' success.

"Geez," Noll said. "I thought it was because we had a good football team."

Lambert was Gerela's favorite player on the Steelers. During the Super Bowl X game in Miami between the Steelers and Dallas Cowboys, Gerela was having a bad game to begin with, and the Cowboys were taunting him. Cliff Harris slapped Gerela upside the helmet, and hollered at him, after he missed one field goal attempt.

Lambert came to Gerela's rescue and accosted Harris. "I thought he was a little intimidating," allowed Lambert. "We're not supposed to be intimidated, we're supposed to be the intimidators." There were other games in which Lambert was a bodyguard for Gerela. Gerela has never forgotten that.

Gerela had gotten hurt on the opening kickoff of that Super Bowl X game, catching a knee in the ribs from Thomas Henderson on the kick return. Gerela was never a run-and-hide kickoff man. He bruised two ribs and cracked another in that encounter. As a result, he missed two field goals he would usually make, and an extra point. But he did end up kicking two field goals that helped win the game, 21-17. It didn't beat the point spread, however, and so a lot of bettors got down on Gerela. In fact, I bet on that game, and I almost never bet on any ballgames. I lost $100 that day, too. It would not be the first or last time Gerela was in the dog house with Steelers' fans. They proved a fickle bunch.

One former Steelers coach once theorized that kickers must have been left alone too much as kids. Paul Martha, who once returned kicks for Pitt and the Steelers, and in more recent years looked after the Civic Arena and its prime tenant, the NHL Penguins, once said, "Goalies in hockey are a lot like field goal kickers in football. They're different than the other guys and they stick to themselves."

Gerela could appreciate that. In fact, he seldom socialized off the field with Steelers, but preferred the company of several Penguins. There was a time when Gerela was the only Canadian in the National Football League. So he was more comfortable with guys who said things like "Crazy, eh?"

He did become good friends with Bobby Walden, a peanut farmer from Georgia, when Walden was a veteran punter for the Steelers. "Bobby Walden and I identified with each other," said Gerela. "Whether you're a punter or a place-kicker, you're one of a kind on a football team. When you only have one at that position, you are a little strange. Bobby was more or less a loner, and so was I."

Walden and Gerela both had great seasons with the Steelers, but hit the downhill slide at the same time. They were both booed.

Teammates think kickers have it easy. Gerela had two nicknames: Good Foot and Easy Money. One was complimentary, one was less than complimentary. As one of Gerela's competitors for the place-kicking job, Rick Snodgrass of Slippery Rock University, once said: "Some of the guys ask, 'How's life in the country club?' Let's face it, we don't work as hard as they do. You can't kick for two hours, or you'd wear out in a few weeks. We're like the Maytag repairman; we have the loneliest job in the world."

On the job, however, there is no place to hide. Nobody has to see the game film to determine how well the kickers do.

"You're like an independent contractor," said Gerela. "The other guys play the game, and you come in to handle the kicking. And it's an insecure job. You never know when they're bringing in another kicker to work out. If you have a bad game, they might lose faith in you.

"The last two-and-a-half years I played in Pittsburgh, I had a groin injury. I probably shouldn't have played. But I never liked to alibi, or talk about injuries. But the coaches knew it, the trainers knew it."

Gerela was placed on waivers when the Steelers made some of their final cuts in late August, 1979. They decided to go with rookie Matt Bahr, another soccer-style kicker who had played at Penn State and was one of two sixth round draft picks. Gerela was available for $100, the same as when the Steelers first got him eight years earlier.

"I got cut by the Steelers a few days after they gave me my one chance to kick in a pre-season game," recalled Gerela, "I kicked two 48-yard field goals and my kick-offs were high and deep when we beat the Jets in New York.

"Joe Greene and the rest of the guys all hugged me and patted me on the back, and they shook my hand. They wanted me to do well. They knew my pro life was on the line. Matt Bahr even came over to me and said, 'Congratulations. Great game. Looks like I'm done.' And I said, 'Don't count yourself out yet.' I knew it was iffy.

"I hurt myself playing in a pre-season game two years earlier. I kicked a field goal and felt like somebody had shot me in the back of the calf. That led to a build-up of fluids in the lymph nodes of my thigh, and I had an infection. It got worse, and I pulled the groin muscle. It was just a twinge, at first, but then it hurt like hell."

Back in 1975, Gerela had suffered a similar painful groin injury which kept him out of the AFC title game. So it was not something he had not experienced before.

Gerela could not follow through on his kicks, and he began hooking his kicks, just like a golfer would if he was not following through on his swing.

In the 1977 season, Gerela attemped an NFL low of 14 field goals and had one mid-season stretch when he didn't try any. He hit nine of those 14 attempts, but totaled only 61 points. The media and the crowds became critical, and some thought the criticism, plus contract problems in 1978, aggravated Gerela's place-kicking problems. As for the fans, Gerela said, "Some of them would boo their own mother." A kicker's mental condition is as critical as his physical condition. "Crazy, eh?" Gerela might say.

The week after Gerela had kicked well against the New York Jets, Chuck Noll called Gerela to his dorm room at St. Vincent College to give him the bad news. "I shook his hand," said Gerela, "and I said, 'Thank you for the years here in Pittsburgh.' Hey, he'd given me two years to get healthy. How could I complain?

"If I see him today, he'll come over to say hello. He'll say, 'How you been? How you doing?' He never did anything to me to make me dislike him or have a bad attitude about my time with the Steelers.

"I think Chuck admires and appreciates everything someone did, but he's not going to come out and say anything. When I had some of my best kicks, or I was coming off the field following a big field goal, and, no matter how big it might be, he'd just sort of nod, or give me a little smile. 'Thatta way to go!' was about the best you got. But there'd be some little mannerism, some look of approval. It was not a whole lot — but it was just something to show he's for you."

Gerela went from the Steelers to the San Diego Chargers. "I bombed out," said Gerela. "I had no desire, no get-up-and-go." After a decade in the NFL, he was done.

Gerela felt he was better than Bahr, but concedes that Anderson is "a complete kicker," and as good as they come. He won't concede that Anderson was better, even though Anderson's accuracy record and distance record was far superior to his.

"Bahr could never kick off. He'd hit the ball to their 15 or 18, at best, and our guys would be so pissed off because the opposition brought the ball back to their 30 or 35 yard line. I never thought his leg was strong enough to be a kicker for a contender," said Gerela.

"But I think when they drafted him they made up their minds that he was going to be their man. Now Gary is very good. You don't mind having someone like him coming in and beating you out when you're at your best. He's very strong, in all phases of the game.

"Kickoff-wise, I think I was one of the best who ever played the game, at getting it downfield high and into the end zone. Inside the 40, before I got hurt, I did extremely well. Beyond the 40, I was very average. Gary is excellent at all distances. If he had competed with me when I was 26, it would have been exciting."

"They're different than the other guys and they stick to themselves."
— Paul Martha

Gary Anderson

Matt Bahr

L.C. Greenwood
on the attack

L.C. Greenwood
"I never wanted to be embarrassed"

L.C. Greenwood's goatee had gone gray, no, make that white, wispy and white. It had been jet black when he played left defensive end for The Steel Curtain defense in its glory days. Can you hear Bruce Springsteen singing in the background?

There was white in the sideburns as well, which only added to his distinguished look, even if it did point up that — at 44 — he was getting older. He had always had a distinguished look, like a proud warrior. He probably noticed that I had gotten grayer, too, but was kind enough to say nothing about it.

The hallway to his office was narrow, and the door in an awkward position, but Greenwood greeted me warmly, as he always did, with a solid handshake and a rich bass word of welcome, and somehow managed to let me slip past in one nimble maneuver. He was always one of the tallest, most agile and cat-quick of the National Football League's defensive linemen. And sweetest. He used his remarkable quickness to fire off the line. He still has the moves.

He still has the same numbers, too. The last four digits in his office telephone number are 6868, which was his jersey number when he played for the Steelers. The last four digits of the phone number for his playing partner Jack Ham happen to be 0059.

Besides his wispy, white goatee, what I noticed next were his hands. They were smooth, almost polished, ebony and absolutely massive. In my lifetime as a sportswriter, mostly on the pro basketball beat, I have shaken hands with Wilt Chamberlain, George Mikan, Connie Hawkins, Julius Erving and Michael Jordan. They could all hold a basketball like it was a softball. Their fingers may have been longer, certainly thinner, but their hands were no larger or more impressive than Greenwood's. When you are 5-8½, and have hands to match, you are always impressed with guys like Greenwood. He always reminded me more of a basketball player than a football player.

Once Greenwood grabbed you, I thought, there was no getting away from him. He had your butt. There is a retired judge in Pittsburgh, over 70, a former Pitt football player who remains in great shape, named Emil Narick. When Judge Narick shakes people's hands he likes to yank them forward, like a collegiate wrestler going for a takedown. They think they have been in an earthquake. I have always wondered why he did that. Greenwood has nothing to prove, he never has, so he holds you with his handshake, like he is genuinely glad to see you again. He does not leave an insignia from his ring on your fingers.

I had been through a series of reunions just before I visited Greenwood, school reunions, family reunions, old friends coming to Pittsburgh to pay a visit, and I had seen a lot of his Steelers' teammates, and spent considerable time with them. Reunions can be very demanding and leave you emotionally drained. But Greenwood has always been such a laid-back, light-hearted, easy-laughing, warm fellow, that he provided relief, not just another reunion.

There is a sign about stress in his office. It says "Stress is the confusion created when one's mind overrides the body's basic desire to choke the living shit out of some asshole who desperately needs it."

As he sat at his desk, he turned sideways, and tugged at his goatee occasionally when he pondered his Pittsburgh Steeler playing days. Sunlight came through the window behind him, and highlighted his huge head and hands and goatee, and gave him an ethereal presence. His was a striking profile.

For some reason, many of the great football players have a theatrical look about them, almost a mask. Franco Harris and Greenwood were like that. A former schoolteacher, a man with far-ranging tastes in literature, the arts and in fashion, Greenwood was always too slim, too urbane to be a football player.

He was known during his playing days with the Steelers as "Hollywood Bags," quite different from Mean Joe Greene, Dwight "Mad-Dog" White and Ernie "Arrowhead" Holmes, or "Fats" Holmes, his linemates on the Steel Curtain's front four.

"I was the first on our team to wear a shoulder bag," he explained. "Every so often, I'd talk about getting in the movies someday. One day, White put the two together. He hollered out, 'Hey, there he goes off to the studio. What do you call that? Your Hollywood bag?' It stuck with me."

Greenwood would not relent, at last, and tell what his initials L.C. stood for. That's private.

He provided some penetrating insights into the Steelers: why he both admired and was critical of his coach, Chuck Noll; the chemistry of the clubhouse at Three Rivers Stadium; why he and his teammates were so upset by the way Franco Harris was turned away by management in his final season; special insights into the psychological needs of teammates such as Ernie Holmes and Lynn Swann; his own failure to get into the Pro Football Hall of Fame so far; the special way he and linebacker Jack Ham choreographed their movements on that left side of the line; the fashion secret behind "Frenchy" Fuqua; what he learned at all those Miller Lite beer commercial reunions; what he learned as the child of a demanding father in Mississippi when he used to chop cotton; and, best of all, what really went on inside those Steel Curtain huddles.

With a theatrical sweep of his hand, Greenwood wants to take you behind the Steel Curtain and closed doors to give you some special insights into the Steelers. With a smile.

Greenwood was wearing a gold diamond-studded pinky ring on his right hand, and expensive-looking diamond-studded gold bracelets on both wrists. Interestingly enough, he wore none of the four Super Bowl rings he earned as a Steeler.

Greenwood always "accessorized" his wardrobe, as he liked to put it. When he was dressed casually, with an open collar, he always favored gold chain necklaces, several of them at a time, as I remember. Listed by the Steelers at 6-6 3/4, 240 pounds, Greenwood was hard not to notice in the first place, but he always absolutely glittered with gold.

His clothes, make that costume, have always been important to him, "since I was six or seven," he says with pride. On this particular day, in his cluttered office, and sitting behind a cluttered desk — such a contrast to his own personal appearance — he wore a long silver tie with a silver tie clip, and a crisp-looking white-on-white dress shirt. He looked elegant.

Some might question whether or not Greenwood was the best-dressed Steeler of his day — some of his choices and combinations broke the ozone barrier — but he takes credit for turning running back John "Frenchy" Fuqua into a fashion plate who gained national recognition for his outlandish outfits. Greenwood would have you know that he was the one who turned Fuqua into a fashion-conscious football player.

Greenwood was always good fun, a fellow who brightened up a room with his gaiety. Greenwood would listen a lot, and laugh a lot, and his laugh was long and low, so rich and hearty, and ever-lasting. His laugh made you laugh. It was beautiful.

During his Steeler playing days, Greenwood was a school teacher early on, then turned to several business pursuits. Greenwood was always all business when it came to football or his career concerns. He had gotten on with his "life's work" when he was a youngster. Back then, he wanted to be a pharmacist. But it is hard to imagine Greenwood wearing a white jacket to work every day and filling prescriptions and being happy with himself. But he has always been a serious student, and serious thinker, behind that ever-smiling mask.

Instead, Greenwood served as president of Greenwood Enterprises, a firm which produces and markets coal — "we like to say we're marketing people now" — and is a partner in Monaloh Basin Engineers, a civil engineering firm which specializes in road and highway design. Both firms shared space in a house on Washington Pike, the main street in Bridgeville, once a booming coal mining community south of Pittsburgh, just below Upper St. Clair, and near other one-time prosperous coal-mining communities called Cecil, Morgan, Beadling, Heidelberg and Muse. This was once a soccer hotbed, with ethnic clubs sponsoring amateur teams.

Those coal mines have long been closed up, but Bridgeville has come back nicely from economic bad times. Through the years, many Steelers have lived there. It is a good buy, one of Pittsburgh's best-kept secrets. There are a lot of white frame houses in Bridgeville, and there is a quaint, old-fashioned look about some of its streets. Greenwood's offices were in a yellow frame home, with brown and white trim — "Frenchy" Fuqua would approve of the colors — which provided quite a contrast to its next door neighbor, the Freyer Funeral Home, on Bridgeville's busiest thoroughfare.

Greenwood has been in the coal business, and has ridden its ups and downs, since 1974, the year the Steelers won their first Super Bowl.

Greenwood gained more national attention as a member of the Miller Lite commercial team of former athletes than he had playing second fiddle to Joe Greene and Terry Bradshaw and Franco Harris when he was on the Steelers' football team.

Greenwood first gained attention for crushing a can of Miller Lite on a bar with his bare hand before the unbelieving eyes of pretty boy quarterback Bert Jones of the Baltimore Colts. Later, Greenwood was the masked wrestler in a who-is-that-masked man? long-running commercial aimed at testing the wits of Miller Lite fans. "I was always in experimental-type commercials," Greenwood wants you to know.

He had already been a part of that Miller Lite team for eight years, but admitted his involvement had been reduced. The advertising theme was over 12 years old and growing thin on Madison Avenue, as thin as Greenwood's goatee, it seems. In short, it was being phased out.

"I've gone from making about 45 to 50 appearances a year for Miller Lite around the country," conceded Greenwood, "to about five to ten a year. I've got one coming up shortly."

It hasn't surprised him, or caught Greenwood off guard. "It's like football: you know what it is when you sign on," he said. "As you get farther away from your high visibility as an athlete, they tend to drop off. I was just trying to cash in on it while the sun was still shining. Now the sun is starting to go down."

Greenwood liked his own line, and let out one of those low laughs that seem to rumble up from the deepest recesses of his still-flat belly.

One night in New York, my wife and I were taken to dinner at the fashionable and so-expensive "21" restaurant by my boss, John Brunelle, at Conde Nast Publications, Inc., when we ran into Greenwood. He was in the company of Ben Davidson, the former villain and arch-rival defensive terror of the Oakland Raiders. They were there, along with some other former pro legendary figures, for one of those famous, or notorious, Miller Lite reunion dinners. Nothing but the best for that bunch.

Had Greenwood played for a similarly-great football team in New York, he would have enjoyed the national notoriety because of his ability and flamboyant ways of a Broadway Joe Namath, and he certainly was more of a genuine article than Mark Gastineau. Greenwood had the name — "L. C." — and the nickname — "Hollywood Bags" — to make it big in the Big Apple. He has no regrets in that respect. "I played for the greatest football team of all time," he proudly pronounces.

"But we enjoyed a lot of good times with the Miller Lite team, too. The best part was when we had those reunions. We'd get together in New York or Los Angeles, and we'd be there for four to five days of shooting. We'd have free time together, and we'd have a big banquet where Bob Uecker and Rodney Dangerfield would provide the entertainment.

"Those four or five days would be really crazy. We'd sit around and drink you-know-what and tell war stories. We had the greats from all different sports, and someone like Mickey Spillane, a great detective mystery writer. We had Red Auerbach from the Boston Celtics, and

great ballplayers from all different sports. It was interesting. Some of the things they did and some of the things that happened. Whatever sport they were in, it was just so crazy. You formed good relationships. In nearly all the cases, these guys were legends, but they were also just good guys to be around."

People have said similar things about his Steelers team. On the wall of his office, there is a poster from the 11th Miller Lite reunion party. Greenwood is way in the back, towering over everyone else. Among those pictured are Davidson, Auerbach, Spillane, Sparky Lyle, Conrad Dobler, Dave Cowens, Boog Powell, Lee Merriweather, Bert Jones, Bob Lanier and Larry Csonka. "We had some crazy times together," gushed Greenwood.

Craziness is a relative term, Greenwood wants you to know. "How do you define it?" he asked. "With the Steelers, we had a lot of guys who had a lot of fun. Hey, Stallworth, quiet as he was, could get crazy. Dwight, as boisterous as he was. Bradshaw . . . I don't know how you can describe him. Terry Hanratty was Mr. Personality, always saying and doing crazy things. Then there was Ernie; now you go to the other extreme."

That set off Greenwood on a subject that was near and dear to him, Ernie Holmes. Holmes had always been a storied character with the club. He had puffy cheeks and slits for eyes, an Oriental look about him, a menacing look about him, which he worked on. Once, he shaved his head, leaving only an arrow on the top of his skull. It pointed him straight ahead. That was funny. Then, on one bizarre day, Holmes was caught firing a shotgun at passing cars on a bridge above a highway in Ohio. That was scary. And sad. The police apprehended Holmes after a helicopter chase, and he ended up in Western Psychiatric Institute, a mental hospital just below Pitt Stadium on the campus of the University of Pittsburgh.

"Mr. Rooney called me at my home," said Greenwood. "I was living in East Liberty at the time. It was during the off-season. Mr. Rooney asked me to go visit Ernie. He told me where he was. I said, 'No, he can't be.' Mr. Rooney said, 'Why don't you go over to see how he's doing?' Now that was not my cup of tea. I was reluctant to go there. But since Mr. Rooney asked me to do it, I had to go. So I went over on a Saturday afternoon.

"I am escorted to this room where Ernie is, along with some of the other people who were there. Ernie's pointing out different people to me, telling me how crazy everyone is around him. Ernie's telling me stories about them. The people there tell me I can take Ernie out, but I have to have him back by eight o'clock. I wasn't too crazy about taking him out of there, either. I didn't know what shape he was in.

"So I take Ernie to my house. I called Hubie Bryant, who had been on our team (in 1970, a wide receiver out of Minnesota and Penn Hills High School). So Hubie stops by the house. He comes in and turns the music up loud, and Hubie's dancing, boogying all over the place, having a good time. Ernie just sat and stared at him. Ernie finally said, 'Hey, Hubie, you oughta be over where I am. You're the crazy one!'"

I told Greenwood I was unable to get hold of Holmes, to interview him. His latest telephone number was disconnected. Holmes had been long gone by the time I came on the Steelers' beat, but I had always been intrigued with his history.

A buddy of mine, Jim Godwin, had just told me a story about how he and Holmes both resided in the Washington Plaza apartments in downtown Pittsburgh at the same time. "I remember being in the lobby one day when the elevator doors opened," said Godwin, "and Ernie was in the elevator, holding a chest of drawers in his hands, well off the floor, all by himself. I'll bet the drawers were still loaded, too. He just smiled at me.

"He was always smiling. I always had the impression he just wanted everyone to like him."

Greenwood nodded his head repeatedly when I told him that tale. "Most people look at Ernie as a wild man, and as an animal," said Greenwood. "But Ernie was a real nice guy. He had his problems, but he was still a good guy. Most guys feared him. Some guys didn't want to be around him.

"If I look at Ernie, as I look back, all Ernie wanted out of anybody was just respect. He just wanted to be one of the boys. He just wanted to be liked.

"Sometimes the way he acted, or because his reputation preceded him, some people backed off. He just wanted to be one of the boys."

I mentioned to Greenwood that Andy Russell had said that Ray Mansfield was the only Steeler who intimidated Holmes. "I don't think anybody intimidated Ernie," said Greenwood. "I just think Holmes respected Ray more than most because he'd been around so long. When Ernie would get too eager in practice, or start slapping helmets and stuff like that, Ray would tell him to lighten up, and get his attention."

I mentioned that Roy Gerela had suggested Preston Person was the toughest guy on the team in those days. "No way," said Greenwood. "I think Ernie was the toughest guy on the team. I don't know too many people who walked that Ernie was afraid of.

"In 1976, after we lost (24-7) to the Raiders in Oakland for the AFC championship, Gene Upshaw came over to us outside the visitors clubhouse just to be friendly. Ernie hollers to him, 'Hey, let's go.' Gene just wanted to shake hands. 'No, no, no,' Ernie's hollering, and calling Gene all kinds of names. 'Let's go, let's get down right here!' He liked to physically beat the guy. Fats challenged him to go back out and play again — just the two of them. Fats hated it when his man didn't hurt after a game. If they didn't bleed or he hadn't knocked them down, he wasn't happy. Gene turned to me, 'Hey, L.C., talk to him. What's wrong with him? Talk to him. The game's over.' Ernie just had that attitude. 'Let's get down, right here.'

"One night I went to some place where I liked to go to relax and have some fun. Ernie was at the door. I started to walk through the door, and Ernie says, 'You big ol' bastard, I'm going to kick your ass.' I said, 'You're not going to kick my ass. You're not going to catch me.' I was in a jovial mood, just walking in. He stopped me.

"He was like a big, physical kid. He says, 'Let's go, let's fight.' I said, 'What do we have to fight for?' He says, 'Where I come from, we go out and party all night on Saturday and drink as much as you can, and you go out on Sunday night and get drunk and get into a fight.' I said, 'I'm not from the same place. I don't know anything about that.' And I walked away. I know I disappointed him. He just wanted to be one of the boys. It was still hard for me to believe when he went off the deep end like he did."

Dwight White remembered Ernie Holmes with blood and sweat on his face in the huddles, happy as hell. Greenwood remembers that and more about the defensive huddles. They were hell in black and gold flames, to hear Greenwood go on about the activity. White said he never spoke to Jack Lambert in the huddle because of a personal feud. "I'm a private person," said Greenwood, "and I didn't know about a lot of things that were going on like that. I know they hardly ever spoke to each other. They'd huff up in each other's faces in the huddle.

"I remember Lambert and Joe Greene getting into it one day at Three Rivers Stadium because of something Lambert said to Joe. The next thing I know, they were at it in the huddle.

"Some of us didn't have much to say in the huddle. Everybody's in there bitching. I'm trying to concentrate on what I want to do next, what I'm seeing on the field. I'm into the game. When I crossed the white line, I just worried about what was happening in front of me. But there was a lot of bitching in the huddle.

"Mike Wagner would just look at me from the other end of the huddle, and we'd laugh at each other. They'd be hollering about who's doing this, or who's doing that, or who's supposed to do this, or who's supposed to do that. It was crazy.

"Lambert was always trying to get everybody quiet. Mel Blount, and Glen Edwards, and John Rowser and Ron Johnson and Jack Ham were always talking. Lambert's trying to get the play in from the sideline. Woody Widenhofer is upstairs sending the call down to George Perles on the sideline. Perles is supposed to signal Lambert. But Woody and George were probably arguing about what was best to do, too. Joe and Ernie would be bitching at one another. Lambert's trying to get the play from the sideline. It was just like mass confusion. It was so chaotic. Everybody was talking at the same time. I used to just stand there and laugh.

"We had a lot of fun on that team. We'd play our touch tag football games where I was the quarterback and Ham was the receiver, and we'd sucker one of the defensive backs, usually Wagner, into defending against my passes.

"We had a game we'd play in the locker room, before practice or even before a game, where we'd pass this ball around. It was great for quickness and hand-eye coordination. Chuck would come into the locker room and get all pissed off. He had no idea what kind of football team he was going to send out on the field that day.

"The assistant coaches were different then. They'd stick up for us. They always stood up for their players. Those guys stood up to Chuck."

He mentioned Woody Widenhofer, George Perles, Rollie Dotsch, Lionel Taylor and Dick Hoak, by name. "They weren't 'yes' men. They've got guys now who are 'yes' men. Chuck tells them to jump and they say, 'How high?' That's hurt them. Another thing, the assistants we had were partying as much as the players. So they weren't on our asses about stuff that didn't matter in the long run.

"Joe Greene would get pissed off at the offense if it didn't score. On the other hand, Joe stuck up for Bradshaw a couple of times with Chuck, and then he'd get on Bradshaw himself a couple of times about the way he was playing. It would go back and forth."

Like most of the Steelers of the Super Bowl era, Greenwood took tremendous pride in his personal performance. "As for me, my philosophy was that I was very serious about what I was trying to do," he said. "I tried to prepare so I wouldn't be embarrassed. I prepared because I always wanted to do it better. I was always giving away 30 to 40 pounds to the guy playing opposite me, so I always wanted an edge.

"I never played a football game in 13 years when I was completely healthy. I wanted to make big plays, but I did not want to do anything that was out of character for our defense. I knew what everybody else could do, and where they'd be, and if I couldn't make the big play myself I was going to make it easier for someone else to do it. I could take a chance.

"I kinda thought I knew what I was doing. I never feared any offense, no matter who we were playing. I was always smaller than the people I played against, as far as weight was concerned. I was also taller, so I could see what was going on back there, and identify offensive formations. I was 228 or 230 pounds, and I had to figure out how I could make a play in my hole going up against a guy who was 270 or 280.

"If Ham and I didn't have faith in doing something the coaches wanted us to do then we just ignored the call and did it our way. Jack would say, 'That ain't going to work.' We weren't going to get embarrassed if we didn't think it would work."

What about Chuck Noll? "I think his non-association with the players has hurt him," said Greenwood. "I like and respect Chuck as a tactician. As a person, I lose a lot of respect for him. With me, it was different, but everybody has different needs. Some guys needed his personal attention, or needed to be encouraged by him.

"You've got kids coming from all over the country congregating here. They were good athletes, but they needed somebody to say something to them. Chuck always said it wasn't his job to motivate people, and that if anybody needed somebody else to motivate them they had a problem. But some people do need that pat on the back, that word from somebody they really respect. But he's not a personable person.

"Steve Furness and I would sit on our stools after a game, and Chuck would come in the locker room, and go over to certain players. It was Furness who opened my eyes to this. Chuck would go around, and he'd stop and say something to Sam Davis, one of our captains, and he'd say something to Bradshaw or Hanratty, whichever one was quarterbacking that day, and he'd say something to Swann, and he'd say something to Joe, and he'd pass by Furness and me and go to Lambert or Ham, and then he'd head out the door."

On more than one occasion, Furness posed a question to Greenwood: "Hey, what's wrong with you? You just played a helluva game, and he didn't say, 'Hey, L.C., helluva game.' He didn't even look your way."

Greenwood wouldn't take the bait. "It didn't bother me. I just wanted to do my job. I knew when I played well. Nobody had to tell me that. I knew what I did. But there were guys who looked up to him, who respected him, who needed something from him. They were just kids. They were coming out of college and they were coming into a new environment. Some of them didn't know how to behave.

"I remember Ron Johnson coming into a huddle one day, and he said, 'Oh my God, L.C. Greenwood, a living legend! And here I am with the Steel Curtain! With Mel Blount! I can't believe I'm here!' But he was in awe, just the same.

"Before us, the Pittsburgh Steelers were just a football team in the NFL. I've been to every state in the United States, and I've met people everywhere who talked about our team. The Pittsburgh Steelers have a lot of respect throughout all the country.

"Now people want to play here. Before we came here, they didn't want to come here. I remember Art Rooney Jr. calling me on the day of the draft, and asking me, 'Are you happy the Steelers drafted you?' And I said, 'Not really.'

"I had been told by the Steelers and the Dallas Cowboys that I could be a first round draft choice. But they found out by talking to our team physician that I had a hyperextended knee. He told them my knee would not hold up. So I ended up being a tenth round draft pick. I didn't even think I wanted to play pro ball. I wanted to be a pharmacist.

"I had a nonchalant attitude. I didn't think I could play defensive line. I wasn't big enough. I thought I might be able to play linebacker. But I also thought I'd get caught up in a numbers game at a pro training camp. I was coming from a small school, Arkansas AM & N (now Arkansas-Pine Bluff), and I had no idea pro football was even on the agenda. I had no intention of playing the game."

Unlike some of his teammates, Greenwood was bypassed in balloting for the Pro Football Hall of Fame. "I'm not the only one," he said. "Hell, our whole defensive unit in '76 was good enough to go into the Hall of

Fame. You take a guy like Glenn Edwards, for instance. I thought he was the best safety in the league. The guy had size, speed, quickness, and he reacted to the ball so well; he was just phenomenal. And he's never even going to get nominated.

"You'd have to put our whole defensive line in the Hall of Fame. Look at the way we shut down the great Dallas teams. Maybe I'll get there by the time I'm 55. I see some guys starting to come to the top of the list, and I don't think they should even be considered.

"There are some other guys on the team I'd rather see get into the Hall of Fame before me. Like Lynn Swann. He deserves to be in the Hall of Fame. Lynn wants it so much. He wants to be in the Hall of Fame. I got out of football what I put into it. Hey, I'd like to be in the Hall of Fame, but if they said to me, 'L.C., do you want to be in, or do want one of the other guys on your team, like Lynn Swann, to be in?' I'd say, 'Take Lynn.' I think it eats him up each time he gets bypassed.

"Lynn was a highlight film player. He went to the moon or to the turf to catch the ball. He won so many games with great catches."

Talking about Swann must have made Greenwood think about Swann's roommate, Franco Harris. And when Greenwood started talking about Franco, he got up out of his chair, and started talking louder.

"They were paying Walter Abercrombie more than they were paying Franco. How do you like that? It was the same way with me. They were paying John Goodman more to sit on the bench than they were paying me. They got Greg Hawthorne, and they got Abercrombie, and now they've got Tim Worley, and none of them play hurt like Franco always did, and none of them have had the success he had.

"I agree with the guys who point to Franco as the guy who turned this franchise around. He came here in 1972 and took us to the playoffs for the first time in the team's history. A guy like Tim Worley has great potential, but he didn't have the immediate impact that Franco had.

"Franco was always hurting. You'd see him in the tank (whirlpool bath) all week, working on his knees, or his ribs, or his ankles, to get ready for Sunday. The guys that have come after him don't play hurt.

"If Franco wanted a million dollars a year, they should have given it to him. If he wanted a million dollars for the following season, and they didn't feel he had it in him to play another year, they still should have given it to him. They owed him that.

"Not only was he a great football player, but he went all over Pittsburgh and did every community service project that came up, and the people of Pittsburgh loved him. All the things he did. Then they treated him the way they did. It wasn't his agent's fault that he ended up going to the Seattle Seahawks. It was management's fault for playing games with him. That really upset me. Why couldn't they pay him?

"Look at the Oakland Raiders. Al Davis is supposed to be such a bad guy. But he always said, 'You play, baby, and I'll pay you.' And he did. Look at the 49ers now! That's why they're so good. Not just because Montana is such a great quarterback. DeBartolo says I want to win, and he pays his players better than anybody else and they win for him."

261

Dwayne Woodruff recalls L.C. Greenwood wearing clothes like he had never seen before. "He'd come into the locker room wearing something I didn't think he could ever top, and then the next day he'd come in wearing something wilder, unreal," said Woodruff.

"Clothing was always my thing," said Greenwood. "Since I was six or seven. When I came to Pittsburgh, I had a lady who made me all kinds of clothes. She'd make me all different kinds of outfits. I was tall and thin and couldn't get what I wanted off the racks. If I did find something that fit, I'd buy it in five different colors, and make up different combinations.

"I was doing a promotion for a clothing store one day, modeling some outfits and talking on the radio, and 'Frenchy' Fuqua came in. I had one with a cape to go with it. It was too small for me. It was a purple jump suit with a cape. He wasn't into clothes at the time.

"They gave him some white shoes and accessorized it for him. Then he started getting things like glass heels with goldfish swimming around in them and, before you knew it, he was getting all kinds of national attention as the team's most flamboyant dresser. He got a lot of p.r. for that. And he wasn't the best-dressed player on the team.

"When I was young and growing up, I'd go out and chop cotton and they'd pay me $2.50 a day. I'd take $2 of that and put it away for my education. I'd take 25 cents out for lunch at school, something like cheese and crackers and some bread and baloney. And I'd take 25 cents out for my clothing allowance. I'd save $1.25 each week for clothes. I'd go to the local men's store and I'd buy stuff, like a shirt, or socks, on a layaway plan. I was always wearing nice stuff."

Greenwood lived in a community called Canton, only this was in Mississippi, not the one in Ohio where the Pro Football Hall of Fame is located. His dad was Moses, and his mother was Eliza and L.C. was one of nine children. Moses was 6-5, and worked hard. He was also hard on his children. "My dad was so tough that I didn't want to be home," said Greenwood. "That's why I chopped cotton; that's why I played football. Anything to be out of the house.

"He'd give me a list of chores to do, and I couldn't get them all done in time, and he'd give me a beating like you wouldn't believe. He'd beat the hell outta me. I don't feel bad about that now. That's just the way it was. It's just what he knew, what he saw others doing before him. It's the way they thought you were supposed to raise kids. He never did anything but work and go to church. He didn't smoke or drink.

"He'd work eight to ten hours at a factory in the day, and then come home and looked after some hogs and animals and some food we raised out in the country. He didn't have a lot of fun.

"So I really grew up fast when I came to Pittsburgh. I had to grow up fast. I was coming from a small town and a small school, and had dealt mostly with black people all my life. But I'm a people person and I got along fine with everybody. And I found out I could play football with anybody and get along with anybody. I've been abused and misused. I'm a trusting person, and I've been told I'm gullible. But I like me just the way I am, and I'm not done playing yet."

262

Ernie Holmes
Lonesome roads

Ernie "Fats" Holmes has always had a tough time dealing with or recognizing reality. He has always operated in another world, a twilight zone. Holmes has had a tough time since he left the Steelers after the 1977 season, but he remains optimistic — even perhaps when he has no reason to be — and thinks tomorrow will be a better day. Tomorrow he will get a better job, one befitting a man of his stature. Tomorrow he will enjoy a banquet.

Holmes has kidded himself for a long time.

Holmes was a menacing figure during his days with the Steelers, both on and off the field. Opposing players feared him. So did teammates. They all thought he was a little crazy. People gave Holmes a lot of space.

Someone close to the Steelers once said that Chuck Noll was an outstanding coach because he could work with an Ernie Holmes as well as an Andy Russell, regarding them as players who worked at opposite ends of the intellectual and behavioral spectrum or rainbow.

Holmes was an eighth round draft choice out of Texas Southern in 1971, and made the team in his second attempt in 1972, splitting time with Ben McGee at defensive tackle. Holmes had been a *Pittsburgh Courier* All-American.

I was unable to interview Holmes for this book because all the telephone numbers provided by the Steelers chapter of the NFL Alumni Association and all the telephone numbers provided by the Steelers provided the same results. The telephone service had been disconnected. In a sense, so has Holmes.

His former teammates told lots of funny, maybe not so funny, stories about Ernie Holmes. He was quite the character, all right. He was, it appears, a disturbed man. He needed help.

But, man, could he play football. He came to the Steelers in 1972 and joined Joe Greene, Dwight White and L.C. Greenwood to form one of the most feared foursomes of all time. They made the cover of *Time* magazine.

Holmes, who turned 43 in July, 1991, has a bizarre record he can not run away from. There was the arrest and conviction for taking potshots at several truck drivers and wounding an Ohio state cop in a helicopter in 1973. He ended up in Western Psychiatric Hospital for a brief stay after that episode.

There was a trial for possession of cocaine in Amarillo, Texas in 1977. He was involved in the Manpower jobs scandal in Pittsburgh in 1978.

There was an assault charge here and a drunk driving charge there.

"I don't know why these problems keep following me around," said Holmes. "Pretty soon, I'm going to be known as Courtroom Ernie."

263

He also had at least two marriage breakups. He has been battling alcohol problems for quite awhile. He had periods of depression.

"It's 9 a.m. . . . In the old days, I'd be starting on my second fifth of cognac by now," he related to sportswriter Ron Cook when he came to Pittsburgh in the summer of 1985 to attend an NFL Alumni Association golf outing.

There are lots of role models chronicled in this book for young people. Holmes is not one of them. But young people might learn from his mistakes. Holmes had it made, as far as professional athletics were concerned, but he could not control himself. Maybe he did not get the help he needed.

Holmes said all his memories of the Steelers were not pleasant ones. I had an opportunity to talk to Holmes on the telephone about ten years back, and he was bitter about a lot of things. He was back in the public consciousness at the time because he was one of the "Redskins" in the American Express commercial that featured Tom Landry, the coach of the Dallas Cowboys.

"I left Pittsburgh without a penny in my pocket," he told me then. "If fair is fair, the whole stadium should sink into the river." Yet he admitted to many that he would probably be in prison were it not for club officials.

"Art Rooney is one guy I don't hold anything against," said Holmes. "He's the greatest man I ever met in Pittsburgh. I played the way I did out of love for him."

Playing the way he did, some insiders say Holmes may have been the best defensive football player on the Steelers in 1974 and 1975, when the team won its first two Super Bowls.

On Holmes' behalf, those close to him always stood by him during his troubles. Club president Dan Rooney, Coach Chuck Noll and several teammates drove to Youngstown, Ohio for one of his trials, and they flew to Amarillo for another, to testify on his behalf as character witnesses.

The Steelers traded him to the Tampa Bay Buccaneers in 1978 after his weight soared and his knees became troublesome. But Noll would never knock him.

"Ernie is very much like Pittsburgh — much better than its reputation," noted Noll.

Joe Greene tries to remember the best of everybody, especially Ernie. "The thing I remember most about Ernie," Greene told Cook at the Steelers' reunion, "was the day he came to the team's Christmas party dressed as Santa Claus. He must have spent $1,000 to $1,500 on toys for the kids."

Trying his best to be a good guy, Holmes bought his high school building in Jamestown, Texas once upon a time and turned it into a youth center. At the same time, he had two boys of his own in Texas and a boy and a girl in California. Not a pretty picture.

"I've had lots of jobs since I quit playing. People ask me, 'What are you doing those lowly things for? You were a superstar. What did you do with all your money? Snort it away.'

"I try to tell them I don't do that stuff. I try to explain what's happened to me. But how do you tell my story?

"People have been manipulating me and my money since I played for the Steelers. I just quit a job not too long ago because of that. I was working double shifts, but I wasn't getting paid for it. I can count, you know? I'm no fool."

He said something about becoming a security guard, or starting his own security guard business. "I'm a licensed specialist with a .357 and a .38. I shoot a .45 pretty good, too," he said back in 1985. Imagine hiring Holmes as a security guard. Maybe he could get that cop he shot in Ohio as a reference regarding his shooting skills.

"I don't know if I had a good time or just a good drunk during my years here," he said. "I don't have any arrows to shoot or axes to chop on anyone's head. I just wish some things could have been different."

Ernie "Arrowhead" Holmes

Jon Kolb
"Successes last only one play"

Jon Kolb keeps surprising people. As an undersized offensive lineman for the Steelers' four Super Bowl teams, he kept the biggest and baddest defensive linemen away from Terry Bradshaw and punched holes and found daylight for Franco Harris and Rocky Bleier.

Kolb was one of the quietest of the Steelers, a strong, silent type, never seeking publicity or the limelight, and thus did not enjoy the notoriety of many of his teammates. He never played in a Pro Bowl, but was regarded by the Steelers as one of their most valued performers.

To a man, they considered Kolb an All-Pro, in every way. At 6-2, 260, he was smaller than most NFL linemen, but the Steelers liked them that way for their trapping game which required quickness and strength above all else. Kolb could always move well, and he could bench press with the best of them in the weight room. He handled opposing linemen as well as weights.

Kolb kept his distance from the media, for the most part, somewhat warily, yet he and Jack Ham were the only players on the team who offered their sympathy when they learned that my brother Dan had died during my days on the Steelers' beat. Kolb's compassion wouldn't surprise those close to him, but he surprised and pleased me that day. It is something about him and Ham I will never forget.

"A lot of our guys had images that were not honest, not the way they really were," said Kolb. "So many of them have been successful beyond football. That's why I don't think many of them wear their Super Bowl rings. They've gone beyond that."

Kolb came to the Steelers the same year, 1969, as Chuck Noll. He was Noll's first No. 3 draft choice, a center and linebacker who had been a second-team All-America selection his senior season at Oklahoma State. Kolb came from Ponca City, Oklahoma, and he has stayed as long as Noll. He is one cowboy that Noll likes.

He played offensive tackle for 13 seasons before joining the coaching staff as a conditioning coach in 1982, and later that year replaced George Perles as the defensive line coach. Kolb has since looked after the special teams, and more recently he resumed his duties as conditioning coach while assisting with the offensive line. Kolb is a company man, and contributes in many ways.

There are days when Kolb has a difficult time saying hello to anyone. He goes about his job and is satisfied to do it well. Get him going in a conversation, however, and he will talk non-stop. You can not keep Kolb from going into an ardent dissertation on the subject, especially if you are talking about blocking techniques, protein, amino acids, any kind of conditioning charts, Christian fellowship, hunting, fishing, weightlifting, football in general, farms or diets.

Then Kolb comes out of the closet. He is a zealot, always out to proselyte non-believers to his side. Kolb can be convincing, whatever the subject. He is like Noll in that respect, as well. After 22 years together, he thought he had come to understand Noll better.

"I've learned not to get alarmed if he hasn't spoken to you in the last week," said Kolb. "I've learned you don't have to start packing your bags. Sometimes he gets so focused. More than anyone I ever met.

"His mind gets locked in on a subject. When he's thinking about something, he'll walk into the locker room and he doesn't even acknowledge you. When he does that, I go into re-wind in my mind. What have I done wrong? Is he mad at me about this? Or is it that?"

But Kolb is the only coach who has been with Noll, as a player and as an assistant, for all of his 200 plus victories. "They say I retired from football," he said, "but I'm involved with football three times as much as I was as a player."

There are times when Kolb has tunnel vision as much as his boss. Once he warmed to the subject, however, Kolb cleansed his soul on several topics relating to his career with the Steelers. He provided some insights into the special existence of the offensive linemen: why they bond together, how they operate in anonymity and fear, for the most part; why their very name is a misnomer, the kinship and "short hand" they develop in their signal-calling after a long time together. He also offered clues about the success of the Steelers' defensive front four during those glory days, especially the intensity that Dwight White and Ernie Holmes, who challenged and taunted him every day in practice, brought to the game, and to the practice field.

Kolb is a deep thinker and, once you open the floodgates, look out.

"Losing teammates always hit me the hardest," he said. "You get close to guys, and then they're gone. People like Larry Brown and Sam Davis knew things about me that nobody else knew. We were that close. The first real shocker to my system came after they announced that I was retiring to become a coach. That same day I walked into the players' dressing room, and the guys were sitting around by my old cubicle, sitting on their stools as we always did, and they were talking away. When a coach would walk up, the communication would either change or stop. And that's exactly what happened when I approached my pals. I couldn't believe it. It had been just one hour since I went from being a player to a coach, and it made that much difference. Mike Webster was one of those guys, and I couldn't believe the way he reacted to the switch in my role.

"Then I went into the coaches' dressing room, a place where I'd been maybe five minutes in my entire 13 seasons with the Steelers. And two coaches were talking about a player. They were discussing his abilities, strengths and weaknesses, and my mouth dropped open. I'm still thinking about him as a teammate. On that day I didn't feel like a player or a coach. I still don't feel completely like a coach yet. As long as guys like Tunch Ilkin, Dwayne Woodruff, Bryan Hinkle and David Little are on the team, I'll feel that way. We played together. They will have to leave for me to make that shift."

267

He offered theories on other subjects close to his heart:

"The defensive linemen are really the offensive linemen," said Kolb. "They can run stunts, and jump around, and attack you or, in short, they can be offensive. Whereas the offensive linemen have to be defensive. In pass blocking, you have to hold your ground. In run blocking, you have to stay with your man, and not let him get away. The worst thing that can happen to an offensive lineman is to get mad or aggressive. You've got to stay cool and keep your head about you. You have to be as cool as an assassin. An offensive lineman cannot allow himself to have a rage."

That was not always easy, Kolb concedes, when it came to practices at Three Rivers Stadium. Kolb and his sidekick, guard Sam Davis, had to go up against Dwight White and Ernie Holmes each day at practice. Their confrontations were wars.

"Those guys never took a play off; they charged hard on every snap," recalled Kolb. "They had such pride in their game. I see Dwight White today and he still doesn't relax when he sees me. He'll say, 'I beat you up all the time.' He lives out in the North Hills near where I live, so I see him from time to time. He'll be fishing at the lake in North Park with his daughter. He'll be wearing an ol' straw hat and looking like Huckleberry Finn. I'd love to be able to say something like, 'How's the fishin'?' or 'Did you catch anything?' But he won't let me; he won't let me up for air. You can't say the first nice thing to him; he won't give you a chance. He's a competitor, and he'll tell me how he always got the best of me. 'Dwight, you never did,' I'll say and then that starts it going. It was like that when we were playing together. We'd be on a bus going to play in the Super Bowl, and he'd try to pick something with me. He wouldn't let me rest. He was like a flea, always finding a place to bite me.

"Now he did me a big personal favor just two years ago, so he treats me right that way. But Dwight took what he did so seriously. I'd get so mad at George Perles because he was coaching that defensive line, and he knew the combination to get Dwight and Ernie going.

"On Friday, we'd go through our short yardage plays. I've never understood why we spend so much time on that because basically it's straight-ahead blocking, and they're coming straight at you, too. It's like a bull rush.

"Now L.C. Greenwood and Joe Greene were the other two in the front four, and they were on the other side so Sam Davis and I didn't go up against them. L.C. generally practiced with a towel around his neck, and he'd take his defensive stance sometimes. He didn't get too serious. Joe was 50-50. I was talking to Joe about it just the other day. He doesn't remember correctly what he did, but Joe would pick his spots. Now that he's a coach, of course, he doesn't want to admit that. Because he wants his guys going hard on every snap. But Dwight and Ernie did it that way every time.

"Sometimes the games on Sunday were a relief. We used to say we had four games a week, on Wednesday, Thursday, Friday and Sunday. There were times when Sunday was the least physical game."

It was mentioned to Kolb that Ray Mansfield, the veteran center, used to scold Holmes or White when they got too vociferous in practice drills. "I couldn't say that," Kolb came back. "I couldn't say, 'C'mon, Dwight, lighten up.' I would never admit to him that he was getting to me. Sam was real quiet, too, and he didn't say much.

"I could read Dwight's stance. He doesn't want to hear that, but I knew when he was coming hard on the inside or the outside, and I could meet him, and stop him. I had his number."

Holmes was harder to stop, on or off the field, than even White. He was not as predictable.

"I remember this time at St. Vincent College when Chuck was fining Ernie for being overweight. He was well over 300 pounds, and Chuck told him he was going to start fining him every day to the tune of $50 for every pound he was overweight. He told him he would be weighing him the next day.

"Sam takes Ernie under his wing, and tells him about liquid protein, which was a big deal then, and how that could help him lose weight. Ernie didn't understand, however, that you took the liquid protein instead of your normal food intake. And there was nothing normal about Ernie's normal food intake. So Ernie took some liquid protein that day. At dinner that night in the cafeteria, Ernie had his usual two or three helpings of everything. He was traced later that night eating at Pizza Hut, the 19th Hole and then Burger Chef. When he weighed in the next morning, he had gained six pounds.

"Ernie was mad and he was mad at Sam. Sam and I were rooming together at the time. Sam was lying on his back in bed, with his hands cupped under his head, staring at the ceiling. All of a sudden, the door was kicked open. It opened with a loud sound and scared me to death. It was Ernie. He had kicked in the door, and he rushed toward Sam and grabbed Sam around the neck and started shaking him. 'I'll kill you!' he screamed. 'I'll kill you!' Sam's legs were dangling all over the place. I'm trying to pull Ernie off Sam, and I'm not budging him. 'That liquid protein didn't work!' Ernie is screaming. Finally, some other guys came to the rescue and saved Sam from being strangled in his bed. Now, that's one side of Ernie Holmes.

"Here's another. I can remember holding a 4th of July picnic at our farm out in Washington County, when I was living out there. I had made a big sand box and a tree house for my son, Eric. I was real proud of it. I always thought a sand box and tree house were important when I was a kid, and I wanted my kids to have them, too.

"Ernie went over and got in the sand box and played with the kids all day. What a contrast! He could be such a madman at times, on the one hand, and, on the other hand, there was such a softness to him at other times."

Kolb let those stories sit awhile, and turned his attention to some potato salad he was eating during a lunch break in the Steelers' offices at Three Rivers Stadium. The team had defeated the Los Angeles Rams,

41-10, in a Monday Night Football Game just the day before. It had been quite a turnaround from a disappointing 27-7 defeat to the 49ers in San Francisco the week before. The Steelers were solid in the first half in that game, and looked like they might pull off an upset at San Francisco, but they made some embarrassing mistakes in the second half to take themselves out of the contest. Now, after the victory over the Rams, they were back in the AFC race again.

Earlier, Kolb had told team president Dan Rooney, who had been having lunch at the same table, that he was pleased by the improved attitude toward adversity that the Steelers had shown the night before.

Gaston Green had returned the opening kickoff 99 yards to enable the Rams to jump off to a 7-0 lead before Al Michaels, Dan Dierdorf and Frank Gifford had a chance to properly introduce themselves on the ABC TV network telecast. It had been the first time in four years the Steelers showed up on Monday Night Football, whereas they had been regulars in the '70s.

"After they got that first TD on us, we went right out on the field with a 'so what?' attitude," said Kolb, "and went on a nice march (8-play 75-yard drive) and scored ourselves. We came right back at them. Our guys came off the field after that touchdown like they haven't come off the field before. They were pumped. They knew they could move the ball on the Rams. Then it was a new game, and we hit hard and we beat them in every way. Last night, we had a bad break on the opening play and we didn't fall apart.

"When we were playing the 49ers, on the other hand, we were down by only three points late in the third quarter, but the 49ers knew they would find a way to win it. They knew something would happen. They knew it, just like we always felt that way when we had the Super Bowl teams. Our guys haven't gotten to that point. That's the difference between a team that knows it's good and a young team that's not sure of itself. People look at the Steelers today and they forget about the struggles we had to go through to find ourselves.

"I think about those times almost daily," claimed Kolb. "We didn't know what we had. You can't either dwell on it or live in the past, but you can work hard to get back to those winning ways. You can build off it.

"I try to look ahead. I have a 19-year-old son, Eric, who is doing well in college right now. I'm so proud of him. I have a 10-year-old son, David, and he's doing well. He wanted to play racquetball the other day. I didn't feel like playing racquetball, but I did. And we had a great time. You can get caught up in this football stuff sometimes, but you have to look beyond it to really enjoy what's out there."

That is for sure. There are no windows in the Steelers' office complex at Three Rivers Stadium. The sun does not shine that much in Pittsburgh, to begin with, but it shines even less in the Steelers' offices. There is a lot of concrete, and a lot of black walls. The gold stripes don't provide much of a relief from the drabness and dreariness of the place. It is still your basic bomb shelter.

The Rooneys and most of the people who work there are pretty pale. I remember one bright afternoon, when I was covering the New York Giants at their camp in Pleasantville, N.Y., talking to team owner Wellington Mara, whose blue eyes were in a permanent squeeze the entire conversation. "The Irish were not meant to be out in the sun," he said. "We were meant to live in caves and peat bogs. I think that's why so many Irish spend so much time in bars where it's dark." It may also offer a clue as to why the Steelers owners always liked being in the bowels of a concrete stadium. The sun was for sissies.

As long as there are barbells in that basement, Kolb can keep himself happy, too. If he wanted to get tanned, he would simply go out in the stadium and run up and down the steps in the sun-streaked upper decks about a hundred times. He and Mike Webster always thought that was a lot of fun in the sun. Their idea of a day at the beach.

"I played for a losing team in college for three years," recalled Kolb. "Then I came here and we were 1-13 my first season. We were a very close team. The struggle brought the closeness. We were satisfied with small successes in those days."

Kolb can trace his Steeler involvement back to Pitt Stadium, where he played as a rookie, and through all the seasons that the Steelers have called Three Rivers Stadium their home.

"I can take you out on the field in Three Rivers Stadium and show you a spot on the 25 yard line, between the hash marks, where I once gave up a sack. I don't remember the team or the player who did it, but I know I was embarrassed. Brad was writhing on the field, like he was never going to get up. You don't want the quarterback to do that. You want the quarterback to bounce up and get back in the huddle. When he's writhing out there like that it just calls that much more attention to what you did, and it only adds to your embarrassment.

"In our first game in Cleveland this year, Bubby Brister got sacked several times, and he was doubling up on the ground. It was no different for me as a coach than it was as a player. I'm still saying under my breath, 'C'mon, Bubby, get up. Don't just lie there.'

"I have tombstones and wreaths on a lot of fields like that. The turf may be different than it was then, but I know the spots. There's one around the 45-yard line out at Pitt Stadium where I blocked Ray Nitschke, who'd been my boyhood hero. We were playing the Green Bay Packers there my rookie year. Mansfield got hurt and had to come out, and Coach Noll sent me in at center.

"I'm looking ahead and I can see Ray Nitschke. He had no teeth, and he was looking right at me. He was the Jack Lambert of his day, in every way, including those teeth he didn't have. I'm going, 'Wow!' My life was complete. I'm 22, and I'm playing against Ray Nitschke and the great Green Bay Packers.

"On the first play, Dick Hoak was the ballcarrier and Nitschke hit Hoakie clean. I never moved to block Nitschke on that first play. Noll started hollering at me, 'What are you doing?' That kinda woke me up. On the next play, I cut blocked on Nitschke, something I seldom did when I was playing, and he went down. I remember Earl Gros was carrying the ball. Nitschke's knees were bad, and he was near the end of his career, and he went down. I remember that play. It made such an impression. It was like it was yesterday."

Kolb claims that the offensive linemen were thought of as a group, whereas running backs had individual identities such as Franco and Rocky, and the wide receivers like Lynn Swann and John Stallworth, and, of course, Bradshaw, the quarterback. "No one mentioned us by name too often," he said. "Our personalities probably had something to do with it, too."

Kolb played for 11 seasons next to Davis, and his last two alongside Craig Wolfley. "I went through two generations, so to speak," he said. "When Sam got hurt in a pre-season game at Dallas, I started playing with Wolfley, whom I didn't really know.

"Sam and I had played together so long, we had sort of a short hand in our signals on the line, as far as who we would be blocking. He might just say my name and I knew what he wanted me to do. Now Craig's making calls, and I'm saying, 'What does it mean?' He was going by the book, by our system, and Sam and I had gotten away from doing it by the book. We were playing it by ear. With Sam and I, there was a game going on as far as the team was concerned, and there was also our game. And sometimes I don't know what was more important to us. We might have Harvey Martin and Randy White of the Cowboys to deal with, and we had to respond in concert. That's where closeness develops.

"I would like to be like Sam Davis. How do you write a book about being humble? Well, I think Sam Davis and Larry Brown could do it. You could look around here and find somebody who doesn't like me, but you'd never find anybody who didn't like those two.

"It was hard getting used to a new partner, but Craig and I were a good combination, too. That was a good year for me, though. You would look at your year by things like how many sacks you gave up. There was a play that year where I got beaten as badly as I've ever been beaten. It happened in Tampa. I still don't know if my guy went inside or outside. He just disappeared right before my eyes. There's no sicker feeling. That's another reason why offensive linemen are so close. Your heart turns to panic. As I turned to see where my man went, I saw Craig catch him and knock him off stride. He just nicked him enough in the knee to knock him down. He saved me. I can remember it like it was yesterday. I had a sick feeling, like when you nearly have an accident in a car. Boy, I hugged Craig so hard. I looked bad enough on the film that week, but he saved me from being embarrassed on the field that day.

"I don't think I ever cut-block too many people. That's a one-shot deal. If you missed your man, then you're dead. Or he could go down and get back up again. If your quarterback is taking time to throw the ball, your man has time to get back up and get after your quarterback. You still look bad. I wanted to stay with my man.

"We had confidence in those days. You knew Larry Brown and Mike Webster would do their job, and you knew Moon Mullins and Sam Davis would do what they were supposed to do. You felt Swann and Stallworth would catch the ball, and that Brad would get it to them. You knew Franco and Rocky would run the ball well and get the first downs.

"So I had a constant panic. You have a bad down, and you messed up everything. You were the one who blew it. We had so many capable people, and you didn't want to be the one to get embarrassed. Successes for an offensive lineman last only one play, and failures last forever."

Kolb was asked about Moon Mullins, who had been a tight end at Southern California, and seemed to be cut from a different cloth than the rest of the offensive linemen. "Moon was different from everybody else," said Kolb. "Moon was always hotter than everybody else; he was always more tired. He was always more frustrated. But he was good for us. I might have felt real sore, but I knew I didn't hurt as badly as Moon did. He was different. These guys are all into Bart Simpson talk now. Moon was saying that stuff 20 years ago. He'd say, 'Hey, man, just trade me.' He was ahead of his time."

I had been told that Mullins and Webster often corrected Bradshaw in his play-calling, or called the play themselves if Bradshaw was struggling to make the call. "Maybe Terry would call 'full right 18 straight,' and everybody knew it was 'full right 19 straight.' So we didn't say anything; we just ran the right play. We knew what he meant."

Kolb did concede that the Steelers changed their "live" color in 1990 for the first time since he had been associated with the Steelers. That color — which had been brown — signalled that there would be an audible call. "If we didn't catch it," recalled Kolb with a smile, "the defensive team would remind us because they would be yelling 'brown' on the other side of the line. We couldn't miss it.

"That 'full right 19 straight,' by the way, was my play. It meant that Franco would be running right over me. But Franco ran over Larry Brown just as often. He ran where he saw an opening.

"Franco, by the way, was a lot harder to block for than Rocky. Rocky hit the hole faster. You had to block longer for Franco, and hold your man longer. You'd feel Rocky running by you. You never felt Franco. I was always conscious of Rocky going by."

What about Bradshaw? What's bugging him? Kolb and Bradshaw had roomed together late in their careers, after Davis got hurt and was not traveling with the team. Kolb was asked to explain Bradshaw's behavior when he was bad-mouthing Pittsburgh, its fans and the Steelers at large, and the front office in particular.

"When I think of Brad, to me, it's like when you had a lot of presents under the Christmas tree, and you didn't know which one to play with. He had so much talent, and he could pick which way he wanted to go. He was my roommate for a few years on the road after Sam was injured. So I got to spend time with him.

"I'd look at Brad and say what if I had been blessed with some of the things that he had. I'd been with Brad in New York, for instance. My wife would go up with his wife — he was married to Jo Jo Starbuck back then — and we'd be walking the streets of New York, and everybody knew him.

"Or we'd be at a rodeo in Fort Worth, and everyone wanted his attention. Everybody was blowing by me to get to him for his autograph, and to talk to him. I felt bad for him. He couldn't enjoy the rodeo. Not too many people in Pittsburgh have ever experienced the public adulation he had. We were at the Wheeling Jamboree once, and everybody was demanding his time. I can understand how he feels now. I think he feels, 'I've given, and I've given.'

"He was the right quarterback for us, that's for sure. He fit into a unique recipe. He fit at the right time with the kind of guys we had. The kind of receivers we had; they fit his talents. Brad was not Joe Montana. He didn't read the coverage and go one-two-three and fire the ball. Brad knew what he was going to do and he just did it.

"He was my roommate, so we'd be watching a game on TV, and he say, 'You can't throw the ball into Cover 2 like that.' So I knew he knew formations. I know he could read the defenses. I watch the game on TV as a fan. Brad has always watched it as a coach.

"Swann might be covered by ten men and he'd just gun the ball to him. He had receivers he could do that with. He could throw into a crowd and get away with it. He also had an offensive line that gave him time to find his receivers. You can look back and you can check the records and he didn't get sacked much. We were usually one or two in the league in that category. And Brad didn't get rid of the ball as quickly as Danny Marino. People were playing a different style back then. Now it's more drop-back and throw the ball on cadence.

"As far as leadership goes, we didn't need a leader on the field. I don't think anybody was looking for a leader. Moon was going to complain whatever we did, and Rocky was going to block, and Franco was going to find an opening, and our offensive line, including the tight end, was going to block. The press wanted to write about a leader, but they were looking for something we weren't looking for. Our huddle was pretty quiet. The defensive huddle, I'm told, was something else. They're different."

When Kolb was playing for the Steelers, he raised cattle on a farm in Ninevah, and he had his own meat packing house in nearby Washington. He would go to the farm on his days off, when his teammates might be out playing golf.

"Everybody knows we have a great quarterback, great receivers and great running backs," he said back then in an interview I did with him for *The Pittsburgh Press*. "I think we're taken for granted on the offensive line. Some people must think they just found us out in an alley.

"Even the coaches, when they're talking about the backs and receivers, refer to them as the 'skill' positions. Like we're just trained to run around and bump into things."

He looked around the clubhouse back then and spoke of his colleagues in the front line.

"Mike Webster has no peer at his position," said Kolb. "He's the best center in the National Football League. Sam Davis — and I don't know how he does it — just keeps playing better every year. Larry Brown, by the end of the season, could be the best tackle in the league. Those three are just exceptional. Larry is starting to dominate people. Mike has been doing it right along, and it's obvious what Sam does."

Pointing toward Gerry "Moon" Mullins, Kolb said, "Gerry's just a good steady player, and he gets his job done."

What about Kolb?

"Jon isn't a press agent; he just shows up," he said.

He was also quick to praise two young reserves, Ted Petersen and Steve Courson.

He took them one game at a time in those days, one play at a time, really. "It's easy," Kolb liked to say, "to go from the penthouse to the outhouse."

Kolb had thoughts on other aspects of the lot of the offensive linemen which he related to me when I was covering the club for *The Pittsburgh Press*:

"If you beat a guy 68 times in 70 plays, you don't get to jump around with your hands up. But if a guy beats you twice in timely situations, he gets the game ball and gets to run around. He might get his butt run over on the next play and nobody notices it.

"If you listen to color men on television, you'd think the tackle is out there just so the defensive lineman can beat up on him. But then our defensive linemen think the same way. I guess that's why they're so successful.

"Normally, our own coaches don't even know were're around as long as we're not making any mistakes."

Or as Davis put it: "If you block three defensive linemen and one gets through to sack the quarterback, the defensive line looks great. Conversely, if four offensive linemen do their job, and the fifth fails, then the entire line looks bad. That's just a job hazard."

Kolb could never get comfortable when he was playing for the Steelers. He was always worried about his status, where he stood with the coaches, whether he would survive the next cut.

"I was in my third year on the team and I was a starter," Kolb told me when I was covering the club, "but I'd had no real communication with Coach Noll. He'd say something to me on the field once in a while, but that was it.

"So I was in my room one day at camp, and there was a knock at the door, and one of the ballboys told me Coach Noll wanted to see me.

"Immediately, I thought I was being cut. At least I hoped I was being traded. I walked to his office, and just before I got there I had to wipe away a tear or two. I tried to put on my best game face before going into his office.

275

"I stepped through the door, and he was sitting, with his back to me, at his desk. He turned around toward me and said, 'Being a farm boy, I thought you might be able to appreciate these.' He handed me a photograph he'd taken, and said, 'This is a pileated woodpecker I caught with my camera when I was in the Florida Everglades.'

"He also showed me several other pictures he'd taken there, like one of an alligator peering out of the water the way they do. Boy, I was so relieved, I flipped through those pictures with such a smile on my face. Oh, man.

"I guess Coach Noll associates farm boys with nature and the outdoors. The thing I'd have to say about the coach is that he's unpredictable. One time a few years back, I was sitting in my room at St. Vincent's with three other guys. One of them had a banjo leaning up against the wall by his bed. Coach Noll walked into the room, picked up the banjo, sat down on one of the beds and played it and sang a song, and then walked out without a word to any of us."

Jon Kolb assists Merril Hoge in pre-game stretching exercises.

Jack Ham
He is still delivering the coal

E ver since he was a young boy, Jack Ham has been in the coal business as well as the football business. Both were in his blood. Jack is from Johnstown, Pennsylvania, best known perhaps for monstrous floods that devastated the Cambria County community in 1889 and 1936 or as the site of a movie in which a 21-year-old Tom Cruise starred in 1983 as a handsome heartbreaking quarterback in "All the Right Moves," about a high school football player from western Pennsylvania who needed a scholarship to get out of a depressed town. The movie might have been about Jack Raphael Ham, a hometown boy who made good as an All-American linebacker at nearby Penn State University and as a Hall of Fame performer for the four Super Bowl championship teams of the Pittsburgh Steelers in the '70s.

He was always at his best in big games, and may be best remembered for the two passes he intercepted in the fourth quarter of the 1974 AFC title game with Oakland.

John Ham, his father, was a mechanic responsible for repairing equipment for Bethlehem Mines. After work and on weekends, John Ham made extra money by hauling coal to homes in the Johnstown area. Jack helped his dad haul that coal to his regular customers.

"You liked it when you could just dump the coal down a window or door into the cellar," recalled Jack, "and you hated it when you had to put it in a wheelbarrow and push it up ramps to get to out-of-the-way cellars or coal bins." It brought to mind images of coal bins in my own homes in Hazelwood, a scene my children will never know.

Then again, maybe those out-of-the-way coal bins helped build strong muscles for the young Ham. It certainly didn't turn him off about coal. When he was playing for the Steelers, he moonlighted — just like his dad in a sense — as a sales rep for Marshall Brown's Neville Coal Co.

When I visited with Jack on a beautiful day in early November of 1990 — temperatures were in the high 70s in Pittsburgh and the fall foliage was spectacular — he was working in his office at Industrial Park, a professional building complex just above the Ohio River and Neville Island, only two minutes from Ham's posh home in Sewickley Heights, one of Pittsburgh's most affluent and fashionable suburban communities. Ham didn't have any business appointments that afternoon, so he showed up casually dressed in tennis whites and sneakers, and he still looked like an athlete in fine shape, even if he was just over a month away from his 42nd birthday. There was more salt and pepper in his hair, especially his beard, than when I had seen him last.

Nowadays Ham can handle coal while wearing tennis whites because he's not loading it into wheelbarrows anymore. Jack was still delivering coal, but he had cleaned up his act and broadened his horizons considerably.

"I sell coal internationally, to Japan, and several European markets, via ports in Philadelphia and Baltimore, and I have some customers in Washington, D.C. I am an exclusive rep for Cooney Brothers Coal Company in Portage." Portage is a town you pass while driving Rt. 219 South from Ebensburg, about five or six miles from Johnstown. Ham first met Paul Cooney when the latter was invited by the Steelers to accompany the team on a road trip.

"When I was playing for the Steelers, Monday and Tuesday were truly off-days, and you could work at something," said Ham. "You could get away from football for awhile, and you could prepare for a professional career after football."

Ham learned how to work hard, and efficiently, and to organize his time schedule from his father back in Johnstown. "When the home coal business waned," he recalled, "my dad got into lawn care, and I remember going with him to cut grass at the Sunnehanna Country Club.

"My dad needed to make extra money. When I was in high school at Bishop McCort, I had an older brother, Ron, going to Villanova University, and an older sister, Connie, going to Duquesne University. My dad was moonlighting quite a bit because he needed the money to pay for two college tuitions. It was a struggle for him, a real drain, but his goal was to make sure we all went to college. I got a scholarship to go to Penn State (one of the last two offered that year by Joe Paterno, almost as an afterthought). That should have helped, but I think I ended up costing my dad more money.

"He went to every game I played at Penn State, even if it was in California. I played in the Hula Bowl, an all-star game in Honolulu, and he went to that. When I was playing for the Steelers, my dad used to go to a high school football game on Friday night, the Penn State game on Saturday, and then come to Pittsburgh to see the Steelers on Sunday."

Jack's mother, Caroline, still comes to some Steelers' games at Three Rivers Stadium.

"My dad died in 1980 (at age 65). It's a shame he didn't get to see me get inducted into the Pro Football Hall of Fame (1988). It's kinda ironic that I ended up in the coal business. If my father knew I was working for a non-union coal organization I think he'd flip over in his grave."

When Ham went into the Pro Football Hall of Fame, the class included two western Pennsylvania products, Mike Ditka of Aliquippa and Fred Biletnikoff of Erie.

In addition, Jack had served as a color analyst on Steelers' preseason telecasts for five years, the first four on WTAE-TV and the 1990 exhibition slate for WPXI-TV. He did the same for Mutual Radio Network's Sunday National Football League broadcasts. As a youngster, he didn't talk much because he had a lisp. He overcame that, however, to become a much-respected radio and TV commentator. He was no longer doing any commentary for college telecasts. "I didn't want to be on the road so much," he explained. "The older I get the more I value my free time at home with Joanne."

Jack Ham

Times change, that's all. Ham told me a story that sounded so familiar, because I had experienced it myself with my own father and brother in my youth.

"When I was in high school, my dad and my brother and I would watch the Steelers' games on television, and the Steelers would lose most of the time, and my dad was so critical of them. We'd drive to Pittsburgh every so often, and we'd go see the Steelers play at Pitt Stadium. They'd beat the hell out of some team for three quarters, but they always managed to lose in the end. In fact, my wife, Joanne, remembers going to see some of those same games, and seeing Gale Sayers of the Chicago Bears returning a kickoff a hundred yards. People had those kinds of days against the Steelers back then.

"So I didn't have the best image of the Steelers. Of course, I have buddies back in Johnstown who didn't have the best image of me. I go back there a lot and there are some guys who went to high school with me who didn't think I was worth a shit and they're still wondering what happened to me."

Ham was a unanimous All-America as a senior at Penn State, but was somewhat undersized as far as professional football standards, at 6-1, 220 pounds.

"When I was drafted by the Steelers, I wasn't too happy," he said. "The New York Giants had told me they were going to take me No. 1. San Diego told me they'd draft me No. 1. Nobody drafted me No. 1. When Dan Rooney called me and told me the Steelers had just drafted me on the second round, I was sick. Steve Smear, one of my teammates at Penn State, and I were appearing at a car dealership in Johnstown when I got the news. I was not too thrilled."

Then when he first reported to Three Rivers Stadium, among the smallest of the new recruits, Ham was chastised by Art Rooney, Jr., then the head of the team's player personnel department. When Rooney spotted the undersized Ham hanging around the clubhouse door, he shouted, "Hey, kiddo, deliveries are down the hall!"

"You don't understand," Ham hollered back. "I'm the linebacker you drafted from Penn State. Remember? Jack Ham?"

If he needed something to lighten him up at that moment, Ham could look to his left where there was a larger-than-life portrait poster of Oprah Winfrey, and to his right, someone had superimposed the head of Fred Rogers of "Mr. Roger's Neighborhood" on Ham's body in a Steeler uniform in his Pro Football Hall of Fame poster. And someone had written in the message, "To Jack Ham, Have a nice day! Fred Rogers."

"I didn't know any better than playing behind a great defensive line when I came to the Steelers," said Ham. "We had a great team at Penn State and we had Mike Reid, Steve Smear and John Ebersole on our defensive line, and they all went on to be starters in the National Football League.

"I came to Pittsburgh and saw a defensive line that was not as good as the one we'd had at Penn State. I'm not sure Lloyd Voss, Chuck Hinton and Ben McGee would appreciate that, but that's how I felt.

"We had a line coach named Dan Radakovich and he didn't waste any time in making changes. He put Dwight White in right away at camp as the starting right end. He put L.C. Greenwood in as the starting left end. He just moved them all in there from Day One. Joe Greene was already there, and Ernie Holmes came in with me. So for the next ten years, I was playing behind another great defensive line."

Ham started as a rookie and was in the Pro Bowl by his fourth year.

Ham came to the Steelers in the draft class of 1971. It was topped by wide receiver Frank Lewis of Grambling, who was outstanding for the Steelers and even better for the Buffalo Bills after he went to them in a trade in 1978. It also included Gerry "Moon" Mullins of Southern Cal, White from East Texas State, Larry Brown of Kansas, Holmes of Texas Southern and Mike Wagner of Western Illinois.

"Look at that draft and look at the draft of 1974, and you'll see how lucky the Steelers were; that's one of the big reasons we became such a great team," said Ham.

That 1974 class, for the record, included Lynn Swann of Southern Cal, Jack Lambert of Kent State, John Stallworth of Alabama A&M ("You have to be lucky when you get a Stallworth on the fourth round"), Jim Allen of UCLA, and Mike Webster of Wisconsin. Donnie Shell of South Carolina State and Randy Grossman of Temple were both signed as free agents that same summer. There could be as many as five Hall of Famers from that class.

"I don't know what would have happened to my career if I had played for the New Orleans Saints or the Tampa Bay Buccaneers. I'm the first guy to tell you I needed help. I played behind L.C. Greenwood and Joe Greene, and alongside Jack Lambert for most of my career. That's why I always admired Andy Russell. He played great football for awful football teams. He and Joe Greene were the only Steelers in the Pro Bowl back in 1971 and 1972. I didn't know what it was like to ever play behind a bad defensive line."

Jack Ham was hurt and unable to play late in the season and in the playoffs when the Steelers were shooting for a fifth Super Bowl championship in late December of 1980. The year before, he had been hurt in the next-to-the-last game of the season, suffering a broken left ankle that finished him for the year. Even so, Ham had been named the best linebacker in the American Football Conference that season. It didn't make up for not being able to play in the Super Bowl. And now, a year later, he was sidelined again just when things were heating up.

"We're gonna miss him," Jack Lambert said. "That's one guy you never want out of your lineup."

Or, as L.C. Greenwood put it, "With the kinda thing Ham does, they don't even run or throw in his direction."

In a story I wrote from San Diego for *The Pittsburgh Press*, Ham said, "Goal-wise, I didn't come into the league to be an all-pro. I sure didn't want to be on a losing team. I never experienced a losing record, and didn't want to in the pros, either, but that's what happened here my first year. I enjoy the team aspect of the game, going for championships in the playoffs and winning Super Bowls. Those are the fun things to me. All-pro . . . that's after the fact.

"After we won the Super Bowl a second time after the 1975 season, I was having breakfast with Joe Greene when we were getting ready to play in the Pro Bowl.

"Joe was just beaming. He'd had a great season, and he'd won all kinds of awards. He had that Coca-Cola commercial smile on his face. And we talked about what really was important to us as players. We agreed that all those individual awards and all-pro stuff didn't come anywhere near what winning a championship did for you."

Ham didn't know he would end up being a radio and TV analyst after his playing days. Back then, such experts didn't carry a lot of weight with him.

"People get reputations for big plays. But I prefer to play consistent, error-free football. If you're doing your job well, and defending your own area, you might not get tested that often, or get a chance to make big plays.

"I don't care what other people say or write about what I've done on the football field. I don't think in individual terms. It's what happens to our football team that's important. Unless the criticism comes from Chuck Noll, I don't think much about it. It's not important. Most people don't know what we're trying to do defensively, or what my responsibility is on a certain play.

"When we go through a film, it's what Noll thinks that's important. I'm only interested in the criticism — positive or negative — when it comes from inside our organization. Others can't comment on my play; at least I don't have to concern myself with it."

Ham did not avoid the media. He would answer questions thoughtfully if approached, but he didn't volunteer much. Sam Rutigliano, when he was coaching the Cleveland Browns, worked with Ham twice in the Pro Bowl, and always referred to him as "the quiet one." It was how Ham struck a lot of people.

"I've been the same way all my life," he said. "I just happen to play football. Sometimes when you're in an occupation everyone just expects you to be outgoing, and to have clever things to say all the time.

"Franco Harris has a bad rap in that respect. He's been a quiet guy all his life. He was like that when we played together at Penn State. He's an introverted guy, that's all. It's not because he has a big ego, or that he's aloof. That's not him at all."

Ham was always the first to extol the virtues of the men around him. "If I had been with another team," he said, "I might not have been thought of in the same light. We have a unique type of defense, and it's honed around the kind of talent we have. I'm not kidding myself.

A 218-pound outside linebacker might get crushed out there if I were surrounded by different people."

One of his close friends was Mike Wagner, the free safety. "Jack just totally controls his area of coverage," said Wagner. "He's always impressed me with his anticipation, and his knowledge of what the other team is trying to do.

"He gets himself into position, and attacks the blocker before they can get to him. Greene and L.C. Greenwood control the line of scrimmage. I used to play over there more, and very little garbage leaked through. Sometimes in our huddle, Jack seems to be sleeping. He's so low key. Teams run at that side because they can't believe it, or they've got to balance their offense. They can't run left all the time."

Loren Toews, a terrific reserve linebacker. said Ham was the player he most admired on the Steelers' squad. "He combined flawless execution of his trade with humility and graciousness," said Toews over the telephone from Santa Clara, California, during the 1990 season. "He imparted inspiration by performance."

Ham has to smile now when he thinks about Tuesdays during the regular season, the day that the team reviewed film of its previous game. "That's the room where you wanted to get respect," said Ham. "If you made or didn't make a play, that's where you'd hear about it.

"If I'd had a bad day in the last game I hated to go into that room. If you got hit good, or missed your man, you were in for it. If you went into that room with a thin skin you were in trouble.

"And you didn't ever offer an excuse, like I slipped, or I fell. They'd be all over you. They'd be hollering, 'Ike, Ike, Ike,' as in 'Alibi Ike.' If you played well, in a subtle way, somebody like Mel Blount or Mike Wagner or Glen Edwards would say, 'Great play, Ham.' Coming from those guys, coming from players I respected, it meant more to me than anything the coaches could say. Blount and Pine (Edwards) were also the toughest critics. Of course, I was always sitting with Lambert and Wagner and they could be tough, too. Especially if you made a mental mistake. They would jump on you so bad."

He also remembers Tuesday as the day he and some of the offensive linemen and defensive linemen would play touch football. "I was always the designated quarterback for both teams," he said. "Moon Mullins was the best player because he was the best athlete of all the linemen. He'd been a tight end in college. Ray Mansfield enjoyed it. Mansfield would play in every flag football game you could organize because he loves competing more than anyone I ever knew. That Tuesday game was for real pride.

"On Saturday, when we'd devote some practice time to the special teams, I wasn't involved. So I'd run pass routes against Wagner or Edwards or Blount, and L.C. Greenwood would always be my quarterback. He'd wait forever until I got into the clear and then heave the ball to me."

He remembers Wednesday as the day the team would go over the game plan. He remembers those sessions with George Perles and Woody Widenhofer, the defensive coaches. "Those guys were insane," said Ham with a smile. "But they were great for us.

"Woody wanted your ideas. He felt the linebackers were not brain dead, and that we had something to contribute. He was willing to listen, especially during the game. He was confident in his own ability, which allowed him to listen to others.

"Woody would stick up for us, too. I saw him and Chuck get into it pretty good at camp a couple of times. It might have been a set-up, I don't know, but it looked like the real thing. George Perles was like that, too. He stuck up for his guys. He also knew how to jump-start his guys if he thought the scrimmages were too tame.

"I never saw guys taking advantage of the coaches, either. Those guys were like us. They used to stay out a lot later than we did at training camp. They'd go out at 11 p.m. when we were coming in. I remember George saying that he went out one time his first summer of training camp, and that he stayed in one time his second summer.

"Their favorite place was called Pete's Tavern. It's gone now. One year, when we were driving up Rt. 30 to Latrobe for our summer training camp, we saw a lot of signs outside the different bars when we got close to the camp that said, 'Welcome Back Steelers,' and stuff like that. At Pete's Tavern, they had a sign that said, 'Welcome Back, George and Woody.' Those guys stopped off and made Pete change the sign before Chuck could see it. He'd have hit the roof. Nobody ever saw Chuck go anywhere when we were at camp. It's always amazed me. Where did this man go?"

Ham found Chuck Noll to be a fascinating study. Then again, he had a coach in college who was very similar in his style, outlook, worldly concerns and conservative life style. That, of course, was Joe Paterno.

"Even so, I never met anyone quite like Chuck," says Ham. "He reminded me of Paterno in a lot of ways, but he was different in other ways. We'd do some little thing over and over again at practice until we got it right. If two guys in a row missed tackles, we'd all be doing proper tackling techniques for the next half hour, to the point where you never wanted to miss a tackle again. He didn't want any bad techniques. It didn't matter who did it, either. He'd work with a guy he knew that two days later he'd be cutting from the squad. He'd be out there with a guy like that giving him all his individual attention. He loved to teach. With Paterno, it was the same thing. Joe saw guys make mistakes from 80 yards away. I think those glasses he wears are so thick so he won't miss anything. They're like looking through a telescope, I think. He'd make you work on little things, too, the basics, until you got it right. They were both big on fundamentals. That's where it all starts."

I told Ham how some newcomers to the Steelers had been so impressed by Noll the previous season, by the way he reacted so calmly

1988 Hall of Fame inductees (from left) include Fred Biletnikoff, Mike Ditka, Jack Ham and Alan Page.

Jack Lambert (58) and Jack Ham (59) combine to make stop.

to the club's first two setbacks, embarrassing losses to Cleveland by 51-0, and to Cincinnati by 41-10. They were used to coaches screaming at everyone, and blaming the ballplayers and assistant coaches for what went wrong.

"When we were 1-4 in 1976, I saw that same side of Noll," said Ham. "He's got that inner strength. The only thing he did was have us go back to basics at practice, and work on blocking and tackling techniques. He stayed the course. I don't think he ever got his just due. It wasn't until last year that he was finally named Coach of the Year. But Chuck could care less about that sort of thing. It doesn't matter to him."

It never bothered Ham that Noll did not have much to say to him. "I always respected Chuck and liked the way he ran the team," said Ham. "After a game, we'd be sitting around on our stools, and he would come by. I don't think he ever said more than, 'Jack, are you OK?' Then, he'd ask Lambert, "Jack, are you OK?' We used to wonder why he didn't just say, 'Jacks, are you OK?' It could have saved him time and a few words."

Many Steelers say Franco Harris was the one who turned things around for the franchise when he came to the team in 1972, Ham's second season with the Steelers. "We didn't win shit before Franco showed up," says Joe Greene.

Ham can pinpoint the game, the third of the 1972 season. "We were playing in St. Louis, and they had a lousy team. But we were losing late in the game. We had played badly. Franco scored a touchdown to win it. Before that time, we'd never done anything like that. We had just won a game when we'd played god awful.

"The Steelers weren't sure, at first, they had done the right thing in making Franco their first draft pick in 1972. Dick Hoak, the backfield coach, couldn't have been impressed with what he saw of Franco in his first training camp. He wasn't like your typical fired-up rookie, flying all over the place. He paced himself.

"He was never much of a practice player at Penn State, either. Paterno had to prod him all the time to get him to do anything.

"We're playing Atlanta in the pre-season and Franco takes a sprint draw and he takes off and runs 80 yards for a score. He outruns two defensive backs, just enough to get in the end zone. We'd never had a running back who could make that kind of impact. Now they all knew we had a big league running back.

"We were 6-8 the year before Franco came to the team, and we were 12-4 his rookie year, losing to Miami in the AFC championship game. Yes, he made a big difference."

Ham said L.C. Greenwood was similarly unenthused about practice sessions. "Greenwood was the worst practice player of them all," he said. "Once, we were together for a week in preparation for the Pro Bowl.

Chuck Fairbanks was our coach. At a team meeting, he told L.C., 'If you have a great Pro Bowl game, I'm going to have to revamp all my coaching theories. You haven't done a damn thing all week.'

"L.C. was something else. We had a great relationship, and played together so well. Some of the things he could do were unbelievable. He could set up an offensive lineman so well. I'd ask him to do certain things to help me out, and he always came through.

"He'd knock a running back off stride or slow him up when he was coming out of the backfield for a pass. I really needed that help toward the end when my legs had gone bad on me. Sometimes he'd overdo it, and get flagged for clotheslining some poor soul with those long arms of his. He didn't play defensive end like any other defensive end ever did. He'd run around blocks, duck under them. He was a real student of the game. I don't think people realized that. He was as prepared for a football game as anyone on our team."

Talking about Greenwood reminded Ham, for some reason, of "Moon" Mullins, an offensive guard on the great Steeler teams, and a good friend of Ham. "He was the chronic bitcher, the only guy who bitched more than Greenwood did," said Ham. "They were always complaining about one ailment or another. They were never a hundred percent healthy.

"Moon was always whelping. 'I can't block him,' he'd say, and meanwhile he was chopping down people. You could never bitch as much as Moon could bitch.

"I remember Moon going up against Ernie Holmes in practice. Moon was the technique guy, and Holmes just tried to fight his way past blockers. I saw blood coming out of Moon's helmet. Ernie loved that. Ernie had more scratches on his helmet than anyone else on the team. He was always butting his helmet into your helmet. He loved that.

"Perles used to jump-start the defensive line. Psychologically, he had all those guys turned on."

So many of the Steelers have stories about Ernie Holmes. He seems to bring out the story-teller in all of them. Ham remembered visiting with Holmes a few years earlier in Beverly Hills, of all places, to do a feature about former Steelers for the pre-season telecast packages.

"At training camp this one year, Chuck wanted Ernie to get rid of the excess weight he was carrying. So Ernie was wearing this skin tight rubber suit, like a skin diver. It covered his whole body. It was 95 degrees most days that week at St. Vincent. It's a wonder he didn't die from heat prostration.

"Ernie was sweating so bad he was actually stinking. You can imagine the odor in the huddle with him in that rubber suit. Chuck would like to see a certain defense against a certain offense, and he'd come into our huddle and tell us what he wanted us to do.

"He'd stick his head in our huddle and back off, the odor was that bad. Our huddles kept getting wider and wider. No one wanted to be near Ernie. This was toward the end of Ernie's career. He was traded to Tampa Bay, and I remember George Perles pleading his case at the end. He didn't want to let him go.

"At his best, Ernie was great. I have a tape of the '74 AFC championship game. I never saw a more dominating player on the field than Ernie that day. He was going up against Gene Upshaw. Upshaw's in the Hall of Fame and he was never any slouch. Ernie was throwing Upshaw back in Ken Stabler's lap that day.

"I always got a kick out of Ernie. He'd come to my house for a party when we were living in Green Tree, and he'd never stop eating. My wife, Joanne, loves to cook, so she loved Ernie. She'd fix him a pyramid of food, and he'd come back for more. There was no one who could eat or drink like him. You name the vice and he was better at it than anyone else on the team. He did everything wrong to his body."

"I'm glad I didn't come to the Steelers when Joe Greene and Terry Bradshaw and L.C. Greenwood were the only players they had on the team," said Ham. "My first year was bad enough. In the very first game I played, we lost by 17-15 to Chicago. Dick Butkus was playing for them then, but he was at the end of the line, and the Bears were a pretty bad ballteam. When the game ended, Joe Greene takes his helmet off and turns around and whips it toward the stands. Thank God it hit the crossbar, or it would have killed somebody in the crowd. His helmet flew apart. That's when I realized how much Joe hated to lose football games. He hated not having anything to play for. So did I."

"I remember Ron Johnson coming to our team (in 1978). He was just overwhelmed by what we had to know and do defensively. As we'd break huddle, Mike Wagner would tell him where to go and what to do.

"In this one game, Wagner went down with an injury. He was being tended to by the trainers and team doctors on the sideline. You would have thought that Johnson was a blood relative the way he was looking after Wagner. He wanted him back on the field in the worst way.

"Now Wags had taken a good shot in the head, and he couldn't go back in. We were good friends, but I saw a bond between him and Johnson I didn't know existed. Johnson needed Wagner to tell him where to go and what to do. Wagner was one of our underrated and underappreciated players. To think that we got him on the 11th round of the draft is mind-boggling.

"Every time I see Roger Staubach, he starts talking about Wagner. Wagner made a big interception against Staubach to help us beat the Dallas Cowboys, 21-17, in our second Super Bowl. Staubach keeps ranting that Wagner was lucky, that he made a good guess, when he stepped up and made the interception. Mike showed Staubach one coverage and played another. I see Staubach at golf tournaments, tennis tournaments, touch tag football games, and Staubach still brings it up. I told Staubach, 'It's over, Roger, it's over.' It still bothers him to this day."

Rocky Bleier
"The good soldier"

Running back Robert "Rocky" Bleier remains one of the most popular of the Super Bowl champion Pittsburgh Steelers. He was adopted as one of Pittsburgh's finest citizens. Fans have always liked him and identified with him for many reasons. They thought he was one of them.

For starters, he was on the small side for a pro football player, at 5-9, 210. He wasn't especially fast. He was handsome, but balding. Imperfect, like most of the fans. He was from Notre Dame, where he had been a member of the 1966 national championship team, and the captain of the football team his senior season. He was Pittsburgh's 16th round draft choice in 1968, so he was an underdog. His hometown was Appleton, Wisconsin, where he lived upstairs of his dad's saloon — just like Art Rooney did in his youth — yet the fans could see him as the boy next door, the kind of guy they would like their daughter or sister to marry. He wore a mustache, and there was always a ready smile under it. He was quick to shake your hand, and it was a firm but not overdone grip, and he would give you an autograph and, seemingly, the cape off his back. He seemed too good to be true.

He had done his duty, and gone to Vietnam. He was wounded there, and had come home with a limp. But he worked hard and, after struggling for several seasons to find a spot on the Steelers' roster, he became one of the contributing stars to all those championship seasons. He came through in the clutch so many times. Steeler fans still talk about how high he jumped — higher than he should have been able to jump — to catch a pass in the end zone to nail down the Steelers' third Super Bowl victory. He finished his career as the fourth leading ground gainer in team history even though he had only five 100-yard games. He blocked for Franco Harris, he did the little things well, and he could pick up tough yards in tough times. He seemed like the sort of guy who'd give up his body for a buddy. On a battlefield or a ballfield. He was, indeed, an All-American boy, if not an All-American football player.

"I am a breathing example of what you can do if you want to," Bleier told writer Rick Telander in an August 11, 1986 story for *Sports Illustrated.*

Philadelphia had its Rocky in Sylvester Stallone, and Pittsburgh had its Rocky in Robert Bleier. Pittsburgh's Rocky was reliable and durable, playing 12 seasons with the Steelers, interrupted early on by an overseas stint in the military service. He was selected as one of the ten outstanding young men in America by the Jaycees in 1979. He was named the NFL's Man of the Year for the 1980 season, his final campaign. He never played in the Pro Bowl and he will never be voted into the Pro Football Hall of Fame. But he has helped others gain enshrinement and no one smiles more at the induction ceremonies than he does. He is not envious or waiting for his due. In his mind, he has done it all.

"People who miss the game didn't fulfill their expectations, the way I see it," observed Bleier. "So they still want to play, or relive those days. I fulfilled my expectations beyond my wildest dreams. For me, everything had fallen into place, with everything I had. I was at the right place at the right time."

That was not always the case. After his rookie season with the Steelers, Bleier was drafted and shipped off to Vietnam.

On August 20, 1969, his platoon was ambushed in a rice paddy near Chu Lai, and Bleier was wounded in his left thigh. While he was down, a grenade exploded nearby, sending pieces of shrapnel into his right leg and foot.

When Bleier was recovering in a hospital in Tokyo, he remembers receiving a postcard from Art Rooney. "I was pleased he took the time," said Bleier. "The card said something like, 'We're still behind you. Take care of yourself and we'll see you when you get back.' That was nice."

Bleier reported to the Steelers' training camp in 1970, and was 30 pounds under his previous playing weight. He could not walk, let alone run, without pain and a noticeable limp.

He was waived on two different occasions by Noll, but would not give up, and hung around until he had a chance to reclaim a spot on the roster. In 1974, after a weightlifting program had bulked him up to 212, he made his opening. He rushed for more than 1,000 yards in 1976 and caught the decisive touchown pass in Super Bowl XIII.

Rocky Bleier has done all right for himself. He is still a well-paid star, only now his stage has shifted to the corporate world where he is a much-in-demand and well-compensated motivational speaker. Bleier gets paid to tell his own story, how he overcame adversity, what he learned from his struggles with the Steelers, what he gained from his teammates on those outstanding squads and from the club owner, Art Rooney, and his coach, Chuck Noll. When he is on the speakers' circuit, he tells amusing inside stories about Terry Bradshaw and Joe Greene and Jack Ham and Jack Lambert, and what they and Chuck Noll are really like.

There were times he wanted to quit when he was fighting for a significant role with the Steelers, but he persevered. He does not paint a profile of courage. He saw no other way than the path he took, as he views it now. In short, he did what he had to do, and he did it as well as his body and soul would permit him to do it. His story has always been an inspirational one. He tells it well. Nowadays, he does it for a living. Whereas Hal Holbrook does an evening with Mark Twain, Robert Bleier does an evening with Rocky Bleier. He was always the good soldier. He was always a very coachable kid. He did as he was told. He did it by the book. So many steps this way, so many that way. It was the only way he could do it and do it well. Now he does it by his own book, "Fighting Back," which was written by Terry O'Neil, a classmate at Notre Dame and later the executive producer of CBS Sports. That became a made-for-ABC-TV movie in 1980 starring Robert Urich as

ROCKY BLEIER
PITTSBURGH STEELERS
MAN OF THE YEAR
1980-81

NFL

Miller
HIGH LIFE BEER

Rocky, Bonnie Bedelia as his wife, Aleta, and Art Carney as Art Rooney. Rocky's story still plays well.

Bleier's ability to inspire effort and commitment from others continues. He was active in the National Multiple Sclerosis Society and served on the International Board of the Special Olympics, and Vietnam Veterans Memorial Fund. Among the awards he has won are the Whizzer White Humanitarian Award, the Vince Lombardi Award and the Most Courageous Athlete of the Decade Award.

There is a need to hold on to a genuine American hero like Bleier. In a period, where so much has gone wrong to disillusion people, such as the savings and loan mess, the wars in the Mideast, the stock market on a roller coaster ride, ballplayers on drugs, Pete Rose spending time in prison, UNLV under constant investigation after it won the NCAA men's basketball title, and news like that in the newspapers, it is no wonder Bleier has a big appeal to so many people.

In the month before we talked, in October of 1990, he had 23 speaking engagements all over the country. His speaking fee is $6500, plus expenses. So he made about $150,000 for the month for speaking, to go with some other business enterprises he gets involved with. It is more money than he ever made in a season playing for the Pittsburgh Steelers. He started out making $18,000 his first season with the Steelers, and $130,000 his last season. "Throughout most of my career, I was usually able to double my income with my outside business activities," he said. "I always felt insecure. I think we all do unless we've inherited money."

I visited him, by coincidence, on Veterans Day. We both missed the parade that day in downtown Pittsburgh, and Bleier was still in bed when I arrived at his home at the appointed time of 10 a.m. He had slept in.

His home is really an estate. It is a huge French Tudor on seven acres of prime real estate in fashionable Fox Chapel, one of Pittsburgh's high-priced suburbs. The Bleiers bought it at a bargain price of $350,000 in 1978, and it has to be worth well over $1.5 million in today's marketplace. It was built in 1928, originally on a 70-acre parcel, by a Gulf Oil executive as a gift for his daughter. It is impressive.

His estate is located just north of the North Side. You travel Route 28, along the Allegheny River, to get there. It is in the toney neighborhood of the Shady Side Academy Senior School and the Fox Chapel Golf Club on Fox Chapel Road. You pass two imposing white pillars and a "No Trespassing" sign at the base of a hill and proceed past some newer homes to the top of the hill. You enter a courtyard, and think you ought to be riding on a horse, clip-clopping on the stone pavement, rather than riding into it in an automobile.

Before Bleier came downstairs to speak to me, I met his house staff. I was greeted at the door by Randy Gomola, 27, who lived in the house, and looked after the heavy-duty chores. He had been with the Bleiers for seven years. Laura Kissel, the housekeeper, was in the kitchen. She had been with them for 10 years. Randy asked me if I would like a cup of coffee, and brought me one in quick time.

Later, when I asked Rocky what Randy's role was in the house, Rocky said, "You know all those things around the house you never have time to do, or you never want to do? Well, Randy takes care of them." Rocky punctuated that sentence with a smile, a Cheshire cat smile. That's when I knew that Rocky Bleier really had it made.

I also met Rocky's personal secretary, or executive coordinator, Gloria Ashcroft, who was in her sixth year of setting up all his speaking engagements, doing the proper homework so he could tailor-make his talks to his audience, and making his travel arrangements.

"He's got about 600,000 frequent flyer miles for USAir alone," said Ms. Ashcroft. "Sometimes these companies send their own planes, or get him a charter, if they have to in order to get him when they want him. The requests for his services are consistent."

Ms. Ashcroft, who lives in the Shadyside section of the city, was wearing a large American University sweatshirt and jeans, and looked like a graduate student. She works out of an office in the Bleier home. "He does about 150 to 160 talks a year," she said.

During the previous month, his 23 speaking engagements had taken him on a cross-country whirl from Williamsburg, Virginia, to San Francisco, to Des Moines, New Orleans, Philadelphia, Orlando and Flemington, New Jersey. "He did two talks a day on a few occasions," Ms. Ashcroft added. "He's quite popular. Companies like him. Rock has a wide appeal. He can do AT&T, Arco and IBM and Garage Door Associates. As you know, Rock is a real down-to-earth guy. You know he's a genuinely nice guy." Ms. Ashcroft does the advance work for Rocky, the way he used to do for Franco Harris, so he knows what to expect, the kind of meeting he is attending, and what he needs to do. In short, she does his homework for him. He does a quick read on the material en route. "He's quite bright, and he picks up what he needs to know pretty fast," she said, proudly. A friend of mine, Bill Haines, a vice-president at Arco, told me Bleier had been a big hit with his staff when Bleier spoke at an Arco sales meeting in Philadelphia. Haines had been familiar with Bleier from his days in a similar executive capacity at Mobay in Pittsburgh. "The guys in Philly are all Eagles' fans, but they enjoyed Rocky," said Haines.

Another marketing administrator wrote to Ms. Ashcroft about an appearance by Bleier to Chelsea Building Products in Oakmont: "While his reputation as a motivational speaker had preceded him to our group, there were still 'skeptics' who didn't look forward to sitting through another sports talk. Without exception, everyone was thoroughly won over by Rocky's exceptional presentation. While sports provided a colorful thread woven through the message, the message was not for athletes but rather for each of us in the room to overcome our obstacles and excel in our individual pursuits."

Rocky's wife, Aleta, and their children were not at home. Their daughter, Samantha, 17, was at Winchester-Thurston, a private school for girls, where she was a junior, and their son, Adri James, 14, was in eighth grade at Shady Side Academy. Aleta had left the house after the kids went to school. She is very active, as is her husband, in the community, and in many charity-related programs. Aleta is used to the good life. Her father, Dr. James Giacobine, was a pioneer open heart surgeon in Pittsburgh, serving at St. Francis Hospital in Lawrenceville. She is a socialite, and has introduced Rocky to many of the better things in life. Just as Joanne Ham likes to tell people that Jack had no knowledge of ballet before they met, Aleta has shown Rocky a different world than what he knew in Wisconsin or Indiana. Many of the Steelers are more sophisticated today than when they first came to town. That is part of growing up.

There is a life-size oil painting, for instance, that was propped against the base of a bookshelf in the gameroom of the home that shows Rocky and Aleta standing at attention in formal horse riding attire, all black complete with top hats, whips at the ready, with horses and hunting dogs about them. His buddies back in Appleton or South Bend would surely get a kick out of the portrait, or the new-look Rocky. Now he is Rocky the rider.

"Me and Charles Barkley," said Rocky, referring to a popular TV commercial for an anti-perspirant deodorant stick in which Barkley, the bad boy of the Philadelphia 76ers, is outfitted in a bright red riding outfit and sits on a horse at the start of a hunt. In the TV spot, Barkley concludes his lines by saying, as a pretty woman rides by him, "Well, it's off to the foxes!"

It is not exactly the uniform one thinks of when one thinks of Rocky Bleier. Then again, Ham has a bocce court in his backyard in Sewickley these days to amuse himself. What would it be like to grow up over a saloon, your family of six — he has two sisters and a brother — sharing a single bathroom with four bachelor boarders (including one nicknamed "Hammerhead"), and now having your own mansion, your own estate? Asked what goes through his mind when he is atop the horse for a hunt, which the Bleiers do with friends at the Sewickley Hunt or Rolling Rock Hunt, Rocky smiled again, and said, "I know I've come a long way from living above the bar in Appleton, Wisconsin. I wish my family and boyhood buddies could see me now."

Some of the real Rocky Bleier may have been lost along the way. He certainly is not the same Rocky Bleier who first showed up at the Steelers' training camp in 1968. Following his playing days with the Steelers, Bleier had a five-year stint as a well-compensated sportscaster at WPXI-TV in Pittsburgh. It was a role he never became completely comfortable with, no matter how much coaching he received. On stage, as a speaker, he was good, very good. On camera, with a microphone before him, he stumbled, didn't read his copy easily, and seemed miscast. But he had speech coaches, and learned how to enunciate and pronounce certain words, and how to posture and how to be animated in his delivery. His voice became deeper, his words better chosen, and he became a bit of an actor. Before he knew it, Rocky was playing the role of Rocky Bleier. These days, he always seems to be on stage. He seems stuffy, or a bit choreographed. There is a lack of spontaneity. That's a shame. Because deep down, he is still a great guy and somebody whose company you know you would enjoy over a beer or two. He has taken on airs, without realizing it. You change, as you grow older, and sometimes it is hard to go home again.

Rocky was not sure how many rooms are in his present home, but said it had 10,000 square feet, for whatever that is worth. All the rooms I saw were large rooms. They all had many accessories about them, like in a decorator's showroom. There was a museum-like quality about the place, especially in the gameroom where the walls are covered with plaques, awards, paintings, posters, photographs, framed magazine and newspaper articles chronicling the career of Rocky with the Steelers. It is an awesome collection, a tribute to a special athlete and citizen of the community. Rocky's rec room is as big as some of the wings at the Pro Football Hall of Fame.

There is a framed poem on one wall about a soldier by George L. Skypeck that starts: "I was that which others did not want to be and went where others feared to go, and did what others failed to do. . ." There was a framed column by Jim Murray of the *Los Angeles Times* with a headline on it that read: "Another Rocky Movie, But It's A True Story." There were two covers of *Sports Illustrated* with Bleier's likeness on them. One had a cover line about "Rocky Bleier's War." with a June 9, 1975 date and a 75 cents price tag on it. Another, dated Dec. 6, 1976 and costing $1, read "The Steelers Storm On — Davis Leads Bleier Past The Dolphins," and shows guard Sam Davis leading Bleier on an end sweep on a snow-covered field.

There was a tear sheet from a Jan. 7, 1980 issue of the *New York Times* showing Bleier scoring the touchdown that clinched the victory against the Houston Oilers in the AFC Championship Game. That brought back a big personal memory.

I was standing in the end zone at Three Rivers Stadium that day as Bleier ran between right guard Sam Davis and right tackle Ted Petersen for that touchdown. The play was a 34-trap. It was a four-yard run with only 54 seconds showing on the scoreboard clock and helped boost the Steelers' lead and the final score to 27-13. It happened about 20 yards away from where I was standing, right next to Joe Gordon, then the team's publicist. And I had a tear or two in my eye, I confess. I had come home to Pittsburgh only ten months earlier, after working out of town as a sportswriter for ten years, and I realized I had made a smart decision. The Steelers were going to the Super Bowl again, and I was going with them. I was happy, despite the tears. "What's wrong?" Gordon asked. "Nothing," I said, smiling. Bleier had scored on a one-yard burst the week before to help the Steelers defeat the Dolphins, 34-14, and he would be part of the winning cast two weeks hence when the Steelers would rally to defeat the Los Angeles Rams, 31-19, before 103,985 fans at the Rose Bowl in Pasadena for the Steelers' fourth Super Bowl victory in a six-year stretch.

When he appeared at the top of the staircase in his home, fresh from a shower, looking smart and satisfied, Rocky reminded me of Rhett Butler in "Gone With the Wind" the way he moved across the balcony and down the stairs. He had that same damn sly smile. His was a grand entry. We tried three different rooms — like Goldilocks and the three bears — before we found a place where we felt just right to talk about his days with the Steelers. One was too hot, one too cool, and the third, if not just right, was OK.

Both of us had cases of the sniffles, probably because there are six cats and five dogs in residence at Rocky's palace. And I am allergic to cats, for sure.

"I think about the playing, the difficult days, the growth of the team, the way it developed in the '70s," began Bleier, who was wearing eyeglasses and began smoking the first of many cigarets. "I think about the attitude that developed, the beliefs that developed, that you can win.

"It's not that we were invincible, but we could beat anybody out there, if we played our game. I think about my ability to play with such superb players, and what made our corps of Super Bowl performers — Ham and Bradshaw and Franco, Lambert, Joe Greene, Mel Blount and Andy Russell — and what made them win was that they were good athletes with a dream to be better.

"Looking back, after ten years away from the game, we grow as individuals, and you ask why it all happened the way it did. You try to figure out why. As far as Chuck Noll is concerned, I never had any problems with Chuck. I had problems understanding Chuck sometimes, but I never had any problems with Chuck. By the time you get to pro football, you have played junior high and high school and college ball, and you were a major force through all those levels. You had to have some natural skills. But people had always given you positive reinforcement, a pat on the back, a pat on the head, or a kick in the ass. Somebody paid attention to you. You had all these little kudos. People were taking you out to dinner, buying you drinks. Chuck Noll is not a people person. He does not have great people skills. He does not empathize with people.

"The reasons why? Chuck's a self-made man. He has great intelligence. He's lived off that intelligence. He's never wanted to be in a position where he sought approval, or where he had to depend on anybody else. He was always a student. He took pride in that. He was analytical.

"After a game, we'd be sitting there in front of our lockers, and he'd come by and say 'Nice game.' I always felt it was difficult for him to do that. But it was something he had to do, not that he wanted to do it. I remember going through training camp with him, and what a startling experience it was. He only spoke to certain people. He'd say something to guys around me and I thought he hated me. It was very difficult. You weren't getting a pat on the back. There was no reinforcement."

"One season I was playing most of the time with a pulled groin, and a pulled hamstring in the same leg. It was high in the sheaths. To play, I had to get novocaine shots. I'd get a shot up my groin, and then in my behind, and then the trainers would wrap it. I couldn't walk on Monday or Tuesday after a game. I could walk through practice on Wednesday, and limp through practice on Thursday. This was during the 1977 or 1978 season, and I was feeling like a warrior. I was going beyond the call of duty. That was partly my problem, too, the way I looked at what I was doing.

"One day Noll comes into the training room, and I'm getting my leg wrapped as usual, and he walks by me, and looks around. Nothing. He didn't say a single solitary thing to me. I thought he might say 'How are you feeling?' And he just went on. Not a word. That's what I mean. It wasn't just me, either. He'd drive guys like Lambert crazy because of the same reason. I remember Jack saying, 'You bust your ass for him and he doesn't pat you on the back, or say anything.'

"Before my last season (1980), I went in to see Dan Rooney and I told him it was going to be my last year. I asked him, 'Dan, do you think I should tell Chuck?' Dan hesitated before he answered, and that's all I needed to know. I didn't say a word to Chuck about my plans."

Bleier took out another cigaret. Maybe talking about Noll made him nervous. He said he started smoking when he was in Vietnam. He admits to being nervous every now and then.

I mentioned to Rocky that I had heard Noll say on many occasions that anyone who was thinking about retiring ought to just retire. As far as Noll was concerned, if the thought had entered your mind you were no longer able to play on his team. I also suggested that he didn't want to acknowledge that Rocky was in the training room that time he walked in and out without a word. Like his old coach, Paul Brown, Noll did not like to see players in the training room. If they weren't on the field, they didn't exist.

"After the season, I never really had a chance to properly tell Noll that was it for me," Rocky continued. "I wanted to thank him for all the things he had allowed me to accomplish. That bothered me. I wrote him a letter, to get it off my chest, but I never mailed it. I felt badly about that, not for me, but for Chuck. I was only one person. This is something I wanted to say. But I never felt his door was open to his players to be emotional.

"We have all learned from different people. I learned a lot from Chuck, especially from his basic, fundamental approach to the game. He acknowledged your best efforts, but you had to look close to pick up the signs. He'd give you that little look. I think about Chuck at times. If I was to be a head coach, my coaching technique would probably be a lot of Chuck Noll. What Chuck taught you is really true. In my talks, I'm probably offering a lot of what is Chuck's coaching philosophy.

"When we first arrived at Notre Dame, they showed us the movie, 'Knute Rockne of Notre Dame.' Knute Rockne, of course, was a real motivator. Chuck Noll always said it wasn't his job to motivate people. It was his job to take motivated people and give them guidance and direction.

"I remember Chuck scolding some players on our team for making noise on the sideline. He didn't want any of that 'Let's go, let's go' stuff. He said it was false chatter and it didn't mean a damn thing. He thought it only lasted so long, and he'd hold his fingers an inch apart to make his point. Noll said that what gets you through, when you're tired and down at the end of a game, are good habits. That's what wins games, he felt, not false chatter."

When Bleier came back from Vietnam, he was not physically able to compete for a spot on the team. I asked him if Art Rooney had gone to bat for him and gotten him a second chance with the team. That's what I had heard, but it turned out that Dan Rooney rescued him.

"Chuck cut me from the team, and Dan Rooney found a way for me to stay with the Steelers," recalled Rocky. "This was before the 1970 season, and the veterans were on strike. I didn't have a contract, and I went and talked to some of the veteran players like Ron May and Roy Jefferson and told them I thought I could only stay on strike with them so long, that I ought to go to camp if I was going to have any chance of making the team. They understood my situation. Dan asked me if I wanted the team doctors to take a look at me, and I said, 'No, I want to practice.' I stayed out about a week with the veterans, but then I reported to training camp. The double sessions were taking a real toll on me. I was limping. I'd have cut myself under the circumstances.

"When the final cut came down, Ralph Berlin, the trainer, told me that Chuck wanted to see me in his office. When I got there, Chuck got up from behind his desk, and said, 'Rocky, we put you on waivers today. I think you should go home and do what you have to do and come back next year and try again.' I begged and pleaded with him to reconsider, and asked him to let me come out to practice that day. But he said that wouldn't be possible. I went to practice that day, anyhow. We were practicing up at a field in the West End section of Pittsburgh.

"I went through practice and all the players were looking at me like I was crazy. They knew I'd been cut. 'What are you doing here?' some of them asked me. I went to my apartment I was sharing with Larry Gagner in Green Tree. I was crying in my car as I drove there. I didn't know what I was going to do.

"Then Dan called, and apologized for how I'd been cut, and he said he had talked to Chuck about my situation. He said he wanted to try and get me on the physically unable to perform list, so that I would not cost Chuck a spot on the roster. He said that maybe I could help the team later in the year. He sent me to see the team doctor, Dr. John Best. He took out some shrapnel in my leg, and he took all the scar tissue in his bare hands and just broke it all loose. He just worked it and worked it with his hands. It hurt like hell. It took me eight weeks till I didn't have any pain. I didn't want to be out of sight or out of mind. So Dan gave me the opportunity to stick around the practice field, and let them know I was still alive."

ocky Bleier comes marching home.

As WPXI-TV sportscaster in 1981

'ith Mayor Caliguiri in United Way
ledge-A-Thon promotion

With "Bullet Bill" Dudley,
another popular Steelers back

Bleier says there are a few questions he is routinely asked when he conducts question and answer sessions at his speaking engagements: What's the problem between Chuck Noll and Terry Bradshaw? What happened to Franco that final season? Is Jack Lambert really as wild as he appeared on the field? What was The Chief like?

"But the No. 1 question, above all others," said Bleier, "is about Bradshaw and Noll. Why the rift? What's behind it? Why can't they settle the dispute or the feud?

"The funny thing is, as I remember it, Chuck was always talking to Bradshaw. Bradshaw had meetings with him every day. Chuck was the quarterback coach as well as the head coach. Bradshaw had more access to him than anybody on the ballclub. Back then, generally, they had a nice rapport. In truth, Bradshaw got more attention from Chuck than anybody on the ballclub. So he can't complain about that.

"Everybody wonders why Bradshaw is really down on the fans. I don't think he really is. I think Bradshaw is afraid. I think Bradshaw is afraid to come back. We all have these fires that build up in our minds. It's difficult to confront those fires. In Brad's case, I think of how they developed.

"The Chuck Noll thing has its beginning when Bradshaw struggled at the start of his career with the Steelers, and how Noll put him on the shelf in favor of Terry Hanratty and then Joe Gilliam. Bradshaw has never forgiven the fans for cheering when he was injured and had to give way to Hanratty in a game. He can't shake that, even with all the success he later had, and all the adulation he had in this town. Brad had great talent, and he could see so much out there on the field. He had an eye, and he was quite the quarterback. Nobody should ever forget that.

"Toward the end of his career, when he had the bad arm, Noll had to put him on the shelf again (in 1982). That hit a nerve. The rift would not have taken place if Chuck had gone over to Bradshaw after he hurt his elbow and couldn't play, and said, 'Brad, I have two guys with no experience (in Cliff Stoudt and Mark Malone) and I'd like you to be there to help them. I need you.' Whether he believed that or not, Chuck should have done that. I think Brad felt abandoned. His career was over. Chuck should have talked to him. Brad is just sitting there or standing there, stewing. Then somebody in the media asked Chuck how close Brad was to coming back to play, and Chuck, with his own brand of humor, said, 'He's closer. But so is Christmas.' That's the kind of stuff that sticks in a player's craw. It's like the 'Franco Who?' line. They've all come back to haunt Chuck. And he didn't mean to be mean in either case. It's just his way.

"Then the animosity was fueled further by the Franco Harris thing the following year (1983). Bradshaw blamed Chuck for Franco's situation. Bradshaw wondered how they could just throw the guy out, or let him go to Seattle. Bradshaw felt that Chuck could have told Dan Rooney, 'Hey, I need Franco. Do whatever you have to, but I need him. Get that contract thing resolved.' So that was just one more log on the fire.

"Then Bradshaw heard others, like L.C. Greenwood and Dwight White, as well as Franco, knocking Noll, or complaining about the way they were treated by their coach, and he knew he was not alone in his feelings. Now Bradshaw had a platform on national TV, with CBS as an analyst, and he said, 'I'm going to take a shot at Noll,' and he did that. Then the Hall of Fame induction came along (1989) and he didn't have anyone from the Steelers introduce him. Brad was never close to anyone in the organization but The Chief, and he had died. He felt close to Verne Lundquist (with whom he worked NFL games at CBS), so he asked him to do it.

"In his acceptance speech, he never mentioned Noll. He ignored Dan Rooney during the ceremonies. Then he came out with his book, in which he was critical of Noll and the Steelers organization and the city and the fans. Then he was on a book tour, and he said he was not coming to Pittsburgh on the book tour. He said he was against Pittsburgh; he said he was against the media here. It just got worse and worse. It's too bad."

Three Rivers Stadium is one place where you won't find Rocky Bleier these days. "I don't go to the games," he explained. "I have ten season tickets, and I use them for business. Do I miss the game? No. I watch them on TV. I follow things, so I know what's going on, but I do so from a different perspective. I visit during the week on occasion.

"Part of the reason I don't go is probably ego. I'm no longer a football player and I'm no longer a sports broadcaster. It's not my arena anymore. I get tired of people saying, 'When are you going to suit up? They need you.' Or, 'Rock, it's not the same ol' Steelers, not without you and the guys you played with. It's not as much fun.' I don't need that anymore."

Nobody knows or appreciates the Rocky Bleier story any more than the master of the house. "I look at my whole life, and think how lucky I've been," he said during our visit. "As far as the Vietnam experience, I was very lucky about what happened to me. I'm glad I went through it. I never look at myself as a military hero. That's a media perception. What happened to me in Vietnam, and what happened throughout my career with the Steelers, is no special story. I didn't do anything that anyone else wouldn't have done under the same circumstances.

"There are people walking the streets today who overcame similar obstacles in their lives that were even greater than I had to deal with. But I went into a high profile business, and was on a team that came under such tremendous national and even international exposure. We won four Super Bowls and my story gained a great deal of attention in the meantime. I think the story appealed to people's basic nature. Most of us are engrained with a sense of honor and duty. There's no glory in being injured in practice. If it's going to happen you want it to happen in a big game. It's where it happened to me that made such a difference. If a hunter shoots himself he doesn't get much glory. The difference is the fields that you play on.

"It was not hard for me to come back as a ballplayer. It was the road of least resistance. The same was true of me going to the Army in the first place. What were my options? Go to Canada? Get into the reserves? Injure myself? Ask for status as a conscientious objector? I couldn't get into the reserve. I got drafted. I go.

"I didn't lose a leg; I didn't lose a foot. I wanted to come back and play. That was my desire. I didn't want to go back and run my daddy's bar. Playing football was the only thing I knew how to do.

"So I spent that first season back on a physically unable to perform list. I made the taxi squad the following season, and got activated a few times, enough to get credit for the year. In the third year, I made the team and played on special teams. I never had to make any decisions.

"After the 1973 season, I decided to quit. I didn't think I'd go back to Pittsburgh. I had been the leading ground-gainer in the pre-season schedule in both 1972 and 1973. I think they were playing me so they could cut me. It was obvious to me that in 1974 the starting backs would be Franco Harris and Steve Davis, with Preston Pearson and Frenchy Fuqua as backups. I was going to be on special teams again, at best.

"I was in Chicago during the off-season and selling insurance. I saw the handwriting on the wall. I thought this might be what the good Lord wants you to do. I thought it was time to get on with my life's work. You have accumulated five years and you will qualify for a pro football pension some day, and maybe it's the best you'll ever do. Maybe it's time. That's the way I was thinking.

"I got a call out of the clear blue from Andy Russell. He was coming into Chicago for a dinner that was associated with the pro football players association. He said, 'Let's get together.' He wanted me to come to the dinner and see some other players. I said, 'Andy, I've decided not to come back. I've decided to quit.' Andy said, 'You can't quit. You've got to come back. You go back to camp and you make them make a decision as to whether to keep you or cut you. Don't make it easy for them.' It made some sense to me. I didn't need a lot of arm-twisting.

"I was the leading ground-gainer in the pre-season for a third year. But I ended up playing special teams again. The backfield pairings worked out just the way I had figured. I didn't play in the backfield in the first two games against Baltimore or at Denver. We beat Baltimore, 30-0, but Franco got injured and couldn't play, and Frenchy went in at fullback with Davis. In the second game, we tied Denver, 35-35. Joe Gilliam was the quarterback. We lose the next game at home against Oakland (17-0). In the fourth game, at Houston, the offense was doing fine, with Bradshaw at quarterback, but just before the half Frenchy got dinged and Chuck puts Preston and I in there together. I'm the fullback. Preston breaks one and went in for a touchdown from 47 yards out and we win (13-7). In the next game at Kansas City, I start at fullback with Preston at halfback. Preston had another big game, God bless him, and we win (34-24). Now Franco is healthy, and Chuck puts Franco back in at fullback, and I'm back to being a swing back. We beat Cleveland (20-16).

"The next game is a Monday night game with Atlanta, and at a team meeting on the morning of the game, our backfield coach, Dick Hoak, says, 'Franco, you and Rock will start tonight.' I couldn't believe it. I drove from the hotel where we were staying to the Stadium to get my playbook. Because I'd been playing fullback and now I'm playing halfback, and I didn't think I knew the plays. We won that game (24-17), and I started the rest of the way. We went to the Super Bowl that year and won. If I had quit, I wouldn't be here today. I wouldn't have won four Super Bowls. I wouldn't have had those super memories.

"Being a pro football player is a great life. It gave me a status different from my peers, and I liked the attention. So I was going to try everything to make it."

George Gojkovich

Rocky Bleier

Steve Courson
A mercenary who needed a new heart

"All the great generals cried. Grant cried, Sherman cried, Lincoln cried, Lee cried, MacArthur cried, Patton cried. Men who say they don't cry scare me."
—General H. Norman Schwarzkopf

Steve Courson's current situation may be the most compelling of all the Super Bowl champion Steelers. He had been one of the most physically impressive of their offensive linemen. Now, at age 35 when we spoke, he was on the waiting list for a heart transplant, and he figured it would be a long wait.

"You usually have to be critically ill to get one," Courson said. "I'm praying for the heart of a 300-pound biker. My support group — my folks, my friends, my girlfriend — has been unbelievable. I was pretty depressed for awhile."

When he was with the Steelers, fans used to gawk at him, and sportswriters used to smile when he would pass them during practice sessions at St. Vincent College. He was unreal. He was always wearing jerseys with cut-off sleeves that showed off his enormous physique. He had a 58-inch chest, 22¾-inch neck, 29-inch thighs, 18-inch calves, 38½-inch waist, and 20½-inch biceps. His upper torso was breathtaking, his shoulders were simply extraordinary. He was so muscular and so bizarre in his choice of costumes, usually looking like the mercenary soldier he envisioned himself to be, that he was comical. He was the Steelers' answer to TV's "The Incredible Hulk."

No one smiles at Courson anymore. They worry about him. He had become a walking time bomb. He was told he had only a few years to live unless he got a heart transplant. "My life is on hold," he said.

Courson is a crusader these days, speaking out against drug abuse, especially the use of anabolic steroids. He went public with his protest in an article in *Sports Illustrated* (May, 13, 1985) when he was still the property of the Tampa Bay Buccaneers, the team he went to when the Steelers traded him. Courson and his doctors are not certain whether or not his own long-term and heavy usage of steroids caused his heart damage, but he has become a self-taught expert on the subject and is all too aware of the peril they pose for young people who resort to using them in the hope of improving their physical appearance, muscular definition, size, strength, speed and athletic ability. "There is tremendous pressure on you to use these drugs," Courson said.

Courson is still a huge man, if not the 6-1, 275 pound, and sometimes larger physical freak he was in his football-playing days. He seemed less ominous when we saw him on November 5, 1990. He seemed kinder, gentler, the sort of young man President George Bush would boost rather than criticize. His dark eyes seemed to beg for understanding and compassion.

It was late in the afternoon, and Courson was sitting across a table talking about what he is doing these days — going to schools and seminars and speaking to youngsters about the pitfalls of drug usage. At times he got too technical, and I thought I was talking to Jon Kolb, one of his old linemates who was a physical fitness zealot and assistant coach with the Steelers, or that I was back in a chemistry class at Taylor Allderdice High School feeling a bit bewildered by all the strange terms. Courson showed me a slide presentation he used in his talks. Again, I felt like I was in a chemistry class. He showed me his computer, where he wrote about drug abuse and related subjects, and was putting together material for his own book, and metal file drawers packed with information and clippings on the subject.

As Courson spoke, my mind kept flitting back to an interview I had earlier in the day with Rocky Bleier. What a contrast between Courson's situation and Bleier's world.

Courson was sick and Bleier was the picture of good health. Courson was dressed casually, as usual, and Bleier had on his Eddie Bauer coordinates. It was Veterans Day when I visited them. Courson saw himself as a mercenary when he was playing pro football, strictly a hired guerrilla, whereas Bleier saw himself as the good soldier, ready to take orders from the high command. Bleier talked about a "thank you" letter he had written to his former coach, Chuck Noll, but had never sent in the mail. Courson showed me a copy of a letter he had written and sent to Noll congratulating him for an anti-steroid remark he had made in a newspaper article during the previous year. He never received a response to his letter. "There are lots of things I philosophically disagree with as far as Chuck Noll is concerned, but I respect him," Courson said. Courson was sitting at a formica table in a kitchenette area, Bleier was sitting at a grand, highly-polished dining room table that seats 12. Courson was by himself in a two-bedroom basement apartment and Bleier was being looked after by a staff of three workers in a mansion, and had his own family. Courson was living in the Crafton-Ingram section of the city, Bleier in Fox Chapel. Crafton-Ingram, about five miles southwest of Three Rivers Stadium, had once been a grand area. It still has some large, beautiful old homes, but not all have been maintained well. The heating bills and maintenance costs became prohibitive for the people who reside there these days, and many of the grand houses have been subdivided, or chopped up into apartments. The area is showing its age. It is what Courson can afford at this stage in his life. He lived a wild life as a bachelor ballplayer, lost much of his money through ill-advised investments, so he is not as well off as most of his Super Bowl teammates in many ways.

Bleier has a purple heart somewhere in his home. Courson had a damaged heart, and he needed help. "Without a heart transplant," he said, "I am going to die." Both were making their living by going out on speaking engagements, but Bleier's requests and fees were certainly more frequent and substantial than Courson's. Bleier got about $6,500 per appearance and Courson about $1,000 at best. Sometimes Courson speaks for free, with a basket being passed for donations, which go into the Steve Courson Medical Trust Fund. He needed about $250,000 for his heart transplant and recuperative care. "Rocky said to say hello," I told Courson. Steve smiled and said, "He did, huh? That's interesting."

Whereas the Steelers' organization remained critical of Courson for his public bleatings about the National Football League, football at large, their coaches and set-up, many of the players had remained supportive of Courson. The Steelers' basketball team, which operates independently, frequently participates in fund-raising games throughout the tri-state area on behalf of Courson. It was only 11 months earlier, on January 6, 1990, that I had served as the master of ceremonies at a fund-raising dinner called "Farewell to Arms," which raised monies for Mike Webster's favorite charity, spina bifida, as well as Courson's heart transplant fund. Among those who appeared on the dais that night were former teammates Jack Lambert, Lynn Swann, L.C. Greenwood, Ray Mansfield, Webster, as well as Bob Golic of the Los Angeles Raiders, sportscaster Myron Cope and local sports banquet jester Jim Meston. At one point in the program, Lambert looked out in the audience in Courson's direction and said, "Steve, you and I had our disagreements (exchanging highly critical letters through the local newspapers about drug usage by athletes), but you were my teammate. And I love you. And I want to see you get this heart transplant and get well again. Good luck, and God bless you."

Courson appreciated Lambert's support, but was still looking for some of the same from the Steelers' organization.

"The Steelers bought a table for that dinner," Courson said, "but none of their top officials showed up. And didn't you think it was odd that I was never asked to come to the microphone and thank everyone?"

Maybe the Steelers get sensitive when Courson talks about the pain-killing drugs he and his teammates were routinely given so they could play, or when he suggests he was not the only Steeler using steroids. Or when he talks about the big lie that big-time sports have become. How the promises are merely charades. "They tell you you'll live to collect your NFL pension," Courson said. "Most people retire when they are 65. The average mortality rate for vested NFL players is 56! It's a dangerous game." Courson has all the charts and studies and bona fide sources to back such statements. "The Steelers are not too thrilled about me shedding the light on several things."

Courson spent six seasons (1978-83) with the Steelers, and collected two Super Bowl rings along the way. He was traded to the Tampa Bay Buccaneers, and played for them for two seasons. He was released in 1985 right after he went public with his anti-drug criticism in *Sports*

Illustrated. He believes he could have continued to play, but that he was blackballed by the league. Courson's crime, he feels, was being too honest. He violated an unwritten code.

A promising back-up performer for most of his years with the Steelers, Courson came into his own in the 1979 season, my first as a reporter on the beat for *The Pittsburgh Press.* He was very impressive that year as injuries to Sam Davis and Gerry Mullins enabled him to start eight regular season and two post-season games. But he missed the Super Bowl with a sprained ankle. He had missed his first season with the Steelers, 1977, with an ankle injury suffered in training camp and spent the year on injured reserve.

"This is the worst week of my life," Courson said before Super Bowl XIV, when he knew he would not be able to play. "To come all this way and to have contributed as much as I have this season, and then to have this (injured right ankle) going into the big game. It's been a real bummer." He would learn later that it was not the worst week of his life. It only seemed that way at the time.

"It's as much drug abuse to take steroids as heroin or cocaine," said Courson when he spoke on June 16, 1990 at a seminar sponsored by Ohio Valley Hospital and WTOV-TV9 of Steubenville. "When most people imagine drug abusers, their thoughts are of street people living in the gutter. Realistically, these people can't afford drugs, but professional athletes and middle and upper class teenagers can. I've seen studies that say 6.6 percent of all high school senior males are using steroids. If I can reach even a couple of those kids, I'll know I've done some good."

As a linebacker at the University of South Carolina, Courson weighed 230 pounds. He said he tried to gain weight through nutritional and weight training programs, but had little success.

Finally, he said a team physician prescribed steroids. Courson said he gained 30 pounds in 30 days. At his peak, he claims he weighed 300 pounds, with just 8 percent body fat. He could bench press 605 pounds, could run the forty-yard dash in 4.65 seconds and was a respected offensive lineman in the NFL.

He had not really recovered from a knee injury when the Steelers sent him to Tampa Bay at the outset of the 1984 season. He required knee surgery in Tampa. Asked to defend the trade back then, Noll noted in *The Pittsburgh Press,* "He was not performing here, this year or last year. I think he could have been. It takes a whole man to perform. His injury was something that goes away. It's tendinitis.

"Life is career-threatening. You've got to want to play the game and do a lot of things. Most people are their own worst enemies. The mind is career-threatening, too. Maybe a change of scenery will help him."

Courson retired after the 1985 season — nobody wanted him anymore — and soon found he was suffering from cardiomyopathy. It is a rare disease that enlarges the heart and weakens the heart walls. His heart simply does not pump enough blood anymore. "Steve's heart is stretched and dilated," said Dr. Richard Rosenbloom, his physician. "It is flabby and baggy and doesn't pump as a normal heart should." Soon after Courson quit playing, he could barely walk up a few flights of stairs without feeling winded. The only long term treatment for his cardiomyopathy is a heart transplant. Courson blames his health problems on his fifteen years of steroid use, though he has no proof. "This disease has educated me tremendously," Courson said. "I feel happier, more fulfilled, than when I played. I'm able to help others and even though I'm in a precarious situation health-wise, I can use this to do good. It's my motivator. I just don't want anyone to follow my lead and take steroids."

He said he first took steroids as an 18-year-old freshman at South Carolina, but then gave them up until he was a rookie with the Steelers in 1978. He said he continued using them throughout his professional career.

He was back in South Carolina, speaking at Furman University on September 20, 1990, to the school's athletes, when he said, "Our generation of athletes never had the benefit of making an informed choice. Our measuring stick for what they do is based solely on their performance, therefore it lends to the predicament of taking a performance-enhancing drug."

Courson said steroid use is widespread in sports and is fueled by "our addiction to sports." He travels across the country delivering his message to young people. He said he did over 100 such programs the past year.

John Lestini, a Weirton, West Virginia-based manager of Olympia Steele, a professional management group, books Courson's speaking engagements, often pairing him with Dr. Charles Yesalis, a professor of exercise and sports science at Penn State University.

Over a two-year period from 1989 through 1990, Courson spoke at Edinboro (Pa.) University, Marquette, California (Pa.) University, Missouri, Alderson-Broaddus College, Maryland, Ferris State, East Carolina, Furman, Marshall, West Virginia Wesleyan and South Florida. He had spoken to students in high schools at Norwin, Monessen, Titusville, Mt. Lebanon, Chartiers Valley, Elizabeth-Forward, St. Anthony's Holy Name in Monongahela and Plum.

He also told his story on most TV networks, CNN, ESPN, CBN, CBS and Fox Network and appeared on Good Morning, America (CBS) with Cathy Sullivan, NBC's Today Show with Bryant Gumbel, HBO's NFL Inside Report with Lenny Dawson, The Larry King Show (CNN) and NBC's NFL Halftime.

His message comes from the heart, even if it is a damaged heart.

"We, as a society, as long as we base the hiring and firing of coaches on winning and losing, are not part of the solution," Courson said. "We are part of the problem. We, as a society, do not want to accept what elements of our sports world do on Saturdays and Sundays for us to be entertained."

308

Courson claims drug-testing is not a solution to the problem, calling the NFL's drug-testing policy "a sad joke."

Courson continued: "Anyone who believes that the 13 positive tests a year ago (1989) are an indication of the size of the anabolic steroid dilemma in pro football still believes in the tooth fairy.

"No athlete can be honest about their drug use without committing career suicide. They have to maintain this conspiracy of silence.

"As long as we continue to feed our addiction to sports then we will not get rid of this problem. Some of the only real solutions, especially at the grade school levels and high school levels, is to start to reduce some of the emphasis on sports.

"The parents and coaches at the peewee level and especially at the high school level need to start teaching that personal excellence and lifetime fitness practices are more important than winning."

Reflecting on his early years with the Steelers, he said, "Some of the older players were role models to the younger players. When I got into the league, there were not many players doing it (taking steroids) at first. Then it became an epidemic.

"The Steelers have been known to have one of the finest weight and strength programs in the NFL. To say that anabolic steroids didn't play a role in the Steelers' success would be a falsehood. But this isn't a Steelers' problem. It's a league-wide problem. It's a problem today in Division I colleges and even in high schools. No one ever told me not to take steroids, or suggested I was killing myself."

In a separate interview, Courson said, "It's business and it's money. You do what you have to do. Do you think I wanted to take that stuff? I did it because it was my job. It's war out there."

It's war out there. Courson says things like that a lot. Or about "battles in the trenches." He compares being an offensive lineman to being in the vanguard in the days of the Roman Empire, when slaves were sent out to absorb the initial attack of the enemy. He is a war buff, one quickly observes by walking around his basement apartment. The book shelves are stacked with books about every war that has ever been fought. There are video tapes about wars. There are miniature military tanks on the shelves. There is an American war helmet next to a German war helmet. There is a Steeler helmet. Some special edition Iron City beer cans with Steelers' likenesses on them. There is a game ball he was awarded while playing for the Steelers (after a 33-30 overtime win against the Cincinnati Bengals on November 25, 1979). There is also a Courage Award from the Tampa Bay Buccaneers that was voted on by the players after the 1985 season. "Why would they vote me such an award, and then the next season management thought I wasn't good enough to play for the team?" Courson asked. "They said I wasn't productive enough. If I wasn't productive, why did my teammates vote me this award. It's a lot of politics."

Courson has testified before Congress about the use of steroids in professional and amateur athletics. He told the Senate Judiciary Committee, chaired by Sen. Joseph Biden, a Democrat from Delaware, that by his most conservative estimate of all NFL offensive and defensive linemen, half of NFL players in power positions use steroids.

Atlanta Falcons offensive guard Bill Fralic, a former All-America at the University of Pittsburgh and Penn Hills High School, estimated that 75 percent of all NFL offensive and defensive linemen, linebackers and tight ends use steroids.

Courson heard the testimony of NFL officials and coaches, including Chuck Noll, whom he believes help create the atmosphere that compels steroid use. "Noll represents the way big-time coaches look at the dilemma," said Courson, that is they refuse to acknowledge their role. Courson later wrote to Sen. Biden of his disappointment.

But what could he expect of a government that appears blind to what is really happening out there in the athletic world. It sickens Courson, for instance, that somebody like Arnold Schwartzenegger is the chairman of the President's Council on Physical Fitness and Sports in this country when Schwartzenegger is an admitted steroid user.

Schwartzenegger once boasted, "I had the dream of being the best in the world in something," and has admitted that he used anabolic steroids to help realize that dream. He doesn't talk about it much these days, however.

"All I saw (at those Congressional hearings) was management trying to absolve itself of liability," wrote Courson. "I saw leading men in the NFL, who are respected intellects, show profound ignorance on the steroid issue that baffles my sense of respect."

In an article in the January 21, 1990 issue of *Time* magazine about sprinter Ben Johnson, who had to surrender his gold medal at the Seoul Olympics after it was revealed that he used steroids to achieve his world-beating performance, it said steroid users are getting younger. A 1990 federal study says 250,000 adolescents use the drugs.

Concludes Courson: "I am deeply depressed for the future of sports."

Courson recalls his early days with the Steelers, when he first came to camp at St. Vincent College in 1977. "I went through a big change when I played football," he said. "I was one of those guys who was basically in awe of professionals and the incredible accomplishments that the Steelers had made before I got there.

"I came after they'd won their first two Super Bowls. The Steelers were the power team in professional football. To a young college player, they were already legends. I was in awe of what I was getting into. I didn't have a mirror on myself, but I didn't see myself being as good as they were. Seeing Franco Harris, Mike Webster, L.C. Greenwood and Joe Greene can give you a case of the shakes.

"As I became an older player, however, I changed. I was less excited and in awe of my surroundings. I developed a more mercenary attitude. You go through a few strike situations, and you see it as less of a game and more of a business. You see friends go, getting cut or traded or retired. You play with injuries, and you take pain-killing drugs, and you learn things about yourself and the business.

"That's why I wore the camouflage outfits, and started doing my unique thing. I saw myself as a gladiator and a mercenary. And I told myself I was going to do the best I could do to win. I've never been a real suit and tie person. I've always been a bit of a renegade. Basically, my attire was my suit and tie for what I chose to do for a living.

"The whole way through, I asked a lot of questions. I came into a game that had win-at-all costs models. I always have to question that. I saw steroid use in college, but a lot more in professional football. The players are older and require it more. They're playing for a paycheck. Steroid use becomes much more pronounced the older you get. You can bounce back faster, and do more physically with performance-enhancing drugs. Hell, when I first came up, amphetamines used to get passed out in the trainers' room like mints at a restaurant. They didn't know how dangerous they were long-term. That doesn't happen these days. The first team to do it was the San Diego Chargers, and guess who was an assistant coach there when that was going on? That's right, Chuck Noll. So he's not dumb about this stuff.

"After the '82 strike, it was less of a game to me. As far as I was concerned, I was going to war. I wanted to win to survive. They don't keep a guy who doesn't pull his own load. You are a marketable commodity and you can get hurt.

"The problem with a lot of athletes, including teammates of mine, is that a lot of us wrap up our self-worth in that game. Jack Lambert took offense at some of the things I said in the article in *Sports Illustrated*. He wrote a letter. I think he misunderstood me. He was speaking to me through the media. Jack is a big anti-drug person. So am I. I've done research in libraries on this stuff. I have busted my ass to get the right information. I've forgotten more about drugs than most of the people who are criticizing me. Don't tell me about this state-of-the-art drug testing. In most cases, it's a waste of time. You can beat the system. I can tell a high school student in 25 seconds how to beat that testing. But the players association seems more open to doing things that will help approach the problem. The pressure to win and survive hasn't changed. Such drug-testing is a way for organizations to morally absolve themselves of blame.

"There's also a lot of hypocrisy out there. Alcohol and cigarets are drugs and they kill more Americans than American drugs. The difference is they are legal. You tell me why they're legal?

"I know that Jack Lambert and Jack Ham, for instance, never took steroids, and that they trained hard and played hard. But I trained as hard as anyone. I spent ten times as much time in the weight room as most of the players on the team. So I wasn't looking for shortcuts. We all have drug prejudices. Some people think alcohol and cigarets are

OK because they're legal. One of the things that's underplayed in my problem is that I was also a heavy drinker. That couldn't have helped my condition.

"There were good times, too, and I won't forget them. We had a real tight-knit offensive line group for one thing. My favorite years were when Rollie Dotsch was our offensive line coach. We had a real camaraderie. We had such an unusual group of dedicated guys. I played between Mike Webster and Larry Brown. That was a great privilege. I played behind Sam Davis and Moon Mullins and learned so much. They were winning and took a lot of pride in what they did.

"Mike Webster is the only one still playing. It's sad for me to watch him. I respect him so much. But why the heck is he still playing? Yet I respect him for the fact that he's still playing. But I think so many of us have our self-worth tied up in being a pro football player.

"I had physical ability, but I was a real raw talent when I first joined the Steelers. Playing against guys like Joe Greene every day in practice made me a better ballplayer.

"I was popular. I was single. Gary Dunn and I were the talk of the dressing room. Most of the other guys were married. The other players took pleasure in hearing about our antics. Yeah, I know they told stories about my shenanigans at the VIP and the Green Tree Marriott, but I was having a good time. I wasn't serious about any woman. The NFL was my wife, my mistress and my girl friend. It was the most important thing in my life.

"We used to go crazy. This is a shot and a beer town, and the fans like to bump elbows with the players. Gary Dunn and I used to get a little crazy, anything to have fun. With the size of us, we could have been destructive. But we weren't; we just wanted to have fun. We wanted to blow off steam, and relieve the pressure that was on us to win. When I got traded, that put a damper on our program. Gary had been the only other single guy among the veterans. His locker was next to mine. We lived near each other in the same apartment complex in Hunting Ridge, down in South Fayette. Ted Petersen was there, too; he still is.

"I've toned down my act considerably. I can't do real heavy exercise. I have a beer once in a while, but that's it. I have to go in and replace my plumbing before I can do much. Once I do that, the doctors tell me I'll be back on the basketball court again. I used to love to play basketball and softball. I want to dunk the ball again.

"Right now, I'm trying to channel my energies. I learned from my earlier athletic activities that if you get knocked down you have to get up and make the best of it. If I sat and thought about some of the setbacks I have suffered, it would only make me angry.

"I want to get better and go back to school. I wanted to be a teacher. When I got sick, a lot of people around me thought it was the end of the world. But I got a lot of support from my teammates and my friends. That was important to me. When I first got out of football, I felt that everything was so unfair. I was a real frustrated case.

312

"Now I have more hope. When I go around to schools and talk to young people, I really enjoy that. I want to continue to work with young people. That's why I have to go back to school. I don't want to talk about steroids the rest of my life. My big passion is history. That's what I want to teach. That's where my heart is."

Steve Courson

Lynn Swann
Doing it gracefully

"Did I ever tell you you're my hero.
You're everything I wish I could be.
I could fly higher than an eagle
You were the wind beneath my wings."
—Bette Midler
"The Wind Beneath My Wings"

This was on the eve of the Pro Football Hall of Fame induction ceremonies in Canton, Ohio, at a dinner in the Civic Center, and I spotted Lynn Swann, the former star receiver for the Pittsburgh Steelers. I had to smile. Whereas most of the former football players who were there were talking to other former football players, Swann was speaking to James Sikking. By the looks on their smiling, animated faces, you would have thought they were old friends.

James Sikking may not be as familiar to you as Frank Gifford, or Lenny Dawson, or Dan Dierdorf, some of the other friendly faces to be found in the same area of the floor, but Sikking is also a TV star. He is an actor who plays the part of the doctor father in "Doogie Howser, M.D.," one of my daughters' favorite TV shows, and he used to be the head of the S.W.A.T. team in "Hill Street Blues."

Swann also posed for a picture with the pageant queen at the Canton event. "This is my new wife," kidded Swann, smiling into the camera. He did not even need a cue to brighten the scene, and put a smile on everyone's face. He is a natural. He was always comfortable in the spotlight.

There are always lots of TV stars, especially sitcom and soap opera stars, invited to participate in the Pro Football Hall of Fame Week activities in Canton. Swann enjoyed seeing these stars as much as the local citizens because he wants to be a TV star someday. And he is well on his way.

Television has always brought out the best in Lynn Swann. Swann starred in four Super Bowls for the Steelers, especially Super Bowl X in 1976 in which he was named the game's MVP, and he made a great touchdown catch in Super Bowl XIV in 1980 to help the Steelers win their fourth NFL title.

He started a career as a sportscaster with ABC-TV even while starring for the Steelers, and has continued to work for them ever since, showing up as a reporter on "Monday Night Football," on various "Wide World of Sports" segments, the 1984 Summer Olympics in Los Angeles, the 1988 Winter Olympics in Calgary, the Kentucky Derby, and other spectacular sports events. He has appeared on and even hosted several TV game shows.

Swann cut his pro football career short at age 30, after nine pro seasons (1974-82), to take a full-time lucrative position with ABC-TV, and some say it may cost him as far as getting into the Pro Football Hall of Fame. The voters seem to prefer players with double digits for years performed, and with bigger numbers as far as passes caught and yardage gained and touchdowns.

Swann was on the doorstep of the Pro Football Hall of Fame in the summer of 1990, as he was asked to introduce his good friend and former roommate Franco Harris, who was inducted along with another former teammate Jack Lambert. "I'm getting close," Swann said to a crowd that included many Steeler fans. "All the fans in Pittsburgh said someday I'd make it to the Hall of Fame. Maybe I'm half way there. But you know in Pittsburgh, we never believed in next year. We believed in today."

He was something less than the six feet, 180 pounds at which he was listed, and something more when it came time to soaring high in the sky to catch a football, or sliding this way or that way to wrap one tightly to his stomach. The renegade likes of George Atkinson and Jack Tatum of the much-hated Raiders tried to break his back and spirit, or take his head off, but Swann would not be denied. Swann was special. Doug Krikorian of the *Los Angeles Herald Examiner* labeled Swann "the premier receiver of the 1970s. In football, you're a Lynn Swann-type if you can go deep and go across the middle and do it gracefully and, most of all, make your biggest catches in your team's biggest games."

Swann is not sorry he stopped playing pro football when he did, as he always wanted to get into the media. Swann's stats are not as impressive as players who stayed for 12 to 14 seasons, such as teammate John Stallworth, but no one made more big money catches in his career. When the opportunity came to get into network TV, Swann simply could not say no. That is what he majored in when he was an All-American receiver at Southern Cal. During the off-season when he was with the Steelers, he worked for KABC-TV in Los Angeles for seven years. No one was any better prepared for his life's work than Lynn Swann.

Though he grew up just outside San Francisco, and was a college star in Los Angeles, and works for a company based in New York, Swann stays in Pittsburgh. He has a home in the posh suburban community of Sewickley, and an office in Gateway Center 2 in downtown Pittsburgh. He always surprised people by sticking around Pittsburgh throughout the year.

"The fans are really behind you here," he explained. "Football is a little more important in Pittsburgh than some places. That makes it enjoyable."

From his office windows in Gateway Center, he can see a slice of Point State Park, where the Allegheny River and the Monongahela River meet to form the Ohio River. He cannot see Three Rivers Stadium, but he is a frequent visitor there, and he is still capable of lighting up the place.

"You have to have a home base," said Swann, when we spoke. "In the TV business, you feel like you're part of a traveling group of homeless people. I thought it was better to have a home here.

315

"Some people think I picked Pittsburgh because people know me here. I picked Pittsburgh because I like it here. I like the quality of life here, the cost of living. You get more for the dollar you make. You make a conscious decision to live somewhere, and then you make it more like your home.

"I'm constantly looking for more business opportunities, but I don't want any that would cause me to move from Pittsburgh. With USAir, I can get direct flights to LA and to New York, and it's going to get even better with a new airport being built here. Besides, I feel comfortable here."

He could catch footballs with the best of them, no matter where Terry Bradshaw might throw them, and he had confidence coming out his ears, and a smile that spanned those ears. It was a star package.

There is a simple sign on the door of his ninth floor office that says "Swann, Inc." It would have been just as appropriate above his cubicle in the Steelers clubhouse. He has always been a versatile performer with a busy schedule.

Swann has been the national spokesman for Big Brothers and Big Sisters since 1980. He serves on the board of trustees of the Pittsburgh Ballet Theater, where he has created a youth scholarship. He had gone to dancing school in his youth, and even appeared in a PBS Special with Gene Kelly, who grew up in Pittsburgh and became one of the world's best known dancers.

Swann was named the 1981 NFL Man of the Year, a prestigious award determined on the basis of an NFL player's contributions to his community as well as his playing excellence. He was also voted to the All-NFL team of the decade of the '70s, and to a first-team position on the Super Bowl silver anniversary team in public balloting in 1990.

Now if he could only get voted into the Pro Football Hall of Fame. . .

Something else I remember from the evening in Canton. When I told Swann I was doing a book about the glory days of the Steelers, and some of the success stories of his former teammates, I remembered him asking me, "What's going to be the measure of success? I think all of them have been successful."

How do you measure success, or a man's measure of his worth? Who enjoys their job? Who feels fulfilled in what they do? Who establishes the rules for that game?

I was waiting for Lynn Swann in the lobby of the Gateway 2 Building, and I was watching two window washers at work. They were cleaning the windows in the atrium lobby, and were both high up on long ladders, so long the ladders bent in the middle, and seemed to sway a little. Over their shoulders, through the atrium, I could see the landmark Christmas tree-shaped decorative lights on the corner of Horne's department store. Swann was late, so I had time to watch the window washers.

I was fascinated by their movements. The oldest of the two was a burly fellow, with a big belly, and it was hard to believe how nimble he was on the ladder, and how he could lean this way and that way without the ladder toppling over on its side. I thought about how Swann was renowned for his high-flying ability, and his body control, and how he credited all those dance classes he went to as a kid for making him graceful and athletic. And here was a window washer who also could do wondrous things in the air, swaying back and forth, applying a wet cloth, then drawing a long rubber blade across the wet windows, and drying them off, with such apparent ease. He stretched as far as his arm would reach, dipped down past his shoetops, and back up again. There was an artistry and a style about him that belied his being overweight.

When the older of the two window washers came down for a break, I thought he looked familiar. "Are you from Hazelwood?" I asked him. He nodded affirmatively. He knew me and he knew my brother Dan, he said. He was a year behind my brother in school at St. Stephen's Grade School. Small world, I thought. His name was Bob Blackburn, and he was 52, and he had been washing windows for 33 years, he said, since 1957.

"Didn't you play football in Hazelwood?" I asked.

"Yes, I did. I played guard for two years for the last two teams of the J.J. Doyles."

What a coincidence, I thought. The J.J. Doyles were the local heavyweight sandlot football team that my dad was always telling me could beat the Steelers when we used to watch the Steelers playing in TV games back in the mid-'50s.

"I washed windows during the day, and played football at night," said Blackburn. "And sometimes on weekends."

This particular atrium had a plaque on the wall dedicating it to the late mayor, Richard S. Caliguiri. It was from the Equitable Life Assurance Society of the U.S. in appreciation for Caliguiri's contribution to Pittsburgh's Renaissance II, the city's second major facelift in the past 35 years, and was dated September 12, 1985.

Caliguiri, in his early 20s, had looked after his father's bowling establishment on Second Avenue in Hazelwood back in the mid-'50s. I used to get bowling scores from him as the 14-year-old sports editor of *The Hazelwood Envoy*. Blackburn, 18 at the time, set duckpins in Caliguiri's bowling alleys. The following year, Blackburn would begin his career working for Penn Window.

He washes windows for all the tall buildings in the Gateway Center as well as the all-glass paneled PPG Building, which is a 40 story window, in a way, or what Blackburn termed "A window washer's nightmare. But there's quite a view from the top of it."

"Did you ever get hurt washing windows?" I asked.

"Yeah, back in 1960. I fell and broke my ankle."

His dad had gotten him into the business, he said, and, at one period, there were four Blackburns washing windows at the same time. Blackburn had started out making $1.40 an hour. The other fellow working with him, I learned, was his 43-year-old nephew, John Blackburn, also from Hazelwood.

"It's a tough job," said Bob Blackburn. "It's tough on the body. You do a lot of stretching up there on the ladder. You can feel it when you get home at night. You have to work in all kinds of conditions, on all kinds of lifts. Sometimes it gets windy up there. But we're careful.

"I love football, but I rarely get to watch Pitt or the Steelers. I'm often working on Saturdays and Sundays. That's overtime, and that's where the money is. Sometimes I see Swann come through here. I've seen Mel Blount down here. I used to wash windows at the homes of Franco Harris and L.C. Greenwood."

Pittsburgh's skyline, especially the PPG Building, are often talked about and are a point of pride to the city. The view of the city's skyline coming out of the Fort Pitt Tunnel always amazes first-time visitors, and brings a smile to the face of locals as well, who never tire of the sight, especially when the buildings are lit up at night, or during the holiday season.

But no one ever thinks about the guys like Bob and John Blackburn who help bring a shine to those buildings, or make it easier for the people in those buildings to see and appreciate the sights around them, like the three rivers, and Point State Park, the stadium, or the inclines on Mt. Washington.

"Yeah, we see a lot of things, too," said Blackburn, "but it's pretty much just a job more than anything else."

The conversation about taking care of the maintenance for those buildings reminded me that the mother of Johnny Unitas, who was a single parent, used to clean offices in one of those downtown buildings.

There was only one boy back in our neighborhood in Hazelwood who went to dancing school like Lynn Swann did. His father owned a saloon — just like the fathers of Art Rooney and Rocky Bleier — and the family lived above a beer distributing business across the street from the saloon. Everyone thought he was a sissy because he went to dancing school. When he was in his 20's, he committed suicide.

Lynn Swann said he never thought of himself as a football player. "My playing football was a fluke," he said. "I only played because my older brother played. Gene Kelly should have been a football player and I should have been a dancer. I never wanted to play football.

"I promised myself I wouldn't play more than five years. Then six came, then seven, then eight and nine.

"I played at USC because I had a scholarship and couldn't afford college without it and I played pro football because I was a first round draft choice.

"If I chose to, I could have played for some time. But I never wanted to be one of those people who lingered on. It was my time."

Injuries had slowed Swann in his ninth pro season, however, and he seemed to be slipping. His production dropped off dramatically. In the first five games of his final season with the Steelers, Swann caught just eight passes for 82 yards. By then, Stallworth had become Bradshaw's prime receiver. It had to make it easier for Swann to walk away

318

from the Steelers when he saw a chance to crack the network TV market. He was hired by ABC-TV initially to work with veteran broadcaster Keith Jackson on USFL telecasts. He knew there was an opportunity to get involved in ABC's Olympic coverage package.

"Emotionally and mentally, I'm ready to leave the security of the sports world," Swann said when he announced his retirement at a press conference in Los Angeles in 1983.

He had often called professional sports "America's greatest part-time job." He explained his remark this way: "It allows you to work at something you enjoy doing, it gives you the opportunity to make a substantial income and it gives you a great deal of time in the off-season to prepare a career. All too often, I see athletes who aren't prepared to make that transition and don't leave football when it's time to."

While in it, however, Swann brought a special blend of talent and attitude to the Steelers, who made him their No. 1 draft pick in 1974, the year they would win the first of their four Super Bowl titles.

"Lynn Swann was a guy who had super confidence, and this was something we needed," said Steelers' president Dan Rooney. "It showed we had to bring in a lot of different personalities to be successful."

He was handsomer than most football players, most people for that matter, and smooth and glib, and he always seemed to be tap-dancing in one manner or another. He was Ben Vereen with shoulder pads.

"I think it's not 'luck' that all the things I've done throughout my life prepared me for what I accomplished as a player and in my professional career," he once said. "My mother made me take dancing lessons and I'm very grateful for that. Tap dancing, modern jazz, ballet. From four until I was a high school senior.

"Dance develops coordination, timing, rhythm. Dance is more than people on stage in tights and slippers. They're athletes and more people should realize that.

"At USC, I did gymnastics and worked on the trampoline a lot. I played basketball all my life. All these things contributed to the body control that went into those catches. Plus concentration on the ball. Some people might call it luck."

He demonstrated some other skills at USC. Once he was asked to give an impromptu talk in class. He talked about how tap dancing really started with the black slaves in the South. Since the slaves weren't allowed to talk while they worked, they tapped a kind of Morse Code to each other. Swann tapped his way through it, and the students bought it. Swann played for USC in two Rose Bowls, was a first team All-American in 1973, and set all-time pass catching records at his school. Swann was only 23, the youngest so honored, when *Sport* magazine selected him as the MVP in Super Bowl X, when he caught four passes for 161 yards and the winning touchdown against the Dallas Cowboys at the Orange Bowl in Miami.

Chuck Noll knew Swann was something special. "I would like to say that we developed Lynn Swann," noted Noll, "but the truth is he was perfectly developed as a football player the first time he stepped out on our practice field."

With Willie Stargell and Franco Harris

In fashion show

Lynn Swann

With Foge Fazio, Franco Harris, George Bush, Marcus Allen,
Dinah Shore, Danny Marino at Hilton Hotel

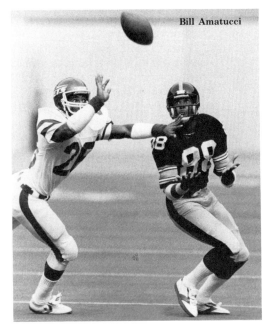

Bill Amatucci

tching shot in back

Catching ball vs. Jets

Steve Fenn/ABC

s ABC-TV Olympics reporter

Joe Greene carries Swann
off the field after he
was KOd by Raiders.

Like Noll, Swann had many interests. He enjoyed skiing, tennis, car racing, hunting, fancied himself a fine amateur photographer, a gourmet cook and a connoisseur of French wine. He liked flashy cars, and tooled around in a silver Mercedes-Benz, a Porsche, and other fine autos. He was married to a beautiful model for a short time. He took lessons to fly a helicopter and an airplane. The sky was not the limit for Lynn. He knew no boundaries. He was just different.

Lynn Swann was born in the aluminum town of Alcoa, Tennessee. Alcoa's headquarters, coincidentally enough, just happen to be in Pittsburgh, where the company was started with the help of Mellon money. Lynn was one of three brothers. His dad was a Delta Airlines porter. His mother was a dental technician. His grandmother was a lifelong domestic for a well-to-do family in Alcoa. The family moved to San Mateo, California early in Lynn's life.

"I went to public elementary school with the kids from my black neighborhood," recalls Swann. "I always played football and because smaller kids like myself were always receivers, I just naturally learned to catch. Nobody ever taught me which way to hold your hands or that sort of thing. I grew up knowing always to catch it with my hands, not against the body. Sometimes with Bradshaw, who threw a real hard ball, you had to catch with your arms or body if it was a wet or very cold day. Sometimes it came at you like a rifle shot, or like it was coming out of a .44 magnum.

"Anyway, I got a scholarship to Junipero Serra, an all-white boys Catholic high school, though I was a Baptist. I was one of four blacks out of 900 students.

"I got my leaping ability from playing basketball. I was able to dunk the ball when I was a junior in high school and I was only 5-10 then. I was the state long jump champion, too, at San Mateo High School and I'd like to think I could have made the Olympics if I had stayed with it.

"I long-jumped 25 feet, four-and-a-half inches in high school. I high-jumped 6-2, I pole-vaulted 13 and a half feet. I ran the high hurdles in 14.9 and I ran the 100-yard dash in 9.7. But leaping is a matter of timing. And timing is something that's inside of you and you just work at it."

Someone overhearing Swann saying all this interjected, "How far did you shot put?"

"About three feet!" Swann said with a smile.

Swann suffered several concussions after taking hard shots, twice during the 1976 season, once in an AFC title game against the Oakland Raiders, and again against the Dallas Cowboys in Super Bowl X.

In the AFC title game, Swann had been knocked unconscious by Oakland's strong safety George Atkinson, and spent two nights in a

322

hospital. He did not think he would be able to play in the Super Bowl in Miami. He felt he had gotten three or four cheap shots from Raider defensive backs in that game, and had been clubbed in the back of the head twice by the same Atkinson during the regular season.

There was a memorable photo of Swann being carried off the field at Three Rivers Stadium by Joe Greene after Atkinson had nailed him.

"Of all the things that happened in my career, that incident still stands out the most in my mind," said Swann. "Here I was knocked cold out there on the field, and Joe Greene runs out and picks me up.

"Now you must understand Joe Greene was nursing a badly pinched shoulder. It was a bitterly cold day, and Joe was in terrible pain. But he still picked me up and I was like a rag doll in his hands.

"A picture of the scene hangs in my home. I look at it as symbolizing the spirit of those Steeler championship teams. It showed that Joe Greene's greatest concern at that moment was for a fallen teammate. Nothing else. He didn't care about his own pain. The guys on those teams genuinely cared for one another and that's one reason why we won so often."

Swann drew diagrams of three plays on the desk between us, showing where he was clobbered from behind, too vehemently in his mind, by Jack Tatum and Atkinson.

"On this one play, just before the half, Bradshaw had thrown a short swing pass to Rocky Bleier at midfield. I was down in the far left corner of the end zone, completely out of the play, and sort of jogging through the end zone. I didn't even know Tatum was there. He drove his forearm right into the base of my neck. He really dinged me. I was still dizzy when I went to the locker room at halftime.

"Then, in the second half, I came across the middle on a cross-over pattern, and caught a pass from Bradshaw. Atkinson collared me pretty good. I fumbled the ball and Tatum recovered it. Atkinson drove me right into the icy field. The only way I know what happened after that was from what I saw on the tape. That was when Joe Greene carried me off the field.

"The following year, I was running a pattern across the middle, about 15 or 20 yards downfield, and Bradshaw threw a pass to the left sideline to Franco. Instead of going after Franco and trying to tackle him, Atkinson instead decks me from behind. Franco nearly scored on that play.

"That's when Chuck made the comment about the criminal element in the league. That's when we knew they had targeted people. That's when I knew there was a price on my head. I had every right to be concerned about my well-being."

The Dallas Cowboys did not share Greene's concern, and certainly not Swann's misgivings. Even if Swann was able to play in Super Bowl X, Cowboys' defensive back Cliff Harris had suggested that Swann might be intimidated easily.

"Any player in the NFL who thinks about his last injury is washed up," said Swann. "Cliff Harris doesn't know Lynn Swann, and he doesn't know the Pittsburgh Steelers.

"It's like being thrown by a horse," added Swann, who has owned horses. "You've got to get up and ride again immediately, or you may be scared the rest of your life."

There were times when Swann considered quitting rather than risking permanent injury, believing the league was not looking after him or any other receivers by permitting such obvious foul play.

"Being physical and aggressive has always been a part of football," said Swann. "It's excessive, though, when you're hitting someone like that whose back is turned — that's not necessary."

In Super Bowl X, one play in particular stands out. Swann out-jumped Cowboys cornerback Mark Washington, for starters, then the ball glanced off his chest, and Swann extended himself to make a diving catch for a 53-yard gain. It was a catch that made all the highlight films that year.

"Discipline," said Swann, when asked how he kept his eyes on that elusive ball. "Having physical ability is great, but if you don't have the discipline to do what's necessary then all that ability goes to waste. Concentration can be learned. It's easy to be distracted. You have to shut out all distractions and just go for the ball.

"I think that most really good ballplayers see themselves as heroes, making great catches and great runs. Then when it happens you say, 'Hey, I knew I could do it!' I'd been wanting to do something super for a long time.

"There was no room for being gun-shy on the Steelers because we ran a lot of patterns over the middle. If you were gun-shy, you weren't gonna be around too long. People know that and they take shots at you."

When he left the Steelers, Swann said he was taking a lot with him, sort of a movable feast. "I take with me most of all the character of the people I played with. It was a great opportunity to grow and mature in Pittsburgh.

"I just want to be remembered as one of several people who played on one of the greatest football teams ever assembled in American sports history, and as someone who gave to his community and his friends above and beyond his athletic abilities."

Noll did not brood about Swann stepping down. "Football is a transitory thing," said the Steelers' head coach. "Most players realize that. Because of that, you always cheer for the person who knows or finds out what he wants to do with his life."

Speaking about Swann, Dan Rooney remarked, "Everybody remembers the great catches he made, particularly the one in Super Bowl X. But that was just one aspect of Lynn.

"The one I remember is the one in Super Bowl XIV. I remember we were down at the half, and we came out in the third quarter, drove down the field and Lynn leaped about as high as the ceiling in this room to catch a touchdown pass that brought us back."

That play came on the first series of downs in the second half. Swann went up between defensive backs Nolan Cromwell and Pat

Thomas, and little ol' No. 88 came down in the end zone with the ball. Looking at a photo of that catch today, you can see that Swann's knees were as high as the shoulders of both Cromwell and Thomas, who both had their shoes planted on the endzone grass at the instant Swann made the catch. A follow-up photograph that has always been a favorite of mine shows Swann being held high by Bennie Cunningham, the Steelers' big tight end, with Stallworth at his side, and Swann is thrusting his arm upward in a victory salute. To a football fan, it was almost as good as the picture of the raising of the flag on Iwo Jima. That TD catch also lifted the Steelers from a 13-10 deficit to a 17-13 lead in what would be a 31-19 victory. Later on, Swann had to leave the game because he was suffering from blurred vision. Stallworth, who would always perform in Swann's shadow, made two spectacular TD catches that day, but finished second to Bradshaw in the MVP voting.

Swann was asked how he wanted to be remembered as a football player.

"I guess as a person who played his best games under pressure," he said. "When the games meant the most and we had our backs against the walls, my teammates could count on me to come through. It seems like the big events always brought out the best in me. Maybe it was fear of failure that made me play better in such circumstances."

Swann also said he wanted to be remembered as a player who spoke out against the violence of his sport in the celebrated George Atkinson lawsuit against Chuck Noll that grew out of a savage Atkinson hit on Swann.

"I didn't sit in a corner and let what I considered a cheap shot go by without saying something about it," he said. "I testified at the trial. I gave my version.

"George Atkinson lost the lawsuit and the league the next season passed the so-called George Atkinson rule. That's when a player can be suspended, or fined, for committing a flagrant foul. I think football today is cleaner because of it. I hope I'm remembered for my contributions in this area."

ABC-TV has found they can count on Swann to be a sportscaster at any kind of sports event. He does not know how to say "no" to any request. He never flinches. He is still going across the middle and risking shots in the back, nowadays from TV sports critics. "I cover anything they assign me to," said Swann.

Whatever Swann covers, he attempts to get some first-hand experience, sort of like George Plimpton, so he can better appreciate what the performers are feeling. "It gives you a perspective that can greatly aid your commentary," he said. "You know what's going on from the athlete's point of view."

He even traveled to Anchorage, Alaska to cover the Iditarod Sled Dog Race, a grueling 1,157-mile race between Anchorage and Nome. "It definitely was something with which I was not familiar," said Swann.

The race is run in the dead of winter, which is one of the reasons coordinating producer Curt Gowdy, Jr., selected Swann for the assignment for ABC's "Wide World of Sports."

"Curt told me," said Swann, "he thought I'd be good at it because I was one of the few announcers who could stand the cold. He said, 'After all those passes you caught in the snow at Pittsburgh, this should be a snap.'

"So I said OK. I mean they weren't going to send Jim McKay to cover an event when it's 50 below zero."

Swann will do anything because he aims to please, and he feels the experience will help him make the climb he pictures for himself in the TV world. He says he won't be completely satisfied until he reaches the top echelon of his field — until he is rubbing microphones with Brent Musburger, Dick Enberg and Jim McKay.

"I think there's an opportunity to do that if I work hard and get the assignments," said Swann. "But you also have to be lucky in terms of those assignments. You have to have something very, very dramatic happen that catapults you beyond the group of people you're in."

He knows he has to wait his turn, too.

"You have to be competitive in a non-competitive way because you're working together as a team. You'll never hear me say I want this particular assignment or this particular role because people's noses get bent out of shape, and they start to think you're after their job. I'm not after anyone's job. I just want my job and to be the best."

His coverage of the 1988 Iditarod won an Emmy, which is the sort of thing that will help advance Swann's career. "If you keep working and improve, the opportunities should present themselves," he said.

"I guess I'm what you would call a goal-oriented person. I always have tried to be the best in anything I do. I'm never satisfied with myself. In my own mind, I never thought I played my best football game. I always thought I could have done better."

Stallworth and Swann take a breather at practice.

326

John Stallworth
"I was blessed with a talent"

John Stallworth is at home in Huntsville, Alabama, even though he grew up and played his high school football in Tuscaloosa, about 150 miles to the south. He went to college in Normal, just outside of Huntsville, starring as a wide receiver for Alabama A&M, and it is where he met his wife, Flo, who grew up near the campus.

At age 38, and three years removed from catching passes for the Pittsburgh Steelers, Stallworth sounded like he was in heaven, to hear him talk about how content and happy he and his family are in Huntsville. His former teammate and twin deep threat with the Steelers, Lynn Swann, regards Stallworth as one of the Steelers' greatest success stories. "John always wanted to go back home to Alabama," said Swann when we spoke before he introduced Franco Harris at Pro Football Hall of Fame ceremonies in Canton, Ohio in the summer of 1990, "and he's doing well there. You can use him for a yardstick of success among the Steelers of our day."

While Swann, who grew up in San Francisco and played his college ball at Southern Cal, lived in Pittsburgh year round during his playing days, and continues to live there while working for ABC television, Stallworth would always go home to Alabama when the NFL season was over.

"That was me," said Stallworth when we spoke in late November, 1990. "Alabama and the things that it conjures up in my mind means so much to me. I have a very special relationship here with friends and family. Not that I didn't have some of that in Pittsburgh. But what is near and dear to me is in Alabama. I just don't fit into that in the North.

"We had about 35 people to our house recently during Thanksgiving Day. My wife's family was here, and my brother and sister, some great aunts and some grandparents, the whole works, were here. When I was growing up in Tuscaloosa, we had all kinds of cousins right in the neighborhood, and I like that. Having a close-knit family is a sign of success, too."

Stallworth is quite successful in his "life's work," as owner and president of MRC — Madison Research Corporation — a research and development firm that works closely in support of several Huntsville-based aerospace industry firms. MRC provides a full range of defense and industrial services. Incorporated in 1986, MRC specializes in the analysis and application of advanced technologies to a wide range of defense mission requirements. Stallworth oversees a staff of 15 engineers and support personnel.

"John Stallworth Day" was held in Huntsville back on April 1, 1988. He was pictured on the program for the affair making that great over-the-shoulder TD catch against the Los Angeles Rams in Super Bowl XIV, his second TD of that memorable day. In the program, among the many letters of congratulations, there is one from Joe W. Davis, the mayor of Huntsville.

"We are proud to have John join our business commmunity as an entrepreneur where he has again established himself as a man of integrity with an interest in the future of this community.

"Not only has John Stallworth achieved athletic excellence, he has provided our young people with a worthy role model, illustrating that strength of character combined with hard work and determination is an unbeatable formula for achievement."

Stallworth's coach at Alabama A&M, Louis Crews, offered in his letter of congratulations, "Recalling our first days when I began to call you 'Spaghetti,' brings back memories of how fragile, humble and graceful you were. No matter how frequently you got hurt, you would always bounce back up rapidly. No matter what we asked you to do for the team, you would say, 'Yes, sir,' and do it. Now matter what you did, you did it gracefully — in the manner of a Tennessee walking horse."

When Stallworth was playing for the Steelers, back in 1983, he returned home to work in real estate and development and went to school to get a master's degree in business with a finance concentration. "I started my own aerospace engineering firm, and we're doing some great work," said Stallworth. "The Marshall Space Flight Center and the U.S. Missile Command are here in Huntsville, and I thought there was a great opportunity in that field.

"At first, it was very difficult. It's very technical and the language was foreign to me. But I felt I could be good at it because I knew what it took to be successful. If ballplayers would apply themselves in business the way they did in sports — with the same enthusiasm, determination, dedication and work ethic — they could be successful in almost any field.

"It's the same way in sports. Or in the National Football League. So many guys played strictly on their ability. Some had the skills and speed and jumping ability, but they lasted only three or four years, and were out of the league. What separates you from the pack? The hard work, that's what I think. I wouldn't have stayed 14 seasons with the Steelers strictly on athletic ability. I worked at my trade. I learned to be a complete receiver."

Stallworth was always regarded as the Steelers' second best receiver during the team's glory years, taking a back seat to Swann, but he had more staying power than Swann. He played five more seasons than Swann. In the end, he finished with 537 receptions to become the Steelers' all-time leader in that category, with Swann a distant second at 336 receptions. Elbie Nickel (1947-57) is third with 329 receptions, Franco Harris fourth with 306, and Louis Lipps fifth with 303, following the 1990 schedule.

Stallworth holds Steelers records for most yards receiving with 8,723 compared to 5,462 for Swann, in most touchdown passes caught with 63 compared to 51 for Swann, and for catching passes in 67 consecutive games.

Such statistics should serve Stallworth in good stead when he comes eligible for the Pro Football Hall of Fame. A player has to be retired for five full seasons to be on the ballot.

John Stallworth

"I try to stay away from thinking about it," said Stallworth. "Yes, I'd love to be there.

"Early in my life, I wanted to do something to be remembered. When I was young, I used to struggle with the subject of death. Don't ask me why. I know it sounds strange. I thought about how some day I wouldn't be around. But I could do something in my life to be remembered.

"I was blessed with a talent for catching a football. I want to be remembered. If I think about the Hall of Fame now, it wouldn't be productive. I can't do anything right now to affect whether I go in the Hall or not.

"When I think about the sacrifices so many guys made on our team, I would like to see them all in the Hall of Fame. I'd like to see Swann in the Hall of Fame. I know his personality, and I know he'd like to be in.

"I have not been to the Hall of Fame to see our guys go in, but I have watched them all on television. My feeling was one of joy. I was happy for them. I know the pain they went through to get there. I remember Joe Greene when he suffered nerve damage to his shoulder. Getting to the Hall must have made him think it was worth it.

"I look at Bradshaw, and I think about the problems he had with injuries, and the problems he had off the field, with the marriages he had. I look at Mel Blount, and the struggles he had on and off the field. I think about the things they had to overcome.

"I've seen them overcome the adversity. That's what you learn. You see how they handled the great times and the tough times. When the hard times or the low times came to me, I had the knowledge of how to handle them.

"I still feel that way. In order to get where you want to be, you have to have a game plan. Whether you're playing for your life or between the lines, it's how you want your family to be, where your kids are, and where you hope they will end up. You have to work hard to get there."

Reflecting back on my days on the Steelers' beat, Stallworth seemed shy, but maybe that was by contrast to his next-door neighbors in the Steelers' clubhouse, J. T. Thomas and Mel Blount, who talked a lot and enjoyed schmoozing with sportswriters.

Stallworth would never seek out a sportswriter to talk about his latest exploits, frustrations or opinions about the opposition. It was not Stallworth's way. He spoke softly and cautiously.

When approached and questioned, he seemed reticent, at first, but he warmed up quickly. There was an ease about him. There were lights on in both of his dark eyes, an enthusiastic gleam once he got into a subject. Sometimes he would positively giggle. There was an inner strength and conviction to his comments, and he was not afraid to allude to the Lord when he reflected on his accomplishments and the source of his strength.

"He makes the way for me, and gives me great patience," said Stallworth. "I feel a great influence in my life."

He was sincere, there was never any doubt about that. His ebony face was smooth and narrow, with high cheekbones, but his smile was wide.

The only time there was tension was if someone pressed him for comparisons with Lynn Swann. He liked Lynn, all right, but he did not want to take a back seat to anybody.

"We had two great receivers," recalled Lionel Taylor, who was the receiver coach early in the Steeler careers of Stallworth and Swann. "We had Swann from Southern Cal, and Stallworth from a small southern black school, and they were different. But I told Stallworth, 'You'll be playing longer than Swann.' I knew Swann had other ambitions."

There was a sweetness about Stallworth, almost a coo in his voice at times. He could kid you once he trusted you and felt comfortable in conversation. He could tease. He laughed easily, sometimes cracking up. There was an absolute joy about John Stallworth when things were going well with him. He seemed to enjoy practice. It seemed like there was nothing he would rather do than run after passes, with those long, loping strides — he was so swift and graceful — and clamp his hands on a football tossed his way. He had strong hands and strong concentration. A scene at St. Vincent College comes to mind. Stallworth and Bradshaw went off by themselves one day, to one of the three football fields laid out on the green campus, the one that was lined by a snow-fence and weeping willows, down by the road that brings the fans from Rt. 30 to see their beloved Steelers up close.

Bradshaw and Stallworth were playing "catch" — but they were playing "catch" as only they could.

Stallworth would snare a bullet toss just before it struck the grass, grabbing it with those two large hands of his, and locking it between them like a vise. I kidded him on one sideline snare. "You practicing your Super Bowl highlight film catches?"

He just smiled and wiped the sweat off his forehead. They threw the ball back and forth, with force when Bradshaw was throwing it, and with more of a lob when Stallworth would return the ball. Both were bareheaded and the perspiration glistened on their foreheads. This was fun, but it was serious business.

I remember seeing the two of them hook up on passes in practice at Three Rivers Stadium, and marveling at the way they communicated with each other without words. Stallworth would explain how his pattern would change — and Bradshaw would recognize it before the snap — just by the way the defensive back lined up, inside or outside of him.

"Sometimes Brad thinks we can outjump everyone, and I wouldn't argue with him about that," said Stallworth. "Most defensive backs are shorter than I am. And I think I can outjump them all. And when Lionel Taylor was the receiver coach here, he said when you get your hands on the ball you should catch it. That helps to think that way. No one's going to stop me."

Bradshaw threw high balls to Stallworth and Swann and the other receivers in practice sessions.

It paid off in the biggest of games.

In Super Bowl XIII in January of 1979 against the Dallas Cowboys, Stallworth was one of the game's top offensive performers, catching three passes for 115 yards and two touchdowns in the first half. He could not play the second half because of leg cramps. In one playoff game against Denver that same season, he set an AFC record with 10 receptions.

"In that Super Bowl against the Cowboys in Miami," said Tom Moore, the Steelers' receiver coach at the time, "we threw a little 10-yard curl to Stallworth and he ran it 75 yards for a touchdown. He can do that on any given play.

"In the Super Bowl against the Rams at Pasadena, those two catches by Stallworth for touchdowns showed the greatest kind of concentration. They were both tough over-the-shoulder grabs; only the great ones get those."

John Stallworth has always seen himself as an underdog, surprisingly enough, and so he has always rooted for the underdog.

Back in the 1979 season, Stallworth was voted the Steelers' most valuable player by his teammates when he caught 70 passes for 1,183 yards. Some thought he should have been named the MVP in the Super Bowl as well when he made two touchdown catches, but Terry Bradshaw won that award. Stallworth was happy with the Steelers' MVP award (which he would win again in 1984). "Just look around this locker room and you'll know why," he said then. "There are so many super players on this team, and if they think you're the MVP it really matters. Then, you've really made it."

Prior to a playoff game that year with the Miami Dolphins, Stallworth spoke to me about why he was never a Dolphins' fan as a young man in a story I wrote for *The Pittsburgh Press*.

"I remember the year (1972) when they went 17-and-0," said Stallworth, who was then a junior at Alabama A&M, "and I did not want them to go 17-and-0. All through high school and college, I was a strong rooter for the underdog."

That is understandable, once you are aware of Stallworth's history. His Tuscaloosa high school team, the Black Bears, did not strike fear into too many hearts. "We never won more than three games a year," said Stallworth. "It was hard for even some of the 'homers' to pick us to win."

At Alabama A&M, things got a little better, but not much. "We didn't have a real good team," he recalled. "We were about a .500 team, though we did win the conference championship in my junior year."

That was the same 1972 season in which the Dolphins posted their perfect record. En route to the first of two consecutive Super Bowl titles, the Dolphins defeated the Steelers, 21-17, at Three Rivers Stadium in the playoffs.

Even though he was not a Dolphins' fan, he did have a great deal of respect for their top receiver, Paul Warfield. He also admired Gene

Washington, the one who played for the Minnesota Vikings and the one with the same name who played for the San Francisco 49ers. "I liked the way Warfield always carried himself, the way he made the clutch catches," said Stallworth. "He looked like a champion, and he played like a champion. But I didn't pattern myself after any of them. I just had my own style. There were some good receivers who came out of Alabama, like Ray Perkins and Dennis Homan, but I didn't try to be like them, either."

Stallworth was never a hero-worshipper, it's that simple. "I remember Speedy Duncan of the Washington Redskins came to our high school in Tuscaloosa, and was signing autographs," said Stallworth. "I didn't want one, but my instructor forced me to get one. It didn't thrill me at all."

One man who did visit the school to see Stallworth was Bear Bryant, the legendary coach of Alabama, whose campus is in the same community. "He sent for films of me, but that's all," said Stallworth.

A fourth round draft pick of the Steelers in '74, Stallworth regarded himself as an underdog when he reported to the Steelers' training camp. For one thing, the Steelers' first draft pick that year was another wide receiver, Swann. Ahead of them were two established receivers, Ron Shanklin and Frank Lewis.

"Lynn and I came in together, and we were competing against the veterans, so we became partners," said Stallworth when he was still playing for the Steelers. "I don't think a do-or-die competitive situation could ever exist between us because of that. I think other people make more of it than we do. It's no big thing at all.

"He likes himself and I like my play," he continued. "I'm not known as a glib guy, but I think I'm pretty good. Until this year, I was competing, not necessarily against Lynn, but against the system.

"The system was getting the ball to somebody else, and I wanted the ball. There were things I knew I could do, and I wasn't getting the chance."

When Stallworth was frustrated, he sulked. He was not disruptive because that simply was not his style. But he brooded.

He recalls being in a weight room after a game at Three Rivers Stadium, and having Chuck Noll stick his nose in the door. "I hadn't caught the ball at all in the game, and I was pissed," said Stallworth.

He recalls this exchange with Noll.

"How do you feel?" asked Noll.

"Physically or emotionally?" said Stallworth.

"Both," came back Noll.

"Physically, I'm OK. Emotionally, I'm pissed off."

"Why are you pissed off?"

"Because I didn't catch any passes."

"But we won the game."

"Yeah, but I'd like to think we could do both."

Stallworth said that was only one of many exchanges he remembers with Noll. He has a good feeling about Noll. "I know he cares about every guy who comes through there," said Stallworth. "He never told me, 'John, I understand,' but I knew he did.

"One game I played with a knee sprain. After I'd catch the ball, I was defenseless. I couldn't do anything except wait till I was tackled. But I made three catches for good gains that day.

"Chuck came out on the field after the game and met me at midfield. He said, 'I shouldn't have played you today. I will never do that again. I will never put you out here when you can't defend yourself.' I remember that. I know he cares."

I recalled a scene at Three Rivers Stadium in September of 1980. Stallworth was wearing dark glasses and walking with the aid of an aluminum cane when he came into the clubhouse the day after he had been a casualty in a 20-17 victory over the Colts in Baltimore.

Noll strolled by, spotted Stallworth, smiled at him and inquired, "Where's your tin cup?"

Stallworth chuckled at first, and then, as Noll walked away, called out, "Et tu, Brutus?"

Stallworth was injured a lot during his stay with the Steelers, especially early and late in his career. Once, even though he was nursing a sore foot, he caught a then career high of eight passes for 134 yards in a 38-10 victory over the New York Jets in September of 1981. He also had a 17-yard end sweep and made a big block on the first of two short touchdown runs by Frank Pollard.

Afterward, Noll told reporters, "John's value to the team is great. He really isn't a hundred percent yet; there's still some pain in his foot. He's still playing with a little bit of pain, but he's playing through it. It hasn't hurt his concentration.

"He has big play ability, and he's got the kind of attitude when he's thinking, 'You throw me the ball and I'll catch it. I'll get it.' And he does."

Noll knew how Stallworth was thinking because they had their talks.

"I'm all too aware of the criticism he's been getting from Bradshaw, and the stuff with Franco and Chuck, and Franco's final year with the team," said Stallworth when we spoke late in the 1990 campaign. "I know about the Franco Who? and the Terry Who? business. But I think I understand the man. Maybe I'm fooling myself, and I may be fooling myself all the way to the grave, but I think he's a very emotional person even if he doesn't show it.

"I think he has goals and convictions about how things should be done. He has it square in his mind as to what he wants to accomplish. Looking at his team, he felt that anything that wasn't a plus shouldn't get in his way. If a player wasn't there, or wasn't working toward a team goal, then he didn't want to acknowledge or talk about that individual. That's just the way he was.

hn Stallworth keeps eyes on the ball

Making over-the-shoulder catch for TD against LA Rams in Super Bowl XIV

"I went to Noll on another occasion. I felt Bradshaw was ignoring me. I felt he had hooked up with Swann, and that they had something going, and I wanted to break into that. I had an opportunity to talk to Chuck a few times. I wanted the ball. It was tearing me down to work so hard in practice and then get overlooked in the games. I was doing all I could and there was a game plan that I wasn't a part of. I thought Bradshaw was definitely ignoring me. Brad said he couldn't keep everybody happy, no matter how hard he tried. I thought Chuck understood me. He knew how I felt. He knew I was a hard worker. He didn't want me to lose the desire to be a part of the Steelers' offense.

"There's another story I remember about Noll. One day in practice, Bradshaw and I and some other players conspired to fool Chuck. Brad called a play in the huddle, and he said he was going to call an audible at the line of scrimmage, but that he'd also call a disregard-the-audible signal. Chuck thought he was calling an audible, and Chuck was wrong. He blew the whistle right before the ball was snapped because he thought Bradshaw made a mistake. We had set out to fool him and we did.

"I fell down on the field at Three Rivers and started rolling around screaming. Like a big kid. We had fooled Chuck. Jim Smith, one of our receivers, saw me rolling around like that and he thought I'd gone crazy. If Chuck had been the monster some people want to make him out to be he'd have come down on me pretty hard for behaving like that. But Chuck laughed it off, too. He could be like that. That's why I don't have any problems with Chuck Noll. And never did."

Stallworth said he was inspired by three people during his stay with the Steelers, mainly team owner Art Rooney, and two of his teammates, Rocky Bleier and Donnie Shell.

Stallworth, Bleier and Shell were among the Steelers' alumni who were present to see the unveiling of a memorial statue of Art Rooney on Sunday, October 7, 1990 outside Three Rivers Stadium. I spotted Stallworth and Shell together, as usual, and spoke with them that day. They had attended a dinner the night before at Art Rooney's former residence near the Stadium, where one of Dan Rooney's daughters and her husband were living at the time.

"I have many wonderful memories of Art Rooney," said Stallworth. "More so than seeing all the guys I haven't seen in a long time, my thoughts this morning are about Art Rooney, and what he meant to the organization, and what he meant to me. And how he carried himself.

"There's a lesson to be learned there, about how you deal with folks, and how you might have climbed the ladder of success, and how you still ought to treat all people like they're important. I believe they are all important.

"I remember the way he used to come into our locker room, and the way he'd inquire about each of us. I remember the way he treated the ground crew, and the locker room staff. Those personal relationships were more important than anything else to him. Those things were coming back to me. And I was glad to see that so many other folks, judging by the great turnout of teammates and fans, felt the same way I did. I didn't need any confirmation of those thoughts, really, but it still felt good to see that scene.

"I've talked to guys on other teams about their owners, and they said the owners only knew you if you were a star on the team. Otherwise, they didn't want to know you. And I remember reading about one owner, a woman out west, who said she treated her players real well, just like she treated her thoroughbred horses. How would you like to be a player on that team? And be compared to horses?"

Then Stallworth spoke about Bleier:

"As far as Rocky is concerned, to me, he was a guy who worked so hard to accomplish his goals. Rocky was a guy you could look to as an example. He was not the fastest guy in the world, and he was not the best athlete. People always questioned his ability, even at the beginning, before he went off to Vietnam. When he returned, and needed a cane to get around, and had trouble keeping up with everybody else the following year at camp, his status was questioned again. But he worked hard to come back from his injury.

"When I was little, I used to like to read books about athletes who had overcome adversity," said Stallworth, which brought to mind my own experience in reading similar books in the school library. "Those type of books shaped a lot of what I thought you had to do to become successful in sports and in life."

He and Shell have always had a special relationship.

"Donnie and I come from similar backgrounds — both ol' southern boys," said Stallworth. "We both have a lot of respect for family and a love for family. We looked around and saw what the limelight could do to you, and how it could take you away from your family, even destroy you. We talked a lot, and we talked about what we wanted to be.

"We had both come from small black colleges, and we know what it meant not to have everything handed to you. In Pittsburgh, you had clean underwear, T-shirts and jocks, and all the other equipment. Everything was not handed to you where we came from. The food and the training facilities weren't too hot in high school or college. So we appreciated what we had here, and we wanted to hold onto it."

He and Shell also influenced young players, especially someone like Dwayne Woodruff. All three of them returned to college and earned master's degrees. They wanted to be prepared when they put pro football behind them.

"We knew what we wanted and what we didn't want. We didn't want all the glitz and the glamour," said Stallworth. "We had a deep personal relationship with the Lord. Donnie helped bring me into the fold, in that respect; he put things in perspective for me."

"When I came to Pittsburgh, I wanted to be a star," said Stallworth. "The first four years I really struggled. I had a lot of injuries those first few years. I didn't complete a full season in the first three years.

"In my first year, I went to the hospital and I was told I had sickle cell anemia. They told me initially that I didn't have the trait, but that I had the disease. I knew you didn't live a full life if you had it. I remember my reaction: My gosh, I've struggled so long, and I'm not going to be able to play football. Instead of thinking that I'd never reach the age of 70, I was worried about my football career.

"It scared me, my wife and the coaches. After that, they didn't play me much for awhile. Lionel Taylor didn't know what they were going to do with me. They were afraid. Then we learned that I had the trait, but not the disease. That's a lot more common among black people, and it hasn't caused me any problems.

"So I'm at peace with my present situation. I'm happy where I am, and what's going on in my life. I'm happy with my new business. The peace comes from having a good relationship with Jesus Christ, the savior. I have my priorities in order.

"When I was growing up in Tuscaloosa, I wanted our family to express more feeling for each other. There was a lot of love in our family, but it was not stated. It was sort of a 'you understand that I love you' feeling. But it was not stated. We didn't know what was missing from that. My emotions cried out for expression, especially from my loved ones."

His dad was David Stallworth, who worked as a heavy machine operator in the construction business, and his mother was Mary, who worked, at first, as a domestic in local homes and later in a local hospital. John had three brothers and a sister. There was also an uncle just down the street, with six kids, whom John considered an extension of his own family.

"When I got married, I got more comfortable with expressing my emotions. I've drawn it out of my mom and dad. Now we know we were missing something. I've learned more about my brothers and sister. I missed the time I was away in Pittsburgh. When I got back, I wanted to know more about them, and what they were all about. Who were they?"

So he is at home in Huntsville with his wife, Flo, who assists him in his business endeavors, and their children, John Jr., who was 15, and Natasha, who was 11 when I spoke with their dad. They live in Brownsboro, a suburb just outside the city.

"One of the things I learned along the way," said Stallworth, "was that no one was going to give you anything. But if you worked real hard, you can attain something.

"One of the things I want for my children is for them to be good at something, to excel in something, to be recognized at being good at something. It's something you can carry with you for the rest of your life. The players who were on the Pittsburgh Steelers came away from that as better people, whatever they choose to get into. They have the right stuff, they know what it takes to win and be successful."

338

Donnie Shell
"You can't play all your life"

Shoes must have been important in the young life of Donnie Shell, the strong safety for the Steelers in their Super Bowl championship years, and a strong candidate for the Pro Football Hall of Fame when he becomes eligible in 1992.

When we spoke in November of 1990, he told me a story about needing the proper shoes to go to church in his youth. Then I checked my files and found a story I had written about him in December of 1980 for *The Pittsburgh Press*, when he was named the Steelers' MVP by his teammates and, ironically enough, he told me a story about a different occasion when he needed special shoes, and worried whether he would get them or not.

In the meantime, he had left big shoes for someone to fill in the Steeelers' defensive secondary. He intercepted 51 passes in his 14 seasons, ten as a starter, with the Steelers, more than any other strong safety in National Football League history at the time of his retirement.

He was a hard hitter with his head, helmet and shoulder pads all screwed on tight. His name fit him as well. He often came out of nowhere, like a nuclear submarine shell to nail an enemy ballcarrier. He once broke the ribs of Earl Campbell, the crushing running back of the Houston Oilers. Howard Cosell loved him, even when others thought Shell was slipping. "They can criticize him all they want," intoned Cosell on a Monday Night Football telecast on ABC-TV. "He hits like a linebacker!"

You have to travel back in time to appreciate Shell's success story. Shell was in the sixth or seventh grade back home in Whitmire, South Carolina, a textile community where most of the adults among the 3,000 residents helped make men's shirts. Donnie needed a pair of shoes for a school play, and he did not know how he was going to come by them.

Shirts were plentiful in Whitmire, but shoes were something else. They were as hard to come by as money in the modest Shell household, where Leon and Aurelia Shell provided for ten children. Donnie was next to the last in that lineup, and one of seven boys. By the time clothes got to him they were well worn. No one in the family had the kind of shoes he needed for the school show.

"I was all worried," recalled Shell, "but my mother calmed me down. She told me not to worry. She said, 'Don't cross the bridge before we get to it.' When the time came for our play, I had the shoes."

Asked how his mother came up with the shoes, Donnie smiled and said, "She took my shoes and dyed them. I needed blue shoes to go with my costume. And she gave me blue shoes."

Shell was 28 at the time he shared that story with us. In his seventh season with the Steelers, he had led the team with a career-high seven interceptions — three of them were game-saving steals — and was a Pro

Bowl pick for the third year in a row. He was so proud to be chosen by his teammates as the Steelers' MVP.

"This is great," he said. "It's something I always wanted; it's an especially great honor because it's from my peers. And I think we have some of the greatest players in pro ball on our team."

Ten years later, over the telephone from his home in suburban Columbia, South Carolina, he had another shoe story.

"The way we came up," said Shell, "sometimes I was afraid to go to church. I didn't have new dress clothes, and I wore mostly hand-me-downs. I had to wear sneakers, and I was concerned about my image. I thought I should be wearing dress shoes to church. My mother told me not to sweat it. She said the Lord didn't care how I looked when I went to church. Being a child, though, I know I was embarrassed. We never had new dress clothes. Everybody else seemed to be dressed up. Being a child, I felt peer pressure. I thought people were looking at me, and thinking we were really poor."

The memories of how he felt as he walked to Bruce's Methodist Church A.M.E. on Sunday stick with Shell like a lingering leg wound. But it is where he also learned what really counts.

Nowadays, Shell knows that his family was really rich, even though his dad worked as a janitor for the city, and there was not always enough money to go around. The family stayed together and prayed together, and Shell counts his blessings.

As a ballplayer, though, he was careful with his money. He wanted to make sure he held onto his money, and that he would not have to worry about his finances or his future. Like his closest buddies on the Steelers, John Stallworth and Dwayne Woodruff, he went back to school while he was playing for the Steelers, and got a graduate degree. He has a bachelor's degree in health and physical education and a master's degree in guidance and counseling.

Many pro athletes and even some former college players find it difficult to cope with life after their active playing careers. Some have fallen on hard times. Some have gotten into drugs, alcohol, marital and family problems, and other kinds of trouble. Some have even committed suicide they were so depressed. They miss the limelight, they miss the big money, they miss the discipline and structure playing big-time sports demands of them. They don't know what to do with themselves.

Like Stallworth and Woodruff, Shell was strong-willed and determined, had a good wife and family who support his efforts, and strong religious beliefs.

"You've got to have a life after football," said Shell. "You can't play all your life."

Tony Parisi was in his 26th year as the Steelers' equipment manager in 1990. I asked him what he remembered best about his dealings with Donnie Shell. "He would wear shoes till they absolutely wore out," said Parisi with a smile. "I used to go to the guys, and get after them to work at breaking in the new pairs of shoes I gave them. You wouldn't want

nnie Shell

Superstars competition lineup (from left) includes Lynn Swann, Jack Ham, Donnie Shell and John Stallworth with ABC-TV's Don Meredith.

Retirement press conference lineup (from left) includes Chuck Noll, John Stallworth, Art Rooney, Donnie Shell and Dan Rooney.

Equipment manager Tony Parisi tightens screws in a helmet.

to play a game wearing shoes for the first time. They'd be stiff and uncomfortable. I'd also ask the players to give me the shoes they'd worn a long time so we could give them to young athletes in the city who needed them and couldn't afford them. But Donnie never wanted to give me any shoes. He hoarded his shoes. I remember he toed in a lot, and he'd wear out his shoes a certain way. But no matter how worn they'd get, he wouldn't throw them out.

"He probably had the best attitude of anybody I dealt with. He was real appreciative of our efforts. He'd come to me before every ballgame and ask me to adjust his helmet and tighten it up. He was a hard hitter and stuck his helmet in there pretty good, and nicked up his helmet quite a bit, so he wanted it to fit him a certain way."

Parisi, a Canadian who played goalie for minor league ice hockey teams as a young man, appreciated Shell's concern about his equipment fitting him properly.

"He never wasted anything. He wore only two pair of shoulder-pads the whole time he was here," Parisi said. "He wore his shoulder-pads so tight. He was easy to work with. He trusted you."

Shell now lives in Columbia, located in the heart of South Carolina. His alma mater, South Carolina State, is located in nearby Orangeburg. Columbia has become the commercial and governmental center for the state, and the University of South Carolina is a source of community pride. Columbia has a tradition-rich heritage. It was one of America's first planned cities, and its historical landmarks include beautiful antebellum homes and stately public buildings. Shell's hometown of Whitmire is 55 miles west of Columbia.

Shell's father, Leon, worked as a custodian in Whitmire for many years, and later as a weaver in one of the local textile mills. So Donnie and his wife, Paulette, and, at the time of our interview, their two daughters, April Nicole, 13, and Dawn, 9, and their son, Donnie Lamont, 5, get to see their grandparents from time to time. Paulette is from Hartsville, and she, too, has family in the area. She and Donnie met in his sophomore year at South Carolina State. They like having relatives and close friends come visit. There were a dozen for Thanksgiving dinner at the Shell's suburban home.

"The family-type atmosphere is very important to me," said Donnie. "We had that with the Steelers, too. The togetherness we shared, on and off the field, was important to me. During Thanksgiving and Christmas, everybody made sure that everybody had a place to eat, and you did whatever you could to keep everyone's spirits high during the holidays, if they were away from home."

That brought to mind how Shell was feeling lonely back in September of 1980 when his family was back home in South Carolina. He was invited to dinner on consecutive nights by Mel Blount and John Stallworth and their wives.

"It was nice of them to look after me that way," said Shell at the time, "but we're all like one big family."

342

Soon after those dinners, Blount, Shell and Stallworth were all awarded game balls for their performances in the 1980 season opener, a 31-17 victory over the Houston Oilers. Blount and Shell each intercepted two passes, and Stallworth was Terry Bradshaw's biggest passing target and made a spectacular leaping catch for a 50-yard touchdown that sealed the verdict.

"The three of us are pretty close," said Stallworth back then. "Mel and Donnie and I are pretty active in the religious aspect of things on this team. It makes you think the Lord is with us. Donnie and I had injuries with our legs, so we've been getting together and praying together."

Shell feels he had a leadership role with the Steelers, especially after Blount left the ballclub and Shell became one of its elders. "I had a knack to motivate people by what I did, especially in practice," said Shell. "And religion was important to me and to other guys on the team, so we shared a lot in that respect, too.

"That all started with my family. My mom always taught me how to pray, and how to depend on the Lord. There was always a way out, and never to give up.

"You had to have good values the way I was brought up. It was a poor environment, and we all wore hand-me-downs. We usually had no breakfast or lunch because we couldn't afford it, but we had a big meal each day around 4 p.m."

Shell gained the respect he desired on the football fields of Whitmire. "I started playing in eighth grade," said Shell. "Jim Brown was my hero. I wanted to be a running back. But I ended up playing offensive guard and tight end on our team, but always wished the coach would put me at running back.

"I played high school ball and won a scholarship to South Carolina State. My self-esteem had grown by then."

Even so, when Shell showed up at the Steelers' training camp in 1974, he still felt like he was not dressed properly, or that he was wearing the wrong shoes. For starters, he had not been drafted by anybody. He signed with the Steelers as a free agent.

But there was a strike in 1974, and the veteran players missed most of the camp workouts. Nine free agents, including Shell, Randy Grossman and Marv Kellum, made the team that year. It was the year the Steelers would win their first Super Bowl.

"I'd set some goals for myself when I came in to camp," recalled Shell. "I had seen my faith in action. I was not in awe of anybody. I was wanting to make an impact."

His remark brought to mind something Keith Willis, a defensive lineman who signed with the Steelers as a free agent out of Northeastern in 1982, had said about Shell helping him out with sound advice in his rookie season. "He told me not to worry about being a free agent; that I was as good as anybody out there," said Willis. "He told me to try and make an impact at every practice, at every opportunity."

Shell was simply doing for Willis what others had done for him in his rookie season.

"I think it was L.C. Greenwood who first encouraged me," said Shell. "He used to talk to me all the time. He told me what to look out for. We had some memorable conversations on the plane. He kept pushing me. He had been a late round draft choice, and had come from a black school in the South like me.

"Sam Davis was another player who pushed me. Sam had signed with the Steelers (1967) as a free agent lineman from Allen University. Allen is also located in Columbia. He was the only guy from his school ever to make it in the NFL. He inspired me. He was a stabilizer. He let nothing affect him adversely. He was an unmovable force. He never wavered. He had an easy, soothing manner about him. You felt comfortable when you talked to Sam Davis. He was also the captain of the offensive team, so it meant a lot to me when he paid me personal attention."

In 1976, Shell was named the first and only captain of the Steelers' special team units.

When Shell retired after the 1987 season, he was third in team history in interceptions with 51, behind Mel Blount (57) and Jack Butler (52). During the 1981 season, I recall seeing Shell intercept three passes in one game against quarterback Brian Sipe of the Cleveland Browns. A check of the record book shows that occurred on November 22 at Cleveland Stadium. He was a game-saver for the Steelers.

Shell joined the Steelers the same 1974 season as Stallworth, and they became friends. "We were especially close," said Shell. "We had played against each other in college. Together, we formulated our ideas about what we wanted to be, and the things we wanted to do, and not do.

"At first, you see all the glitz and glamour in pro sports. There is peer pressure. The temptations were there. You have to keep in mind your individual goals. We kept focused. You have to take a stand for what you believe. We were not going to let others lead us in the wrong direction.

"You have to learn to say, 'Thanks, but no thanks.' The other guys may look at you a little funny, at first. In the beginning, John and I would go down the road with the guys after practice, and have a drink with them. But after that first year, we very seldom went down. By then we were comfortable to stay in the dorms at night. Or we'd go out to Wendy's and have a hamburger and a soft drink. Training camp was boring, and it was hard on your body, so going out, I guess, was kind of an outlet. The guys wondered why we didn't come down to the bars and nightclubs anymore. Personally, I had no energy after two-a-day practices.

"I succeeded on the field and I have succeeded off the field, by having the same attitude and work ethic. I have good work habits. I'm a perfectionist. I want to do it right. I try to correct my mistakes as soon as possible."

In the summer of 1990, Shell spent a month as an observer with the coaching staff of the Cleveland Browns. Bud Carson, the second-year head coach of the Browns, had been the defensive coordinator for the Steelers when Shell started his pro career. There was a lot of mutual respect. "He's a good one," Shell said of Carson.

In earlier summers, Shell had spent a week with the Steelers in a similar observer's role, back when Tony Dungy, who had been one of his best friends when they were teammates, was the defensive coordinator and defensive backfield coach of the Steelers.

Shell says he wants to be a coach someday, but not right now. He wants to spend time with his family. He knows coaches have a crazy schedule, so he is postponing his career plans. He knows it is a risky business. That was brought home when Carson, with another season still left on his contract, was fired at mid-season by Browns' owner Art Modell. Shell has done some career counseling for young athletes since he left the Steelers, but has not made the kind of career commitment that his friend John Stallworth has made. "I want to be flexible," he said. Shell says he can afford to bide his time. "Eventually, I want to pursue coaching," said Shell. "It's something in the future."

The year before, Shell had served as a defensive backfield coach at Spring Valley High School in Columbia, a team that had been ranked 25th in the nation for awhile. He also has gone out to high schools and lectured to the students about setting goals, staying drug-free, and taking control of their own destiny. Shell seemed to be sampling what might be out there for him.

"I took good care of my money, and I can choose what I want to do," said Shell. "Today, you need to be diversified. I don't want to work for some company that's going to send me to Japan or someplace like that. My priority is my family. Coaching takes a lot of time; I've seen that on every level. I want to spend time with my wife and kids and make sure they are raised properly. I'm sacrificing now for my family. I want to stay associated with sports, and in a teaching aspect. I want to be close to home. Right now, I'm working at my home."

That is in Meadow Lakes, a residential community in the suburbs six miles to the north of Columbia. The Shells have been there for 14 years. "It's nice and quiet, and we're settled in to the community," he said. "But, eventually, I'd like to live farther out. We have some property 20 miles out. We might build out there someday. I'd like to get closer to nature."

Shell does more than talk about his family. During the 1980 season, Shell received a game ball for making his second game-saving interception in a four week span in a 23-17 victory over the Minnesota Vikings in Bloomington. When he got back to the Greater Pittsburgh Airport, I remember he presented his wife, Paulette, with a single red rose. Paulette came to the airport along with their daughter, April Nicole, who was four at the time. "I wanted to show them how much I appreciated having them on my side," said Shell. The Steelers were 4-1 at the time, and Shell had three game balls to his credit. Talk about fast starts.

345

When the Steel Curtain was at its best in the '70s, Joe Greene and L.C. Greenwood were leading the charge, and when the opposing passer did complete a pass, menacing types like Mel Blount and Donnie Shell made the receivers wish they had dropped the ball. Their trademark was to leave bruises.

The Steeler defensive backs, iron-fisted folks like Glen Edwards and John Rowser, and J.T. Thomas, Mike Wagner and Ron Johnson, made people pay from the moment they left the line of scrimmage seeking a pass until it came their way. They would bump-and-run, run-and-bump opposing pass-catchers to distraction and the disabled list.

The Black and Gold turned their foes' bodies Black and Blue. After the Steelers won their third Super Bowl, however, the National Football League altered its rules.

Commissioner Pete Rozelle and the rules-makers changed that, banning the bump-and-run style which teams such as the Steelers and Raiders played to perfection, and with great relish, and turning the game into the sort one used to find only at the company picnic.

"The old way was the way I liked to play," said Shell. "I liked to bump 'em."

When Shell was starring, he was reluctant to talk about it, even after he intercepted three passes by Brian Sipe in a victory in Cleveland in 1981. "I can't let up," said Shell. "When you take time to look at what you've done, you have to look back. Somebody might beat me to the end zone for a pass."

Shell still smiles when he thinks back to his early days with the Steelers. "Right from the start, Joe Greene made you feel a part of the team," he said. "The system made a distinction about free agents in the NFL, but not with them. And I followed their lead later on when I was the veteran, and we had free agents coming in to camp with us.

"We had a lot of leaders on that team. Mel Blount really stood out. He'd take me out to dinner and talk to me. He'd see me when I was down, and get after me. I wanted to play more, and I was just seeing action on the specialty teams. He told me, 'You have a role. Do that role. Don't lose sight of your goals, but accept your role.' It was good advice, as usual.

"Chuck Noll also had a good influence on me. He was a tremendous leader. Regardless of the situation we were in, he always came up with the right words.

"Bud Carson was a great fundamentalist, and he made you a sound player when he was our defensive coordinator.

"Now Tony Dungy is the defensive coordinator for the Kansas City Chiefs, and he had the same responsibility with the Steelers for several seasons. I never knew he wanted to be a coach. We were roommates for two years, and I learned a lot from him.

"When he got traded to San Francisco, it was very difficult for me. It was hard for me to swallow. That's when I woke up and saw the business side of football. I guess they had reasons for doing it, but I couldn't see them back then. It was tough. We thought a lot alike. He didn't hang out, and he went to church and he had the same values. It ended up working out well for both of us.

"Playing in the Super Bowl makes you spoiled. I thought we should do it every year. I'd get perplexed when we didn't. If you came in and made the sacrifices and dedicated yourself to the right goals, I thought we could do it every year. But it's difficult. Everybody has to be on the same page, as Chuck Noll always liked to say, going for a common goal.

"I did pretty much everything I wanted to do in football. I think it was awesome. I was blessed and fortunate to be around a Mr. Rooney. I don't think a lot of organizations had that, the kind of relationship we had with him. To be around people like Joe Greene, L.C. Greenwood, Jack Lambert, Tony Dungy, Mel Blount, Franco Harris and John Stallworth and so many others. I'm a fortunate person. It helped shape me.

"I wish every person could experience that. The people I was surrounded with — like Chuck Noll and Dan Rooney — it was just great. It was a great opportunity for me and my family. Football was a big part of my life, and it always will be."

Donnie Shell, Mike Webster and John Stallworth

Gary Dunn
"Always Eddie Dunn's boy"

Tavernier is a little town in a place called Plantation Key in the upper portion of the Florida Keys. It is about four or five miles north of Key Largo, a town made famous by Bogie and Bacall and a popular song of the '80s. It is where you can find Gary Dunn these days.

Dunn was a defensive lineman for the Steelers for 11 seasons, and he is back where he feels he belongs, "in a little house by the bay."

He was born in Coral Gables, just outside Miami. Dunn drives to Homestead, which is south of Miami, where he began working in early 1991 as a national account sales manager for Budweiser. Before that, he had been selling commercial real estate, sometimes residential, for Mike O'Connell Realty in Miami. It had been two years since he had been released by the Steelers. "I'm getting my feet wet," said Dunn.

When Dunn was playing for the Steelers, the Florida Keys were his off-season retreat, a place to go fishing and to relax in the sun. He bought a piece of property on Plantation Key during his last season with the Steelers. "It's an old house in a nice neighborhood on the water," he said. "I'm going to hold onto it for awhile, let it appreciate in value."

Dunn has always been happy in South Florida. "I always went back there in the off-season," he said. "I stayed the whole year just once in Pittsburgh, and that was a long year. The winter's just too long. I kept looking up and wondering when the sun was going to come up again."

In Florida, there is family. His mother is there four months a year, and there are plenty of relatives and friends from his college days at the University of Miami. He goes to the football games when Miami is at the Orange Bowl, but he does not take in the Dolphins games farther north at Joe Robbie Stadium.

At age 37, he admitted he missed playing pro football. "I get a little frustrated at times, if I'm having problems or difficulties." He has filed for workmen's compensation over injuries suffered as a member of the Steelers. This annoys some front-office people with the Steelers. They feel he is suing the Steelers. Dunn does not see it that way.

"My knee, shoulder and back all give me trouble," he said. "I feel like a former football player, that's for sure. But I have no problem with the Steelers. I've been up to see Dan Rooney and Joe Gordon and they were fine with me.

"I watch all the games that are on television, and I also talk to Tom O'Malley, who ran the Steelers basketball team and roomed with me for ten years. He keeps me up to date on what's going on."

In Pittsburgh, he was just Gary Dunn, a valued defensive lineman for the Steelers. He started 15 of 16 games in the 1979 season, his fourth of 11 seasons (1977-87) with the Steelers, including Super Bowl XIV at the Rose Bowl in Pasadena. He was a dedicated, versatile performer who eventually succeeded Joe Greene in the middle of the line.

His advice to young players: "Work hard and never think you have made it. And don't let (trainer) Ralph Berlin tape your ankles."

In Miami, he was always known as Eddie Dunn's boy, and it was a big thrill for him when he went back home during the 1980 season and had his only start of that season against the Miami Dolphins at the Orange Bowl.

His grandfather had served as the president of the University of Miami from 1926 until 1952. Gary's father and brother both played football for the Hurricanes. Eddie Dunn, his dad, was one of the school's finest running backs.

"Probably one of the best things I ever did," declared Gary Dunn, "was bringing my whole family to Pittsburgh back in 1978 when we were playing the Houston Oilers in the AFC championship.

"It cost a little money, but it was worth it. I brought my mom and dad, my brother and his wife, and my sister up there. It was the only way my whole family could come together.

"We won and, well, you should have seen my dad after the game. He was never a pro football fan, mind you. He coached at the University of Miami for 15 years, two as a head coach, and he was still a college football man. He didn't like some of the things we did in pro football.

"My dad came in the locker room, and he was lit up like a Christmas tree. He was grinning from ear to ear. He was crying. He hugged me. And it felt so good.

"That was the year we went on to play Dallas in the Super Bowl in Miami. So we went down there, and that really made the year for my family."

That was Super Bowl XIII. The Steelers defeated the Cowboys, 35-31, to win their third National Football League title in five years. A year later, they beat the Los Angeles Rams, 31-19, to win an unprecedented fourth Super Bowl title.

That, says Dunn, was the biggest game of his life.

"I started that game," he recalled, "and it was an unbelievable feeling. To go out and be introduced to that large crowd. To know it was on television around the world. Starting in the Super Bowl . . . that was something in dreamland. Something you always wanted to do. Something you were pointing to . . . for so long.

"It doesn't hit you until the dang game is over. Then it comes home. It's a real emotional experience. Knowing people were watching. How big the game was."

No one in Dunn's family was there for that game. They were all in a hospital room back home in Coral Gables, at Eddie Dunn's bedside. He had cancer real bad. He had been battling it pretty good, but he was getting weak now, and it was only a matter of time.

"They had a Super Bowl party in the hospital," said Dunn. "They were waking up the whole wing, I hear, screaming and yelling. I called my mom after the game. She said my dad was up, getting out of his bed, and having a good time.

"She said the doctors couldn't believe it. But he'd had a couple of operations, and they were saying he was going to die. He was 64 when he died; it happened in March, soon after the Super Bowl.

"He was an All-American at Miami. He still holds records there. I just received the new Miami football brochure, and he has some records that even Earl Foreman and Ottis Anderson couldn't break."

While Gary was born and grew up in Coral Gables, near the University of Miami campus, both of his parents were originally from Pittsburgh. That is also true of several of the early leaders in the Miami athletic department, men like Jack Harding and Andy Gustafson. For many years, Miami's football program recruited heavily in Western Pennsylvania. So it pleased his parents to see Gary playing for the Steelers.

His mother grew up on the North Side of Pittsburgh, on California Avenue, not far from Three Rivers Stadium. Gary remembers taking a drive one day through the Liberty Tunnels and going up to Brookline. His dad pointed out places where he and his buddies had pulled off some shenanigans as kids. "He showed me his old house; it wasn't too big, in a long row hanging off the side of a hill," said Gary. "He liked doing that."

Gary remembers something else about his dad, something Eddie Dunn told him once, when Gary was frustrated with football, and all the hard work. It is something that helped him through the two-a-day practice sessions at St. Vincent College in the latter summers of his pro career. "No matter what you think," he said his dad told him, "it's all worth it."

It is not easy being a defensive lineman in the NFL. More often than not, you get lost in a wall of bodies, or beneath the bodies. It is not a glamour position. It was important for Gary to keep his dad's message in mind. "If you have a bad day, it's frustrating, yes," said Gary. "If I didn't make the proper play. But if I stuffed my blocker and got down the line and did what I was supposed to do, well, then I felt good. I didn't feel as good as I did when I made the tackle, but I felt good." When you're an inside lineman, you don't make ten to 15 tackles a game. You've got to get your satisfaction other ways.

Dunn once split the position of tackle with Steve Furness, but Furness was traded to the Tampa Bay Buccaneers before the 1981 season, and Dunn had an opportunity to start.

To him, lining up next to Joe Greene meant that he had arrived. "Joe's a leader," Dunn said back then. "I know since I've been here, every year he's been helping everyone. He sort of runs things. He's got a big name, but he's a team player all the way. He's not out for Joe Greene. That rubs off on the rest of us.

"I always heard of Joe Greene. When I first got here, I couldn't believe how he was working with everybody. He wasn't stuck on himself. He was always only for the team.

"That's the way my dad thought it ought to be. So I felt pretty good playing next to a great player like Joe Greene. When we lived in Miami, my dad was a sports celebrity wherever we went in the city. Every time we went out, everyone knew him. I always thought that was nice. Maybe now they'll know his boy did all right, too."

Gary Dunn

Eddie Dunn of U. of Miami

Tunch Ilkin (62) and Craig Wolfley (73) are close friends.

Tunch Ilkin
The Turk who became a Christian

The sun was orange hot, and it was not even noon yet. The humidity was high. It was a killer day. The Steelers were going through their morning walk-through workout, players moving around in shorts, most of them bare-chested, in a robot-like manner, going through their maneuvers. Some of them seemed to be sleep-walking. Tunch Ilkin was off by himself, unable to practice with the others because both of his shoulders were still sore from off-season arthroscopic surgery.

Players who are injured are often treated like lepers at pro football training camps, isolated until they are healthy again and useful. Coach Chuck Noll does not even discuss injured players, like they do not exist. He does not pay bedside visits.

Like most of the Steelers coaches and players, Noll was never quite sure how to say his name, anyhow. For the record, it is pronounced TOONCH ILL-kin. Not Tunch, as in Punch. It is a Turkish name. Tunch was born in Istanbul, and moved to Chicago with his family when he was two years old.

Now Tunch was nearing his 33rd birthday, and his 11th season in the National Football League, and he was eager to get back into the thick of things. He had been to the Pro Bowl the previous two years, but he knew he could not afford to rest on his laurels. Not with Noll.

Trying his best to function productively in that twilight zone, trying to keep busy, trying to stay in some semblance of shape, Ilkin was running up a steep hill that ran alongside Bonaventure Hall, where the Steelers stay at St. Vincent College, and just above the field where Noll was conducting the workout.

Up and down, up and down, Ilkin kept his head down and dug in to go up the hill, again and again. He would stop just short of the cornfield that rimmed the top of the hill, a cornfield that bordered all the ballfields on the western side of the campus. He would ease himself down the hill, as if it were an icy surface, and then he would turn and head back up the hill.

Ilkin often has a pained expression on his face, like a man whose shoes fit too tightly. So he did not look out of character. Up and down he went. The Greek myth about Sisyphus came to mind. Sisyphus was a legendary king of Corinth who was condemned to roll a heavy stone up a steep hill in Hades, only to have it roll down again as he neared the top. Ilkin, the only Steeler to play in the two previous Pro Bowls, had become a sympathetic figure in the Steelers' training camp picture. There was concern about his career.

"I'm not thinking when I'm running up and down that hill," said Ilkin with a chuckle. "My mind just blanks out."

The field where the Steelers were working out is used for both baseball and soccer by the teams of St. Vincent College. There is a batting cage, and benches and, at the base of that hill where Ilkin was running, there is a baseball scoreboard.

Seeing that baseball setting and seeing the cornfield nearby brought the movie "Field of Dreams" back to mind, as it often did when I was watching the Steelers practice. I had read the book, "Shoeless Joe," by W. P. Kinsella several years before the movie was made, and I loved the story from the start. Ilkin had also seen the movie.

Most men who have seen that movie end up crying at the finish, when the deceased father of the main figure in the movie, comes back to play catch with his son — as played by actor Kevin Costner — on a baseball field the son had built in the middle of a cornfield in Iowa. The son had been urged by voices to do it. "Build it and he will come," the voice said. At first, some of the great baseball players of the past, including "Shoeless Joe" Jackson, his image ruined by a gambling scandal involving him and his teammates on the ill-famed Chicago Black Sox, emerge from the cornfields and play ball. It is not till the end, however, that we realize the one who will come is the father, not the famous ballplayers. It took a long time for Ilkin to realize that his father, who had always been a strong, formidable figure in his life, was willing to let him be his own man.

There have also been times in recent years when Ilkin saw images on the Steelers' practice fields that brought back to mind some of his former teammates, the players who had been on the team when he first reported to camp in 1980, right after the Steelers had won their fourth Super Bowl. Just like in "Field of Dreams."

That rookie class of 1980 included No. 1 pick Mark Malone, Bob Kohrs, John Goodman, Bill Hurley, Craig Wolfley, Frank Pollard and Tyrone McGriff. Ilkin was the No. 6 choice. Ilkin continues to have close relationships with several of them, as well as some of the Steelers who had already been on the squad for several years.

Malone and Ilkin used to call each other from rival camps, and during the 1990 season Ilkin and Wolfley were on the phone a lot, encouraging each other. They have all suffered setbacks and they look out for each other. When he was unable to perform in a pre-season scrimmage with the Washington Redskins in the summer of 1990, Ilkin found his mind playing tricks on him as he witnessed the action at nearby Latrobe High Stadium.

"We were all running around, and I saw a No. 73. And I thought of Craig Wolfley. The guy had big biceps and wide shoulders, but he was taller than Craig. I saw Jon Kolb and Larry Brown. That happens now more than ever before. I think this year I'm feeling more lonely than ever before. Most of my friends are gone."

Later in that same day that Ilkin made these comments, he was seated at a special outdoor barbecue that has become an annual event at the team's training camp. He was seated near Joe Greene, one of the assistant coaches, on a grassy knoll just below Bonaventure Hall.

Tunch Ilkin

"I miss my buddies," Ilkin continued, picking up on his earlier conversation. "I miss Ted Petersen and Tom Beasley. I keep seeing those guys. Then I realized they weren't there. I was daydreaming. At Latrobe, because I wasn't playing, I was daydreaming. From across the field, I was imagining that all my old buddies were there. I was like playing a game with them."

When Greene got wind of what Ilkin was saying, he later related privately, "I can see what Tunch is going through now. Last year, he missed Mike Webster and this year it's Wolfley. He loved Webby and Wolf. That's what makes guys retire. When you look around and you don't know anyone. So you feel out of it and you retire."

Greene's words came to mind following the fifth game of the 1990 season, when I came upon Ilkin the morning after a satisfying victory over the San Diego Chargers. Ilkin was relaxing in the lobby of the Steelers' offices at Three Rivers Stadium. Ilkin was playing again, was coming off a personally upbeat performance, was doing a local radio show of his own on WTAE, and seemed to have the world at his heels, rather than on his shoulders, as he looked that day when he was running up and down the hill at St. Vincent's.

He was doing lots of good things in his community. I had appeared during the off-season with him and former Pirates' relief pitcher Kent Tekulve to read to children at the Upper St. Clair Library during a special program aimed at encouraging youngsters to read. Ilkin's five-year-old son, Tanner, stood next to him as he read to other children.

Ilkin was wearing a T-shirt that had Arizona State Fellowship of Christian Athletes across the chest. That, too, points up an interesting insight into Ilkin as an individual.

Ilkin was also speaking frequently at local churches, relating how he had become a convert to Christianity from being a Muslim, offering "witness," so to speak. He was willing to share, to speak up about his newfound outlook on life and The Lord.

Again he grew reflective. He talked about driving his auto past the playing fields of Upper St. Clair, where he and Wolfley and Noll all live, even though Wolfley was now winding up his career with the Minnesota Vikings. "I saw all these kids playing soccer," he said, "and I thought about how neat it will be when I'm able to watch Tanner doing his athletic things. I'm looking forward to that." He also has a daughter, named Natalie, who had just turned 2.

"But don't get me wrong," Ilkin added. "I love what I'm doing now. I'm in no hurry to quit playing pro football."

It took a long time for Ilkin to gain respect with the Steelers, and with the National Football League. He wanted to hold on to that. "In my rookie year, I had survived training camp and now we were back in Pittsburgh getting ready for the next pre-season game," Ilkin recalled. "We had so many good offensive linemen, and I was kinda hoping they'd put me on the injured reserve list. I was definitely the odd man out.

"Chuck called me in. My buddy Bill Hurley had just been put on I.R. (injured reserve list) and I figured I was going the same route. Chuck said he had to ask for waivers on me. I still didn't realize that I had been cut from the squad. I had played in three exhibition games, and now I was done. It was a shocker.

"I went back home to Chicago, and was recommended for a job with a marketing firm. I had my degree. And I was offered a job as a sales rep for a furniture company. A friend of mine thought I'd do a good job. When I found out people wanted to hire me, I got nervous.

"I didn't take that job. I still wanted to play pro football. So I took a job at $3.50 an hour to work in a health club. I cleaned windows and bathrooms, and you know what, from 10 to 10 every day, six days a week. I was living on my buddy's porch in Chicago. It was an enclosed porch and we put a cot in there. He said I could stay with him. I'd work out whenever I got a chance, and took advantage of all the facilities of the health club.

"The Steelers got hit with a rash of injuries in the offensive line, and I was re-signed in mid-October and came back to the team. I played in ten games that year."

It was a long way from that near-miss to representing the Steelers in the Pro Bowl in Hawaii in 1989 and 1990.

"It was really a thrill for me," said Ilkin. "I saw Mel Blount and Terry Bradshaw on the sideline in 1989. I'm the only one there from the Steelers, and it was my first Pro Bowl. I didn't even know they would be introducing the new class for the next Hall of Fame induction.

"Now I thought the world of both of those guys. I played with Mel and Brad for four years. My heart started thumping. I couldn't believe I was actually going to play in the Pro Bowl. I felt just like I did when I first came to the Steelers' training camp. I'm saying, 'What am I doing here?'

"We were standing in two lines, each conference all-star team facing the other, and the newest Hall of Fame guys were walking between us in pre-game ceremonies. I stepped out of line, and shook hands with Mel and Brad to congratulate them. I felt so great to be able to do that. I'm thinking as they walked around, 'Hey, those are my buddies.' They were guys I had good times with.

"I did the same thing this last time with Lammie and Franco. I played with them both for five years. Franco is just such a special guy. Franco was one of the nicest guys I ever met. I was really excited for Franco, especially because of the things that transpired at the end of his career with the Steelers. Lambert was special, too.

"I was thanking God. Geez, it was great to be there. I wish I could have been at the Hall of Fame when they all went in."

Now that he has twice played in the Pro Bowl, Ilkin's dream is still alive to someday play in a Super Bowl, to bring home a Super Bowl championship ring like the rest of those guys he admired.

"Sure, I'd love to have one of those rings in the worst way," he said. "But I don't feel cheated. I'm just so thankful I got to play for the Steelers. It's such a great organization. I learned from these people. They were great role models. I thank God I was here. I was part of the Super Bowl football teams, in a way, because I was a teammate of those guys with the Pittsburgh Steelers."

Ilkin has been playing football since he was in seventh grade. He played his college ball at Indiana State University. His wife, Sharon, was a cheerleader at Indiana State. In fact, Sharon once appeared on the cover of *Sports Illustrated,* standing next to Indiana State's most famous athlete, Larry Bird, now of the NBA's Boston Celtics.

"Some of our relatives want to know how come I've never been on the cover of *Sports Illustrated,*" Tunch likes to tell people, "since my wife was."

The women in the Ilkin family have always enjoyed a higher public profile than the men. Tunch's mother was Miss Turkey in 1950. He says she is still a beautiful woman.

I read in a book about the Middle East called "Tribes With Flags" that few Muslims in Turkey ever become Christians. Tunch has had a storybook career in the National Football League. His success story is a riveting one, as is his tale of conversion to Christianity from being a Muslim.

He shared these stories with members of Westminster Presbyterian Church at a Saturday breakfast meeting in the spring of 1990. "He was tremendous," said Walter Stockdale, among those who attended the session. "I'm glad there were young people present to hear about his life. It was inspirational stuff."

It is some story. Ilkin's father managed a textile factory and their family lived well when they were in Turkey. Tunch was an only child and the Ilkins had a beautiful home with servants. Yet his father wanted the family to move to America, and did so in 1960, coming to Chicago.

"My parents had it pretty good in Turkey," he said. "But my dad thought we should come to America. We had a one bedroom apartment. My parents' bed came out of the wall. I slept on a cot in the kitchen. I remember my mom saying, 'So this is America!' It was an ethnic neighborhood, lots of Italians, Cubans, Polish, on the near North Side, right off Lawrence on Beacon. I've only been back to Turkey once. When I was seven, I spent the summer of 1964 there. I have foggy memories of Turkey."

When he was at Indiana State, Ilkin said other students tried to interest him in Christianity, but he constantly ignored their efforts. "I thought Christians were wimpy guys," he said, "and I was into sports and being strong then. I also had led a sheltered life.

"When I joined the Steelers, they had 19 players on the roster who had been in the Pro Bowl," recalled Ilkin. "But they had even more than that who actively participated in a prayer group and a Bible study group.

"The Steelers had a special spirit for community involvement and social service activity because of the team's owner, Art Rooney. Certain players on the team, like Jon Kolb and Donnie Shell and Craig Wolfley, had a special impact on me. Here were all these really tough, macho guys who were great football players, yet they walked with The Lord.

"They turned over their problems and, indeed, their lives to The Lord. Little by little, I wanted to be with them. When I converted, I was afraid to tell my parents. My mother was a religious woman and she really flipped out when I told her. It took me three years to tell my dad.

"Actually, he finally asked me about it. 'Son, how come you didn't tell me you converted to Christianity?' he asked me one day during a football game. I told him I had been afraid to tell him. He said, 'Hey, you know I'm a free-thinking open guy.' I couldn't believe it.

"So the Steelers have not only had great football players all these years, but they've had terrific people, too. I was so lucky to come to a team like that."

Ilkin can remember those first days at St. Vincent College, especially Photo Day when the veterans reported and everybody assembled in game uniforms to have their pictures taken. He talked about it following football practice one day at St. Vincent in the summer of 1990, holding an icepack to one of his shoulders as he sat in the hallway outside the Steelers' locker room, still sweating from an afternoon workout.

"I was totally awestruck," Ilkin recalled, "after I first saw the lineup coming out of the locker room. Five thousand people were here on Photo Day when the vets came in. We were lucky to draw that many at Indiana State for our home games.

"I saw this big sign on the front of Bonaventure Hall that said 'Welcome Back Four-Time Super Bowl Champion Steelers.' That was an eye-opener, and it made you feel like you were, suddenly, in a different land. This was not Indiana.

'How am I going to compete with these guys?' I thought more than once. What am I doing here? Just seeing those guys was something. How many Hall of Famers were in that group? If I was not here to try out for the team, I'd have been going around asking for autographs.

"I was one of the first in line at the lunchroom that day. I was starting to eat my food when I saw Steve Courson. Look at that guy! Look at that build! I felt puny next to him and his muscular physique. Then I was seeing L.C. Greenwood, and Mike Webster, and Jack Lambert and Franco Harris.

"Then Terry Bradshaw made his appearance. Brad was talking to everybody. He was talking about his latest movies and TV shows and about being on a show with Barbara Mandrell. These guys are scary, I thought."

He found a friend who was just as nervous in Wolfley. During their second or third year, Ilkin is not sure which, Wolfley's dad was dying from leukemia. "I was still on the bubble, as far as making the team, and he was my biggest booster," Ilkin recalled. "We had started to room together. We did a lot of things together."

I recalled a day I was at the wave pool at South Park with my family and spotted Ilkin and Wolfley and their wives there together, really relaxed in each other's company. It looked like one big family. Ilkin nodded at the memory, and resumed his story.

"Wolf was a starter. Then his father took a turn for the worse. He was expecting him to pass. It was remarkable how calm he was about it. Boy, I was not a Christian at the time, and I thought he must have some tremendous inner strength, that this Christianity must be something. I was almost flipping out, and he was calm as can be. His father died right after we both got married. We both cried about that.

"It's really tough going through training camp without him. We used to be so close. It's not the same without Wolf. Outside of my wife, I was closest to him."

Ilkin said Wolfley tells a great story about rooming with him at St. Vincent College.

"One of the first nights we were rooming together, one eerie night, the moon was full and the light from it was streaming into our room. In the middle of the night, I bolted up in the bed. I started talking, and I was talking in Turkish. I sat up and started yelling something in Turkish. I scared the hell out of him. He thought I was freaking out."

Myron Cope cannot hear that well anymore — he has a bum ear — but he was particularly puzzled and perplexed when he could not make out what Tunch Ilkin was saying at a Steelers' press conference at Three Rivers Stadium late in the 1990 season.

Cope was sitting right next to Ilkin at Cope's reserved seat, usually at Chuck Noll's right elbow, and Ilkin was just following instructions to say something to test the microphone before the interview was to start.

Ilkin started speaking in Turkish, to the delight of everyone but Cope. "What's that you're sayin'?" Cope cried.

"That's Turkish, Myron," Ilkin came back, "and you don't want to know what I was saying. It had something to do with a donkey."

"Oh, yeah," said Cope, as if he comprehended. "What's that old saying about talking Turkish?"

"It's about talking turkey, Myron," someone interjected.

"Oh, yeah, that's right, let's talk turkey," Cope came back, giggling at his own gaffe.

It had been that sort of weekend with the Steelers. They had played in San Francisco the day before and blundered their way to a 27-7 defeat, helping the 49ers considerably to retain their perfect start in the NFL campaign.

The season was seven games old, and the Steelers were struggling to find their true identity. The defeat had been a difficult one because there were times the players and coaches seemed to be communicating in Turkish.

Ilkin was introduced about 15 minutes before Chuck Noll's usual weekly press conference. Steelers' public relations director Dan Edwards had hustled the media away from their luncheon tables early because the Steelers had an annoucement to make.

The team had nominated Ilkin for The Travelers NFL Man of the Year Award, acknowledging his off-the-field contributions to the Pittsburgh community. The favorite charity of each team's nominee receives a $1,000 donation from The Travelers Companies Foundation, and Ilkin chose the Light of Life Rescue Mission on Pittsburgh's North Side as his beneficiary. It is a retreat for the homeless.

The idea behind the award is to boost volunteerism across the country. Deeply concerned with the needs of the less fortunate, Ilkin has channeled much energy to help the homeless. He and former Steelers' teammate Weegie Thompson organized the "Steelers Shootout," a celebrity-amateur trap-shooting contest at the Millvale Sportsmen's Club to benefit three Pittsburgh homeless shelters, including the Light of Life Rescue Mission. The event raised $16,000 in 1989 and $20,000 in 1990. "There are so many golf tournaments, but this was something different," he said. "And about 20 Steelers or so participate." Ilkin also organized a draft-day event which netted another $5,000 for the shelters.

"The homeless situation is something I've had a heart for through the years," said Ilkin. "It's something I've tried to be involved in."

Ilkin frequently visits area schools and churches, addressing youngsters on drug and alcohol awareness, the value of education and religious values, and the need for self-esteem. He actively supports the March of Dimes, Allegheny General Hospital's "Drinking, Drugs and Driving" assemblies, Big Brothers/Big Sisters and the Athletes in Action football camp. Ilkin also joins other Steelers to conduct Christmas food drives for the needy.

Ilkin was among the Steelers who had sub-par performances in San Francisco, but he had not left his heart out there. He was coming off successive seasons in which he had been named to the NFL's Pro Bowl and this award was meaningful to him.

"When there's somebody in need you'll see a Steeler there," he said. "Community involvement has always been a priority with the organization. This is a real reflection of The Chief's life," he said in reference to Art Rooney, the late owner of the Steelers. "It's been handed down.

"I've been blessed to join the Steelers' organization. I could see it from the beginning. Guys like Franco and Mel Blount and Mike Webster and Jon Kolb. These guys were always recruiting the rookies to go to charity-related functions. Craig Wolfley went to so many places. Robin Cole . . . I remember seeing Robin at functions nobody had even asked him to attend. He was just always there, where he could help.

"It's a credit to the organization. Sure, there were times when you said, 'Wow, I've got to go here and there tonight, and I'm short on time.' But when you go you drew a lot more than you gave. You feel good when you're able to do something positive for other people."

Asked if he felt athletes had an obligation to give of themselves to such community activity, Ilkin replied:

"If you're in a position that athletics gives you, you feel like you've accomplished something. It's a privilege instead of an obligation."

During the 1990 season, Ilkin was injured again. This time he suffered a separated elbow. It happened on November 2, as the Steelers were preparing for a home game against the Atlanta Falcons. When he was wheeled on a stretcher out of Three Rivers Stadium during a practice session, he looked like he was in sheer agony.

"Nothing ever hurt as much," said Ilkin after he had been on the injured reserve list for four weeks, and was ready to return to action. "My elbow was just dangling. It really killed. That was about as intense a pain as I've ever had."

Ilkin knew it was serious when, as he fell, he glanced at his left forearm and saw it dangling at an odd angle.

"I was laying on the ground and heard everybody going 'Ahhhhhhh!' and then I knew I shouldn't look.

George Stewart, the special teams' coach, was so sickened he walked away. Running back Warren Williams had a worse reaction. He fainted.

Ilkin had to wonder whether it was all worth it, anymore. He had considered retirement, he now admitted, during training camp. But he felt the Steelers could possibly go all the way, and he still wanted to play in a Super Bowl before calling it quits.

Ilkin recovered, with a lot of hard rehabilitation work, and was eager to resume playing, especially with a big game at home with the Cincinnati Bengals, and first place in the AFC Central on the line.

I mentioned to Ilkin that someone in the media ranks had asked a question about him at that Monday afternoon's press conference with Chuck Noll at Three Rivers Stadium. They had asked if Tunch Ilkin would be activated for the big game at home with the Cincinnati Bengals that coming Sunday.

"What'd he say?" asked Ilkin. "Did he say 'Tunch who?'?"

As it turned out, the Steelers had their chances at beating the Bengals, but came up short. Ilkin came out of the game with a strained back, and gave way to second-year pro Tom Ricketts. The loss hurt, his back hurt, and the Steelers appeared to blow a chance to determine their own destiny and improve their playoff bid.

Ilkin seemed to be running out of time in his bid to grab the ring.

Mike Webster
"Last of the Mohicans"

Mike Webster was one of the bigger boys at Bearskin Lake, whose ice-covered surface each winter was a place where Webster and his friends could play football. Webster was always pretending he was Jim Taylor, the fearsome hard-nosed fullback of the Green Bay Packers. This was back home in Wisconsin in the mid-60s when the Packers were the greatest thing since popcorn, dominating the National Football League, and setting standards for teams such as the Steelers to chase after in later years.

Webster went to see the Packers play in Green Bay only once, and that was an exhibition game. "We lived on a farm 120 miles from there," Webster said in an interview with me for *The Pittsburgh Press* when he was playing for the Steelers. "You couldn't get tickets to Green Bay games; you still can't. But my dad was a big fan and we never missed a game on TV or on the radio."

That is why games with the Green Bay Packers were always special for Webster, whose hometown was Tomahawk, as well as teammate Rocky Bleier, who hailed from the Wisconsin community of Appleton. The Steelers won all four of those encounters with the Packers while Webster was playing for them.

"I can still see the green and gold," Webster said, "the way kids around Pittsburgh talk about the black and the gold. We played football in our farm field with some of our neighbors, and we'd go off in the winter to a place on an island that was owned by some friends of our family. There was a big muskie lake — Bearskin Lake — that would have ice four feet thick in the winter. We'd tackle each other in the snowbanks. It was all in good fun."

Vince Lombardi's team was Webster's team back then. He knew all their names, with Jim Taylor as his favorite. "They were always present in my thoughts," Webster said. I met Mike Webster's father, Bill, at a Steelers' practice session at Three Rivers Stadium. Webster's dad had the same wrinkled face, with furrows in his forehead as if they had been plowed there by farm machinery. He had rugged good looks. His face had felt the sting of many Wisconsin winters.

"If he had to do it all over again," said Mike, "my dad would have been a football coach. When I was growing up, he was the kind of guy who was like Vince Lombardi, a real butt-kicker. He was a tough disciplinarian and he taught me good values, and how to be mentally tough. He was affectionate, but strong and tough, too."

Home for the Websters then was a 640-acre potato farm. "It was the biggest waste of my life," Bill Webster said with a shrug, but Mike said he didn't really mean it. "When we'd have a good crop, so did everyone else and the price would be down. But we never had a crop failure."

Mike Webster remembered those days well. "It was always a struggle," he said. "There were five of us kids, and my dad sometimes worked two jobs. He'd have a night job to make some extra money. But he never complained. We always had something to eat and clothes on our backs.

"I remember during the summer we'd get up at 7 in the morning and, when I was 7 years old, I got to drive the tractor. Plowing the field was a real thrill to us. I think a farm is the only place to raise kids. It was a hardy upbringing and I benefitted from it."

So did the Steelers. The team got real lucky when it drafted Webster, an under-sized center out of the University of Wisconsin, on the fifth round in 1974. They got themselves a special person. It was a draft to beat all drafts as the Steelers also selected Lynn Swann, Jack Lambert, and John Stallworth in the first four rounds (they had no third pick). Lambert is already in the Pro Football Hall of Fame, and Webster, Swann and Stallworth are good bets to join Jack there. The Steelers also picked up free agents Donnie Shell and Randy Grossman that summer and ended up winning the first of their four Super Bowls at the end of that memorable season.

Webster stayed for a club record 15 seasons with the Steelers, from 1974 until 1988, and played in 220 games for them, another club record. He played in 177 consecutive games, and gained a reputation as an "iron man," but came up short of the Steelers' record of 182 straight games set by Ray Mansfield, whom he succeeded as the team's starting center. Webster missed only four games in those 15 seasons, and became known as "Iron Mike." Webster played in nine Pro Bowls. "Mike Webster played the best center that's ever been played," said his coach, Chuck Noll, which was high praise, indeed.

Webster was 6-1½, 225 pounds when he reported to the Steelers' training camp in the summer of 1974. He quickly built himself up to 260 pounds, and became one of the team's strongest players. Soon after Webster showed up, Mansfield felt his starting job was in jeopardy. "You knew he was special," said Mansfield.

"He has the toughness I like. Not a macho toughness, where you've got to strut it around, but an inner toughness, the John Wayne type who doesn't complain."

No one worked any harder in the weightroom than Webster, or ran up as many steps at Three Rivers Stadium as Webster, though his buddy Jon Kolb came close. The two of them dominated several NFL weight-lifting competitions.

"The main function of strength for a lineman is usually to move somebody," Webster said. "In football, strength can only succeed when mixed with agility, balance, speed and intelligence about what's going on around you. But, without strength, I wouldn't be here.

"Patience is also a big part of me. I was fortunate because I didn't have to wait too long. I had a full-time spot in 1976. Now, the older I get, the more patient I become. Playing every day is now your business and there are others very anxious to compete for what you enjoy doing.

"In college, the coach's job is on the line. When you are a pro, I think you feel the same kind of pressure."

Webster became identified for wearing short sleeves, baring biceps that made grown men gulp. A fund-raising dinner held to honor him and Steve Courson in 1989 was billed as "A Farewell to Arms." Those lead pipe arms of Webster were intimidating, for sure. Webster swears it was not an ego trip.

"It's purely a technical thing," Webster insisted. "It's tough enough blocking big opposing linemen, so I don't want to give them anything extra to grab. The more a lineman can grab, the better his chances of manhandling you."

Wisconsin was not a winning situation, so Webster was apprecia- tive of the opportunity provided him in Pittsburgh. "The Steelers are the first winning team I've played for and there's a big difference," he said. "Good teams hang together. You learn to deal with pressure and turn it to your advantage. It becomes a motivational thing rather than fear. You can't play scared. You have to play with confidence.

"Personally, I don't want to lose sight of the fact that I've been incredibly lucky to be with this team and have so many great athletes around me. I have to admit that a lot of it has to do with being in the right place at the right time."

To the end with the Steelers, Webster still had his sights on win- ning another championship. "You always think you have a chance to go to the Super Bowl," he said. "And to be a part of those great teams of the '70s has built, I guess, a foundation for this franchise that makes getting to the Super Bowl a goal. Anything short of that has never been the goal for Chuck and his way of thinking."

All good things must come to an end, however, and that happened when Webster was left unprotected and became a Class B free agent follow- ing that 1988 season. Most thought that he would retire as a player and stay with the Steelers as an assistant coach—that was a rumor making the rounds — but for some reason it did not work out that way. When he announced his retirement from the Steelers, Webster was all set to sign up as an assistant coach with the Kansas City Chiefs.

At a press conference at Three Rivers Stadium, Webster paid spe- cial tribute to Art Rooney and Chuck Noll, as well as former Steelers' offensive line coach, Rollie Dotsch, who had died from cancer.

Webster said of Noll: "He's one of the most important and special people in my life. And it's important that people know the impact that he has far and above playing the game of football. We talked about tech- nique all the time, about winning and losing and about character. Character starts with the real basics of life, and Chuck has had such a profound and positive impact, not only on myself but on a lot of other players.

"I think a great deal of him. I always will and I'm deeply indebted to him for the things he has meant in my life. His impact on this team,

Mike Webster

this community and each individual player is far and above what we could ever have from a won-lost standpoint."

On another occasion, he said of Noll: "Chuck has said each player can have a positive or a negative impact, and the only way I know to have a positive impact is by contributing."

Webster also cited his special teammates.

"You can't imagine the closeness you get with people when you're down there on your own two-yard line and your back is to the wall," he said. "Or when you're down, 45-3, like we were in the Thanksgiving Day massacre in Detroit. And the most important thing is you want the man across the line of scrimmage to know what your name is when the game is over."

At that press conference, some suggested that Webster had served as a role model for his teammates and for youngsters who followed the team during his storied stay with the Steelers. He was always the first one on the field and the last one off the field for practices. He always led the way in the grueling 350s (running around the outline of the football field). "Basically, you lead by example, by your performance," Webster said.

"Athletes are not heroes because they have not gotten to the point in their life where they have learned enough about what a hero really is. A hero is someone who changes for the better, someone who is willing and has the courage to take things maybe he believed were wrong and change them and do what is right.

"That's something I would like to be someday. A hero. Not for myself, but for my kids. Throughout my life I've had people ask me what is a hero or say to me that I'm a hero. Parents have to realize that the hero their kids want is their own mother and father. They don't want the athlete to be the hero as much as they want the people who are the most important to them to be their hero."

Like it or not, Webster was a hero for many of the younger Steelers offensive linemen. Take Tunch Ilkin, for instance. Hear him out on the subject:

"Webby is the consummate leader," Ilkin said. "Webby is a guy who is the standard, not only as far as the Pittsburgh Steelers are concerned, but as far as the whole National Football League is concerned.

"When I first came here, one of the first things that hit me was Webby's presence. Here was a guy who is a great player, a diligent worker and a hard-nosed person. Here's a guy who's always playing hurt, never complaining, always doing his job and who is so knowledgeable it's like having another coach on the field.

"This is the kind of guy you want to emulate. You talk about a role model, you can't get any better than Mike Webster. One of the most incredible things I ever saw was what Webster did in my rookie year. He got hurt on a Sunday. He tore cartilage in his knee and was on crutches all week. We played on a Thursday night in Houston. He couldn't even walk. They taped him up, he went out there and couldn't work. He went back in, retaped it and went out there again, and played the whole game and played the last three games like that. Then he went to the Pro Bowl and played, came back and got operated on."

Then llkin thought of another Webster story. "In 1985, Webster was listed as questionable for a game with the Houston Oilers. I would have bet my house on Webbie playing. One of our young linemen came up to me during the week and said, 'Webbie's hurting. He probably won't play, huh.' I just told him, 'Are you kidding? How much money do you have? Bet it all on Webby playing.'

"We're not dealing with a mere mortal. Without a doubt, he's the best offensive lineman in pro football."

Or, as quarterback Mark Malone, put it: "There's a 90 percent chance Webby would come off his death bed to play a football game."

Craig Wolfley, who played guard alongside Webster, expressed his admiration this way:

"He'll recognize a defense and turn around and suggest an audible. You don't see that very often. It's actually depressing. You take seventy or eighty snaps amd make maybe seven mistakes, and you're feeling pretty good about yourself. Then you watch what he did on the game films and you realize you're worlds apart.

"Every offensive lineman wants to grow up to be like Mike Webster. But when God made him, He used a different kind of material. There will never be another like him. If anyone has a bigger heart than Mike Webster, I want to see him.

"L.C. Greenwood once put it best. He said anyone can play football when they're healthy. It's those who play when they're hurt who are special. That's Mike Webster. He embodies what pro football is all about."

Bill Meyers, the offensive line coach at the University of Pittsburgh in recent seasons, had worked with Webster in a similar position with the Steelers in 1984, and came away a Webster admirer.

"His training habits are the most outstanding of any player I've ever been around," said Meyers, who also coached at Green Bay, Notre Dame and at Stanford. "There aren't very many players who are going to push themselves up those steps like he does. And in practice, he won't take water. He'll go 12 or 15 plays in a row just to train himself for the long drives in a game. No matter how hot it is, he won't take water. Nobody else does that."

Webster's always had excess energy on the field, and Meyers admires that as well. "Watch any other lineman in the league," he said. "They all saunter up to the line of scrimmage. Mike sprints to the line on every play. That's intimidating. He whipped your butt on the last play, and here he comes sprinting up there to do it again. The defense breaks its huddle, the linemen turn around and there's Webster standing there waiting for them. Grinning. I'll guarantee you that shakes people up."

Webster says he's not trying to intimidate anyone when he does that. But he also smiles when he says that.

367

"I'm just excited," he said. "I can't wait for the play to start. I'm like that all day before a game. The alarm rings in the morning and I sprint to the breakfast table."

When Webster and his wife, Pam, and their five children lived in McMurray, a suburban community south of Pittsburgh, Mike had a weight room in the corner of his house, and a blocking sled in the front yard.

"Maybe I'll bronze it and make it a memorial," Webster said, "to the stupidity of man."

Jon Kolb, who frequently worked out with Webster, said, "I wouldn't be surprised if he had a football field behind his home."

Gary Dunn, a noseguard who went up against Webster daily at practice, said of Webster: "He frustrated me all week. The hardest time I had all week was in practice and then I'd take the day off on Sunday. His dedication, his work habits, he developed such good techniques — all those things together. He's the hardest-working football player I've ever seen, off-season and in-season."

Noll was more to the point: "Mike has been the thing I work around," he said. "It's the one position I never had to worry about."

Webster nearly retired in the mid-80s to take a coaching job with the Green Bay Packers. After the strike season of 1987, he got into a spat with the Steelers over payment for games during the strike, and announced his retirement. He recanted two days later. The day after he changed his mind, and said he would be playing again, I remember walking through the hallway outside the locker rooms of the Steelers and Pirates at Three Rivers Stadium with Joe Gordon, on our way to lunch at the Allegheny Club, when we were overcome by a fast-moving Mike Webster.

It was a bitter cold February day in Pittsburgh, and Webster was wearing a black and gold tassel cap, pulled down over his ears, a black turtleneck, and lots of warm sweatshirts and sweatpants. He started clapping his black gloves as he got close to us. His face was already reddened, and he was on his way into the stadium where he would be running up and down the steps. "It's time to get back to work," Webster said with a smile as he passed us in the hallway.

He retired again following the 1988 season, when he was left unprotected in the Plan B free agent draft. Webster was the last remaining player of the 22 players who had played on all four Super Bowl teams. "I'm the last of the Mohicans," Webster said. Club president Dan Rooney regretted saying goodbye to Webster, but felt it was one of those difficult decisions the team had to make.

"We're trying to create a new dynasty, a new team of the '90s," related Rooney. "I think everyone knows what we're trying to do. We have to get on with young people."

That left Webster, at 36 and the oldest player on the Pittsburgh roster, as the odd man out. Webster said he understood back then.

"I played for one of the greatest organizations in football, on one of the greatest teams in football history, and I hope I'm not doing anything to tarnish that.

"My special feelings for Pittsburgh will always be there. I have no complaint at all with the Steelers. They've done the right thing. They have been very good to me, and I have nothing but good things to say about them.

"After wearing the black and gold for so long, I just couldn't look at any other jersey and imagine myself wearing it. Pittsburgh and the Steelers have meant too much to me. The last 15 years have been very special. I didn't want to tarnish that by going someplace else. I guess, more than anything, my decision is out of loyalty and gratitude to Pittsburgh, and the Steelers."

Five weeks later, he decided to play center for the Chiefs, and put his coaching assignment on hold. He was simply better than what the Chiefs had at center, and the Chiefs wanted him to continue playing. In 1990, he ended up playing for Marty Schottenheimer, a former Pitt center/linebacker from McDonald, Pennsylvania, who had an unsuccessful stint at a Steelers' summer training camp under Noll. Former Steelers recall that Schottenheimer was always asking Noll a lot of questions during chalk board sessions.

It is no wonder Webster switched his mind so quickly. As a 16-year veteran, the minimum salary the Chiefs would have to pay him would be $300,000. Assistant coaches do not make that kind of dough in the NFL, or in any other league for that matter. Many head coaches do not make that kind of money.

Webster was among the Steelers who showed up at the Melody Tent outside Station Square on a stormy Sunday, June 10, 1990, for a reunion of the 1978 Steelers' team — thought to be one of the best teams in the history of the NFL.

Webster stole the show in the next day's newspapers by painting a critical picture of the Steelers' organization. In a month's time, he would be going to his second summer camp as a player for the Chiefs, preparing for his 17th pro season.

Suddenly, he seemed bitter about being cut loose two years earlier by the Steelers, as a player and as a potential assistant coach, quite a turnabout from the thoughts he had expressed at the press conference announcing his retirement from the Steelers. His tune had changed considerably.

"It's not the way it should have been done," Webster was saying two years later. "But that doesn't really matter because that's the way they do things.

"You've got to question the way they've done it over the years. If that's the way they want to do it, well then . . ."

Ed Bouchette of the *Pittsburgh Post-Gazette,* Mike Prisuta of the *Beaver County Times* and Ron Musselman of the *Valley Dispatch* in

Webster and Chuck Noll at "retirement" announcement   Mike Fabus

Webster gets set to pass block.   Bill Amatucci

Tarentum surrounded Webster that day inside the tent, and pressed him for more comments about his dissatisfaction with the Steelers' organization. It hardly seemed like the appropriate occasion for such an outburst.

Joe Gordon, the business manager of the Steelers, and his wife, Babe, had come to the barbecue to have a good time, but Webster had tossed some hot sauce into the reunion that ruined the meal somewhat for Gordon. "It's a shame Mike feels that way," he said, "but Mike never let us know what his intentions were when we were making our plans. We never got a clear indication of what he wanted to do."

Webster made references to how some of his former teammates were unhappy with the way their careers ended with the Steelers, including L.C. Greenwood, John Banaszak, Terry Bradshaw, Gary Dunn and Franco Harris, to name a few. Webster felt the Steelers' organization could have handled things better. It might interest him to know there are people on the Steelers' front-office staff who share his feelings.

"I don't rely on them for everything anyway," he said. "There's a lot of other things in life and we still accomplished quite a bit when I was there.

"That's the way they do things. And it didn't bother me that they did it that way. If you go back over their history, the way they operate the front office . . . but I'm not going to get like everyone else."

He said his difficulties were all with Dan Rooney and Chuck Noll.

Webster took his work habits in stride, as if it were all second nature to him. "It's just something I feel I have to do," he said. "From the time I was six years old, I had to go to work. I'd complain and moan about missing cartoons on television, but I developed good work habits."

This explains why he was so devoted to conditioning, why he thought nothing of running seven miles a day, running up and down 25 sets of steps in stadiums, doing all the weightlifting he does.

"You never know how long you're going to be able to play. I want to get everything out of it I can while I'm still here. You never know when your time is coming."

With Webster, that was for sure.

"The season's 20 weeks long, hopefully 24 weeks long," Webster said. "You have to program yourself for the whole thing. You have to be able to get the job done when you don't feel like doing it, when you're feeling badly.

"I've found that the human body and mind are capable of doing much more than people expect. No matter what you're up against, the No. 1 ingredient in life is that you continue to fight with everything you have. You have to fight the word 'can't.' You have to fight the word 'failure.' You can never give in to that."

When Webster spoke like that, he had a habit of changing his voice, and sounding a little like his favorite Hollywood hero, John Wayne. Webster shares a passion for John Wayne movies with Mansfield, and he loves to quote lines from Wayne movies.

"There's some great lines in them," Webster said, "appropos to offensive linemen like, 'My hide's tougher than boot leather, but no man wants to be called high-smelling and low-down.'"

One Wayne line Webster wanted to be able to say and mean it, goes like this: "I'm retired . . . relieved . . . and rejoicin'."

Bill Amatucci

Mike Webster

The Spirit of the Steelers
Library is a magic spot

After Art Rooney died, the Steelers were not sure what they were going to do with his office at Three Rivers Stadium. It would not have been right to turn it over to anyone else. So the decision was made to turn it into a library, where students of football or Steeler lore could come and do research.

There was a renovation to give it a special and appropriate look. The outside wall of the office was torn down and replaced by a clear glass panel, one that ran at a slight angle away from the door to the library. Visitors to the Steelers' office complex could stop in, and browse through the bookshelves, and check out some of Mr. Rooney's personal mementos. Everything remains but the cigar smoke and ashes.

One that caught the eye was the 1975 Dr. Martin Luther King Citizens Award which was presented to Mr. Rooney by Hand in Hand, Inc. There are two bronzed hands touching one another, and a $1 bill is stuck between the fingers of one of the hands. Written in ink on it is this message: "Thanks, Mr. Rooney: Love you like a dad. Terry Bradshaw 6-19-90."

Many of the books in the two sets of shelves in the room were sent to Mr. Rooney by the authors, with personal inscriptions. One, for instance, from former *Washington Post* sports columnist Bob Addie had this inscription: "For Art Rooney, God made gentlemen in the mold of gold." Another book was signed by Hall of Famer Paul Brown: "To my friend, Art Rooney. The grandest man in all of sports."

When I was doing research for this book, going back through the players' files and combing clippings from magazines and newspapers for notes, quotes and anecdotes, one of the Steelers' public relations representatives, Pat Hanlon, suggested I do my work in the library.

I did not like the idea, at first, because it was a brightly-lit room — like an operating room in a hospital — and passersby always looked in, and I felt like I was in a fishbowl. But, after using it a few times, I changed my mind. It was a magic spot — you could sit there and, suddenly, the Steelers' world came to life about you.

What better place to work on a Steelers' book than in Art Rooney's office, I thought. Better yet, I was sitting in his old chair and doing some writing at his desk. Framed photographs of his favorite friends and former ballplayers and some of the city's celebrated sports figures — like boxers Billy Conn, Harry Greb and Fritzie Zivic — were on Art Rooney's personal Wall of Fame. Plus, and you can call me crazy if you will, but I swear I started getting good vibes in that room.

I browsed through books that had belonged to Art Rooney. Most were about football, some on baseball and boxing and horse racing — his favorite sports — and some were about Pittsburgh, politics, priests and Ireland. Some had bookmarks in them, some had as many as three bookmarks in them. The bookmarks were memory cards or mass cards, the kind you pick up when you sign your signature in the guest book at a funeral home. A religious figure is portrayed on one side of the card, with the name of the deceased and birth and death dates and an appropriate prayer. Some books had as many as three memory cards jutting out of them. I came across hundreds of these cards and did not recognize a single name.

Some of the names were Roy P. Smith, Edward A. Emmerling, Frank L. Sunseri, John S. Cuda, John B. Mastrangela, Irma McAnulty Bandi, Carol L. Goble and Joseph M. Deemer, Sr.

One of his old friends, Bill Burns, who had been an anchorman at KDKA-TV for over 30 years, came by one day while I was doing research. Burns had broken his hip, and was using a walker. He had been retired for several years. "It's not the same coming over here anymore," said Burns. "Geez, I miss The Chief."

When I mentioned to Burns about all the memory cards from funerals I had found in the books, he smiled and said, "He went to more funerals than most undertakers in this town."

I could feel Art Rooney's spirit still there, maybe because there were so many reminders. When I covered the Steelers, I used to visit Art Rooney as often as possible, just to talk to him. There are different portraits of him in the library, and I swear you can sense his presence.

I never felt this more than I did when I was doing some work in the library on Friday, November 30, two days before a big game between the Steelers and Cincinnati Bengals who were tied, along with the Houston Oilers, for first place in the AFC Central with 6-5 records. While I was reading clippings and taking notes, I could check out the passersby. Bob Trumpy, the former tight end for the Cincinnati Bengals and now an analyst for NBC-TV, was there to review tapes. He would be working the upcoming game with Don Criqui, and he was there early to do his homework. Joe Greene, one of the Steelers' assistant coaches, and a former adversary of Trumpy, walked by as well.

People would stop in to say hello, and I would hit them with a question or two to fill some gaps in my work, like trainer Ralph Berlin, equipment man Tony Parisi, and player personnel director Dick Haley, TV-radio broadcaster Myron Cope, who have all been on the Steelers' scene more than a quarter century. I felt like a priest hearing confessions on Friday afternoon.

Then Chuck Noll stopped by. I had reading glasses perched at the end of my nose. "You look studious," he said for openers. "Are you working on your doctorate degree?"

I told him some of the discoveries I had made about his former ballplayers, what they had in common such as similar backgrounds, two parent families, big families, mothers and fathers who both worked — not in the yuppie sense, but just to make ends meet — families with a sense of values, religious spirit, great expectations, and what remarkable decisions they had made and achievements they accomplished in their youth. Noll was interested, he looked intrigued at times, and pressed for more information. I had hit the right button, it appeared.

Noll had been the subject of many lengthy newspaper stories that week because he would be going for his 200th victory in regular and post-season games. "It's just a number," he said. "I just want to win this game. It's an important game right now. Besides, I've already won more than 200 games. Don't they count the pre-season games? Why not? I do."

Then Noll moved across the front of the desk — the desk of Art Rooney, remember? — and took a seat, and started offering some of his own theories about what makes a great football player. Noll seemed to be so at ease and relaxed.

At that moment, as I looked across the desk at Noll, I could see Art Rooney behind him. I swear I could see him smiling, looking over Noll's shoulder. It was like an apparition, the way you have seen them in "The Christmas Carol" when they show the ghosts or spirits of Christmas past, present and future, or the way they were described in Henry James' novel, "The Turn of the Screw."

I must have smiled. I did not say anything to Noll about it. Maybe he would think I was crazy, too. After all, Pat Hanlon told me not to tell anyone about this when I related this to him.

Three things went through my mind at once. That was the first time I saw Art Rooney's life-size image on the glass wall like that. It was a reflection of an oil portrait on the adjoining wall.

I recalled conversations I had in the past with Tom Jackson, the ESPN football analyst who once played linebacker for the Denver Broncos, Art Rooney and several Steelers from Noll's Super Bowl teams.

When I had gone to Canton, Ohio in August for the induction of former Steelers Franco Harris and Jack Lambert, I had talked with Jackson. He was all excited, telling me about how he had visited the Steelers' office in advance to do a pre-Hall of Fame feature for ESPN on Harris and Lambert, and how he had visited the Steelers' offices. He had mentioned that Art Rooney's long-time secretary, Mary Regan, had shown him into the library, and how she had him stand in a certain spot where he could see Art Rooney, looking as if he were actually in the room. Now I knew what he was talking about. I had not noticed that reflection of Art Rooney earlier, not until Noll sat across from me.

I remembered how Art Rooney had once told me — "just between you and me" — that Noll had never just sat in that chair, and talked to him in a casual way, only about business. Noll was so charming this day, and so at ease in conversation, that I wondered how in the world some of his players could complain so much about him and his manner. In my dealings with him, even at difficult times, I always thought he was pleasant enough, even if he was a bit reserved at times, and stubborn at other times. He still seemed like a good guy.

Just as people had told me that Noll was not just a football coach, many of his former players were adamant about impressing people as more than football players, or even former football players.

"All through school people have held them in a certain light, that's why," noted Noll that day. "In school, people always regard football players as being a bunch of dummies. So they want to prove how smart they are. I'll bet you learned that their mothers were the dominant figures in their upbringing. There is usually a strong matriarchal influence or forging. It was that way with me, I know. My dad was sick a lot. The mother tends to be the dominant factor. It's not an absolutism, but you find it quite a bit in their background.

"That's why college coaches always recruit the mothers. They have the most influence on their children."

I remembered that Noll once remarked to an Air Force test pilot, "Do you know what the toughest job in the world is? It's being a housewife and a mother. We need to pay more tribute to these women. We need more of them."

I suggested that, after reading this book, Noll and his scouting department might want to check back even further when investigating possible draft choices. "It was like that with Moon Mullins," said Noll. "Walt Hackett, one of our assistant coaches back then, knew Mullins as a kid, back in grade school, and he knew his family, and that's why we took him, on the basis of his recommendation.

"You learn a lot of things about the people you have. Big kids have a problem in that they're not naturally aggressive. They never had to be. People backed down from them because of their size. No one wanted to fool around with them or challenge them. The little guys were the aggressive ones in school. You put a football uniform on those big guys and they're still not aggressive; they never had to be.

"Football is a game when you have somebody in front of you, challenging you all the time, more so than with most sports. Somebody is over you, threatening you, and he's going to hit you, and try to hurt you. It's one of the things you have to overcome to be good."

When I mentioned something to him that I thought was special about John Stallworth, Noll smiled and tapped his head and his heart, as if "signing" to a deaf person, before he said anything. "You have to be smart," he said, tapping his temple, "and you have to have it here," he added, tapping his heart. "You can't measure those in the scouting reports. It's something you learn when they're around you. It takes awhile for you to determine that.

"People who tell you they hate football, and what it's all about, tell you more about themselves than they do the sport.

"To be a successful athlete, you have to have a high regard for yourself. You have to see yourself as superior, not in a cocky, arrogant way, but you have to feel you're the best before you can become the best at anything. You have to believe you're going to get the best of your opponent.

"I get so ticked off when someone brings their son to me and says the kid could be such a good player, but he needs a coach to motivate him. I hate that. He doesn't want to be a football player. It's something the father wants."

Chuck Noll's folder in the Steelers' archives is the fattest one of the Steelers' current cast. The clippings go back to 1969.

Shortly after he had arrived to take over the team, in February of 1969, Noll said, "It's the function of a coach to get his players to perform to the best of their ability. You don't have to scare a guy. You can't have him more scared of his coach than his opponent.

"If you're asking me 'Am I going to run the team like the Marine Corps?' the answer is no . . . We're going to put it on a man-to-man basis that the job has to be done. And we're going to expect these men to do it."

Pat Livingston, the sports editor of *The Pittsburgh Press,* wrote in his column of September 21, 1969: "Noll's quiet approach, his soft sell to his players, raises the question as to whether these tactics will work with the swashbuckling, self-centered, fire-breathing animals who play with the pros."

Only Chuck Tanner, the former manager of the Pirates, could have been more of an optimistic leader of a sports team in Pittsburgh.

Back on October 5, 1970, after the Steelers' 16th consecutive loss under their second-year coach, Noll said, "We knocked the daylights out of Cleveland. Our defense did a fantastic job, overpowering them and shutting the door on them. We got 100 percent out of our people. They were aggressive and really hit hard." The Steelers won four of their next five games.

Early in the 1989 season, the Steelers lost their first two games by a combined 92-10 score. Asked later in the season how he managed to work his way through that difficult start, Noll said, "I was upbeat, really, the whole time. You're stunned a little bit, but for the most part, I felt good about these people."

After the Steelers reached the playoffs that year, quarterback Bubby Brister said of Noll: "He didn't freak out. He didn't go crazy and throw stuff and start cutting on our players and pointing fingers. He told us what we needed to do. We had to work harder. We had to stay longer. We had to get here earlier. That's one reason we're in the playoffs. He kept us together. He always believed in us and let us know what we needed to get the job done."

Dan Rooney
"We want to do it right"

"Always do the right thing. It will gratify some folks and astonish the rest."

— Mark Twain

Steelers' president Dan Rooney drove to work the same way he has every day since the Steelers moved to Three Rivers Stadium in 1970. He lived in one of the city's finest suburban neighborhoods, Virginia Manor in Mt. Lebanon, about six miles south of the stadium. It took him about 15 to 25 minutes, depending upon the traffic. He traveled along Rt. 19, the same as Chuck Noll, who lived in neighboring Upper St. Clair, just three more miles to the south.

This was Friday, Dec. 14, 1990, and as Rooney made his way down Rt. 19 North, and approached a certain stretch on Banksville Road — about a mile before the Fort Pitt Tunnel — he thought about the bad accident he had been involved in there ten years earlier.

"It doesn't come back to me every day that I drive that road," Rooney said, with a smile, "but, yes, I do think about it from time to time. In fact, I thought about it this morning."

I had come to Three Rivers Stadium the same route, and had thought about Rooney's close call a decade earlier. I often thought about it, so I figured Rooney did, too. I'd been in a bad auto accident as a three-year-old on the Glenwood Bridge near my boyhood home, and I have never crossed that span that I didn't think about how lucky I had been. It seemed like a natural thought process to me.

It was on a Wednesday, the day before Thanksgiving in 1980, when Rooney lost control of the station wagon he was driving when it hit an icy patch on Banksville Road, spun around crazily and struck a utility pole. Four other autos were involved in a chain-reaction collision.

Rooney suffered facial lacerations and a broken right hip. He was already afflicted with rheumatoid arthritis — which pains him on bad days and stiffens his gait — so there was concern about how that might complicate matters. He underwent surgery for 3½ hours and a steel pin was inserted in his hip bone. He looked far worse than anybody on the Steelers' injured reserve list. While members of his family were counting the lacerations on his forehead, he was counting his blessings.

The Steelers had gotten off to a great start for the 1980 season, the year after they had won their fourth Super Bowl in six years, with a 4-1 record. Then they lost three in a row and four of seven before Rooney's auto mishap.

"Accidents happen to people every day," Rooney told those who suggested his accident was the latest in a string of Steeler misfortunes. He would think that a bit melodramatic. Dan was 48 at the time, but feeling a lot older.

378

Ross Catanza, a photographer for *The Pittsburgh Press,* was on the scene soon after the auto accident. Catanza said Rooney's head was bloodied to the point that he didn't recognize him. "The window was shattered on the driver's side, and there was a bubble in it where his head had obviously struck it," recalled Catanza. "There were bloody towels all over the place. It was bad."

Art Rooney Jr., who headed the Steelers' scouting organization at the time, stayed overnight in a hospital suite with his injured brother, and their mother and father made several visits. Dan's wife, Pat, and their nine children were frequent visitors. It is not the way Dan would have chosen to spend Thanksgiving, but such holidays have always been special in his family, and they were this time as well.

He could see their faces. He was alert. He smiled and talked with them. To him, it was still a special day.

Thinking back on it ten years later, Rooney reflected, "You hope you're in the hands of the Lord. You have to believe in another power. It's one time I was really in a situation where I felt helpless. I knew I had no control. I was spinning around, and there was no way to stop it. When I was a kid, I thought I was the greatest driver. I learned that day that you're very mortal."

Dan Rooney was 58, his hair had gone completely gray, and fell casually on his forehead. After that auto accident, he had never appeared to be quite as strong or as vital as he had looked before.

But his enthusiasm was still keen for his responsibilities as president of the Pittsburgh Steelers and as one of the leading executives and movers and shakers in the National Football League. He put in long hours at his tasks. He was determined as ever to develop winning teams. And he was in control, something that is important to him, whether he is driving his car, flying his airplane or setting the Steelers' course for the future. He's not big on cruise control.

There was still a vision in his blue eyes of going after the NFL's Holy Grail again. There were four Vince Lombardi trophies on display in the lobby of the Steelers office complex, just down the hall from his office. His teams had won four Super Bowl rings in the '70s. He wanted another, and the sooner the better. "I never liked that 'one for the thumb' stuff," Rooney remarked, "but I have wanted to win another championship."

A week earlier, I had spoken to Dan Rooney in a room next to his that used to be the office of his father, Arthur J. Rooney, the founder and chairman of the board of the Steelers, but had been turned into a memorial library.

When he spoke then, Dan had his hands wrapped around a huge bronze trophy that had been given to his father, as well as everyone else associated with the Steelers, to mark the franchise's first 50 seasons.

"I've been raised to win," declared Dan Rooney when asked what drove him. "My father had a great desire to win. He had great horses.

He played ball himself. I grew up wanting to win, wanting to do it right, wanting to have good people around us, wanting to help people be the best they can be.

"Motivation is something that comes from within yourself. I believe we want to win and we want to win with good people. Basic people. Good people. We want to do the right thing.

"I'm not saying every player, every coach and every front-office person has the same energy, background and knowledge, but we try to get those people who are all pointing in the proper direction.

"You're not going to change that with a speech. You're not going to motivate each and every one of them with a Knute Rockne-like pep talk. You have to show them that you expect to win."

Rooney released the bronze trophy, and moved past the twin set of bookshelves in the middle of the room and toward a wall that was covered with framed black and white photos of his father's favorite Steelers, and other Pittsburgh sports personalities.

"See these pictures up on the wall?" asked Rooney, revved up, as if he had been challenged to defend the story of the Steelers. "These are all good people. The Steelers have always had good people. Some of these guys are better known to the public because they're in the Hall of Fame, but they were all good football players.

"Look at these people. Pat Brady. Chuck Cherundolo. Armand Niccolai. 'Bullet Bill' Dudley. Elbie Nickel. Bobby Layne. Dick Hoak. John Henry Johnson. Lou Michaels. Byron 'Whizzer' White."

I suggested to Rooney that there were greater expectations today because the Steelers had won those four Super Bowls in the '70s, that the standards had been elevated.

"Our stated goal in the '60s was to win a title," he snapped. "We wanted to be the best team in the National Football League. We wanted to do things right. That was always there."

In a separate interview, Rooney was asked if he hadn't taken more of an active role in the management of the football team in the late '80s. "I've gotten much more involved . . . because I think it's something that helps the Pittsburgh Steelers. You can't be satisfied with less than victory.

"Do I think there are tough decisions to be made at the end of this year? As a leader, you have to make decisions every day."

When Art Rooney was inducted into the Pro Football Hall of Fame in 1964, he had begun to turn over much of the operation of the team to his oldest son, Dan, who had worked in every aspect of the organization.

Dan was in charge when the Steelers made several moves that completely changed the face of the franchise, and contributed in a big way to its ultimate success.

In 1969, Rooney hired Chuck Noll to coach the team. The Steelers made two significant changes in 1970. With the merger of the National Football League and American Football League, the Steelers were one of three franchises from the old NFL — the Cleveland Browns and Baltimore Colts were the others — who moved from the NFL's Century Division to the new AFC Central Division. The Steelers also moved into a new home as Three Rivers Stadium was opened.

Prior to the building of Three Rivers Stadium, the Steelers played home games at Forbes Field from 1933-57 and at both Forbes Field and Pitt Stadium from 1958-63 and at Pitt Stadium exclusively from 1964-69.

In 1975, Dan was named the president of the Steelers. The 1990 season was his 36th year with the Steelers in an official capacity. In truth, he had been with them all his life.

At 58, Rooney remained one of the most active NFL executives and one of Pittsburgh's most civic-minded leaders.

Among his community activities, Rooney is an officer and board member of The United Way, The American Ireland Fund, The American Diabetes Association, The Pittsburgh History and Landmarks Foundation, and Duquesne University.

He has served on several NFL committees over the past 16 years. He has served on the board of directors for the NFL Trust Fund, NFL Films and the Scheduling Committee. He was appointed chairman of the Expansion Committee in 1973, which considered new franchise locations and directed the addition of Seattle and Tampa Bay in 1978. That year Dan was also named chairman of the Negotiating Committee, and in 1982 he contributed to the negotiations for the Collective Bargaining Agreement for the NFL owners and the Players Association. He was also a member of the six person Management Council Executive Committee, the Hall of Fame Committee, the Super Bowl Ring Committee, the NFL Properties Executive Committee. He is chairman of the World League of American Football Committee.

"I view what I do and what I must do and what I think is necessary, the things that are right, as things that I believe in," said Rooney.

"I don't have any set thing, one thing that we're trying to do. We just operate in a certain way."

The Steelers were the last team to sign its No. 1 draft choice for the 1990 campaign. When Eric Green, the 6-5, 275 pound tight end from Liberty University, was still holding out as the team was breaking training camp at St. Vincent College, the local media said the Steelers should have signed Green by then, and would have if they had operated on the same economical scale as other teams in the National Football League.

"The Steelers are special; we do things our way," Dan Rooney declared in defense of his club.

When I called on Rooney in his own office at Three Rivers Stadium on Friday, December 14, he began the conversation by mentioning how Ron Cook, a columnist for the *Pittsburgh Post-Gazette,* had criticized him for making that statement.

"Cook said we were arrogant . . . but I believe that," said Rooney. "It comes through in all issues. I have no problems believing we're special. Throughout the organization, throughout the locker room and these offices, everyone who works here should all feel we're special. If they don't, they shouldn't be here.

"People are important. We treat people the way they want to be treated. People are important to Chuck Noll. He cares about them."

That being the case, I asked Rooney how he could account for the criticism lodged at the Steelers, most loudly and most publicly by Terry Bradshaw, and by Franco Harris, L. C. Greenwood and Dwight White, among others.

Many of them have blasted Rooney and Noll, and other members of the organization, for the cold-hearted manner in which they and some of their teammates were released by the Steelers. Many former Steelers stay away from the team's offices because they feel uncomfortable or unappreciated. "We could do a better job in that respect," conceded one team official in the personnel department. "That's why the guys don't come around. That's bad. They should want to come here, and our current players could benefit from the association."

Rooney realizes the criticism is out there, but he insists the Steelers care and do the best they can. "Terry Bradshaw is Terry Bradshaw," said Rooney. "I consider him a Steeler. I'd have no problem meeting him anywhere to try and iron out any differences. In fact, I just wrote a letter to Terry Bradshaw this morning."

I asked Rooney if he was sensitive to the criticism.

"You're sensitive and you're not sensitive," he said. "Separation is a problem. It's a problem with your children leaving home. The players are like that."

Why are they like that?

"It's the money they make," said Rooney. "The money they make today — it's the same way with the Pirates — changes everything. The players today have a difficult situation, going from making a lot of money to making not very much money. But go see Andy Russell. He comes around often. He likes coming over here.

"Everyone thinks you should take care of them. Terry blames it on Chuck Noll. The separation today is difficult because of the money involved. We still believe we treat our players well. I consider them like my family, but my kids don't like everything I do either. They don't always agree with me. Joe Greene told me the best thing I ever did for him was when I said 'No' to something he asked me.

"We had a kid try out here, and when we let him go he came over and thanked us. A lot of teams say, hey, the paternalism has been broken, and they blame the unions and the contract battles, and all the money for that. But we think there is still room for paternalism in Pittsburgh. This kid said, 'It's really something, to be honored, to be with the Steelers.' He said, 'You know something, the smart kids, they think there are only two teams that genuinely care about their players. The Steelers and the Raiders.' When he said that, I knew he was being honest. If he had said the Giants or the Bears, I wouldn't have taken much stock in it. But that's one thing I know about the Raiders, they really care. We've always had a fierce rivalry with them, but I know they care."

Kent Tekulve, Chuck Noll, Dan Rooney, Chuck Tanner at Three Rivers

Pat, Art Jr. and Dan with Bishop Donald Wuerl

With San Francisco 49ers owner Eddie DeBartolo Jr.

With Raiders' Al Davis

With agent Les Zittrain and Terry Bradshaw

Art Rooney always had a strong relationship with Al Davis and his family, even though he disagreed with some of the things Davis did to cause turmoil with Commissioner Pete Rozelle and the rest of the NFL owners.

"When I was growing up," said Dan Rooney, "A lot of people would say to me, 'You're just like your dad.' But I'm not. I don't have the humanistic ability he had, the ability to talk to people. He was amazing. He could make people feel so special. He never really retired. The one thing he did was represent our organization in every sense of the word. He really earned his keep. Because of what he did for the organization, for the public, for the community, for every worthwhile cause. For what he did for our players and all the people who work in this stadium.

"Every day when he came in here, there'd be an uplift in the atmosphere. Sure, we miss him. The thing I really miss is I could go and talk to him, and it wasn't as if I was going to ask my boss what to do, or ask my father what to do. I was going to ask someone with tremendous experience.

"Just missing that soundness, that you could go and get this advice. It wasn't employer-employee, or father-son, it was someone who had the experience. That's where we miss him.

"The things he did for the Steelers were really significant in those later years. It would have been easy to say he was just there, but he really provided us with a sense that everyone in this organization was important. He could go around the locker room and talk to the players and make them feel they were important and wanted, and belonged."

And now Dan does that, but in a different way.

"But you have to be yourself. Chuck Noll has to be himself. You have to be true to yourself. The ballplayers can uncover a phony faster than anybody.

"We all want to be understood. Is every player who leaves here happy? Some people don't have as good an experience as others. After they get out and go somewhere else they may realize we have something special here.

"Take Dirt Winston, for instance. He came back here last year and the year before that, and he said the guys here don't know what they have. We respect people here. We have never done a lot of trading. We like to work with our own people. We had Super Bowl teams here where every player got his start with the Steelers.

"But we're not in college here. We don't have the same responsibilities toward looking after all the needs of our players. This is a job, a profession, and it doesn't last forever."

What about since those Super Bowl successes? Does it still work?

I had read where Rooney was not sure the Steelers ought to keep the Super Bowl trophies on display in the lobby anymore. He was not sure whether their presence was inspirational, or whether it had become a burden for the current cast of Steelers.

"I don't know that it works or doesn't work. I know this team is itself. I'm not looking for one for the thumb. I never liked it. That's past. It's great, but it's history. And we have a great history. It didn't start

386

with the Super Bowls, either. We're talking about Whizzer White, who went from being a running back for the Steelers to being a judge on the Supreme Court. We're talking about Johnny Blood, who was way before his time. We're talking about Big Daddy Lipscomb and Bobby Layne. We had some great people here. Like Jim Finks. Those people on the wall I showed you. That's our history.

"These kids . . . when they win the Super Bowl . . . it'll be great. It'll be theirs, and theirs alone. We're getting away from the Super Bowl era now. It's a new situation. Let them enjoy their day. They hope they can get to that.

"They have to believe we have the right organization to win; that's important. Starting with management and Chuck Noll, we're committed. Our goal is to win, to be the best we can be in every department. That's now. We talk about this all the time at our regular meetings.

"We had maybe the greatest team that ever played right here. It's an honor."

Art Rooney and Dan Rooney and all the Rooneys became celebrated folk in American sports when the Steelers won all those Super Bowls. It had to feel good. Dan was asked how he felt in the '80s, when the Steelers went into decline and became mostly a mediocre team.

"I wasn't thrilled," he said. "But I have never been unhappy being here."

It reminded us of how his dad used to say, when asked how he was able to stand the difficult days of the franchise, that "there were no bad days." Dan smiled when he heard that because it had a familiar Rooney ring to it.

"I've never been unhappy being engaged with the players who are here. I consider it an honor to be in this position. The Steelers being a part of the National Football League has been something the Pittsburgh Steelers have been proud of."

There are times when Rooney seems to be so devoted to the Steelers that he has no time for anything else, but that is hardly the case. He is usually so pale it doesn't appear that he's ever out in the sun.

"I enjoy doing a lot of things," he said. "I enjoy flying, and I have my own plane. I enjoy skiing, but can't seem to find the time to do it. I love traveling with my family, anywhere. I enjoy traveling to football functions. I enjoy my faith, and going to church. Seeing my kids grow up. The problem is I don't have the time to do some of those things as much as I'd like. I probably don't have any hobbies as such, but I do have other interests.

"I try to do things for Ireland. Ireland is great and the Irish people are special. I have a position with the United Way that I find most rewarding. I've headed up the local fund-raising campaign and now I have a national board position. It's interesting and they're sincere in helping people.

"Our association and the success of the Steelers has given us a great opportunity to do things here in the community. My wife, Pat, and I, as you know, are very involved in this community in the American Diabetes Association.

"I take great pride in seeing our players making contributions to this community, and seeing them doing that. I thought what Tunch Ilkin said this year was very important about how our players learn to give something back.

"That's just part of the spirit of the Steelers' organization, I think. That's part of the thing, why this is so special. Nobody says 'Do it.' They just recruit each other through the years to go out and become a part of the community. I'm not saying there aren't some wise guys here, or guys who just do their own thing. We have them, yes. But they learn, too.

"You have to get the players, and you have to get their commitment. You have to have their willingness to do what it takes, to be the best they can be, to put it all together. As Chuck says, if you can get them pulling together, they can be better than the sum of their parts. I think Chuck gives them the wherewithal to do it."

Dan's wife, Pat, went to graduate school at the University of Pittsburgh in recent years and obtained a master's degree in education, and teaches at Robert Morris College in Coraopolis. Like the rest of the Rooneys, there is no posturing with Pat. If she gets into a project, she will get her hands dirty. I recall seeing Pat playing tennis at two different NFL owners' meetings, one in Maui and one in Palm Springs, that point up how unpretentious she and all the Rooneys are, and why they are so easy to relate to, even though they are richer than the rest of us.

In Maui, many of the wives of the NFL owners and coaches went to great lengths to make sure they had brought a beautiful line of tennis togs with them for the annual tennis competition. Some of the women wore pastel coordinates, and changed into new outfits between matches on the same afternoon. Others wore enough jewelry to bankroll a student in college for four years.

Pat Rooney showed up wearing sweatpants, the gray variety, the real sweatpants. They may have come out of the Steelers' equipment room. She wore a large and loose T-shirt. "It's Dan's shirt," she said. "I borrowed it from him."

Pat doesn't play tennis often, or take daily tennis lessons like so many of the other women, yet she competed well, just with her natural athletic ability and competitive spirit.

At a beautiful tennis complex in Palm Springs, some of the women were complaining about the hardcourt surface. Carrie Rozelle, the wife of then commissioner Pete Rozelle, and the host for the women's tennis competition, said to Pat in my presence, "The court at my home is Har-Tru surface, so I'm used to a softer surface, too. How about yours?"

Pat simply smiled and shrugged off the remark. Then she turned to me and said, "My boys play baseball and football in the backyard, and that's about it."

The Steelers have the lowest payroll in the National Football League, and have the reputation for keeping a lean, mean staff. The Steelers aren't big on titles, either, and those they have are often confusing for an outsider to appreciate, but Rooney knows everyone's responsibilities.

"Yes, I believe in a small staff," said Rooney. "I think people are more efficient that way. We're not as lean as some people think. We're about right in the middle as far as staffing is concerned with NFL teams. There are teams who have a lot more, and some who have less."

What about the players? What are the demands on the players to perform?

"We ask each player to make a commitment to this team. If he doesn't do it, he's gone."

Several former Steelers have complained about the abruptness with which they were put out to pasture, while some Steeler watchers believe the team hurt itself by keeping some of its greatest players too long.

"There's no question we kept some guys too long," remarked Rooney. "The most famous case perhaps was Dwight White. Some people think we should have kept Dwaine Board rather than Dwight White for the 1979 season. We liked Board a lot. He's still with the 49ers and helped them win three Super Bowls. But we won the Super Bowl the year we kept White, so it was worth it. I didn't think it was a mistake."

L.C. Greenwood and John Banaszak were both cut at the summer training camp before the 1982 season. Both felt betrayed. Were they given any warning as to what was coming?

"Greenwood was told before the camp that he would have a difficult time making the team, that we were looking to make a change, and that he would have to make the team in camp. It was his choice to come to camp. I know how he feels. I know how Dwight feels, and I know how he feels about other guys on the team, and what happened to them. Dwight White has nothing to complain about, or nothing to say. He was kept longer than might have been prudent. Things don't have to happen the way they did. The person involved is part of it, too. It wasn't easy for Banaszak to let go, either. It never is. It's a hardship; it's difficult for everyone."

I mentioned to Rooney that several players I had spoken to expressed disenchantment in particular with the way Franco Harris was dealt away to the Seattle Seahawks when he was holding out for an improved contract before the 1984 season.

"I understand what they're saying, and I think very highly of Franco, too," said Rooney. "But Franco had something to do with it, too. It also comes back to separation."

The toughest separation had to be when he told his brother, Art Rooney Jr., that he wanted him to relinquish his duties as player personnel director prior to the 1987 season. Their father was deeply saddened by that breach, and retreated to his Maryland farm in the aftermath of the move. Art Jr., who remains a vice-president and owner of the team, now looks after the family's real estate interests, and does some scouting on his own, out of a beautifully-furnished office in Upper St. Clair. Firing his brother had to be difficult for Dan.

"It was the same thing," said Dan. "I'm not going to tell you anything I haven't told everyone else. It didn't have to be that way. No, it didn't have to be that way. He had other options. When you let coaches go, which I also felt I had to do, they felt they shouldn't have been let go.

"What you do, you try to say what the situation is, and act on what you believe is best for the franchise. If people don't appreciate that, you can't worry about that. My job is to be management. My job is to say, 'This is the way we're going to do it.' I'm not going to feel like I have to keep everyone happy."

Since his dad died, Dan seems to be quicker to express his opinions publicly, pro and con, and has been critical of many aspects of the football team. Asked what he feels his role is in regard to the team itself, he smiled.

"I don't call the plays," he said.

So you don't feel qualified to coach the team?

"Maybe I'd like to coach the team, but I don't," he said. "My job is to make sure we have the best coaches we can have, and that they have the tools at hand to do the job. Whatever they need."

How involved is he in the team's college draft?

"I'm involved in the draft only to the extent that I ask questions about the players we're picking. It's important who we pick. I want to know why we think a particular player can help us.

"I talk to Chuck a lot about the team. You have to look at the situation. We've had some coaches here before Chuck Noll that I had to work differently with than I do with Chuck Noll. People are different.

"My job is to try and help people in this organization to do their job. I don't have a diagram or a map, or something I use as a guidepost. We want to do it right in all ways. We want to treat players right, we want them to do their jobs right, and make the right decisions every day.

"The Pittsburgh Steelers are an organization that does try to do it right. We want to be something special to our people. That's how we view the Steelers; they are special. The specialness comes in looking at people, getting the right people, and knowing what our mission is."

When Dan Rooney sets foot in his father's former office, now a memorial library, it makes him realize that he was not always the boss of the Steelers. It is a legacy that was passed on to him by one of the most popular men in the history of sports and certainly in the history of Pittsburgh.

His father was a man who played football with Jim Thorpe, was quite an athlete in his own right, and genuinely enjoyed people. His father was demanding of them, and the five boys all feared him to different degrees. Art Rooney challenged each of them. Their father led the league in personal loans to players, coaches, friends and anybody who got close enough to put the touch on him.

Before the Steelers hired Chuck Noll, Art Rooney told a sportswriter friend, "My boys, Danny and Artie, told me, 'When you pick a coach this time, put friendship on the bottom of the list.'"

Dan had seen coaches make too many mistakes in the past. When he was the senior quarterback of the North Catholic High School football team, he was beaten out for the All-City Catholic team by a junior from little St. Justin High School named Johnny Unitas. He kept a close eye on Unitas at the Steelers' training camp in 1955 at Duquesne University. "Our club never gave him a chance," Rooney remarked of Unitas, who became a Hall of Famer for the Baltimore Colts, and one of the game's greatest field generals.

Dan Rooney recognizes the differences between him and his famous father who liked to say, "Winning is it. When you don't win you're too dumb to come in out of the rain. When you win, you get smart in a hurry. That's why winning is better."

"All this, the whole organization," said Dan Rooney, "my father really made it possible for us. But I realize I'm going a different route from him. I really never felt I was the same as him. Maybe I never had the same desires or approach. I want to make my contributions differently.

"I believe in being businesslike. I think a person has to do his job, hold up his end. My father always worried about everyone's feelings — constantly, sometimes it infuriated me. But that's the type of person he was. He was a humanistic man. He tried to think of everything in its relation to people. Money didn't mean that much to him. He tried to be good to people rather than be a good businessman or a successful club owner."

In an interview in 1981 with Bob Oates Jr. of Los Angeles for a book called "The Pittsburgh Steelers: The First Half Century," Dan Rooney reflected:

"It was probably a coincidence, but we learned how to win just as Pittsburgh could get the most out of a winner.

"It made my Dad happy, I know. He's really a politician, to tell the truth. That's how he started out, and he still thinks like the politicians of his day, like the ward leaders, whose major role was always to try to do things for their people. Even now, whenever we have a decision to make, his first thought is, what will the public say? He always wants everybody to be happy, to do things with people.

"And that has set the tone for the way the organization runs. We have always tried to treat people as individuals, to relate to them as human beings, and to try to help them with their problems.

"And this is why we were so lucky to get Chuck Noll. He's not only a good coach, but he fits here. He fits Pittsburgh and he fits the Steelers. He comes from a simple, hard-working background, and he's not looking for a fancy lifestyle or an easy road. He goes well in this town, and he knows it. He appreciates it. 'Pittsburgh is one of the best-kept secrets in the country,' he says.

"And his approach to people is the same as ours. I found this out right away with Rocky Bleier. I thought we were going to have to force Bleier down Noll's throat — to get him to agree to keep Rocky around while he tried to recover. But Noll just said yes immediately. If the Rooneys want to look at individual needs, so does Chuck Noll."

391

Bryan Hinkle
"Tradition is important"

Bryan Hinkle was standing in the lobby of the Steelers' offices at Three Rivers Stadium, waiting for a ride. This was Monday, December 17, the day after the Steelers had defeated the New Orleans Saints, 9-7, in the Superdome to stay alive in the playoff chase with two games left in the 1990 schedule.

It had been, as coach Chuck Noll had described it only an hour earlier at his weekly press conference, "a hard-fought, very physical football game, the kind you like to come away from with a win."

Hinkle had the look of a linebacker who had been in such a football game. His knuckles had fresh scabs on them, and a fresh dark purple wound was evident at the left corner of his mouth. He looked tired, and this was supposed to be a day off for the players, but he had consented to go to New Kensington for an interview for a sports cable outlet. He was waiting for Bill DiFabio, an enterprising one-man media conglomerate, who has been on the Steelers' scene for over 15 years. DiFabio would arrive in a chauffeur-driven white limousine to make the trip a little more palatable for Hinkle, though Hinkle hardly seems like the limo type.

Hinkle was surrounded by the history of the Steelers. Squad photos of the four Super Bowl championship teams were on the one wall, along with freshly-printed photos by Mike Fabus from the New Orleans game, a new feature in the lobby this season. Before him were the four gleaming silver Lombardi Trophies the Steelers had won — no other team could make such a claim. Behind him, on the other wall, were pictures of people like Bert Bell, Walt Kiesling, Johnny Blood, who had been with the Steelers, and were now in the Pro Football Hall of Fame, and more recent Steelers such as Jack Ham and Jack Lambert, two linebackers who had set the standards for all linebackers like Hinkle to follow. Hinkle also looked upon Ham and Lambert as good friends as well as mentors when he first came to the Steelers in 1981.

"I think it's good to have this tradition here," said Hinkle, "like the Super Bowl trophies and pictures of the past greats. It's good for the young guys to see this. I don't think about it much, but we should look proudly upon these displays."

I mentioned that Dan Rooney questioned whether the Super Bowl trophies should remain on display, whether they are still a positive presence or whether they have become a burden for today's Steelers.

"The players should look upon it as an accomplishment. It's a reminder of one of the greatest teams ever assembled and you should strive to do the same thing they've done. These are not only guys who played on championship teams, but they have also been so successful in their careers since leaving football."

392

Has Hinkle found himself saying things to young players that guys like Lambert and Ham had said to him when he was coming along? Hinkle had to smile.

"Sure, you remember what they said to you when you were young, and you relay it to the next generation. You just carry it on. You have to look up to those guys, and what they did, and what they accomplished.

"After being here for 10 years, and seeing how tough it is to be on top makes you appreciate what they accomplished. To do what they did, to win four Super Bowls. I didn't really appreciate it when I first got here. They made it look easy, but it's not easy. After you've played a few years, you realize that. What you strive for is to win another Super Bowl. The attitude about that hasn't changed in the 11 years I've been here. Chuck Noll won't let you forget. He's instilled that in the players every year. They prepare us to win. The bottom line is winning. Chuck comes out, every single day, every single year and prepares us to win football games. He never wavers."

Hinkle has a big role on the Steelers' defensive unit, one that really shined during the 1989 and 1990 seasons, after rough starts both years. Hinkle has had his share of injuries, and he has played when he was not at his best. But half a Hinkle is better than none, according to Dave Brazil, defensive coordinator.

"I want him in the game as long as he can stand up," said Brazil. "I hate to take out his production and his leadership. It's guys like him — Keith Willis, David Little, Dwayne Woodruff — who have enabled our young defense to play like a bunch of veterans."

Hinkle, who had been the Steelers' MVP in 1986, had a great game in the Steelers' 21-9 victory over the Atlanta Falcons at Three Rivers Stadium in 1990, with 11 solo tackles, and forced a fumble and recovered that same fumble at a critical point in the contest.

The victory put Pittsburgh into a first-place tie (5-4 record) with the Cincinnati Bengals in the AFC Central. "I don't even remember the last time we were in first place," said Hinkle, who admits he is not big on remembering past exploits.

Hinkle would have gotten along great with the players in Pittsburgh in any era. He is a throwback of sorts. He married his college sweetheart, but they were divorced. He is not out for personal glory, he does not like too much attention, and he represented himself in his last contract negotiation. Then, too, he wears a patched-up practice jersey that is a leftover, according to equipment manager Tony Parisi, from when the Steelers practiced at South Park back in the '60s. Parisi has tossed away the jersey on more than one occasion, but Hinkle has found it in the trash can and recycled it. "It has a different cut," pointed out Parisi, "and Hinkle says it's comfortable." He probably takes pride in wearing a patched-up jersey. He's a good-looking guy, but he wouldn't want to look like a pretty boy.

"If you have any kind of competitiveness inside, you think you can get it done," said Hinkle. "It may not be pretty, but it's a team sport; it's not an individual thing. You pull your weight and other people pull their weight and, collectively, you get it done."

Nearing the end of the 1990 season, Hinkle had a year to go on a three-year contract that paid him $400,000 a season. Former teammate Mike Merriweather sat out the 1987 season and refused to sign with the Steelers in a salary dispute. He was traded to the Minnesota Vikings, where he was making $750,000 a year.

Hinkle said he would never hold out like that. "If I did that, I'd probably be down at Dairy Queen, scooping ice cream," said Hinkle.

"You pay me what you feel is right, and that's what I'm going to play for," Hinkle told his Pittsburgh bosses.

"I guess I'm different the way I think about my role or about professional football. I love to play football. Most players get into the glory thing, going to supermarkets and getting noticed. I'll go into the supermarket with a hat and sun glasses on because I don't want anybody to even look at me and say, 'Hey, that's Bryan Hinkle.'

"Jack (Lambert) wanted to go into a bar and drink and not be bothered. People always bothered him. I guess I'm the same way. I don't like to be bothered."

Hinkle spent his 1981 rookie season on injured reserve, but he said it was not a wasted year. "I was watching all those guys — Jack Lambert, Jack Ham and Loren Toews. They were real successful, and I just kept learning from what they'd done to be successful."

Lambert liked the blond linebacker from Oregon who had a degree in business administration. Lambert and Ham and Toews all had their college degrees, which also set them apart from the pack. "He's kind of like the old guys," Lambert allowed when discussing Hinkle. "He doesn't say much, but he goes out and does it."

Said Ham: "He gets the job done without any fanfare. He makes the big play and nobody notices. He's not a flashy guy."

The feeling is mutual. "Jack Ham was one of the best linebackers I ever saw," said Hinkle. "I love to watch the old films of when he was playing.

"I played with the Hammer for two years. We're still close friends. Jack and I were similar in size (Hinkle reported at 6-1, 214 pounds). I'd look at him and tell myself that's the kind of player I want to be. I'd pattern myself after some of the things he did, and I'd pick up the nuances of the game from him."

On a Monday Night Football game, ABC-TV's Joe Namath introduced Hinkle in 1985 as "the next Jack Ham." Hinkle had to cringe when he was told about Namath's remark.

"Those are big shoes to fill," he said. "Ham was a great player. I try not to listen to that sort of stuff, good or bad."

To Hinkle, it was like going to graduate school to play behind Ham and Toews, and alongside Lambert.

"From Hammer, I learned how to read (the offensive formations) and some things about covering a receiver. And from Lambert, I learned how to use my body to fight off guards and tackles and get to the football. Loren was so intelligent. From him, I learned that intelligence

394

is an important part of the position. Gradually, I've learned how to play the position. It's all paid off."

In his early days with the Steelers, when Hinkle would come to the sideline he would stop and check with Ham as to how he was doing. "If I can do it like him," Hinkle said then, "I know I'm doing it right. Every time I go to the sideline, I talk to him and ask him if I'm doing it right."

Bryan Hinkle

Roots
"Imagine doing that today?"

P at Livingston was having lunch in the men's grill at the Rolling Hills Country Club in McMurray, about 15 miles south of Pittsburgh, and talking about the Pittsburgh Steelers, a life-long interest of his.

He had retired six years earlier from his post as sports editor of *The Pittsburgh Press*. He had been associated with the Steelers in one fashion or another for over 50 years, going back to his student days at St. Francis of Loretto.

Livingston had been my boss when I came back to Pittsburgh in 1979 and covered the Steelers for nearly five years. The beat had belonged to Livingston for 23 years, from 1949 until 1972. Before he joined *The Press*, he was a publicist for the Steelers, then a scout when Jock Sutherland coached the team, and he did a stint in the U.S. Navy.

Livingston, who was inducted in 1979 as a member of the media segment of the Pro Football Hall of Fame, may have been the first scout in the National Football League. He would like to think so, anyhow.

Pat is a Pittsburgher all the way. He grew up in an area called the Hill District, was graduated from Central Catholic High School, St. Francis of Loretto College and Law School at Duquesne University. He appears to be a nervous sort, yet he was a navy frogman who defused underwater mines in his military service during World War II. Maybe that is why he appears nervous. He was at ease at the Rolling Hills Country Club. Everybody there seemed to know him.

At 70, he was still doing some writing, and tinkering around with computers, also a personal passion, and playing golf, something he loved to do, and something he did more often with Myron Cope, since Cope cut back on his broadcasting schedule that year at WTAE. Livingston was looking forward to spending time with family and friends at Christmas. At the same time, Livingston was complaining about the cold weather which was keeping him off the links. But he was also looking forward to a football game in two days between the Steelers and Browns. With two games to go in the 1990 schedule, the Steelers still had a shot at the division championship and a playoff spot. Which meant, they still had a shot at another Super Bowl. That is the logic Livingston has always brought to the business.

But he did not think they were good enough to do that. "Unless Bubby Brister comes up big," said Livingston.

By coincidence, Livingston had paid a visit to Chuck Noll just two days earlier at Three Rivers Stadium. As usual, Livingston had told Noll what was on his mind, whether Noll was interested or not.

"I offered him my congratulations," Livingston said with a warm smile under his salt and pepper mustache. "I said, 'I think you've done one of your best coaching jobs this year, especially for a team without

Jack Butler

John R. McGinley, Steelers' vice-president and minority owner, presents Mel Blount with Steelers' 1983 NFL/Miller Man of the Year award at Three Rivers Stadium.

Former Pittsburgh Press sports editor Pat Livingston presents "Football Executive of the Year" award to Art Rooney.

a quarterback.' Noll did not care for that remark and looked a little miffed. He said, 'I'm not going to comment on that.' He got a little hot. But that's the way I see it."

Livingston likes Noll, and has always enjoyed their verbal jousts. Livingston believes he knows why Noll has been so successful.

"His resoluteness," said Livingston. "He sets his mind to do something and it's done. It doesn't matter how much advice he gets from guys like us, he sets his course and goes straight as you can go. It takes a long time for him to make a final decision, but he makes damn sure it's the right one.

"The big tenet of Noll is that he has not lost many good football players. The only players he ever lost were when he had a surplus of talent.

"I don't think he's complicated at all. I think he'd be a good neighbor."

Livingston also likes Noll's boss, Dan Rooney. "But he's no Arthur J. Rooney," Livingston added. "None of the five boys are the same as their father. They each have a little bit of him, but not the whole man."

No one would know that any better than Livingston. "The whole Rooney family is very special to me," he said. "I've known five generations of that family. I knew Art's mother and father, and I know some of his great grandchildren.

"I don't know five generations of my own family. I have two daughters, but no grandchildren, and I didn't know my grandparents. One time when I was at the Rooneys' home on the North Side, one of Art's boys, Timmy, told me, 'You're not company. You're family.'

"I spent an awful lot of time with Art back in the old days. We'd go on road trips together. Maybe we'd drive down to Washington, D.C. for a ballgame with the Redskins. I'd ride with him, and we'd go to the race track together. Hell, we'd share the same suite at the hotel.

"It would be Art and Ed Kiely in one room, and me and Jack Sell (the beat writer for the *Pittsburgh Post-Gazette*) in the other room. Joe Tucker might be in another part of the suite with whomever was working with him on the radio.

"We'd go out to Los Angeles a few days early, and fly from Los Angeles to Las Vegas for a night. It was different in those days.

"I had worked with them right out of school in their publicity department. When they hired Sutherland in 1946, he wanted me to go scout college players. He told me, 'You've seen pro football players. You know what they look like.' Before Sutherland, nobody could get a scout on a college campus. But he had been a big man in the college game at Pitt, and he had all the connections. He'd call ahead to his friends and tell them I was coming, and to treat me right. And they did.

"My first association with the Steelers was when I was a student at St. Francis, and they held training camp there in 1938. I was working in the college publicity department, and Jim Leonard was the A.D. and football coach there at the time. He later coached the Steelers for a season (1945). Art came up to check out the facilities. They also promoted some fights up there. They had a raffle one night for $1,000, and my mother won it. When I sent her the money, she called and said there was only $980. I told her I had to buy the fellows a drink, so they didn't think we were cheapskates.

"I couldn't take Jock Sutherland, though. He was a great coach, but he was tough to get along with. He was overbearing. He was always having these bad headaches, but he wouldn't see a doctor. I told the Rooneys I thought something was wrong with him. I quit after the 1947 season, and he died soon after. I quit in February and he died in March, from a brain tumor."

After Sutherland's death, the Steelers went into a tailspin, and became a mediocre football team again.

Livingston believes that moving into Three Rivers Stadium in 1970, the year after they had hired Noll as the coach, was significant in the club's climb to greatness.

"That meant a lot to them," he said. "Up until then, they had never had a practice field to call their own, or facilities that truly belonged to them.

"Before that, a lot of times they were practicing under sandlot conditions. When they were playing at Pitt Stadium and Forbes Field, they were practicing at South Park. There were some other teams in the NFL that practiced under similar conditions back then, but not many. They just had to throw their things up on hooks; they didn't even have lockers," he recalled.

"For lunch, they were on their own, and they'd go to Gorsek's or the South Park Inn for hamburgers and beers."

One of Noll's favorite football players from those days, Dick Hoak, remains as one of Noll's assistant coaches. "He looks like a cadaver," laughed Livingston, "but he was some football player."

Livingston always liked Terry Bradshaw in the team's best days. I asked Livingston what was bugging Bradshaw that he was saying all those bad things about Noll, Dan Rooney, the Steelers, Pittsburgh, you name it.

"I don't think anything is bothering Bradshaw," said Livingston. "I think he's getting a lot of attention by not getting along with anyone here. Somebody must have told him at the network to get all the attention he can."

Jack Fleming was feuding with Myron Cope in the comical way that was part of their repertoire on radio broadcasts of the Steelers' games. The Steelers were leading the Cleveland Browns, 35-0, with four minutes left to play, the same score they led by at halftime when the outcome had already been determined. Cope thought it was time to lighten up a little; this runaway, after all, was the last home game of the season, and so he started reading a poem a Pittsburgher had sent him that made fun of the nickname of the rival team. What's a Cleveland Brown? That was the question posed by the poem. Cope kept reading the rather lengthy poem, as only Cope can, and Fleming found it rather tiresome. "You know, Cope, there is a football game going on here?" said Fleming. Cope kept chattering away, mocking Fleming for being serious over a game that was, for certain, over and done with. Fleming wanted to do his play by play. "Let's get serious, Cope," he kept protesting.

That's Fleming for you. To him, football is a religion, whether he was providing play-by-play for his beloved alma mater, West Virginia University, or for the Steelers. He's serious.

During the 1990 season, Fleming was 64 and Cope 62, but both were wearing well and remained institutions in their profession. Cope calls Fleming "a legend in the business," and Fleming protests once more. "No, you're the legend," he says with a hearty laugh. Off the air, Fleming laughs a lot. Fleming has been fortunate in the broadcast business because he has endured.

After all, Fleming was finishing his 33rd consecutive season of doing Steelers football games (even the legendary Bob Prince didn't do Pirates games that long), and he had been the "Voice of the Mountaineers" for a total of 38 seasons.

Fleming was an Air Force navigator during World War II and broke his jaw parachuting into France. The jaw healed just fine, and when he returned to Morgantown, he began broadcasting for his hometown university in 1948. His tenure there was interrupted only once, when he went to Chicago in 1970 for a four-year stint broadcasting the Chicago Bulls' games in the NBA.

At WVU, Fleming has called the action for both basketball and football teams that nearly won national championships, but came up short. In 1959, a Jerry West-led WVU basketball team lost to California, 71-70, in the NCAA championship contest. In the outset of 1989, the Major Harris-led WVU football team was defeated by Notre Dame, 34-21, for the national championship at the Fiesta Bowl. In the mid-'50s, Fleming broadcast WVU football games when the team had such future NFL standouts as Sam Huff, Chuck Howley, Bruce Bosley, Joe Marconi and Fred Wyant. In basketball, he called the shots for such as West, Hot Rod Hundley, Rod Thorn, Ron "Fritz" Williams and Wil Robinson.

With the Steelers, Fleming had called four Super Bowl triumphs. His oft-repeated call for Franco Harris's 1972 "Immaculate Reception" gained him national notoriety. He had done numerous college bowl games, the 1960 Olympics in Rome, NCAA Final Fours and even some of Jerry West's high school games. In short, he has done it all.

One of Fleming's fans was Joe Gordon, the Steelers' front-office executive and long-time publicist. "Jack has an amazing God-given gift . . . I truly believe he was put here to broadcast football and basketball," said Gordon. "I believe most announcers are like athletes in that they can't go on forever and do it well. Jack is the exception. He's the George Blanda of the broadcast booth.

WTAE's Myron Cope and Jack Fleming are all smiles.

"I believe in his prime he was the best at both basketball and football. His voice is exceptional. It's one you can take for 30 years and not get tired of it. It's so clear, yet captures so well the excitement of the event."

Fleming felt blessed to possess those prized vocal chords, and the jobs he held. "I don't care if I'm doing a high school game — and I still do some during state tournament time in West Virginia — or the Super Bowl, I love it," he said.

"People used to say to me, 'You must have hated doing the Steelers when they were losers.' Nothing could be farther from the truth. I was just like a kid in 1958, because I couldn't believe I was here.

"I do the West Virginia games on Saturday, and I can't wait for Sunday morning to get to the Steelers' game. I listen to WTAE's pregame show on the way in, and I feel good when I see the stadium from the bridge.

"I was so elated when I got this job; it's never left me. Some of the guys in our business will laugh about me saying this, but it's true — I dearly love this work. I'm known as a 'house man' (an incorrigible booster), but I regard that as a compliment. These are my teams. I'm rooting for them to win."

Sometimes at Steelers' games, Fleming took a back seat to Cope, who had provided the "color," or analysis to his play-by-play call for 21 years. Cope, of course, was the more colorful figure. "I just sat down in the booth in 1970 and started hollering and screaming, and it was an understandable shock to Jack," claimed Cope, noting that Fleming had previously teamed with less flamboyant pros such as Joe Tucker and Tom Bender.

"He'll get pumped up and start waving his hands and his face will turn all red," Fleming said of Cope, "and he'll just take over. I've gotten used to playing second fiddle to Myron here. It's my role.

"There are times I'm with Myron and I just get completely ignored. Someone will say to me, 'Who are you?' And I say, 'I'm his bodyguard.'"

For sure, Fleming looks the part. He's a big guy, much bigger physically than the 5-foot-6 Cope.

"I never had enough guts to be a football player, and I didn't have enough talent or speed to be a basketball player," said Fleming. "This is an ideal life for a non-athlete who always wanted to be involved in athletics."

The football press box at Three Rivers Stadium may be one of the most informal in the National Football League as far as gaining admission. But it is also one of the best. It is all business, and the Steelers' publicity staff provides all the information the media needs to do its job, and then some. There are two levels of seats located at midfield, about half way up the stadium. There is a wall behind the second level of press box seats. There is a walkway behind that wall, and it's there that you come upon some interesting people who are most familiar with the history of the Steelers.

Before the Browns' game, for instance, I came upon Jack Butler, Jackie Powell, Baldy Regan, Tom O'Malley Jr., and Ed Kiely, and they can all tell stories about the Steelers from first-hand experience.

I had known Regan since I was 14 and I accompanied the coach of the Hazelwood Steelers to buy our uniforms at the Pittsburgh Sports Shop, where Regan was working. Regan had always been involved in sports, promoting one thing or another: boxing, football and basketball. He had started and managed the Steelers' basketball team that played in benefits and fund-raisers during the off-season.

Regan had recently been elected as a City Councilman. He knew how to keep his name in the newspapers, and was heralded as a "champion of the people." He was from the North Side, and always boasted about that. He once was known as "the mayor of the North Side." He had always been close to the Rooneys, and had learned a lot about public relations from Art Rooney. Before Regan was elected to City Council, he used to run the copying machine in the press box. So he knew all the sports media. His constant companions included Bernie Stein, a former Golden Gloves boxing champion, and Paul Tomasovich, a local legend for his home run hitting prowess in softball. Regan had his critics, but nobody was going to mess with Baldy Regan with Stein and Tomasovich at his side.

Regan is a likable guy. And he has always been good for a laugh. I remember him in the midst of a cream pie-slinging session at a bachelor party for Paul Martha during Martha's Steeler playing days. It was Regan who brought the pies to the party. Regan likes to tell stories. "I remember my mother wanted to buy a big calendar and put it on our refrigerator one year," he was saying. "My dad said we didn't need it. He said our refrigerator was a calendar. He said, 'When you look in it at the beginning of the month, it's full of food. When you look in at the end of the month, it's out of food. So what do we need with a calendar?' "

Tom O'Malley Jr. is the son of an advertising executive at *The Pittsburgh Press* with whom I worked as a copy boy on weekends back in high school. Tom O'Malley Sr. is also the mayor of Castle Shannon. His son has succeeded Baldy Regan in running the copying machine in the Steelers' press box, and in managing the Steelers' off-season basketball team.

O'Malley, 36, is a sales representative for the Bob Purkey Insurance Agency in Bethel Park. Purkey is a former Pirates and Cincinnati Reds pitcher.

O'Malley roomed with Gary Dunn, a defensive lineman for the Steelers, for ten years in an apartment complex called Hunting Ridge in Bridgeville. "It was a trip, to say the least," said young O'Malley. "I used to run with Gary and Steve Courson a lot. To say the least, they were very popular.

"They got a lot of attention in a hurry because of their size, just being athletes. They weren't the bully types, but everybody respected their presence. Guys like Mike Wagner, Mike Kruczek and Moon Mullins used to hang out with us before they got married, and they were better looking. But Dunny and Courson had a way of getting attention.

They might tear off their shirts and assume a musclebuilder's stance, flexing themselves. They stirred up things pretty good, but they were good at keeping the peace. They enjoyed themselves."

O'Malley remembers being in the Steelers' offices one day, and having Chuck Noll call out to him. "Do you have a minute?" Noll asked him. "Come into my office. I'd like to talk to you."

"I thought, 'oh, oh, what did I do wrong now?'" recalled O'Malley.

"So I went in, and sat down. Chuck said, 'How's the basketball team doing?' I told him we were doing fine, and a little bit about what we were doing. I didn't know he even knew I had anything to do with the basketball team.

"He said, 'You know, I used to play for the Browns' basketball team. We had that going pretty good. There were some nights we made $50 or $60.' I told him I thought that was pretty good.

"He told me how you run a basketball team like that, and what opportunities were out there to promote such games. He had some good ideas. Just then, John Banaszak stuck his head in Noll's office to ask him something.

"Chuck asked John if he was playing for our basketball team. Banny said, 'Oh, yeah, we're doing pretty good. We make between $150 and $175 a night now.' Noll just looked at me, and smiled. He seemed to be acknowledging that I was doing a pretty good job booking games and getting them money.

"Banny told him he was meeting somebody at the Allegheny Club about an opportunity to work with a trucking company. Chuck told him he had once worked for a trucking company when he was playing for the Browns. And he told him something about that business.

"Chuck Noll knows something about everything, I swear. He used to tell Gary Dunn, who was into boats, about boating and sailing and what the oceans were like. About tides and stuff like that. He truly is a Renaissance man."

Ed Kiely was a constant companion of Art Rooney for many years. Kiely, 72 when we spoke in 1990, had been the Steelers' public relations man from 1945 until he retired in 1987. He handled all the p.r. for the team until Joe Gordon joined the organization in 1979, and media responsibilities were divided between them for awhile, and then Kiely eventually gave way to Gordon in many areas. But he had good national contacts, and he was always a plus for the program.

Kiely was as close to Rooney as anyone, and accompanied him to most banquets, luncheons, business meetings and, above all else, to hospitals and funeral homes to comfort friends.

"He was politically-oriented as a young guy, and he always knew that people remember when you came to visit at a funeral home or at a wake," recalled Kiely.

"Joe Carr, our ticket manager, had grown up near Art on the North Side, and he knew all the people that Art knew. Carr would read the obituary notices in the newspaper each morning, and he knew which ones Art ought to attend, and he would tell Art about them.

"We'd go to a funeral home to see somebody specifically, but if three or four other people were laid out in the same funeral home, Art would stop in and see everybody. He knew people would appreciate it. But if people would fuss over him, or recognize him right away, he'd ask me on the way out, 'How do they know me?' I think he honestly meant it. He never thought he was any big deal.

"A lot of the old-time politicians went to funerals. Now some politicians made stops just to be seen, and they'd do a hit-and-run job. Art wasn't like that. He'd stick around and talk to people. I'd want to go — I'd get antsy — but he'd insist we stay. I was always amazed how he could say, 'What was your sister's name?' And then he'd say, 'Oh, yes, I knew her,' and he could tell them something about a relative he'd met. He had a way with people.

"Another throwback to old-time politicians was his practice of sending people postcards from wherever he went. Wherever Art would go, he'd buy a lot of postcards, and he'd buy a lot of postage stamps. He'd eat early, and retire to his room early. He'd write postcards during the evening, maybe about ten or twelve, and then he'd do the same thing again in the morning. And he always made a lot of phone calls to friends he knew in those places."

In my lifetime, there were three people who sent postcards to me wherever they traveled, and they included Art Rooney; Angelo Dundee, the great boxing trainer; and Marques Haynes, one of the original members of the Harlem Globetrotters who was billed as "the world's greatest dribbler."

"There were times when he'd asked me to write a guy a letter, and I always urged him to do it himself. He thought I was trying to duck some work, but I knew what an impact a personal note from him meant to people. He was always dropping notes and letters and postcards to sportswriters he knew in New York and Chicago, and places like that."

I mentioned to Kiely that Frank Thomas, the former home run hitter of the Pittsburgh Pirates, had told me a story about how Art Rooney had stood outside in the snow in a long line to attend the funeral of Frank's daughter, who was killed in a weird accident, falling down an elevator shaft.

"He wouldn't go ahead of people," said Kiely, nodding to affirm that story. "He'd stand out there. He thought that people would be upset if he went to the front of the line. He waited his turn. He didn't want any of that nonsense.

"There was never any set plot. He was never ever a running politician, except once, and he really wanted to be with these people in their time of grief. He'd talk to the widow, and tell her it was a time when she had to be strong. He'd boost the kids' spirits."

I recalled Mr. Rooney coming to my brother Dan's funeral, and how he went around the room and shook hands with everybody, talking in a whisper to everybody. "He'd stop and say hello," said Kiely. "He always had a nice word for you. I was there at your brother's funeral, so I know.

"If he was out of town, or couldn't make it himself, he didn't tell anyone else to go. You couldn't be a surrogate for him. He knew that didn't mean as much. But he'd ask Mary Regan (his secretary) to send a mass card, or something like that."

I asked Kiely which of Art's five sons was most like him. "None of them is completely like him," said Kiely. "You can see some of him in all of them. But he's not reincarnated in any of them. Timmy is close in some ways; like his interest in horses, and his easy laugh. But nobody completely. They all have the genes, but they don't have the full genes. Pat has always said, 'There's only one of my father.' I think John would go along with that."

Kiely contends that Art Rooney really became appreciated, and had more opportunities to do good things, after the Steelers started being a successful football team in the '70s.

"A lot of his personality was there, but it never got to full growth until the team got good," said Kiely. "He'd be on TV, and more guys would write about him, and they would write about the unique man he was. He started to get a lot of attention. People on a national basis got to know him. We'd travel by airplane, and we always rode coach. I was always siting on the outside so he could read, or get some sleep. But people would come up and ask him to sign something, and he always did.

"When we started winning Super Bowls, he became a well known person in the sports world. And people just loved him, and what he stood for. He did that TV commercial for United Way, and it was the biggest commercial United Way ever did. People could see what kind of guy he was with kids. And that only added to his image. He met every con man in America, but the guy he would help was the guy who needed help.

"He always wanted an open organization, and the media appreciated that. Guys would come in here from New York and LA, and they couldn't believe the access they had to our people, and the way they were treated. That started at the top, with Art, and the rest of us, Joe Gordon and I, took our cue from him. I always thought it was the best way, too. Art wanted us to have it as open as possible. 'Be open and honest,' he always said. And people talked about it."

Dan Rooney hired Chuck Noll. But Art Rooney believed Dan had done the right thing, even after Noll turned in a 1-13 record his first year.

"That's right," Kiely came back. "He told me, 'He's going to be OK.' I said, 'How can you say that?' He said, 'He's lost games, but he hasn't lost the team.'"

I asked Kiely why Rooney was often in the company of priests, and religious people. What was the attraction?

"Above all else, he had tremendous faith. And, out of that, he just respected the people who were involved in the Catholic faith, priests and nuns. He'd go out of his way to talk to them. His brother was a priest, and he'd been to the seminary himself in his youth."

I don't know what prompted me to ask Kiely about tough guys on the team, but he said Joe Greene and Dwight White were as tough as they came. It was Kiely, according to White, who also recognized that he had some smarts.

Kiely was kind of the club intellectual in residence, always reading books, and newspapers like the *New York Times, Washington Post, Boston Globe, Wall Street Journal* and magazines like the *National Review.* He encouraged White to check them out, and often quizzed him on current events and economic developments during road trips.

"But the baddest guy on the team had to be Ernie Holmes. 'Fats' was something else. The other guys were more afraid of him than Greene. Ernie lived on another planet. I was alone in the office the day (in 1973) Ernie started shooting that rifle at cars passing on the turnpike below. He didn't hit anybody, thank God. But the state trooper called, and said, 'We have a guy here named Holmes.' And I'm thinking, 'This can't be our guy.' The trooper tells me, 'He's from Texas.' Then I knew it was our guy. It was the Ohio state police calling. Ernie had been shooting at cars with a rifle. He had just flipped out.

"I remember another occasion when he was real moody, and Jack Lambert didn't like the way he was looking. Jack said to me, 'I'm getting the hell outta here. He's the only guy who's ever scared me to death.' He was a schizophrenic; he was a different guy.

"My kid, Timmy, worked at the training camp. 'Fats' talked in a strange language. He'd tell Timmy to do something, and Timmy was so scared he'd go out and never come back. 'Fats' referred to Art Rooney as 'The Big Man.' He'd come to me and want to borrow some money, or ask me to see if I could get him a raise. 'You're tight with The Big Man,' he'd say. 'See if you can get me some dust.' Noll was a good coach because he could have guys like 'Fats' — with his skull shaved to an arrowhead — and Andy Russell, a Phi Beta Kappa — and he could put them all together."

Jack Butler heads up the BLESTO NFL scouting combine, out of an office in downtown Pittsburgh. He grew up in Oakland, near Forbes Field, and had been a student in a seminary before sports won out over a religious life.

Butler was one of the best defensive backs in Steelers history, holding forth at cornerback from 1951 through 1959, and setting records that remained on the books until Mel Blount came along and broke most of them in the early '80s.

"You belong in the Pro Football Hall of Fame," Pat Livingston told him earlier in the season at a breakfast before the unveiling of Art Rooney's statue, "but you're never going to make it."

For too many years, Livingston pushed for Butler's induction into the Pro Football Hall of Fame, but was never successful in convincing enough of the other members of the selection committee to vote for Butler on their ballots.

Butler's 52 interceptions were the Steelers' standard for 24 years until Blount broke it with 57. But Blount required 14 seasons, compared to nine for Butler. Butler's single season record of 10 in 1957 stood up until Blount broke it with 11 in 1975. But Blount did that in 14 games while Butler did it in 12.

Butler still holds records for most interceptions in a game, with four on December 13, 1953 against the Washington Redskins, and for most yards interceptions returned in a career with 871, with Blount second-best with 736. Butler also shares records with Tony Compagno (1946-48) with three interception returns for touchdowns in a career, and for two TD returns on interceptions in a season with Compagno and Sam Washington (1984).

After Butler stopped by to say hello to old friends, he went to the private box of his best friend in football, Art Rooney Jr. Jack's wife, Bernie, is close with Kay Rooney, the wife of Art Rooney, Jr., and they frequently travel together.

Jackie Powell was, like Baldy Regan, a Damon Runyan character. Powell was standing in the walkway in the press box, standing in the same spot where he stands for all the Steelers' home games at Three Rivers Stadium. "I try to stand where I'm outta everyone's way," Powell pointed out.

Powell used to be a go-fer for Jack Sell, a sportswriter for the *Pittsburgh Post-Gazette*, who had died a few years earlier. Back then, Powell had a first row seat, right next to Sell. I had first met Powell and Sell when I was a student sportswriter at the University of Pittsburgh in the early '60s, when Powell would accompany Sell to cover Pitt basketball games. All the *P-G* sportswriters in those days had their own sidekicks at sports events they covered.

Sell was best known for covering the Steelers. He had a writing style all of his own. He always referred to Pitt as "Skyscraper U." and to the Panthers as "the Jungle Cats." He called the Steelers "Rooney U."

A lead paragraph for one of his stories might go like this: "Rooney U. is scheduled to take on the Maramen in an arc light scrimmage in the Gotham this coming Sabbath." That meant the Steelers were playing a pre-season exhibition against the Giants, owned by the Mara family, in a night game (or under the lights) in New York on Sunday.

Sell had grown up on the North Side, had been a boyhood friend of Art Rooney, and covered the club from its inception in 1933 till 1973. Sell retired, ironically enough, the year before the Steelers won their first Super Bowl. "Art Rooney took him to the Super Bowl anyhow," recalled Powell. "They were very close."

Powell, at 78 in 1990, had been an egg buyer for the A&P Supermarket chain before he retired. That was his job. At night, he moonlighted with Sell at sports events all over the city.

When we spoke before the Steelers' last home game of the 1990
schedule, against the Cleveland Browns, Powell was still the goal judge
for National Hockey League games at the Civic Arena, where the Pittsburgh Penguins play. "I'll keep at it as long as my blinkers are good,"
said Powell. He had been the goal judge for the Pittsburgh Hornets of
the American Hockey League at Duquesne Gardens in Oakland, starting that assignment in 1938.

He always wears a hat, an old-fashioned fedora. He wore it because
he was bald, and most of the buildings he worked in as a goal judge
had always been cold. "We used to wear a topcoat, too, when we worked
at Duquesne Gardens," he said. "Heck, the players wore sweaters."

Powell was a teenager in Shadyside and a student at Schenley High
School when Sell first asked him to accompany him to sports events to
help him out. "I remember telling him I'd have to ask my mother for
permission," said Powell.

He has lived in Lawrenceville just about ever since. "I remember
a night game in 1935 against the Chicago Bears at Forbes Field," he
said, "when the great Bronko Nagurski got hit by two Steelers on the
sidelines and was hurt.

"Jack wanted me to find out what Nagurski's health status was
at halftime. They didn't have all the sophisticated communication systems and information for writers that they do now in the press box. You
had to keep your own play-by-play and stats. It was different then. So
Jack sent me down to the Bears' locker room.

"George Halas came to the door to see what I wanted. I told him
'Mr. Sell sent me down to see how Nagurksi was doing and if he'd be
able to play in the second half.' Mr. Halas told me, 'He's down at the
other end of the locker room. You go down there and ask him for yourself.' I went down and Nagurski told me his shoulder was hurting, but
that he'd be back in there. 'It hurts a little bit when I breathe,' Nagurski told me, 'but I'll be in there.' Imagine doing that today?"

During the fall of 1989, I was watching my daughter, Rebecca, 12 at
the time, playing in an age-group soccer game in Upper St. Clair. A fellow came over and introduced himself as Bill Barry.

He and I had been talking to each other on the telephone, but had
never met each other. I had contacted him initially as a representative
of our Upper St. Clair-Bethel Park Rotary Club because we were going
to have a fund-raiser to assist the Barry family.

Bill's only son, Michael, an eighth-grader at Fort Couch Middle
School, the same school where Rebecca was a student, was suffering terribly from the ravaging effects of leukemia. He was dying, and Bill knew
that. But Bill didn't want to talk about that. Enough was enough. It
hurt too much. He wanted to talk sports. He needed a break.

We discovered that we were the same age — 47 then — and that we had both attended Catholic grade schools — he in Mt. Oliver and I in Hazelwood — and that we might have played against each other for our school football teams.

Bill knew that I had covered the Steelers. "I want to tell you a story about Art Rooney," he said, smiling.

"One day I was outside Three Rivers Stadium, and I saw the Steelers' sign outside their offices, and thought I'd see if I could meet Art Rooney. I had heard that he was really great with people, so I thought I'd give it a shot.

"I saw a security guard walking along in front of the office, and I asked him if he thought I could come in and say hello to Mr. Rooney. He said he'd see, and he went in and spoke to a secretary, and he came back out, and held the door open and told me to come with him.

"He escorted me to Mr. Rooney's office, where I met a secretary. She ushered me in to see Mr. Rooney. He told me to sit down, and we talked for quite a while. I was originally from the North Side, and he knew my uncle and cousins, and he started telling me stories about them. He offered me a cigar. We talked for about fifteen minutes. Now where else in this country could I get to see the owner of a pro football team like that? As I was leaving, he handed me four tickets to the Steelers' next football game. He said he'd see me then.

"At first, I didn't know what he meant. But when we got to the stadium, we checked with ushers to see where we were supposed to go. The next thing I know, I'm walking into a private box. It belonged to Mr. Rooney. He started introducing me to Tom Foerster and Pete Flaherty, who were County Commissioners then. He introduced me to them like I was an old friend of his. It was unbelievable. I'll never forget that."

In a similar vein, Bob Scott, who has published *Point* magazine, which promotes Pittsburgh to visitors and conventioneers in the city, told me about an experience he had at Three Rivers Stadium.

He was getting onto an elevator before a Steelers' game and noticed an older gentleman wearing a bright green jacket. "We rode up on an elevator with him. We were talking about how we didn't know exactly where our seats were," said Scott.

"Suddenly, the guy in the green jacket gets off the elevator with us, and starts explaining to us where our seats are. We must've looked confused because he ended up taking us to the area where we should be, like he was an usher or something.

"I thanked him and introduced myself. He introduced himself. It was John R. McGinley, the vice-president of the Steelers. I mentioned that I was from New Kensington. He told me he knew Tom Tannas, who was from New Kensington and promoted boxing and was the manager for Ezzard Charles, the heavyweight boxing champion. Mr. McGinley and Mr. Rooney had been in boxing promotions together. I was struck by what a quiet, unassuming gentleman Mr. McGinley was. And how nice he was to us. He was just like another Art Rooney."

410

Merril Hoge
"The Stormin' Mormon"

Merril Hoge was the most popular Pittsburgh Steeler of them all when it came to representing the team at sports dinners and luncheons, fund-raisers, autograph sessions, community service activities, hospital visits, you name it. His buddy, Bubby Brister, who dubbed him "the Stormin' Mormon" because he is a clean-living Mormon from Pocatello, Idaho, may have been more in demand, but none of the Steelers made as many public appearances as Hoge did.

Louis Lipps and Gary Anderson came close, according to Pat Hanlon, the former Steelers' community relations coordinator who fielded all the requests and made the assignments, but Hoge was at the head of the class. "He's a pleasure to work with," said Hanlon. "He's a beaut."

Hoge was a lot like the young Rocky Bleier in that he was white, with an All-American hometown boy appeal, humble as all get out, good-natured, and he had a nice sense of humor. He was a tenth round draft choice in 1987. He wasn't the fastest guy in the world, but what he did with his 6-2, 230 pound body made the opposition nervous. Fans liked his fire, and he liked their company. He handled himself well with a crowd, and had an impish lopsided grin.

"When I first came here from Idaho," Hoge was telling a crowd one night at a banquet at St. Agatha's Catholic Church in Bridgeville, just south of Pittsburgh, "I was asked to fill in at the last moment for one of our guys who had been scheduled to speak at a sports banquet. Pat Hanlon told me it was for a midget football league team. I remember thinking, 'Geez, I can't believe how big football is around Pittsburgh. They even have a football league for midgets.'"

To hear Hoge tell the story, you were not sure whether it was a joke, or just an honest revelation from a naive kid from the Rockies come to the big city.

Hoge had caught on in a hurry with Pittsburghers ever since his second season when he started to show signs of being able to contribute to the team's attack in many ways, as a never-say-die running back, as a reliable receiver, as somebody who will block for a teammate, and as a fierce, hard-working competitor in every capacity.

There was a lot of Bleier in him, there was a lot of his position coach, Dick Hoak, in him. In only his fourth pro season, and he did not see all that much action as a rookie, Hoge moved from 17th to 12th in team history for career rushing yards with 2,106. He passed some familiar and honored names in Steeler history in doing so: Joe Geri (1,500), Bill Dudley (1,505), Sidney Thornton (1,512), Earnest Jackson (1,921), and Lynn Chandnois (1,934).

In 1990, Hoge rushed for a career-best 772 yards, leading the Steelers in that statistical category for the first time, and he scored a career high ten touchdowns (seven rushing, and three on pass catches).

He was second to Lipps among receivers on the team, with 40 catches to Lipps' 50. Two years earlier, Hoge had made 50 catches himself, eclipsing a club record of 49 for a running back, set by Frenchy Fuqua in 1971. His 50 tied him with Lipps that year for the team leadership.

Hoge was something of an unknown in the National Football League before the Steelers qualified for the playoffs in 1989 and Hoge had two great nationally televised outings that put his name in the headlines, and educated people that his name is pronounced as Hodge.

In a wild-card playoff game against the Houston Oilers on December 31, Hoge gained 100 yards. A week later, at Denver, Hoge had the game of his life, rushing for 120 yards on 16 carries, with a personal best 45-yard touchdown run, and a career-high eight receptions for 60 yards. He became the first Steeler to rush for 100 or more yards in consecutive playoff games. Even Franco Harris had never done that.

In the Steelers' highlight film from that season, there is a segment showing Dennis Smith, a defensive back from the Broncos, declaring in a huddle, "That damn Hoge is kicking our ass." You can't get a better compliment than that in the NFL.

Bubby Brister could appreciate a remark like that. It sounded like one of his own. No one is higher on Hoge than Brister, or "the wild stallion," as Hoge called him.

"I expect him to do that every time out," Brister said, reflecting on Hoge's performance at Denver, in what was a disappointing defeat. "I expect him to run, catch and block.

"He's my roommate, my buddy. We talk about it all the time. It wasn't just a fluke. He's capable of doing that week-in and week-out. Maybe not a spectacular game like that, but he's capable of being steady, 80 to 120 yards, and making some catches. He's durable as hell and he's blocking better, too, this year."

At the outset of the 1990 training camp session, writers wanted to talk about that game at Denver with Hoge, but he was not eager to do that. "This is a whole new year," he said, sounding like a star student in the Chuck Noll School of Press Conferences. "I don't like to reflect on things. I think when you do that you get yourself in trouble because things aren't the same.

"You can't go out and say the same thing's going to happen as last year. It's not. It's just not going to happen."

Following Hoge's heroics in the 1989 playoffs, however, he was honored in his hometown of Pocatello, Idaho, where he had once been an all-Big Sky performer for Idaho State University. They did not hold a Merril Hoge Day in Pocatello. They had two days set aside to pay tribute to a native son. "If we won the Super Bowl," he said, "they might have a Merril Hoge Week out here. I hope so." The special days were Feb. 1-2.

Idaho Governor Cecil Andrus tried to explain the significance of the ceremony. "You folks in Pittsburgh are just getting to know Merril," he said. "I can't think of a finer American to be an ambassador for us in your part of the country. The way Merril lives his life with character and dignity and fairness and humility, he's an excellent example to young citizens everywhere."

Brister tagged along with his pal to Pocatello. "This is good for Merril," he said. "He's a good guy and he deserves it. He doesn't drink or smoke. He's very religious. He deserves everything that's happening."

Hoge told the assemblage, "Some little kids asked me if they were going to get out of school for 'your days.' I said no. They said it wasn't official then. Maybe when we win the Super Bowl they will be."

Overlooked, of course, was the fact that the Steelers had come up short that otherwise glorious day in Denver, dropping a 24-23 decision to the Broncos, who went on to play in the Super Bowl. The Broncos were embarrassed by the San Francisco 49ers, but the Steelers believe they could have gotten to the Super Bowl if they had gotten by the Broncos. So the defeat at Denver was a heart-breaker. The Steelers had come so close.

Chuck Noll, the Steelers' coach, said of Hoge's performance that day: "I have seen people run for more yards and have greater stats, but I have never seen anybody run with greater effort and determination. He exemplified the spirit of our whole team.

"You saw him breaking tackles and getting stuff on his own, and that's really the test of a good running back. He's one who will take it beyond what your blockers get for him."

That was an honor for Hoge, the supreme compliment, because it came from a coach he admires so much.

"I think everybody dreams of something like that, where everything comes together in a big game on TV," said Hoge. "I felt good about that. It's something that will stick with me.

"It was a dream, but all it did was make me work harder. We're not finished yet."

Hoge finished the season on a high note, with seven touchdowns in the final six weeks. But he remembered how it was at the start of the season, when nothing was going right, and that is why he admires Noll so much.

"Chuck Noll is the strength of this team and organization," he said. "Everybody was ready to write him off last year, but he was our only source of strength when we got beat 51-0 (by Cleveland) and 41-10 (by Cincinnati).

"We all walked into the locker room and thought, 'Wow. What's wrong with us?' But Coach Noll told us basically we just had to get back to work and things would get better. He had faith. He's the greatest coach I've ever seen, I know that."

That bad start in 1989 may have helped the Steelers steady a rocking, possibly sinking ship, at the start of the 1990 season. Joe Walton had come to the Steelers as the offensive coordinator and put in a whole new system. The Steelers could not seem to get the hang of it, and many, especially Brister, used it as an excuse when the Steelers' offensive unit failed to score a touchdown in the first four games of the schedule, and lost three of those games.

"Everybody was a little discouraged," said Hoge. "Everybody was throwing around the blame. We had to realize that players make the plays."

Asked if he was confused by the new offense, Hoge said, "I'm a lot more comfortable with it. I know the first couple of weeks it was like they snapped the ball and 'Uh, where do I go now?' You shouldn't be doing that."

Hoge remembered how Noll stuck with Walton, and supported him and his system. He remembered Noll squelched any revolt on the part of the players. He would have none of it.

"He just kept saying, 'This is what we're going to do. I believe in it. We've all got to believe this or this is not going to work.' That was part of the change-around. Chuck made us believe in that. He stood up to us and said, 'I don't care. You guys can moan all you want, but this is what I believe in and we're not going to fire Joe and we're not going back to the old system. We're going to change a few things, but you guys have got to make it happen.'

"He's an amazing coach, he really is. He's a unique individual," said Hoge, continuing to cite his coach's virtues. "His mental approach is amazing to me. He instills faith in everybody at times when you really may not have it. You question, 'Does he not see all our problems?' He saw them. He's stern and he's got faith and he knows what he's doing. He knows about this game."

After the Steelers beat the Browns at Three Rivers Stadium in the last home game of the season, Hoge was interviewed by Sam Nover on the "Fifth Quarter" show on WPXI-TV. It was mentioned to Hoge that Chuck Noll had been given a game ball, for the second week in a row. Noll had gotten it the week before after the Steelers beat the New England Patriots for his 200th career victory.

"He's the strength of our team," said Hoge, explaining why the Steelers had given him the game ball. "It's through him that all these things are accomplished. Giving him the game ball is like saying it was a team effort."

After a 27-7 loss to the 49ers in San Francisco at mid-season, Hoge said, "I watched them play. I watched how hard they play. I watched how they capitalized on our mistakes — and they didn't make many themselves — and how that's got to be done to be a winner."

Hoge had an idea of the legacy he wanted to leave behind in Pittsburgh. He was very active in the Pittsburgh community, including serving as honorary chairman for the Junior Achievement Bowlathon in 1989 and the Multiple Sclerosis Ugly Bartender Contest. He was co-chairman in 1990 with teammate Carnell Lake for Blue Cross Caring Team, and was involved with the Epilepsy Foundation and the Steelers' Christmas food distribution.

"The image I want to create is being an all-around back and an all-around contributor to the community and its needs," he said. "I think this offense is going to make me the kind of player I want to be, a complete running back. I know I have the ability to play a long time in this league.

"I'm very sold on the situation we have here. I have a better feeling than I've had since I've been here. I can feel it all around the team, too."

He feels that he and Tim Worley can work out the problems that have nipped at them, and that they can be one of the best running tandems in the league.

"Tim and I look at each other as a good backfield, one that wants to get better, and we are not going to compare ourselves to Franco and Rocky, for they were tremendous when they played, and we don't want to be compared to them.

"We just want to be the best that we can. As long as we can be that, and push each other, we will be a good backfield. You just have to go out there and be your own self, and not try to be somebody else, for when you do that you get into trouble. You can only take care of yourself, and only be yourself. So there is no sense in us trying to be Franco and Rocky, for we aren't.

"We have the ability to be two great backs. Both of us pull for each other. We block for each other. We make each other better."

Hoge has a big fan in Hoak, the Steelers' backfield coach. "I think he's only going to get better," said Hoak. "He's a good, tough player. He does all the right things — he can block, run well and break tackles. He's not a great speed guy, but he does all the things you ask of him."

Before the 1989 season, Hoge handicapped himself this way: "I guess I'm a little bit of an overachiever. I'm under-rated a lot of times. But I know one thing. There's not a running back in the league who can do more than I can do. I've just got to work harder at it. I'm tremendously quick for my size. I use my power and quickness to my advantage."

Hoge had a difficult time at the start of his career with the Steelers. For one thing, he had played on a losing team (2-9) at Idaho State, and did not attract the attention of many scouts. That is why he was drafted on the 10th round.

During his second season with the Steelers, he screwed up a lot as the up blocker on the punt teams, and had to share the blame for four blocked punts by Harry Newsome. Hoge's base salary was $70,000 that season, so the Steelers didn't have a lot invested in him. But Noll stuck with Hoge and it had paid off.

"I want to establish myself as someone they have faith in that they can count on no matter what," said Hoge.

When Hoge talked about being a hard worker, he was being honest. He took a little break at the end of the season, and started working out

415

four days a week in earnest, and then stepped that up to five days just before the opening of the summer training camp.

"I think you paint a picture of what the NFL is like," he said. "You think it's all glory and stuff. I knew there was going to be a lot of hard work, but you don't realize how much behind the scenes work there is.

"None of that is new to me. I've always been a hard worker. It has kind of been my trademark. I learned a long time ago if you're going to get anywhere in life, you have to pay the price."

Merril Hoge

Dick Hoak and Dick Haley
Loyal Steelers Sons

It only seemed that Dick Hoak and Dick Haley had been with the Steelers forever. But they both had been associated with the Steelers all but a year or so apiece since the team resided at Three Rivers Stadium, going into the 1991 season, and they remember what it was like when the Steelers played at Pitt Stadium.

Both also played at Pitt Stadium as collegians, Hoak as a backup quarterback and running back for Penn State, and Haley as a starting running back and defensive back for the hometown Panthers. Both were from Western Pennsylvania — Hoak from Jeannette and Haley from Midway. Their success surprised some people.

Both were undersized as far as football players were concerned, about 5-10 or so. Both were strong, silent types, not given to telling war stories, just providing loyal service to the organization. They have had opportunities to go elsewhere, and had been tempted at times, but in the end they stayed, through thick and thin.

"I was told I was too small, too slow," said Hoak of his playing days. "So I figured I better learn what we're doing, and make sure I'm in the right place."

They were the sort of individuals team president Dan Rooney had in mind when he spoke about the Steelers having "good people" in the organization. They were company men.

During the 1990 season, Hoak had been with the Steelers for 30 seasons, 20 as the offensive backfield coach. He played 10 seasons with the Steelers, his last in 1970 for a second-year head coach named Chuck Noll. Hoak was named the Steelers' backfield coach in 1972 after one year as a high school coach in Wheeling. Hoak was the only assistant coach remaining from the four Super Bowl championship squads.

Haley had a total of 25 seasons with the Steelers, four as a player (1961-64) and the previous 21 as the director of player personnel. He was named to that position in 1971.

He had worked in Pittsburgh for the BLESTO scouting combine since 1966, and after five years with that group he joined the Steelers' front office. He was there through the drafts that developed the Steelers' Super Bowl teams.

They were both members of the Steelers' 1963 team that went into the final game of the season with a shot at the NFL's Eastern Division title, but lost to the Giants at Yankee Stadium, 33-17.

That was as close as they came to being champions until they were part of the organization that dominated the league in the decade of the '70s.

Both have a special affection for Franco Harris, whom they regard as the key guy who got the Steelers over the hump and into the playoffs and Super Bowls.

There was a framed print of a drawing of Franco Harris hanging on the wall opposite the desk of Dick Haley in his office in the middle of the personnel and scouting department segment of the Steelers' complex at Three Rivers Stadium.

When I asked Haley who was the best draft choice the Steelers made during his tenure, he quickly responded, "Franco Harris had to be No. 1. Jack Lambert came close. There was a long debate about the attributes of Harris versus some other prospects. It was not a clear-cut choice by any stretch of the imagination. Getting him wasn't easy. It was a delicate issue. It turned out to be the right choice."

It is a matter of record that Noll was holding out for Robert Newhouse, who eventually became a very solid running back for the Dallas Cowboys. "Franco clearly turned things around for us. He was the final piece in the puzzle. He had to play. You knew he had to play. He put us over the top. The Steelers had made good first round draft picks before I came on board in Joe Greene and Terry Bradshaw, and they had people like L.C. Greenwood, Mel Blount, Andy Russell, Ray Mansfield, Rocky Bleier and Jon Kolb and had built the foundation. But I feel Franco is one we weren't sure about, and we made the right pick."

Because of the outstanding success of some of those draft choices, however, most of the draft classes since the Steelers started winning Super Bowls have been held up to scrutiny and criticism, as if the Steelers' scouting department was not doing as good a job anymore.

"We're not the first organization to have to go through that," countered Haley. "It's a learning process. No matter who you are or how good you are, you have to prepare for that.

"There are different ways to cope with it. Because the standards were so high, it's difficult to keep coming up with good classes. The better you get and the higher you finish in the standings, the later you start picking in the draft. You don't get the same shot at quality players you know will be successful in the NFL. A lot of the time they're gone before your turn comes. We had so many good players here, and won so many games. It looked like it was easy. And it's not."

Haley was asked if there also was a lot of luck involved when the Steelers selected so many good players in the draft. The 1974 draft, for example, included Lynn Swann, Jack Lambert, John Stallworth, Jim Allen and Mike Webster in the first five rounds.

"I agree," said Haley. "You've got to have some luck going for you. No matter how well you prepare, you've got to have some luck. We talked with John Stallworth, for instance, and we thought he might be a good first round pick. But we also thought we could get him later. We took that chance. We got him on the fourth round. That's being lucky. The thing that really makes that 1974 draft stick out is that we had no third round choice. We had two fourth round picks. And we were picking around 20th. It's hard to imagine that you could do better than that.

"There's some luck involved when a Lynn Swann, who was our No. 1 pick that year, turns out the way he did. You never know guys are going to turn out that way. You have to guess a little bit."

418

The Steelers didn't always draft the way most other teams did. They often went for smaller offensive linemen, looking for quicker, mobile blockers who could play Chuck Noll's trap-blocking offense. They had one of the best linebacking groups in the history of the game, yet they were smaller than most. Haley said Jack Ham was about 207, Jack Lambert 202 and Andy Russell 210 or 212 when they were drafted.

"They were good in college," said Haley. "That factor overrides everything else."

That accounts for how the Steelers drafted Jerry Olsavsky, an undersized linebacker at Pitt, who has been a terrific performer on special teams and as a reserve linebacker in recent seasons. Olsavsky comes from a tough town, Youngstown, Ohio, that has always turned out good football players.

He follows a tradition of lightweight linebackers with the Steelers. Noll, himself a former lightweight lineman and linebacker, always has said scouts put too much emphasis on size and speed and athleticism and too little on whether a guy can play.

"There are guys like Jerry O who manage to win at everything they do," said Noll.

"Jerry's probably an ideal example of that," said John Fox, the Steelers' defensive backfield coach who was at Pitt when Olsavsky was there. "When we took him, people probably didn't give him much of a chance. He's been through that since the beginning of his career and he's proven himself at the highest level."

There are limitations, however, Haley insists. "No matter how good you are," he said, "you can't be 5-10 and play defensive tackle. But if a guy is a great college football player, he has a chance."

Haley was a 5-10 halfback at Pitt, yet he was able to play professional football. "He was a great athlete at Pitt," recalled Henry Suffoletta, a teammate at Pitt. "He could play every sport so smoothly. He was a terrific baseball and basketball player, too. I remember once we were in a tough football game at Nebraska, and our quarterback couldn't get the play out in the huddle he was so emotionally caught up in the game. Haley didn't hesitate to make the calls in our huddle. He was such a quiet guy, but he was a leader just the same. And a cool competitor."

I asked Haley how come the Steelers had not selected more Pitt players during the previous decade. During the Steelers' early years, Art Rooney and his coaches were always picking Pitt and Duquesne players to fill out their draft lists. But they managed to miss a good one in the mid-50s, a linebacker named Joe Schmidt, who went on to a Pro Football Hall of Fame career with the Detroit Lions.

In addition to Dan Marino, Pitt had produced the likes of Tony Dorsett, Bill Maas, Chris Doleman, Jimbo Covert, Bill Fralic, Jim Sweeney, Jeff Delaney, Russ Grimm, Mark May, Rob Fada and Carlton Williamson, to mention a few who ended up playing in the NFL.

Were they too close to Pitt to be objective in their scouting?

"That's a good question," said Haley. "I don't have the answer for it. We never had a chance on the great ones that got away, but we missed a few. Certainly we missed on Marino. We didn't think we needed a quarterback at the time. If you knew he was going to be that dominant you certainly would have taken him no matter who else you had.

"We had him come down here to the Stadium and we worked him out. Everybody liked him. Steve Fedell was helping us with our scouting that year, and he had been a teammate and good friend of Marino's at Pitt. Maybe we were looking too much to find faults. We got Gabe Rivera with the 12th pick on the first round that year, and Danny went to the Dolphins on the 27th pick. So nearly everybody passed on Marino in that first round. Five other quarterbacks were taken before him. Bradshaw was saying he was going to play five more years, and that ended up being his last year. But who knew?"

Haley felt Marino may have profited from a change of scenery because some Pittsburghers had soured on him during his senior season, and Haley also felt Marino benefited from having a coach like Don Shula, and playing in a tropical city like Miami. "He got the shot to play there right away," said Haley, "and that had to help him."

The Steelers' 1990 draft class was considered a risky one, starting with the No. 1 pick, Eric Green of Liberty University. After all, Liberty University is not Notre Dame.

"We didn't consider that a big reach," said Haley. "He had great talent. We worked him out ourselves, and we had a lot of help as far as recommendations were concerned. His coach was Sam Rutigliano, who had been the head coach in Cleveland."

As the head coach of the Browns, a team that had a terrific tight end for so many years in Ozzie Newsome, surely Rutigliano recognized a talented tight end when he saw one.

"Plus, one of the assistants at Liberty was Bob Leahy, who had played here with us," said Haley, "and he gave Green high marks in most every category.

"There are questions people like that can answer for you. What was he like? What kind of person is he? Will he accept the challenge?"

I mentioned to Haley how I had learned so much about the early backgrounds and upbringing of the great Steelers from the Super Bowl years, and how there seemed to be many common denominators relating to family and early influences.

"We're more into that now," said Haley. "The more people you can talk to about a guy the better off you're going to be. You have to find people who really know them. As someone who started out as an area scout (for the NFL's BLESTO scouting combine), I know how important contacts can be. You go to the position coach, and you talk to the trainer, the weight coach, anyone who can give you some insight. You want to know if there's any negative stuff."

There were some other players the Steelers picked in the early rounds in 1990 that some might consider reaches, but Haley didn't see it that way. "We had a couple of drafts where we reached, and didn't go with basics," he said. "I think we've gotten back to basics."

Mike Wagner

Jerry Olsavsky

Steelers' scouting staff in 1980 included (back row left to right) Bob Schmitz, Art Rooney Jr., Dick Haley and (front row) Joe Krupa, Tom Modrak and Bill Nunn Jr.

One of the best players Haley has ever secured for the Steelers was Gary Anderson, the team's highly productive place-kicker. Anderson is as good a kicker as there has ever been in the National Football League. How the Steelers managed to get Anderson shows how much luck is an important factor in finding the right players.

Going into the 1982 draft, Haley and the other Steeler scouts, were high on Anderson, a senior at Syracuse University. But he was drafted by the Buffalo Bills before the Steelers thought of selecting him.

Haley went to see one of the Bills' pre-season games that year. He was sitting in the stands, with his wife, Carolyn, when a field goal kick by Anderson sailed wide by a foot. That is when, ironically enough, Haley knew he had found the kicker of his dreams. He turned to his wife and said, "I think we'll get him."

A week later, in September, 1982, the Buffalo Bills gave up on Anderson, and put him on waivers. He had been 0-for-5 as a field goal kicker during the pre-season schedule. So they kept Mike Nick-Mayer, and let go of Anderson whom Paul Zimmerman of *Sports Illustrated* has written: "might be the best field goal kicker ever."

The Steelers knew Pitt's David Trout was not the answer. He had been so inconsistent during the 1981 season.

Anderson is now the Steelers' all-time leading scorer and has moved ahead of Roy Gerela in all the significant field goal and extra-point placement categories. In a hard-fought 9-6 victory over the New Orleans Saints at the Superdome during the 1990 schedule, Anderson accounted for all the Steelers' points, including a game-winning 26-yard field goal with 1:06 left to play.

"He wasn't our draft pick," said Haley, "but he has to be one of the most important players we've ever brought here. We wish we would've drafted him."

Anderson did not get off to the best start with the Steelers, either. The ball slipped through his holder's hands on his first extra point attempt. Two defenders slipped through to block his first field goal attempt. This was on Monday Night football, no less.

But Anderson made three field goals that night, one with two minutes remaining, to clinch the victory, 36-28 at Dallas. "Coming through that tough time, I'll always remember," Anderson said. "Lambert, Bradshaw and Franco were guys I'd watched in college, and now they were giving me a game ball, and I couldn't believe it. Things went from bad to pretty good in half a game. I was fortunate."

Ask Noll about Anderson and he'll say, "We just got lucky. Better to be lucky than smart."

Haley agrees: "It helps when you can sign some free agents, or get people who can help you in the late rounds of the draft. Guys like Glen Edwards. He was a free agent, and he really played great ball for us (1971-77). In the low round of the draft, if you can find one or two people it's a real achievement.

"Mike Wagner was a great low pick (No. 11 in 1971 from Western Illinois. More recently, John Jackson was a great low pick (No. 10 in 1988 from Eastern Kentucky)."

Haley could have added L.C. Greenwood, who came before Haley was working in the player personnel department, who was a 10th round draft pick out of Arkansas AM&N (now Arkansas-Pine Bluff) in 1969.

Some of the Steelers' No. 1 picks the previous few years had come under fire from the media and many of the fans. The early returns by Tim Worley (1989), Aaron Jones (1988) and John Rienstra (1986) were not good. Everybody was much higher on Eric Green (1990), Rod Woodson (1987) and Louis Lipps (1984). Darryl Sims (1985) was the biggest bust of the bunch.

"The best players get three or four looks from your different scouting people," said Haley. "In the last rounds, only one or two scouts have seen them.

"We think we have to take the best players available from now on. You have to stay away from filling out a roster. You have to stay with people who have some ability.

"Over the last four years, we have gotten 36 new players. A high percentage have come through the draft. We've had higher picks the past few years. When you get the 7th or 9th pick in the first round you should get some quality people. We've done a pretty good job in the middle and later rounds."

As examples, he mentioned Carlton Hasselrig, a 12th round nose tackle from Pitt-Johnstown (wrestling team); Justin Strzelczyk, an 11th round offensive tackle from Maine; Merril Hoge, 10th round running back from Idaho State; Richard Bell, 12th round running back/receiver from Nebraska. "They are all quality football players," said Haley.

Haley was asked if the Steelers made the mistake of holding onto some of their superstars from the glory days beyond their best years. "Maybe we kept a few guys we shouldn't have kept," he conceded.

One of the most famous situations of that kind was when the Steelers held onto Dwight White for the 1979 season when they were enamored with Dwaine Board, a fifth round defensive end from North Carolina A&T whom George Perles had picked as "the sleeper" in that summer's camp at St. Vincent.

Dan Rooney always defends that decision by reminding people that the Steelers won the Super Bowl at the end of that season, so that no one should second-guess the makeup of the squad. Board ended up being one of the best pass rushers in the NFL for several Super Bowl-winning San Francisco 49er teams. The Steelers spent high draft choices the next few seasons trying to find a pass rusher.

They thought they had one in 1983 when they passed on Pitt's Danny Marino to grab Gabe Rivera, a defensive lineman from Texas Tech.

"If you don't let Dwaine Board go, and if you don't get Gabe Rivera hurt. . ." said Haley. "And if you don't go after a Darryl Sims. . ."

Sims was a defensive end at Wisconsin whom the Steelers selected with their No. 1 draft choice in 1985. He was a bust, as was Keith Gary of Oklahoma in 1981. "We felt we had to get a defensive lineman," Haley said in explaining those choices that went awry.

"The bottom line in grading a draft is still how well they play. If you have great physical traits and you don't play well, who's at fault?

"When we had the great players, we took more chances in the draft. We didn't need marginal players, so we reached. We took some chances. If he comes through, he'll improve us. But that hurt us; there's a real danger there. The best route is still to take the good football player."

Hoak, the Steelers' running back coach, recalls that Franco's first impression with most people in the Steelers' organization was not a positive one. "We thought we had a real dud on our hands," said Hoak. "In his first pro start, he gained 35 yards and fumbled twice in a loss at Cincinnati in the second game of the season."

Midway through his rookie season, Harris turned it on. He had six straight 100-yard games (equalling Jim Brown's NFL record). The Steelers won nine of ten games to get a playoff berth for the first time in the 40-year history of the franchise.

In the AFC playoffs, Harris made the play that will never be forgotten, catching a deflected pass and thundering 42 yards for the game-winning touchdown against Oakland in what was labeled "The Immaculate Reception." Harris was always so productive in the playoffs, and was the MVP in Super Bowl IX.

Hoak was a high school football star at Jeannette, leading the Jayhawks to a WPIAL title as a quarterback, and has lived in neighboring Greensburg ever since he started playing football for the Steelers. He is at home there. "My family is there, and my friends are there, so I'm happy there," he said. "I've always been able to come home every night."

When we initially spoke at mid-season, he mentioned that his mother, Regina, was still living there, but was "real sick." She died on Friday night before the Steelers were to leave the next day for New Orleans. Hoak stayed behind for the funeral. The Steelers awarded him a game ball after they beat the Saints, 9-6, in a thriller.

Hoak said he left his home at 6:45 a.m. each day. He said it took him about 70 to 75 minutes to get to the Stadium. No one is closer to the team's camp at St. Vincent in Latrobe. "I can get there in ten or 15 minutes from my house," he said.

Asked why he had never left the Steelers for other job opportunities, including a chance to be the head coach of the Pittsburgh Maulers in the United States Football League, he said, "I never felt anyplace else would have been as good as what I had here," he said. "I enjoyed working for the Rooneys and Chuck Noll. I had talked with assistants elsewhere, and I knew I had a better situation here. Chuck doesn't burn out his assistants. We have a sane schedule.

Dick Hoak as Steelers' halfback

Steelers' 1963 backfield included Dick
Hoak (42) with John Henry Johnson (35),
Ed Brown (15) and Bob Ferguson (46).

Comparing notes are coaches Joe Paterno of Penn State, Hoak and Chuck Noll.

"I like working for Chuck. He wants to win, but his family and your family come first. He doesn't believe in staying in the office until one or two in the morning, or sleeping in the office.

"When Chuck comes in in the morning, he starts working on football. He has no time to answer all the calls, or answer all the mail. With him, it's football business right from the start. We don't sit around waiting for him to join us.

"I enjoy working here. I've stayed because we have been winners, because we won four Super Bowls. I've stayed because of the people and the organization I work for. I've stayed because I've loved every minute of it. This is where I'm from. This is where I've spent 30 years."

Sometimes Hoak looks as if he has spent 300 years with the Steelers. He has a tired, bored look about him. Each year he has the worst photo in the team's press guide. It looks like he was stirred from his coffin to pose for the shot. "He looks like a cadaver," says Pat Livingston, who covered the Steelers for *The Pittsburgh Press* when Hoak was playing for them, and loves the guy. Hoak has a way of cocking his head, and angling his pitch-black eyebrows that suggest a guy checking you out under a microscope.

Looks are deceiving. Hoak has a fire in him, and it still burns. He wants to win. He likes to work with winners. He helps them get that way. He is most supportive.

When Noll was asked once why he hired Hoak, who had posted a 1-9 record in his one season as the head coach at Wheeling Central Catholic, Noll said, "Because of Hoak's attitude as a player, and his interest in football. And because he is smart."

Asked what he considered to be his strengths as a coach, Hoak said, "I can get along with players. I understand them and they know where I'm coming from. I played the game not too long ago, and I know what they're going through. I understand some of the things that are happening to them on the field.

"I think you have to pat them on the back and you have to kick them in the butt, but you can't do it every day. It means more when you do it at the right time. You have to know the people you're working with. I think they believe in me.

"Loyalty is another of my strengths. That's another thing. I know what Chuck wants. Being with him so long, I have learned a lot about the running game through Chuck."

Hoak demonstrated that loyalty he was speaking about when asked if he thought Noll was still fired up about football. "He hasn't lost any of his enthusiasm for the game," said Hoak. "He's always looking for new things, things that will help us win. Whether it's offense or defense or special teams, he's always looking for an edge. He'll come in here talking about something he saw in a college game on TV, and he'll be all excited about it."

I mentioned to Hoak how John Fox, the Steelers' second-year defensive backfield coach and Tom Ricketts, a second-year offensive tackle, who had both come from Pitt to the Steelers said they were amazed at how calm and supportive Noll remained when things were not going right, a real contrast to their experience with Mike Gottfried at Pitt. Gottfried would get after everybody in the program after a setback, and blame everybody for what went wrong.

"I have never seen Chuck do that," he said. "Hey, Chuck will get upset, but he's not going to yell and scream at everybody in the room. He's never lost his composure. I've never seen him fly off the handle in a blind rage.

"He's the best I've seen as far as leadership goes. He never lets them believe that they can't win. This year, when things got off badly, he just kept telling them they could still win, that we had to work on some things, and get things right.

"Some people want to be accountants or salesmen. Others want to be politicians. That work never interested me. All through school, I looked ahead to the day when I could coach football or teach. That was my life."

"I remember when Chuck first came," said Hoak. "It was all business. It was completely different from what I had experienced before. You knew from the first couple of meetings that it was going to change."

Before was Buddy Parker and Bill Austin and South Park and mostly disappointment, though the players enjoyed themselves, and their good fortune in being professional football players.

Hoak is one of the few people still on the Steelers' scene who spent time at South Park when the Steelers practiced there. "The move to Three Rivers Stadium was very important in the development of this team," he said. "I can't imagine how we survived at South Park. We'd go out at lunchtime and be on our own to get a meal. Guys would have hamburgers and a few beers. We'd go back and they'd be showing us film, and guys couldn't even stay awake. It was primitive. Thank God we're not there any longer."

As Chuck Noll's 200th career victory was in reach late in the 1990 campaign, Hoak reflected on that first year. Noll's first victory as the Steelers' head coach came on Sept. 21, 1969 — a 16-13 decision over the Detroit Lions in the season opener. That would turn out to be the Steelers' only win of the season. They were on their way to a 1-13 record.

"I didn't play in that first game because I was hurt," Hoak said. "But I'll never forget that game. The pressure was on Chuck because he was the new guy in town and everybody was still calling us the 'Same Old Steelers.' During the game, you could see things weren't going to be the same under Chuck. We hung in there to win. But it was the way we won that had people talking. I was excited and I know the players were. It didn't turn out to be a great season. If you look at the record. We lost 13 in a row. But the players knew things would be turning around. We lost to some good teams. Some were close. But nobody beat us bad."

Hoak's memory may be questioned in that regard. There were some close ones, for sure. The Steelers lost to the New York Giants (10-7 and 21-17), Cleveland (41-31), Washington (14-7), Green Bay (38-34), Dallas

(10-7) and New Orleans (27-24). But there were also some blowouts to Philadelphia (41-27), Chicago (38-7), Minnesota (52-14) and St. Louis (47-10). How had Hoak forgotten?

Hoak played one more season, in 1970, when the Steelers won five games, before he retired as a player. "I was almost sorry I was retiring," said Hoak. "There was a new, positive atmosphere around here that we hadn't had before. But it was my time."

Hoak came back in 1972 to be an assistant coach. "I saw a great difference when I came back after being away a year. "Joe Greene and Terry Bradshaw were already here. George Perles and Bud Carson came as coaches. And we drafted some good players; one of them was Franco Harris.

"What impressed me right off was the players. They were bigger, faster, more talented than the guys I had played with. This was Chuck's team. You sensed positive things were going to happen. The next year, we put it together. We added more good players. And Chuck kept it up. He was a disciplinarian. And he wanted to win."

Why has Noll been so successful?

"Chuck Noll came in here and knew what he wanted to do and how he wanted to do it. He didn't let people talk him out of it or change his mind," said Hoak.

"Chuck made decisions. And he kept going until he got the players he needed to play this game his way. It's always been that way. Chuck never changes.

"I think the big thing Chuck does is judge people. He stayed with players when other people were critical. But those guys paid off. He was good at recognizing talent and staying with them.

"Rocky Bleier was just one of them. Rocky came back from Vietnam and he could hardly run. Chuck saw the quality in Rocky, so he stuck with him. Rocky Bleier went on to become a fine player. He wasn't the best we had, but he played a big role for us in winning four Super Bowls. Some coaches would have given up on Rocky. Chuck didn't. He gave him a second chance.

"And there was L.C. Greenwood. He was 6-7, but he weighed only 225 pounds when he came to training camp. People looked down on L.C., but Chuck saw the potential nobody else saw. He knew L.C. was strong, and fast. And he knew L.C. could put on weight. So Chuck stayed with L.C. The rest is history."

Hoak's theory is that Noll has not tried to please other people, and has continued to do it his way, which he believes is the right way.

"Chuck is Chuck. He hasn't changed much in the way he does things. And you have to admire him for that. He operates on an even keel. You don't see him sky high one week and way down the next week. He never loses his players."

Of all the backs Hoak has worked with, Franco Harris had to be his favorite. "It's unfortunate what happened to him at the end," he said. "I hated to see that. It never should have happened."

Franco Harris

Rocky Bleier

Favorites of Dick Haley and Dick Hoak were Mike Webster (52), Rocky Bleier (20) and Franco Harris (32).

429

When I mentioned to him that several of the outstanding Steelers had said Franco was the one who made the biggest difference in the team, Hoak shook his head affirmatively. "I believe that," he said.

"We needed a big, strong back and Franco was that man. I wasn't here when they drafted him. They got him early in the year and I came in April. He was unique. He weighed 225 pounds, but he ran like a 195 pounder. He had the power of a big man. He had great vision. He could break tackles. We never had a player like him.

"Rocky would hit the hole quicker than Franco. But a lot of times there wouldn't be a hole, and Franco would find one. They (the offensive linemen) may have enjoyed blocking more for Rocky, but Franco made them a good offensive line. He made them look good even if they didn't open a hole.

"Soon after he got into the starting lineup in 1972, I recall we had a draw play to the left, and there was no hole there. He came back to the right and went 70 yards to the two-yard line at Three Rivers Stadium, and we scored soon after."

Why was Franco so special?

"Franco wanted to excel. Whatever he did, he wanted to be a great football player. He wanted to be the best there was. Every day I'd tell myself, 'Don't overcoach him.' If Franco had to hop to do a particular move, then you let him hop. He was different. He didn't want anybody hitting him or tackling him at practice. He didn't want to take a beating. He wanted to preserve himself. Every time he'd take a handoff at practice, he'd run the ball 40 yards. He wanted to get used to running for long touchdowns. He had great acceleration, but it was the vision that set him apart. It was like he knew where everybody was on the field, and he found a way to avoid them.

"You try to tell the guys today how he ran down the field on every handoff. These guys stop after five yards. But he'd run all the way. He got used to scoring touchdowns. He did it every time he took the ball in practice.

"He never asked for any special favors. He didn't act like a star. It's like no one ever told him he was a star. I'd love to coach a million like him."

That is what people used to say about Dick Hoak when he was a player. After the 1990 season, he still ranked fifth among the Steelers' all-time rushers. His best season was 1968 when he finished fourth in the NFL in rushing with 858 yards and he played in the Pro Bowl that year. He completed seven of 16 passes for 188 yards as the Steelers could pitch the ball to him and let him run the option play. He had a game that year at Pitt Stadium in which he gained 166 yards on 16 attempts, including a 77-yard touchdown run in a 16-12 loss to New Orleans. Bobby Layne, the Steelers' quarterback then, said, "You take all those guys with the fast feet and their long strides. Give me a half dozen guys like Hoak, guys who like to hit."

430

When you ask Hoak what kind of players he prefers, he says, "We look for a guy who wants to hit, a team player, someone who wants to win. If he is willing to block, to learn, his physical stature may not be as significant.

"We know we can't teach them how to run. That's natural. But we do spend a lot of time in blocking and pass catching drills. Those are two phases of the game that most outstanding backs in college don't know. They were never required to block or receive, and they are behind in those areas."

Dick Hoak is happy in Pittsburgh. "When I was a player, and I'd had a couple of good years, and people used to ask me, 'Don't you wish you were playing for the Green Bay Packers or the New York Giants?' And I would say, 'No.' I was comfortable here. I liked Mr. Rooney. Dan was just getting involved, and I liked him. I always was proud to be a Pittsburgh Steeler. I've always been comfortable here."

The Monroeville Dapper Dan Club in 1968 honored these Pittsburgh sports celebrities (left to right): Fritzie Zivic, former welterweight boxing champion; Ted Kwalick, Penn State All-America; Dick Hoak, Steelers' running back; Zeke Shumaker, Pitt assistant coach; Paul Martha, Steelers' defensive back; Joe L. Brown, general manager of the Pirates.

Art Rooney Jr.
"No one is The Chief"

Art Rooney Jr., 55 during the 1990 season, has his own private box at Three Rivers Stadium, and usually has Jack Butler, 62, and Bill Nunn, 65, in it with him during the Steelers' home games. Butler, the head of the NFL's BLESTO scouting combine, and Rooney have scouted college players together for years. Nunn retired several years earlier after working in the Steelers' personnel department for 18 years. He and Art and Dick Haley and Tim Rooney, Art's cousin, headed up the Steelers' scouting department during the team's glory decade of the '70s.

Sometimes Art's brother, also Tim Rooney, comes in from Yonkers, New York, where he heads the family's harness racing track there, and sits in the box. Rip Scherer, a high school football coach for many years, is usually there, along with invited high school coaches. Art Jr.'s wife, Kay, sits with other family members in another box. There are no women in his box. "Women corrupt serious football," said Art Rooney Jr.

"She sits in my dad's old box with members of the family and the clergy. My dad's gone, but the clergy remain."

Art Jr., the second oldest of the five Rooney boys, was fired in a shocking move by his brother Dan, the team president, on Jan. 6, 1987. Art looks at those about him in the box and says, "We're history now."

Dan had wanted Art Jr. to bow out gracefully, to go quietly in the night, as if the new assignment was something he had sought and would be pleased with, but Art Jr. wouldn't go along with that. He was upset and objected to the transfer, and voiced his displeasure in the local papers. There was a rift in the Rooney family, and Art Jr. wanted everybody to know it. He resented what was going on. He went to his father to intercede, but got nowhere. That had to hurt.

Asked why he didn't go along with Dan's request to go without any public complaint, Art Jr. said, "I'm not going to talk about that. It's family business. It's too personal."

Art Jr. has not stirred up any controversy, or been critical of his brother, since he shifted offices. He has been quiet.

For whatever reason, Art Jr., rubbed Chuck Noll the wrong way, and had too much to say to the media to suit some in the organization. When the move was made, it depressed his dad who retreated to the family horse farm in Winfield, Maryland, about 35 miles west of Baltimore, to mourn the separation.

Art Jr. retains his financial interest in the team, still draws a salary and expense money, and looks after the family's real estate and some of its business interests, as well as some of his own business interests. He does some scouting, mainly for his own amusement. It is a habit that has been hard for him to kick. He is well off. He lives in a large home in Mt. Lebanon, and the family has a get-away place at a resort area in Deep Creek, Maryland.

Frank Lewis of Grambling, Steelers' No. 1 draft pick in 1971, with Art Rooney Jr.,
then head of Steelers' scouting department.

But he is a changed man. And he is continuing to change, trying to wean himself away from football. "Football is addictive and it's difficult to give up," he said. "This was the first year I didn't review tapes of college prospects. I had somebody else do it."

That person was Paul Roell, a student from the sports management program at Robert Morris College, a student of mine who wanted to be a pro scout. I had put Paul in touch with Art Rooney Jr. They were both happy with the relationship they had forged over the past year.

Art Jr. has changed in other ways, too. He is 6-0½ in height — "as measured by NFL scouts" — and back on August 27 of 1989 he weighed 305 pounds. That is when his doctor ordered him on a diet. "You're old enough now to get serious about your weight," the doctor told him.

When I visited his offices in suburban Upper St. Clair on January 4, 1991, right after the holidays, he was down to 179 pounds. I didn't think he looked so good. He had a lot of loose skin about his freckled face. But he was proud of his weight loss. He was smiling.

He had a four-room suite on the third floor of the Southmark Building, a relatively new complex about two miles from his home in Mt. Lebanon, and about a half-mile, ironically enough, from Chuck Noll's home. He shared the office suite with a secretary and some scouts.

His is a warm, handsomely-furnished office with several windows. "I can see the sun when it's out, and I can see the change of seasons," he said. "Our offices at Three Rivers had no windows, and you had no idea of what was going on in the world outside. It was claustrophobic. I find the change of scenery agrees with me.

"Some of our staff at the Stadium have come out here, and they tell me I have nicer offices than anyone with the Steelers. I tell them not to say that too loud. But I like it here."

One of his sons, also Art, popped his handsome face in the door to say something to him. Art is a dentist, educated at Pitt. He was 28 then, the oldest of four children in the family.

This prompted Art to mention that one of his brother Dan's daughters, Rita Rooney Conway, who was living in the family's old mansion on the North Side, has a degree in engineering from Brown, and in law from Pitt, and is married to a doctor. He said it with pride. "I'm envious," he said.

"Family is family," he said. "When Dan is at family functions he acts as if nothing ever happened between us. I don't want to be bitter. Life's too short."

Art Jr. has always been a Civil War buff, and he had enjoyed a special PBS series on the Civil War that had aired a few months earlier. "There was a scene when General Robert E. Lee was out exercising his horse after the war was over, and a lady in Lexington, Virginia, points out the damage that's been done to her farm, and shows him bullet marks on a nearby tree. The woman asks General Lee, 'What should we do about it?' And General Lee says, 'Cut the tree down and burn it and go on with the rest of your life.' That's what I'm trying to do. But there are a lot of trees to be cut down. I'm trying to find some sanity and peace."

434

He is not bitter, he insists, but the fires still smolder from what he felt was an injustice by his brother. "He's not The Chief," said Art Jr. "I'm not The Chief. We all got 28 chromosomes from our father, and 28 chromosomes from our mother. She (Kathleen) was a McNulty. We all have McNulty blood in us, too. There was only one Chief. But I'm a Rooney. And the Steelers belong to the Rooneys."

The Rooneys he was referring to are the five sons of Art Rooney, the founder of the franchise. Dan, the oldest, was 59. He was born in 1932, the year before his father bought the NFL franchise. Art Jr. was 56. Tim, the president of Yonkers (New York) Raceway, was 54. Twins John and Pat were 52. Pat was the president of the Palm Beach Kennel Club, a greyhound race track, and John, who had just sold a gas and oil company, served as vice-president of the track. The Rooneys also own the Green Mountain Raceway, also a greyhound track, in Vermont. The five sons produced 30 children. Dan had a daughter, Kate, die from lupus a few years earlier, and John lost a son, Jimmy, in an auto accident.

Dan has a son, Art II, 39, a partner in the Pittsburgh law firm of Klett, Lieber, Rooney and Schorling, with offices in Oxford Centre, whom he appears to be grooming to succeed him as club president some time in the future. "It's an Irish custom," said Art Jr., "to name your first-born son after your father. My dad's secretary, Mary Regan, is his godmother. I'm Art's godfather."

Quite often, Art Jr. behaves as if his father is still alive, still somebody he has to please. That, too, is an Irish custom.

"I go to church every day, and pray that I will only remember the good things about my father," he said. "Why do I do that?"

Art Jr. sends lots of congratulatory and condolence letters, just like his dad. He had a letter on his desk from a coach who had recently lost his job as a head coach in the National Football League, and who was thanking Art Jr. for his kind thoughts at a difficult time.

I mentioned to Art Jr. about how I found all the memory cards or mass cards used as bookmarks in the books left behind by his father in his old office at Three Rivers Stadium. Art Jr. smiled, and started pulling out some of his books, and booklets, and thumbed through them. "See," he said, showing how he, too, used the same cards for bookmarks. "I guess you pick up habits without even realizing it.

"We used to take our family and visit my dad and mom at their home on the North Side on Sunday afternoons. My wife, Kay, and the kids enjoyed it. But, almost invariably, no sooner would we get there than my dad would want me to go with him to a funeral home or hospital to visit somebody he'd heard about. He wanted me to chauffeur him to funerals and hospitals. We'd be gone for hours. Finally, my wife protested, and said we wanted to visit with the family on Sunday, but not if I was always going to be taken away. I think my dad was hurt by that."

I mentioned to Art Jr. that I had been with my mother earlier in the day for lunch, that we tried to get together for lunch at least one day a week.

He closed his eyes, and wagged his head on that note. "You know, that's something I'll always regret," he said. "When I was working at the Stadium, my mother was just a few blocks away at our house. I often thought about going up to the house to have lunch with her. But I didn't think it was a manly thing to do."

On the football business side, Art Jr. was asked about the thinking that went into some of the drafts that produced the likes of Joe Greene and Terry Bradshaw and Franco Harris.

"Noll joined us just before the draft in 1969," he said. "We had about five guys identified as people we were interested in with our No. 1 pick. We got extremely lucky. We liked Leroy Keyes of Purdue, for instance, but he got picked third, right before we drafted, and he turned out to be a so-so back with the Philadelphia Eagles.

"That was the year O.J. Simpson came out of USC and everybody knew Buffalo would take him first. Then Atlanta took George Kunz, a lineman from Notre Dame, whom we liked a great deal. He became a Pro Bowl player.

"Of all the players Noll had seen in some of the all-star games, he liked Joe Greene. That went along with our thinking, too, because the other guys were gone. Joe became the cornerstone of the franchise."

Bradshaw was something else. I was working for *The Miami News* in 1970 and saw Bradshaw star in the North-South Game that was played at the Orange Bowl in Miami. I still have a postcard I received around the same time from Art Rooney of the Steelers. "We're not sure what we're going to do with our No. 1 pick," he wrote on the back of a team picture of Noll's first squad. "We might trade the pick. Whatever we do, I hope we do right."

Dan Rooney won a coin flip with the Chicago Bears to get the first pick in the draft as the Bears and Steelers had tied for the worst record (1-13) in the league in 1969.

Art Jr. admitted that Noll and the staff gave strong consideration to trading the pick. "Noll thought we needed a lot of players and might be able to help ourselves in a hurry," he recalled.

"People called with some phenomenal numbers, like ten players. But usually it was a lot of nothing. The Raiders offered us some good people, so did the Cardinals. Atlanta made us an offer. My dad was more involved with the team back then, and he told Atlanta, 'You give us George Kunz and Claude Humphrey and we'll give you the rights to Bradshaw.' But the guy in Atlanta told my dad, 'We can't do that. We're trying to build a championship ballclub.' My father thought about that, and he said, 'That's what we want to do, too.' After that, my father cooled on the idea; he wasn't interested in trading away the pick.

"Jack Butler told us he thought Bradshaw was a once-in-twenty-years pick. My dad thought that's what we needed."

The pick of Franco Harris in 1972 wasn't as clear cut. "He'd had a so-so senior season, but only by comparison to his own super junior

436

season," recalled Art Jr. "Noll, at first, liked Robert Newhouse of Houston, who went on to be a very good back for the Cowboys. There was lots of debate about what we should do that year.

"Getting Franco was like the Battle of Midway. Before that, we never won anything. After that, we won everything."

The draft of 1974 when the Steelers picked up, in order, Lynn Swann, Jack Lambert, John Stallworth, Jim Allen and Mike Webster may have been the best group they got in one year. "Give Noll credit," said Art Jr. "He really liked Stallworth, and said he was worthy of a No. 1 pick. But the scouting department convinced Chuck we could get Stallworth with a later pick. Anybody would like the credit for calling all the shots in that draft, but it wasn't like that. George Perles had a good friend, Chuck McBride, who was an assistant coach at Wisconsin, and he pushed Webster to Perles. That connection turned out to be a great one for us. Webster was small in college, but he was knocking bigger guys off the line pretty good, and, with us, he got bigger."

Dan Marino, like Franco Harris, had a so-so senior season, but only compared to his unbelievable junior season. He was at Pitt, and Art Sr. had seen him play on several occasions. "We've got to find a way to keep that kid in Pittsburgh," the Steelers' owner often said.

"Noll loved Marino," recalled Art Jr. "He worked out for us, and he looked terrific. But Chuck just made the decision that we had built the team of the decade on defense, and we should do it again.

"We looked strong at quarterback, so we went with Gabe Rivera of Texas Tech, whom we thought would be a great defensive lineman. But he got his back broke in a car accident as a rookie, and we'll never know. But my dad used to give me the business about not taking Marino. I thought the thought process was sound that we used that year. I thought The Chief was unfair in his criticism.

"The whole series of draft picks from Joe Greene until we started getting ordinary drafts had a lot of luck in them, too. We worked very hard, but so did a lot of teams. We spent a lot of money, but so did a lot of other teams. We worked intelligently, but other people worked intelligently, too.

"I told my dad that people thought we were just lucky in the draft. He told me not to mind those people, or the criticism. As for luck, he said not to knock it. He said a lot of guys had great jobs and a lot of money, but were never happy. But he thought lucky guys smiled a lot, and that things always seemed to work out for them. He used to say he'd rather be lucky than good."

I mentioned to Art Jr. that I had learned a lot of things about the kind of people the Steelers had drafted and built their team with when they were so successful in the '70s, and how I had discussed my findings with Noll.

"Did he tell you about his theory that strong mothers produced the strongest sons?"

I nodded affirmatively. "He said it was certainly true in his case," I said. "He said his mother was the main force in his formative years."

"OK, good, if he told you that. He used to be on me all the time, telling me that strong fathers tended to produce weak sons. I think he was trying to tell me something.

"I'll tell you who else used to espouse that theory. Buddy Young used to say that."

Buddy Young was one of the first prominent black players in the modern era of pro football, a little guy, just 5-6, who was a running back for the Colts out of the University of Illinois.

I mentioned that many of the Steelers from the glory days were blacks from the South who had grown up in rural settings with two parents, often with both working to make ends meet because they had large families, and that the Steelers themselves had worked as youngsters. There was also a strong religious bent, with a strong sense of family, and values and morals preached to them during their upbringing.

I also mentioned that I had been reading a book called "Staying The Course" in which it said one of the best predictors of success in later life is working hard as a youngster.

Several college coaches said they preferred to recruit blacks from the South versus inner-city blacks from the North who frequently have not grown up in a family where work was a high priority.

"Sport is life and is not Camelot."
— Howard Cosell

"With The Chief, it was Camelot."
— Art Rooney Jr.

Art Jr. stood by a window in his Southmark Building office, and watched as another tenant pulled out of the parking lot in a Mercedes-Benz. "Boy, that's a big one," he said in admiration. "My dad never would have let us buy a car like that. When I came out of the Marine Corps, I bought a real nice MG, and my father scolded me for doing that. He said, 'The guys who build those cars don't buy any tickets. The steelworkers do. You're going to put them out of business buying those foreign cars.' So I got rid of it and I never got another one. That was back in 1959. Those poor guys in the Pittsburgh steel mills went out of business anyhow."

There is a story that's made the rounds about how Art Sr. frowned upon anyone in the family driving a Cadillac. His son, John, had one once, and was driving his dad somewhere in Philadelphia. "Hey, this is a nice car," said the father. "What is it?" John didn't fumble that one. "It's an Oldsmobile, Dad. One of their best models."

Art Jr. explained the background on that car business. "It was against my Dad's psyche and being a North Sider to have a Cadillac.

He didn't want to show off, or try to look like a rich guy. He'd have a Buick loaded up with every possible extra feature. They were nicer than most Cadillacs."

Old fears are difficult for Art Jr. to overcome, however. He and his wife, Kay, had invited some friends from out of town to accompany them to the unveiling of the statue of Art Rooney on Sunday, October 7, 1990 outside of Three Rivers Stadium.

"My wife wanted to get a limo," said Art Jr. "I said we'd have to squeeze in. 'That's not our style,' I said. As in most matters, she won. So we pulled up to the stadium in a limo. When we went in a small tunnel near the box office at the Stadium, I jumped out of the car and ran, so no one would see me in that limo. I didn't want anybody asking me, 'What are you doing in a limo?' I was waiting for my dad to walk across — even in his bronzed state as a statue — and give me hell for riding in a limo. That was The Chief and his Cadillacs.

"He was funny about stuff like that. One time my mother dressed up all us boys in football jerseys to go somewhere. The Chief scolded her. He said, 'We don't advertise our business with our kids.'

"He was very strict. A very strong Catholic. No matter where we'd go, he'd find a church so he could go to mass. I go to mass every day but Saturday. I take Saturdays off. We had rules for everything. The amazing thing is that none of us boys ever really revolted or were rebellious. I was probably the most rebellious, but it was a mild revolt.

"I wanted to be in the theater, as an actor. I did shows in college at St. Vincent, and then I went to Carnegie Tech after that, and I studied in New York at the studios there for a few years. Then I went into the military service. When I got out I got married, and never went back to the theater. It was football from then on."

Art Jr. is smart enough to realize he was part of a very special period in pro football history. Everything fell into place for the Pittsburgh Steelers in the '70s. They were, indeed, the team of the decade. They won four Super Bowls in a six-year period. It may never happen again.

"With The Chief, it was Camelot," said Art Jr. "Something was there for a time, and it's gone. Dan doesn't have to try to emulate that. All he has to do is his job, and win more than you lose and not do anything obscene.

"The Steelers from 1972 to 1980 were special. My dad was King Arthur, and it was King Arthur and his court. You can't expect to duplicate that. Just run a good organization.

"When he was younger, my dad was a goer. He went everywhere for big fights, big horse races, big games of all kinds. Even when he got older, he liked to be where the action was. He was a fan. He went to nearly every Pirates' game at the Stadium. When the Stadium first opened in 1970, he walked from our house to the Stadium and back just about every day. We were always worried that he was going to get hit by a car, or get mugged. Later on, he walked to the office, and somebody would drive him home.

"When my mother was alive, after he turned 70 and relinquished running the operation, he used to go home around 3 o'clock. After she died, he hung around the office later, until 4:30 or 5 o'clock. He bounced back from my mother's death pretty good. Being at the Stadium with the Steelers and all those young ballplayers was pretty strong medicine.

"The Steelers were always so much a part of our life. You went from an infant to a child to a teen and to middle age, and you were associated with the Steelers all the time. You went through every age and the only thing that stayed the same were the players. You're getting older, but they kept you young. For us, they were like the Mississippi River was for Huckleberry Finn. We grew up with it."

As someone who had once thought of being an actor, Art Jr. was asked if his dad had been a tough act to follow. "You're foolish to ever try," he said. "I was smart enough not to try."

The Rooney brothers (left to right) are Dan, John, Art Jr., Pat and Tim.

Wall of Fame
"We're a new breed"

M ost of the 1990 Steelers were strangers to me. I had been on the Steelers' beat for *The Pittsburgh Press* for four years, from 1979 to 1982, and there were only a handful of players and assistant coaches remaining from that period. I am good at faces, but I could not pick most of the Steelers out of a police lineup.

Those I had dealt with back then were Dwayne Woodruff, David Little, Gary Anderson, Tunch Ilkin, Bryan Hinkle and Keith Willis, and their smiles were reassuring when I walked into the clubhouse, and gave me a credibility of sorts when I introduced myself and spoke to younger Steelers who didn't know me at all.

Everybody in Pittsburgh knows Bubby Brister, and all Steeler fans are familiar with the faces of Merril Hoge and Carnell Lake. I had worked the banquet circuit with that trio in recent years, and gotten to know them.

Brister was sitting on a stool where Cliff Stoudt used to dress, just to the right as you enter the clubhouse, and Hoge, his best buddy on the ballclub, was way down at the end of that same strip, in the last stall in the corner, where Franco Harris used to hide. Willis was where Lynn Swann used to live, in a short strip just to the left upon entering the clubhouse. The layout of the large clubhouse was the same, only many of the names above the dressing stalls were different from the days when I was there on a daily basis.

Other recognizable figures in the Steelers' clubhouse were Louis Lipps, who came the year after I left the beat, Rod Woodson, John Rienstra, Rick Strom and Tim Worley. I had been introduced to John Jackson and Hardy Nickerson at several sports promotions in which we had participated around town, especially the Pittsburgh Sports Garden at Station Square.

I knew Lorenzo Freeman, Jerry Olsavsky and Tom Ricketts from their days as students at the University of Pittsburgh. They were the most respectful of the Steelers in my presence, a holdover from our previous relationship. I left *The Pittsburgh Press* in 1983 to take a position at my alma mater (Class of 1964) as assistant athletic director and sports information director, which I held for four years. To me, big as they are, they were still nice kids.

As far as the assistant coaches go, I had worked with Ron Blackledge, Joe Greene, Dick Hoak and Jon Kolb. I knew John Fox from our days together at Pitt when he was on Mike Gottfried's first staff, and more recently as a neighbor of mine in the Trotwood Hills section of Upper St. Clair. I had gotten to know George Stewart, the friendliest of fellows, who liked to talk basketball with me.

Tunch Ilkin, who also lives in Upper St. Clair, was the only player in the locker room on a Monday afternoon following the Steelers' 9-6 victory at New Orleans in the 14th game of the 16-game season. Ilkin did not know I was in the doorway.

He had just emerged from the showers and was walking around the clubhouse with a white towel wrapped around his midriff, kidding around with Rodgers Freyvogel, who was in his 11th season as the Steelers' field manager, since he succeeded Jackie Hart in 1980.

True to tradition, Freyvogel was from the North Side and had attended North Catholic High School, the same as Dan Rooney and Jim Boston and Richie McCabe and so many others associated with the Steelers through the years.

Ilkin was in on his day off because he required treatment for an assortment of nagging injuries. It had been the most difficult of seasons for Ilkin. Following his second straight Pro Bowl appearance, Ilkin underwent surgery on both of his shoulders, and they had taken longer to heal than had been projected. He had a lingering back problem. He had been on the injured reserve list for four weeks at mid-season after suffering a painful dislocated elbow, and he had sprained an ankle two weeks earlier. Plus, he was still suffering from the separation from some of his closest friends, notably Craig Wolfley, Mike Webster and Mark Malone. "The neighborhood has changed some," Ilkin cried out to Freyvogel, who was helping equipment manager Tony Parisi pick up after the players who had been there earlier. "Geez, I miss Malone and Webby and Wolf."

"Ah, screw all those guys!" Parisi screamed from the equipment room, having some fun at the expense of old friends, and getting tired of Ilkin's bellyaching.

"Ah, Tony, how can you say that?" Ilkin came back. "This area over here used to be Park Avenue."

He pointed out the dressing stalls that flanked his and were once occupied by Ray Pinney, John Goodman, John Banaszak, Wolfley, Ted Petersen, Steve Courson, Tom Beasley, Gary Dunn, Jack Lambert and Jack Ham. "God, they were like brothers."

Rod Woodson is a sleek individual, lean and mean looking until he favors you with a smile under that thin mustache of his. He seems to lean forward when he walks across the clubhouse, clothed only in a towel wrapped around his midriff. He looks like an athlete, aeronautically designed. He is six feet tall, about 195 pounds, and, man, can he run.

He was a world-class high hurdler at Purdue University, as well as a two-way performer, an All-American defensive back and a respected wide receiver, and a much-feared kick returner. He won't be satisfied till he does all those things for the Steelers, too, but coach Chuck Noll has not given in to Woodson's well-publicized desire to play wide receiver as well as the other duties he performs with distinction for the Steelers. I had known and been friendly at Pitt with Roger Kingdom, who had come to Pitt from Georgia to play defensive back for the football team when it was coached by Foge Fazio, but ended up giving up football to concentrate on track and field, and won the gold medal in the 110-meter high hurdles in the 1984 and 1988 Olympic Games. King-

Rod Woodson

Mike Fabus

dom wants to do it all, too, always talking about competing in the decathlon, and Woodson seems to be cut from the same competitive mold.

Woodson felt he could have competed on an Olympic level in the 110-meter hurdles, too, and threatened to hold out in favor of track when the Steelers came up short on his original contract demands when they drafted him No. 1 in 1987. Woodson has always wanted more money. And it seemed like he was about to get it, when we spoke on the Friday before the Steelers were to play the Cleveland Browns at Three Rivers Stadium just before Christmas in the 1990 campaign.

Two days earlier, it had been announced that Woodson was selected to play in the NFL's Pro Bowl in Honolulu for the second year in a row, as both a cornerback and kick returner. He and linebacker David Little were going to be the Steelers' only representatives in the Pro Bowl. "I played a little better this year than last year," Woodson said. "This is only my third year playing corner, so I still have a lot of improvement to do."

Fox, the defensive backfield coach of the Steelers, took pride in Woodson's selection. "I wouldn't trade him for anybody," offered Fox. "He's not a finished product. I think he's going to get even better than he is right now."

The Steelers were willing to bank on that. Woodson was in the final year of a four-year contract worth $2.068 million, and the Steelers had recently offered him in the neighborhood of $3 million for three years. No wonder he was smiling, and seemed so easy to talk to. Woodson believes he's worth the big bucks. He has a rare combination of speed, quickness, size and hitting ability. He was named the Steelers' co-MVP, again along with Little, in his first full season of 1988, and a Pro Bowler the following year. He won the NFL's kickoff return title in 1989 to become the first Steeler since Lynn Chandnois in 1951 and 1952 to lead the league in return average.

In Chandnois, Gary Ballman and Larry Anderson, the Steelers have had some terrific kick returners in their history, but Woodson returns them as well as anybody ever did. The same can be said of his punt return ability. Again, the Steelers have been blessed with the likes of Louis Lipps, Theo Bell, Glen Edwards, Rick Woods, Lynn Swann, Chandnois and Bill Dudley, but Woodson may also set new standards in that category. Woodson was sidelined for a few series of downs at New Orleans, and was thought he had hurt his ankle enough to keep him out of the remainder of the game. "The trainers told me he was out," noted Noll at his weekly press conference the Monday after the game. "But he came back. He's one tough football player."

Noll was asked if Woodson's speed makes it all right for him to give ground, and retreat initially when returning punts, in order to find daylight on the sideline. "Yes, you have to have great speed to do that," acknowledged Noll, "and it's fine as long as he keeps gaining the kind of ground he does and getting us good field position."

Woodson was sitting in front of his stall, one once occupied by J.T. Thomas, in a stretch of stalls where John Stallworth, Mel Blount,

Dwayne Woodruff, Thomas and Sidney Thornton once dressed in the last of the four Super Bowl seasons.

Wherever Woodson strolls in the Steelers complex at Three Rivers Stadium, he sees Steelers' memorabilia, footballs from special games marked up with Roman numerals and such in trophy cases in the clubhouse, photos on the walls in the hallways and in Art Rooney's old office, and especially in the lobby, where the Vince Lombardi trophies — all four of them — from the Super Bowl days, the salad days, are always glistening.

"It's not bad, it's good," Woodson said. "The tradition of the Steelers is a great tradition, and it's one you should be proud of. It symbolizes the success they have had here. But it's also one of those things you can't harp on. The past is over.

"They truly set some high standards here. Those were guys I admired and respected when I was a kid, just starting to play ball. I knew all about Mean Joe Greene and Franco and Bradshaw and Mel Blount and those guys. Franco has come in this locker room since I've been here. Swann comes in. Blount comes in. In fact, Blount was on the airplane with us when we went to New Orleans last weekend. When I got here, Mike Webster and John Stallworth were still here, and it was a shock for me to be standing next to them.

"They had so much talent on that team. It's no wonder they won four Super Bowls. When you look back, there was probably not a man you could mention that somebody didn't know, if they were a real football fan. I know that will make me feel prouder when I play in my first Super Bowl. As a kid, seeing Mean Joe Greene in that Coke commercial, tossing his shirt to a little kid . . . all that was super. It's a good feeling. You know you're with an organization that has pride and is respected.

"And The Chief was the type of guy who went forty years without a real winner, and hung in there till this team became the best in the business, and everybody told me how humble he was when he came around here. He brought this franchise from nothing to the Super Bowl.

"It's a different game now from when those Super Bowl guys were playing. They've changed the rules; they've changed the game. Today's game is offensive-minded, and everything is set up for the offensive aspect of the game. Mel Blount was 6-4 or 6-5, 220 pounds, and so fast, and he just dwarfed all those receivers. He could run with any of them, even somebody as fast as Cliff Branch of the Oakland Raiders. He could bump them as they ran alongside each other, and we can't do that. He and I have gotten to know each other. We've talked. He's helped me."

Woodson was sitting in the stall to the right of Woodruff, another of Blount's disciples. "Dwayne has helped me a lot, too," Woodson said. "He emphasizes what it takes. I know what Dwayne went through. He has told me all the stories, about all the horrors and about all the fun when they were winning. You need someone to lead you, and teach you how to understand things. What you need to do. He's taught me a lot."

Woodson was warned that if he didn't watch out he would end up being an attorney, just like Woodruff, who went to and was graduated from Duquesne University's Law School while playing for the Steelers. Woodson smiled. "We've talked about that, too," he said.

Switching signals to the present, Woodson said, "All that tradition is great, but after awhile we have to set some new standards here of our own.

"If you live in the past, you'll die in the past. We're a new breed. We have to win our own championships. If tradition would win for us, we'd have won four more Super Bowls.

"That's why we're working so hard to get to the playoffs again, to continue to improve our team. That's our goal. We need to play consistently well. We don't play consistently well. We're a roller-coaster team. We're close. We're not totally there yet. We need about three or four more key players. I think we're heading in the right direction."

David Little shared Woodson's optimism, but like Ilkin, Hinkle, Woodruff and Willis, he worried that he might be running out of time to play in a Super Bowl.

Then again, there were times he thought that no matter how well he played, he would never play in a Pro Bowl, either. Or be anything but Larry Little's little brother.

Once, after a sportscaster in Pittsburgh introduced him as Larry Little, David shook his head and said, "Do you believe that? When are they going to get it right?"

Only a week earlier, with three games to go in the 1990 schedule, his tenth season with the Steelers, Little had allowed, "I think I'm a pretty good player. But even in Pittsburgh, when I get recognition, it's not for being a good linebacker. It's for being here for ten years or for being the guy who replaced Jack Lambert."

Steelers' president Dan Rooney had said Little "might be the most important guy on the team."

Apparently, at last, there were others in the American Football Conference who shared Rooney's regard for Little, and it couldn't have come at a better time for Little, whose contract would run out at the completion of the 1990 season.

This was Friday, and two days earlier, Little had learned that he had been selected, along with Woodson, to represent the Steelers in the Pro Bowl.

Little had a dressing stall in the farthest corner of the clubhouse. Little likes his privacy. He was the strong, silent type — off the field anyhow. He spoke in a hoarse whisper.

He was asked if being picked for the Pro Bowl gave official certification to something he already felt in his heart. "Probably, yeah," said Little. "Right along, with many of the players here and many of the players and coaches around the league, I had been recognized. Before and after games, coaches and players would come up to me and tell me that.

"But now it's public, now it's official."

Little was asked how he regarded the legacy he had inherited in following in the footsteps of the Steelers and the Dolphins, two of the finest teams of the '70s. He has always been asked to meet standards set by Jack Lambert, his predecessor as the inside linebacker and defensive quarterback of the Steelers, and Larry Little, his big brother and an All-Pro guard in their hometown of Miami with the Dolphins' finest Super Bowl teams. Larry would be a Hall of Famer.

"To me, it's a good thing," said Little. "I'm trying to get to where we can get some of our own Super Bowl trophies. We have to win our own Super Bowls. We can't live off the laurels of their awards. It's something to work for.

"I've always wanted to go to the Super Bowl as a player ever since I went there on tickets that were provided by my brother. I was proud of his accomplishments and that he was one of the best in the league.

"Some people think we are close to going to the Super Bowl. But we haven't gotten there yet. It's something to work for. We came close a couple of times. You have to work so we get the chance. The first step is getting to the playoffs."

Ralph Berlin has been there. He joined the Steelers as team trainer in 1968, one year before Chuck Noll was hired as coach. He shared offices with Fran Feld, his assistant, who was the head trainer at Pitt during my stay there. It was a warm, friendly office.

Berlin was finishing up his 22nd year as trainer for the Steelers, and his 30th as a trainer. He had experienced the climb to the Super Bowls, the fall afterward, and the attempts to put a winner back together again. For all those years, he had been helping to put Steelers back together again.

He had some interesting insights to share. Berlin, who is called "The Plumber," had created a stir in the Steelers' office among his co-workers that week by sending out Christmas cards that showed him strolling the sideline and taking note of some scantily-clad dancing girls. The Steelers are the one team in the NFL that does not have dancing girls on its sidelines. There are no answers to the Dallas Cowboy Cheerleaders in Pittsburgh. The Steelers had cheerleaders for a few years — they were co-eds from Robert Morris College led by the irrepressible Mossie Murphy, a friend of the Rooneys who had been a cheerleader at Duquesne University — but they were quickly abandoned when the Steelers moved into Three Rivers Stadium.

Berlin said the two Steelers who stick out in his mind for shunning his services through the glory years were Joe Greene and Mike Webster. To them, the training room was to be avoided.

"Joe came to us in 1969 and I don't think I saw much of him at all in the trainers' room until he suffered that shoulder injury in 1975," Berlin observed. "His sheet in my office was always clean. I never had any notes on him for treatment rendered. We chart that stuff to keep tabs on their treatment. Joe just never got any treatment.

447

"He just never came in. He never got his ankles taped. He didn't tape his ankles himself, either. He didn't use tape. He didn't use hip pads, thigh pads, or knee pads. It was just Joe out there in shoulder pads and helmet. That was enough for him.

"And Mike, well, they called him 'Iron Mike' for a reason. In the latter stages of his career, I looked after him a lot, but not early on. I remember once when he dislocated three fingers in a game. He didn't even come out. He just put them back in place himself.

"Another time, he tore a cartilage in his knee. He couldn't fully extend or bend his leg. He just had us tape it tight, and he played three games and in the Pro Bowl before he had surgery on it.

"Then there was Jack Lambert. He liked certain kinds of equipment, mostly stuff from the old days, stuff they didn't make anymore. One of the guys in the clubhouse, Frank Sciulli, threw one of his forearm pads away once, and Lambert raised hell, and Frank and Rodgers Freyvogel went into the trash bin outside and fished it out."

Freyvogel remembers that incident. "Jack was going crazy, saying he was going to have to retire," said Freyvogel. "I had to go into the dumpster, just before they were going to crush the garbage in it, and there were rats in there and everything, to get those pads. We still have them."

Remembering Lambert brought a smile to Berlin's face.

"In our first Super Bowl in '74, Lambert came out in the first quarter, and he was bitching to me," said Berlin. "He told me I was the worst trainer in America, that I didn't tape him right. He said his ankle was bothering him. It was my fault.

"Dr. John Best checked him out, and said Jack had fractured his ankle. Jack said, 'Give me something for it so I can play in the second half.' Big John just smiled and said, 'No, I'm not going to do that.' Jack wanted me to tape it up, so he could go back and play. But that was out of the question. But it shows you how badly he wanted to play."

Franco Harris had a reputation for sitting in the whirlpool bath, or the tub, a lot during his heyday with the Steelers.

"Franco spent a lot of time in the training room," said Berlin. "He was very conscious of his condition, especially anything pertaining to his lower legs. Franco played hurt a lot. He nursed himself pretty good, but he was always there on Sunday. Whatever was available to make him feel better, he utilized it."

L.C. Greenwood said he was seldom a hundred percent healthy through most of his career. He said, "It's easy to play football when you're healthy. What separates the pack is the guys who play when they're not feeling so hot."

Berlin had to smile. "L.C. on Tuesday looked like death warmed over," recalled Berlin. "On Wednesday, he'd be limping around. On Sunday, he'd give you a Pro Bowl performance.

"Dwight White was a guy who never got hurt. Collectively, those guys were a tough group."

What about Ernie Holmes?

Berlin nearly choked on his ever-present cigar, one of the joys he shared with Steelers' owner Art Rooney.

"Ernie was Ernie," he said after some thought. "He was moody, as you know. Of the four defensive linemen, Ernie was the one I had the least contact with. He wanted to belong. He liked being one of the fellows, but in a lot of ways he was a loner.

"Ernie had some weird ideas about what was fun. A lot of people were afraid of him, or what he might do."

I asked about Tunch Ilkin, who seemed to be having a most difficult year, both physically and mentally, and might be considering retirement, even though he had a year left on a three year contract.

"It's been one thing after another for Tunch this year," said Berlin. "Tunch is a leader, on and off the field. He's been a great asset to the Pittsburgh Steelers. He really represents us well in the community in so many ways. He's hurting; both shoulders, an ongoing back problem, dislocated elbow, ankle, you name it.

"It's the same with his buddy, Wolfley. He had back problems here, and he was on injured reserve this season for the back again with the Vikings. I know those guys miss each other. They were so close."

Craig Wolfley's figure stood out on the horizon. It was sundown and he and his two children were on their way to a park near their home, just a block from my house in the Trotwood Hills section of Upper St. Clair. He was flanked by his children, and he was holding each of them by the hand. Megan Elizabeth was 5, and Kyle Jacob, or "Jake" as he was called, had just turned 3. I was canvassing the neighborhood, going door to door to sell tickets for a chicken barbecue the Upper St. Clair-Bethel Park Rotary Club was sponsoring to raise money for two children in the neighboring communities whose families needed help with excessive expenses for bone marrow transplants to combat leukemia. One was an eighth grader named Michael Barry, the other was a kindergarten student named Jennifer Erny.

When I saw Wolfley walking to the park, I thought I would skip his house the first time around and catch it on the way back. I had always been successful at selling tickets, magazine subscriptions, Christmas seals, you name it, when I was in grade school, but this was the first time since then that I had gone door to door like this. And it wasn't going well this particular evening. I was getting $3 per house, instead of the $25 and $30 sales I was accustomed to on such forays. I was thinking about going home early, and calling it quits. But I had made myself a promise to stay out a certain time, and to get at least $200 before I went home. That was my goal each night out.

When, at last, I went to the Wolfleys' house, I was greeted by his wife, Beth, but told that Craig had not yet returned from the park. He had come home from practice and taken the kids to ride on the swings, even though it was dark out. There were lights in the park. I said I would come back, but Beth invited me into their home.

I had noticed that their stone slab steps leading to their door were out of kilter. I kidded Beth about that. "I hear Craig can bench press about 500 pounds," I said. "How come he doesn't fix your steps?"

In 1982, Wolfley finished second in the NFL's strongman competition. But Beth came to Craig's defense right away. "He has a bad back," she said. "It has been bothering him the last three years. He's had back spasms and it gets pretty bad."

When Craig came home, he introduced his children to me. Jake came to me and gave me a big hug and a kiss on the cheek. He is a friendly little fellow.

"Well, you came to the right house when you're talking about leukemia," said Craig.

He then told me how difficult it had been to see his father die from leukemia, being ill and fading over a five year period, starting when Craig was playing college ball at Syracuse University, and ending in his second season with the Steelers. Not only was Craig competing for a job on the Steelers, but he was trying to boost the spirits of his brother Ron, now a running back for the Phoenix Cardinals, and Dale, who was an offensive lineman at West Virginia University.

Craig asked Beth to get his checkbook. He wrote out a check and told me more about his father, and what the family had experienced when he became ill and then when he died. He folded the check and handed it to me. It was not until I got home that night, and held the check under a light, that I saw it was the biggest contribution anybody had made during the Rotary fund-raiser. It was a check for $250. I later learned that he had sent a separate check for $100 for another appeal for Michael Barry's fund.

So I was disappointed, like a lot of our neighbors, when Wolfley was left unprotected by the Steelers in the Plan B free agent draft. The Minnesota Vikings claimed him and signed him. They had been encouraged to do so by Tom Moore, their new offensive coordinator, who had held a similar position with the Steelers when Wolfley was with them.

I telephoned Wolfley one night at his home in Minnesota, and mentioned to him that his buddy, Tunch Ilkin, had told me how much he missed him.

"Oh, I know," said Wolfley, who had spent ten seasons with the Steelers and had come to the team in the same 1980 draft as Ilkin and Mark Malone, another close friend. "It was like a separation of Siamese twins. It was more difficult than most people can probably realize.

"I felt so funny the first time I suited up in a Vikings' uniform. The first time I picked up a purple helmet and pulled down a purple and white jersey it felt real strange. And being in a locker room at the Metrodome. The only familiar face, at first, was Mike Merriweather, who had been a teammate for six seasons with the Steelers.

"It was so different. There was a completely different look to the clubhouse. Different players. It was so new. I felt a real sense of loss. I feel respected here, though. When you've been in the league as long as I have, when you've paid your dues, the players appreciate that. I came in with the attitude of working hard to find my place here. It's been going very well. I just came off an injury, but things are looking up. I've started some games."

I asked him if it helped that he knew Tom Moore, who left the Steelers to become a top assistant to Jerry Burns in Minnesota, and Mike Merriweather, a former Steelers linebacker.

"Tom Moore was one of the big reasons I came here, so that's helped me to adjust. There's no question I feel good here. They have some splendid people. And Mike and I have something in common. I have found some good and caring people, something I'm used to, having been with the Steelers."

Louis Lipps had been sidelined for two games, with New England and New Orleans, and was hoping he could return to action against the Cleveland Browns. This was a big game, the Steelers still had a shot at the playoffs, and he had been sorely missed in their passing attack. The Steelers lacked a strong cast of receivers.

During the '70s, they were four deep and then some at the wide receiver slots. Now Lipps alone had proved himself to be a Pro Bowl caliber receiver. Lipps had caught a lot more passes in his first few seasons with the Steelers when John Stallworth was in the other slot.

When Bubby Brister needed a big gainer, he looked for Lipps. But Lipps had taken a shot in the back after making a catch against the Cincinnati Bengals and had not been able to practice or play since then.

"He's the best receiver we've always had since I've been around here," said Brister. "It just gives everybody a lot of confidence when he's in there. We know he's going to make his share of big plays."

Despite missing the past two games, Lipps still led the Steelers in receiving with 44 catches for 602 yards, and three touchdowns. Combined, the other wide receivers had just 46 catches and one touchdown.

Lipps was the Steelers' first round draft choice, out of Southern Mississippi, in 1984. "The first time I walked into this locker room, I knew I was with a class organization," recalled Lipps, when we spoke to him before the game he would miss at New Orleans. "They accepted me with warmth, and everyone wanted to help me right away.

"John Stallworth and I really got close my second year in the league. We were roommates after my first year both at training camp and on the road.

"When I first came here, I wouldn't talk to anybody. I was shy and quiet. I didn't get close to anybody. John helped me find my place here. He told me some of the things he did to improve himself here, and the way he worked at conditioning. Just watching the way he played and practiced helped me.

"I wouldn't say I tried to pattern myself after him, but as far as work ethics go, you couldn't find a better role model than John Stallworth. The kind of patterns he ran, so precise, and the way he adapted to situations. And, personally, he was such a class individual,

451

not only the stuff he did on the field, but what he did off it. He wasn't stuck on himself."

It took awhile for Lipps to find himself as a football player, back in the beginning, back in New Orleans. "Baseball was my first love," he said. "I'd run to the TV to catch a baseball game before I would a football game. I was big on the Los Angeles Dodgers.

"But whatever season it was that was the sport I played. When I got interested in football, I liked receivers like Elmo Wright and Otis Taylor. In fact, Taylor came to scout me when I was at Southern Miss, and I told him he had been one of my favorites when he was with the Kansas City Chiefs.

"I had no idea I'd get a scholarship to Southern Mississippi. I had no idea I'd get drafted. And then to come to a team that had one prime time receiver after another prime time receiver.

"When I first got here, everybody was saying 'he's another Lynn Swann.' That's the kind of stuff I had to blank out of my mind. I had to be Louis Lipps. I couldn't be anybody else.

"It's tough. They've always had a winner here. They won all those Super Bowl championships. It helped to have some of the players from those teams here when I came here. I'll never forget that. I'll never forget the advice John Stallworth has given me, about football, and about life in general.

"I never realized how big football was on a professional level. I didn't realize how the people come after you, the way they mob you and go for your autograph. I came here worrying about making the football team. A lot of people were telling me not to worry about it; you've got it made. But I never felt that way."

He mentioned that Swann had worked out with him on occasion, did some running with him, and talked to him.

"It all helps," said Lipps. "But they had their own identity. You can't try to emulate somebody else. Just be the person you are. Stallworth was a super person. I liked Calvin Sweeney, who was here when I came. I learned from him, too. We were close.

"That's what the team of the '70s had. That's why they were successful. They were like brothers; they cared about each other. The guys that were still here from that bunch tried to make me realize — and they did — what they went through, and why it was worth it."

Ray Mansfield was a guest of Bruce Keidan on a pre-game radio show on WTAE prior to the Steelers' last home game with the Cleveland Browns. Asked to rate the current club, Mansfield offered, "They don't have a homerun hitter. Maybe two times all year, they have scored on a long touchdown pass. You've got to be able to do that."

Mansfield made fun of the predictability of the Steelers when he was playing for them. "Everybody knew what we were going to do," he said. "But they couldn't stop us anyhow. That's when you know you're good."

452

Explaining what life was like as a center, he said, "Life in the trenches is not a nice place. You have guys trying to hurt one another. So you want to be contemptible."

Mansfield had some questions of his own. He was puzzled by how John Rienstra, the fifth year guard who had been the Steelers' No. 1 draft pick in 1986, was languishing on the bench, largely ignored.

"Rienstra was really coming on," said Mansfield. "I'm really mystified by what's happened there. He was hurt, and I know he's had some problems in the past, but he must be in somebody's doghouse. It may not be Noll's, but it might be the position coach's doghouse. Noll never operated that way when I was on the team."

Well, maybe things have changed in 20 years, suggested Keidan, but Mansfield refuted that quickly.

"Chuck Noll is still the same guy he was in 1969."

Mike Fabus

Louis Lipps

Tim Worley

David Little
He has played in big shadows

It took awhile, but David Lamar Little made a name for himself with the Steelers. It has always been difficult for him to live up to the legendary leader of the Steelers' defense who preceded him at middle linebacker, namely Jack "Splat" Lambert. Before that, he was constantly reminded that he was the kid brother of Larry Little, an All-Pro guard with the championship Miami Dolphins of the early '70s.

But, by his tenth season, Little had settled in comfortably as the defensive captain and leader of the Steelers' defense. In 1988, he was honored by being named co-MVP of the team along with defensive back Rod Woodson by their teammates. Only three other Steeler linebackers had been so honored — Andy Russell, Jack Lambert (twice) and Bryan Hinkle — so he was keeping good company. "You have to be yourself and play your own game," declared David, who shunned comparisons with Lambert, and references to being the little brother of Larry Little who'd go into the Hall of Fame in 1993.

I had known his brother from when I covered the Dolphins in 1969 for *The Miami News.* Larry played on the offensive line for 14 years in the National Football League, first with the San Diego Chargers and mostly with the Miami Dolphins. He was 14 years older than David. Larry was the head football coach of Bethune-Cookman College.

"I think I had quite an influence on him," said Larry Little. "I'm quite a bit older than David, and I was playing here in my hometown where I could keep an eye on him. I went to his high school football and basketball games whenever I could. My mother did the same, and she went to his college games. We're a family that believes in supporting each other.

"Ours was more than just a brother-to-brother relationship. He was raised without any father being there. There were four under me, and he was the baby. He had it easier than me in some ways. But it's very difficult for a kid growing up in the same city as his brother, the pro football player."

In a December, 1984 interview with Bill Utterback in the *Beaver County Times,* David Little said, "I remember all the excitement and hoopla and success my brother had in his career, and I want some of that for myself. I want to go to a couple of Super Bowls, and I want to be known as the best linebacker in the league."

At 6-1, 220, Little was undersized as linebackers in the league go, but he took heart from the fact that Lambert and Ham were on the light side weight-wise, but made up for it by their approach, intelligence-wise and intensity-wise. He aimed to do the same.

"I can read offenses pretty well, especially the offensive linemen," said the Steelers' Little. "I can tell when they're going to drop back. I guess I picked it up from my brother. He taught me how to read the guards. I can read their hands or their feet or their eyes. They give things away if you know what to look for. It can be a big advantage."

David Little

Mike Fabus

Little was asked what he had learned from Lambert.

"Jack was a great role model for me. He taught me about the toughness that a linebacker has to have. I learned from his blood-and-guts attitude. I saw the way he pushed himself, even when he was tired and beat up. He never stopped working. He never quit. That's what I learned from him. It's an attitude."

Little has always been quiet and rather shy off the field, but fanatical on the field. He did not growl like Lambert, but he made his own noise. "He's a totally different person on the field," teammate Robin Cole commented a few years back. "He's a fiery guy. His passion for the game comes through. He loves the violence of the game. He loves the intensity."

Little likes to play hard and dish out punishment. "Where I come from you had to be tough to survive," he said. "If you weren't tough, someone would beat you up and take your money. That's just the way it was. My mother taught me good manners and we went to church every Sunday. But on the street, good manners only got you a good beating."

As he gained experience and started leading the Steelers in tackles, and gained more recognition for his efforts, Little learned to live with the shadows in which he performed right from the start of his football-playing days.

"My whole family was athletic," he said. "Two of my sisters (Connie and Joy) were swimmers and one (Linda) played tennis. But Larry was the star.

"If people didn't know about my brother, I didn't tell them. I never had my own identity. I tried to get away from that. I tried to reject it. I didn't want to be known as anybody's brother. I wanted to be known as David Little."

It was just as hard to take the place of Lambert in the Steelers' lineup. Some fans have never been satisfied.

A scene comes to mind from the summer of '85 at St. Vincent College in Latrobe. Little came off the field for a breather during an intrasquad scrimmage. A vocal fan on the nearby hillside who had too much to drink and too much sun started to get on his case.

"What are you doin'?" the fan hollered out for all to hear. "Hey, David Little, you can't afford to sit down. Jack Lambert never sat down. You get back out there. You'll never fill Lambert's shoes. You'll never be good enough."

Then, too, there were signs at Three Rivers Stadium saying similar things, like "BRING BACK JACK" and that had to hurt Little, who was looking to be accepted. He knew he was doing his best, and that was not bad.

"I'll always be in Lambert's shadow," he said in resignation one day. "I've learned to live with Jack's ghost.

"Sure there's a little pressure. The tradition of Pittsburgh football is the good linebackers. A lot of people want to see if I can do well or if I'll mess up.

"That's natural to compare me with Jack Lambert. It's natural

456

that people will look at me and say, 'Jack didn't do it that way.' Or Jack would have made that play or Jack would have done it differently.

"Replacing Jack won't be all that new to me. I've been replacing people all my life. Hey, Jack was a role model for me as far as the way he took command, how he knew where everybody was on the field, and as far as being aggressive.

"Jack was a great player with great accomplishments in a great era. But everything changes. I'm glad people have their history to fall back on. But this is a new day.

"Sometimes, it seems like I'm just out there. Like a picture hanging on the wall. I don't make as much impact as I should. I think my teammates knew I could do the job. I think I proved myself to them."

The inside linebacker of the Steelers is the quarterback of the defense, and he has to recognize the offensive sets and know the proper defense to call instantly. If he did not make the right calls, Little knew that veterans such as Donnie Shell and Robin Cole and Dwayne Woodruff would know it. Even later, he knew players like Keith Willis would know, that Bryan Hinkle would know. "I've had to earn their respect when I make a call," said Little. "They trust me; they have always trusted me."

1990 was his seventh season as a starter, but he had not yet been named to the Pro Bowl. He had also learned to live with the lack of recognition. "I accept that, no complaints," he said. "My first priority is making it to the playoffs again, then to the Super Bowl. If we do that, I'll be happy. The other stuff doesn't matter.

"It's the story of my life. I don't worry about recognition. I don't pay much attention to all-star stuff. As long as I'm satisfied with the way I'm playing and my coaches are satisfied, and my teammates are satisfied, then I'm happy."

A week after we talked to him, on Wednesday, December 19, 1990, Little learned that he had been one of three inside linebackers voted to the American Conference team for the Pro Bowl. Once again, he was joined in an honor by Rod Woodson, with whom he had shared team MVP honors in 1988.

For Woodson, being picked for the Pro Bowl was a repeat, for Little it was league-wide recognition, at last.

"It's about time," said Dave Brazil, the Steelers' defensive coordinator. "I don't think any selection to the Pro Bowl has made me happier."

Hardy Nickerson, a Steelers' linebacker who started next to Little, said, "It's long overdue. Since I've been here, he's played better than anybody in the league. Yet it's still taken nine years to get the recognition he deserved earlier in his career.

"A lot of guys get in there because of their name. David got in because of the way he played."

Little had been overlooked so many times in the past, he was not looking to make the grade in 1990, either. "I stopped thinking about it," he said. "I'm just trying to get in the playoffs right now, go to the Super Bowl, if possible."

His wife, Denise, was much more thrilled by his selection. "She screamed," he said. "She was pretty excited."

David Little, Pro Bowl linebacker

The Big Game
"The last one to walk away is a winner"

It was a big game, a "must" game, maybe the biggest game for the Steelers in a decade. It was the 16th and final game of the 1990 schedule, and the Steelers were playing in the last game of the final Sunday of the season. They were playing the Houston Oilers at the Astrodome, and it would be nationally televised on ESPN.

"It always comes down to Pittsburgh," said former Oilers coach Bum Phillips, who during the '70s often said that "the road to the Super Bowl went through Pittsburgh."

The season was at stake. If they won, the Steelers would be undisputed champions of the Central Division in the American Football Conference, and have the home field advantage for the first round of the playoffs. They could win their division outright for the first time since 1984, and have a 10-victory season for the first time since 1983.

If they lost, their season was over. They would finish in a three-way tie for first place in the AFC Central with the Oilers and Cincinnati Bengals, all with 9-7 records, but would not qualify for the playoffs because they would come up short in the tie-breaking categories. The Bengals would be in as a wild-card entry. Win and the Bengals would be done for the year. The Oilers would be the wild-card team.

The Bengals had beaten the Browns earlier in the day, and the Seattle Seahawks had beaten the Detroit Lions, thus eliminating any long-shot possibilities the Steelers had of making the playoffs as a wild-card team. The folks at ESPN had to love it. The Oilers-Steelers' match-up had been rated a five-star "must see" game, the only game of the weekend given such status, in *USA TODAY.*

On "NFL Report" on HBO, Lenny Dawson, Nick Buoniconti and Cris Collinsworth all confidently predicted that the Steelers would win the game.

So the assignment was a simple enough one. If the Steelers truly had their sights set on the Super Bowl, as so many of them had said all season, they had to beat the Oilers and the opportunity for another title was in their hands. In a sense, this game was bigger than the Super Bowl.

Like many of the Steelers' fans, I found myself wishing and hoping. It had helped before. On the previous Sunday, as I was driving away from Three Rivers Stadium, I had been doing the same. The Steelers had just beaten the Cleveland Browns, 35-0, and everybody was already talking about their chances against the Houston Oilers.

The Oilers were so tough at the Astrodome, and their quarterback, Warren Moon, had been on a torrid tear, and was throwing the football better than anybody else in the National Football League.

But during the game, it was announced in the press box that Troy Aikman, the quarterback of the Dallas Cowboys, had suffered a separated shoulder and would be sidelined the rest of the season. Joe

Montana, the quarterback of the defending Super Bowl champion San Francisco 49ers, was being held out of action because he was nursing some wounds.

I wondered what would happen to the Oilers if Moon got hurt. After all, NFL quarterbacks had been biting the dust in recent weeks in alarming numbers. It looked like Bubby Brister of the Steelers might be the only able-bodied starting quarterback still standing when the playoffs got underway.

Almost on cue, the sportscaster on the radio related that Moon had suffered a dislocated thumb on his throwing hand in the late going of an Oilers' victory over the Cincinnati Bengals.

The next day, as expected, Chuck Noll did not say anything to indicate that the Steelers were taking any joy or heart from the news that Moon would be unable to play against them. Noll, true to form, talked about Cody Carlson as if he were the second coming of Sammy Baugh.

Whereas Warren Moon had thrown a league-leading 33 touchdown passes in 15 games, Carlson, his backup, had thrown but one TD pass. Nor was Noll interested in hearing what the Oilers' coach Jack Pardee was saying about his team: "We're in pretty bad shape physically..."

Noll was not buying into any of that. "If we think the Oilers will be anything less as a team, we're in trouble," he said. Noll gets miffed with the media when they start asking questions such as, "Don't you think it improves your chances..." or "With Moon out, how will this affect the Oilers' offense?"

In Noll's mind, you always respect your opponent, no matter what their record, no matter what the circumstances coming into the game. Just go about your business, and play as well and as hard as you can play. Don't assume anything.

It had been raining a lot in Pittsburgh that week, and water was dripping down from the ceiling directly in front of the receptionist's desk in the lobby of the Steelers' offices at Three Rivers Stadium. There were two buckets catching the dripping water. It was not a good omen.

Cody Carlson was talking confidently as he approached the challenge of his first start of the season. If the Oilers won the division, there was a million dollar bonus for Warren Moon. It was up to Carlson to make sure the incentive clause in Moon's contract would be realized.

Cody Carlson vs. Bubby Brister sounded like a wimps' arm-wrestling contest, considering their cutesy names, but they were both talking confidently before the game.

"I'm confident of my ability to match up with anybody in this league," Carlson said over the telephone from Houston in a mid-week interview with the Pittsburgh media, as he assessed what he thought he could do in his sixth pro start.

"There's not a throw in this game I can't make. With my limited experience, and not playing with the (first) team, I haven't had a chance to polish anything.

"I know what's going to be at stake Sunday night. I'm going to be called upon to make things happen. There's no doubt in my mind that I can do it.

"I feel there's enough pressure for me just preparing for this game and going out to play it. I don't have to get wrapped up in it. I'm not Warren Moon, but I know what I've been called on to do. So I'm just going to concentrate mostly on the game.

"There's a lot riding on this game. It's a great opportunity for me. It's a great challenge. I don't need to necessarily prove anything to myself, or my friends, or my teammates, because they know what I can do. But to everyone else out there, I can prove something.

"It's a do-or die situation for us, and I have to go out there and perform. I'm confident, very excited about it. On the other hand, I definitely don't think I'll be getting a whole lot of sleep the next few nights."

In Pittsburgh, Bubby Brister was on the spot. Steelers fans were confused by Brister during the 1990 season. They never knew which Bubby Brister was going to show up. In three games during the season, Brister had thrown four touchdown passes — something he had never done before in a game in his career.

In seven of the Steelers' previous 15 games, it was pointed out in more than one pre-game report, the offensive unit had failed to generate a single touchdown. They had not beaten a team with a record above .500 all year. In the only other games that had been labeled "must-win" games, the Steelers had twice come up short against the Bengals.

Yet somehow the Steelers were going into this final game alone atop the AFC Central standings for the first time in five years, and were in a position to win their first division title since 1984.

The defense had a lot to do with the Steelers' success and the 9-6 record. It was the No. 1 rated defense in the NFL going into the big game.

"I think it's kind of neat," said defensive line coach Joe Greene. "After 15 games, it's a one-game season."

And Brister would be the key.

"We're going to win the division title," Brister assured everybody who approached him for a pre-game assessment.

"The division championship is on the line; it's the last game. That's the way it should be. The last one to walk away is the winner."

He sounded a little like his old hero John Wayne with that line.

"The whole world's going to be watching Sunday night," Brister said. "It's the only game in town and we gave them a helluva show last year. Carlson will be feeling the butterflies, until he takes a couple of licks.

"Any way you look at it, it's not going to be an easy night for either of us. There's a whole lot at stake, a lot to think about."

In a separate interview, Brister was just as bold, playing up to his image. "We're going to win a division title and it's going to be a lot better and it's going to tickle me to death because of the people who wrote us off," Brister said.

Aware that he and the Steelers had a rap for not being able to win the big game, Brister did his best to shoot down that theory.

461

"It's right there for the taking. Now it's time for us to say, 'Yes, I can.'"

Brister said he wasn't concerned about the noisy crowd and hostile atmosphere the Steelers were sure to encounter at the Astrodome.

"I like it loud, with people cursing you and throwing beer," said Brister. "I like going into a place where you're not supposed to win. Going into the 'House of Pain.' I like it."

Among the Steelers who believed in Brister and the team's ability to win the big one was Eric Green, a big one himself, and a rare rookie who became an "impact player" early in his stay with the Steelers.

"When Bubby's clicking, we're clicking," said Green. "He's the type of guy who loves this pressure. He'll do well; he'll do well. The big players are going to rise in the big game. I love it. I just love a challenge."

And the Steelers just loved Eric Green, a giant of a tight end at 6-5, 283 pounds, who had proved the Steelers were smart in risking their No. 1 draft pick on a player from little Liberty College in Lynchburg, Virginia. Before the big game, the Pittsburgh Chapter of the Professional Football Writers of America announced that they had voted Green the Steelers' rookie of the year.

Green was fighting the flu that same day and was unable to join his teammates for practice at Pitt's new indoor practice facility. The weather had turned cold and ugly in Pittsburgh, so the Steelers decided to go indoors and practice, better preparation for playing in the Astrodome and a chance to practice under more comfortable conditions.

Green received the seventh annual Joe Greene "Great Performance" Trophy presented by Pittsburgh National Bank.

It was an acknowledgment of the outstanding season Green had put together after a late start. He was the last No. 1 pick in the NFL to sign a contract, and missed the entire training camp and the first two games of the regular season.

Back then, an angry Chuck Noll told the media to "forget" Green, because he wouldn't be any help to the team in the coming season.

When Noll was reminded of that, after Green started making lots of touchdown catches, Noll smiled and said, "Everybody can make a mistake." The coach continued, "We're very, very pleased with Eric Green. He's become an important part of our football team. He's demonstrated a desire to get the job done. He wants to win very badly, just as we all do."

Green had forgotten about Noll's negative position in the preseason. "That was a long time ago...the past," said Green when someone brought up the subject late in the season. "I don't dwell in the past."

As for being named the Steelers' top rookie, Green did want to reflect on that.

"Winning an award named for Joe Greene would make any player humble," said Eric Green. "I know I am. That man set some high standards to attain."

Eric Green

Bill Amatucci

As the Steelers headed for Houston, the site of some of the team's outstanding victories in the past, one of the assistant coaches, Jon Kolb, recalled a game there 18 years earlier when he had a stomach virus and was ill before the game, and when the Steelers were missing many of their top players.

That was in the next-to-the-last game of the 1972 schedule. Steelers president Dan Rooney thought it might have been one of Joe Greene's greatest games.

Greene single-handedly set the tone for the game, and terrorized the Oilers from the opening kickoff. He had five sacks and forced several more hurried passes, and led the Steelers to a hard-fought 9-3 victory. That game launched the Steelers on a run of eight consecutive playoff seasons and four Super Bowl triumphs. Like Eric Green said, Joe Greene had set some high standards to attain.

It was Monday, the day before Christmas, six days before the final game of the season at Houston. Tim Worley was alone in the locker room. He had come in for treatment. He had missed the game the day before with the Browns because of the flu.

He had missed five games because of injury and illness. He had missed nearly all the training camp because of an ankle injury. He had missed training camp the year before as a holdout after the Steelers had made him their No. 1 draft choice.

At the outset of the 1990 season, it was hoped that Worley, a 6-2, 228 pound back, would team with Merril Hoge to give the Steelers a solid 1-2 running tandem. After all, they had finished the '89 season as one of the NFL's finest combinations. "We get Worley going and a lot of things will change," said Brister. "When we were winning last year, the running game carried us. Merril and Tim can get it done. They've been there."

At the outset, Worley was positive. "I know what it takes to play in the league now," he said in September. "You can't half-step in the NFL. You have to give 100 percent, not 90, not 95. If you half-step, you get hurt. Everybody is good in the NFL, so you have to be the best you can be.

"I've got a fresh start this year, and I'm ready. I feel great. I'm looking to make something happen."

But the season turned sour for Worley pretty fast. Worley was among those who were constantly griping about how difficult it was to grasp the new system installed by offensive coordinator Joe Walton. His agent was quoted in the newspaper early in the schedule saying the Steelers should trade Worley if they weren't going to use him properly.

For most of the season, Worley was an unhappy camper. He was never happy with the way he was used. He never thought he got the ball often enough. He griped publicly and showed his displeasure several times in outbursts on the sidelines, by slinging his helmet into the bench. He was always bitching. He was hurting. He said little about his

464

inability to break into the clear, or shake off a tackler, or about his penchant for fumbling the ball at the worst times.

"It's frustrating," Worley would say. "Damn, I know I'm not that bad of a running back. I can help the team out some way. But not when I'm sitting on the bench.

"I just want to win some games. I want to be like the Steelers. I want to win some games and make something happen. The offense hasn't scored any points in three games (the streak would stretch to four games before the offense scored). Something is wrong. Something is definitely wrong. Oh the system's fine, and the plays are good. I'm serious, it's great stuff. We just have to learn it. But we have too many formations.

"When Bubby audibles, everybody has to stop and think about what we're going to do. And, bang, the play starts. There's confusion. Nobody knows what they're doing . . . the quarterback, the backs, and the offensive linemen. And that's bad because if the offensive linemen don't know what to do, we can't run . . . we're going to get killed."

Even when the Steelers won, beating the New York Jets, 24-7, in Giants Stadium, Worley was unhappy. He came off the field at one point and slammed his helmet angrily against the bench. "I can't make things happen if I'm not in there," he said.

It never dawned on Worley that he was not making things happen when he was in there, which is why he was being yanked so often. "Go ask them," said Worley, when asked what was wrong, motioning toward Noll and Walton. "When they call my number, I go in. But it's not done much."

When the media would quiz Noll about Worley or Hoge, Noll tended to reply without mentioning Worley about how you had to earn playing time, and how you had to earn being given the ball in clutch times. Noll did not point fingers. It was not his style. He tried to make general comments. But it was obvious he did not think Worley had earned the respect he so badly and desperately desired on the Steelers' team.

"The guy you go to is the guy that is producing," said Noll. "There's no question Merril has been our producer. He's the guy, who when called upon, gets it done. Merril's the guy everyone has confidence in now. That's something you earn; that's not a gift. Nobody gives it to you. That's something you make happen."

At a separate press conference, Noll said in response to a question about Worley: "He has the ability to be a good back. Right now, he's a diamond in the rough. And we're trying to get the rough off it."

After leading the Steelers in rushing as a rookie with 770 yards, Worley had only 413 going into the game against the Oilers. "I think there might be a sophomore jinx," said Worley. "I'm very disappointed. Nobody wants to be hurt. It's just something I have to deal with. I've never been hurt so much in my life."

Besides a bad ankle, he had also been troubled with a sore knee and a bum shoulder.

Dan Rooney stopped by Worley's locker on the afternoon of Christmas Eve and shook Worley's hand, and wished him a Merry Christmas.

Worley smiled and wished his boss the best as well.

I wonder if Rooney noticed that Worley's hand was on the small side as he gripped it. As Worley was sitting on his stool in front of his locker, I noticed that his shoes looked small. I have small feet, and Worley's did not look much larger than mine. "You've got small feet," I said, saying something I don't think I ever said to an athlete in my life.

Worley looked up and extended both of his hands toward me, palms out. "Small feet, and small hands," he said.

The comment shot right through me like a sword. "I wonder," I thought to myself, "if that's why he has such a tough time holding onto the ball. I wonder if the Steelers scouts knew he had small hands."

Scouts measure and weigh the top prospects personally, and time them in the 40-yard sprint, and measure their vertical jump, and so forth. But I wondered whether they measured a prospect's hands. Or had them take eye tests? Or reading and retention tests?

Worley was looking forward to the final game of the regular season, and hoping to make a contribution.

Worley wanted to play well for the Steelers. He grew up in Lumberton, North Carolina as a big fan of the team. He had little choice in the matter. His mother, Nettie Worley, made it for him.

"My mother was always a Steelers fan," he told us. "She had her pick of the Dallas Cowboys, Washington Redskins or the Pittsburgh Steelers. She loved Joe Greene and Franco Harris and Terry Bradshaw. She had five boys, so she had to watch sports. When I was a kid, I wanted to play for Pittsburgh. And look where I am now.

"I didn't start running the ball until my junior year in high school. I was always over what you could weigh and be a running back in those age-group leagues, so I was always playing linebacker or in the line until I was a junior."

He was asked how soon he realized that great things were expected of him in Pittsburgh.

"The one thing I learned here quickly — from the media and the fans in Pittsburgh — is that since Franco Harris was here they have had a history of No. 1 picks at running back who have not produced, like Greg Hawthorne and Walter Abercrombie, and I'd like to change that.

"Coming in as a first-rounder, people expect a lot out of you," said Worley, who signed a $3 million contract when he came to the Steelers from the University of Georgia. "And when you don't reach those expectations, you're going to get a lot of flak from everybody.

"I haven't lost faith in myself. This year I have been injured all year. It's been a rough year.

"People here are so used to winning. They won four Super Bowls. And now the Steelers have gone a long time without winning big. People get impatient.

"I think we've taken a big step in the right direction. And I want to be part of a winner here. I've never been to a city where people appreciate football like they do here. People here love their football."

With his second season nearly completed, Worley was already disappointing the local fans. "If you measure up, they love you," he said. "If you're messin' up, they hate you. Bubby has told me they'll be back on my side when I start producing better.

"I think it's a positive influence, having all the pictures and trophies from the past teams around here. As a rookie, you see that, and you say, 'Wow. Maybe I can do that, too.' Like they say, 'Let's get one for the thumb.' We're starting to turn this team around. Maybe we can do that."

Franco Harris used to dream of long runs, and successful games. I asked Worley if he did the same.

"I dream," he said. "I try to picture myself, and I try to put in my mind, the things I can do. I can picture myself in a game where I break off a run of 70 yards for a touchdown. I always think about big stuff.

"Dick Hoak, our backfield coach, is a good man, and he works with us. He wants us to concentrate. He says, 'No mistakes.' He believes in us."

The Steelers kicked off to the Oilers at the Astrodome, and Cody Carlson threw a pass and completed it on the very first play. He threw a few more passes and completed them. Only a penalty and a botched field goal prevented the Oilers from scoring on their first offensive series.

The Steelers started their first series at their own 37 — good field position. Worley took a handoff from Brister and plowed straight ahead for three yards. Then he was hit and he fumbled the ball. Nobody put a helmet or a hand on the ball. Worley let it get out of his grasp, and he was staring at his hands — those small hands — like he could not believe what had happened. In all, Worley would run the ball three times for five yards before being benched in favor of Warren Williams. Louie Lipps went largely ignored and caught three passes for 34 yards.

The Oilers moved through the Steelers once more with little resistance and scored on a one-yard plunge by Lorenzo White. Carlson completed some more passes. The Oilers led at halftime by 24-0. The game was over. The Oilers scored on five of their first six possessions.

The crowd of 56,906 at the Astrodome went crazy, and the prime time audience ESPN provided had to wish it had a better ballgame to watch to close out the day.

"They helped me get into the groove," Carlson said of the crowd and his coaches after the blowout. "It was actually easier than it looked probably." Carlson completed 22 of 27 passes for 247 yards and three touchdowns. He did this against a defense that had allowed six touchdown passes in 15¼ games, none in the 16 previous quarters.

"He didn't just play good, he played great," offered Warren Moon.

"He didn't surprise me," said Chuck Noll. "He may have surprised a lot of other people."

Asked about how he felt his team would do in the playoffs, Houston coach Jack Pardee wagged his bald head, and said, "We haven't given it any thought. We were just concerned about today. Without today, there is no next game."

467

In short, the Oilers approached this as a playoff game. The Oilers ripped through the Steelers and dominated line play offensively and defensively. It was never a contest. Gene Collier, the columnist for *The Pittsburgh Press*, wrote that the Steelers had "strictly a hit-and-miss offense" all season, "and what their defense had accomplished was largely at the expense of substandard challenges and they hadn't beaten a team with a winning record."

Collier called the Steelers a "definitely overrated team."

Merril Hoge scored two touchdowns in the second half to make the score look more respectable as the Steelers lost 34-14. They had performed poorly, and it ruined the holiday season for Steeler fans back home in Western Pennsylvania.

For those looking for some ray of hope, Eric Green looked great. He had a big night with seven catches for 105 yards. Brister looked better in the second half, but he didn't get anything going in the first half when the Steelers needed to answer the Oilers' offensive firepower.

Brister was not all worked up after the game, like he normally was after a disappointing showing. He was not swearing up a storm. Nobody was too visibly upset.

"I thought we had some of our best practices," was the best Brister could do. "I was very confident. We weren't flat. We just ran into a buzzsaw."

David Little, the inside linebacker for the Steelers, was upset, but in his usual hoarse whisper way. "We have to learn to win big games," he grumbled. "We had a lot of good things happen this year, but when it came down to the game we had to win, we didn't play well. It's really sad, because you never know when you'll get a chance like we had this year. You can't say, 'We'll get them next year.' You never know."

Noll credited the Oilers for an outstanding effort, praise he would repeat the next day at his final press conference of the season at Three Rivers Stadium.

"We played less than we were capable off," said Noll. "There's no reason for it. This is the biggest game we've played in a long time. We had to be ready. Houston just did a good job. They looked like they had a team that wouldn't be denied."

At Noll's press conference, Myron Cope brought up a sore subject with Noll, as he was wont to do. He mentioned that there had been bad signs all along during the season that maybe the Steelers could not win a big game.

The Steelers were 9-1 against teams who came into their game with a losing record, and they finished up 0-6 against teams with a winning record.

Noll had opened his brief press conference with a smile, and saying, "Happy New Year" to the few faithful media that bothered to attend the last go-around. He finished it by answering Cope's question in a classic manner. "We beat somebody with a winning record," he said with a smile. "We beat ourselves a few times."

468

Before the game at Houston, Dwayne Woodruff was asked the inevitable question by those on the Steelers' beat. Would this be his last season with the Steelers? Would he be retiring?

This was the end of his 11th season with the Steelers, and he would turn 34 in two months.

Woodruff was the last link on the playing field to the Super Bowl era. He said he would like to go out the way he came in — with a Super Bowl ring.

"It's very important," he said as the Steelers approached the game with the Oilers. "It would cap off a very successful and happy career. To come in and win one and — if this happens to be my last year — to go out and win one. I couldn't think of a better story than that."

Woodruff was right in that respect.

But Woodruff refused to read the handwriting on the wall. The Steelers weren't good enough to go all the way, for one thing, and he was making $350,000 a year, a figure the Steelers were unlikely to want to pay to a reserve for yet another year. It was pointed out he would not be the first Steeler who wanted to stay after management had told them that it was time to go — players like L.C. Greenwood, John Banaszak, Franco Harris and Mike Webster wouldn't acknowledge their time was up.

"When you lose your job and you're not ready to go, it's the same feelings as if you were laid off from the steel mills," Woodruff said. "It's tough. But life isn't easy."

Woodruff had never taken the easy way out. After all, he had attended Duquesne Law School at night, and was a practicing attorney with Meyer Darragh Buckler Bebenek Eck and Hall in Pittsburgh.

"Dwayne's prepared for a second career," ventured Joe Greene, a good friend whose second career had been as the coach of the Steelers' defensive line after failures in the restaurant and TV business. "Sometimes it's very traumatic to leave the game. Sometimes, guys recognize it's time to do something else.

"I think Dwayne's bright enough and intelligent enough to know when that time is. He's also stubborn and determined enough not to be pushed."

After the loss in Houston, Woodruff was again routinely approached by reporters for a notebook item in the post-mortem section on the Steelers' season. This time he was a little more adamant about his thoughts on the subject.

"I've been talking about it with my wife all week," he said. "I've decided that this time I'm going to be a little bit more aggressive about seeking an opportunity with another team."

The Steelers had left Woodruff unprotected under Plan B for the previous two years, meaning he was free to negotiate with any of the league's 27 teams. He had been upset, and felt betrayed, both times he was left up for grabs.

"Obviously, my future isn't with the Steelers," he said after the season finale. "I don't know if I'll play with the Steelers again, but I think I have a couple of good years left.

"If I had the opportunity to stay, it would be something I'd consider. There are a lot of great people here, but I don't think I'm in their plans."

Two days later, Tim Worley was feeling the same way as Woodruff. He had heard that Chuck Noll had said at his weekly press conference that he wanted to get Merril Hoge and Barry Foster on the field at the same time, and that Hoge might have to shift from fullback to halfback. Halfback is where Worley works.

"That's telling you I'm not needed here," said Worley, always willing to pop off at the slightest cue from anyone covering the club. "If that's the case, what the hell am I doing in Pittsburgh then?"

Worley, who led the team in rushing as a rookie, finished second behind Hoge in his second season with 418 yards rushing on 109 carries for a 3.8 yard average, down from 770 yards on 195 carries and a 3.9 average. "I just had a bad year," he said. "I was hurt and there's nothing I can do about that. They act like it's my fault."

What about that fumble on the first play from scrimmage in Houston?

"I make one little mistake; it's like a world-sized mistake. To tell you the truth, I don't think they like me down there (in the front office) — just the way they act."

Worley was benched during a game for the third time during the season. "No one said anything to me," he said. "They just didn't put me back in. I was being punished, I guess. If you're going to take me out of the game, tell me why. Don't just let me sit over there and say nothing."

What would Nettie Worley think about what her son was saying about her favorite team?

"I know what I can do," he said for a parting shot. "I think next year I'll be a better ballplayer. I've got something to prove to myself and shut the people up around here. I get tired of hearing all this stuff.

"When I come back and do what I can do, I don't want to hear from anybody. I'm a good ballplayer and I'm going to prove that."

Woodruff's next-door neighbor in the Steelers' clubhouse, Rod Woodson, came in for some post-season honors, but it was hard to feel good about it, as it was announced the day after the disastrous season-ending loss at Houston.

Woodson was named the Steelers' 1990 most valuable player for the second time in a voting by his teammates. He was the third cornerback in team history to be so honored. Woodruff had won the award in 1982, and Mel Blount won it in 1975.

Woodson started all 16 games, and led the team in interceptions with a career-high five steals. He returned 35 kickoffs an average of 21.8 yards to rank third in the AFC, and broke the Steelers' all-time career kickoff return yardage record of 2,866 yards by Larry Anderson, finishing with 2,886. With 121 kickoff returns, Woodson was one short of Anderson's team record. Woodson's 23.9 yard career kickoff return average was the fourth best in team history.

He also returned 38 punts for a 10.5 yard average to rank second in the AFC and fifth in the NFL. His 116 career punt returns rank second in team history to Theo Bell's 139, and his 1,021 career punt return yards ranked third behind Bell (1,259) and Louis Lipps (1,212). Woodson had returned a punt 52 yards for a touchdown in a win over Houston in the second game of the season.

Inexplainedly, Woodson said something that week that was a complete turnabout from something he had told us in an interview only a week earlier.

"You get tired of hearing about the old Steelers, even though, it's a great tradition," Woodson told a Houston sportswriter. "This is a new team that is playing with new talent."

Woodson had come a long way since joining the Steelers. He grew up in a difficult environment in Fort Wayne, Indiana. He was a bit of a hood. In his early days with the Steelers, he seemed hell-bent on self-destruction, getting arrested for petty crimes and mischief.

But he has matured and grown, similar to the way another defensive cornerback, Mel Blount, who was thought to be a bad actor early in his career, but came on to be one of the classiest of the Steelers.

J.T. Thomas and Larry Brown
Southern hospitality

At first glance, J.T. Thomas and Larry Brown appear to be a bit of an odd couple. They do not seem to go together.

J.T. was a defensive back, to begin with, and Larry Brown an offensive tackle with the Steelers in the best of times. A study of the species would indicate that there is a real difference in the makeup and personality of players at those positions. Without benefit of any sociological studies, suffice to say they are just different. Strange as it sounds, good defensive backs tend to be offensive in their approach and demeanor while offensive linemen must be defensive and cautious and calculated in their actions. Maybe opposites really do attract.

Brown is a big guy, to begin with, even if not nearly as big as he was when he was playing right tackle for the four Super Bowl winners. Back then, Brown was 6-4, 270 and his teammates called him "Bubba." They said it with reverence. Now he weighed about 230. Thomas probably weighed a little more than he did when he was a lean, mean 6-2, 196.

Brown is the strong, silent type, somebody who would have gone largely unnoticed in the Steelers' clubhouse if he had not been so big, and such a beautiful fellow. Thomas called Brown "a silent doer."

Thomas wears tinted designer eyeglasses that hide bright eyes. His hair and mustache were always cut to precision, and he liked to accessorize his sharp-looking clothes. He had high cheekbones and well-chiseled features.

Brown has a beard that accentuates the long oval features of his face. He has a thoughtful look about him, an easy smile and a hearty laugh. There is a big teddy bear quality about this man.

Bill Nunn Jr., the club's assistant player personnel director back in the '70s, said, "You never know Larry Brown is in the camp until he takes the field. He never causes you any trouble; he never asks for any special favors. He never makes any noise."

Thomas, on the other hand, is a non-stop talker. Once he gets excited about a subject, it is tough to turn off the faucet. When he used to lecture a young player like Dwayne Woodruff, the player would have to beg off, or say to Thomas, "OK, J.T., I get your point!"

But Brown and Thomas, who turned 42 and 40 in 1991, respectively, have been close for a number of years, and have been involved in several restaurant ventures since they retired from football. They are both from the Deep South, and have similar heritages, and a strong sense of their roots.

Thomas grew up in Macon, Georgia, and Brown in Starke, Florida, and both remember all too well where they came from. They were raised by good, hard-working parents to do things right, to have common sense, to be responsible, to put their shoulder into their work, to overcome adversity and disappointment, and to succeed.

In that sense, they were like a lot of the Steelers from those Super Bowl years. They were co-owners of Applebee's Neighborhood Grill & Bar, a national franchise outlet located in the Bourse Shops in Green Tree. They were also partners in another Applebee's in the North Hills, and two Burger King franchises, in Penn Hills and in North Versailles.

One day, I took my sister, Carole Cook, who lived nearby in Green Tree, to Applebee's. She was excited to meet two members of the Steelers team that had given her and her family such thrills. She stood alongside Brown to get an idea of how big he was, as fans will, and he suffered the sizeup amicably. Thomas and Brown both exchanged pleasantries with us.

"I wonder," she said, when they departed, "whether they were always that nice, or did they get that way because they were so successful with the Steelers?"

I suggested they were that way to begin with and, like so many of us, picked up some polish from being surrounded by Steelers of similar background and character. Brown began his pro career as a tight end for the first six seasons, and then switched to right tackle where he became a permanent fixture as a starter before retiring after the 1984 season. He was a fifth round draft choice out of Kansas in 1971. He was chosen once (1983) to play in the Pro Bowl, an honor long overdue him in the opinion of so many of his teammates.

Thomas was the Steelers' No. 1 draft choice in 1973 out of Florida State. He became a starter in 1974. He was a standout in the 1977 Pro Bowl, when he was a late replacement for the injured Mike Haynes of New England. Brown and Thomas have more in common than first meets the eye.

Thomas made one of the great comebacks in Steelers' history after he had to sit out the 1978 season with a life-threatening viral illness called Boeck's Sarcoidosis. His play had suffered during the 1977 season following off-season surgery on his nose that was caused by his illness. He had not been able to train properly prior to the 1977 campaign, and it showed up, as he simply did not have the speed and stamina that had previously characterized his stellar play.

His illness was a hush-hush affair for quite awhile, and referred to as a blood disorder in official Steeler news releases, and media guides.

He came back from a year on the sidelines to make a major contribution to the Steelers winning their fourth Super Bowl after the 1979 season. He started every game in the secondary that season at left cornerback, playing opposite Mel Blount, with Mike Wagner and Donnie Shell at the safety positions. Ron Johnson and Woodruff were reserves in the defensive backfield.

Dr. David S. Huber was the head team doctor who discovered what was wrong with Thomas. Signs of the viral infection first showed up in chest x-rays done as part of the team's annual physical examination before the 1975 season.

473

Thomas had become a starter in 1974 and helped the team win its first Super Bowl. "I went in for a physical when we came to camp the next year," he recalled. "I felt great. Dr. Huber saw something in the x-ray he didn't like. He put me in a hospital. He took a biopsy from under my arm. My wife was pregnant with our first child. I'm 24, and I have my Super Bowl ring, and I had my Super Bowl check, which I hadn't spent, and I wanted to run out of that hospital and spend it all in one great big final fling."

Dr. Huber had Thomas hospitalized for several days. "Doc Huber came to me, at last, and told me he had some good news and some bad news," recalled Thomas. "He said, 'You don't have cancer, Hodgkin's Disease or leukemia, which were possibilities. You have Boeck's Sarcoidosis.' I wanted him to level with me, and he said, 'There's no cure for it. It can kill you. But I don't think it will. Some people have it for a month, and some for years. There's no way of telling how it will affect you.' He treated it with medication and each month I had an x-ray.

"The problem started for me during the 1976 season. I had a good season, too. But it started to act up on me. I had lymph nodes in my nose. I had a sniffle, and I thought I had a cold. I went to Ralph Berlin (the Steelers' trainer) and he gave me some Afrin, a nasal spray that is supposed to be effective within 18 hours.

"But I just kept using it. I got addicted to my medication. I went to the Pro Bowl after the '76 season, but I was suffering, and having a hard time breathing. Dr. Huber checked me out, and said, 'Your nose is the worst nose I've seen. It was like I had cotton balls stuffed up in both nasal passages. 'How do you play football breathing out of your mouth? Nobody can do that.' He told me he bet I had that nasal spray in my car, in my locker, in my medicine chest at home, and he was right. I was hooked on that stuff.

"I came back and played in the 1977 season. I gave up five touchdown passes and got beat deep a lot that year. But I never worked out in the off-season. The doctor wouldn't let me work out until June. I had always trained year round, and now I was starting two weeks before camp opened. I had been lifting weights, so I looked great. But I was in terrible shape. Bud Carson, who was our defensive coach, could see right away that something was wrong with me. I struggled all season long. I had a bad season. In the playoffs in Denver that year, I woke up in the morning and my throat had swollen up.

"I went back in the hospital in July of 1978. They had sent me all over the country to different specialists to find out what was wrong with me. I had a chronic problem. They kept it quiet, but they went out and drafted Ron Johnson and Larry Anderson early in the draft. People wondered what was going on. Mel Blount thought they were going to trade one of us. I couldn't say anything. Finally, it was announced at training camp that I could not play. I was ordered not to have any physical exertion.

"I sat out that season. It was probably my greatest season with the Steelers. Suddenly, I was on the outside looking in. I could see what

J.T. Thomas

was going on, what happened on a pro football team. I had gotten caught up in the arena, but now I was able to step back and see things differently. My perspective changed. I rearranged some priorities.

"I think Dan Rooney thought I was through. When I came back the next year, Donnie Shell and Terry Bradshaw both told me they wished they knew what I knew from sitting out a season. I had been resurrected. All athletes die twice, they say, once when their playing careers come to an end, and once when they die like everybody else. But I came back from the dead, so to speak. I could appreciate how lucky I was to be a pro football player.

"I learned a lot. I appreciated what I had. I had been worrying about the wrong things. When I was playing, I was paranoid. I always thought I was one play away from retirement. I knew that one play and you could be gone.

"I did come back, though. I had lost a big percentage of my lung capacity, but I had started jumping rope in the off-season, and I did it with gusto. I came back in 1979 and ran my fastest 40 yard dash ever.

"I ran it in 4.5. Dick Walker was our defensive backfield coach that year, and he was so ecstatic. He was going crazy. He told Chuck Noll what I had done. Dwayne Woodruff was a rookie and Larry Anderson was in his second season. Noll said, 'Put the old man in the middle, and let's see what he can do.' So I lined up between Anderson and Woodruff. I was the first one off the mark and got a great jump on them. But they caught me at the end and passed me.

"Anderson did 4.44, Woodruff was clocked at 4.46 and I ran 4.48. I also did better than players like Bradshaw and Stallworth in the stress test on the treadmill. I was as good or better than any of the guys on the team.

"I came back and played in Super Bowl XIV. By that time, people with Boeck's Sarcoidosis were coming out of the woodwork to talk to me about it, wherever I went. I got letters and phone calls from people all over the country. All of a sudden, I was a medical expert."

Larry Brown said that he and J.T. became friends while playing for the Steelers and that they once lived in the same apartment building, Mt. Royal Towers, in Squirrel Hill. Then they became roommates at the Steelers' training camp at St. Vincent College, as well as when the team was traveling on the road.

Brown said Starke, Florida is about 40 miles west of Jacksonville, and about 26 miles east of Gainesville. It is a small community of about 8,000. Lumber was a local industry of note. His father worked for DuPont in a local mine, extracting minerals for use in making paint.

"I worked as a kid," said Brown. "When I was 12, a friend and I invested in a lawn mower, and we worked the neighborhood. I cleaned up a dairy store for a year. I always had summer jobs."

Were there expectations at home that he should have some part-time jobs? "The expectations were there, for sure," Brown said with a smile. "My dad found those jobs for me. I was one of seven kids. My two sisters both worked at home, helping out and cleaning what they could, and all the boys had jobs. My mother worked. The money we earned was used to offset some of our personal expenses. My family also had a strong sense of religion."

His background was typical of so many of his teammates on the Steelers. When I told him so, Brown did not appear to be surprised. "We all talked about some of these things," he said, "so I knew where most everybody was coming from."

Brown said he was struck, as a young football player, when he learned of the death of Ernie Davis, an All-American at Syracuse, who played briefly for the Cleveland Browns before dying from leukemia. "People asked, 'Is he going to be as great as Jimmy Brown?' And then he was gone. I was also shocked when I learned that Willie Gallimore, a running back for the Chicago Bears who had played at Florida A&M, was killed in an auto accident. It brought things home to me. It made me realize that you can't take playing football, or even living, for granted. It's a gift that is given to you."

Because he started out as a tight end, Brown was smaller than most offensive tackles when he initially switched line positions. But he added 20 pounds between 1979 and 1980. "He's a stud," said Dick Haley, the team's player personnel director, when he saw Brown in action at the Steelers' training camp the summer after the team had won its fourth Super Bowl.

Mike Webster said back then that Brown was the best pass blocker on the Steelers' offensive line. His teammates were always praising Brown. They still are. Yet he never received much national recognition or acclaim. In that respect, he was a lot like Jon Kolb and Sam Davis, two other exceptional offensive linemen. All the Steelers simply could not be in the Pro Bowl. There were always eight or nine Steelers in the Pro Bowl back in those days. But the acclaim from his teammates meant a lot to Brown, and it still does.

"That's where I got my greatest satisfaction," he admitted. "In any profession, there are tough endeavors. It's very competitive. You need some self-confidence. You also need some feedback. It gives you some sense of credibility. You need that validation. I didn't get much of that from outside. You still need something to feed off. You need to know there is respect from your peers."

J.T. Thomas directs a choir at Ebenezer Baptist Church at 2001 Wylie Avenue in the heart of the Hill District. He said it is the oldest black church in the city of Pittsburgh. His friend, the Rev. J.V.A. Winsett, is the pastor. J.T. plays the organ and piano and sings. He mentioned with pride that his group had recently performed at the African United Baptist Association (AUBA) Conference. "It's the same church I grew up with back home in Macon," he said.

"I went to a Catholic grade school, and on Sunday I'd go from mass to Sunday school at my family's Baptist church. In the South, you go to church all day long on Sunday. You don't play ball. You went to church all day and you'd get home in time for the Ed Sullivan Show.

"I played with a lot of guys on the Steelers who were from the South. The South was different. I grew up with the integration process. I remember when I was 12, back in 1963, and I was riding in the front of a bus for the first time, and it was the biggest thrill of my life.

"I sat in the seat right behind the bus driver. I sold 120 pop bottles for a penny apiece to get the money to go see a movie. I was going to see Tarzan beat up a thousand natives. Tarzan was one of my childhood heroes. Tarzan talks to all the elephants, and his chimpanzee, and then he beats up on all the natives who have been in the jungle for thousands of years. So I was a little mixed up as a youngster. They even had special theaters for blacks in Macon in those days.

"I went through a lot of marches, and racial situations. When I was in kindergarten, I remember going into a downtown department store one day, and I couldn't read the signs by the water fountains, and I went to a fountain for white people and I put my mouth around the faucet. Some woman snatched me away, and told me that I wasn't to drink from that fountain. I remember going to the back of a Burger King to get a hamburger, and now I'm a Burger King franchisee. I was the first black football player at Florida State. But I could handle it. For me, it was old hat. As a youngster, I had a strong sense of will. I wanted to get a good education.

"I was one of the first 17 blacks who integrated the public school system in Macon back in 1965. I had gone to a Catholic grade school, St. Peter Clayver, and I was the valedictorian of my class. But, in ninth grade, I wanted to go to the public school. The black leaders selected the black students who would be integrated. They wanted to make sure they succeeded in school. Most of the black children, supposedly, weren't thought to be up to doing the work in the formerly all-white schools. I went to the public school and signed myself in, against my mother's advice. Nobody selected me. I just wanted to go there.

"I was in a protest demonstration there in Macon once. We were singing a church song that went like this: 'Before I be a slave, I'll be buried in my grave, and go home to live with my Lord.' Dr. King had just come through Macon, and he was preaching non-violent protest. But you wanted to retaliate for what they were doing to you.

"They put the dogs on us. Ronnie Thompson was the chief of police then. He had a gospel quartet then, and he had let my group sing on a TV show he had in town. So I knew him and he knew me.

"In 1975, after we had won our first Super Bowl, I went back to Macon. They were having a J.T. Thomas Day to honor me. I was given a key to the city by the mayor. The mayor was Ronnie Thompson. He later ran for governor.

"When I got the key, I told the city council, 'America is a great place. In 1963, they put dogs on me in this town. In 1975, they give me a key to the city.' Mayor Thompson came to the affair, and I wanted to remind him about that. The theme in Macon then, and now, was 'Macon is on the move.' It's moving, all right, but not fast enough.''

I mentioned to Brown that when Mel Blount was one of nine former Steelers selected to the 25th anniversary all-Super Bowl team he had expressed a wish that the entire Steelers team could be honored at half-time of Super Bowl XXV. I added that Terry Bradshaw said the only thing that would get him to return to Three Rivers Stadium would be if the entire Super Bowl cast came back to be honored.

"I felt that kind of kinship," said Brown. "There was a collective sense of accomplishment. As young men, our perspective isn't what it would be now. Now you can see just how lucky we were."

It would do no good to tell young players today about that, according to Brown. "It's the kind of thing older people have been telling you all your life," he said. "You may say something today that someone, it could even be your children, may hear and not act upon, but if it's a valid point they'll draw on it later.

"As much as I'd like to tell you that as an 18-year-old I formed my life's philosophy, that simply isn't so. But those things are built into you. Those values. What you think is right. What I will do or won't do. Those things are shaped in you early. We're a product of every step we've taken along the way. Certainly, I grew a great deal during my days with the Steelers. And not just in a physical sense.

"I knew what I wanted to be. If I ever have a legacy, I want it to be that I never intentionally hurt anyone.

"I think there was something special about the Steelers' teams I played with. It's special when you have a gathering of that kind of talent. But other teams had talent. On paper, some other teams looked so powerful. But they lacked something. Nothing is perfect, but we came close to it.

"The organization, the coaching, the players, and our ability to work together. That was special. You could look around that locker room and see so many great players. You didn't worry about it when somebody in the starting lineup was missing because of an injury. You knew you still had a great team on the field. You always felt the team could get along without you. That was humbling. We won Super Bowls with key players out. You wouldn't want to live without them too long, but you could win without certain players."

Asked whom he admired the most on the Steelers in his playing days, Thomas came up with a surprise choice. "Terry Bradshaw. I remember we were having a beer in the sauna after a game in which we had our butts kicked. He was always talking philosophically. And he said, 'T., I stunk today.' And I said, 'Hey, we all stunk.' But he wasn't satisfied. He said, 'You guys can lose with me, but you can't win without me.' He liked that, and he started kicking his legs around, and he hollered, 'Hey, T., write that one down. That's a good one.' And you know what? He was right.

"They called him dumb, but I'm telling you there were a lot of quarterbacks you could set them up for an interception. You couldn't do that with him. He threw the ball so quickly and so fast. The ball moved too fast for you to fool him as to your whereabouts. He'd throw to Swann in practice and he'd kill me.

"He wasn't stupid. He could handle a crowd booing him. He could handle all the personalities on the team. His personal life was in the papers. The average person couldn't have handled that. He persevered through all that.

"He was like a Christian thrown to the lions sometimes at Three Rivers Stadium. He had problems with receivers, too, but he overcame that. Stallworth and Frank Lewis felt they were overlooked. Lewis, by the way, was probably one of the greatest who came through here. Stallworth went to Bradshaw and he went to Noll, and he complained about Bradshaw always throwing the ball to Swann. 'Throw it to me or trade me,' Stallworth told Noll. Stall was a gem. But he was unhappy. But he spoke up. Terry started looking left. Before that, Terry had blinders on. It helped Terry.

"I played Swann every day in practice. And he was good. But I didn't want to play Stallworth. He had stuff he never even used. Ask Mel Blount. He did things that just blew your mind. When Stall came to my side in practice, it bothered me. More than any receiver in the NFL. He bothered me more than Isaac Curtis, Kenny Burrough, Fred Biletnikoff. He was the next guy I respected the most on our team.

"Mel was my best buddy. Even though he didn't talk to me as a rookie. Only John Rowser talked to me. There was another very talented guy. He was so knowledgeable. He taught me a lot. So did Mel once he started talking to me."

Asked whom he admired the most among his teammates, Brown became quite political. And honest. "You admired them for different reasons," he said. "It might be for sheer talent. It might be for the way they conducted their personal life. Frank Lewis and I were roommates at the beginning, and I thought the world of him, as a player and as a friend. Lynn Swann's locker was next to mine, and he was special. So were Stallworth and Shell.

"So was Jon Kolb. I worked out with him, and he taught me a lot about weight-lifting. He took me on as a personal challenge when I needed to build myself up as an offensive lineman. We worked as long as we had to work to get what we needed to get done. Mike Webster worked as hard as anybody I ever worked with. When you look back to Willie Mays, you know there are people who may have stayed too long. Maybe Mike has done that, but he worked so hard, and put in so much time and effort, I guess it's his call when he wants to give it up. I guess he's earned that.

"There were guys like L.C. I looked up to him a lot. I worked out every day against L.C. It was a combative situation. He made me work that much harder. Maybe Ernie and Dwight were more unpredictable than L.C. and Joe Greene, but L.C. gave you an honest workout. Dwight may have been more intense, and maybe L.C., because of his size, felt he had to save himself for Sunday. But he was tough.

480

"I saw him once go up against Bob Brown of the Raiders. Brown weighed over 300 pounds. He was awesome. L.C. was about 230 then. Every play, L.C. never gave up. He just kept coming at the guy. He didn't try to avoid him. His stature just started to rise with me after that.

"That's the beauty of football. You really see what the guys around you are made of. You could see this in your teammates. This guy answered the call.

"And, at the top, you had to admire Chuck Noll. You have to give Chuck credit as a manager and as a coach. He deserves credit. He dealt with a lot of different personalities and changes, and there were some tough decisions to be made, and you had to respect that. He kept a handle on the club.

"How blessed and lucky we were, when it all meshed together. It's not something you should dwell on, not something you should brag on. It tells you that you were fortunate to be a part of that. At the same time, it doesn't define your life.

"It can be part of a very important segment of it. You can draw upon it now, and all those experiences. You were stretched to the limit, physically and emotionally, and you lived through it.

"You tend to have more hope that you'll survive this, too. You look at tough things ahead of you. You don't have to let it overwhelm you. People have to go back to basics, and remember what they did to get where they are today.

"I was always nervous, always before a game. If I didn't feel it before the game, it would bother me. If I didn't take a guy seriously; if I saw film and I didn't think he could deal with me, I'd find myself struggling and have a difficult game. I'd get banged up when that happened. I was better when I respected my opponent. You always should."

As a youngster, Thomas thought sitting in the front of a bus was heaven. When he played for the Steelers, though, I recalled that he always sat in the last row of seats on the plane, on the left side. He had the seat on the aisle and Swann had the seat by the window.

The Steelers were a superstitious lot when it came to riding on airplanes. Most of the veterans staked claims to seats and they rode in the same seats for every trip, chasing rookies and stray sportswriters away from their domains. The same Steelers played cards together each trip, the same ones listened to music or read books or magazines.

Why did Thomas choose the back seat of a plane when the front seat of a bus had been such a big deal to him?

"I did that because of something Tony Parisi, our equipment man, told me," Thomas said. "When I was in college, Wichita State's football team was wiped out in an airplane crash. That bothered me. Tony told me, 'When you see a plane crash, what do you see? You always see the tail-end of the plane sticking out. To me, that's the safest place to be on an airplane.'

"So I always sat back there. Swann sat next to me. He sat there because he liked the media. And the media all sat in the back of the

481

plane. Elmer sat between us. If you asked if the seat between us was occupied, we'd tell you that Elmer was sitting there. For eight years, we did that. Elmer was a fictitious character we dreamed up so we could keep the seat empty between us."

I mentioned to him that he used to smoke a pipe on the airplane trips. "I did that in college, too. But I quit after I came back from being sick. I figured I better watch what I was doing, and be good to myself health-wise."

And he would wear a headset and listen to music. And smile a lot. He liked being in the back seat of the Steelers' plane almost as much as sitting in the front seat of the bus back home in Macon.

Larry Brown

482

None for the Thumb
A sober night at The Saloon

T he Saloon on Washington Road in the heart of Mt. Lebanon's business district was always a favorite haunt of the Steelers in their salad days.

"We had some crazy times in here," said Steve Courson. "I got insane in here more than once. But it was all in good fun; we never caused anybody any trouble."

Courson told war stories of how he and Gary Dunn, his running buddy when they were Steeler teammates for six seasons (1978-83), used to put the backs of their heads on the bar and drink Kamikazes at The Saloon. "Until we were half-blind," Courson says with a smile over his Fu Manchu mustache.

I didn't ask him what goes into a Kamikaze drink; I just figured it was self-destructive.

That sort of sums up Courson's life, and helps explain why, at age 35, he was an endangered species.

Courson confesses to abusing his body with too much alcohol, too much anabolic steroids, and too much night life. It has left him in jeopardy. "But we don't know what happened to my heart," he said. "Hell, Arnold Schwartzenegger used ten times as many steroids as I did."

But it's Courson whose life is imperiled.

"My life is on hold," he says. "Without a heart transplant, I am going to die."

Courson said he was keeping busy. That week he was a guest panelist about drugs in sports on Ann Devlin's "Pittsburgh's Talking" show on WTAE-TV. A war buff, he admitted "I've been glued to watching CNN the past two weeks, keeping up with the war in the Mideast. It's frightening."

Courson needed over $150,000 to pay for a heart transplant. There have been several fund-raisers held on his behalf by friends and former teammates over the past three years. None of them have raised a lot of money. But every little bit helps the fund grow.

Jimmy Sheppard, the owner of The Saloon, and Sue Duffy of Dormont, who has been working there as a waitress for 12 years, hosted a fund-raising night for Courson. It was promoted by Tom O'Malley Jr., of Bob Purkey's Insurance Agency in Bethel Park. O'Malley moonlights as a manager for the Steelers basketball team. O'Malley rounded up the former Steelers who served as celebrity bartenders at The Saloon.

They included Larry Brown, Ted Petersen, Bill Hurley, John Banaszak and Craig Wolfley, who had just returned to Pittsburgh after playing for the Minnesota Vikings during the 1990 campaign.

John Steigerwald of KDKA-TV was there to interview Courson and some of his teammates. Steigerwald noted how slim Brown appeared.

"He was up to 290 when he was playing for the Steelers," said Steigerwald. "You think he doesn't see Courson in his condition, and wonder if he's safe from the aftereffects of steroids. Nobody abused steroids more than Rocky Bleier, and he had admitted as much. It's ironic to see some of these guys and how much weight they have lost since they quit playing football."

Franco Harris and L.C. Greenwood would have been there, but they were among the nine former Steelers who were in Tampa to be honored as members of the Silver Anniversary All-Super Bowl team.

Wolfley came to Courson's side and told him that Tunch Ilkin wanted to come, but had a schedule conflict. "Tunch loves you, and he's praying for you," Wolfley told Courson. Then Wolfley leaned forward to get his head on the same level as Courson, who was sitting in a cramped booth, and hugged him warmly. It was cold as can be on the sidewalks outside The Saloon that late January night, but it was a lot warmer inside.

Wolfley also offered regards from Mike Webster, whom he said he had spoken to on the telephone that day.

This fund-raiser was held three nights before Super Bowl XXV. These Steelers all said they were happy that the San Francisco 49ers got bumped off in the NFC title game and would not be in the Super Bowl. After all, the 49ers had a shot at winning three straight and their fifth NFL title, and that would give them a Super Bowl record superior to the Steelers and another ring. They didn't want Joe Montana to have one for the thumb.

They were happy that a former teammate, Matt Bahr, booted the field goals that erased the 49ers and put the New York Giants in the big game against the Buffalo Bills.

It was 11 years earlier that most of them were in Pasadena, California, a few days away from beating the Los Angeles Rams in Super Bowl XIV for their fourth Super Bowl title.

Courson's former teammates, his friends and his fans all embraced and hugged him at The Saloon. They told him how good he looked, and wished him well.

Former teammate and weightroom advocate Mike Webster, who had been with the Kansas City Chiefs the past two seasons, sent a check for $500. It boosted the total take for the night to $1,520.

Courson seemed pleased. "It's important for me now to have this support," Courson said. "It's nice just to see all my teammates and friends having a good time together. There was never this kind of closeness when I was in Tampa. With the Steelers, we won more than Super Bowls."

When Courson was traded by the Steelers to the Tampa Bay Buccaneers in 1984, he felt estranged. But Courson is not a shy guy, so he aggressively pursued good times in Tampa Bay, the kind he had enjoyed in excess in Pittsburgh.

484

He tried to recreate the kind of environment he had with the Steelers. "I tried to get the guys in Tampa to get together after practice, and to get together for a few beers, and let their hair down. To get to know and appreciate one another better. But they weren't interested. There, it was more of an individual thing."

Courson spotted Wolfley on the other side of the bar, and nodded in his direction when he added, "Wolf says it was kind of like that in Minnesota. Maybe we were just outsiders . . . who knows? But they didn't seem to have much contact with one another off the field."

In Pittsburgh, besides The Saloon, the Steelers whose company Courson enjoyed used to hold Friday "team meetings" at Ron Dempsher's The Wheel Restaurant in Bridgeville, and they'd get together on weekdays at a bar in Mt. Lebanon called The Sunken Cork. On Sunday nights, they would go to the Marriott or Holiday Inn in Green Tree.

"We had some offensive line parties you wouldn't believe, where we'd use all the money we had paid out in fines for allowing sacks, or getting penalties," Courson said.

"We had a good time; we really enjoyed each other, and we cared about one another. I was the only single guy on the offensive line, so Dunn would come, even though he played on the defensive line, just to keep me company."

Courson and Dunn could fill up a room just by themselves, and they were just as capable of clearing a room. "We were usually the peacemakers, though," Courson said. "Half the time, they'd come to us if somebody was disturbing somebody or giving somebody a bad time. We should have been paid to be bouncers.

"I don't know how many times I had to step in between some guys and say, 'Hey, guys, I know you're having fun, but the party's over.'"

He looked to where Larry Brown was standing. "He's a class act," Courson said. "I was privileged to play between guys like Brown and Webster. I'm doing fine. Pretty soon, I should be able to go out in the woods and do some hunting, or go to the Florida Keys and go fishing with Gary. I'd like that. But I don't think I'll be making any comebacks in football. There are not too many 35-year-old offensive linemen. They're here for me; that's the main thing. It gives us a chance to see each other."

It was only a decade since Courson was a member of a Steelers team that won its fourth Super Bowl. He had started eight regular season games and two post-season games, but had to sit out the Super Bowl with a sprained right ankle. That was a bummer.

"It was full speed ahead for me in those days," Courson said. "I liked to party and have fun. Being a single guy, I had a wide open field. But it's changed since then. I've had to go to AA (Alcoholics Anonymous) for treatment."

I noted that Courson was sipping on a soda with a lime twist.

"I don't drink much anymore. I have a beer every now and then. Sometimes I'll have three or four in an evening, but that's a rarity more than anything anymore. I find I can still have fun. I was drinking real heavy back then and I wasn't really happy."

I had always heard that Courson and Dunn did just fine as far as finding women who wanted to keep company with them. At The Saloon, two good-looking women both sought Courson's attention. He was pleasant with them, but not interested in following up on their leading lines. One asked if he would sign his autograph on the front of her Steelers T-shirt ("I can't get the guts to ask you to sign my T-shirt," she said), and he obliged her. She also asked him to pose for pictures "You're not shy in front of a camera like me," she said). Another introduced her husband to Courson, but later made passes at Courson when her husband was no longer around. Courson just smiled a can-you-believe-this? smile at me. I figured he must have been an even greater magnet when he was playing ball for the Steelers, and showing up on all the TV screens at The Saloon. Wolfley and Courson compared notes on something else that was different between the Steelers and the Vikings and the Steelers and the Buccaneers.

"Those other teams don't do much contact work during the week," said Courson. "Chuck Noll is from the old school. He has to see guys go at each other for three days each week, and pound away at each other. I'm diametrically opposed to that. By then, you know what you're supposed to do on a football field, and you don't need to be hammering away.

"Wednesday and Thursday were always put-on-the-armor days — or what we called heavy days — and we'd ease up a little at Friday's practice. That's the way they did it with Paul Brown in Cleveland and with Sid Gillman in San Diego. They did some other funny stuff in San Diego when Noll was there, as far as amphetamines were concerned. They were available like candy mints in their clubhouse. So Noll is not as ignorant about drug usage in the NFL as he maintains.

"All the other teams have better-paid players, too. When Franco was trying to get a career-ending contract from the Steelers for $400,000 a year Tampa Bay was paying Hugh Green over $600,000 a year.

But both liked Pittsburgh the best. "It's a big small town," Courson said. "There are a lot of good fans here. You can have fun with the people, like the people who are here tonight. They looked forward to us coming. We livened up the place.

"But if I lived my life all over again, I don't think I'd play football. I liked it and I enjoyed it, but I'd devote more of my time to more intellectual pursuits."

Steve Courson

Heroes and Friends
Remembering those days with the Steelers

"Your heroes will help you find good in yourself,
your friends won't forsake you for somebody else."
—Randy Travis
country singer

In December of 1990, nine former members of the Pittsburgh Steelers were voted to the Silver Anniversary Super Bowl team in fan balloting conducted by the National Football League. It certified what Steelers fans had felt right along, that in the '70s they cheered on the greatest football team ever assembled.

Six of those players were members of the Steel Curtain defense, the heart of four championship teams. They were defensive tackle Joe Greene, linebackers Jack Lambert and Jack Ham, and cornerback Mel Blount — all members of the Pro Football Hall of Fame — and defensive end L.C. Greenwood and safety Donnie Shell.

Other Steelers selected were Hall of Fame running back Franco Harris, wide receiver Lynn Swann and center Mike Webster. The players were honored at the Super Bowl on January 27, 1991 in Tampa, Florida.

Quarterback Terry Bradshaw finished a distant second behind San Francisco's Joe Montana, a native of Monongahela, Pennsylvania, getting 134,584 votes to Montana's 747,801.

Vince Lombardi, who won the first two Super Bowls with Green Bay, was named the coach. Incredibly, Chuck Noll, the only coach to win four Super Bowls, was fourth in the voting, behind Lombardi, Bill Walsh and Tom Landry.

Soon after the announcement was made, Blount was traveling with the Steelers to New Orleans, and he was asked about its significance.

"It's a nice honor," he said, "but what about the rest of the guys? What about Larry Brown and Sam Davis and Jon Kolb and Bennie Cunningham and Randy Grossman and Glen Edwards and Mike Wagner? Do you want me to go on? I think our whole team was the greatest team in that 25-year period. We should be in it as a team. They ought to bring our whole team to Tampa to pay tribute to it."

That gives you some idea of why that team was so successful in the first place. They looked after each other, and Noll was successful in getting them to make individual sacrifices for the good of the team.

The only member of the Steelers' last Super Bowl champion team who was in the lineup on Super Bowl XXV was Matt Bahr. He had not gotten any bigger than when he was the littlest guy in the lineup with the Steelers, but now he was a Giant. A New York Giant.

It has been ten seasons since he was a Steeler.

He did not win the Super Bowl MVP award — that went to Ottis Anderson, the Giants' running back who, at 34, was the same age as Bahr. But Bahr provided the winning margin with the second of two field goals he kicked in the contest.

He kicked five field goals to account for all the Giants' points, including the game-winner in the final seconds, in a 15-14 victory over the San Francisco 49ers in the NFC championship game. Then, a week later, Bahr booted two field goals in a 20-19 victory over the Buffalo Bills in Super Bowl XXV.

Several Giants got down on their knees in a group on the sideline as Bahr lined up his field goal attempt at San Francisco's Candlestick Park. "Make it, please," one of them said. "Lord, let him make it."

"I was really happy for Matt Bahr, the way things worked out for him," said Joe Gordon, the Steelers' long-time front-office executive. "He was one of my all-time favorites. He was always a class act.

"When he was here, he obtained a master's degree (in industrial administration) from Carnegie Mellon University. I really liked him. He always had his head on his shoulders.

"You could see that the way he acted when he kicked the game-winning field goal against the San Francisco 49ers in the NFC championship game. Everyone else around him was going crazy, and Matt was standing out there like he was just kicking in warm-ups."

The one-point victory over the Bills was the closest margin of victory in the history of the Super Bowl. The Bills' Scott Norwood missed a 47-yard attempt in the last seconds of the game, or else Norwood would have been the hero.

When he was playing for the Steelers, Bahr worked as an engineer in the off-season at Westinghouse Electric.

During his second and last season with the Steelers, Bahr was blamed for at least three setbacks that season, two to Cincinnati and one to Cleveland. He also threw the Steelers off stride in a game with the Raiders.

"It's easier to play down my role in a win," Bahr once told me before a ballgame in Tampa in November of 1980, during his second and last season with the Steelers, "than it is to perk up after a defeat. When I miss a kick, and it comes back to haunt us, and we lose . . . that hurts me.

"I didn't contribute as much as I could. All I want to be is a part of the team and, to do that, I have to make my contribution."

The year before, Bahr had kicked some big field goals that won several games for the Steelers.

"My finest moment was going to the Super Bowl," Bahr said back then. "I couldn't have asked for more. Just being on the team.

"Kicking is funny. It's one of the few black-and-white situations in football. There are only two results. Only one needs an explanation. If you miss, people want to know what happened."

When we were talking in Tampa ten years before Bahr came back to be a Super Bowl hero, he was standing on the balcony of his hotel room, and he surveyed the beautiful blue water of the Gulf of Mexico and it sparked a thought:

"I've learned that when you lose, the sun still comes up in the morning, and when you win time doesn't stand still," said Bahr. "You always look ahead. I just want to help the team. I know it sounds redundant, but I'm a company man."

Then he thought better of that, and blushed. He apologized in parting. "I'm sorry," he said. "I'm not very interesting. I'm just an engineer at Westinghouse."

Ten years later, Bahr became the toast of the town in New York City with his football heroics. At the end of the 1990 campaign, he was the only Steeler still standing.

Like most kickers, Bahr was different, which helps explain why he regards the personal highlight of his Steelers' career — as did Randy Grossman — as "seeing myself on a bubble gum card." Right behind that was winning Super Bowl XIV against the Los Angeles Rams in his rookie season, and kicking a game-tying and game-winning field goal against the Browns earlier that season.

Bahr said it was interesting to experience the fierce rivalry between the Browns and Steelers from both sides, and it was a thrill being part of the Browns finally winning at Three Rivers Stadium after not doing so for a decade.

Super Bowl XXV Weekend was a disappointment for Lynn Swann. In the *USA Today* special preview edition that came out on the Friday before the game there were two items about Swann, one at the top of the sports section, and one in the People section of the nationally-distributed newspaper. Lynn was the first player listed, followed by L.C. Greenwood, among the 15 finalists in the voting for the 1991 class of the Pro Football Hall of Fame. Neither one of them made the final list of five enshrinees, however, that was announced the following day. It broke a four year chain in which former Steelers had been so honored.

There was also an item that Swann was being replaced by Alex Trebek as the host of the "To Tell The Truth" game show. Swann also drew the toughest assignment on Sunday on ABC's telecast of the Super Bowl when he had to interview the key figures from the losing Buffalo Bills team: coach Marv Levy, quarterback Jim Kelly, and the goat of the game, placekicker Scott Norwood, none of whom was a happy camper. To make matters worse, Swann was criticized in the next day's *USA Today* for addressing the Bills' coach as "Lev-ee" rather than "Lee-vee." Oh well, Swann has bounced back from adversity before. In fact, a few weeks later, he was a judge in the internationally-televised "Miss U.S.A." contest, and back in the spotlight again with Dick Clark and Barbara Eden. Swann was smiling from his frontrow seat.

Randy Grossman, who grew up in Philadelphia and went to Temple and was a fan of the Philadelphia Eagles, once listed his greatest thrill as making the National Football League in the first place.

The highlights of his Steelers' career, according to Grossman, who marched to the beat of a different drummer, was "making the team as a long shot free agent, and seeing myself for the first time on a football trading card."

His most cherished memory was "being a part of both historic events and a historically significant group of athletes and coaches."

The player he most admired was Andy Russell. "He was prepared and focused," said Grossman.

Grossman shared the tight end position with Bennie Cunningham. Cunningham had been the Steelers' No. 1 draft choice out of Clemson in 1976, and was 6-4, 247 and was a bigger and better blocker, which suited the Steelers' scheme of things. Grossman made the Steelers as a free agent in 1974. He was 6-1, 215. He possessed a great pair of hands, and was a reliable and resourceful receiver.

He left his mark. He started in 44 of the 118 games he played for the Steelers and caught 118 passes for 1,514 yards and five touchdowns during the regular season, and in playoff competition he caught 15 more for 186 yards and one touchdown.

"I'd like the fans to remember me for what I did," he said, "and for doing what I was asked to do when I was called upon."

When he retired after the 1981 season, Grossman was just 29. "It's really been a fairy tale," he said then. "Now I guess I'm officially stepping into the real world."

Grossman got involved in several business ventures while he was still playing ball, mostly investment and real estate projects, and continued to do so when he retired. He was an owner of a Bobby Rubino's Ribs restaurant at Station Square immediately upon retiring, then in real estate development at Seven Springs Mountain Resort, and more recently as a broker for Kidder, Peabody in downtown Pittsburgh. During the 1990 season, he was also doing daily reports on the stock market activity for WISH Radio in Pittsburgh.

He found a home in Pittsburgh, specifically Squirrel Hill, one of the nicest and best-preserved communities in the inner-city. He has had his ups and downs, successes and failures, since he left the Steelers with four Super Bowl rings in his collection, but he has done OK.

When I talked to many members of those Steelers' championship teams, several of them were aware that one of their teammates, Glen Edwards, who had put in seven seasons with the Steelers (1971-77), and had two Super Bowl rings of his own, was having a difficult time.

He was still wearing those rings. He said people tell stories that he was so bad off that he had to sell his Super Bowl rings, or that the IRS took them away from him, but Edwards shows the rings to visitors to put those stories to rest.

Randy Grossman

Sam Davis

Bill Amatucci

Bennie Cunningham

"People are going to believe anything they want, anyway," he told Bruce Lowitt of the *St. Petersburg Times* during the 1990 season. "People want to see you do bad. It's the nature of man."

Edwards, at 43, was making $1,300 a month and living from paycheck to paycheck as a jailer in the Pinellas County Juvenile Detention Center in Clearwater, Florida. He dealt with difficult youngsters who have run afoul of the law in his native state.

He used to make close to six figures a year when he was playing defensive back for the Steelers and then the San Diego Chargers in the National Football League. He had a condo in San Diego, and drove a Mercedes-Benz.

Now his 21-year-old marriage had fallen apart, his car had been seized by the IRS, his driver's license had been suspended. He was living in a small house in St. Petersburg with the oldest of his four children, 18-year-old Landrick, and trying to make ends meet. Edwards said he owed the IRS more money than he can ever hope to earn.

He has had as many as three jobs at one time, trying to get out of the hole. He reads the Bible, trying to find solace for what has happened to him. He feels like he is already in hell.

"I tell guys now that there's three steps in football — they get you, they trade you and they get rid of you for good. Until a guy experiences that third step, you never know what it's like. If your age doesn't get you, your salary will. They'll either tell you you're too old or not worth it."

Another Steelers defensive back, Dwayne Woodruff, was feeling in a similar mood after both the 1989 and 1990 seasons when he thought the Steelers were no longer interested in his services.

It was difficult to feel sorry for Woodruff, however. After all, he had been with the Steelers for 12 years, and had played 11 seasons with the Steelers. He sat out the entire 1986 season with a knee injuury, but was paid for that season as well. In 1990, he was making about $350,000 to $400,000 a year. He would have to be paid as much or more if the Steelers retained his services. He had become a reserve on the team, a reliable reserve, but a reserve just the same. He turned 34 shortly after the 1990 season.

Steelers' management had opened doors for him at Duquesne University's School of Law, which he had attended at night for several years to get his degree, and had opened doors for him with a local law firm where he was employed. If, indeed, his days were over with the Steelers, why couldn't he walk away feeling the Steelers had been pretty good to him, and supportive above and beyond the call of duty?

The Steelers are proud of what Woodruff has accomplished, as a player, as a citizen, as an attorney, and they would like to think he would be as proud of his past association as they have been.

For the previous few years, Woodruff had been talking like he was wronged by the Steelers somehow. They left him unprotected in the

Plan B free agent draft, but brought him back for the 1989 and 1990 seasons when no one else offered him a contract. If he is not happy with how he was treated by the team, how can anybody else be expected to look back with a kind eye on his experience? Certainly Dwayne Woodruff owes the Steelers some thanks. Conversely, he had been a model citizen and had represented the Steelers in a first-class fashion.

About a week later, on February 1, Woodruff's name was, indeed, on a list of 15 players the Steelers did not protect on their 37-man Plan B list. Those not protected were free to sign with any team they chose until April 1. After that, their rights would revert to the Steelers.

Key veteran players also left unprotected included John Rienstra, the team's No. 1 draft choice in 1986, Keith Willis, Mike Mularkey, Terry Long, Brian Blankenship and Bryan Hinkle and players with promise such as Tyronne Stowe and Derek Hill.

"Just because they're on the list doesn't mean they're unwanted," said Tom Donahoe, the director of pro personnel and development. Hinkle, Willis, Mularkey and Blankenship had all told Donahoe they had no plans to sign elsewhere.

"I won't be leaving the Steelers," said Hinkle. "I told them if they need to put me on (unprotected list) in order to keep someone else, that's fine with me."

Hinkle was offered new and longer contracts by other clubs, with a signing bonus, but said he would keep his word. "I want to stay in Pittsburgh," said Hinkle.

Mike Webster felt wronged when he left the Steelers. He wanted to continue to play, and they felt he had played long enough. There might have been an opportunity for him to stay as a coach, but they could not get a good reading, they said, on exactly what he wanted to do.

Webster was among the most admired of the Steelers' Super Bowl cast. When I polled members of the supporting cast of Steelers' teams since the club moved to Three Rivers Stadium in 1970, Webster was among those most often mentioned in that respect on the questionnaires they returned.

Emil Boures, a backup center and guard for five seasons (1982-86) after coming out of Pitt, put it this way: "Webster was a team player, very unselfish, who would help rookies trying to take his job. But, most of all, he was a friend."

Steve Furness, a defensive lineman for nine seasons (1972-80), was a neighbor of Webster's in McMurray, and they lifted weights together. Furness was hired in February as a defensive line coach with the Indianapolis Colts after serving as an assistant coach at Michigan State, working for George Perles, who had been his coach with the Steelers.

"I admired Mike Webster because he was a self-made player," said Furness. "He was not blessed physically as some were, but he had a hundred percent determination and mental toughness."

Furness felt the highlight of his Steelers' career was "the first time I was introduced on defense in Three Rivers Stadium."

In early March, just before his 39th birthday, and following his 17th season in the National Football League, Webster announced in Kansas City that he was retiring as a player. For real. He would be eligible for the Pro Football Hall of Fame in 1996.

Ray Pinney, a commercial real estate broker back in Seattle where he played offensive line for the University of Washington before he joined the Steelers in 1976, wrote of Webster: "He trained hard, practiced hard and got the most out of the talent he had."

A cherished memory for Pinney was a comical one: "When (defensive backfield coach) Dick Walker got poked in the butt with a yard marker in Cleveland in 1978 during a play that ended up in a big pileup on the sidelines. Walker had to leave the game, get stitches, and stood up on the bus all the way back to Pittsburgh."

Rod Woodson, the Steelers' MVP for 1990, was honored at a banquet at the Vista International Hotel in mid-February. He was able to watch a personal highlights film, hear his coaches praise him, and he received a gold watch from the Pittsburgh Chamber of Commerce, and discussed how he could soon become a million dollar a year ballplayer.

But his mind, like a lot of other people's minds, was elsewhere, on a war in a strange land. "My oldest brother is in the Middle East now," he told the audience at the Vista. "Talking to him on the phone puts everything in perspective."

Joe Jay Woodson, 29, is a sergeant in the first platoon of the U.S. Marine Corps. He was stationed at the time in Saudi Arabia, and was involved with tanks.

Terry Hanratty had fun when he played for the Steelers, even though he never realized the personal goals he had set for himself after coming back home — he was born and raised in nearby Butler — following an All-America career at Notre Dame.

"I think ballplayers ought to step back from football and take a broader look, to see the big picture," he said when we spoke shortly after Super Bowl XXV. "I don't think they realize how lucky they are. I don't think enough of them give back to the community.

"They should lighten up a little. We won only one game in 1969, but we enjoyed each other and the camaraderie was great. It seems like there's no fun in football anymore. People don't go out in the community anymore and enjoy themselves and the fans."

He pointed to the Pirates as to how ballplayers have changed, how sports have changed. "I used to know every one of the players on the 1960 Pirates," he said. "Now the names and faces change so much from one year to another. Now everyone is after the best deal — I can't blame them in a way — but sports is not what it used to be. Maybe that's age talking; I hope not. I'm still just a young pup."

Hanratty, at 43, was at his desk at Sanford Bernstein at 59th and Fifth Avenue in midtown Manhattan, where he was an institutional broker. His clients included Mellon Bank, PNC and Federated Investors, to name a few, and this enabled him to get back to Pittsburgh on business trips about every two months.

It sounded hectic as hell in the background. "There's Mellon Bank now," I heard Hanratty saying to someone else, as we spoke over the telephone. "Hey, will somebody pick up on Mellon Bank for me?" It sounded like he was on a telephone from the floor in the middle of the New York Stock Exchange.

Hanratty said he learned things during his days at Notre Dame and with the Steelers that serve him in good stead today. "Just the importance of teamwork," he said. "Being able to get along with your teammates. We have 15 brokers here, and we're in close quarters. You have to be able to get along with your fellow workers."

The best of times for Hanratty happened during the 1972 season. "Terry Bradshaw separated his shoulder in a game with Cincinnati at midseason, and I suffered broken ribs in relief of him in the same game. But I was able to play, and I was the starting quarterback for the next four games. We won three of them.

"It felt good to be in control of the club. Having the team at your command. I was not a good relief pitcher. I sprained my wrist in Cleveland in about my fifth game, and Terry was able to take over again.

"I had great expectations for myself in Pittsburgh. But, in the end, the best quarterback won out of all of that."

I mentioned to him that some of his Steeler teammates felt Joe Gilliam got the short end of the stick from the Steelers when he was bumped in favor of Bradshaw during the 1974 season.

"Joe was not running the offense the Steelers wanted to run," recalled Hanratty. "Joe wanted to throw the ball. On every down. He went in there and ran one play they called, and then he went boom, boom, boom.

"You can't win that way. It's been proven. The New York Giants this year are the best example of the kind of team that wins. They had a boring offense, but their defense was great and gave them good position, and they knew how to get it into the end zone."

His most cherished memory came after the Steelers won their first Super Bowl. "Seeing Mr. Rooney up there on the stand accepting the Lombardi Trophy from Commissioner Pete Rozelle was a great sight," said Hanratty. "Mr. Rooney had the map of Ireland on his face, and the look of the aged people of all places in Pittsburgh, the look of the blue-collar worker. He was up there for a lot of people who never thought they would ever be winners."

As for the Steeler he admired the most, Hanratty said, "I'd have to say Ray Mansfield. Oh I admired Franco Harris and Lynn Swann and players like that, but Mansfield the most.

"I don't think I ever knew of a guy who had more heart than he had. He played through painful injuries. You couldn't get him out of there. He could suck it up better than anybody. Today, on size and athletic skill, he might not even get a shot. To be calling all the shots in the offensive line the way he did always impressed me.

"I'm in awe of him. Every time I see him, I tell him that."

Punter Craig Colquitt who spent six seasons with the Steelers, kept company with Matt Bahr, but Jack Lambert was his favorite. "He initiated team leadership by his presence and field efforts," commented Colquitt. Reserve defensive back and kick returner Rick Woods (1982-86) also looked to Lambert for his "no-nonsense" and "tough style."

In the "most admired" category, Lambert, Jack Ham and Franco Harris got the nod from Bahr. "They did their talking with their actions," said Bahr.

Gregg Garrity, who also graduated from Penn State, also tabbed Harris as the Steeler he most admired. "Because not only was he a great player and leader on the field, but he's a great person off the field," said Garrity. "No one was too small or insignificant for him to spend time with."

John Banaszak, a defensive lineman for seven seasons (1975-81) with the Steelers who was close to Furness and Webster, cited Joe Greene as the "most admired" player. "Joe exemplified exactly what a professional football player should be like, both on and off the field," said Banaszak, a businessman in McMurray.

"From my experience with the Steelers, I learned to be a champion in all aspects of my life. For the Steelers were champions before Mr. Rooney received his first Lombardi Trophy."

Gerry "Moon" Mullins, a starting offensive lineman during the decade of the '70s who continues to reside in McDonald, Pennsylvania, and sells commodity minerals, also pointed to Greene as the player he most admired. "He was a great player, a team leader on and off the field, and an exceptional human being," said Mullins.

Tony Dungy, a defensive backfield coach on Marty Schottenheimer's staff with the Kansas City Chiefs, has fond memories of his two seasons (1977-78) with the Steelers as a reserve defensive back and his eight seasons (1981-88) as an assistant coach.

"I admired Larry Brown," said Dungy. "We had so many guys who were dominant at their positions, but Larry Brown and Jon Kolb were great players who never got any fanfare. And Larry was the nicest, humblest person you would ever meet. Only the players on our team knew how great he was."

Dungy's highlights included "making the team in 1977" and leading the team in interceptions with six after "jokingly saying in training camp that I would get more interceptions than Mel Blount."

Loren Toews looked to fellow linebacker Jack Ham. "He combined flawless execution of his trade with humility and graciousness. He imparted inspiration by his performance," said Toews.

Bennie Cunningham's hero was John Stallworth — "a real perfectionist and a sincere friend."

Rocky Bleier was the "most admired" by several Steelers, including Stallworth. Randy Reutershan, a special teams performer and defensive back from Pitt for one season (1978) with the Steelers, wrote: "I knew how hard it was for me to make the team, but Rocky Bleier had so much more to overcome. And he was able to reach and maintain such a high performance level."

J.R. Wilburn Jr., a record-setting receiver for the Steelers from 1966-70, seconds the motion. "Rocky Bleier overcame extreme disabilities to not only make the team, but to go on to star in Super Bowl games."

John Brown, an offensive tackle (1967-72) who was now a district manager with Pittsburgh National Bank, said the highlight of his career was "being there at the beginning of the maturation of the great Super Bowl teams." He said Bleier was the player he admired the most: "He made the most of his talents."

Sam Davis, who played 13 seasons for the Steelers as a guard, was a great blocker for Bleier and Harris, and somebody other players and sportswriters felt comfortable confiding in. "I admired all my teammates," declared Davis, a North Hills businessman, "because each had their own uniqueness, their own special way of handling things."

Remember Mark Malone said he and his wife were going to Lamaze Method classes during the Steelers' summer stay at St. Vincent?

The Lamaze Method focuses on controlled breathing and resultant control of pain. You learn about the labor process, mind-conditioning and pattern-paced breathing. Best of all, you feel like a team. You are in it together, or at least that is the idea.

I told Malone he might want to check with Jon Kolb, one of the Steelers' assistant coaches, and a former teammate of Malone, for some additional advice on the subject.

Kolb was regarded as one of the strongest players in the National Football League, and was a legend in the team's weight-lifting room, when he participated in a birthing process during the 1980 season.

I recalled that Kolb completely blanked out in the delivery room, and could not remember whether his wife was supposed to be inhaling or exhaling at the start of contractions. It was his job to coach her in that respect, to help her relax, but he froze.

He tried to support his wife's back, and said afterward that his arms were never so sore before. And this was a guy who could bench press 550 pounds.

I called Malone late in the season to see how things had worked out for him and Mary Ellen. They'd had their share of tough times. Both came from broken homes, and while Mark was playing for the Steelers, it was discovered that Mary Ellen had thyroid cancer. But they overcame their setbacks.

I wanted to know how they had come through their Lamaze Method experience.

"We never got to do it," Mark said. "We ended up not using the Lamaze Method. She had to have a Caesarean section delivery. We had twins, a boy and a girl, Austin James weighed 8 pounds, 1 ounce, and Shelby Lynn weighed 6 pounds, 1 ounce. It's great. Everything's super."

Many of these Steelers also have cherished memories of Art Rooney. Bahr mentioned "the continued friendship with The Chief and the other Rooneys after I was released" as being important to him.

Dungy knows that Art Rooney kept in touch with players who were sent elsewhere. "My most cherished memory was Mr. Rooney's letter to my parents after I was traded to the San Francisco 49ers. He wrote them and said he had enjoyed meeting them and appreciated having me on the team. That was special coming from him."

Boures said his most cherished memory was "getting to know Art Rooney, Sr. It was fun sitting in his office, or in the locker room, and talking to him. He knew more about you than you knew about him."

Colquitt recalled that "Art Rooney Sr. signed and wrote a personal note on a baseball to my son, Dustin, writing 'You will be a star someday.' It was great stuff."

Sam Davis lists his most cherished memory as "presenting the game ball to Mr. Art Rooney after the first Super Bowl."

For Furness, it was "watching Mr. Rooney stroll the sidelines during practice, smoking his cigars."

Ted Petersen's career with the Steelers was interrupted when he was sidelined for several seasons with a hip problem. It hurt him whenever somebody hit him there. He had a tumor there, and it was feared it was cancerous. But it turned out to be benign.

He is thankful for that. Petersen played for the Steelers from 1977 to 1983 and again during the 1987 season.

He admired Art Rooney Jr. and Jon Kolb, a fellow offensive lineman. "Jon was such a great competitor as well as a great man," said Petersen. "Jon helped me considerably as a player."

Petersen was hired in 1990 as the head football coach at Trinity High School in Washington, Pennsylvania, where he also served as assistant athletic director and a health teacher.

"Playing under Chuck Noll was a great help to me now that I am coaching high school football," Petersen said. "I see myself acting and reacting just like he did. It's scary!"

John Luckhardt, the highly-successful athletic director and football coach at Washington & Jefferson College, about 30 miles south of Pittsburgh, provided some interesting insights into the Steelers and the Rooney family.

"Merril Hoge and Hardy Nickerson work out in the off-season at our weight room at W&J," allowed Luckhardt. "And Craig Wolfley still comes around. They are the best kind of guys you'd ever want to meet.

"I've been there for ten years, and I got to know some of the Steelers who used our facilities back then, like Mike Webster, John Banaszak, Larry Brown, Jon Kolb and Steve Furness.

"They are the types of people you want your young people to be exposed to. They emanate such great personal characteristics, and reinforce all the things you talk about as a coach and educator. They provide tremendous models for how you ought to live your life."

Luckhardt played his college ball under Jack Mollenkoff at Purdue, and later served as an assistant coach at the University of Illinois. "I remember going to the College All-Star camp one year in Chicago," recalled Luckhardt, "and Jon Kolb was a 215-pound center and Larry Brown was a tall, skinny tight end who couldn't catch a cold.

"And I coached against Wisconsin when Webster was sharing the starting center spot with another player. He, too, was about 215 then. Kolb and Brown became bookend tackles for the Steelers, and Webster has had a great career as a center in the NFL.

"They were all misfits, and the Steelers had a lot of them. Noll took a lot of undersized centers and made them guards and tackles. Tunch Ilkin was a college center, too. He liked players who were quick on their feet, and agile for his trap-blocking schemes.

"But they have all been successful. I'm a believer that people who are successful are multi-dimensional, so I am not surprised that they have been successful following their football careers."

Several members of the Rooney family have been associated with the football program at W&J during Luckhardt's tour. They are all grandsons of Art Rooney. Alumni of his program include Mike, the son of Art Jr.; Dan, son of Dan; and Sean, son of John. Going into the 1991 season, Luckhart listed three sons of Pat, namely Chris, Tom and Brian. So he has had the sons of all the Rooney brothers except Tim.

"What I have always admired about the Rooneys is that they start at the bottom and work their way up," said Luckhardt. "Dan, the president of the team, started out picking up the laundry, and that included jockstraps, when he was a kid.

"The kids were not given everything. All of them have been asked to work. They have all worked as ballboys or in the equipment room. They don't walk in looking for you to take care of them, as they might, coming from a family that owns the professional football team in town. They are great kids."

The Steelers' season was over. A few sportswriters, not many, were in the Steelers' office for Chuck Noll's final press conference of the season. So was Lynn Swann, but not in an official capacity. He had simply stopped in to say hello to some of his close friends in the organization, and to wish everyone a "Happy New Year."

He was speaking to some secretaries, as he used to do when he was playing for the team. He was wearing a brown leather aviator's jacket, blue jeans, and a brilliant smile. 1990 had been a good year for Lynn Swann.

In addition to all his ABC-TV sportscasting duties then, he was also hosting a game show on NBC-TV called "To Tell The Truth."

"In the future you might be seeing me on all the networks before I'm through," he said.

When Swann peeked his head into the media room where TV cameras were already set up to tape Noll's weekly press conference, Swann whispered, "Is this the post mortem?"

Asked to size up why the Steelers came up short in such a big game against the Oilers, Swann smiled. "The defense, which has been great all year, is expected to perform on that level, but it didn't. You have to do it again and again to go all the way.

"You have to have an offense coming on strong and sharing its responsibility, and they didn't move the ball until it was too late. And you can't let a young quarterback (the Oilers' Cody Carlson) with talent feel very confident early. You can't let a team take off on you like that and run up points.

"It's never easy to get to the playoffs or the Super Bowl. It's easier today with the new expanded field for the playoffs, but it's nothing you can take for granted."

I questioned Swann about his visit to the Steelers' offices on the afternoon of New Year's Eve. Was it the pork and sauerkraut for lunch that drew him back?

"I don't come over here very often," said Swann. "Professionally, I have no reason to be over here. Another reason is that I don't think the guys really want to see the players of the '70s strutting through here like they all own the place.

"If I have a reason to come here, it's to say hello to people like Ralph Berlin (the trainer), Tony Parisi (the equipment manager), or Rodgers Freyvogel (the field manager). For the present team, it's not that beneficial to be seeing us. People are always comparing them to the old Steelers. They must get sick of it.

"We can do nothing to alter what we did here, but the memory of what we did is embellished by time. I jumped over a car here once. It was a promotional car sitting in the end zone. I was going deep for a pass and couldn't stop my forward momentum. So I leaped over the hood of the car rather than run into it. I thought that was pretty good. But before long, I had jumped over a car length-wise rather than across the hood. Then it became a truck that I jumped over. That's what I mean. Everything gets embellished.

"I like the guys on this team, but I choose to give the players space to make their own history. All the old timers want to hold on to what we did. It's why guys stay associated with their alma maters. Why they belong to alumni groups. It gives them a feeling of youth. There's a certain segment of our society that doesn't want to get old.

"But we can't do anything to add to what we did, or all that we accomplished from 1970 to 1980, when we won our last Super Bowl, or the building of this franchise. We can't add to the legendary stories, like Mean Joe Greene throwing his helmet against the goal post.

"Or Terry Bradshaw losing his hair, trying to become a quarterback. Franco Harris can't make another 'Immaculate Reception.' John Stallworth and Bennie Cunningham and I . . . we can't catch another touchdown pass. Mel Blount can't make another interception. Donnie Shell can't nail anybody. Frenchy Fuqua can't wear another cape. L.C. Greenwood can't have another dress-off with Frenchy. Dwight White can't intimidate anybody. Larry Brown can't have another Pro Bowl season and still go unrecognized. Mike Webster can't snort and see his breath in the cold anymore, at least not in a Steelers' uniform."

I mentioned to Swann that a front office official of the Steelers suggested the organization could have done a better job in handling the separation of its players, and that he wished more of the former ballplayers would come around, that they could be a good influence on the younger players.

Only two weeks before, when Mel Blount hitched a ride with the team to New Orleans, Blount had told a reporter, "I'm one of about five guys who still can come back, who still enjoys a strong relationship with the Steelers."

Swann shrugged that one off. "Everybody has different reasons for why they do what they do," he said. "Even when I was a player, I was always more comfortable at this end of the building than most of the ballplayers. Some guys never came back here to the offices."

He was standing in Art Rooney's old office, where I pointed out the Rooney's reflection in a glass pane. Swann also showed unusual insight in recognizing what Rooney was all about. "He was in a tremendous situation, or position, when I came here," said Swann. "Dan was running the operation, and Mr. Rooney had time to be a good guy. He was like just a nice man.

"Art walked around here, smoking his cigar, saying hello to everybody. He knew everybody's name. He would ask, 'How's your mom and dad?' He was in a position where he could afford to be more concerned about people than winning or losing, or money, unlike an owner like Al Davis. But let's not make any mistake; he taught Dan how to run this business. And he didn't believe in giving the house away to the ballplayers. They still don't.

"I didn't know Mr. Rooney at all when I was drafted. But our quarterback coach at Southern Cal, Craig Fertig, told me all I needed to know about him. Fertig was drafted by the Steelers (on the 20th round in 1965) after playing quarterback at USC. He got a signing bonus. But before he reported, John McKay made him an offer to stay at USC and coach the quarterbacks. Fertig decided to forget about pro football, and he returned his bonus check to the Steelers.

"Craig told me he heard from Mr. Rooney, who told him that nobody had ever returned a bonus check before when they didn't have to. Now Craig Fertig was a cigar smoker. Every year, Craig told me, Mr. Rooney sent him a Christmas card and a box of cigars."

501

Jim Clack

Jim Clack
"Super Bowl strategies for a championship life"

Just call Jim Clack the comeback kid.

He has had more comebacks than Muhammad Ali, Sugar Ray Leonard, Frank Sinatra, Elvis Presley and Lazarus combined. Those who care about Jim Clack can only hope he does not have to make any more comebacks.

He has overcome a lot of adversity in his life. He suffered several setbacks, some self-imposed, but he has always been able to find strength somewhere and to work his way back to the top, or pretty close to it.

Clack was a starting guard for the Steelers in their first two Super Bowls (IX and X), and was later the captain and offensive MVP for the New York Giants.

Not bad for a fellow who it was felt was too small, at 6-3, 215 pounds, when he came out of Wake Forest University to ever make it as a professional football player.

Clack, in fact, failed in his first two training camp trials to stick with the Steelers, but made good on his third try and became a key contributor and inspirational force for two championship teams.

Throughout his life, Clack simply has refused to stay down when others might have called it quits.

He has faced and overcome incredible obstacles, from devastating athletic disappointments and defeats to crushing business failures, to a drug usage arrest, and an automobile accident in which he was nearly killed in 1985. Clack has always come through, persevering and winning.

Nowadays, Clack is an in-demand motivational speaker as the director of special projects for The Brooks Group in Greensboro, North Carolina, near his hometown of Rocky Mount. Like former teammate, Rocky Bleier, he has good stories to share with others, true stories about his own life and a series of struggles and successes. It is called, fittingly enough, "Super Bowl Strategies For A Championship Life."

Comments Clack: "I've been very fortunate to play football so long. I always enjoyed playing the game. There's nothing like winning the Super Bowl."

His boss, Bill Brooks, believes that the key to future success often lies in studying the past.

"While many of the obstacles we encounter in this extremely busy world are new, how we react can be predicted by studying how people with characteristics similar to ours reacted to the challenges in their lives," said Brooks, a writer, speaker and founder of The Brooks Group, a sales training and consulting firm.

"I have always been enthralled by what motivates people, and what inspires a few to a high level of sustained performance," said Brooks.

"By understanding that, I can find ways to help others motivate themselves."

Jim Clack is an ideal case for somebody like Brooks.

There have always been obstacles in Clack's case. "The death of my father in high school," he recalled over the telephone, "the making of the Steelers' team after the third try, the trouble I had when I got out of football in 1982, and the wreck on July 17, 1985 are all true experiences in my life.

"I was fortunate to have a strong family base that taught me strong value structures," he said. "Those principles have helped me survive through some very impossible times. I regret that my father never saw me play high school, college or professional football. He died when I was a sophomore in high school. My mother has been by my side through thick and thin. She is the best."

Clack does a program on focus, teamwork and commitment in which he tells football stories that relate to business situations and career growth. Having been a vital cog in the development of playoff teams in Pittsburgh and New York, he knows what he is talking about.

In February, 1991, Clack was inducted into the Wake Forest University Hall of Fame. He was one of four former Deacon athletes honored at halftime of an exciting basketball game with Duke, which Wake Forest won. He choked up when he made his acceptance speech, and could not hold back the tears. "It meant a great deal to me," said Clack.

Clack's career had a storybook start. He was a bona fide hometown hero at his high school in Rocky Mount. He gained All-American honors as a football player back then, and scored the winning basket when his high school team won the 1962 4-A state championship game. You have to understand how big high school basketball is in North Carolina — close to the hysteria of Indiana, if you remember the movie "Hoosiers" — to appreciate the significance of being a schoolboy star in Rocky Mount.

He went to Wake Forest in Winston-Salem where he started on the football team for three years, playing linebacker as a sophomore and junior, then offensive tackle in 1968, his senior year. That season he received the "Bill George Award," presented annually to the team's top lineman.

He tried out for the Steelers as a free agent in 1969, but was cut and ended up playing for Norfolk in the Continental Football League. The next season he was a member of the Steelers "taxi squad," practicing with the team, but never dressing for a game.

In his third attempt, he made the team and was a contributing member of a team that made six straight playoff appearances. He played center and guard for the Steelers, and snapped on punts, extra points and field goal placements.

He split time with Ray Mansfield at center, and mentions Mansfield as the player he most admired on the Steelers. "Even though we were fighting for the same job," recalled Clack, "Mansfield was still trying to help make me a better player. He defined what giving 100 per cent is all about."

Clack also cites the Steelers' organization as a model in professional sports. "We were like one big family," said Clack. "The relationships and times off the field are among my most cherished memories. It's something that can never be taken away. It was not only a great team, but it was a great bunch of people. Real friends. The association with the organization and The Chief was special.

"The money was not always the best, but I guarantee you that the Steelers' organization run by Mr. Rooney and his family was one of the greatest sports franchises of all time."

When Clack was playing for the Steelers, he always had something going on the side. He owned an antique shop in Washington, Pennsylvania, where he and his wife Becky lived, and he was a sales representative for a trucking firm. He even took a fling at politics in Washington County.

He was a center when he first signed with the Steelers. Because of injuries, he was forced to play guard and he did a good job. Then the Steelers traded away Bruce Van Dyke to the Green Bay Packers and Clack shared a guard spot with Sam Davis.

The Steelers back then had a most versatile offensive line and many of the players had been centers to begin with. At one time when Dan Radakovich was coaching the offensive line, there were four centers in action at once. That would be Clack, Mansfield, Mike Webster and Jon Kolb. Of course, Radakovich was a center in college at Penn State. "If you can block with the ball, you can block without it," said Radakovich. "It makes sense."

Sometimes they slipped into old habits, however. Centers traditionally are the building block for an offensive huddle. Clack forgot once that he was playing guard and not center. "I put my hand up to signal for the huddle," recalled Clack. "The guys didn't know who was playing center. Finally, Ray Mansfield told me to put my hand down."

Clack recalled another incident when he got dinged in the head. "Chuck Noll sent Ray Pinney in to replace me," recalled Clack. "But Pinney said the wrong thing when he entered the huddle. Mullins was supposed to move into my spot. And Pinney was to play where Mullins had been. Pinney told Mullins he was replacing him, and Mullins thought he was supposed to go out, and he refused to. So Pinney went back to the sideline. We scored a touchdown on the next play, but Noll still screamed at us when we came off the field. Mullins got real mad about that. Even when we scored a touchdown, we couldn't always please Chuck."

Clack could play either guard position or center, and was a valuable player for the Steelers. In fact, he was the answer to a trivia question they had at the Pro Football Hall of Fame to test visitors.

One question called for the name of the only offensive lineman ever to play three positions in a regular NFL game. The answer was Clack, who played both guard slots and center, against Baltimore in the 1974 opener.

Clack became more than just the answer to a trivia question, however. He had built himself up to 250 pounds.

"I had never been on a weightlifting program in my life before I came to Pittsburgh," said Clack. "Physically, it was demanding, but that didn't bother me as much as the mental depression that went with it. I mean there I was watching guys my age lift and press almost twice as much weight as I could. I felt like a weakling, but in six months I put on 30 pounds and got a lot, lot stronger.

"In fact, when Artie Rooney (then the Steelers' chief scout) saw me for the first time since the draft, he didn't even recognize me because I had matured so much physically.

"Then, later on, when I became a guard, I had the advantage of having to face Joe Greene and Ernie Holmes in practice every day and they were the best pair of tackles going. When you went up against Holmes, you learned to stay low because if you didn't block him from the knees down, he clubbed you to death. That was no fun, either, except for him. As a lineman, all you do is get clubbed, mugged, clawed and scratched every week. At least as a guard I could be the attacker. At center, you get attacked. So I wasn't sorry when they switched my position."

He joined the Giants in 1978 after he was traded away by the Steelers.

During the pre-season of 1980, it seemed that Clack's career was in jeopardy. He had required surgery on both knees, and it appeared he was finished. But he stuck it out for all 16 regular season games.

The pre-season of 1981 seemed to indicate that Clack might have to call it a career. His shaky knees finally crumbled. He had played 12 seasons, and it seemed like the right time to say goodbye.

He walked away, telling coach Ray Perkins he did not think he was up to playing another season. Perkins told him he hoped he could call him if he needed him later in the schedule. Clack, then 34, left the door open. In early November, Perkins placed a call to Clack to come back to the Giants. Because of injuries, Perkins needed Clack at center. The next Sunday. To go all the way.

Clack had been playing basketball in Rocky Mount about three or four times a week with friends. He was hardly ready to play a whole game in the National Football League. But that is exactly what he did.

"Going back when I did really wasn't that tough," said Clack, "because I had felt good about the way I had adapted to the 'real world.' I think a lot of athletes don't prepare themselves well enough for that day when their body says it's time to quit. I've always been a hustler about my business interests, working hard to set up some things I wanted to be involved in. I knew I could play football for six weeks."

The Giants finished strong and knocked off the Dallas Cowboys in sudden death overtime in the season finale and, to many people's surprise, made the playoffs for the first time in 18 years.

"The feeling I had beating Dallas that way and going back to the playoffs had to rate as one of the greatest thrills and periods of time in all my football experiences," he said.

"It had become one of those stories you always read about. It was like a dream.

"Six weeks before, I was sitting at home, having a good time doing my thing. Then here I was going back to the playoffs, not with a team like the Steelers who were expected to be there every year, but with a team and town that was cherishing every moment of the experience because it had been so long coming."

As it turned out, the Giants lost to the Super Bowl bound San Francisco Giants the next week, 38-24. The loss caught Clack off guard, and bothered him more than he might have anticipated.

"The feeling that came over me after we lost to San Francisco was maybe one of the worst feelings I've ever experienced," Clack said.

"And not just because we had a good chance to win that game and go on, but because, after making the commitment to myself that there would be no next year, I realized that there wasn't going to be another time like this one.

"I looked around the locker room at the younger guys and they were disappointed, but they knew we had a good team and that they would be back. I went off to the back of the locker room and just got lost. I couldn't really even talk to them."

During his playing days with the Giants, he owned two restaurants, two sporting goods stores and a uni-sex hair salon back home in Rocky Mount.

Then one night, Clack did something really stupid. He did a line or two of cocaine with an acquaintance, gave him a couple of toots to take with him, and one day, six months later, he was arrested. Because he had been so popular, because he had been such a big local success story, Clack became a headline story for his indiscretion.

For a long time, Clack had a hard time making eye contact with anyone in Rocky Mount. Phil Musick, who had covered Clack when he was playing for the Steelers, but was now writing a general column for *The Pittsburgh Press*, put it this way: "He moved to the mountains, sold his sporting goods stores and came to a keener understanding of the term loner." He had to sell the sporting goods stores. "The schools quit coming around . . . you know," he explained.

Clack admitted, "It took awhile to believe people were not talking about me all the time."

He managed somehow to hold on to two restaurants on the shore at Nag's Head, and his hair styling salon, and he opened a new restaurant. He also lost about $100,000 in a limited partnership invest-

507

ment that cost former teammate Gerry Mullins in a similar manner. But Clack managed another comeback.

"Don't get me wrong," Clack conceded to Musick. "I know what I did was wrong, but. . ."

When I brought up the same subject in a discussion in March, Clack said, "That business happened at the beach, and it really set me back. I was at a party with a man and I had some coke. I gave a vial to him and his date. His date was an officer of the law. I was very wrong, but. . ."

But. In 24 hours following the 1982 coke bust, Jim Clack, one of the community's leading citizens and all-time heroes, was a name mentioned mostly in infamy. He had let down a lot of people. "I got cruel calls at the store," he said. He ended up with a sentence of three years probation. It helped wreck his first marriage.

Then he and his second wife were nearly killed in an auto crash in July of 1985.

His wife, Pattie, was driving their 1983 Mercedes-Benz when she made a turn on the road in front of an oncoming GMC truck. The driver of the truck said he was too close to the intersection to avoid the accident.

Pattie and Jim both ended up in the intensive care section at Nash General Hospital. Pattie came out of there a lot sooner than Jim. He suffered a fractured pelvis, collapsed lungs, broken ribs and a concussion. He underwent surgery for removal of a damaged spleen and to repair his other injuries.

Somehow, Clack came out of it alive.

"That nightmare is still with me," said Clack. "I was in intensive care for 15 days. I learned later that Art Rooney was leading the people at his parish in praying for me. He sent me several mass cards. That's something that has really stuck with me. The date of that accident was July 17, 1985. I was a goner. One night they told my mother I wasn't going to make it. 'He can't live,' they told her. They had me on life-support systems.

"I still have a lot of pain in my body, but I had a lot of pain in my body to begin with, from football. But I learned from football that you have to be a battler to be successful. My doctor had played for Woody Hayes at Ohio State. He said that football saved my life. He said, 'He's a fighter, and he's fighting for his life. He knows what that's all about.' I know I'm just grateful I survived it."

Clack continues to fight for his life. Every day.

Robin Cole and Ron Johnson
No one messed with these big city slickers

M ost members of the Steelers, especially during those glorious Super Bowl seasons, came from small towns, mom 'n' apple pie communities, or rural roots, mostly Southern, thank you.

More than one coach on the club said he preferred it that way, too, and I have heard college coaches in the Northeast say the same thing, because the kids were more coachable, had better values, had parents who worked and expected them to work as well, and were not as spoiled. They were also more into teamwork; they were brought up that way, that's why.

So you had Mike Webster from Tomahawk, Wisconsin; Jack Lambert from Mantua, Ohio; Edmund Nelson from Live Oak, Florida; John Stallworth from Tuscaloosa, Alabama; Dwayne Woodruff from Bowling Green, Kentucky; Sam Davis from Ocilla, Georgia; Rocky Bleier from Appleton, Wisconsin.

Robin Cole and Ron Johnson were exceptions to the rule. And they would not have had it any other way.

To them, Pittsburgh is a small town, a city you can hold in your hand and still form a fist. It is a mom 'n' pop stop. It is a city, all right, but a lot more manageable than their hometowns.

Cole came from Los Angeles and Johnson from Detroit. Now those are big cities. They grew up in the ghetto, and learned to take care of themselves and hold their own on mean streets. They could match tall tales with any of their teammates and then some. They could strut with city slickers and never get out of step, and they took pride in coming up the hard way.

Both came from big families and had older brothers to back them up in arguments. Looking at an old notebook with chicken scratch comments from both of them, it is interesting to note that Robin related:

"Nobody messed with the Coles."

And, a few pages later, from Ron:

"Nobody messed with the Johnsons."

They never did, that's for sure, when Cole and Johnson played for the Steelers.

Both had to crack a talent-rich roster, but both found their way into the starting lineups and became stars in their own right. Robin was with the Steelers for 11 seasons, from 1977 to 1987, and then put in one more season with the New York Jets under Joe Walton. Ron spent seven seasons with the Steelers, from 1978 to 1984.

Both were No. 1 draft choices, Johnson out of Eastern Michigan in 1976, and Cole from New Mexico in 1977. Johnson was the first rookie to start for a Super Bowl winner, replacing the ailing J.T. Thomas all season long and going up against the Dallas Cowboys in Super Bowl XIII.

509

"People thought I had a chip on my shoulder when I first came here," Johnson said. "I didn't try to act that way. We had a lot of defensive backs that came to camp that year. They weren't too happy about me in the beginning. I thought I had a lot to prove. I didn't have time to go around and make friends."

Johnson had seemed arrogant to some. Cole had come off that way, too, at first. They often talked a better game than they played, but that is part of the big city intimidation bit, and they both enjoyed some great moments in black and gold. In the end, you had to like them both, once you got past the tough-guy-from-the-ghetto act.

They talked and walked like guys from the big city. They came across that way on the field, too. They were two of the hardest hitters on the Steelers' defense, liked to make the big play — the shocking stops — and had some showboat in their muscular, well-conditioned bodies. In short, no one wanted to mess with Cole or Johnson.

Not if they were smart.

"I never had a fight when I was a kid," claimed Cole. "Maybe some pushes on the football field, but I never had to fight. If I could avoid it, I'd avoid it. I was always busy, working to earn some money. I had no time to get into trouble. Some of the kids I grew up with got into trouble, some bad trouble. That's where my grandmother came into play. She kept us all on the straight and narrow. We always went to church on Sunday. I thought stealing was the worst thing you could do; that you'd die from it. I had to work for things."

Johnson played football, as a defensive lineman, mind you, at Northwestern High in Detroit. That is the same school that produced Willie Horton and Alex Johnson, major league baseball stars, and Ron Johnson, who starred at Michigan and with the New York Giants in football. While at Northwestern, the Steelers' Johnson (no relation) was also a sportswriter on the student newspaper, and the president of his senior class. See, he really was an exception to the rule.

"In my sophomore year in college, I worked in a Cadillac factory," Johnson said. "I worked on the fenders, to see that there weren't any kinks in the fenders. I bought one and sold it. My father worked there, too. He always drove a new Seville."

Cole was an industrious kid, too. "When I was about nine, I used to ride in a car with my brother and help him deliver newspapers," recalled Cole. "Then I got my own route later, with the *L.A. Times*. I'd get up at two in the morning, and deliver the papers. We went through some tough neighborhoods.

"My route went through an area called Taco Flats. Even I was afraid to go in there. It was a Spanish-American community. You learned what you had to do if you were going to go in and out of there. It was the kind of place where you'd have to pray before you went in. If the kids didn't get you, the dogs would. I got a couple of dog bites on my ankles and worse.

"I liked to play basketball back then, too, and baseball. Sandy Koufax of the Dodgers was my favorite player. I liked Don Sutton, Wes

Ron Johnson

Parker. I was good at sports, and I stayed out of trouble. I was good at public relations and dealing with people. I was the candy man; I could sell more candy than any of the other kids at school. I'd sell chocolate bars for 50 cents to raise money for our basketball team, or for Little League. I won a gift certificate; I sold more than 300 other kids. That was the first time I ever won anything. I figured out I had to work to win. I can sell; I'm a hustler."

When you are a child, you do not know any better. You accept your surroundings because that is all you know. You never feel poor unless somebody tells you you're poor, or you see something better on television. To Cole and to Johnson, that is the way it was.

"I guess we had a tough school," Johnson said. "When you're in it, you don't pay much attention. When I look back, I could have been in all kinds of things. If you were the kind of guy who followed the crowd. I remember just walking to school and seeing people fighting all the time. It just wasn't my nature.

"I was always involved in organized sports. When school was on, I always had to go to practice. My brothers paved the way. I wanted to play the game, though, like Lem Barney, who was a great cornerback for the Detroit Lions. I wanted to be like him."

An NFL scout once said of Johnson: "There's a bit of thug in him. And you need guys like that in pro football."

One day in practice at St. Vincent College, in Johnson's second season (1979) with the Steelers, he squared off briefly with John Stallworth. One of the coaches broke it up, and Johnson said to the coach, "John's not too big, otherwise I'd beat the hell outta him right here. But we need him for the season."

The coach, of course, smiled when he told that story.

Cole believes he learned a lot in his L.A. heyday. "All those lessons pay off now," he said. "Too many kids I know who went to high school with me don't have much going for them these days. One of the ones voted most likely to succeed didn't succeed at anything. Simply because of lack of discipline.

"Throughout my life, I wanted to work. That was something I wanted to do. You won't find success in the street. It's a dead end, believe me."

Robin Cole was in training, learning the retail automobile business, at Benson Lincoln-Mercury on Rt. 51 in Whitehall in 1991. He had spent the previous year at Sewickley Lincoln-Mercury. He was looking into investing in his own dealership. At 35, he and his family live in Eighty Four, Pennsylvania.

"I've always liked working with people, and being with people, and I've always been good at selling," commented Cole on the first day of March. "The automobile business is a people's business."

I mentioned Ron Johnson to him, and he said that, coincidentally enough, he had just visited with Johnson while on business in Detroit.

Robin Cole

"We're friends," said Cole. "I'm friends with anybody who wants to be friends. Heck, I was friends with guys on the team who weren't interested in being friends. That's my nature.

"I felt like a leader on that team, and my only regret was that I was never the captain. But I know I can lead people, I know I can direct and manage people to be successful, and to work as a team.

"I'm like a lot of people who played in the NFL, looking for what kind of work they can do now that they are finished playing," continued Cole. "Where do I go from here? When you were playing ball, or when you're in the entertainment business, people put you up on a pedestal.

"Now you've got to get back on level ground again and begin from the bottom to build something else. Some people think you made so much money playing ball you don't need to work. Well, I played before the money was that big, and I've got to work. I want to work. I want to be productive at something else.

"You've changed and you've grown since you first came to the Steelers. You should have learned something along the way to help you. Life is about struggles. That's the way it should be. If you're not struggling, you're not working.

"Success is a journey, not a destination."

Ron Johnson has always looked upon playing football as an opportunity to improve yourself in all ways. He looked at it that way on all levels — high school, college and pro ball.

"John Stallworth and I were talking on the telephone just the other night," Johnson said, "and he asked me if I had seen the list of salaries in *USA Today*. Today's ballplayers are making the kind of money where they can just focus on being the best athlete they can be. If they take care of their money their money will take care of them later on down the road.

"But I still believe that an athlete ought to graduate and get his degree. After you've made some money it's more difficult to come back and finish school.

"That was high on my list of priorities when I was in college. Once you have a scholarship there's no reason for you not to get a degree. You may have more pressures on you than the average student, but one you don't have is the responsibility to finance your education. You're fortunate. You have to keep things in perspective."

Johnson was graduated from Eastern Michigan with a degree in speech communications, with a minor in marketing. "That's what I always wanted to do," Johnson said.

In 1991, at 35, he sold educational programs for Nystrom Company in seven counties of Michigan, including half of his hometown of Detroit. He goes back to his old school, Northwestern High.

"A lot of the inner-city problems are caused by peer pressure," Johnson said. "Most of these kids are being raised in single parent families. It's difficult when a father isn't at home to be involved with them. I'm involved with a lot of inner-city youth programs in Detroit.

We live right here in the city, and my son, Ron Jr., is ten and I manage in the Little League. The kids call me 'Coach Ron.'

"I use my communications and marketing background in everything I do. There's nothing else I wanted to do, except maybe coach."

Johnson also sells insurance and he does some scouting for the Steelers, concentrating on the Big Ten and Mid-American Conference. "Maybe the people in Pittsburgh don't realize it," he said, "but George Perles has had a No. 1 draft choice every year that he has been at Michigan State."

Perles was the defensive line coach, and later the defensive coordinator when Johnson was playing for the Steelers.

In addition to seeing Perles, Johnson said he had recently seen John Rowser, another former defensive back of the Steelers, as well as John "Frenchy" Fuqua, a running back who works in circulation at *The Detroit News*. "In fact, the three of us all got together this past year," Johnson said. "I took some pictures. They weren't with the Steelers at the same time I was, but we feel like teammates.

"We were part of the same organization. That is a reflection of the Rooney family. Everybody wanted to play for Mr. Rooney.

"I was a Steelers fan coming out of college," Johnson said. "I'm still a Steelers fan."

"I think a lot about being drafted by the Pittsburgh Steelers, and how lucky I was. I'm proud of the fact that I was a No. 1 draft choice of the Steelers. It's not just because of the championships we won, either. It's because there were so many great people, so many down-to-earth solid people. Some teams had some wild people on their club, and they were known throughout the league. Our guys were more settled.

"Mel Blount sort of took me under his wing. He helped me quite a bit. I used to break up the guys at practice and at Bible study when I'd start screaming about how I couldn't believe I was on the same team as Mel Blount. But you have to understand that he was already in the league nine years when I joined the team. I was in ninth grade when I was watching Blount play for the Steelers on TV.

"And in my rookie year, I'm starting at left cornerback opposite Mel Blount in the Super Bowl," said Johnson.

He had a special regard as well for Stallworth and Donnie Shell. "They were our inspirational and spiritual leaders, along with Mike Webster and Jon Kolb. They were down-to-earth superstars.

"They were channeled. They were interested in winning football games and taking care of business. I enjoyed the day-to-day challenge. We had a close-knit football team. We'd come back to training camp each year and we'd all embrace like we hadn't seen each other in a hundred years instead of just four months back.

"The player I admired the most was Mike Webster. I watched Webby work out a few times. He'd run up and down the steps at the Stadium.

I remember he once checked himself out of a hospital to play for us. He had been in traction. He went back to the hospital after the game. Webby is what really epitomized the Steelers. When I go around to the city schools and speak to the students I often tell them about Mike Webster. He was a small guy when he came to the Steelers, but he showed us all what you have to do if you want to be a great athlete."

After seven seasons with the Steelers, Johnson said he went through a difficult period of adjustment before he got himself in gear again.

"It took me awhile to get football out of my system. I had been playing football since I was nine. My career ended abruptly. I found out I was finished with the Steelers about four weeks before I was planning on going to camp. I didn't know I was finished.

"That first year away from football I was like a fish out of water. Then I realized I better get on with the rest of my life."

"When the Steelers went to Houston for the final game last season, I didn't expect them to get beat," Johnson said. "When they knew that they could win their division and go to the playoffs by winning, the Steelers should win.

"I think once these players today realize who they are and who they play for they will be better off. That was something I learned in high school. Our coach used to tell us about the guys who had built the program, and how they had paved the way for us. We had a reputation as a team that we had to play up to.

"It's the same with the Steelers teams. When I joined them they already had a reputation as the fiercest football team in the league. I remember scolding the veterans in a game once, telling them they weren't playing like the Steel Curtain defense.

"They have to understand that when people see those black and gold uniforms coming they expect to get beat. There were people who feared us. They have to realize they are still the Pittsburgh Steelers.

"They have linebackers who really hit, and they have one of the speediest secondaries in the league. They won't have any trouble winning in the future. Bubby Brister has as strong an arm as Terry Bradshaw, but he's not yet as good a leader as Brad was. With their defense, they have the nucleus to be a Super Bowl caliber team again. They have to recognize it now.

"They have to recognize and realize who they are. Maybe they need to look at old films."

Mike Wagner
"It's nice to be remembered"

Mike Wagner was walking through the aisleways at the Auto Show in the David L. Lawrence Convention Center in February when an older woman started making a fuss over him. "She was just an ol' Steeler fan and she was just so excited about seeing me," said Wagner. "She said, 'I just wanted to say hi to you. You remind me of so many great times. You bring back a lot of memories of good times for football in this town.' She just made me feel good. It's nice to be remembered that way."

Wagner was always a favorite with the fans. He was tall, curly blond, handsome and had an easy smile. He was always willing to spend time with people, and he made them feel comfortable in his company. He was never a prima donna, and he always remembered where he came from — Waukegan, Illinois, just outside of Chicago. He worked hard and achieved more than anyone thought possible at first glance.

In 1991 he was living in Hampton Township, a suburb just north of Three Rivers Stadium, and he had an office at nearby Two North Shore Center, along the Allegheny River.

He wore the black and gold proudly for ten years, from 1971 through the 1980 season. He came to the Steelers as an 11th round draft choice out of Western Illinois University, and went on to become a starting safety for the Steelers in four championship seasons, twice getting picked for the Pro Bowl — in 1976 and 1977 — and he was one of the team's big success stories. He still ranks among the team's all-time interception leaders with 36.

In 1975, Wagner had two interceptions against Oakland in the AFC championship game. He had an interception against Dallas which led to a key fourth quarter score in Super Bowl X, and one against Minnesota in Super Bowl IX.

Today, he serves as executive vice-president of the RRZ&G Capital Group Limited, a corporate finance unit of Russell, Rea, Zappala & Gomulka Holdings, Inc., and is largely involved in the acquisition of small companies.

Andy Russell, one of the principals of the company, of course, is a former teammate on the Steel Curtain defense. Dressed in a business suit, Wagner could be a model.

Wagner regards two comebacks from injuries as the personal highlights of his career with the Steelers. He suffered a broken neck in the third game of the 1977 season against the Cleveland Browns and made a marvelous comeback to contribute to the team winning its third Super Bowl the next season. He was sidelined after the eighth game of the 1979 season by an upper leg and hip problem which required surgery.

"Those were the toughest challenges I faced in my pro football career," recalled Wagner.

517

Following the 1980 season, Wagner decided his body was not up to another season, that the injuries were piling up and that it was time to step aside. Doctors warned him that he might not walk again if he were reinjured. This is when he gained real insight into the Steelers' organization, and Art and Dan Rooney. He was eager to share these insights.

"I read something recently about the team being cheap, and not paying the players that well, and I found myself bristling," said Wagner, who was 42, and 11 years removed from his playing days with the Steelers.

"I believe the Rooneys paid top dollar to us. They paid for a championship team. The money we made pales by comparison to the salaries today, but we were well rewarded for what we did in those days.

"There were two incidents in my career where the Rooneys were very generous to me. One year it was announced that I had been picked for the Pro Bowl, and then I was removed. The league office said an error had been made in the vote count. Dan Rooney was very upset by it.

"He called me into his office, and he told me that he considered my season to be a Pro Bowl caliber season, and that he was going to pay me the Pro Bowl bonus that was in my contract. He didn't have to, but he did.

"Then, after the 1980 season, I went to Dan and told him I was retiring. I told him I couldn't stay healthy anymore, and that it was time to try something else, that I had other opportunities I felt I should look into.

"A few days later, I get a call from The Chief. He wanted me to keep playing. He said, 'I'll tell you when to quit.' But I told him I was just getting beat up, and it was time.

"Two days later, I get a call from Jim Boston at the office, and he tells me to come in, and that he has something for me to sign. I told him I was serious about retiring, and that I wasn't just using this as a negotiating ploy. He said he understood, but told me to come in anyhow.

"They had a two-year or three-year contract for me to sign, and it had a signing bonus. 'Just sign it,' Dan Rooney told me. And they gave me the bonus. 'Good luck,' Dan Rooney told me. 'This is our going-away gift.' I wanted to share this story because the Rooneys always did things very quietly, and didn't get credit for it. The public doesn't realize what went on behind closed doors. Dan is not one to beat his own drum."

Coincidentally enough, I heard a story the same week as Wagner made this remark that was of a similar gesture. Ralph Cindrich, the Mt. Lebanon-based attorney who represented the team's 1990 No. 1 draft choice, Eric Green, revealed to reporters that Rooney had just given Green a bonus check.

Green had an incentive bonus in his contract that called for near-

518

Mike Wagner

ly $10,000 if he led the Steelers in passes caught. He finished third with 34, 16 less than team-leader Louis Lipps.

But Green had missed the first three games of the season because of a contract dispute. Rooney sent him a note saying he was a big factor in turning the team around after a 1-3 start, and wanted to give him the bonus anyhow.

"In all my years in this business," commented Cindrich, "I can only recall one other instance that happened, and that was also with the Steelers. Fans may think it happens frequently, but it doesn't."

True to form, Dan Rooney refused to comment on the bonus.

"My most cherished memory of my association with the Steelers," said Wagner, "was just learning the Rooney legend, and being part of the so-called family, and being treated fairly, and being appreciated by all of them. I was a low round pick, and I was fairly cynical about the Rooneys and pro football organizations when I came up. So, seeing what they did for the community and what they meant to the city of Pittsburgh was really edifying and gratifying.

"It's a private business, but Dan and Mr. Rooney were able to really make the team a part of the city. They knew the town well and they won over the players to be a part of it. I really would have played for free, but I went for the going rate. They really made me into a Pittsburgher.

"The Rooneys have tried to do what they can to give to the city and to the community. You have to try and give once in a while, and make yourself available."

Wagner was a cut above most athletes intelligence-wise and a clear thinker and rational performer on a defensive team that needed a balance between an emotional and mental approach.

"L.C. and Jack Ham and I were the quiet ones on the defensive unit," he said. "Jack Lambert and Dwight White and Glen Edwards were always hollering and trying to get everybody pumped up. Lambert would be hollering at Joe Greene to get him going, and it was bedlam. White and Edwards were the loudest in the huddle. We were all different. Once the ball was snapped, though, we all had the same intensity.

"The neat thing about our team was that we were probably one of the closest teams in sports. Winning begets that. But I think the players really cared about each other. When we get together, you still see a lot of emotion. There's a real genuine closeness.

"We all owed a lot to someone. I owed a lot, for instance, to John Rowser. He was my corner when I was a rookie. He helped me a lot. He was a hard-nosed veteran and he knew what had to be done. Rowser helped Mel Blount a lot, too. Blount was on the bench, to begin with, a highly-talented athlete who just had to learn how to play his position in the pros."

Wagner is a big fan of Chuck Noll, and credits Noll for molding many personalities into a single unit, a force that dominated pro football during the '70s.

"Noll came back from coaching in the Pro Bowl in 1972, and he told us, 'I had the best players in the league to work with. And I didn't see any players any better than what we have right here in this room.' Noll wasn't one to exaggerate. When he made a comment like that it hit home.

"We had barely lost to Miami (21-17) in the AFC championship game. Nobody knew we were a championship team, but everybody started believing in themselves more. That's what has to happen with the current Steelers' team. They have to believe how good they are.

"In the middle '70s, we felt we dominated the fourth quarter. We and our fans knew we were going to find a way to win. In the '80s, we didn't have that intimidation factor. And we became average. This current team has the talent again to go all the way. They just have to believe in themselves.

"Our team was able to become champions under two different sets of rules. We felt the league changed the rules to restrict what the Steelers were able to do, and other teams couldn't do. But that didn't stop us from winning.

"We won our first two Super Bowls with a dominating defense. We were different in the last two Super Bowls. It wasn't hard to win when we were putting 35 points on the scoreboard and we still had a solid defense."

Wagner was among the former Steelers who were approached by network sports reporters a few years back, and asked if he thought the game had passed by Noll, that it was time Noll retired.

Wagner would not buy any of that. "Who could you replace him with in this situation?" he asked, in turn. "Chuck is masterful for putting together a team. His strongest point was getting you ready for Sunday. He knows how to prepare a team for a game better than anybody.

"Chuck coached our linebackers at the beginning, and I remember he used to sit next to me in the film room, and he'd whisper things to me. He was always telling me something, always teaching me more about football.

"My dad always told me as long as they're yelling at you it's OK. It's when they stop yelling at you that you better worry. Chuck can make young players uncomfortable because he's difficult to read at times.

"I think the smartest move Noll ever made was to shift his concentration to the offensive team instead of the defensive unit. We had a bunch of renegades on our defensive team. They were uncoachable. Even the quiet guys I mentioned — Russell, Ham and L.C. — thought they knew best what to do. They did it their own way. Chuck turned over the defense to some defensive coaches, and cut us loose.

"I lived a block away from Noll in Upper St. Clair for ten years and it wasn't until I retired that I was invited to his house for the first time for a party to meet his son and future daughter-in-law. It was after I retired that his wife, Marianne, called and talked to me about things concerning retirement and wished me well."

There was a time when Wagner thought Noll wanted him to retire following his first season with the Steelers.

"I came into the clubhouse during the off-season and Noll came by, and we started talking. He started asking me about my future goals, and what I planned to do after pro football. He had me worried. Here I was 22 years of age, single, and thinking about nothing but football, and my coach wants to know about my career plans. I started thinking that maybe I didn't fit into his plans for the next season.

"You were always worried about running into Noll when you came to the clubhouse to work out in the off-season. If he'd see you he'd have you in a room for an hour with the projector going, pointing out different things that he saw on film from the previous season. Hey, it was the off-season and the guys wanted to get away from that stuff for awhile. But Noll was so intense. I know someone in the organization told him to stay out of the clubhouse during the off-season, that he was driving the players away.

"I go to the Stadium from time to time, and I take my son, Farrell, who's 3½ with me, and he gets real excited about it. I like to take friends and neighbors down there now with their kids. It's hard to tell who gets a bigger kick out of it — the dads or their kids. It's interesting to see how outsiders view it, and what it means to them to meet some of the Steelers. Now I'm seeing and am able to appreciate the Steelers from another slant.

"I will drive around the Stadium in my car every now and then. I feel good over there, but I don't want to be hanging around. I like to stop in and see Chuck. I'm comfortable being around him now. When you're a player for Chuck Noll, you're so wary of him. We didn't get to know him in that football environment. You see a different side of him now.

"I'm just getting to know Chuck Noll and it's interesting. As a coach, he has to influence and control you. And he's careful what he says around you. He's detached. It's much easier for me to go into his office now. He's so warm and friendly, and seems happy to see me."

"What I miss the most, and what was so great about professional sports, is the day to day demand on your mind and body. You always knew where you stood. Somebody was always keeping score.

"But I'm enjoying aspects of professional football now that I was never able to enjoy as a player. For instance, I had one of the greatest times I ever had at a neighborhood party two years ago when the Steelers played at Denver in the AFC playoffs. It was a thrilling game and we were really cheering and getting into it.

"As a player, when the game was over, we were always too tired physically and emotionally to go to any parties. By the time, we were able to switch gears most of the partying was over.

"The only good thing you had was the doing. That's what Noll used to talk about. He said nobody really liked practice, or watching film, or studying assignments. The game is the doing. The game itself is the best thing.

"The games are more fun for us now, when we get together at reunions, and talk about those games. Part of the fun now is the reliving. We probably cherish the game more. As you get older, you cherish the memories of what you did.

"The best fun is getting together with the players and discussing the old days. The players take great pride in what we did.

"I think the bonding was tremendous on this team. We played in a town where there weren't a lot of distractions. There's no beach in Pittsburgh, or very many bright lights. I'm not putting down Pittsburgh, either.

"Pittsburgh is a blue collar, high work ethic community. We began to think like Pittsburghers and take pride in the way we worked. I felt it was the perfect situation for us. It was like playing football in Green Bay. You were able to concentrate on the game, and the fans here made it all so important with the support they provided.

"I felt the Rooneys and Noll always drafted smarter people and better people. They tried to bring in class people. And some of them might have fooled some people. I always had respect for Dwight White, for instance. He's a bright guy. He'll always be a success. But on the football field he was a madman. I think it was part of his method. He wanted to scare people.

"Lambert was like that, too. I was entertained by Lambert. Then we had two other linebackers back then, at the start, in Russell and Ham, who had little to say, and went about their business in a quiet way. But they performed with the same passion for excellence. It takes all kinds to make a football team, I guess, and we had them all."

Mike Wagner (23) intercepts pass.

George Gojkovich

Words of Praise

*"As the precocious editor and publisher of **Pittsburgh Weekly Sports** in the early 1960s, Jim O'Brien was a trend setter. He provided a forum in Pittsburgh for a new breed of literate, humorous, hard-hitting sportswriters. Subsequently, during his years with **The Miami News** and **The New York Post**, O'Brien clung to his roots. Pittsburgh was always in his blood, and since returning here in 1979 he has been a knowledgeable observer of the scene. Like his previous books, **Hail to Pitt** and **City of Champions, Doing It Right** is a valuable addition to the archives. Part history and part memoir, it follows the Pittsburgh Steelers of the Super Bowl decade into the 1980s and their post-football lives, enriching the folklore."*

—Roy McHugh
Columnist/Sports Editor
The Pittsburgh Press

*"**Doing It Right** can best be described as a unique behind-the-scenes story of what sets the Steelers apart from the pack, yesterday and today. Football fans and non-football fans alike are bound to benefit from the insight into how these men strived for excellence on and off the playing field. Jerry Kramer's **Instant Replay**, which chronicled Vince Lombardi's great Packer teams of the 1960s, has always been my favorite football book. Until now. This is the best football book on the market today."*

—Matt Marsom, Editor
The Football News

*"Jim O'Brien makes it easy to recall the glory days of the Pittsburgh Steelers. **Doing it Right** is loaded with colorful insight into the players, coaches, and management of that championship franchise. Painstakingly researched, O'Brien interviewed just about everybody associated with the team at that time."*

—Nikolai Bonesso
Pittsburgh City Paper

*"What **Doing it Right** gives us is not so much the concrete and beams of the dynasty; rather, we get the flesh and blood. O'Brien has not put on paper X's and O's, much as a coach or quarterback chalk up winning plays. Instead, he chose to dip his pen into the heart of this team and its city. Couched within a 'sports book' is a 'feel' for Pittsburgh — its people, its tradition, its pride, its heart. It's a feel provided by one of its sons. You come away liking that feeling."*

—Taylor Scott
Point Magazine

What readers say about "Doing It Right"

"Our whole family enjoyed it. Anybody who's a Steelers fan would love this book."
—Lisa Holmes, Pleasant Hills, Pa.

"Having been raised in Oakland (Lawn Street), the names were very familiar to me and brought back many fond memories."
—Bill Lindner, Danbury, Conn.

"These last few days have been pure bliss, reading your book, and remembering all those great moments with the Steelers then and now. Your book is a masterpiece. Your portrayal and description of Art Rooney, Dan Rooney, Chuck Noll, the other coaches and players was so revealing and genuine. If people want to know what the Pittsburgh Steelers' organization is all about, they should read your book!"
—Don Siebert, Hastings, Pa.

"It's a good read. I'd recommend it heartily."
—Doug Hoerth, WTAE Radio

"I have read that marvelous book, 'Doing It Right,' and found it absolutely superb reading. I have recommended it for all the fans over here who get my biweekly Steelers' newsletter."
—Gordon Dedman, Fareham, England

"It's like a family album of the Pittsburgh Steelers. It is full of wonderful stories and, in a sense, they are all parables to help us in our own lives. I believe you did it right."
—Rev. Laird Stuart, Pastor
Westminster Presbyterian Church
Pittsburgh, Pa.

"It is so interesting to come face to face with these Steelers personalities, to see the other side of their lives, past and present, to know them without their shoulder pads."
—Vaughn Gordy, Mt. Lebanon, Pa.

"Congratulations to you and Marty Wolfson on your great book, 'Doing It Right.' Your hard work and energy were well spent. I know that Father would be very excited for you men."
—Frank W. Gustine, Jr., Pittsburgh, Pa.

"Your book was the perfect gift for my husband. It's about the men behind the names of the greatest team in history. It is a cherished possession."
—Barbara J. Carey, Bellevue, Nebr.

527

"I've enjoyed your recent book on the Steelers, particularly finding out how the players have used their athletic success to carry them to a career after their playing days."

—Pat Nixon, Pittsburgh, Pa.

"Once you start it, you can't put it down. The joy of the book . . . it brings back so many good times."

—Ralph Conde, WHJB Radio, Greensburg, Pa.

"It is not a normal football history book, but a personal view with a personal touch. The book looks at the people, not the x's and o's of football. That's doing it right, too."

—Les Harvath, North Huntingdon, Pa.

"The people that I have given it to as gifts have raved about it. They were great Christmas gifts for my customers. We had all the faith in the world that your book would be successful."

—Tom Hayes, Pittsburgh, Pa.

"It brought back so many memories, just looking at the photos. Also thanks for the bookmark. I could not believe it when I saw who it was! How could you know that Jack Lambert is, was, and always will be my favorite football player? ESP???"

—Mary Lou Winters, Canton, Ohio

"You certainly know how to tug at the skirts of Mother History and compel her to come out and play. It's interesting and pleasant reading."

—John G. Brosky, Senior Judge
Superior Court of Pennsylvania

"I was born at McKeesport Hospital. I ended up playing for Vince Lombardi and the Green Bay Packers in the last world championship (Jim Brown's last game in 1965) and the first two Super Bowls. So I can appreciate these stories about a similarly great team, the Pittsburgh Steelers."

—Robert A. Long, Waukesha, Wisc.

"I am a huge Pittsburgh Steelers fan and enjoy anything I can get on the Steelers. I absolutely loved it. Your writing brought the players and organization closer to me, and now I feel like I know both better."

—Ricky Wilson, Independence, Va.

*"I enjoyed '**Doing It Right.**' You did a wonderful job in writing about the Steelers. I felt as though I was reading about my friends."*

—Philip Ahesh, Canonsburg, Pa.

*"I am the son of 'the first professional football player,' and really enjoyed your book **'Doing It Right.'** Since I was born and raised in Latrobe, I enjoyed your comments about the Steelers training camp at St. Vincent. I don't think I ever drive past the school that it doesn't bring back memories of my father."*

—Dr. John K. Brallier, Ligonier, Pa.

"I wanted to commend you on an outstanding effort to capture the image of the Pittsburgh Steelers. It brought back fond memories, especially of Art Rooney. He was a legend and he was truly one of a kind."

—D. Michael Fisher, Harrisburg, Pa.
Pennsylvania State Senator

*"I just finished reading **'Doing It Right,'** and it is worthy of a national award. I'll read it more than once, which is rare. We have read all of your previous books, and look for more."*

—Tom Carroll, Reisterstown, Md.

*"A sequel would be in order and I would be pleased to have my name included on any waiting list. You have given me many a smile in reading **'Doing It Right.'** I worked in the front office of the Steelers for many years, and it brought back some great memories."*

—Catherine Kosack, Los Angeles, Calif.

"I'm not a good reader, but I just couldn't put your book down. It sure brought back many, many good memories that all Steeler fans have of those great years. I really enjoyed the different insights on the players and was happy to hear so many still live in Pittsburgh."

—Bob Krozely, Nashville, Tenn.

"I loved the book, but I may be prejudiced. My father really enjoyed it. I learned things about my teammates I didn't know."

—Jon Kolb, Pittsburgh, Pa.

Words of Praise For
"Whatever It Takes"

"Nobody has a passion for a community or its sports team any more than Pittsburgh-area journalist Jim O'Brien. This is reflected in his latest book entitled **Whatever It Takes,** *a humanistic look at the glory days of the Pittsburgh Steelers. The real appeal of O'Brien's well-researched and documented effort is the personal touch. He relates upbeat stories about the Steeler families, upbringing and early influences, and even Noll's theories on child-rearing! This is a must book for all Steeler buffs and any fan of professional football and would make a great Christmas gift."*

—Doug Huff, Sports Editor
The Wheeling-Intelligencer

"I think the most interesting story in the manuscript is the author's own. His personal journeys through the Pittsburgh sports scene of the 1950's and 1960's, long before the successes of the Super Bowl '70s, are wonderfully detailed and quirky. He has a special awareness of and feel for the way in which the Steelers have fit into the fabric of this city's neighborhoods. I'd like to read a book by O'Brien about **Sports in Pittsburgh Then and Now.**"

—Review for University of Pittsburgh Press

"Jim O'Brien is a one-man cottage industry. He writes books. He publishes them. He markets them. He autographs them. He distributes them. He promotes them. He promotes himself. His topic is the Pittsburgh Steelers. More to the point, his subjects are athletes who played for the Pittsburgh Steelers during their glory years. O'Brien has taken the public's infatuation with the Steelers and turned the infatuation into two books about the team and a job for himself."

—Richard Gazarik
The Pittsburgh Tribune-Review

"This poignant story grips the reader right away, and leaves many readers with the impression that **Whatever It Takes** *is a better book than* **Doing It Right.** *The story is a Pittsburgh effort from beginning to end. The printing was done by Geyer Printing in Oakland. Typesetting for the book was done by Cold Comp on Penn Avenue, Downtown. The distribution is being handled by Central Wholesale on the South Side. His books are a part of Pittsburgh's present and its history."*

—Andrew Wilson
Allegheny Business News

"You are doing a tremendous service for sports fans. It's important that these stories be saved for future generations. You have to talk to these people before it's too late. I am a hero-worshipper, so I envy you your assignment."

—Pat Williams, President
Orlando Magic
Former Minor League Baseball Executive

"O'Brien's portrayal of the coach who molded the individuals into four-time Super Bowl champions, Chuck Noll, is particularly enlightening. O'Brien has long been regarded as one of the most knowledgeable observers of the Pittsburgh sports scene, something he clearly demonstrates in **Whatever It Takes.** *And that's not only true of the players and coaches, but also of the people of the city."*

—Chris Carr
The Football News

"With **Whatever It Takes,** *Jim O'Brien picks up where he left off with last year's* **Doing It Right.** *This is another delightful collection of anecdotes and follow-ups of the champion Pittsburgh Steelers. Filled with memorable stories and priceless photographs, both books are a must for any football fan, especially the die-hard Steeler fans who remember the lean times that sandwiched the Super Bowl years."*

—Nick Bonesso
The City Paper

"It's done with compassion by O'Brien, a guy who probably knows Pittsburgh sports and its people as well as anyone in Western Pennsylvania.
—Jim Lane, Sports Editor
Altoona Mirror

"Jim O'Brien has done it again. Last year at this time I was recommending his book on the Pittsburgh Steeler Super Bowl teams, **Doing It Right,** *as a neat Christmas gift for pro football fans. Now O'Brien has done a splendid sequel called* **Whatever It Takes.** *Besides plenty of interesting reading, there are also photos galore of past and present Steelers."*

—Brian Herman, Sports Editor
Monessen Valley Independent

*"***Whatever It Takes** *is a perfect sequel to the first Steeler book, which we recommended last year."*

—Steve Kittey, Sports Editor
The Latrobe Bulletin

What Readers Say About Books About Pittsburgh Steelers

"I have recently finished reading your books, **Doing It Right** *and* **Whatever It Takes,** *about the Steelers of the '70s. I have always considered myself a loyal fan, but after reading your books, I almost feel as though I've known these players all my life. You've given them a depth and humanity all too rare in sports histories.*

"You have helped me understand something of their backgrounds and core beliefs, which in turn creates a greater understanding of what drives these men in their pursuit of excellence. It also helps explain how such a seemingly disparate group can come together for a common purpose.

"I have always sensed that there is something special about the Pittsburgh Steelers, and now I know I was correct. Thank you for a splendid history of the greatest football team of all time."
—Sean P. Duffy
Wheeling, West. Va.

"Thank you for writing two such superb books on the Pittsburgh Steelers glory years. Your insights and appreciation for those teams — the players, the coaches and the management/ownership — is truly remarkable. I appreciate your effort and the quality of your writing."
—Andy Russell
Steelers (1963, 1966-76)

"I just finished your book **Doing It Right,** *which my sister Kay Gariglio of Ford City, Pa., gave to me. I'm not a good reader, but I just couldn't put your book down. It sure brought back many, many good memories that all Steelers fans have of those great years. I really enjoyed the different insights on the players and was happy to hear so many still live in Pittsburgh."*
—Bob Krozely
Nashville, Tenn.

"Congratulations on a terrific job from a Steelers die-hard fan. I was from Ellwood City and, ironically, my first baseball hero was Frankie Gustine. I moved to Erie in 1948 when I was 13 years old, but I never gave up on my Pittsburgh teams."
—Sam Garwig
Erie, Pa.

"You help to take me back to a great time in my life."
—Bob Trimble
Sportscaster, WKBD
Detroit, Mich.

"I want to be a member of Jim O'Brien's Sports Book of the Year Club. I want to thank you for writing these books. Every Steelers fan should have them. I have enjoyed them immensely."
—Gerald Kostley
Latrobe, Pa.

"Thank you for caring so much about Western Pa. My husband and I are so proud to be the children of coal miners here in Western Pa."
—Arlene and Wally Borish
Pittsburgh, Pa.

"I was a teenager during their championship reign, and am now in my early thirties. I cannot tell you enough how much of a joy it is to relive those thrilling moments and also to find out what the guys are up to these days."
—Mary Senich
Monessen, Pa.

"It was a pleasant surprise to learn that I (in my own small way) helped to contribute $20,000 to the Art Rooney Scholarship Fund from the proceeds of your book. I guess 'The Chief' had a way of rubbing off on all of us."
—Michael A. Cibulas
Alliance, Ohio

*"Thank you for writing **Doing It Right** and **Whatever It Takes**, the best books I have ever read."*
—Andy Ondrey

"This is going to be a 'must-read' book in our house. The photos are superb and the team signatures a treasure. Thank you for all the work put into this book, but I'll bet you enjoyed every minute of it!"
—Alice S. Langtry
House of Representatives
Commonwealth of Pa.

*"Jan Kaefer, my daughter-in-law, presented your book, **Whatever It Takes,** to me as a Christmas present. It's been a long time since I enjoyed reading a book as much as I did yours. Your focusing on the life after the athlete's stardom is not only interesting, but should be of great value to the young athlete considering college and or professional experience. I'm looking forward to your book about the 1960 Pirates, and any other books you write in the future."*
—Charles H. Kaefer
Bradford, Pa.

Steelers' Super Bowl History

IX

New Orleans
January 12, 1975

Pittsburgh 16
Minnesota 6

X

Miami
January 18, 1976

Pittsburgh 21
Dallas 17

XIII

Miami
January 21, 1979

Pittsburgh 35
Dallas 31

XIV

Pasadena
January 20, 1980

Pittsburgh 31
Los Angeles 19

Acknowledgements

Iam most grateful to my wife, Kathie, who knows this book by heart. She served as my editor. She is my best friend, my toughest critic and the best proofreader in our home.

I also applaud Marty Wolfson, who nursed the original book through the development and production stages, and once again demonstrated his dedication to doing it right.

Thanks to Stanley Goldmann and Bruce McGough of Geyer Printing and Ed Lutz of Cold-Comp for their efforts above and beyond the call of duty to bring this book to life. Ed Ryan was a special patron.

Thanks to the Rooney family and the Pittsburgh Steelers who shared their stories, and especially to the public relations staff of Joe Gordon, Dan Edwards, Pat Hanlon and Lynn Balkovec, as well as team photographer Mike Fabus, and Teresa Varley of *Steelers Digest.* George Gojkovich and Bill Amatucci also provided outstanding photographs.

In recent years, I have learned the importance of having loyal friends. They played many roles, but most of all they prayed and pushed, and made sure I did this book. They include Mike Ference, John Fadool, Bill Priatko, Gordon Small and Richard Newton.

Supporters of this project included Christopher Passodelis, William Haines, Bill Baierl, Dave Brown, Ed Harmon, Ted and Barbara Frantz, John Bruno, Frank Fuhrer, Steve and Charlie Previs, John Williamson, Tom Hayes, Stan Stein, Carl Moulton, Alex Pociask, Frank Gustine Jr., Paul Halliwell, Vince Scorsone, Jeffrey Berger, Tom Mariano, Andy Russell, Rocky Bleier, Marshall Goldstein, Renny Clark, Andy Komer, Rolf Hilden, Michael C. Linn, Gayland Cook and John Williams.

Thanks to *The Pittsburgh Press* and the University of Pittsburgh which have provided wonderful opportunities for me at several stages in my life. Angus McEachran, the editor of *The Press*, gave me permission to reprint portions of articles I had written as a staff member of *The Press.* PNC Bank and 84 Lumber were special patrons.

Special thanks to these patrons: Ajmani & Associates, Alcoa, Anlauf's Atlantic Service Center, Blue Cross of Western Pennsylvania, Anthony Crane Rental, Inc., Baierl Chevrolet, Bayer, Community Savings Bank, Continental Design and Management Group, H.J. Heinz Company, Integra Financial Corp., Investment Corp. of Palm Beach, Mascaro Inc., Meridian Exploration Corp., Mutual of Omaha Insurance Co., Pittsburgh Trane Sales Agency, Russell, Rea, Zappala & Gomulka Holdings, Inc., Tedco Construction, Westinghouse Electric Corp., Merna Corp. and West Penn Wire Corp.

Thanks to the late Arthur J. Rooney for letting me use his desk and chair to work on this book. That helped. I also think he sent me an Irish leprechaun and an archangel from heaven to assist me on this project when I needed a boost. Thanks to the Pittsburgh Penguins for winning the Stanley Cup championship, and to the Pirates for making us feel once again like citizens of "The City of Champions."

—Jim O'Brien

Pittsburgh Proud Sports Book Series

Here is information relating to the highly-successful series of books about Pittsburgh sports subjects by Jim O'Brien that are available to you by mail order.

PENGUIN PROFILES — Pittsburgh's Boys of Winter

Stories reflecting on the history of hockey in Pittsburgh. Interviews with many of the current stars, from Mario Lemieux to Jaromir Jagr and Kevin Stevens, and Penguins of the past. 448 pages, 200 photos. Hardcover: $24.95. Softcover: $14.95.

REMEMBER ROBERTO — Clemente Recalled By Teammates, Family, Friends and Fans

Pirates Hall of Famer recalled by those who knew him best. Interviews with his wife and sons, and his celebrated teammates during his 18 seasons in Pittsburgh. First adult book on Clemente to come out in over 20 years. 448 pages, over 220 photos. Hardcover: $24.95. Softcover: $14.95.

MAZ AND THE '60 BUCS
When Pittsburgh And Its Pirates Went All The Way

Interviews with all the living members of the World Series champion Pirates of the 1960 season, and five of the key members of the New York Yankees. Chapters on every one of the Pirates of that season. 512 pages, over 225 photos. Hardcover: $24.95. Softcover: $14.95.

DOING IT RIGHT — The Steelers of Three Rivers And Four Super Bowls Share Their Secrets For Success

Tales of the glory days of the Pittsburgh Steelers. Interviews with the stars of the '70s, as well as players from the early days of the franchise, and those who followed the championship seasons. If you've wondered whatever became of some of your favorite Steelers, here are the answers. Terry Bradshaw, Franco Harris, Rocky Bleier, Jack Lambert, Jack Ham, Mel Blount, Lynn Swann, Mike Webster, Ernie Holmes, John Stallworth, Chuck Noll, L.C. Greenwood are all chronicled here. 536 pages illustrated. Hardcover only: $24.95.

WHATEVER IT TAKES
The Continuing Saga of the Pittsburgh Steelers

More stories about Steelers from the earliest days of the franchise through its most successful seasons, right up to the retirement of Chuck Noll and the new era established by hometown sensation Bill Cowher. This book is now out of print, but will be available in 1996. Indicate with your order for any of the books above that you also are interested in obtaining a copy of this book.

For more information or to place an order please call Jim O'Brien at his home office (412-221-3580). Or write to: James P. O'Brien — Publishing, P.O. Box 12580, Pittsburgh, PA 15241. Pennsylvania residents add 6% sales tax to price of book, and Allegheny County residents should remit additional 1% sales tax, plus $3.50 for postage per book.